No Stress Tech Guide To Microsoft Works 7

By Dr. Indera E. Murphy

Tolana Publishing
Teaneck, New Jersey

No Stress Tech Guide To Microsoft Works 7
(Previously published under the title No Stress Tech Guide To Works 7)

Published By:
Tolana Publishing
PO Box 719
Teaneck, NJ 07666 USA

Find us online at www.tolanapublishing.com
Inquiries may be sent to the publisher: tolanapub@yahoo.com

Our books are available online at www.barnesandnoble.com

ISBN-10: 0-9773912-2-1
ISBN-13: 978-0-9773912-2-6

Library of Congress Control Number: 2006902442

Printed and bound in the United States Of America

Cover design by Mary Kramer, Milkweed Graphics, www.milkweedgraphics.com

V2.0

Dedication

This book is dedicated to my mother. She doesn't understand why I stay up all night, but she supports what I do. Hopefully, this book will explain why I stay up all night. I can't ask for more than that!
Thank you mommy.

Why I Wrote This Book

I know that many books claim to have "step-by-step instructions". If you have tried to follow books that make this claim and you got lost or couldn't complete a task as instructed, it may not have been your fault. When I decided to write computer books, I vowed to really have step-by-step instructions that actually included every step.
This includes steps like which file to open, which menu option to select, when to save a document and more.
In my opinion, it's this level of detail that makes a computer book easy to follow.

About The Author

Dr. Indera Murphy is an author, educator and IT professional that has over 20 years of experience in the Information Technology field. She has held a variety of positions including technical writer, programmer, online adjunct professor, consultant, web designer, course developer and project leader. Indera has designed and developed software applications and web sites, as well as, manage technology driven projects in several industries. In addition to being an Executive Director, she taught courses in a variety of areas including project management, technical writing, information processing, Access, HTML, Windows, Excel, Dreamweaver and critical thinking.

Titles In The Series

	ISBN
ACT! 2007	978-0-9773912-5-7
ACT! 2009	978-1-935208-07-5
ACT! 2010	978-1-935208-09-9
ACT! Pro 2011	978-1-935208-13-6
ACT! Pro 2012	978-1-935208-17-4
Using Crystal Reports 2008 With ACT! 2010 Databases	978-1-935208-10-5
Crystal Reports XI For Beginners (2nd Edition)	978-1-935208-00-6
What's New In Crystal Reports 2008	978-1-935208-01-3
Crystal Reports 2008 For Beginners	978-0-9773912-9-5
Crystal Reports 2011 For Beginners	978-1-935208-15-0
Crystal Reports Beyond The Basics	978-1-935208-18-1
Crystal Reports For Visual Studio 2005	978-0-9773912-6-4
Crystal Reports Basic For Visual Studio 2008	978-0-9773912-8-8
Crystal Reports For Visual Studio 2010	978-1-935208-12-9
Crystal Xcelsius 4.5	978-1-935208-02-0
Xcelsius 2008	978-1-935208-05-1
SAP Crystal Dashboard Design 2011 For Beginners	978-1-935208-11-2
OpenOffice.org 2 Writer	978-0-9773912-4-0
OpenOffice.org 3 Writer	978-1-935208-08-2
Microsoft Office Starter 2010 (Word & Excel)	978-1-935208-14-3
Microsoft PowerPivot For Excel 2010	978-1-935208-16-7
Microsoft Works 7	978-0-9773912-2-6
Microsoft Works 8 & 8.5	978-0-9773912-1-9
Microsoft Works 9	978-0-9773912-7-1
Windows XP	978-0-9773912-0-2

Coming Soon

Alpha Five Desktop Applications For Beginners	978-1-935208-20-4
Crystal Reports For Sage Peachtree Accounting	978-1-935208-19-8

TABLE OF CONTENTS

Section 1 Overview

Section 2 Word Processing

Section 3 Spreadsheets

Section 4 Databases

Section 5 Organization

INTRODUCTION TO WORKS 7

Welcome and thank you for purchasing this workbook!

The fastest and easiest way to overcome an obstacle is to have someone that has been there, to be by your side every step of the way. That is the purpose of this workbook - to be by your side every step of the way through learning Microsoft Works.

A hands-on approach is usually the best way to learn most things in life. This workbook is a visual guide that has over 600 illustrations that practically eliminate the guess work and lets you know that you are doing the steps correctly.

At the end of each lesson is a "Test Your Skills" section to further ensure that you are learning the topics that are covered. The exercises in this section allow you to practice what you learned in the lesson.

The table of contents takes the "How To" approach, which makes it easier to find exactly what you are looking for. This workbook will guide you through the highways of Microsoft Works 7 and get you up to speed.

Microsoft Works is an integrated software package that includes a word processor, spreadsheet, database and other tools. This workbook is divided into five sections - Works Overview, Word Processing, Spreadsheets, Databases and Organization.

Turn the page and let's get started!

LESSON 1

What's Covered In Each Section Of The Workbook

The lessons in this workbook cover all of the major components of Works. While the topics are covered thoroughly, they do not go into long drawn out explanations. I teach college level computer classes and have "discovered" that many people want to cut to the chase as they say, and not have to read a lot of theory or long explanations. I have tried my best to stick to that philosophy.

Section 1 provides an overview of the entire Microsoft Works 7 software package. The features of each application are discussed to help you get acquainted with the terminology. You will also learn how to use the templates that come with Works.

Section 2 covers the Word Processor. You will learn how to create and edit letters and other documents, how to create templates, set up a mail merge, design a newsletter and create a Table of Contents.

Section 3 covers Spreadsheets. You will modify existing spreadsheets and create new spreadsheets. You will learn how to format spreadsheets by changing column widths, add borders and shading, headers and footers, protect data, add formulas, use functions and create several types of charts.

Section 4 covers Databases. You will create databases, learn how to sort records, design a data entry form, create and use filters, convert data to spreadsheet format and create reports.

Section 5 covers the Calendar and Project Organizer. These tools will help you manage your day and keep your work organized.

All of the web site links in this workbook are listed on this page on our website: www.tolana.com/books/works7/works7links.html. You can go to this page and click on the link that you want instead of having to type the link in. See how nice I am. If you plan to use this web page, it is probably a good idea to bookmark it, so that you can get to it quickly.

Conventions Used In This Workbook

Works, like many other software packages has more than one way to complete a task or get to an option. To expose you to a variety of ways to accomplish a task, I decided to demonstrate several ways so that you would become more familiar with the menu options, which have all of the features, as well as, the toolbars and shortcut menus which are a subset of the options on the menus. I designed the following conventions to make it easier to follow the instructions in this workbook.

- ☑ The `Courier font` is used to indicate what you should type.
- ☑ **Drag** means to hold down the left mouse button while moving the mouse.
- ☑ **Click** means to press the left mouse button once, then release it.
- ☑ **Double-click** means to quickly press the left mouse button twice, then release it.
- ☑ **Right-click** means to press the right mouse button once to open a shortcut menu.
- ☑ Click OK, Click Save, Click Close, Click Next, Click Yes, Click Add and Click Finish means to click the button on the dialog box or window.
- ☑ Press **Enter** means to press the Enter key on your keyboard.
- ☑ Press **Tab** means to press the Tab key on your keyboard.
- ☑ **SMALL CAPS** are used to indicate an option to click on or to bring something to your attention.
- ☑ This NEW icon represents a new or modified feature in this version of Works.
- ☑ This icon indicates a tip or additional information about the topic that is being discussed.
- ☑ When you see "**YOUR SCREEN SHOULD LOOK LIKE THE ONE SHOWN IN FIGURE X.X**", or something similar in the exercises, check to make sure that your screen does look like the figure. If your screen does not look like the figure, redo the steps that you just completed so that your screen does match the figure. Not doing so may cause you problems when trying to complete other exercises in this workbook.

☑ "Save the Term Paper document as L4 Term Paper" means to open the Term Paper document and save it as L4 Term Paper. "L4" refers to the lesson number. Doing this lets you keep the original file.

☑ **INSERT ⇒ MEDIA ELEMENT ⇒ SHOCKWAVE AUDIO** means to open the **INSERT** menu, select the option **MEDIA ELEMENT**, then select the option **SHOCKWAVE AUDIO**, as shown in Figure 1-1.

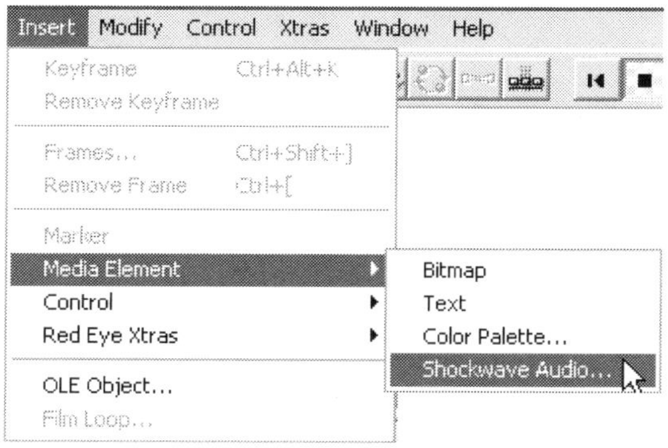

Figure 1-1 Menu navigation technique illustrated

Assumptions

(Yes, I know one should never assume anything but . . . .)

☑ That you have Microsoft Works and all of the components installed on your computer. If you are not sure that you have all of the components installed, follow the instructions below in the section "How To Check For A Complete Installation".

☑ You know that the operating system used to write this workbook is Windows XP Professional. If you are using a different version of Windows it is possible that some of the screen shots may have a slightly different look.

☑ You are familiar with the Windows environment including Windows Explorer and are comfortable using a mouse.

☑  You know that this button will minimize the open window and place an icon for it on the Windows taskbar. When you want to view the window again, click the button on the taskbar and the window will reappear.

☑  You know that this button will open the current window to the full size of your computer screen.

☑  You know that this button will close the window that is open.

☑ That you have access to the Internet to download the practice files for this workbook.

Lessons 1 and 2 will explain the key concepts and components of Microsoft Works. You will be given a tour of the software. Works is an integrated software package, which means that all of the applications (word processor, spreadsheet and database) work together. Don't be overwhelmed by the size of this workbook because Works is really easy to use. Most lessons can be completed in 60 minutes or less.

How To Check For A Complete Installation

The purpose of this exercise is to make sure that you have all of the necessary components of Works installed before you start going through the workbook. If Works came pre-installed on your computer, you may not have all of the components installed.

1. Click the Start button on the Windows Taskbar and select **ALL PROGRAMS** or **PROGRAMS**, as shown in Figure 1-2.

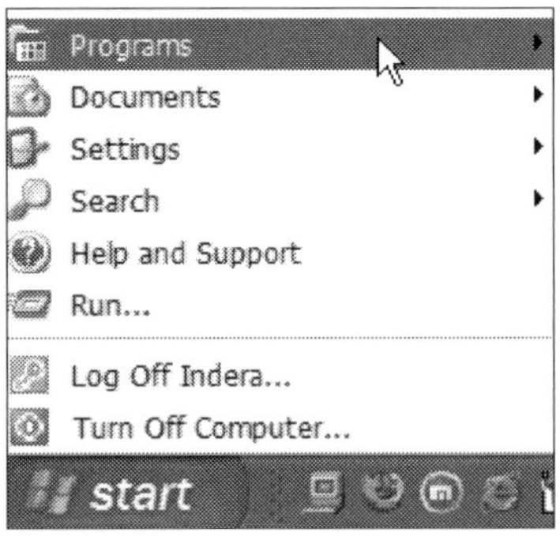

Figure 1-2 Start menu illustrated

2. Select the group Microsoft Works. If you see all of the options shown on the right of Figure 1-3, you have a complete installation. If you have a complete installation, go to the section "Major Components of Works". If you do not have all of the options shown in Figure 1-3, go to the next section, "Re-Installing Works".

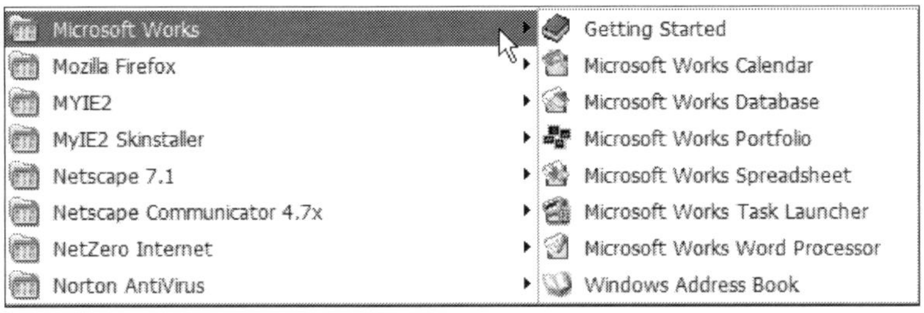

Figure 1-3 Microsoft Works complete installation

Re-Installing Works

The instructions below will walk you through re-installing Works so that you will have all of the software necessary to complete the exercises in this workbook. You should only complete this exercise if you do not have a complete installation of Works. If your installation is complete, please skip this exercise. Depending on how Works was originally installed, you may need the installation CD. This would be a good time to pull out the Works or Works Suite CD.

1. Click the Start button on the Windows Taskbar and select Control Panel if you have Windows 2000 or Windows XP. If you are using Windows XP and the Classic view (which looks like Windows 2000) select Settings, then Control Panel. The Settings option is shown above in Figure 1-2.

2. Double-click on the **ADD OR REMOVE PROGRAMS** icon in the Control Panel shown in Figure 1-4.

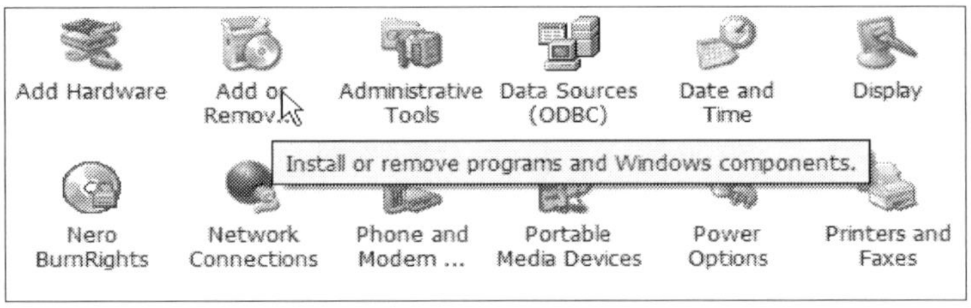

Figure 1-4 Add or Remove Programs icon illustrated

3. Scroll down the list and click on the option **MICROSOFT WORKS 7.0**, as shown in Figure 1-5, then click the **CHANGE** button. You will see a Welcome window that says to wait a few moments. Please wait until you see the next Welcome window shown in Figure 1-6 before going to the next step.

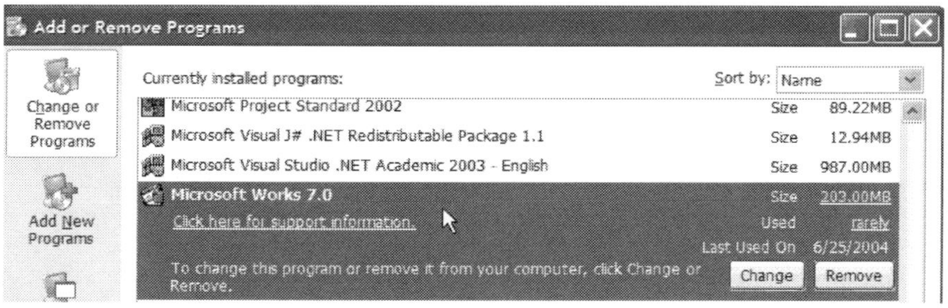

Figure 1-5 Microsoft Works 7.0 option selected

4. Click Next on the Welcome Back window shown in Figure 1-6, then select the **CHANGE INSTALLATION** option shown in Figure 1-7. Click Next.

Figure 1-6 Welcome Back window

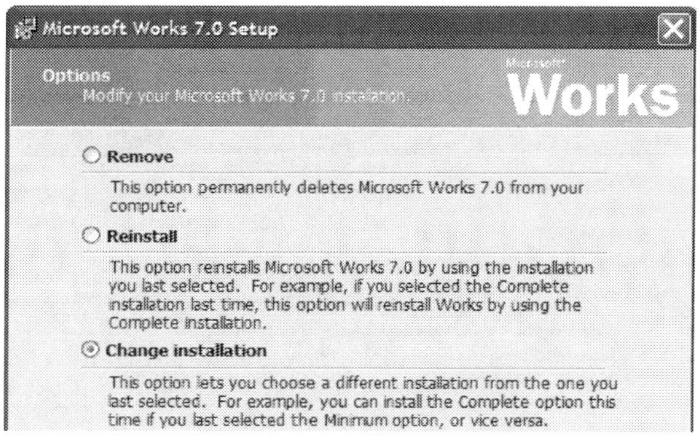

Figure 1-7 Setup options dialog box

Yes, I see the **REINSTALL** option in Figure 1-7 above. The problem with selecting this option now is that you may not know how Works was installed before, so it is safer to select the **COMPLETE INSTALLATION** option.

5. Select **COMPLETE INSTALLATION (RECOMMENDED)** and click Next.

6. Follow the instructions to complete the installation. Once the installation is complete, close the Add or Remove Programs dialog box and the Control Panel. When you are finished, refer back to Figure 1-3 to make sure that you have all of the software installed.

Major Components Of Works

Word Processor

The word processor allows you to create text based documents like letters, proposals, labels, memos and legal documents. Figure 1-8 shows a document created with the word processor. You can also insert different types of files in a word processing document. This is known as linking and embedding.

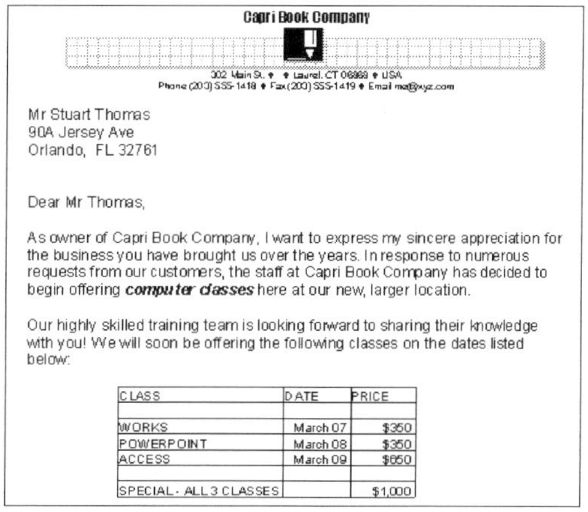
Capri Book Company

302 Main St. • • Laurel, CT 06868 • USA
Phone (203) 555-1418 • Fax (203) 555-1419 • Email ma@xyz.com

Mr Stuart Thomas
90A Jersey Ave
Orlando, FL 32761

Dear Mr Thomas,

As owner of Capri Book Company, I want to express my sincere appreciation for the business you have brought us over the years. In response to numerous requests from our customers, the staff at Capri Book Company has decided to begin offering ***computer classes*** here at our new, larger location.

Our highly skilled training team is looking forward to sharing their knowledge with you! We will soon be offering the following classes on the dates listed below:

CLASS	DATE	PRICE
WORKS	March 07	$350
POWERPOINT	March 08	$350
ACCESS	March 09	$650
SPECIAL - ALL 3 CLASSES		$1,000

Figure 1-8 Word processing document

Document Views

Document views determine what portions of a word processing document are visible on the screen. There are three views as discussed below.

① **NORMAL** is the default view in the word processor. This is the view that you use to create and edit documents.
② **HEADER AND FOOTER** allows you to add, edit and view information in the header and footer section of the document.
③ **PRINT PREVIEW** allows you to see how the document will look like when it is printed.

Spreadsheets

Spreadsheets are usually used to calculate data like balance sheets, sales forecasts and budgets as shown in Figure 1-9. Spreadsheets have rows, columns and cells. Cells are where the numbers, text and formulas are entered. If you change a number in a calculation or formula, the spreadsheet will automatically be recalculated. You can create your own formulas or use the built-in functions like AVG or SUM. You can also create charts based on the data in a spreadsheet, as shown in Figure 1-10. Works allows you to create a variety of charts including pie, bar and line to name a few.

Databases

Databases allow you to store related information in one place. Examples of databases are an inventory or customer database. You can sort all of the records in a database or select specific records based on criteria. You can also create reports using the data in the database. Databases store the information in fields. For example, in the products database shown in Figure 1-11, you would store the following pieces of information: Product Number, Product Name, Qty On Hand, Price and Cost. Each of these pieces of information is stored in a separate field. All of these fields make up a record. In Figure 1-11, you see several records in the database.

	A	B	C
1	CLASS SCHEDULE FOR MARCH		
2			Students
3	CLASS	DATE	Enrolled
4			
5	WORKS	March 07	20
6		March 09	12
7		March 10	8
8		March 20	19
9	POWERPOINT	March 08	15
10		March 12	19
11		March 15	14
12		March 25	10
13	ACCESS	March 09	18
14		March 23	13
15		March 28	10

Figure 1-9 Spreadsheet document

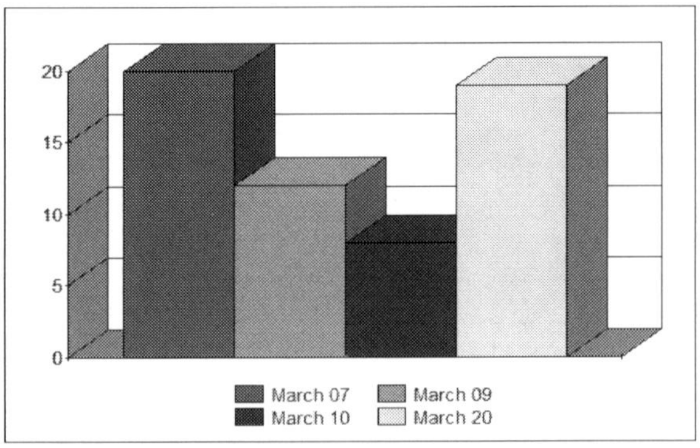

Figure 1-10 Bar chart

✔	Product Number	Product Name	Qty On Hand	Price	Cost	Date Ordered	Qty On Order
1	CH-007	Aladdin	800	$14.95	$6.95	2/1/2004	25
2	CH-100	Cinderella	100	$12.95	$4.50	2/1/2004	30
3	CH-101	Tom and Jerry	100	$12.95	$5.50	2/6/2004	25
4	CH-220	Bugs Bunny	0	$12.95	$5.50	1/20/2004	25

Figure 1-11 Products database

Database Views

There are three views in the database that you can use as described below.

① **LIST VIEW** as shown above in Figure 1-11 displays many records at the same time. You can also add or modify data in this view.
② **FORM VIEW** will display one record at a time, as shown in Figure 1-12. You can use this view when you are adding or modifying data in the database.
③ **FORM DESIGN VIEW** allows you to create and modify forms as shown in Figure 1-13. You cannot add or modify data in this view.

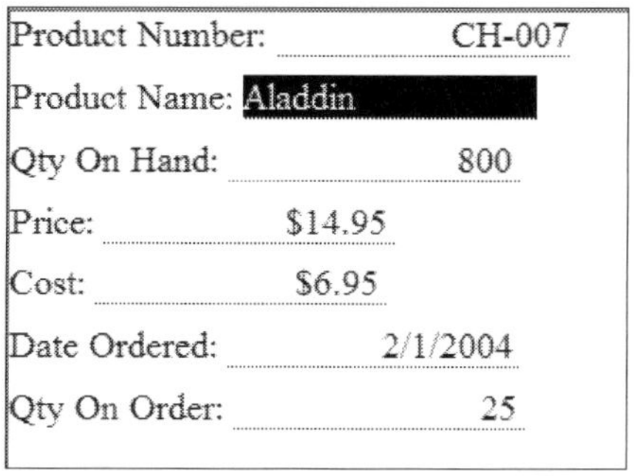

Figure 1-12 Form view

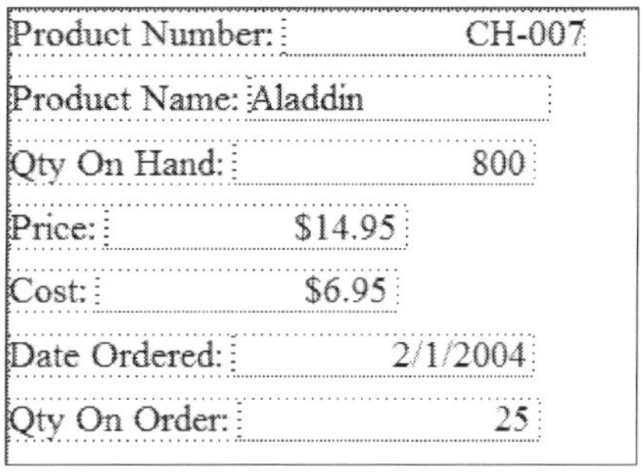

Figure 1-13 Form design view

Other Tools That You Can Use

In addition to the main software packages (the word processor, spreadsheet and database), there are other tools that you can use to further enhance the documents that you create. Some of these tools are discussed below. These tools are not part of Works. Many of them are integrated into Works, when Works is installed. You should already have them installed on your computer because they come with Windows.

Clip Art Gallery

The Clip Art Gallery is an application that lets you manage and organize the clip art that is on your hard drive. Works comes with clip art that you can add to the Gallery. If you reinstalled Works earlier in this lesson, the clip art that comes with Works was installed, if it wasn't already on your hard drive. You can also use other clip art that you already have installed on your computer, in documents that you create in Works.

Word Art

Word Art lets you change the appearance of text. You can use Word Art to add borders, shading or rotate text.

Note-It

Note-It lets you add notes to a document.
The note is not visible in the document.
You insert a graphic in the document that lets the reader know that there is a note attached to the document. The reader of the document double-clicks on the graphic to read the note as shown in Figure 1-14.

Figure 1-14 Document with Note-It feature added

Microsoft Draw

The application lets you create drawings free hand, as shown in Figure 1-15. You can add your drawings to word processing documents or database forms. Microsoft Draw can also be used to create logos.

Insert ⇒ Picture ⇒ New Drawing, will open this application, if the word processor application is open.

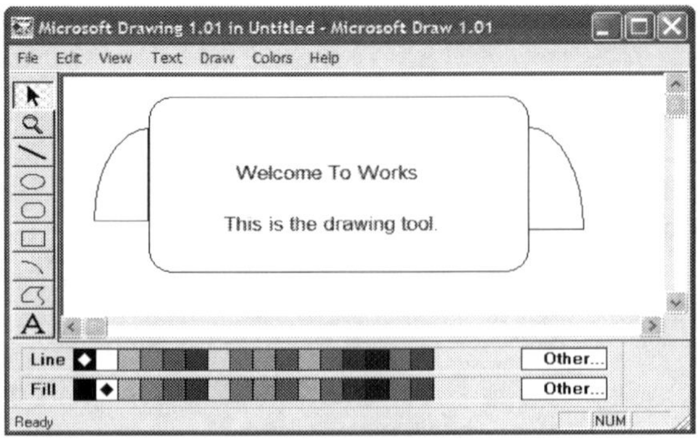

Figure 1-15 Microsoft Draw software

NEW Format Gallery

The Format Gallery shown in Figure 1-16, unlike the other tools discussed in this section, comes with Works and is a collection of pre-made formats that you can easily apply to text in a word processing document. If there are formats or styles that you use on a regular basis that aren't in the gallery, you can create your own formats and save them in the Format Gallery.

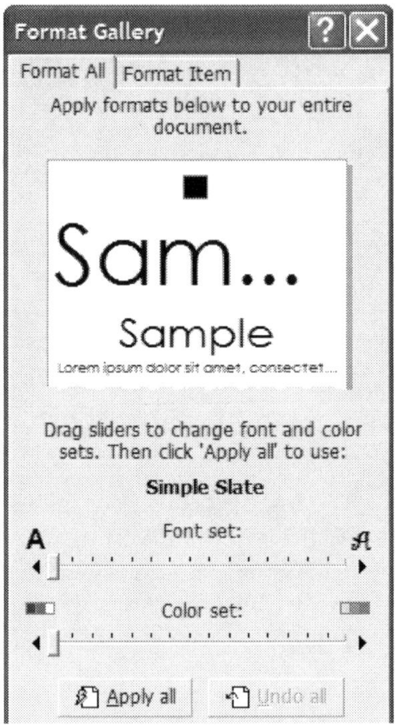

Figure 1-16 Format Gallery dialog box

Works Terminology

Microsoft Works defines everything you do by using the terminology below, therefore I think that it is important to understand these terms.

Program Works comes with the following applications (programs): word processing, spreadsheet, database, calendar and the project organizer. Each program has a specific function.

Task Works considers everything that you do a task, from creating a letter, to scheduling an appointment, to creating a chart.

Documents Are the files that you create which are based on tasks that you need to complete.

Wizards Are helpers. You select the type of document that you want to create, like letterhead, a proposal or invoice. The Task wizard lets you select a few options about the type of document that you want to create. Once you have selected the options, the wizard will create a document based on your choices.

Templates Works comes with several templates that you can use. Templates look like a regular document. The difference is that when a template is opened, only a copy of it is opened. You use the copy instead of the original. Templates that you create can be used over and over again, without having to select any options like you do when you use a wizard.

A good example of when to use a template is for a fax cover page. When you use a fax cover page, you do not need to change the layout. You type in the information that you need, like who the fax is going to and the fax number that you will send the fax to. You will create a fax cover page template later in the workbook.

NEW Works Task Launcher

Think of the Task Launcher as the starting point for everything that you can do in Microsoft Works. Figure 1-17 shows the Task Launcher. The first thing that you may notice about the Task Launcher is that it looks more like a web site than a standard software window. The Task Launcher is covered in more detail later in this lesson. I like to think of the Task Launcher as the control panel for Works because the Task Launcher allows you to go from one application in Works to another.

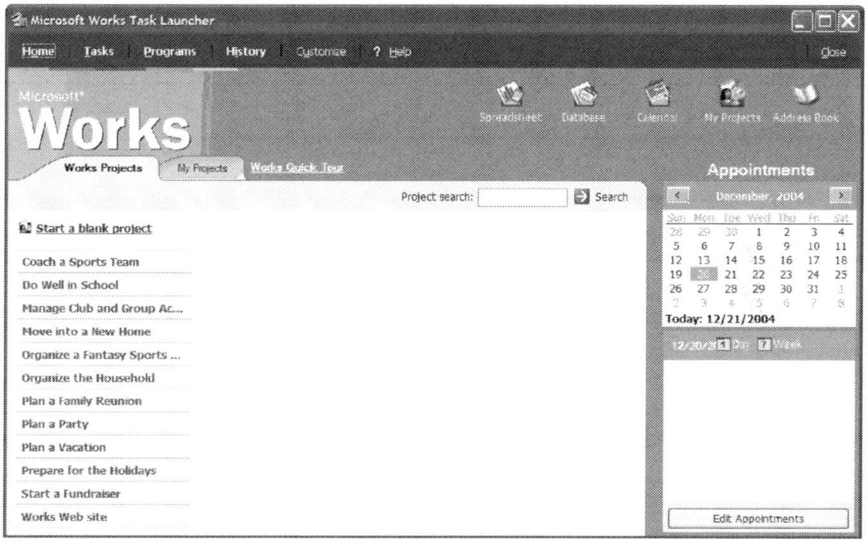

Figure 1-17 Works Task Launcher home page

Interesting Observation

While writing this workbook I needed to uninstall and reinstall Works a few times. What I noticed is that the icons in the upper right corner of Figure 1-17 shown above on the Task Launcher changed, each time I installed Works.

In addition to the icons shown in Figure 1-18, which are the same as the ones shown above in Figure 1-17. The icons shown in Figure 1-19 and Figure 1-20 appeared during different installations.

Figure 1-18 Larger view of the icons shown above in Figure 1-17

Figure 1-19 Icons on the Task Launcher

Figure 1-20 Icons on the Task Launcher

How To Start Works

Now that you have read a little about Works, I'm sure that you are ready to open the software and get started.

1. Start ⇒ Programs or All Programs ⇒ Microsoft Works ⇒ Microsoft Works Task Launcher. If this is the first time that you have opened Works, you will see a dialog box asking if you want to see a demonstration. Click Cancel. You can view the demonstration later by selecting Help ⇒ Getting Started, from any window in the Task Launcher.

> You will need the free Adobe Reader to open and view the Getting Started manual. If you do not have the Adobe Reader, download it from this page. Once you download it, you have to install it. http://www.adobe.com/products/acrobat/readstep2.html

2. Close or minimize all open windows before starting the next exercise.

How To Create A Shortcut For Works

This exercise will show you how to create a shortcut for the Task Launcher because it allows you to get to every program and feature that Works has. Doing this is optional. If you want to create a shortcut on your desktop for Works follow the steps below.

1. Right-click on a blank space on your desktop. New ⇒ Shortcut as shown in Figure 1-21.

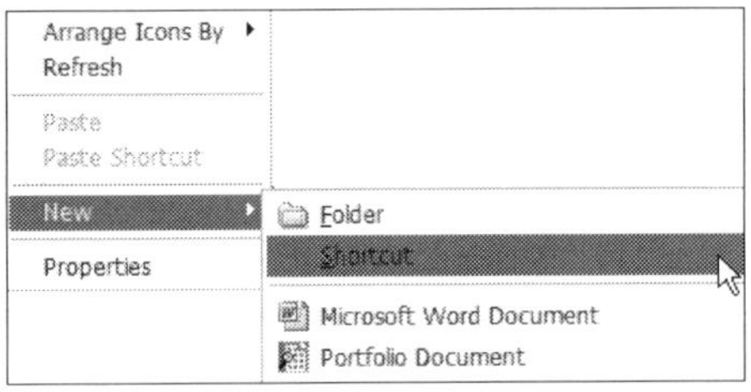

Figure 1-21 Menu options illustrated

2. Click the **BROWSE** button on the Create Shortcut dialog box. Navigate to and click on the plus sign next to the folder C:\Program Files\Microsoft Works.

The C drive is under the **MY COMPUTER** folder as shown in Figure 1-22. "C" is the drive that most people have their software installed on. If your software is installed on a different drive letter, select that drive letter instead. You will see different folders on your C drive, then the ones shown in Figure 1-22.

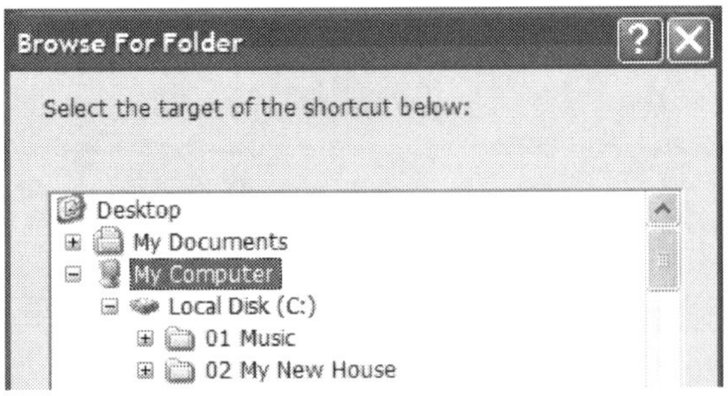

Figure 1-22 My Computer folder illustrated

3. Scroll down the list of files and click on the file **MSWORKS.EXE**, illustrated in Figure 1-23. Click OK, then click Next.

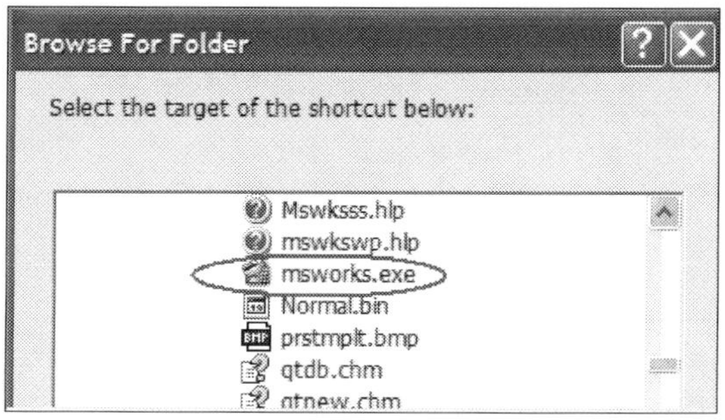

Figure 1-23 Microsoft Works program file

4. Type `Microsoft Works` in the field shown in Figure 1-24. This will be the text that appears with the icon on your desktop. You can type whatever you want here. Click Finish. You should see an icon on your desktop, like the one shown in Figure 1-25.

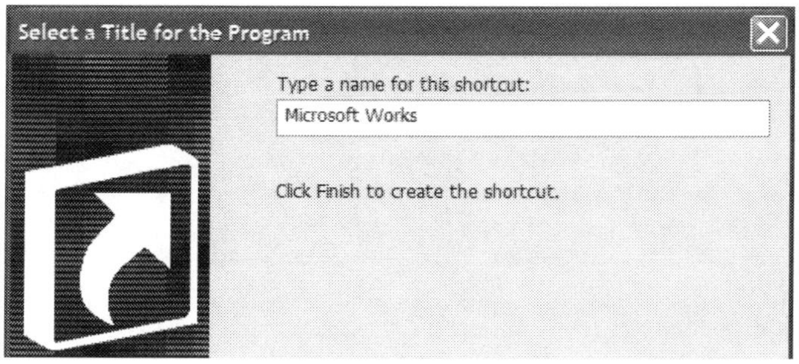

Figure 1-24 Name for the shortcut

Figure 1-25 Microsoft Works shortcut on the desktop

A Quick Tour Of Microsoft Works

Works is a tasked based suite of tools. Unlike "Office" suites, which contain several separate software packages, all of Works packages are accessible from one interface. The easiest way to have constant access to all of the tools in Works is through the Task Launcher. I suspect that the reason Works considers everything you do a task, is because of the Task Launcher.

In addition to being able to create word processing documents, spreadsheets and databases in Works, you can also send email via the email software that you are currently using and surf the Internet using Internet Explorer, right from inside of Works. Works also has a portfolio tool that allows you to organize files. The project organizer lets you manage projects by entering all of the tasks and their due dates.

The word processor, spreadsheet and database applications in Works are scaled down versions of Microsoft Word, Excel and Access. These packages are the core of the Microsoft "Office" suite. In the future, if you have a need for more features, the transition to the "Office" products will be smoother, if you are already familiar with Works.

Home Page

The Home page is the default page of the Task Launcher.

1. If you do not already have Works open, you can double-click on the icon on your desktop that you created earlier in this lesson, or you can open Works by opening the Programs menu, illustrated earlier in Figure 1-3.

The Works Task Launcher should be open and you should be on the Home page, as shown earlier in Figure 1-17. From here you can use the wizards, open existing documents, as well as, create new documents. The features under the **CUSTOMIZE** and **HELP** links at the top of the Task Launcher will be covered in the next lesson.

2. The **WORKS QUICK TOUR** link on the Home page provides an overview of the major components of Works. Click on this link now. When you are finished reading, close the Quick Tour window.

Tasks Page

1. The wizards are on the Tasks page. Click on the **TASKS** link now. The wizards will walk you through creating a document by having you select a few options.

2. Click on the Letters & Labels link. Your window should look like the one shown in Figure 1-26. You can use these wizards to create envelopes, labels and stationery, among other things.

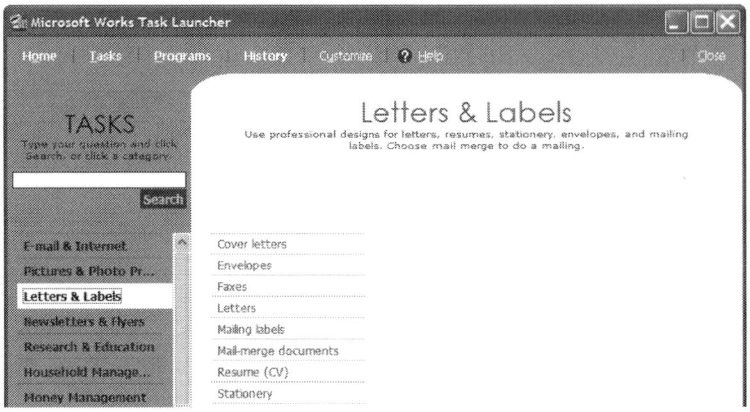

Figure 1-26 Letters & Labels wizard options illustrated

The options on the left side of the Tasks window are the categories. The options on the right are the tasks for the category that is selected. The options in each category are templates that come with Works.

You can also create your own templates. When you create templates, they are saved in the **PERSONAL TEMPLATES** category, which is on the Tasks page. If you have not created any templates yet, you will not see any in the Personal Templates category illustrated in Figure 1-27.

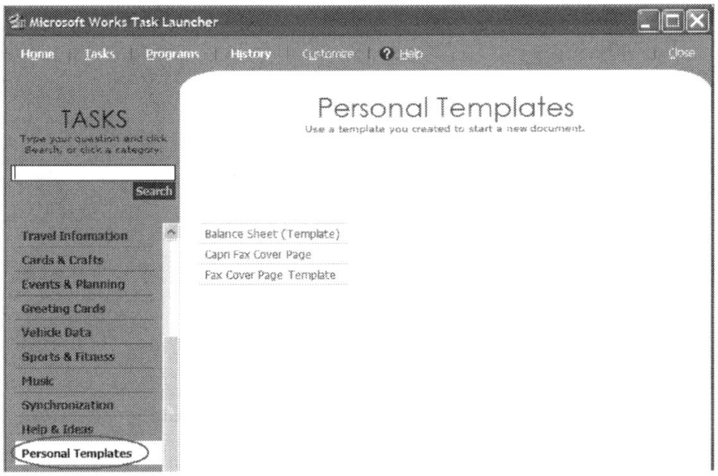

Figure 1-27 Personal Templates category illustrated

Programs Page

The links on the Programs page shown in Figure 1-28 allow you to open the word processor, spreadsheet and database applications, as well as, many other tools. The **MSN PHOTOS** link shown in Figure 1-28 will take you to Microsoft's web site, where you can upload photos to the Internet and share them with friends for free.

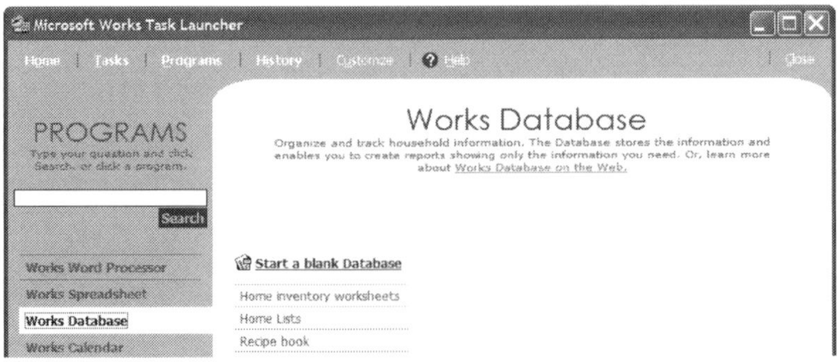

Figure 1-28 Programs page

The **MSN** link will take you to Microsoft's Encarta web site, which you can also use for free. Encarta is an online encyclopedia. If you have never opened any of the applications, click on the link for one now.

The Programs and Tasks pages in the Task Launcher have a **SEARCH** field. The search feature is useful if you are looking for a task. For example, type `budget` in the Search field on the Programs page, then click the Search button. Works will retrieve all of the tasks that are budget related, as shown in Figure 1-29. From here you can click on the task that will best meet your needs.

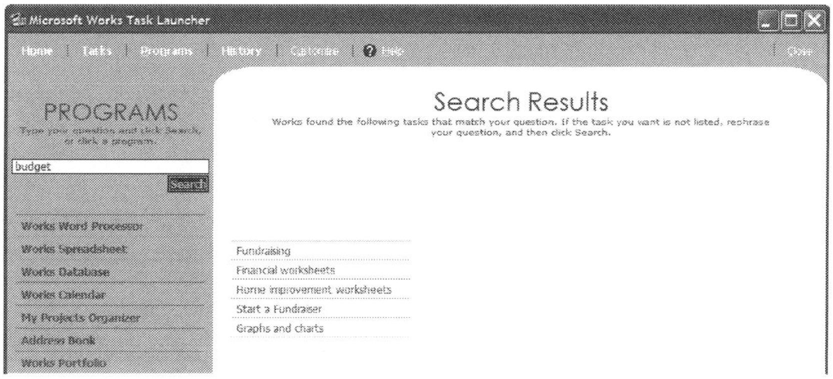

Figure 1-29 Result of the search

History Page

1. Click on the **HISTORY** link. Your History page should look similar to the one shown in Figure 1-30. The History page displays the documents that you last used. You will not see any files listed if you have not created or opened any yet.

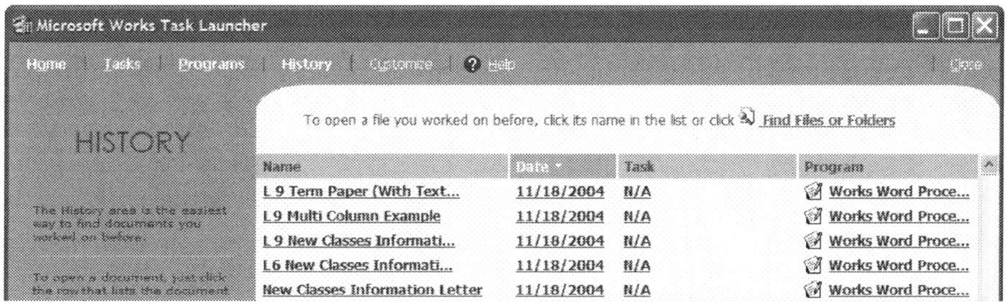

Figure 1-30 History page

2. If you see the document in the list shown above in Figure 1-30 that you want to open, click on it. The **PROGRAM** column on the far right tells you what type of document it is.

> The History page will display the last 500 files that were opened. Once you have opened file number 501, the oldest file by date will automatically be removed from the History page. The file is still on your hard drive, just not on the History page.

3. If you do not see the file that you want on the History page, click on the **FIND FILES OR FOLDERS** link, shown above in Figure 1-30. This will take you to a window that will let you search for the file.

This feature did not work for me. Hopefully it will work for you. When I clicked on the Find Files or Folders link, I get the message shown in Figure 1-31. I posted several messages over the months that I was writing this workbook to find out why this feature did not work for me. I did not get it resolved by the time this workbook went to print. If it works for you, you will see the Search window that is part of Windows.

Figure 1-31 Error message

Other Tools In Works

Now that you have reviewed the Task Launcher tools, it's time to explore other tools that Works has. The remainder of this lesson will provide an overview of the calendar, project organizer and portfolio.

The Calendar

The calendar is a useful feature because it allows you to keep track of your appointments, as well as, create reminders.

1. Click on the **HOME** link, then click on the **CALENDAR** icon. If your email software opens, close it and the calendar will open. You should see the calendar shown in Figure 1-32.

   If you have already used the calendar, you may have a different view showing then the one shown in Figure 1-32.

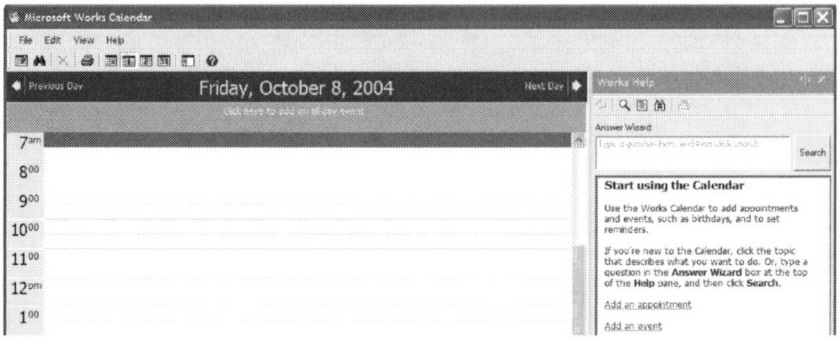

Figure 1-32 Works calendar

2. File ⇒ Exit, to close the calendar, then click on the **PROGRAMS** link.

3. Click on the **WORKS CALENDAR** option. You will see the calendar options shown in Figure 1-33. The first two options on the right are shortcuts to the most used calendar options. You will learn how to use the calendar in Lesson 18.

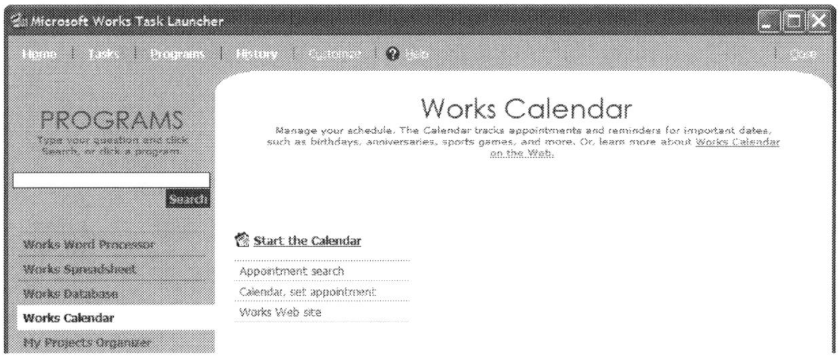

Figure 1-33 Calendar options

The Project Organizer

I like to think of the Project Organizer as a blueprint for a project or event that has a lot of steps to it. You can create your own project or you can use a project template that comes with Works.

Figure 1-34 is a project template that comes with Works. You will learn how to create and edit projects in Lesson 19.

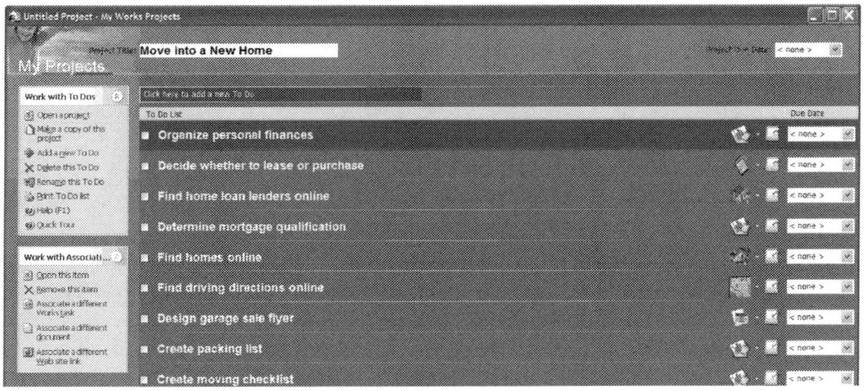

Figure 1-34 Move into a new home project template

Projects allow you to incorporate documents that you have already created, add items to your calendar, create to do lists and more. Once you create a project, you will see it on the **MY PROJECTS** tab on the Task Launcher home page.

The Portfolio

The Portfolio allows you to organize text, documents and pictures in one place, which Works refers to as a **COLLECTION**. Usually, you will group items together because they have something in common.

For example, you would create a portfolio to store documents and photos that are related to a fundraiser that you are working on.

Whatever you can do in the Portfolio to organize files, you can do in Windows and have more options at your disposal. Figure 1-35 shows the Portfolio options on the Programs page. Figure 1-36 shows the Portfolio in the Gallery view.

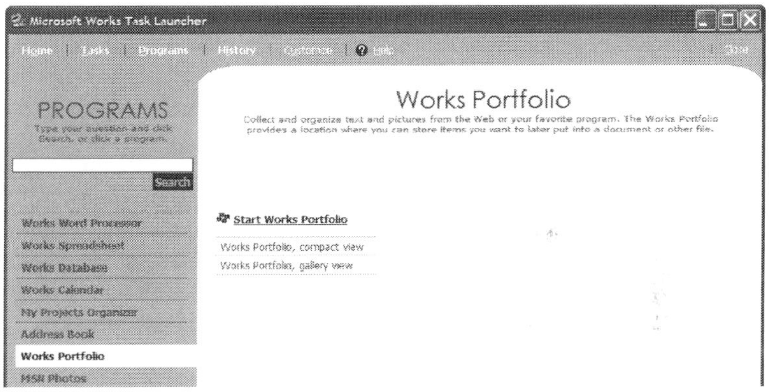

Figure 1-35 Portfolio options on the Programs page

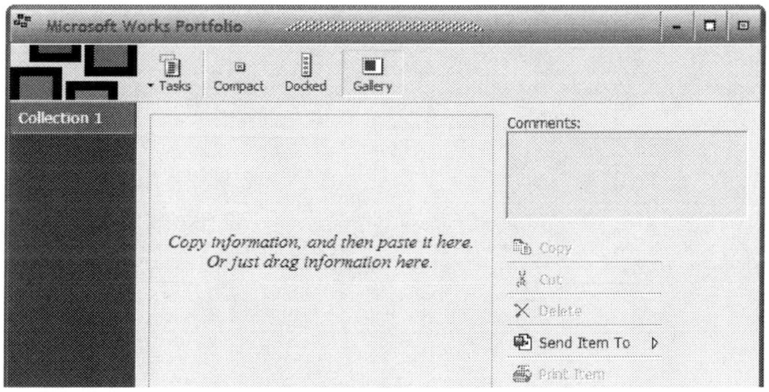

Figure 1-36 Portfolio in the Gallery view

Test Your Skills

1. Where can you view a list of the files that you have opened in Works?
2. If you create a template, where is it saved?
3. What option allows you to access all of the tools that come with Works?

GETTING STARTED

In this lesson you will be introduced to the common features of the applications in Works like toolbars, selecting menu options, dialog boxes and how to navigate to a different folder. Using these features are the same in the word processor, spreadsheet and database applications.

When you are more familiar with Works you can come back to this lesson and customize the software more. You will learn how to do the following:

☑ Create a folder to store the files in that you will create and use in this workbook
☑ Download the practice files for this workbook from the Internet
☑ Check your settings in Works
☑ Use the Help System

LESSON 2

Toolbars

Each application in Microsoft Works has its own toolbar. A unique feature of Works is that the first 13 buttons shown in Figure 2-1 on the Formatting toolbar are the same on the spreadsheet and database toolbars. Table 2-1 explains the purpose each of the buttons. The other buttons on the Formatting toolbar are specific to the application and are covered later in the workbook.

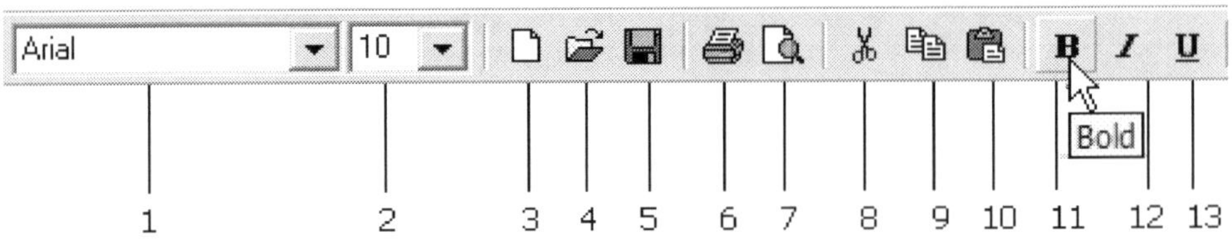

Figure 2-1 First 13 buttons on the Formatting toolbar

Button	Purpose
1	Lists the fonts that are installed on your computer.
2	Lists the font sizes available for the font that is selected.
3	Opens a new file.
4	Opens an existing file.
5	Saves the file.
6	Prints the file.
7	Preview the document.
8	Cuts (deletes) the selected text.
9	Copies the selected information to the clipboard. (1)
10	Inserts the contents of the clipboard into the document. (1)
11	Makes the selected text bold.
12	Makes the selected text italic.
13	Underlines the selected text.

Table 2-1 Common formatting toolbar buttons explained

(1) The clipboard is not visible. It is part of the computers temporary memory.

In previous versions of Works, the word processor also had the same 13 buttons on the Formatting toolbar. Now, Works has these 13 buttons spread out on two toolbars in the word processor. The word processing toolbars are covered in Lesson 4.

The buttons on are toolbars are shortcuts for the most used menu items. Instead of opening the Format menu and selecting Font to make text bold, you can click on the button with the "B" on the toolbar, as shown above in Figure 2-1. You will also see the word **BOLD**. This is known as a **TOOL TIP**. If you move the mouse pointer over a button on the toolbar, a tool tip will appear that gives you a brief description of what the button does.

Menus

Menus allow you to select commands. Selecting a command causes an action to happen. The commands on a menu are related. For example, the commands on the word processing Format menu relate to formatting a document, as shown in Figure 2-2. You will not find formatting commands on the Tools menu.

To select a command, open the appropriate menu by clicking on it and then selecting the command. Figure 2-3 shows the word processing Edit menu and its commands. To the right of many of the commands on this menu you will see keyboard shortcuts.

There is a **KEYBOARD SHORTCUT** next to several of the commands on the Edit menu including the Undo AutoCorrect, Paste and Find commands. You can use the keyboard shortcuts instead of opening the menu and selecting the command. To use the keyboard shortcuts, press the key combination next to the command that you want to use. I have always wondered how many people have really memorized more than two or three of these keyboard shortcuts. The only three that I use, when I can remember them is Cut, Copy and Paste.

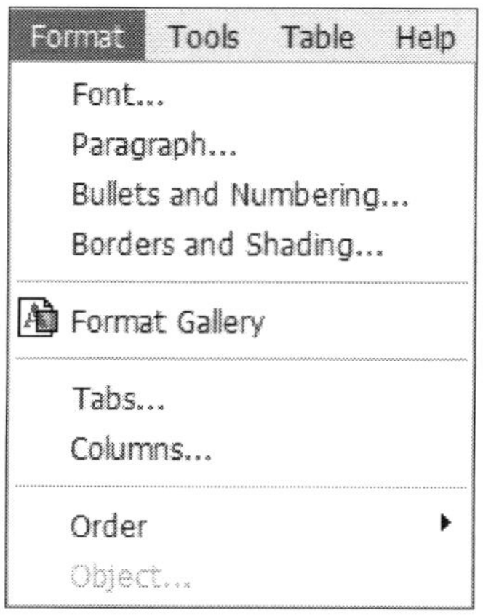

Figure 2-2 Format menu options in the word processor

As shown in Figure 2-3, some of the commands (Can't Redo, Cut, Copy, Clear, Edit Links and Edit Object) are dimmed out. This means that these commands are not available for the task that you are currently working on.

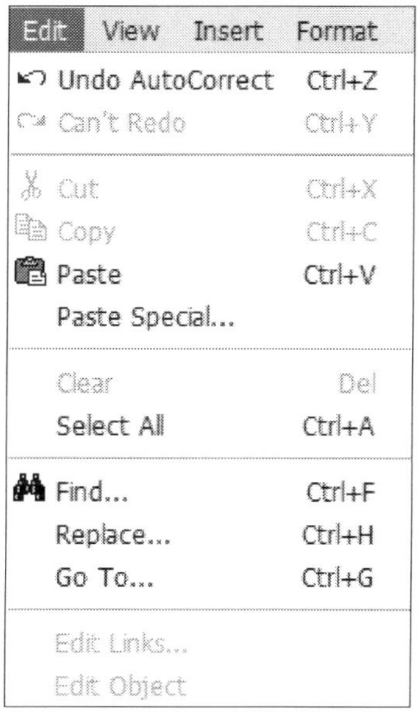

Figure 2-3 Edit menu options in the word processor

Dialog Boxes

Dialog boxes are used to get more information from you about the command that you have selected. A dialog box will also appear any time that you select a command that has an **...** (ellipsis) at the end of it.

In Figure 2-3 above, the Find and Replace menu options are some of the commands that will cause a dialog box to open.

Figure 2-4 shows the Print dialog box in the word processing application. Dialog boxes have many different options that you can select to customize the task that you are working on.

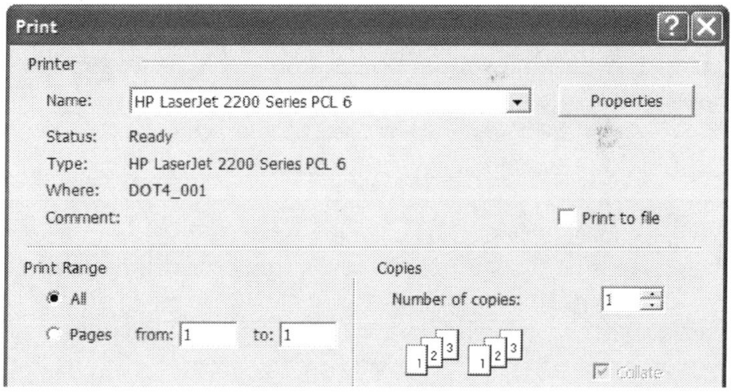

Figure 2-4 Print dialog box

Text Boxes

Text boxes let you type in the information. In Figure 2-4 above, the **FROM** and **TO** fields are text boxes. Text boxes are often called Fields.

Option Buttons

Option buttons are grouped together. You can only select one button in an option group. The **PRINT RANGE** section on the Print dialog box is an option group. You can select **ALL** or **PAGES**, but not both, as shown above in Figure 2-4.

List Boxes

List boxes let you select an item from a list. You can only select one item in the list box. The field, **NUMBER OF COPIES** shown above in Figure 2-4 is an example of a list box. You can click on the arrow at the end of the list box to increase or decrease the number of copies that you want to print.

Combo Boxes

Combo boxes are similar to list boxes. Click on the arrow at the end of the combo box and you will see the options that you can select from. The top of Figure 2-5 shows the **NAME** combo box opened.

Combo boxes are commonly known as **DROP-DOWN LIST BOXES**.

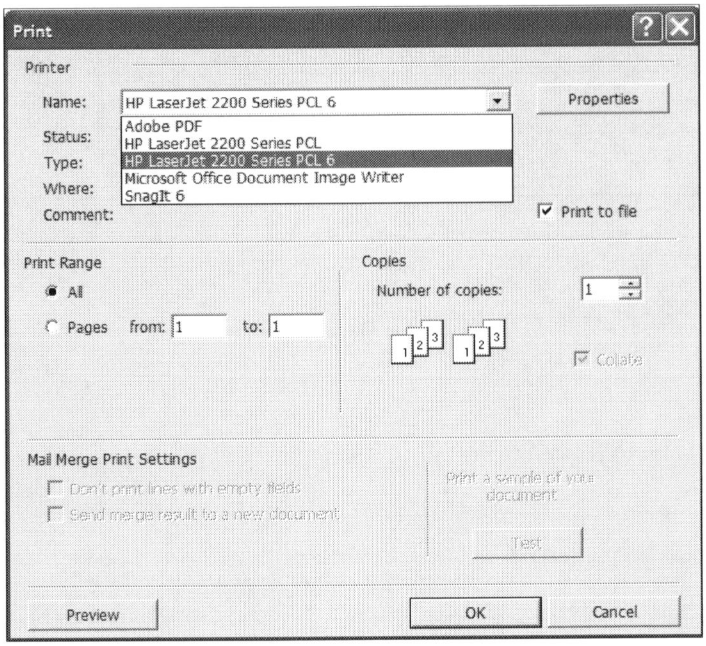

Figure 2-5 Name combo box illustrated

Check Boxes

Check boxes are options that are turned on and off. To turn an option on, click in the box so that a check mark appears. In Figure 2-5, the check box next to the **PRINT TO FILE** option has a ✓ (check mark) in it. The ✓ lets you know that the option is turned on. To turn the option off, click in the box and the ✓ will disappear.

Command Buttons

Command buttons cause an action to happen. **PREVIEW**, **TEST**, **OK**, **CANCEL** and **PROPERTIES** are the command buttons on the Print dialog box shown above in Figure 2-5.

In other Microsoft packages that I have used, command buttons that have an ellipsis, will open another dialog box. The **PROPERTIES** button shown above in Figure 2-5 will open the dialog box shown in Figure 2-6. The Properties button should have an ellipsis, but for some reason it doesn't.

Notice that the **DETAILS** button shown in Figure 2-6 has an ellipsis. The Details button will open another dialog box.

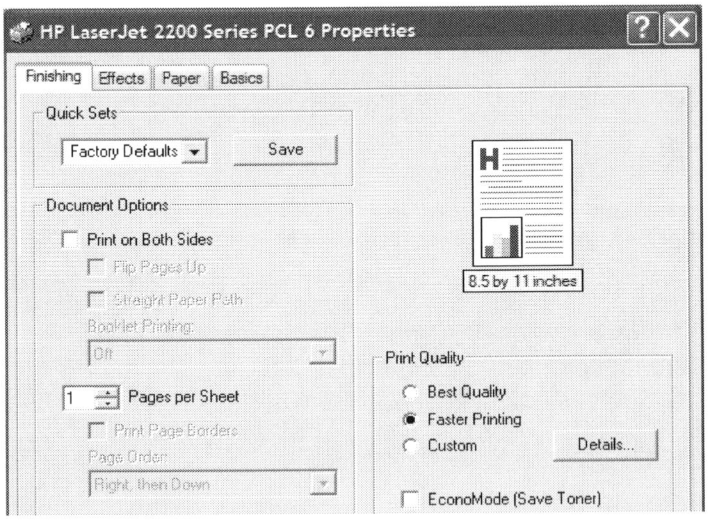

Figure 2-6 Printer Properties dialog box

> You may have different tabs and options on your **PRINTER PROPERTIES** dialog box then the ones shown above in Figure 2-6. The tabs and options will be different, depending on the brand and model of printer that you have.

The Difference Between Save And Save As

The **SAVE** command will save the file that is currently open, with the existing file name. The **SAVE AS** command will let you save a file for the first time or you can save an existing file with a new name. This means that you will have similar information in two documents, unless you delete one of the documents.

When you create a new document and select the Save command on the File menu or click the Save button on the toolbar, the Save As dialog box shown in Figure 2-7 will automatically open.

Works knows whether the current document has already been saved or if it is a new document. If you have a document that you want to save with a different name, open the document and select "Save As" on the File menu. Then type in the new name for the document. The original document is still there.

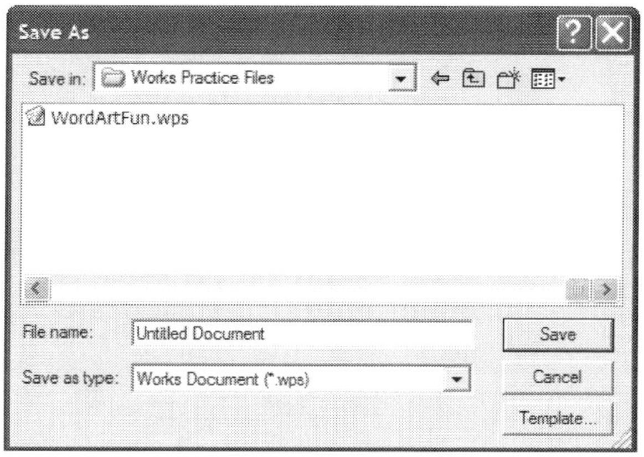

Figure 2-7 Save As dialog box

Keeping Documents Organized

Often, you may want to keep certain documents together. A good way to do that is to keep them in the same folder. Suppose you are working on a mailing for a fundraiser. You may create flyers, form letters and databases for the project. The best way to keep all of these documents together is to put them in the same folder. You will learn how to create a folder on your hard drive from inside of Works in the next exercise.

Another way to keep certain documents organized is to use the Portfolio feature, which you read about in Lesson 1.

How To Create A Folder In Works

The folder that you create in this exercise will be the one that you store all of the files in that you create in this workbook, as well as, the practice files that you will download. These files will be used as the basis for many of the exercises that you will work on.

1. Open the Word Processor.

If you have the Task Launcher open, click on the Programs link, select the Word Processor link, then click the **START A BLANK WORD PROCESSOR DOCUMENT** link.

If you do not want to create the folder under the **MY DOCUMENTS** folder, navigate to the place on your hard drive where you want to create the folder after selecting File ⇒ Open, in step 2.

2. File ⇒ Open. Click the **CREATE NEW FOLDER** button illustrated in Figure 2-8. You will see a folder named **NEW FOLDER**, as shown in Figure 2-9.

Figure 2-8 Create New Folder button illustrated

Figure 2-9 New Folder illustrated

3. With the New Folder text highlighted, type `Works Practice Files` in the field and press Enter.

Unless stated otherwise, all of the files that you create in this workbook should be saved in the folder that you just created. I will refer to this folder as "your folder" throughout the workbook.

How To Download The Practice Files To Your Hard Drive

The steps below will show you how to download the files that are used in this workbook.

1. Open your web browser and go to www.tolana.com/d/works7/index.html.

2. Right-click on the first file, Actual vs Projected and select the **SAVE TARGET AS** option if you are using Internet Explorer. If you are using a different browser, select the option that will let you save a file to your hard drive.

3. Open the **SAVE IN** drop-down list and navigate to your folder and double-click on it. The **SAVE AS** dialog box should look like the one shown in Figure 2-10. Notice that your folder is in the Save In field at the top of the dialog box.

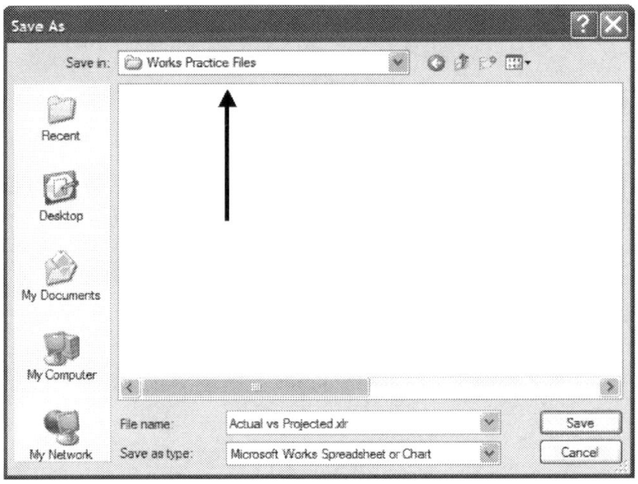

Figure 2-10 Works Practice Files folder

4. Click Save. The file will now be saved in your folder. Repeat these steps to download the remaining files on the web page. When you have downloaded all of the files, close your browser.

Check Your Settings In Works

Some of the settings in Microsoft Works will change how some of the applications look and work.
To ensure that your version of Works will look like the figures in this workbook, you should go through the steps in this section and make any changes that are needed. This is known as "Customizing the software". Make sure the options on your dialog boxes and menus match the figures.

For example, if the figure shows that the right margin is 1.25" and your dialog box shows the right margin as 2.50", change the right margin to 1.25". Don't worry, most of the settings used in this workbook are the preset defaults that are set up when Works is installed.

If you have already customized Works, you may want to write down any settings that you change.
That way when you have completed this workbook, you can put the settings back to the way you have them now.

Check Your Word Processor Settings

1. Open the Word Processor, if it is not already open. File ⇒ Page Setup. On the **MARGINS** tab, you should have the settings shown in Figure 2-11. If not, make any changes that are needed. Figure 2-12 shows the settings that should be selected on the **SOURCE, SIZE & ORIENTATION** tab.

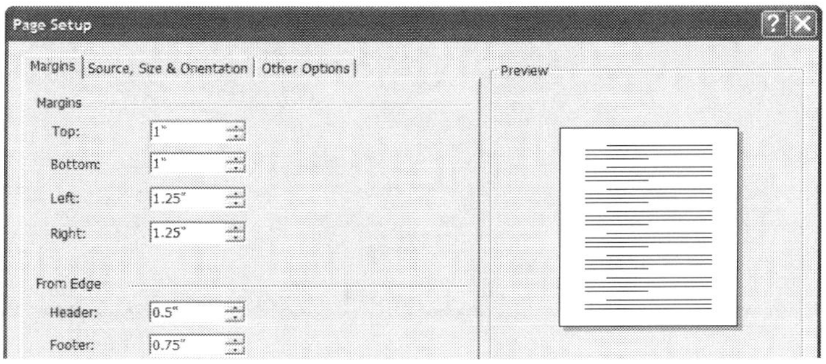

Figure 2-11 Margin settings

To change the margin size, click in the box that you want to change. Delete what's there and type in what you want. The other way to change the margin size is to click on the arrow at the end of the field to select the margin size. The options on the Margins tab determine how much available space a page will have.

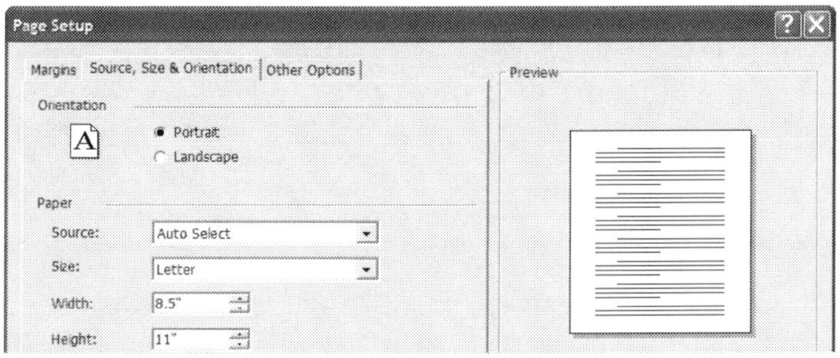

Figure 2-12 Source, Size & Orientation settings

The options on this tab let you select the size of paper that you want to print on. An example of **PORTRAIT** orientation are the pages in this workbook. The page layout shown above in the Preview section of Figure 2-12 also illustrates the portrait orientation. You can also print in **LANDSCAPE** orientation which would be turning a piece of paper on it's side, as shown in the Preview section of Figure 2-13.

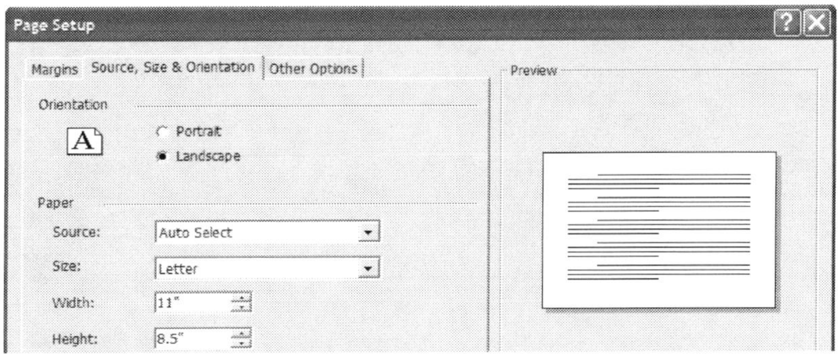

Figure 2-13 Landscape orientation illustrated

2. Figure 2-14 shows the settings that should be selected on the **OTHER OPTIONS** tab.

The options shown in Figure 2-14 allow you to override the default starting page number, header and footer settings.

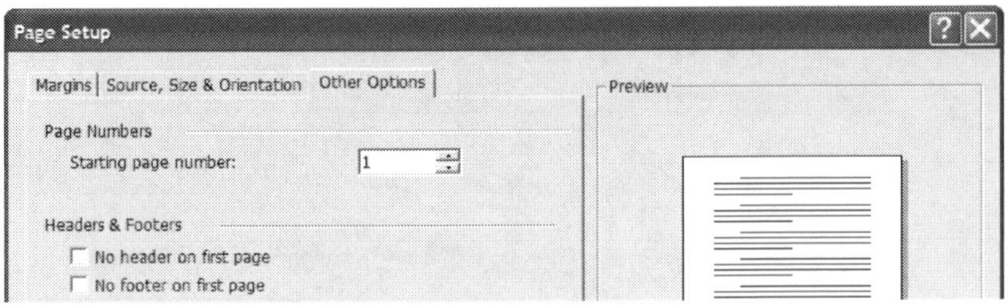

Figure 2-14 Other Options settings

3. If you made changes on any of the three tabs on the Page Setup dialog box click OK, otherwise, click Cancel.

4. Open the View menu. If there is no check mark next to the **RULER** and **STATUS BAR** options, click on the option now.

5. Open the View menu again. If the symbol in front of the option, **ALL CHARACTERS** is recessed like the Status Bar option is, click on the option to turn it off. Your View menu should look like the one shown in Figure 2-15.

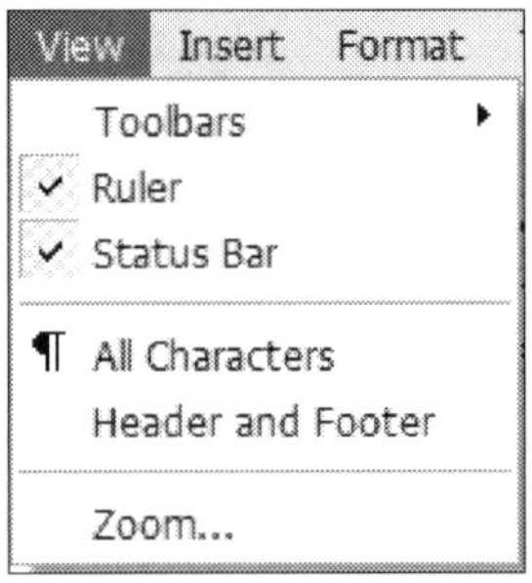

Figure 2-15 View menu options

6. Type `Qween` in a new word processing document, then click the **SPELLING AND GRAMMAR** button on the toolbar. It is the seventh button from the left on the Standard toolbar (the top toolbar). You should see the dialog box shown in Figure 2-16.

7. Click the **OPTIONS** button. If the **BACKGROUND SPELL CHECKING** option is not checked, click in the box in front of it. Your dialog box should have the options selected that are shown in Figure 2-17. Click OK.

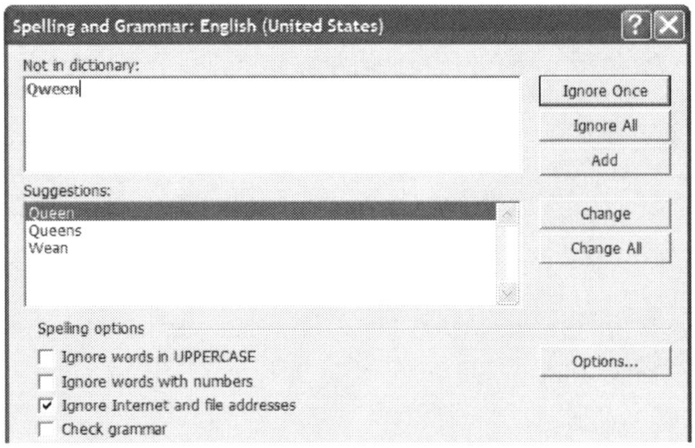

Figure 2-16 Spelling and Grammar dialog box

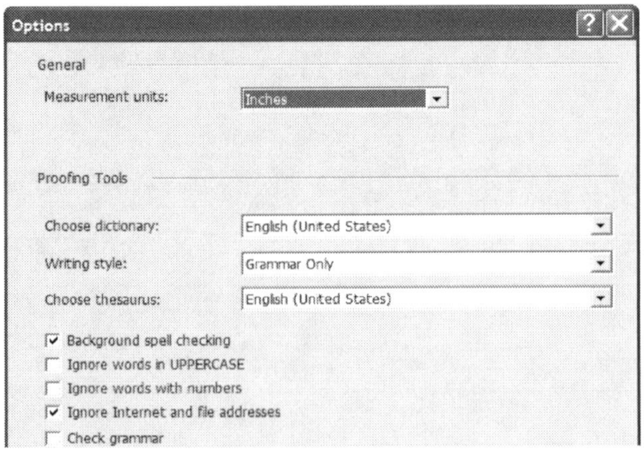

Figure 2-17 Spelling options illustrated

8. Click Close on the Spelling and Grammar dialog box. Close the document (File ⇒ Close). When prompted to save the changes, click No.

Check Your Spreadsheet Settings

Click on the **HOME** link on the Task Launcher window, then click on the Spreadsheet icon.

1. Open the Spreadsheet application. File ⇒ Page Setup. These options work the same way they do in the word processing application. The Margins tab should have the settings shown in Figure 2-18.

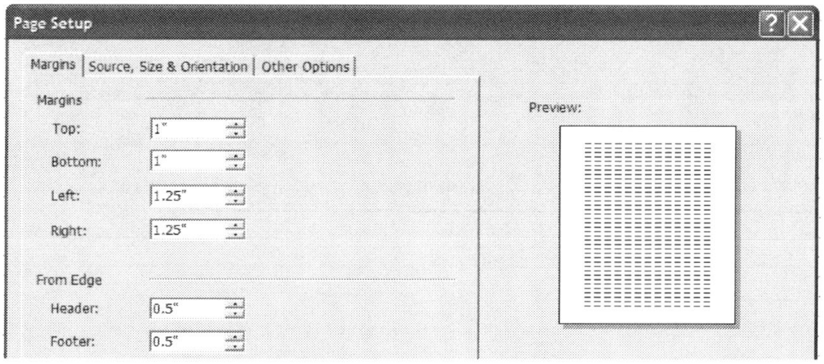

Figure 2-18 Margin settings

2. Figure 2-19 shows the settings that should be selected on the Source, Size & Orientation tab. Figure 2-20 shows the settings that should be selected on the Other Options tab. Click OK.

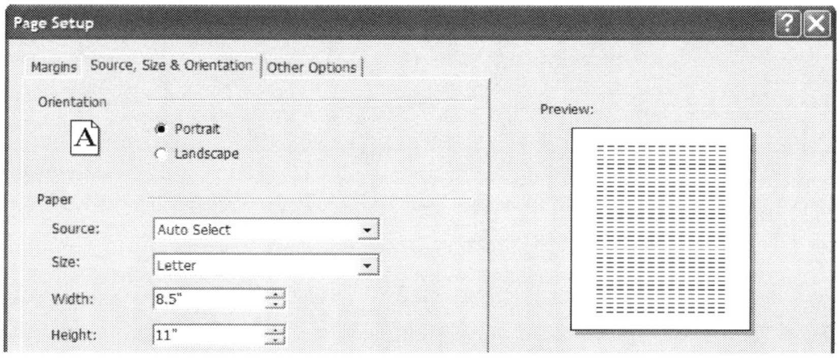

Figure 2-19 Source, Size & Orientation settings

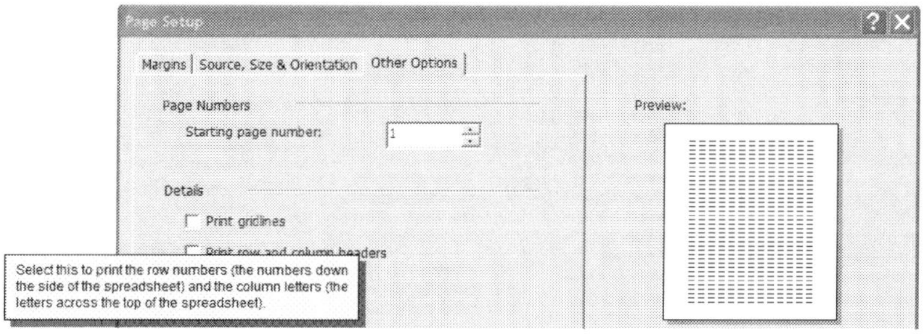

Figure 2-20 Other Options settings and Tool Tip illustrated

> If you want to find out what the **PRINT GRIDLINES** or **PRINT ROW AND COLUMN HEADERS** options mean, click on the question mark in the upper right corner of the dialog box. Then click on the option that you want to know more about. You will see a Tool Tip like the one shown above in Figure 2-20.

3. Close the Spreadsheet application (File ⇒ Exit). If asked to save the changes, click No.

Check Your Database Settings

1. Open the Database application.

   If you open the database application from the Database icon on the **HOME** page, you will see the dialog box shown in Figure 2-21. For this exercise, select the **BLANK DATABASE** option, then click OK. If you open the database application from the **PROGRAMS** link, a new database will open automatically.

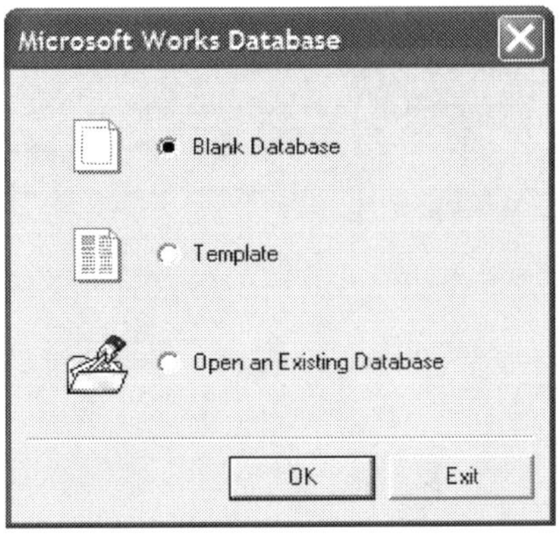

Figure 2-21 Database options when opened from the Home page of the Task Launcher

2. Click the **ADD** button shown in Figure 2-22, then click Done.

3. File ⇒ Page Setup. Figure 2-20 shown earlier, shows the settings that should be selected on the Other Options tab. Click OK.

4. Tools ⇒ Options. Figure 2-23 shows the settings that should be selected on the General tab.

5. Figure 2-24 shows the settings that should be selected on the View tab.
   Figure 2-25 shows the settings that should be selected on the Data Entry tab.

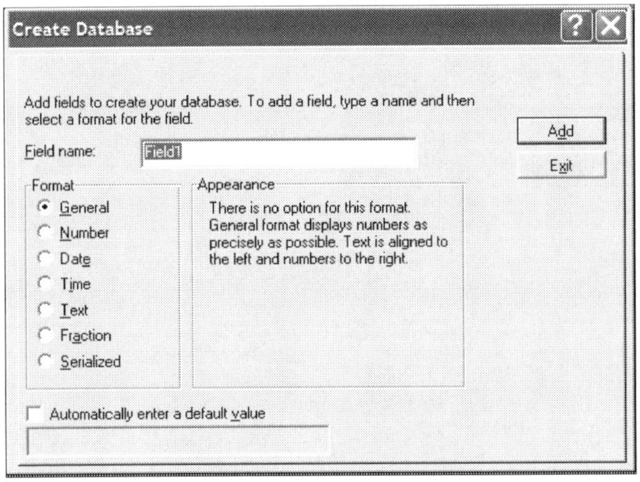

Figure 2-22 Create Database dialog box

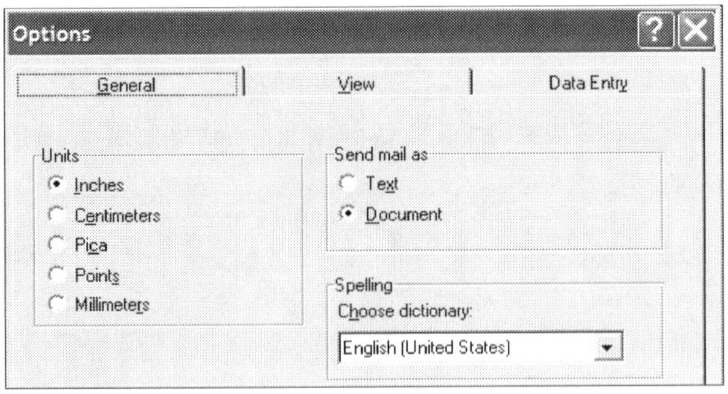

Figure 2-23 General tab options

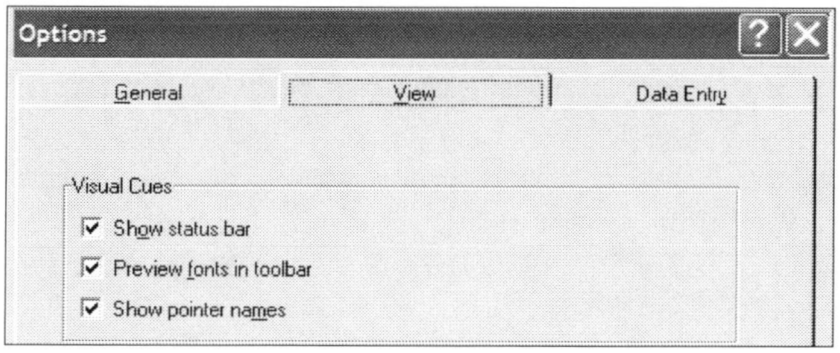

Figure 2-24 View tab options

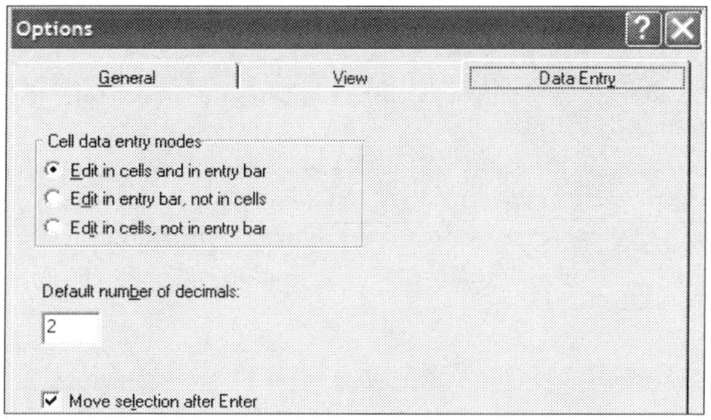

Figure 2-25 Data Entry tab options

6. Click OK, then close the database application, but do not save the changes.

Customizing The Task Launcher

There aren't many options available to customize the Task Launcher.

1. Click on the Home page link on the Task Launcher, then click the **CUSTOMIZE** link. Your dialog box should have the settings shown in Figure 2-26. If not, make any changes that are needed and click OK.

If checked, the **TRACK HISTORY** option causes the files that you open or create to appear on the History page that you saw earlier in Lesson 1 in Figure 1-30.

If you want to remove all of the files that are displayed on the History page, click the **CLEAR HISTORY** button shown in Figure 2-26. This button only removes the files from the History page. It does not delete the actual files off of your computers hard drive.

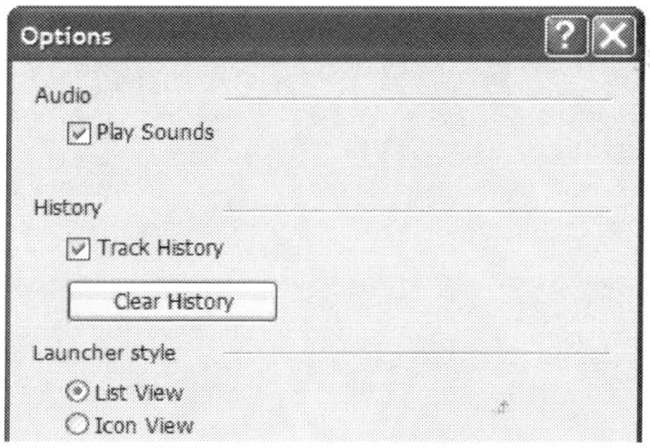

Figure 2-26 Task Launcher customize options

NEW The Icon View

This new Task Launcher view will allow you to display icons on the right side of the pages in the Task Launcher instead of links. Figure 2-27 is an example of the Icon view.

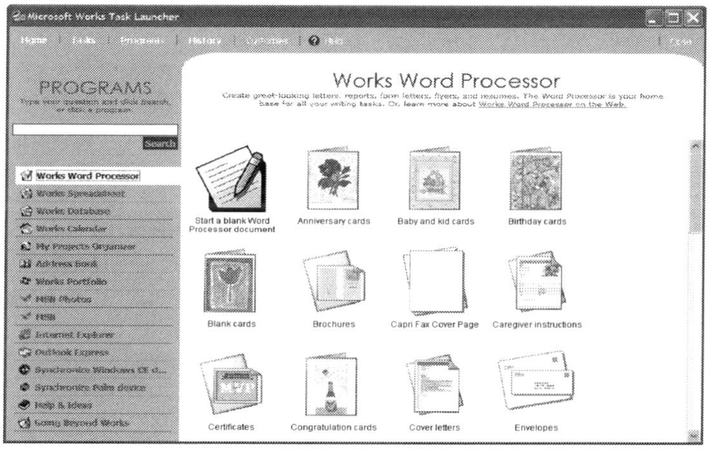

Figure 2-27 Icon view of the Programs page

The Help System

The Help System is quite extensive in Works. Many topics provide step by step instructions, which should be very helpful.

1. To start the Help System from the Task Launcher, click the **HELP** link at the top of any page in the Task Launcher and select **MICROSOFT WORKS HELP**. The Help System will open on the right side of the window that you have open, as shown in Figure 2-28.

> Note the Question Mark illustrated at the top of Figure 2-28. This question mark will open the Help System for the application that you have open at the time that you click on it. Even though each application has its own help system, they all work the same.

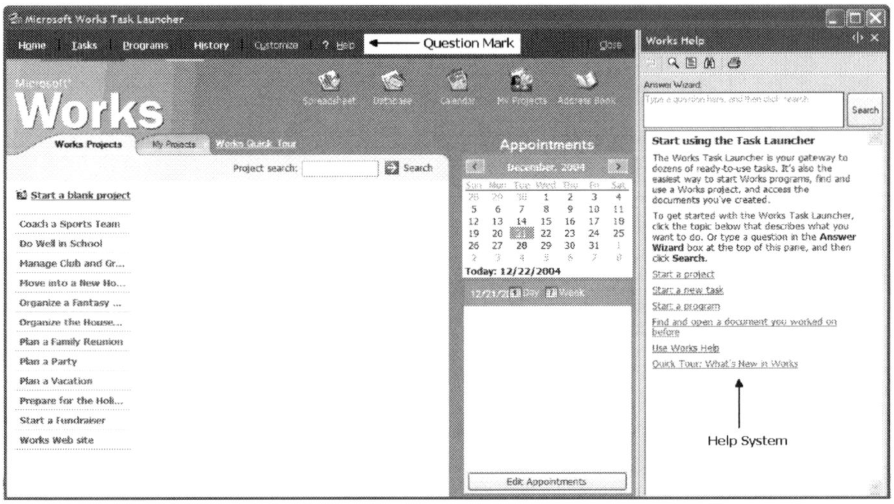

Figure 2-28 Works Help system illustrated

There are five buttons at the top of the Help System portion of the window. The toolbar buttons shown in Figure 2-29 are explained below.

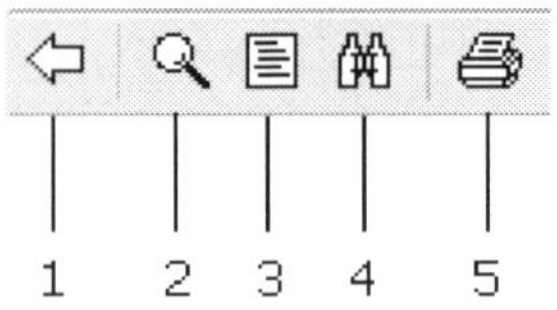

Figure 2-29 Help System toolbar buttons

① The **BACK** button takes you back to previous windows that you viewed. This option is only available after you have viewed at least two help topics.
② The **ANSWER WIZARD** button allows you to type in a question and retrieve documents that are related to your question. It may be me, but I don't find this feature all that helpful. The Answer Wizard is different from the Search field on the Tasks and Programs windows. The Answer Wizard does not locate tasks, it searches the Help database.
③ The **CONTENTS** button will display the table of contents of the help system for the application that you currently have open. For example, if you click the Contents button while in the Task Launcher, you will see the Table of Contents shown in Figure 2-30. If you click the Contents button in the Database application, you will see the Table of Contents shown in Figure 2-31.
④ The **INDEX** button will let you type in the topic that you want help on. The topics that match what you enter will be displayed in the **TOPICS FOUND** section, as shown in Figure 2-32. When you click on an option shown at the bottom of Figure 2-32, you will be taken to that topic.
⑤ The **PRINT** button will print the help topic that is displayed.

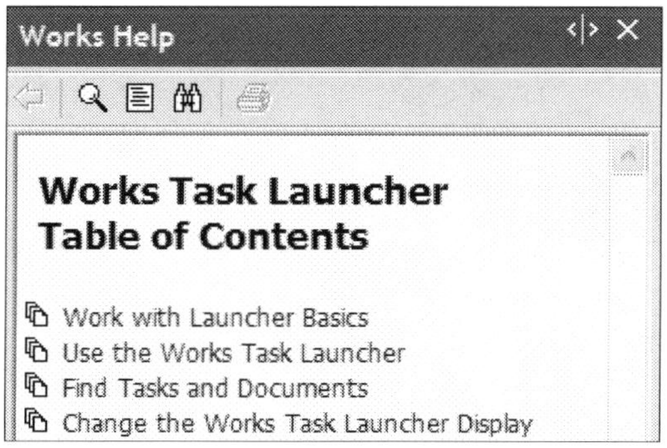

Figure 2-30 Table of Contents for the task launcher

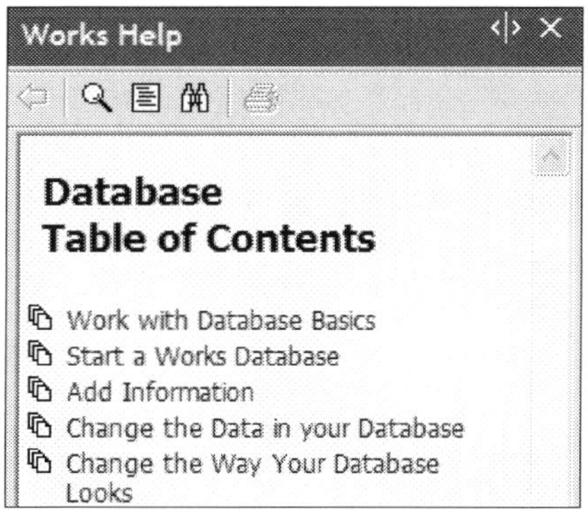

Figure 2-31 Table of Contents for the database application

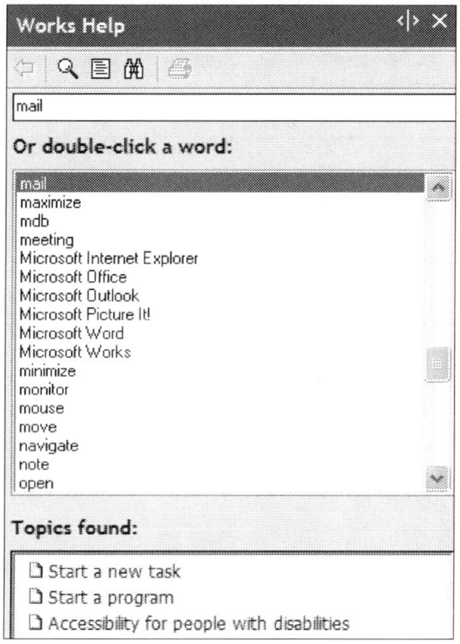

Figure 2-32 Help topics index window

2. Select the category that is closest to what you are looking for. You will then see a list of topics as shown in Figure 2-33.

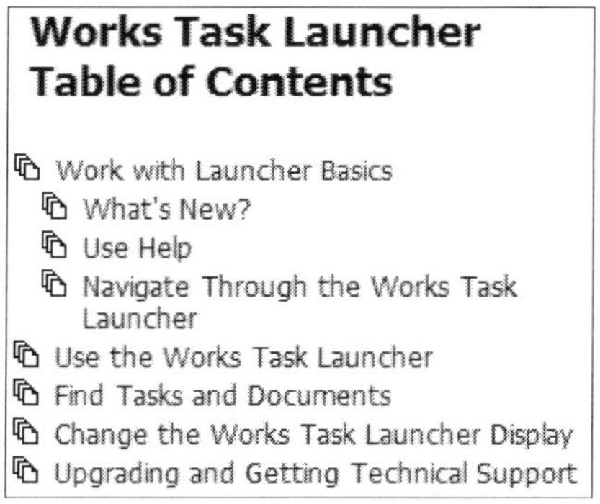

Figure 2-33 Task Launcher help topics

Help System Options

The **RESIZE HELP** button, which is across from the words "Works Help" in Figure 2-34, will let you change the size of the Help section in the application window. You may want to do this when you want more room in the window for the document that you are working on.

If you place the cursor in the position illustrated in Figure 2-34 (where you see the double arrow on the left), you can also resize the help window. Click the **RESIZE HELP** button again to restore the help window to it's original size.

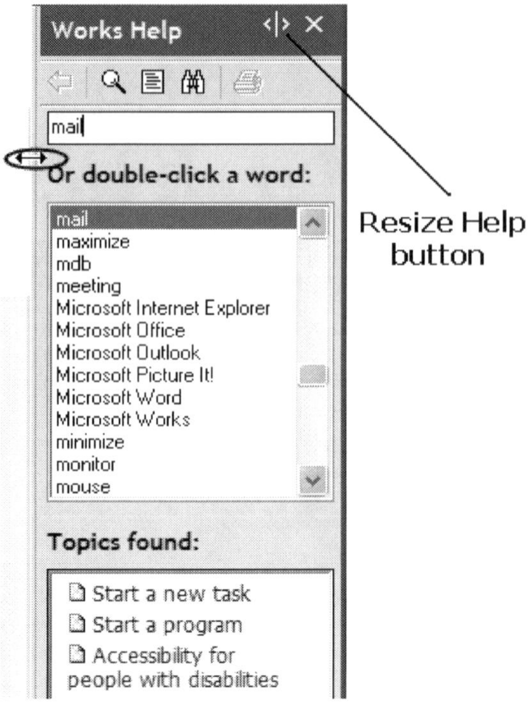

Figure 2-34 Help window made smaller

How To Use The Help System

1. Open the Word Processor, then click the **CONTENTS** button on the Help window. Click on the second option, Start a Works Word Processor Document as shown in Figure 2-35.

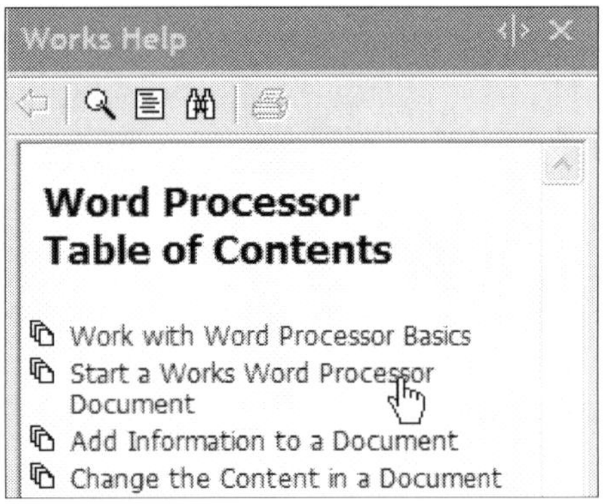

Figure 2-35 Help option selected

2. Click on the first option Open A Document, then click on the topic, **OPEN AN EXISTING DOCUMENT**. You should see the help topic shown in Figure 2-36.

Step-by-step instructions are displayed that will show you how to open an existing document.

Below the instructions, you will see a section called **RELATED TOPICS**. These are topics that may also help you complete the same task. If you click on a link in the **RELATED TOPICS** section, you will be taken to that topic.

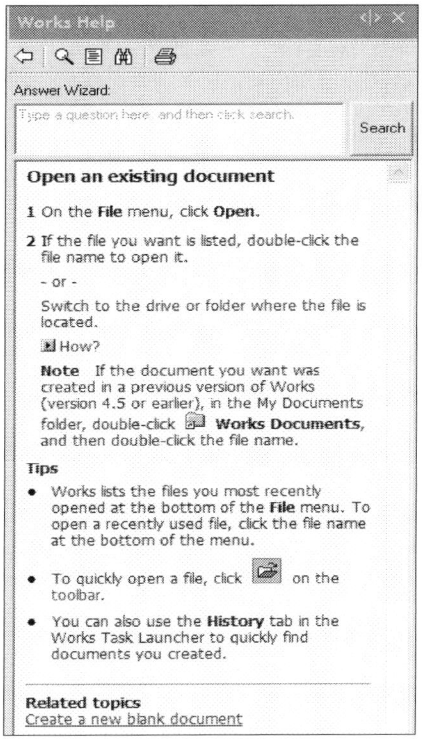

Figure 2-36 Help topic selected

3. Close the word processing application.

Backing Up Your Work

I cannot stress how important it is to save and back up your work frequently. Doing so will save you frustration in the event a power failure occurs, or if your computer freezes, or if you have a hardware failure. The majority of times that you lose work, it can't be recovered or if it can, it may cost you a few hundred dollars to recover it.

If you aren't already, you should also be saving your work to an external source like a CD, DVD, external hard drive or USB drive. Windows has a backup utility that you can use. I tell my students this and it never fails that in each class, at least one student loses some, if not all of their work. Don't say that I didn't warn you <smile>.

Other Sources Of Help

Below are additional sources of help if you have a question about Works.

Works Home Page

The link below is for the home page for Microsoft Works. From time to time, you may want to visit the web site to see if there are any software updates available. You can also download templates, <yes, they are free> sign up for the Works newsletter and more.

http://www.microsoft.com/products/works/default.mspx

Getting Started Manual

To read the Getting Started manual that is on your hard drive, you need the free Adobe Reader. Works should have installed the Adobe Reader if is wasn't already on your hard drive. If not, you can download it from http://www.adobe.com/products/acrobat/readstep2.html. Once you download the file, double-click on it to install the free reader. You can download the installation file and save it on your desktop to make it easier to find. To access the Getting Started manual, open the Help menu on any Task Launcher window and select Getting Started.

Newsgroups

If you have questions that you can't find the answer to in the help system, the newsgroup for Works should help you get an answer to your question. There are newsgroups on the Internet that are specifically for Works. The most popular one is listed below. You will be able to post questions and receive answers. You will also learn how other people are living with and using Works.

The newsgroup host is **MSNEWS.MICROSOFT.COM**.
The name of the newsgroup is **MICROSOFT.PUBLIC.WORKS.WIN**.

You will need to have a newsgroup reader like the one in Microsoft Outlook Express installed to use the newsgroups. You can also access the newsgroups online at Microsoft's web site. The web site address is http://www.microsoft.com/communities/newsgroups/default.mspx.

Using Email Software To Access The Newsgroups

Many people prefer to use email software like Outlook Express (which you already have on your computer), that has a newsgroup reader to access the newsgroups instead of logging on to a website to access them. If you want to do this, the link below provides instructions for setting up Outlook Express to use newsgroups. Don't worry, its not painful to set up.

http://www.microsoft.com/communities/guide/newsgroups.mspx

> If you plan to participate in newsgroups either from the web site or using software like Outlook Express, you should not use your real email address. Most people that use their real email address suddenly start receiving a lot of spam email. My advise is to set up a free email account. If your ISP offers multiple email accounts, you can create another account under your primary account and use that one for newsgroups.

Test Your Skills

1. What dialog box would you open to change the margins?

2. What does File ⇒ Save As do?

3. How do you clear the items on the History Page?

WIZARDS AND TEMPLATES

Earlier in this workbook I said that you could access all of the components of Works from the Task Launcher. This includes the wizards and templates.

In this lesson you will walk through some of the wizards that come with Works. Wizards prompt you through creating the "layout" of a document. When you get the layout the way that you want it, you can save it as a template. If you save the file as a template, you will not have to use the wizard again to create the same layout.

The wizards covered in this lesson are some of the ones that you may want to use. You will learn how to create the following:

- ☑ Mailing labels
- ☑ Fax cover page
- ☑ Brochure
- ☑ Newsletter
- ☑ Weekly planner
- ☑ Conventional mortgage worksheet
- ☑ Monthly home budget
- ☑ Video/DVD collection

How To Create Mailing Labels

The mailing labels that you will create in this exercise will use names and addresses from a database. There are three types of labels that you can create as discussed below.

① **MULTIPLE-ENTRY LABELS** let you type in the names and addresses or whatever information you want on each label. This is a free form type of label.

② **RETURN ADDRESS LABELS** let you create an entire sheet of labels with the same information on each label. You can also use this type of label for something other than a return addresses.

③ **MAILING LABELS** let you create labels based on information that is stored in a spreadsheet or database. To use this option you need to have the names and addresses already entered in a spreadsheet or database.

An option that I wish were included in the label utility is the ability to print on specific labels on the sheet. This would be useful when you have some labels on a sheet that were left over from a previous label printing task because it would keep you from wasting labels. I have seen this feature in other label printing tools, so I know that it is possible.

1. Open the Task Launcher if it is not already open, then click on the **TASKS** link.

2. Select the Letters & Labels category. You should see the window shown in Figure 3-1. Click on the **MAILING LABELS** task, then click the **START THIS TASK** link.

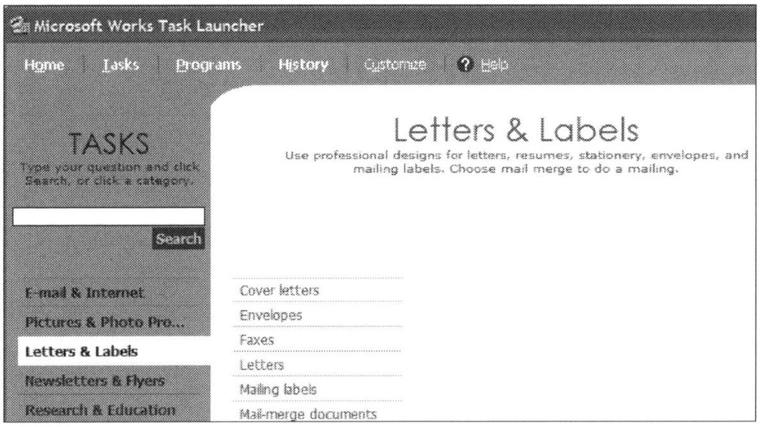

Figure 3-1 Letters & Labels category

3. On the Labels dialog box select the **MAILING LABELS** option illustrated in Figure 3-2, then click OK.

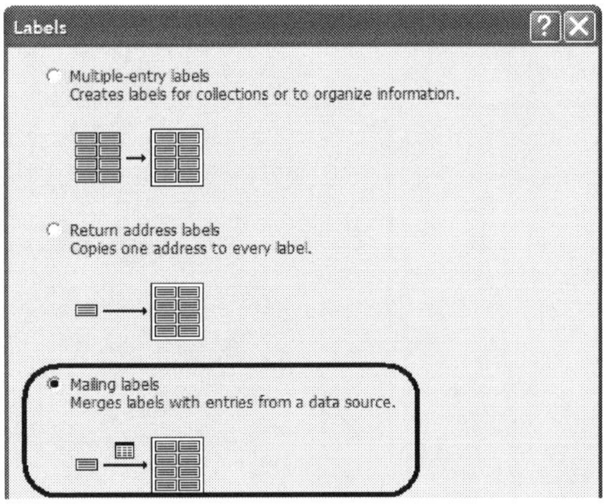

Figure 3-2 Labels dialog box

Label Setting Options

The Label Settings dialog box has the following options:

① The **PRINTER INFORMATION** option lets you select the type of printer that you will use to print the labels.
② The **LABEL PRODUCTS** option lets you select the brand of labels that you want to use. The default label brand is Avery. I remember a time when the only options were Avery and custom. All of the other label brands printed the Avery equivalent on their boxes of labels so that people would know which Avery label size to select. I'm happy to see that other brands of labels are now included in the list.
③ The **PRODUCT NUMBER** is based on the brand of label that you select. If you open the Label Products drop-down list and select a different brand of labels, you will see the options in the Product Number list change. When you select the product number, the dimensions of the label will appear to the right of the Product Number list, as shown in Figure 3-3.
④ The **CUSTOM** button allows you to create a custom sized label. I have never had to use this option and there is a good chance that you won't either. If you want to see what the custom options look like, you can click the Custom button now. You will see the dialog box shown in Figure 3-4.

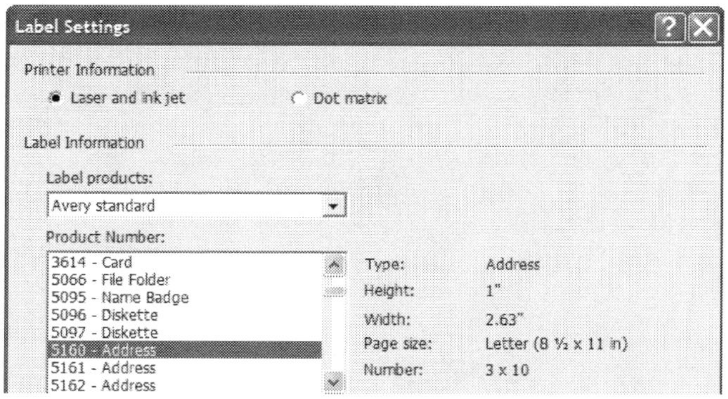

Figure 3-3 Label dimensions illustrated

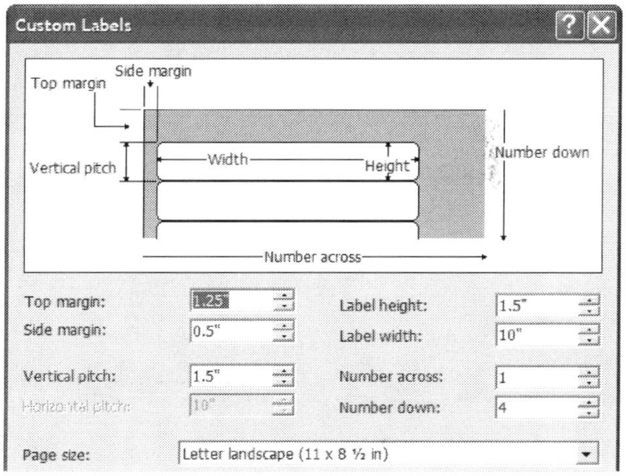

Figure 3-4 Custom label options

Select The Label Settings

1. The first step is to select the type of printer that you will use. If the **LASER AND INK JET** option is not selected, select it now.

2. The second step is to select the brand of labels that you will use. Select **AVERY STANDARD**, if it is not already selected.

3. The third step is to select a label size. Scroll down the Product Number list and select **5160 - ADDRESS**. Your dialog box should have the options selected that were shown earlier in Figure 3-3.

Select The Data Source

The data source is the file that you will use to get the names and addresses from to print on the labels. You can get the names and addresses for the mailing labels from your electronic address book, a spreadsheet or a Works database. In this exercise, the data is stored in a Works database.

If the data source that you are using had a thousand names and addresses and you only wanted to print labels for a subset of the names in the data source, you would create a filter that would only print labels for the names that meet the criteria of the filter. You will learn how to create filters later in the workbook.

1. Click the **NEW DOCUMENT** button. You will see the dialog box shown in Figure 3-5.

As the name of the dialog box suggests, you will select the file that has the names and addresses that you want to print labels for. The address book that is referenced in Figure 3-5, is the one associated with the email software that you are using.

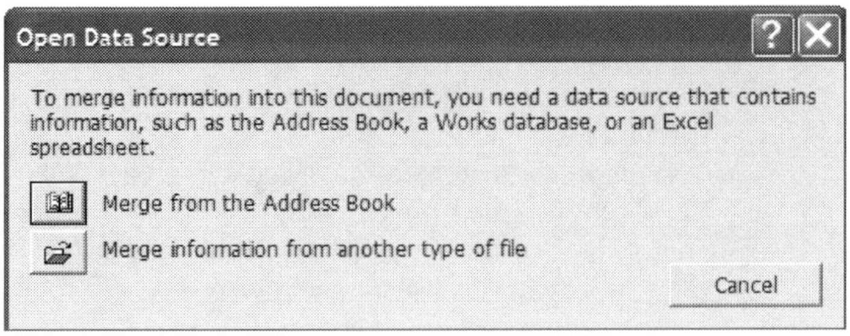

Figure 3-5 Open Data Source dialog box

2. Click the **MERGE INFORMATION FROM ANOTHER TYPE OF FILE** button.

3. On the Open Data Source dialog box, open the **LOOK IN** drop-down list and double-click on your folder. Your dialog box should display the databases shown in Figure 3-6. Double-click on the Customers Database file. You will see the dialog box shown in Figure 3-7.

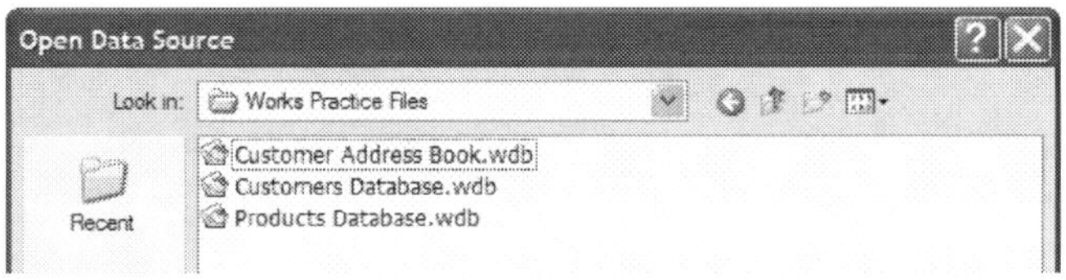

Figure 3-6 Database files in the Works Practice Files folder

Select The Fields To Print On The Label

The fields shown in Figure 3-7 are in the database that you selected. You do not have to select all of the fields. You only select the fields that you want to print on the label.

You can double-click on a field in the dialog box or select the field, then click the Insert button to add the field to the document.

Don't boo me, but in previous versions of Works there was a **NEW LINE** button that would move the cursor to a new line on the label. Why it was removed, I don't know.

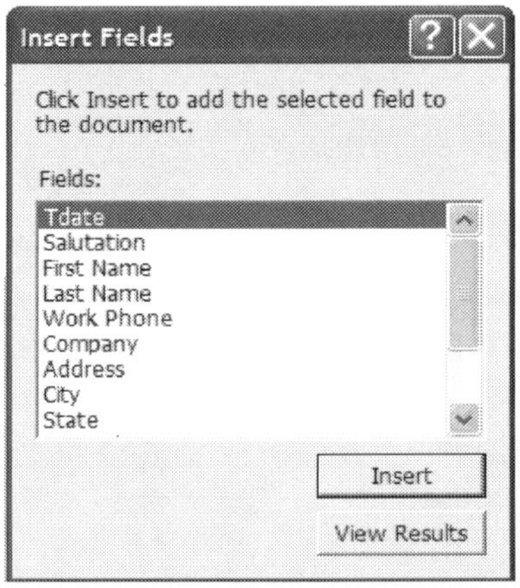

Figure 3-7 Insert Fields dialog box

1. Add the First Name field to the document. The First Name field should now be in the label template on the left side of the document on the screen.

2. Add the Last Name field. Place the cursor after the Last Name field on the label template, if it is not already there, then press the Shift and Enter keys. The cursor should now be on a new line.

3. Add the Address field. Move the cursor to a new line on the label document and add the City field to the label.

4. Type a comma after the City field, then press the space bar. This will cause a space to be printed after the comma and before the State field.

5. Add the State and Zip Code fields to the same line that the City field is on. Don't forget to add a space between the State and Zip Code fields.

6. Go back and add a space between the First and Last name fields. Your label layout should look like the one shown in Figure 3-8.

«First Name» «Last Name»
«Address»
«City», «State» «Zip Code»

Figure 3-8 Label layout completed

View The Labels

1. Click the **VIEW RESULTS** button on the Insert Fields dialog box. You should see the label for Tina Jones, as shown in Figure 3-9.

Tina Jones
30 Long St
Ft Laud, FL 32991

Figure 3-9 Label for Tina Jones

2. Click the right arrow button on the View Results dialog box shown in Figure 3-10, to view data from the next record.

To me, what would really be cool is if you could preview an entire sheet of labels here. You could do this in previous versions of Works. For the life of me, I can't figure out why they took this feature away. What's also missing in my opinion, is a graceful way to close the View Results and Insert Fields dialog boxes. Did you notice that neither of these dialog boxes has an OK or Close button?

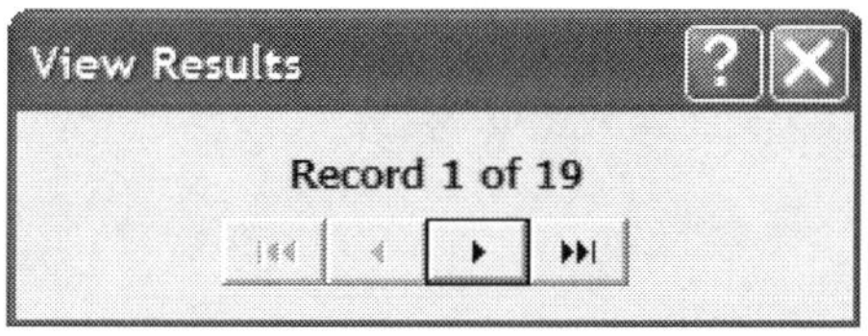

Figure 3-10 View Results database navigator dialog box

3. When you are finished viewing the labels, click on the X in the upper right corner of the View Results dialog box to close it, then click on the X in the upper right corner of the Insert Fields dialog box to close it.

You just viewed the names and addresses one by one. You can view all of the labels by clicking the **PRINT PREVIEW** button on the toolbar.

4. Click the Print Preview button. Your label document should look like the one shown in Figure 3-11. If you needed to, you can make changes right on the label document. You can also add things like a graphic or logo to the labels.

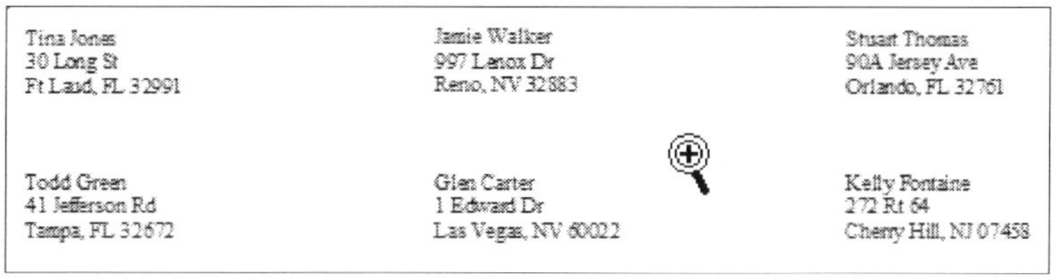

Figure 3-11 Labels in print preview with the cursor in magnify mode

5. Place the mouse pointer over the labels. The pointer will change to a magnifying glass with an X in it, as shown above in Figure 3-11. Click on the labels document to make the page larger.

6. Click the labels document again to return the page to its original size, then click the Close button.

   Another way to make the labels appear larger or smaller in the Print Preview window is to open the **ZOOM** drop-down list shown in Figure 3-12 and select a different size.

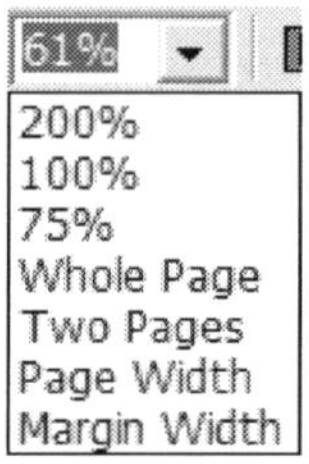

Figure 3-12 Zoom drop-down list

Save The Label Document

1. Click Save and navigate to your folder.

2. Type `Customers Labels` in the File name field, as shown in Figure 3-13, then press Enter or click Save.

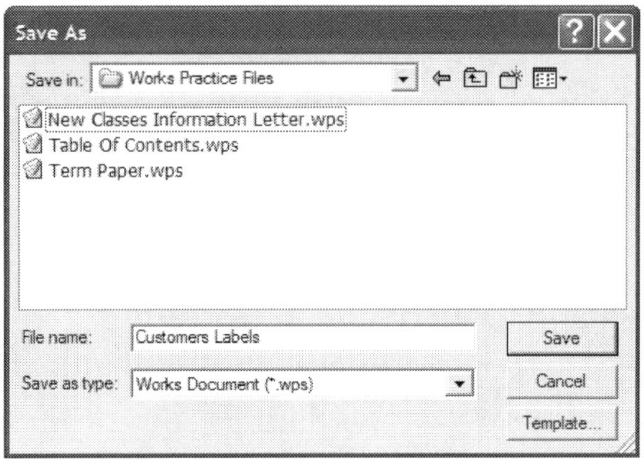

Figure 3-13 Save As dialog box

How To Test The Labels For Printing

If you need to test the labels, it is probably a good idea to print the test labels on a sheet of paper instead of using a sheet of labels. Once you print the test labels on paper, hold the paper up to the sheet of labels to make sure that they are lined up correctly.

1. Click the Print button if you want to print the labels. Make sure that your printer is on.

2. When you are finished printing the labels or are finished viewing the document, close it and save the changes if prompted.

Create A Fax Cover Page

In this exercise you will create a fax cover page using a wizard.

1. Open the Task Launcher. (There should be an icon for it on the Taskbar at the bottom of the screen.)

2. Click on the Tasks link, then click on the Letters & Labels category.

3. Click on the Faxes link, then click on the Start this task link.

4. Click on the Yellow Circles Fax Sheet layout shown in Figure 3-14. This is the only option that you have to select to create a fax cover page from the wizard. Click Finish. You will see the Fax cover page shown in Figure 3-15.

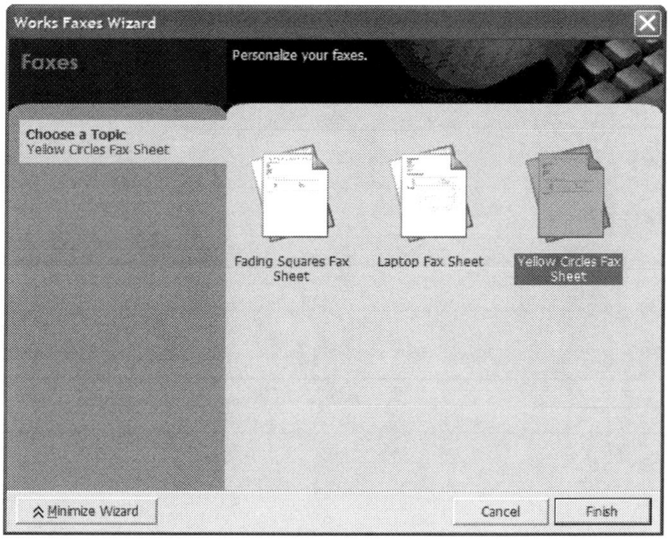

Figure 3-14 Fax Wizard

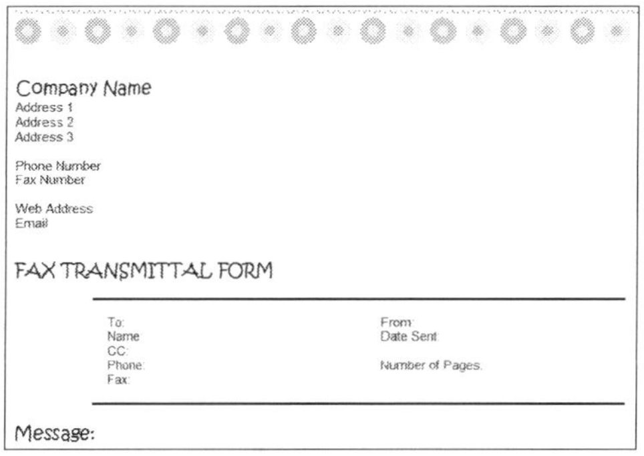

Figure 3-15 Fax cover page

Modify The Fax Cover Page

You could use the fax cover page as it is shown above in Figure 3-15, but it would be more efficient if you saved your information on the fax cover page and created a template. That way, every time you use the fax cover page, you will not have to enter this information when you need to create a new fax cover page document.

1. Highlight the words **COMPANY NAME** in the document and type `Capri Book Company`.

2. Highlight the company name and open the font drop-down list and select Tahoma. If you do not have this font, select a different one.

3. Highlight the Address 1 field and type `320 Main Street`, then highlight the Address 2 field and type `Laurel, CT 06868`.

4. Delete the Address 3 field. Add the phone number, fax number, web address and email address information shown in Figure 3-16 to the document.

Figure 3-16 Information to add to the fax cover page document

5. Click to the right of the **FROM** field and press the space bar, then type your name across from the word **FROM**. This would be a good time to save the fax cover page as a template, which you will do in the next exercise.

Save The Fax Cover Page As A Template

1. File ⇒ Save As or click the **SAVE** button on the toolbar.

2. Open the **SAVE AS TYPE** drop-down list at the bottom of the dialog box and select Works Template, as shown in Figure 3-17.

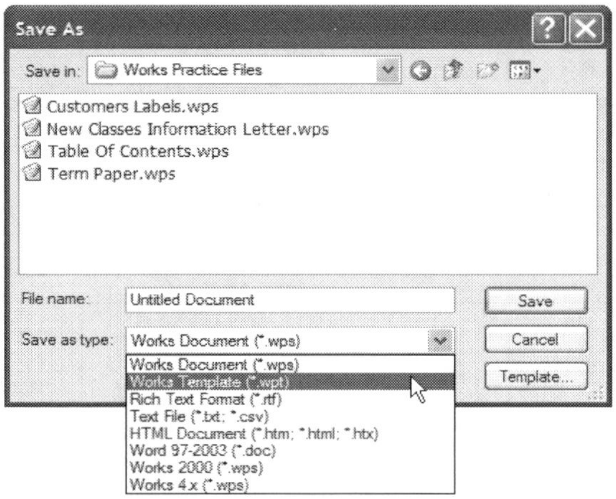

Figure 3-17 Save As Type drop-down list options illustrated

3. Open the **SAVE IN** drop-down list at the top of the dialog box and navigate to your folder, if it is not already displayed in the field. Type `Capri Fax Cover Page` in the File name field, then click Save.

4. File ⇒ Close. The Task Launcher window should be visible. If not, click on the Task Launcher button at the bottom of the screen. Click on the **PERSONAL TEMPLATES** option. You should see the Capri Fax Cover Page template as illustrated in Figure 3-18.

If you have created other templates you will also see them in the Personal Templates section.

If you open the Capri Fax Cover Page template, you will see that all of the information that you added to the template is already filled in for you.

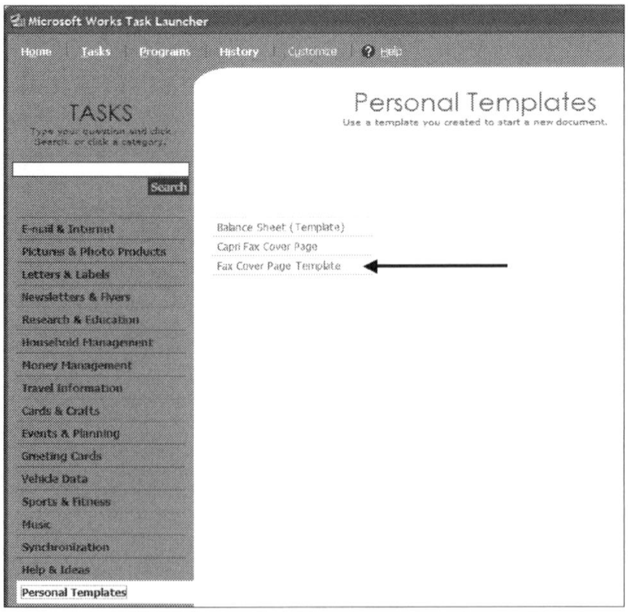

Figure 3-18 Personal Templates

You do not have to save any of the templates in the rest of this lesson unless specifically instructed to do so. If you want to customize a template, save it in your folder. Otherwise, close the document after completing the last step of each template exercise.

Create A Tri-Fold Brochure

1. If the Task Launcher is not already open, open it now and click on the Newsletters & Flyers task.
2. Click on the Brochures wizard, then click on the Start this task link.
3. Click on the **TRI-FOLD COOKING** layout, then click the Finish button. You should see the brochure template shown in Figure 3-19. You can add content to the brochure.

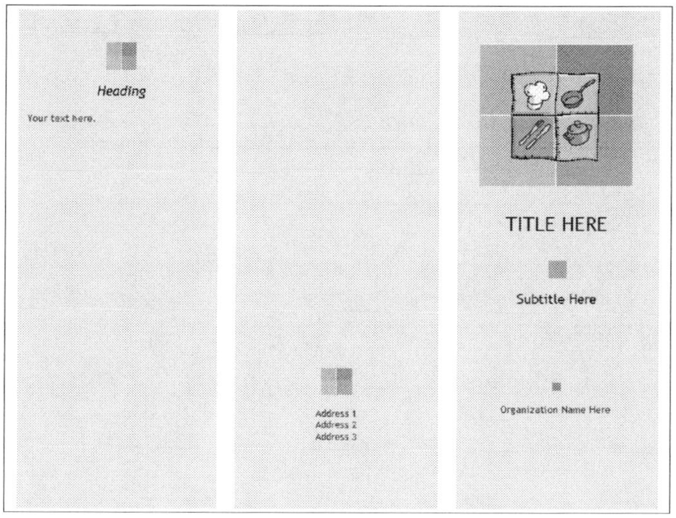

Figure 3-19 Brochure template

Create A Newsletter

1. If the Task Launcher is not already open, open it now and click on the Newsletters & Flyers task.
2. Click on the Newsletters wizard, then click on the Start this task link.
3. Select the first **2 COLUMN WIDE NEWSLETTER** layout in the second row, then click the Finish button. You should see the newsletter template shown in Figure 3-20. From here you can add content to the newsletter and modify the layout if needed.

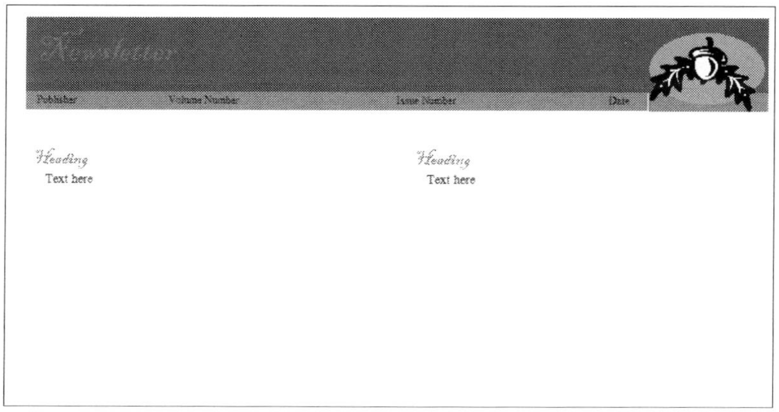

Figure 3-20 Newsletter template

Create A Weekly Planner

A weekly planner is like a to-do list.

1. If the Task Launcher is not already open, open it now and click on the **HOUSEHOLD MANAGEMENT** task.
2. Click on the **CHORES AND ERRANDS LISTS** wizard, then click on the Start this task link.
3. Scroll down and select the Weekly Planner layout, then click Finish. You should see the spreadsheet shown in Figure 3-21.

   You can print the weekly planner and hand-write the items in or type the items in and then print it.

Figure 3-21 Weekly planner template

Create A Conventional Mortgage Worksheet

1. If the Task Launcher is not already open, open it now and click on the **MONEY MANAGEMENT** task.
2. Click on the **FINANCIAL WORKSHEETS** wizard, then click on the Start this task link.
3. Select the Conventional Mortgage Qualification option, then click Finish. You should see the spreadsheet shown in Figure 3-22.

> If you enter the information in the worksheet, you will be able to determine the maximum mortgage amount that you qualify for and what you can spend per month on a mortgage payment.

Create A Monthly Home Budget

If you started filling out the mortgage spreadsheet in the previous exercise, but couldn't fill in some of the information, the monthly home budget that you will create now may help you.

1. If the Task Launcher is not already open, open it now and click on the Money Management task.
2. Click on the Financial Worksheets wizard, then click on the Start this task link.
3. Select the Monthly Home Budget option, then click Finish. You should see the spreadsheet shown in Figure 3-23.

> If you enter the information in the worksheet, you will be able to determine what your monthly expenses are and see where your money is going.

Create A Video/DVD Collection Database

1. If the Task Launcher is not already open, open it now and click on the Household Management task.

2. Click on the Home Inventory Worksheets wizard, then click on the Start this task link.

3. Select the Video/DVD Collection option, then click Finish. You should see the database shown in Figure 3-24.

4. Save this database in your folder. Type `Movie Collection` as the database name. Close the database.

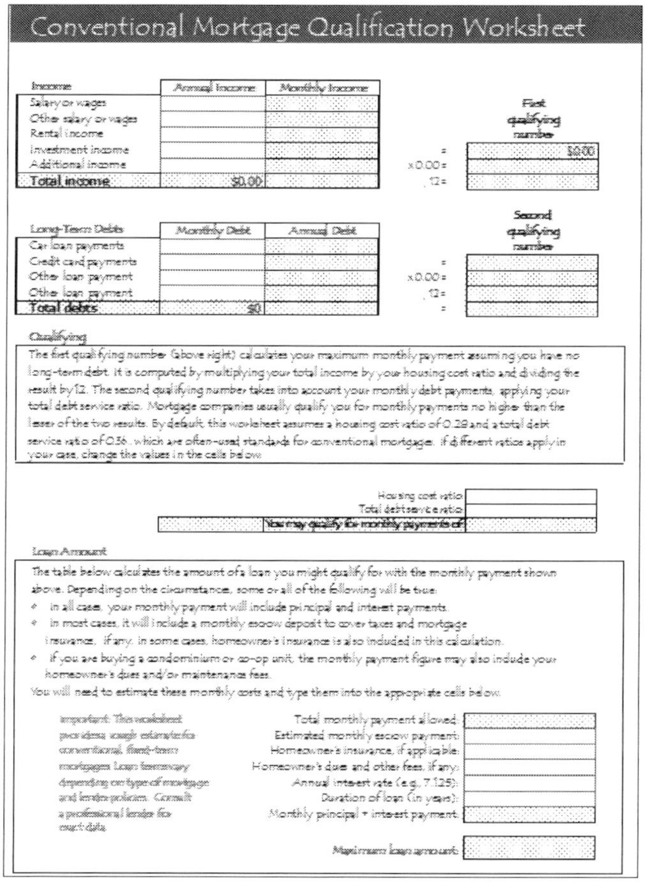

Figure 3-22 Mortgage qualification worksheet template

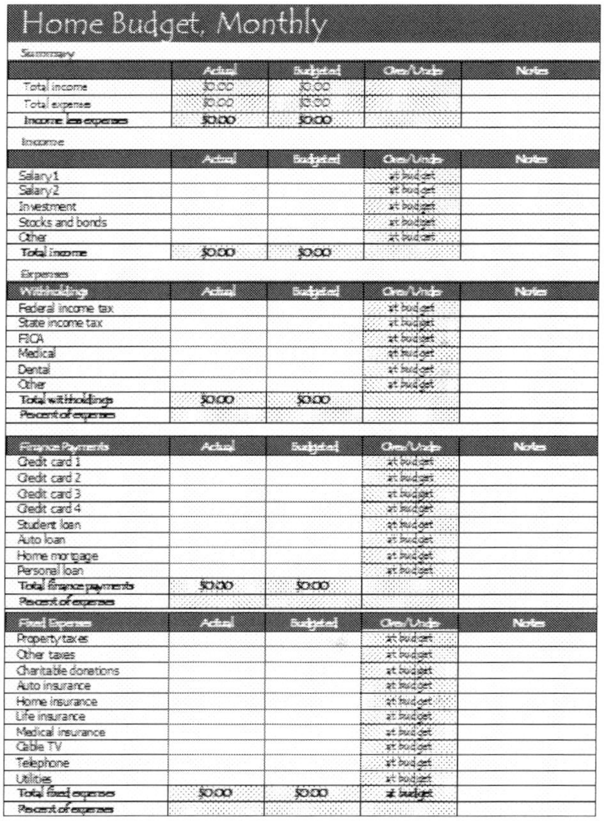

Figure 3-23 Monthly home budget worksheet template

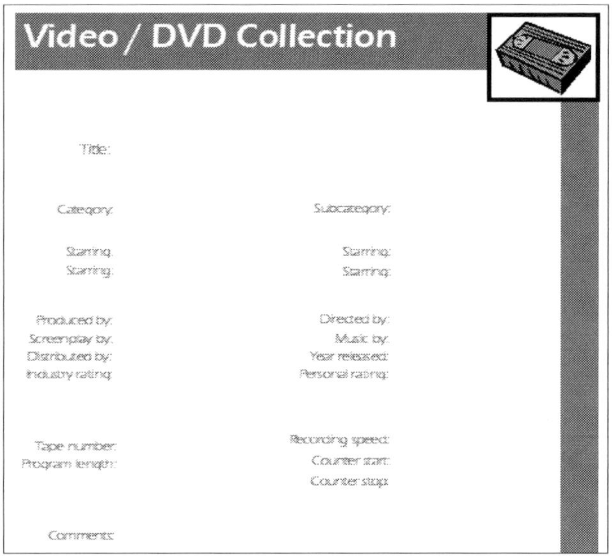

Figure 3-24 Video/DVD Collection database template

Wizards and templates provide the foundation for you to create documents faster with more consistency. The advantage that templates have over wizards in my opinion, is that templates do not ask you to select any options.

Test Your Skills

1. List two options for data sources for mailing labels.
2. How can you view data while creating labels?
3. What Task category has the mailing label wizard?

WORD PROCESSING BASICS

In this lesson you will learn basic word processing formatting techniques including the following:

- ☑ Changing the margins
- ☑ Changing fonts
- ☑ How to bold and underline words
- ☑ How to create a bulleted list
- ☑ Using the Format Gallery
- ☑ Spell check a document
- ☑ Using grammar check
- ☑ Printing options

As you go through the exercises, you may find it helpful to keep the History page of the Task Launcher open at all times. Doing this will allow you faster access to many of the files needed to complete the exercises.

LESSON 4

Word Processing Menus And Toolbars

You should familiarize yourself with the word processing menu and toolbars. If you want, you can open the word processing application to follow along. Table 4-1 explains the word processing menu options.

Menu	Purpose
File	Open, save, create and print files.
Edit	Modifying documents.
View	Change how the document is displayed on the screen.
Insert	Add page numbers, charts and other objects to the document.
Format	Change fonts, add borders and columns to documents.
Tools	Spell checking and the thesaurus. Create envelopes, labels and form letters.
Table	Create tables like this one.
Help	Opens the Help system.

Table 4-1 Word processing menu options explained

Formatting Toolbar

In Lesson 2, you learned about the first 13 buttons on the Formatting toolbar that are common to the word processing, spreadsheet and database applications. You also learned that these 13 buttons are on two toolbars in the word processing application.

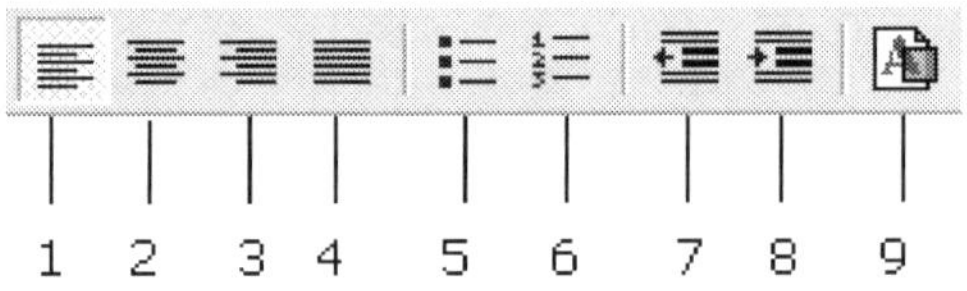

Figure 4-1 Word processing Formatting toolbar

The buttons shown above in Figure 4-1 are the remaining buttons on the Formatting toolbar in the word processing application. Table 4-2 explains the purpose of each button.

Button	Purpose
1	Left aligns the selected text. This is the default text alignment.
2	Centers the selected text between the margins.
3	Right aligns the selected text.
4	Justifies the selected text between the left and right margins.
5	Creates a bulleted list.
6	Creates a numbered list.
7	Decreases the amount of space that a paragraph is indented.
8	Increases the amount of space that a paragraph is indented.
9	Opens the Format Gallery.

Table 4-2 Formatting toolbar buttons explained

Standard Toolbar

The Standard toolbar shown in Figure 4-2 contains the options that you are most likely to use when working on word processing documents. These options can also be found on the menus that were discussed earlier in this lesson. Table 4-3 explains the purpose of each button.

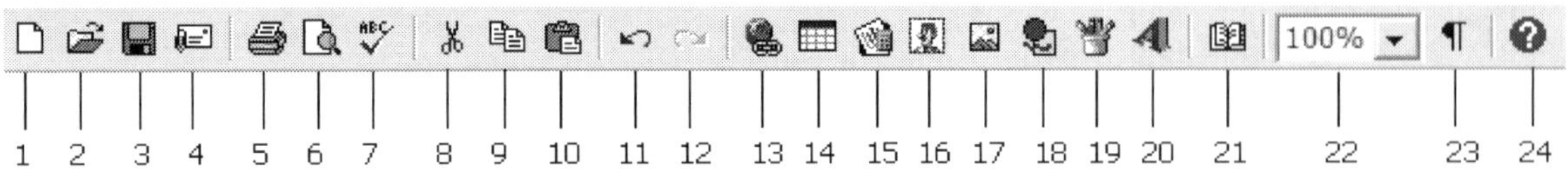

Figure 4-2 Word processing Standard toolbar

Button	Purpose
1	Opens a new document.
2	Opens an existing document.
3	Saves the current document.
4	Opens your email software.
5	Prints the current document.
6	View the document as it will look when printed.
7	Check the spelling and grammar of the document.
8	Cuts (deletes) selected text from the document.
9	Copies selected text to another part of the same document or to a different document.
10	Inserts what you have copied into a document.
11	Reverses actions or deletes entries that you type. You can undo the last 100 actions.
12	Repeats an action. You can redo the last 100 actions. This button will change to Can't Redo when there is not anything to "Redo".
13	Add a hyperlink to the document.
14	Create a table, which is similar to a spreadsheet.
15	Insert a new spreadsheet into the word processing document.
16	Opens the Clipart Gallery shown in Figure 4-3.
17	Opens the Insert Picture dialog box shown in Figure 4-4.
18	Opens the Microsoft Drawing application that comes with Windows.
19	Opens the Microsoft Paint application that comes with Windows.
20	Opens the Word Art application.
21	Opens the address book associated with the default email software on your computer.
22	Controls how small or large a document appears on the screen.
23	Show or hide the paragraph marks as shown in Figure 4-5.
24	Opens the Help system.

Table 4-3 Standard toolbar buttons explained

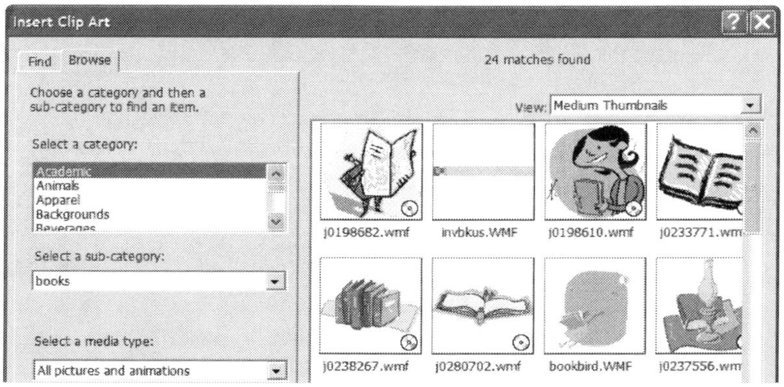

Figure 4-3 Clipart Gallery dialog box

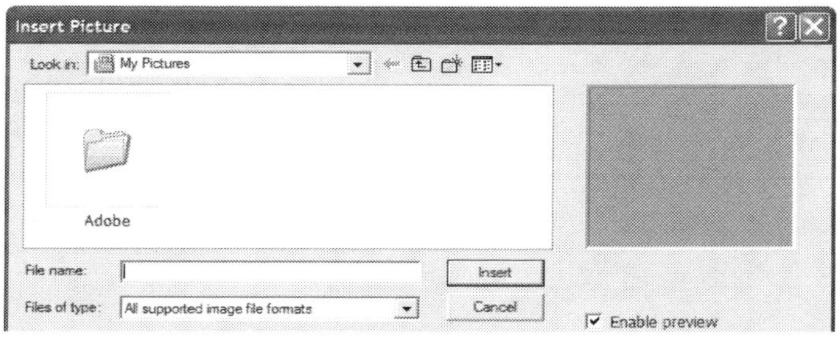

Figure 4-4 Insert Picture dialog box

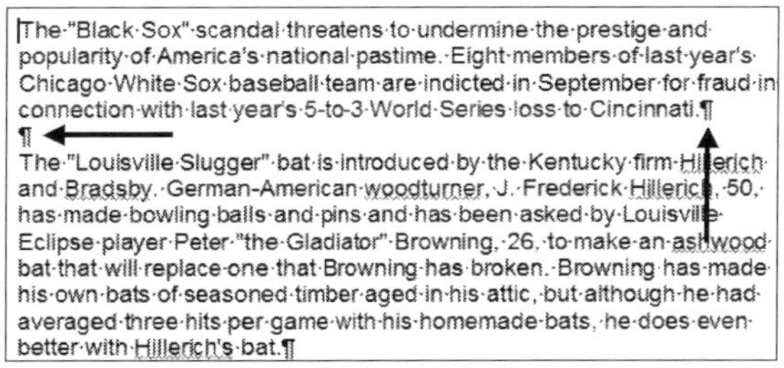
The·"Black·Sox"·scandal·threatens·to·undermine·the·prestige·and·popularity·of·America's·national·pastime.·Eight·members·of·last·year's·Chicago·White·Sox·baseball·team·are·indicted·in·September·for·fraud·in connection·with·last·year's·5-to-3·World·Series·loss·to·Cincinnati.¶

¶

The·"Louisville·Slugger"·bat·is·introduced·by·the·Kentucky·firm·Hillerich·and·Bradsby.·German-American·woodturner,·J.·Frederick·Hillerich,·50,·has·made·bowling·balls·and·pins·and·has·been·asked·by·Louisville·Eclipse·player·Peter·"the·Gladiator"·Browning,·26,·to·make·an·ashwood·bat·that·will·replace·one·that·Browning·has·broken.·Browning·has·made·his·own·bats·of·seasoned·timber·aged·in·his·attic,·but·although·he·had·averaged·three·hits·per·game·with·his·homemade·bats,·he·does·even·better·with·Hillerich's·bat.¶

Figure 4-5 Paragraph marks turned on

How To Select Text In A Word Processing Document

You can read through this section to become familiar with the terms. In the next exercise you will be able to practice selecting text.

1. Place the cursor in front of the first word that you want to select. In Figure 4-6, the cursor is in front of the word **classes** on the last line of the paragraph. Hold down the left mouse button and drag the cursor to the right, until what you want to select is highlighted, as shown in Figure 4-7.

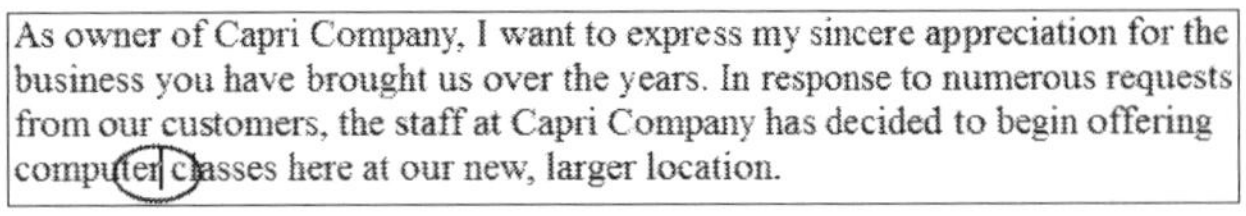
As owner of Capri Company, I want to express my sincere appreciation for the business you have brought us over the years. In response to numerous requests from our customers, the staff at Capri Company has decided to begin offering computer classes here at our new, larger location.

Figure 4-6 Cursor in position to start selecting text

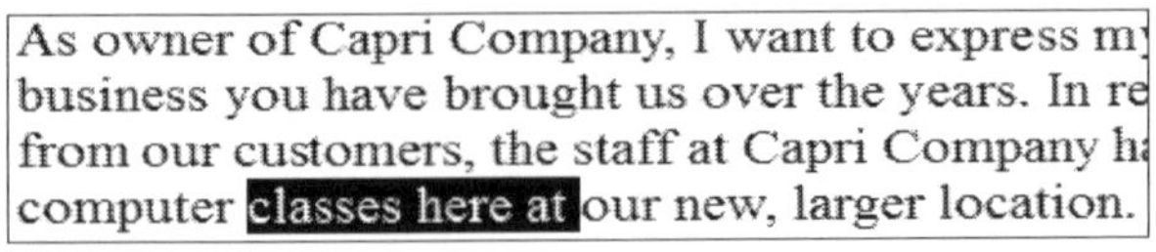
As owner of Capri Company, I want to express m
business you have brought us over the years. In re
from our customers, the staff at Capri Company h
computer classes here at our new, larger location.

Figure 4-7 Text selected

2. Now you can change the font or make the text bold.

The word processor in Works, like every other word processor that I have used has a built-in **WORD WRAP** feature. Unlike a typewriter, you should not press the Enter key to go to a new line in the word processor. You should only press the Enter key when you need to start a new paragraph.

Changing Fonts, Font Size And Margins

You can change the font, font size and margins to make the document look better. Just don't get too carried away. I know how tempting it can be.

1. Open the word processor by clicking on the **PROGRAMS** link in the Task Launcher.
2. Select the Works Word Processor option, then click on the **START A BLANK WORD PROCESSING DOCUMENT** link.
3. File ⇒ Open. Navigate to your folder and double-click on the New Classes Information Letter.
4. File ⇒ Save As. Navigate to your folder and type `L4 New Classes Letter` as the file name, then click Save.

Modify The Document

1. Click in front of the word **DEAR**. Hold down the left mouse button and drag the mouse down until the entire letter is highlighted, as shown in Figure 4-8.

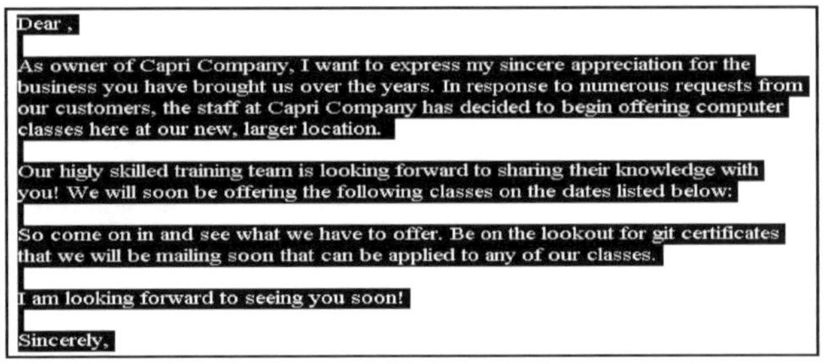
Dear ,

As owner of Capri Company, I want to express my sincere appreciation for the business you have brought us over the years. In response to numerous requests from our customers, the staff at Capri Company has decided to begin offering computer classes here at our new, larger location.

Our higly skilled training team is looking forward to sharing their knowledge with you! We will soon be offering the following classes on the dates listed below:

So come on in and see what we have to offer. Be on the lookout for git certificates that we will be mailing soon that can be applied to any of our classes.

I am looking forward to seeing you soon!

Sincerely,

Figure 4-8 Text in letter highlighted

2. Open the Font drop-down list and select the Arial font. With the text still selected, open the **FONT SIZE** drop-down list and select 12.

3. To change the margins, File ⇒ Page Setup. Change all four margins to 1.25", as shown in Figure 4-9, then click OK. Click on a blank space on the letter to deselect the text. Your letter should look like the one shown in Figure 4-10.

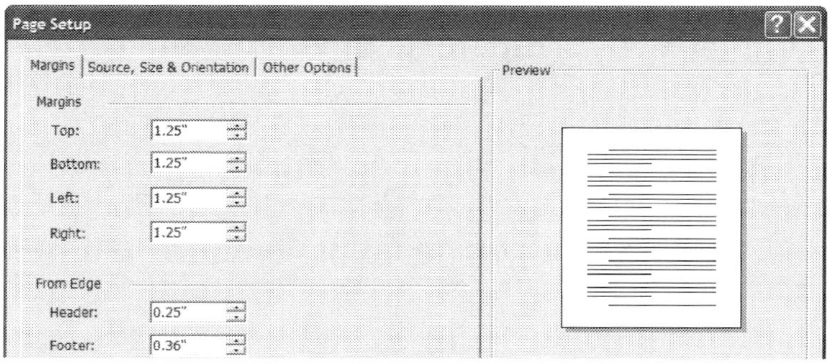

Figure 4-9 Margins changed

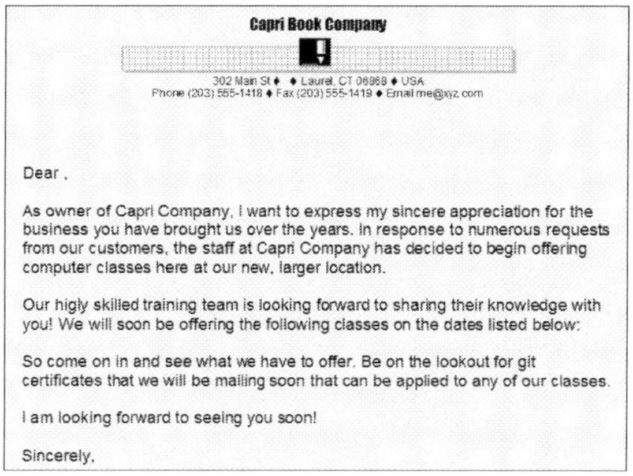

Capri Book Company

302 Main St ♦ ♦ Laurel, CT 06868 ♦ USA
Phone (203) 555-1418 ♦ Fax (203) 555-1419 ♦ Email me@xyz.com

Dear ,

As owner of Capri Company, I want to express my sincere appreciation for the business you have brought us over the years. In response to numerous requests from our customers, the staff at Capri Company has decided to begin offering computer classes here at our new, larger location.

Our higly skilled training team is looking forward to sharing their knowledge with you! We will soon be offering the following classes on the dates listed below:

So come on in and see what we have to offer. Be on the lookout for git certificates that we will be mailing soon that can be applied to any of our classes.

I am looking forward to seeing you soon!

Sincerely,

Figure 4-10 New classes letter

Using The Bold, Italic And Underline Formatting Options

1. On the last line of the first paragraph, highlight the words **COMPUTER CLASSES**. Click the Bold button, then click the Italic button. Click on a blank space on the letter to deselect the highlighted text. Your letter should look like the one shown in Figure 4-11.

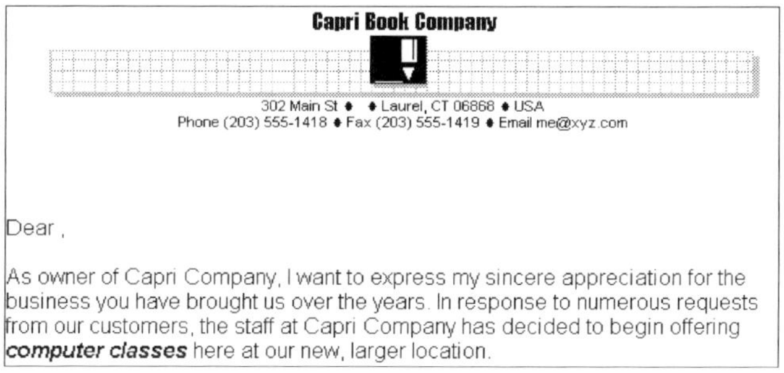

Capri Book Company

302 Main St ♦ ♦ Laurel, CT 06868 ♦ USA
Phone (203) 555-1418 ♦ Fax (203) 555-1419 ♦ Email me@xyz.com

Dear ,

As owner of Capri Company, I want to express my sincere appreciation for the business you have brought us over the years. In response to numerous requests from our customers, the staff at Capri Company has decided to begin offering ***computer classes*** here at our new, larger location.

Figure 4-11 Bold and italicized words illustrated

2. Move the mouse pointer to the blank line above the word **SINCERELY** and press Enter.

3. Press the Tab key once and type,
`Don't wait until the last minute to get the training you need.`

4. Press Enter. Select the sentence that you just typed and click the **UNDERLINE** button. Your letter should look like the one shown in Figure 4-12.

5. Delete the last line of the letter, "Your name goes here".

6. Place the cursor on the last blank line of the document as shown in Figure 4-13, then press the **BACKSPACE** key until the cursor is on the line below the word "Sincerely".

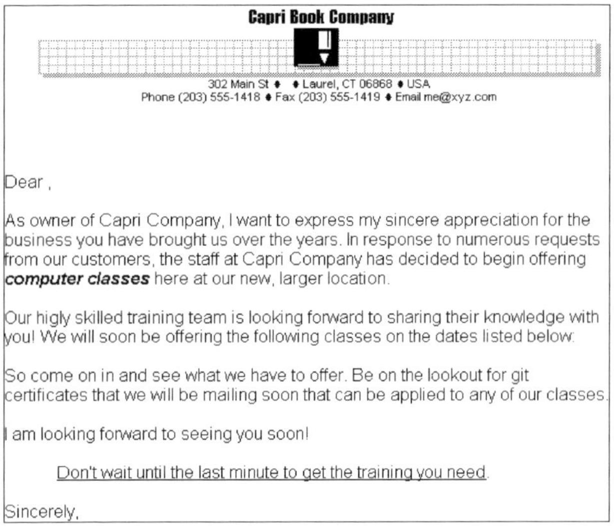

Figure 4-12 Underlined text illustrated

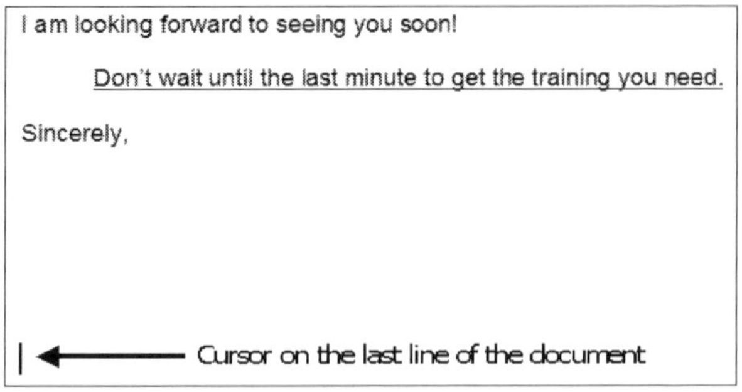

Figure 4-13 Cursor on the last line of the document

The Undo Command

This command will allow you to undo (remove) the changes that you just made.

> This command will only undo one change at a time. If you need to undo five changes (which are called **ACTIONS**), you have to click the Undo button five times.

1. Delete the first word in the first paragraph of the letter, then type the words `I am` at the beginning of the first paragraph.

2. Click the **UNDO TYPING** button three times. The word "As" has returned and the words "I am" are gone. If you pressed the space bar after typing the words "I am", click the Undo Typing button four times instead of three.

Bullets

Bullets are often used to make lines of text stand out in a document. They are also used to create lists.

Two Ways To Create A Bulleted List

① Position the cursor in the document where you want to place the first bullet. Click the Bullets button. Start typing the items for the list. Press the Enter key after each item. When you type the next item a bullet will appear. After you type the last item, press the Enter key. When the bullet appears, click the Bullets button to remove the last bullet.

② The second way is to type the list of items first, then select all of the items and click the Bullets button.

> To remove the bullets, highlight the bulleted list and click the Bullets button.

How To Create A Bulleted List

1. Move the cursor to the line above **I AM LOOKING FORWARD TO SEEING YOU SOON**, then press Enter. Press the Tab key and type `Introduction To Multimedia`, then press Enter.

2. Press the Tab key and type `Introduction To Web Page Creation`, then press Enter. Press the Tab key and type `Introduction To Networking`, then press Enter.

3. Highlight the three lines that you just typed and click the Bullets button. Your letter should look like the one shown in Figure 4-14.

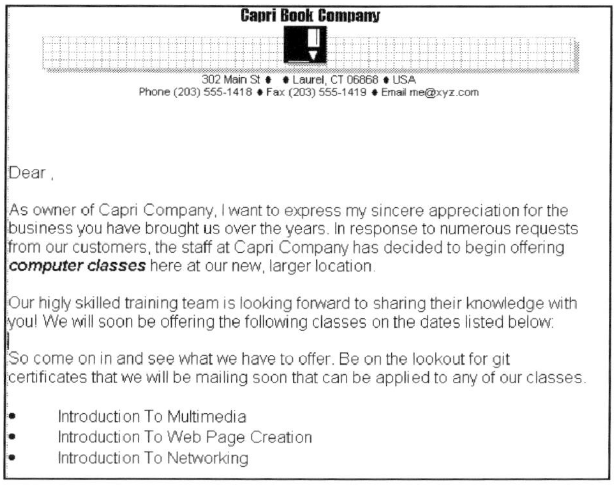

Figure 4-14 Bulleted list added to the letter

How To Change The Bullet Style

There are several bullet styles that you can select from. The bulleted list that you just created used the default bullet style. In this exercise you will learn how to change the bullet style.

1. Select the three bulleted lines, if they are not already highlighted.

2. Format ⇒ Bullets and Numbering. You should see the Bullets and Numbering dialog box. Click on the Bullet style that is selected in Figure 4-15 and click OK. Your letter should look like the one shown in Figure 4-16.

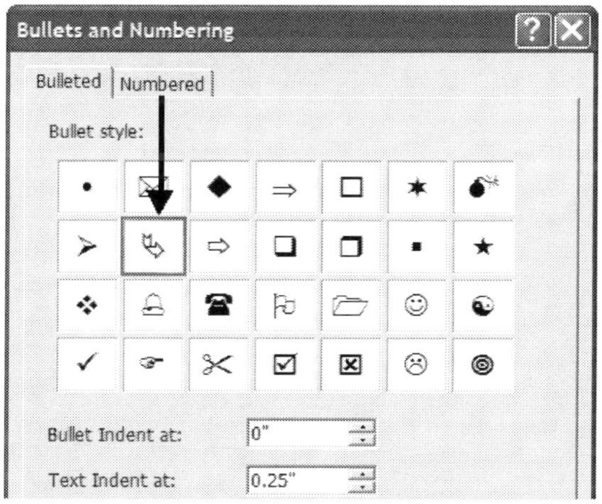

Figure 4-15 Bullet style options

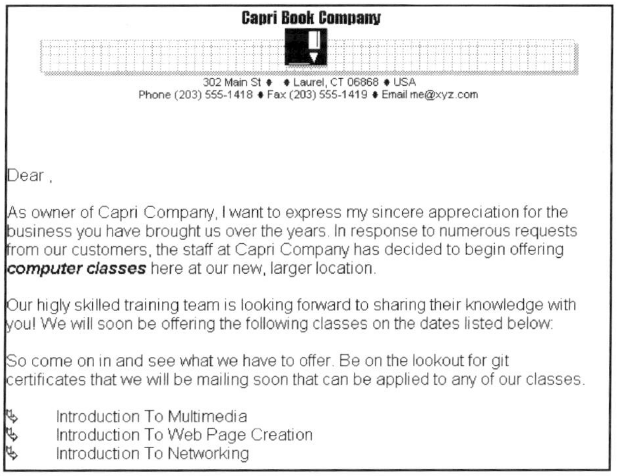

Figure 4-16 Bullet style changed

3. Click Save and leave the document open.

NEW The Format Gallery

If you have used a previous version of Works, you may remember a feature called Easy Formats. While that feature was more powerful, it has been replaced with the Format Gallery. Works comes with several font and color sets that you can use to easily format your documents.

You can also create a new formatting style, save it in the Format Gallery and use it over and over again. To use one of the formats, type or select the text that you want to apply the format to and complete the steps below.

How To Create Your Own Format

The easiest way to save a new format is to create it first, then add it to the Format Gallery.

1. File ⇒ Save As. Type `L4 Format Gallery` as the file name.
2. Highlight the sentence that is underlined in the document. Format ⇒ Font, then select the font, Myriad Web. If you do not have this font select a different one.
3. Change the font color to red and check the **SHADOW** effect shown in Figure 4-17, then click OK. The sentence should now be red, underlined and have the shadow effect as shown in Figure 4-18.

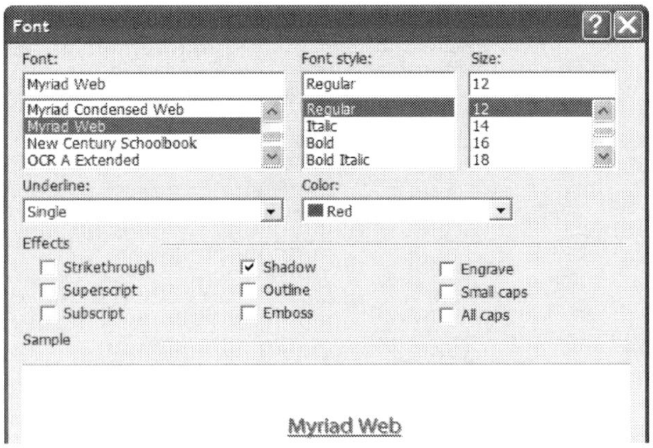

Figure 4-17 Font and effect options selected

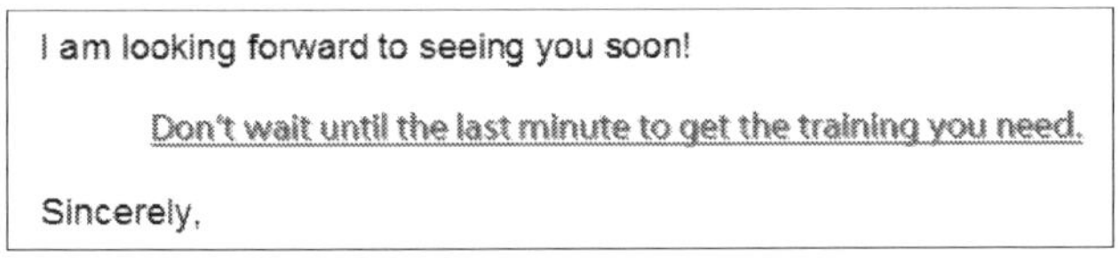
I am looking forward to seeing you soon!

Don't wait until the last minute to get the training you need.

Sincerely,

Figure 4-18 Text formatting changed in the letter

How To Add Your Format To The Gallery

In this exercise you will add the format that you just created to the Format Gallery.

1. Highlight the sentence that is underlined, then click the **FORMAT GALLERY** button on the Formatting toolbar.
2. Click the **ADD** button shown at the bottom of Figure 4-19. Figure 4-20 shows the default Color Sets that you can select from. The options on the **FORMAT ALL** tab shown in Figure 4-21 will allow you to format the entire document at the same time.

Figure 4-19 Format Gallery dialog box

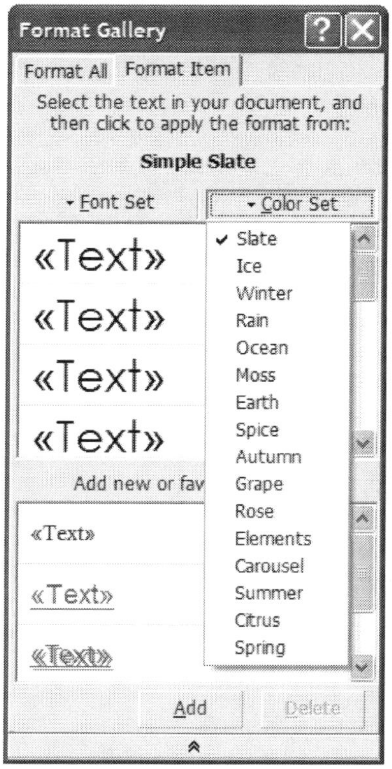

Figure 4-20 Format Gallery Color Set options

Figure 4-21 Format All tab options

Shrinking The Format Gallery Dialog Box

If you plan to use the Format Gallery on a regular basis, you may find it helpful to shrink it and leave it open. To do this, follow the steps below.

1. Open the Format Gallery dialog box if it is not already open, then click on the arrow shown at the bottom of Figure 4-21 above. The dialog box will shrink, as shown in Figure 4-22. You can move the dialog box up near the menu and toolbars to keep it out of the way, as shown in Figure 4-23.

Figure 4-22 Format Gallery dialog box

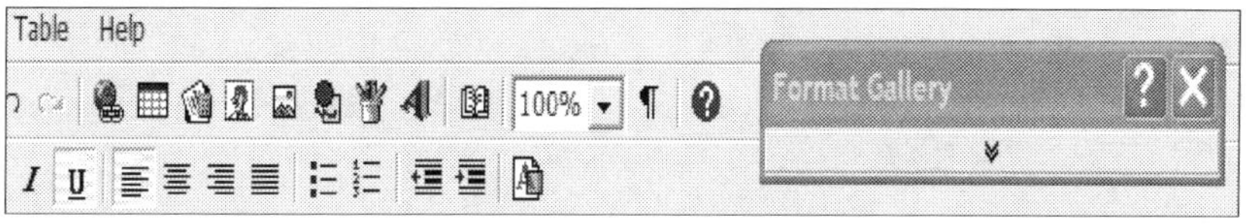

Figure 4-23 Format Gallery dialog box moved up near the menu and toolbars

The Format Gallery dialog box will stay where you place it, even when you close and reopen Works.

Apply Your Custom Format To Text

1. Highlight the third paragraph in the letter, then click the Format Gallery button on the Formatting toolbar. If you shrunk the Format Gallery dialog box, in the previous exercise, it will expand.

2. On the **FORMAT ITEM** tab click on the Format that you created, which is at the bottom of the Format Gallery dialog box.

3. Close the Format Gallery dialog box or shrink it. The third paragraph should now have the same formatting as the last sentence of the letter. Save the changes and close the document.

You can use the format that you just created in any word processing document that you create or modify.

The Replace Command

This is a useful command when you need to change the same text in several places in the document. This command will search the entire document, or any part of it that you highlight. Every occurrence that matches your search criteria will be replaced with what you specify.

The letterhead of the New Classes Information letter has the company name as Capri Book Company. Look through the letter and you will see the company name written as Capri Company twice in the first paragraph. Instead of looking through the document to find out where the company name needs to be changed and typing the word **BOOK** in every occurrence, you can use the Replace command.

1. Open the L4 New Classes letter. Edit ⇒ Replace. You will see the Find and Replace dialog box.

2. In the **FIND WHAT** field, type `Capri Company`.

You may be thinking that you could just type Capri or Company and not both words in the **FIND WHAT** field. If you did that, the search would find these words in the letterhead and add the replacement text there also. This is not what you want.

3. Press the Tab key and type `Capri Book Company` in the **REPLACE WITH** field. Your dialog box should have the fields filled in as shown in Figure 4-24.

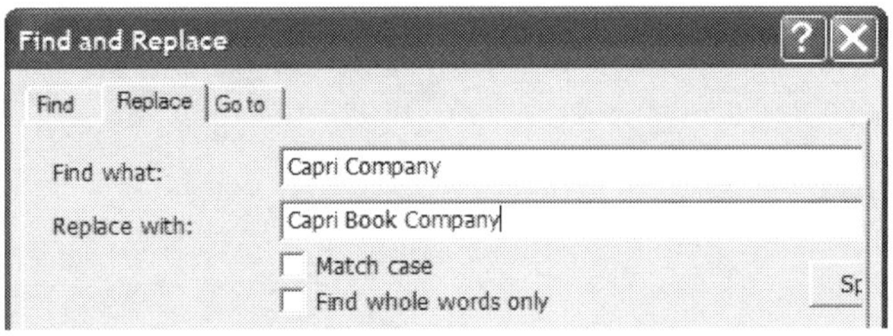

Figure 4-24 Replace options

On the right side of Figure 4-24 above, is a button labeled **SPECIAL**. Hopefully, it is more visible on your dialog box than it is on mine. This button opens the menu shown in Figure 4-25. The options on this menu provide additional items that you can search for. A similar menu is also available on the Find tab.

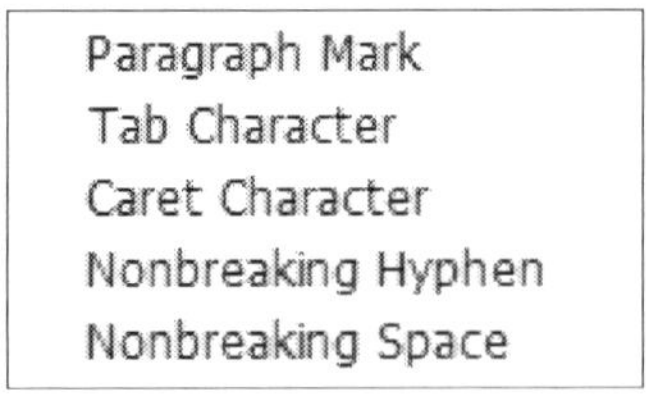

Figure 4-25 Special characters menu

4. Click the **REPLACE ALL** button. You should see the message shown in Figure 4-26. Notice that the message tells you how many times the text was replaced. Click OK and close the Find and Replace dialog box. Save the changes and close the document. The text has now been replaced twice in the first paragraph.

Figure 4-26 Confirmation of replacement message

The Find And Go To Commands

As you saw earlier, you can also look for a specific word or go to a specific location in the document. These features are useful, especially in long documents when you know what you are looking for.

Using The Find Command

If a document had 50 pages and you needed to find the word Brooklyn, it could take a while to visually go through all 50 pages of the document. Instead, you could follow the steps below to have Works find each occurrence of the word for you.

1. Open the Term Paper document.
2. Edit ⇒ Find. Type `Brook` in the **FIND WHAT** field.

The **MATCH CASE** option if selected, will only find words that are in the same case (upper, lower or a combination of both) that you enter in the **FIND WHAT** field. If you type "brooklyn" in the Find What field and select the Match Case option, the word Brooklyn would not be retrieved because it is in a different case then what you typed in.

The **FIND WHOLE WORDS ONLY** option if selected, will only find words that have all of the characters that you type in the Find What field. If you type the word "Brook" in the Find What field and select the Find Whole Words Only option, the word Brooklyn will be retrieved.

3. Select one of the options and click the **FIND NEXT** button. Did you get the results that you expected? You can play with these options to get a feel for how they work, then close the Term Paper document.

The Go To Command

The Go To Command has five options that will help you navigate through a document and find exactly what you are looking for. These options are more helpful in long documents, but you can use them in any document that you want. The options are discussed below.

① The **PAGE** option will take you to a specific page in the document. Select this option and type in the page number that you want to go to on the right, as shown in Figure 4-27, then click the **GO TO** button.
② The **FOOTNOTE** option will take you to a specific footnote in the document, if you know the footnote number. Footnotes are located at the bottom of the page.
③ The **ENDNOTE** option will take you to a specific endnote in the document, if you know the endnote number. All Endnotes are usually located at the end of the document, which is why I'm not sure why this option is necessary.
④ The **FIELD** option will take you to a specific field in the document, if you know the name of the field.
⑤ The **TABLE** option will take you to a specific table in the document, if you know the table name.

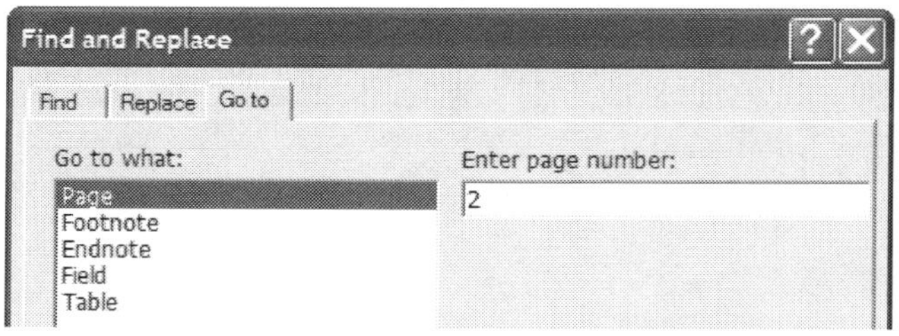

Figure 4-27 Go To options

The Spell Checker

Once you have finished working on your document it is a good idea to check the spelling. To activate the spell checker, you can use one of the following three options.

① Click on the Spelling and Grammar button on the toolbar.
② Press the F7 key.
③ Tools ⇒ Spelling and Grammar.

By default, the spell checker is turned on. You will see a red squiggly line under words that are not spelled correctly, based on the spelling options that you selected.

1. Open the L4 New Classes Letter document and click in front of the word Dear.

> I usually put the cursor at the beginning of the document before spell checking it. I do this because the spell checker will only have to go through the document once. Doing this is optional.

2. Start the spell checker. You should see the dialog box shown in Figure 4-28.

   You will see that the misspelled word is highlighted in the document, as shown in the upper left corner of Figure 4-28. This is helpful if no words are suggested because you may not know what the word should be, without being able to see it in the document.

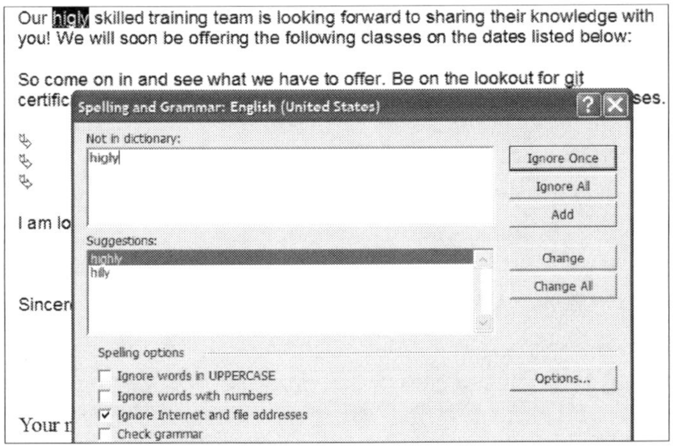

Figure 4-28 Spelling and Grammar dialog box

3. Click the **CHANGE ALL** button to change the highlighted word in the document to the word that is highlighted in the **SUGGESTIONS** section of the dialog box.

The reason that you may want to use the **CHANGE ALL** button instead of the **CHANGE** button is because you may have misspelled the same word, the same way, more than once. Change All will change the word every place that it is misspelled the same way in the document.

The next misspelled word should be **GIFT**. If all you saw was the misspelled word in the **NOT IN DICTIONARY** section of the dialog box, you probably would not know what to change it to.

4. Look in the **SUGGESTIONS** list to see if the word that you want is there. If it is, select it and click the **CHANGE ALL** button. If it wasn't there, you would type "gift" in the **NOT IN DICTIONARY** field and click the **CHANGE ALL** button. Click OK on the Spelling check is complete dialog box, then save the changes and close the document.

An Alternate Way To Use Spell Check

I think that most people use the Spelling dialog box that you used in the previous exercise. There is another way to find suggestions for the misspelled words. Initially, this method does not have all of the features that the Spelling dialog box has, but you may find it convenient sometimes. Follow the steps below to use the spelling shortcut menu.

1. Open a new word processing document and type the word `higly`.

2. Right-click on the word that you just typed. You will see the shortcut menu shown in Figure 4-29.

At the top of the Spelling shortcut menu are the suggestions for the word that you are spell checking. Notice that they are the same suggestions as the ones shown above in Figure 4-28.

If you see the word that you want, you can select it from the menu. If you need spelling features that are not on the shortcut menu, select the **SPELLING** option at the bottom of the menu shown in Figure 4-29 and the Spelling dialog box shown above in Figure 4-28 will open.

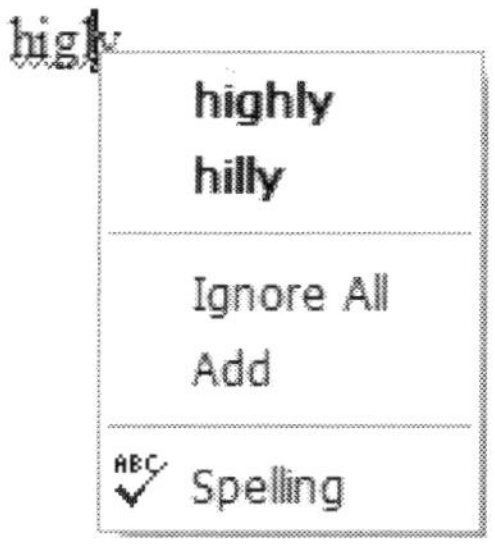

Figure 4-29 Spelling shortcut menu

3. Close the document, but do not save the changes.

Spell Check Button Options

The options explained below are the buttons on the Spelling dialog box shown earlier in Figure 4-28.

① **IGNORE ONCE** If a word is not in the dictionary and you want to use it, you can click this button and the word will be skipped during the spell check process.
② **IGNORE ALL** This button will skip the same word every time that it is in the document, opposed to one time like the Ignore Once button does.
③ **ADD** If a word is not in the dictionary, but you know that it is correct, you should add it to the dictionary. Adding a word to the dictionary means that from that point on, the word will not be marked as being incorrect. A good use of this option is adding peoples names and street names to the dictionary. The dictionary that you add words to is called the **PERSONAL** dictionary and is separate from the dictionary that the spell checker uses. The Spell Checker also uses the Personal dictionary. The Personal dictionary is shared by many software packages that have a spell checker.
④ **CHANGE** Click this button if you want to change a word that has been marked as not being spelled correctly.
⑤ **CHANGE ALL** Clicking this button will change the same word every time that it is found in the document, instead of only changing the current occurrence of the word like the Change button does. I use this option instead of the Change option because it can save time.
⑥ **OPTIONS** Clicking this button will open the dialog box shown in Figure 4-30.

As you can see, there are not many spelling options that can be modified. The options selected in Figure 4-30, are the ones that I feel are the most useful.

Tools ⇒ Options, will also open the Options dialog box.

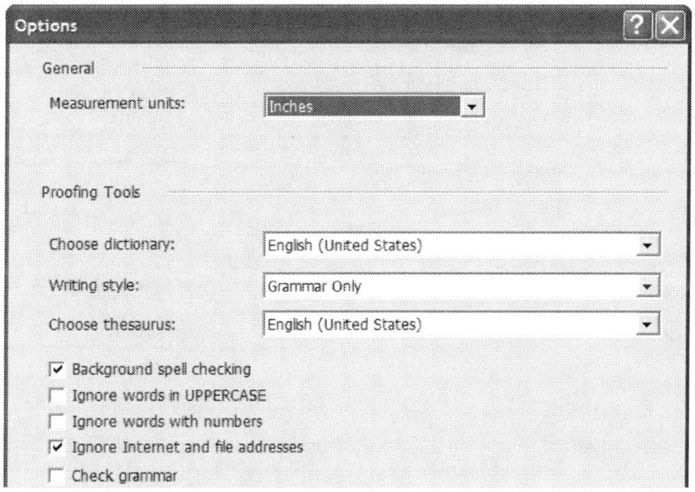

Figure 4-30 Spelling Options dialog box

If you add words to the custom (personal) dictionary, you may want to back up this file. That way if something happens to the file, you can restore it. The file name is custom.dic. The path to it is C:\Documents and Settings\Account Name\Application Data\Microsoft\Proof\custom.dic. Replace "Account Name" with your Windows login account name. If you cannot find the file in this location, search your hard drive for the file. Each person that has a login account on your computer has their own personal dictionary.

If you buy a new computer and have added words to this dictionary, copy this file from your old computer to the new computer and place it in the path shown above. When prompted to overwrite the existing file, click Yes. The existing file should be empty unless you added words to it.

The personal dictionary, just like the one that the spell checker uses is used by the word processor, spreadsheet and database applications. It is also used by other Microsoft applications, that have a personal dictionary, like Microsoft Office.

Spelling Options

The section below explains the options on the dialog box shown above in Figure 4-30.

① **BACKGROUND SPELL CHECKING** If this option is checked, the spell checker will check for spelling errors as you type. Selecting this option is what will cause the red squiggly lines to appear in your document.

② **IGNORE WORDS IN UPPERCASE** If this option is checked, the spell checker will not check words that are in all capital letters.

③ **IGNORE WORDS WITH NUMBERS** If there are words that have numbers and this option is checked, the spell checker will ignore the words with numbers.

④ **IGNORE INTERNET AND FILE ADDRESSES** If this option is checked and your document has a web site address like www.tolana.com, it will be skipped during the spell check process.

⑤ **CHECK GRAMMAR** If this option is checked, the grammar will be checked in addition to the spelling.

Grammar Options

The **WRITING STYLE** field shown above in Figure 4-30 contains two grammar styles: Grammar Only and Grammar & Style.

Figure 4-31 shows the Grammar Checking dialog box. To activate the Grammar checker, you have to select the **CHECK GRAMMAR** option at the bottom of Figure 4-28 shown earlier.

The **OPTIONS** button on the Grammar checking dialog box shown in Figure 4-31 opens the same Options dialog box shown earlier in Figure 4-30.

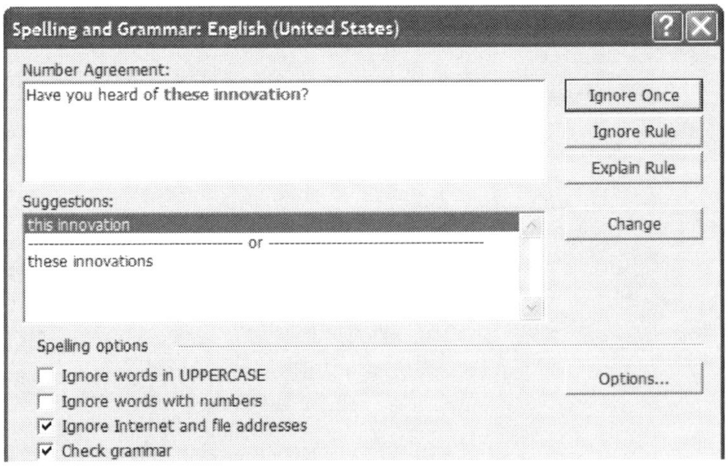

Figure 4-31 Grammar checking dialog box

If you are not sure why a phrase has a grammar error, click the **EXPLAIN RULE** button shown above in Figure 4-31 and you will see a message similar to the one shown in Figure 4-32. The information on this dialog box will explain the grammar rule that has been violated and will offer suggestions on how to fix the problem.

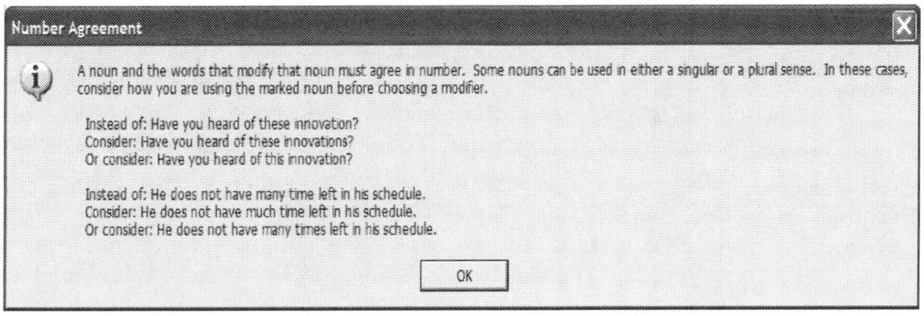

Figure 4-32 Grammar rule explained

Printing Options

There are several printing options that you should be aware of. They are discussed in the next few sections of this lesson.

Print Preview

Print Preview allows you to view the document as it will look when printed. Like the applications in Works, the Print Preview window has it's own toolbar as shown in Figure 4-33.

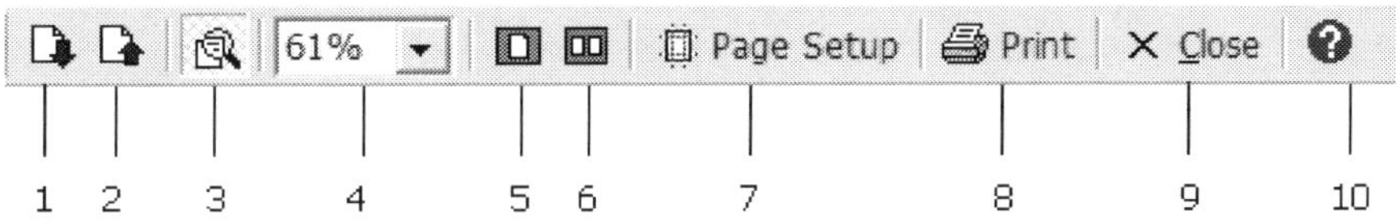

Figure 4-33 Print Preview toolbar

Table 4-4 explains the purpose of each button on the toolbar.

Button	Purpose
1	Displays the next page in the document.
2	Displays the previous page in the document.
3	Used to magnify (enlarge) the document. (Only on the screen)
4	Opens the Zoom drop-down list.
5	Displays one page of the document in the Print Preview window.
6	Displays all of the pages in the document at one time, in the Print Preview window.
7	Opens the Page Setup dialog box.
8	Sends the document directly to the printer. You do not get to select any options that are available on the Print dialog box. (File ⇒ Print)
9	Closes the Print Preview window.
10	Opens the Help System.

Table 4-4 Print Preview toolbar buttons explained

1. Open the Table of Contents document and preview it.

2. To see the document better, click on the document or open the Zoom drop-down list and select a larger percent. To return the document to it's original size, click on the document again.

3. Click the **MULTIPLE PAGES** button. Your Print Preview window should look like the one shown in Figure 4-34. When you are finished viewing the document, File ⇒ Close, then close the document.

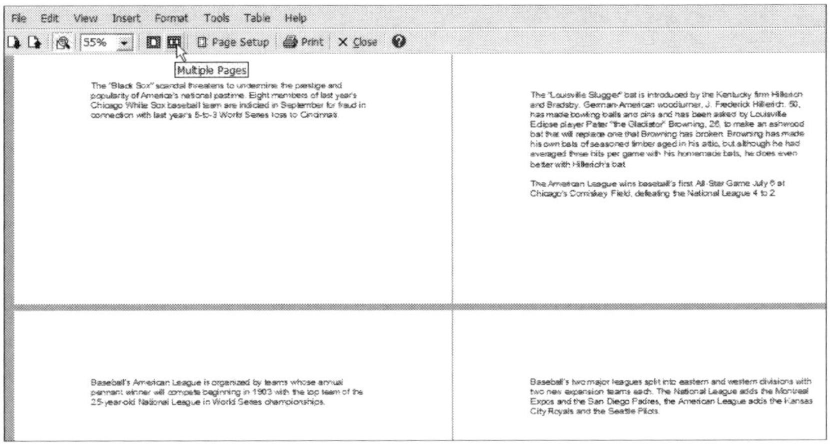

Figure 4-34 Multiple pages visible at one time in the Print Preview window

Printing A Document

Now that you have created, edited and spell checked your document, you can print it.

What Is The Difference Between The Print Button And The Print Command?

The Print button on the toolbar will send the document to the printer using the current print options. You do not get a chance to select any print options if you use the Print button on the toolbar. To me, it would make sense to have the Print button on the toolbar open the Print dialog box also.

The Print command is on the File menu. Selecting this command will allow you to select print options for the document, like the number of copies that you need to print.

1. Open the L4 New Classes Letter document. File ⇒ Print. You will see the dialog box shown in Figure 4-35.

Print Range Examples

If you only need to print some of the pages in a document, type the range that you need to print in the Pages **FROM** and **TO** fields.

If you only need to print page 5 of a 20 page document, you would type 5 in the **FROM** and **TO** fields. If you left the **TO** field empty in this example, all of the pages after page 5 would also print.

If you need to print pages 3, 4 and 5, you would type 3 in the **FROM** field and 5 in the **TO** field.

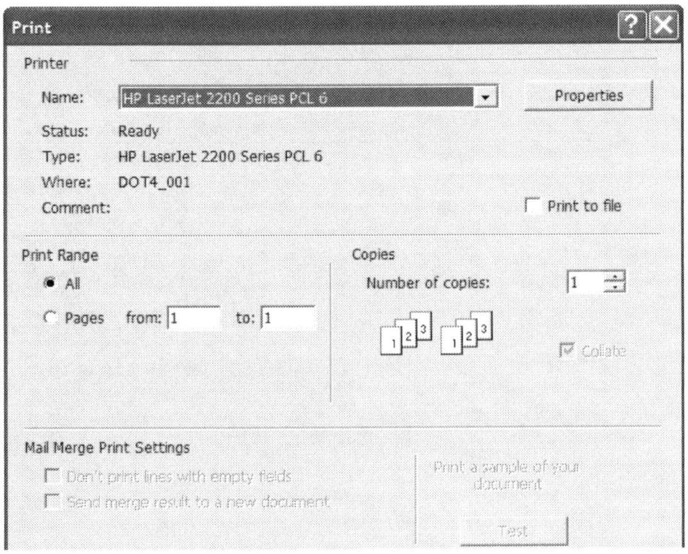

Figure 4-35 Print dialog box

2. None of the options need to be changed. Click OK to print the letter or click Cancel to return to the letter. Close the document when you are finished.

Inserting Page Breaks

Page breaks allow you to force part of the document to start on the next page. This feature is useful when you want more control over where text will print on a page.

1. Save the Term Paper document as `L4 Term Paper (with page breaks).`

2. Place the cursor under the first paragraph. Insert ⇒ Break ⇒ Page Break as shown in Figure 4-36. The only part of the document on page 1 should be the first paragraph.

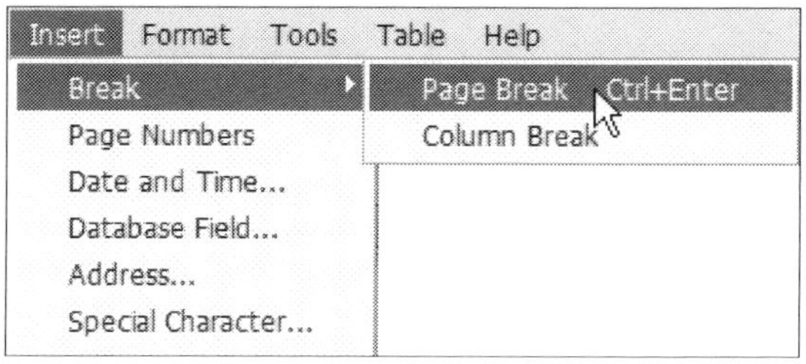

Figure 4-36 Page Break menu options

3. Insert a page break after the second paragraph on page 2. The second paragraph starts with the words "The American League".

4. Insert a page break after the third paragraph on page 3. The third paragraph starts with the words "Cy Young". Save the changes and leave the document open.

Your document should now have four pages. You can check by looking in the lower left corner of the word processing window. You should see "Page 4 of 4" as shown in Figure 4-37.

Figure 4-37 Page number that you are currently on and total number of pages

How To Count Words In A Document

There could be times when you need to know how many words are in a document. The steps below will show you how to find out how many words are in a document.

> If you only want to count the words in specific sections of the document, highlight the section(s) and then follow the steps below.

1. The L4 Term Paper (with page breaks) document should already be open. If not, open it now. Tools ⇒ Word Count. You will see the message shown in Figure 4-38. This message tells you how many words are in the document.

   Previous versions of Works would also count the words in the header and footer, as well as, in the footnotes. This may explain why the message says that it did not count the words in these sections of the document.

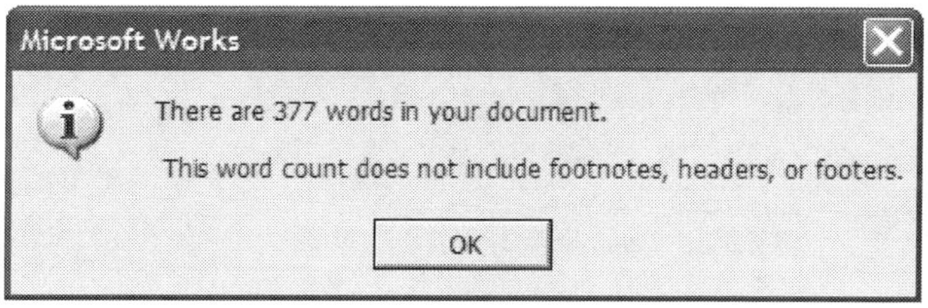

Figure 4-38 Word count information message

2. Click OK to close the message window.

Symbols And Special Characters

There are symbols and special characters that you can add to documents. Follow the steps below to learn how to add symbols or special characters to a document.

1. Place the cursor in the document where you want to insert the symbol or special character, then Insert ⇒ Special Character.

Some of the symbols that you can add to a document are shown in Figure 4-39.

You can select symbols in different fonts.

The special characters that you can add are shown in Figure 4-40.

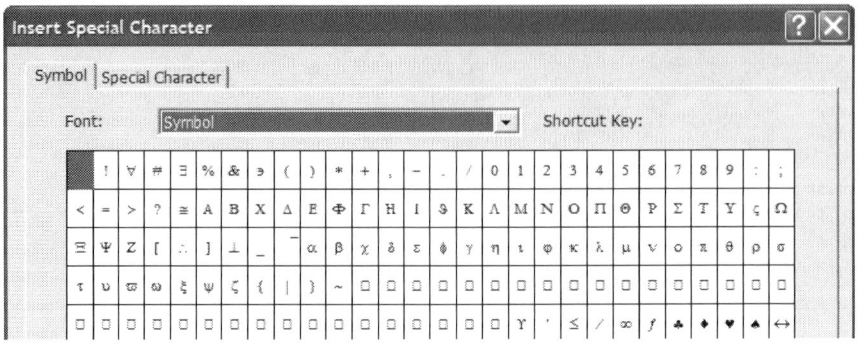

Figure 4-39 Symbols that you can use

If you select a different font like Wingdings, you will see other symbols that you can use.

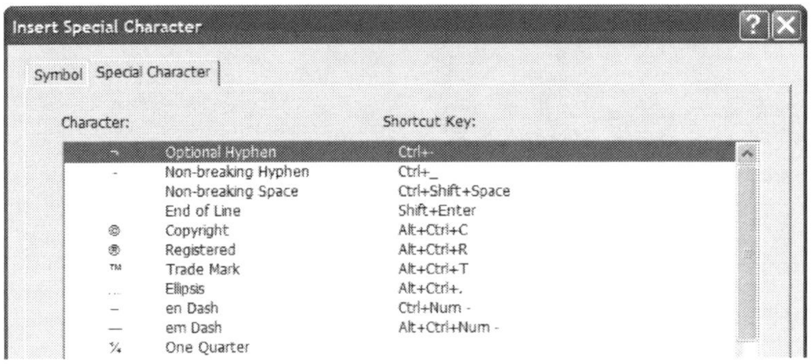

Figure 4-40 Special characters that you can use

2. Select the symbol or special character that you want to add, then click the **INSERT** button. Click Close.

The Thesaurus

The thesaurus will let you find a synonym, antonym or similar word for the word that you have selected. Follow the steps below to use the thesaurus.

1. Highlight the word in the document that you want to find another word for. Tools ⇒ Thesaurus. You will see the dialog box shown in Figure 4-41. The word that you highlighted in the document is in the **LOOKED UP** field on the dialog box.

The options available to replace the word that you selected are in the **REPLACE WITH SYNONYM** list.

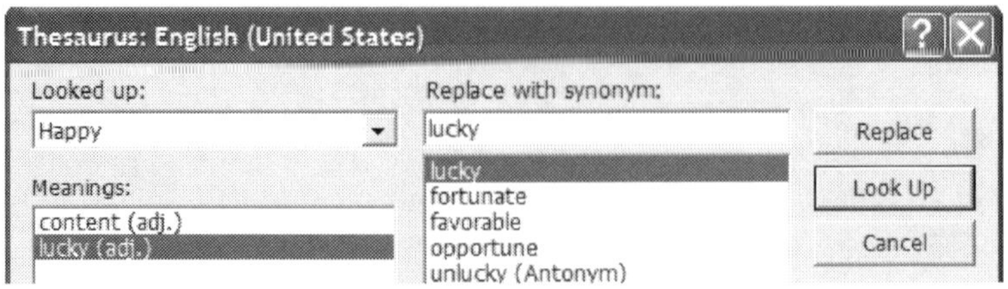

Figure 4-41 Thesaurus dialog box

2. Select one of the options in the **MEANINGS** list. The words in this list let you select the meaning of the word that is in the Looked Up field. In this example, I selected "lucky" as the meaning, as shown above in Figure 4-41.

3. When you find the word that you want to use, select it and click the **REPLACE** button. The word will be inserted in the document. Close any documents that you have open and do not save the changes.

Images

Earlier in this lesson you learned a little about the Clipart Gallery. Works supports a variety of image formats as discussed in Table 4-5. This is not the entire list of image formats that Works supports. The letters in the Format column in the table are the extension for the image type. Knowing the extension will help you identify the type of image that you have selected to work with. Images are also called clip art or graphics.

Format	Description
BMP	BMP stands for Bitmap. This use to be a popular image format. The downside to using this image type is that the file size is very large, when compared to the other file types discussed in this table.
GIF	GIF stands for Graphics Interchange Format. This is one of the most popular image types for graphics that are used on web pages. You can also use them in documents that you create in Works.
JPG	JPG stands for Joint Photographic Experts Group. This file format is often used for photographs. You may also see this file format with the extension JPEG.
PNG	PNG stands for Portable Network Graphics. This file format is primarily used for web graphics. It is one of the latest file formats to be introduced. It is gaining in popularity because it supports a high compression rate.
WMF	WMF stands for Windows Metafile. This file format is popular because it can be used in almost all Windows based programs.

Table 4-5 Image formats explained

Test Your Skills

1. Create a format that uses the Emboss effect and Arial font size 12. Add this format to the Format Gallery.

2. Save the L4 New Classes letter as `L4 (skills)`.

   - Change the bullet style to a ☑.
   - Apply the format that you created in number one above, to the second paragraph.

3. Where would you find the Thesaurus option?

HEADERS, FOOTERS AND OTHER FEATURES

Headers and footers are most often used to print information that you want to appear at the top or bottom of pages in the document. When printed, headers print at the top of the page and footers print at the bottom of the page. Items commonly placed in headers and footers include page numbers, the date, copyright information or the document name. In addition to learning how to create headers and footers in this lesson, you will learn the following:

☑ How to attach spreadsheets and charts to word processing documents by embedding and linking them
☑ Moving (drop and drag) text
☑ Paragraph alignment
☑ How to set the line spacing in word processing documents

LESSON 5

Headers And Footers

You can put almost everything in the header and footer sections of a document that you can put in the main portion of a document, including clip art. The header and footer sections of a document are enclosed in a dotted line box as shown at the top of Figure 5-1.

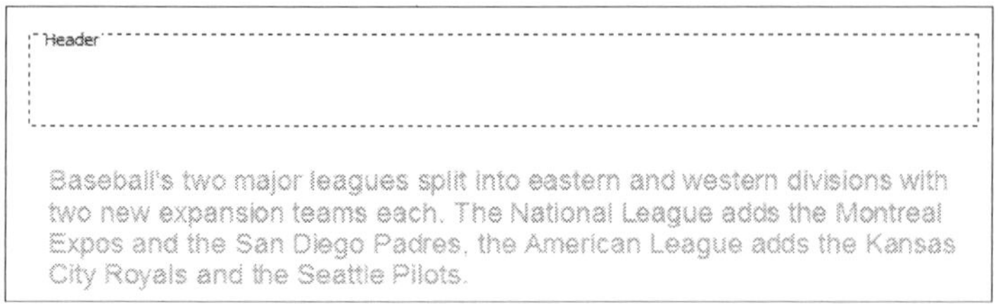

Figure 5-1 Header section illustrated

Header And Footer Toolbar

Headers and footers have their own toolbar. Figure 5-2 shows the buttons on the Header and Footer toolbar. Table 5-1 explains the purpose of each button.

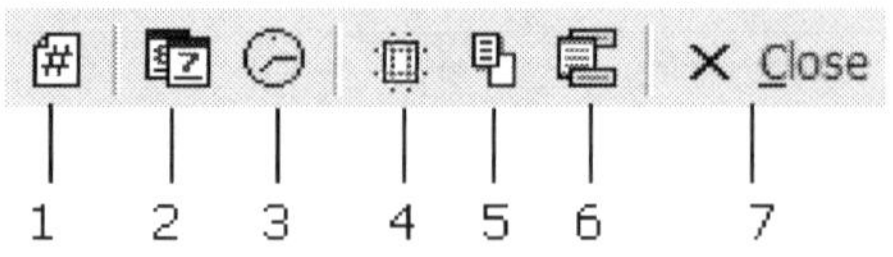

Figure 5-2 Header and Footer toolbar

Button	Purpose
1	Inserts the page number.
2	Inserts the current date.
3	Inserts the current time.
4	Opens the Page Setup dialog box.
5	Inserts the document name.
6	Lets you switch between the header and footer sections of the document.
7	Closes the header and footer toolbar.

Table 5-1 Header and Footer toolbar buttons explained

How To Add Page Numbers To A Document

1. Save the L4 Term Paper (with page breaks) document as `L5 Term Paper (with header and footer).`

2. View ⇒ Header and Footer. Click in the header section of the document, then press the Tab key until the cursor is at the four inch mark.

3. Type `Page` and press the space bar, then click the **INSERT PAGE NUMBER** button on the Header and Footer toolbar. The header section should look like the one shown in Figure 5-3.

Figure 5-3 Page number added to the header

How To Add The Document Name To The Footer

You may have a hard copy of a document but can't remember what file name you saved it as. To help solve this issue, you can include the document name in the header or footer section of the document.

1. Click the **SWITCH BETWEEN HEADER AND FOOTER** button on the Header and Footer toolbar.

2. Click the **INSERT DOCUMENT NAME** button on the Header and Footer toolbar.

While inserting the file name is a good idea, you may not know what folder it is in. You could search your hard drive to find it, or you could type the folder name in front of the file name. Doing this is known as inserting the path of the file.

3. Press the Home key so that the cursor is in front of the filename, then type `C:\Works Practice Files\`. Your footer section should look like the one shown in Figure 5-4.

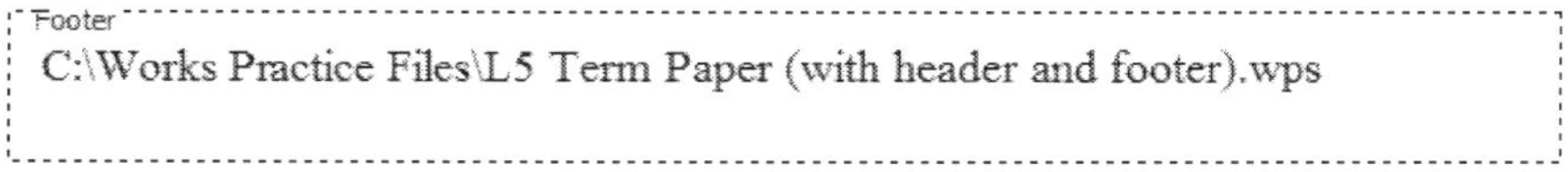

Figure 5-4 Path and document name added to the footer

> If your folder is under the My Documents folder, type `C:\My Documents\Works Practice Files\`. If your folder is someplace else on your hard drive, type in that location.

How To Make The Font Size Smaller

The font size of the information in the footer section is very large. The document would look better if the information in the footer was smaller. Follow the steps below to change the font size of the text.

1. Highlight the text that you want to change the font size of. In this case, highlight the information in the footer section.

2. Open the Font Size drop-down list and select 8. The path and file name in the footer should be much smaller.

How To Add The Date And Time To The Footer

Adding the date to the footer is a good idea, especially if you are working on a document that will be changing and is printed often. Adding this information will let you know which printed copy is the most recent.

There are two ways to add the date and time to a document. You can add the date and time together as one field. If this is what you want to do, you should use the option on the Insert menu.

If you want to add the date or the time, or both, you can. One reason that you may want to add the date and time separately is because you may not want them to be side by side. You may want the date in the left corner of the header and the time in the right corner of the footer.

1. Press the End key so that the cursor is at the end of the file name in the footer, then press the Shift and Enter keys. The cursor should be on the next line in the footer.

2. Insert ⇒ Date and Time. You should see the dialog box shown in Figure 5-5. Select the (highlighted) third option, which lists the day and date. (In the figure, you would select Sunday, January 9, 2005).

> You will see different dates in the dialog box because Works uses the current date and time on your computer.

Depending on the type of document that you are working on, you may or may not want the date or time to be updated. If you want the date to update, (change every time you print the document) make sure the option, **AUTOMATICALLY UPDATE WHEN PRINTED** is checked. If you do not want the date or time to update, clear this the option.

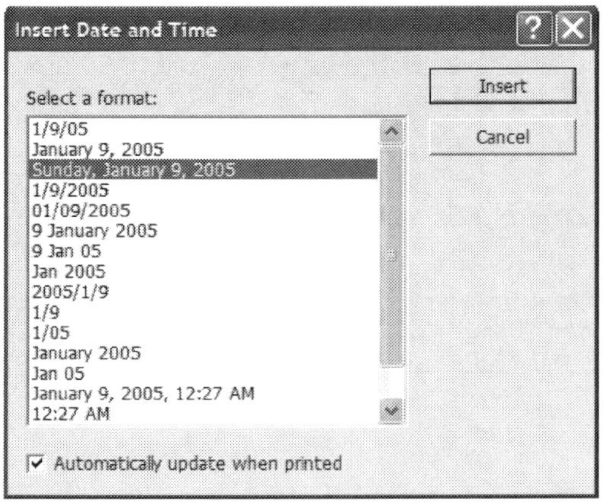

Figure 5-5 Insert Date and Time dialog box

3. Click the Insert button. Your footer should look like the one shown in Figure 5-6. Preview the document, then save the changes and close the document.

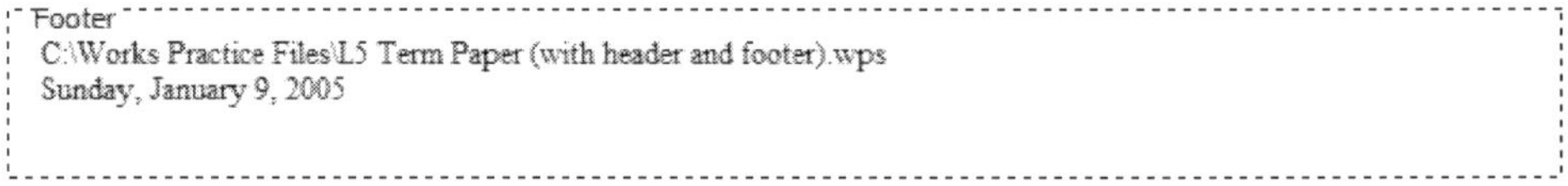

Figure 5-6 Completed footer

Footnotes

Footnotes are used to give more information or provide the source of information in the document. When you create a footnote, a marker is placed in the document. The footnote text that you enter prints at the bottom of the page.

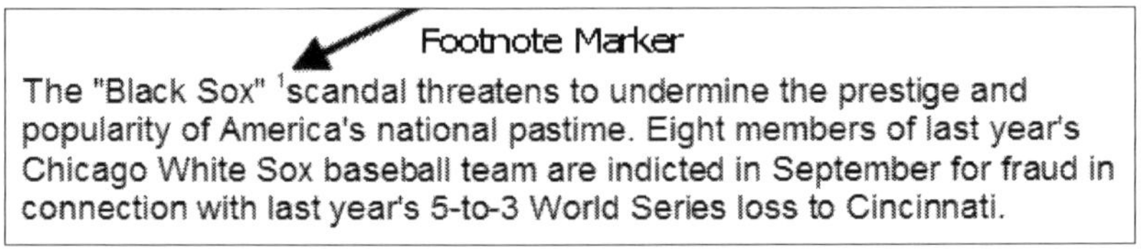

Figure 5-7 Footnote marker illustrated

You can add formatting to footnotes, like changing the font or making it bold, just like you can in the main section of the document. Figure 5-7 illustrates the Footnote marker.

Footnote Styles

There are two types of Footnote styles: Auto Number and Custom Mark.

① The **AUTO NUMBER** style assigns footnote numbers in sequential order.
② The **CUSTOM MARK** style allows you to type in the mark that you want.

How To Create Numbered Footnotes

1. Save the Term Paper document as `L5 Term Paper (with footnotes)`.

2. Place the cursor in the first line of the document after the words **BLACK SOX**. The cursor should be after the quote. Insert ⇒ Footnote. You should see the dialog box shown in Figure 5-8.

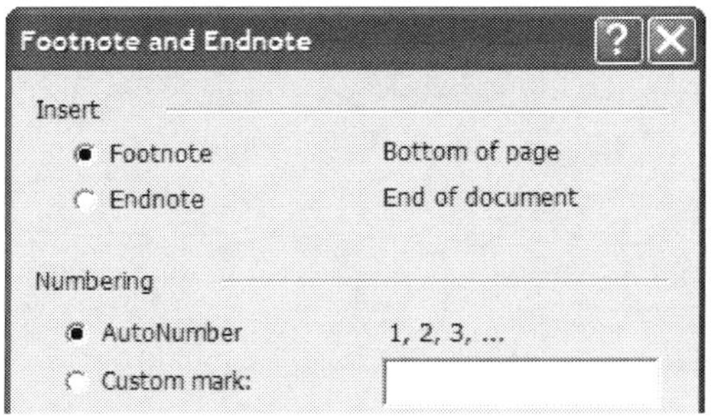

Figure 5-8 Footnote and Endnote dialog box

3. Select the **AUTO NUMBER** option, if it is not already selected, then click OK. The footer portion of your document should look like the one shown in Figure 5-9.

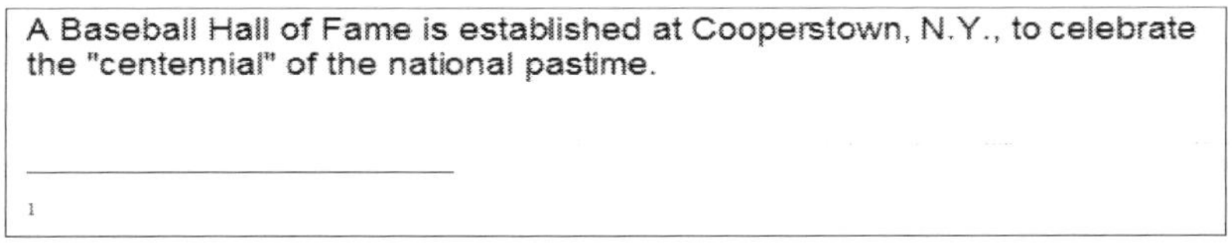
A Baseball Hall of Fame is established at Cooperstown, N.Y., to celebrate the "centennial" of the national pastime.

1

Figure 5-9 First footnote added

4. The cursor should be in the footnote section of the document.
   Type `The Black Sox's are a baseball team.`

5. Create another numbered footnote for "Louisville Slugger" in the second paragraph. You can follow the steps above. Type `Louisville Slugger is a brand of baseball bat.` in the footnote section. The footnote section of your document should look like the one shown in Figure 5-10.

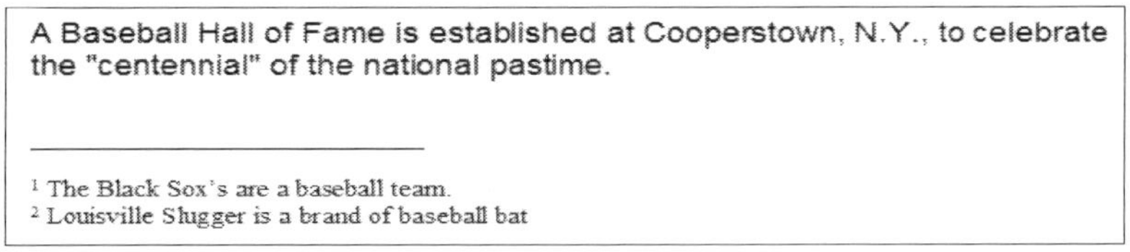
A Baseball Hall of Fame is established at Cooperstown, N.Y., to celebrate the "centennial" of the national pastime.

1 The Black Sox's are a baseball team.
2 Louisville Slugger is a brand of baseball bat

Figure 5-10 Footnote section of the document

How To Create A Custom Mark Footnote

A custom mark footnote will allow you to use any character that you can type into the field. I haven't seen this feature used much, but wanted to let you know that it exists and how to use it, should the need arise.

1. Place the cursor after the word **ECLIPSE** on the fourth line in the second paragraph, then Insert ⇒ Footnote. Click on the **CUSTOM MARK** numbering style option.

2. Click in the text box across from the Custom Mark field and type a `#` (It's on the 3 key), then click OK.

3. Next to the # in the footnote section, type
   `The Louisville Eclipse is a baseball team`. Save the changes.

Create Another Footnote

1. In the next to last paragraph on page 1, place the cursor after the word **EXPOS** on the third line. Insert ⇒ Footnote and click OK.

2. Type `The Montreal Expos are based in Canada`. The footnote section of your document should look like the one shown in Figure 5-11. Save the changes and close the document.

Notice that even though you added a custom mark for the third footnote, that the fourth footnote still kept the numbering sequence. If you were to rearrange the sentences that contain footnotes, the footnote numbering sequence will automatically be renumbered also.

[1] The Black Sox's are a baseball team.
[2] Louisville Slugger is a brand of baseball bat.
[#] The Louisville Eclipse is a baseball team.
[3] The Montreal Expos are based in Canada.

Figure 5-11 Completed footnote section of the document

Linking vs Embedding

Linking and embedding allows you to place a portion or an entire document inside of another document. You can link or embed any of the following types of objects in a word processing document: a table, chart, spreadsheet or other objects.

Linking

When you link information, the document that has the linked information will be updated when you modify the source file. Linked data is stored in the source file. The file where you place the data only stores the location of the source file.

Use the linking option when you think the source file will change and you want the changes to be updated in the second document. For example, you prepare a weekly report which includes invoices from vendors. You only need to show the invoice amount in your report for each vendor, which will change every week. You would want to link the information, so that you would not have to make the changes manually in the report.

It is important that you understand that if you use the linked feature and want to share the document with a co-worker or anyone that will not use your computer to open and view the documents, that the files have to be on a shared drive. In the workplace, this shared drive is known as a server. If you want to share the files with someone in your house that uses a different computer, you would have to grant access to your hard drive, or put the files on a drive that is functioning like a server.

Linking is usually done in the workplace, while embedding can be done from home, as well as, the workplace. To accommodate both needs, you will learn how to create linked and embedded documents in this lesson.

Embedding

When you embed information in a file you are placing a copy of the information in another file. The embedded object becomes part of the other file. If you modify the source file of the embedded object, the changes will not be reflected in the document that has the file embedded in it. Use the embedding option if you do not need to see the changes that are made to the source (original) file in the file that you embedded the object in.

The main difference between linking and embedding is where the data or information is stored and how it is updated after you add it to another file. If you are sitting there shaking your head, the next few exercises will show you the differences between linking and embedding.

How To Link A Spreadsheet To A Word Processing Document

Usually, you will want to link or embed information from an existing document. To do that, you must open the document that contains the information that you want to link to and select the content that you want to link or embed. In this exercise you will link a portion of a spreadsheet to a word processing document.

1. Open the spreadsheet application, then open the New Classes Spreadsheet file.

2. Click in cell A4. Hold down the left mouse button and drag the mouse over to cell C4, then drag the mouse down to cell C10. Your spreadsheet should look like the one shown in Figure 5-12. In the upper left corner of Figure 5-12, you should see the range A4:C10. This is the range of the spreadsheet that you want to link to.

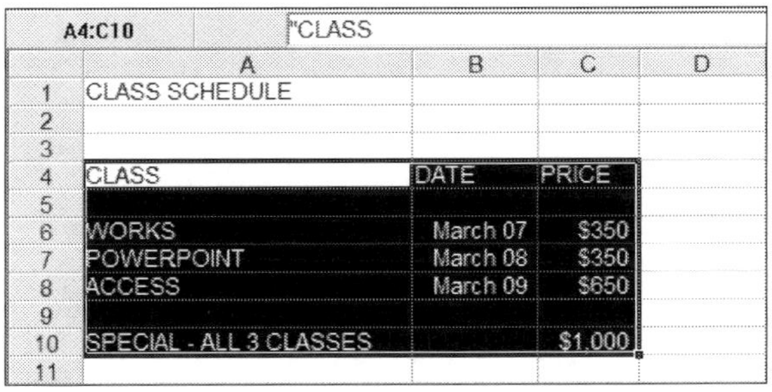

Figure 5-12 Range of the spreadsheet that you will link to

3. Right-click in the highlighted portion of the spreadsheet and select **COPY** as shown in Figure 5-13.

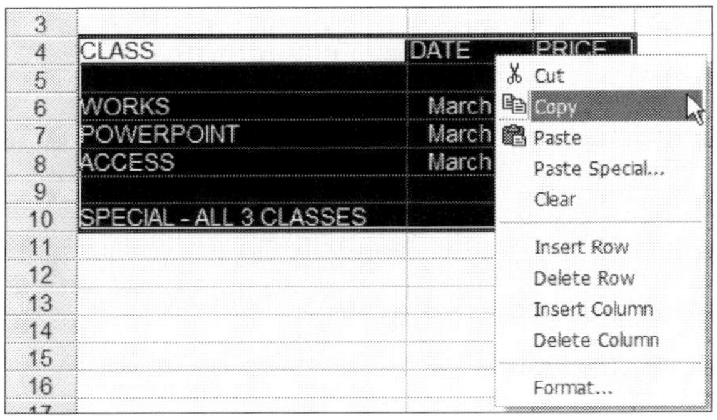

Figure 5-13 Spreadsheet shortcut menu

4. Click on the Task Launcher icon on the taskbar at the bottom of your screen.

5. Click on the History link, then click on the L4 New Classes Letter as illustrated in Figure 5-14.

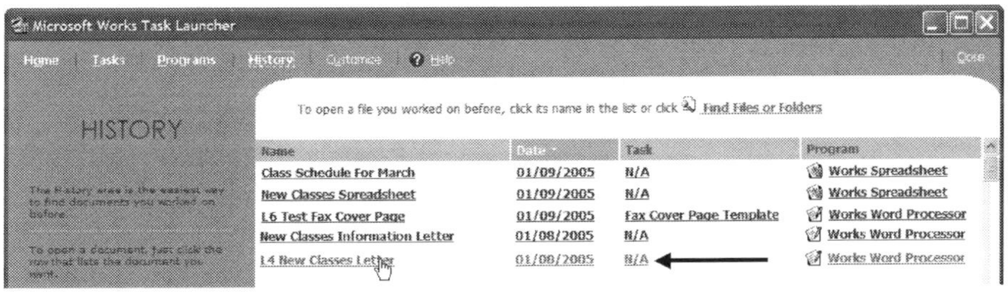

Figure 5-14 Document selected to open on the History page

6. Click on the blank line after the second paragraph in the L4 New Classes letter and press the Enter key, then press the Tab key twice.

7. Edit ⇒ Paste Special. You should see the dialog box shown in Figure 5-15.

Paste Special Dialog Box Options

① Select the **PASTE** option if you are going to embed the document.
② Select the **PASTE LINK** option if you want to link the document.
③ The **RESULT** section explains what the option means.

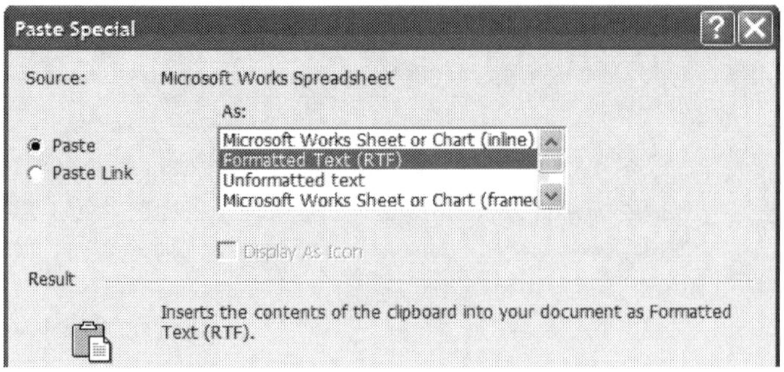

Figure 5-15 Paste Special dialog box

8. Select the Paste Link option. Notice that the explanation in the **RESULT** section of the dialog box changed from what is shown above in Figure 5-15. Click OK.

9. Click in front of the paragraph under the chart and press the Enter key. Your document should look like the one shown in Figure 5-16.

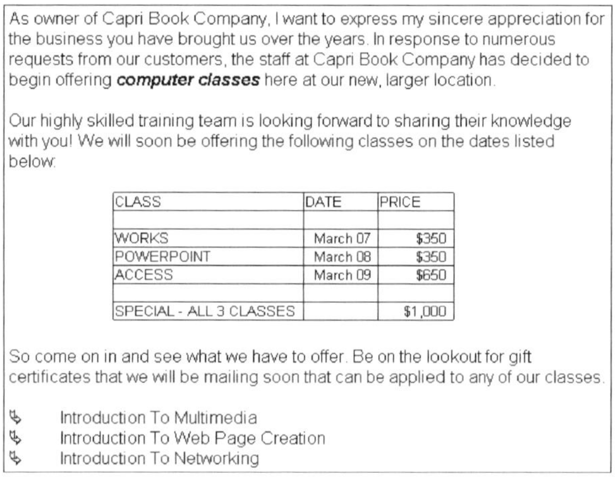

As owner of Capri Book Company, I want to express my sincere appreciation for the business you have brought us over the years. In response to numerous requests from our customers, the staff at Capri Book Company has decided to begin offering ***computer classes*** here at our new, larger location.

Our highly skilled training team is looking forward to sharing their knowledge with you! We will soon be offering the following classes on the dates listed below:

CLASS	DATE	PRICE
WORKS	March 07	$350
POWERPOINT	March 08	$350
ACCESS	March 09	$650
SPECIAL - ALL 3 CLASSES		$1,000

So come on in and see what we have to offer. Be on the lookout for gift certificates that we will be mailing soon that can be applied to any of our classes.

- Introduction To Multimedia
- Introduction To Web Page Creation
- Introduction To Networking

Figure 5-16 Spreadsheet linked in the word processing document

10. File ⇒ Save As. Type `L5 New Classes Letter (linked)` as the file name.

11. Close the letter, but leave the New Classes spreadsheet file open.

How To Embed A Spreadsheet In A Word Processing Document

If the range A4:C10 is not highlighted in the New Classes Spreadsheet file, highlight the range now.

1. Open the L4 New Classes Letter (**HINT**: Open the File menu and select it or click on the History link on the Task Launcher.), then move the cursor down to the blank line after the second paragraph and press Enter. Press the Tab key twice.

2. Edit ⇒ Paste Special, then select Paste on the **PASTE SPECIAL** dialog box, if it is not already selected.

3. Select the option, Microsoft Works Sheet or Chart (inline), if it is not already selected, then click OK. The letter looks identical to the letter that you linked the spreadsheet to in the previous exercise. Click in front of the paragraph under the chart and press the Enter key.

4. File ⇒ Save As. Type `L5 New Classes Letter (embedded)` as the file name. Close the letter and leave the New Classes Spreadsheet file open.

While the charts look the same in the word processing documents, the difference is that the information in the "linked" spreadsheet will change if the data in the New Classes Spreadsheet file changes. The change would not appear in the L5 New Classes Letter (embedded) document.

How To Create A Link That Uses An Icon

If the letter that you have been working with is a letter that is going to be distributed to your co-workers, you may not want to show the spreadsheet in the letter. Instead, you may want to place an icon in the document that represents the spreadsheet. If the reader needed to see the spreadsheet they could click on the icon. The icon created is a shortcut, that when clicked will open the linked document.

In this scenario, the linked document is the spreadsheet. There are two ways that you can create a link and use it as an icon. One way is to do it with the document already open that you want to create the icon for. The other way is to use the Insert Object option. In this exercise you will learn both ways.

1. Click on the New Classes Spreadsheet document icon on the Taskbar. If the cells are not highlighted as shown earlier in Figure 5-12 highlight them, then right-click on the highlighted cells and select Copy.

2. Open the L4 New Classes Letter word processing document, then click on the blank line after the second paragraph and press Enter. Press the Tab key twice.

3. Edit ⇒ Paste Special. Select the option, Microsoft Works Sheet or Chart (inline), then select the **DISPLAY AS ICON** option. Your dialog box should look like the one shown in Figure 5-17. Click the **CHANGE ICON** button. You will see the dialog box shown in Figure 5-18.

You will see the icon that will be added to the document instead of the actual spreadsheet, above the Change Icon button on the Paste Special dialog box.

Clicking on the Change Icon button will let you select a different icon.

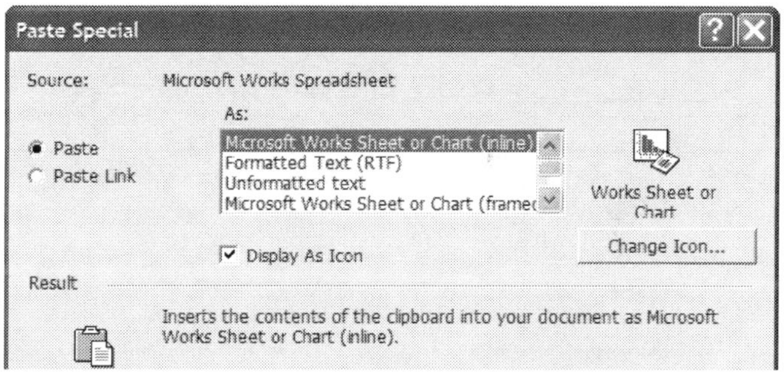

Figure 5-17 Paste Special options selected

You should see the icon that was on the Paste Special dialog box highlighted on the Change Icon dialog box, as shown in Figure 5-18. The three icon options that you see are the ones that come with Works. If you want to use a different icon you can, by clicking on the Browse button and navigating to the location of the icon that you want to use.

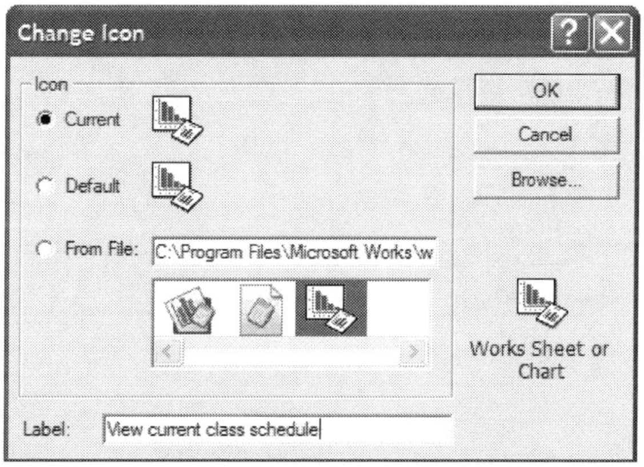

Figure 5-18 Change Icon dialog box

4. Type `View current class schedule` in the **LABEL** field at the bottom of the dialog box. Your dialog box should look like the one shown above in Figure 5-18.

5. Click OK to close the Change Icon dialog box. Click OK to close the Paste Special dialog box. You should see the icon in the document as shown in Figure 5-19.

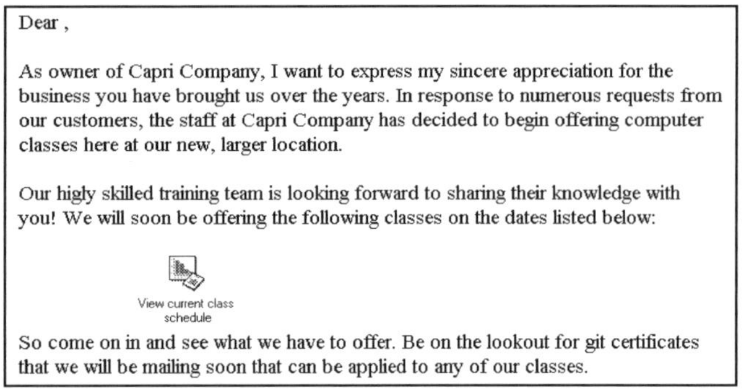
Dear ,

As owner of Capri Company, I want to express my sincere appreciation for the business you have brought us over the years. In response to numerous requests from our customers, the staff at Capri Company has decided to begin offering computer classes here at our new, larger location.

Our higly skilled training team is looking forward to sharing their knowledge with you! We will soon be offering the following classes on the dates listed below:

View current class schedule

So come on in and see what we have to offer. Be on the lookout for git certificates that we will be mailing soon that can be applied to any of our classes.

Figure 5-19 Icon added to the document

6. File ⇒ Save As. Type `L5 New Classes Letter (icon)` as the file name. Close the letter and the spreadsheet. When prompted to save the changes to the New Classes Spreadsheet, click Yes as shown in Figure 5-20.

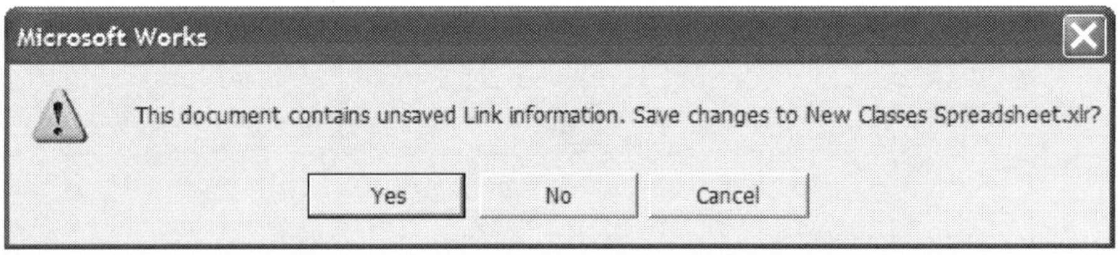

Figure 5-20 Prompt to save the changes to the spreadsheet

The reason that you are prompted to save the changes to the New Classes Spreadsheet even though you did not change it, is because you created a link to data in the spreadsheet. The "link" has to be saved so that if any information in the spreadsheet is changed, Works will know that the changes have to also be updated automatically in the L5 New Classes Letter (linked) word processing document.

7. Click on the New Classes Spreadsheet file in the Save As dialog box. The reason that you are doing this is to save the linked information in the same spreadsheet as discussed in the tip box above. Click Save, then click Yes to replace the spreadsheet.

How To Change The Font Attributes On An Icon

If you think the text is hard to read on the icon that you just created, follow the steps below to change the font attributes.

1. Open the L5 New Classes Letter (icon) document, then right-click on the icon and select Font. Change the font size to 10 and click OK.

2. Save the changes and leave the document open.

Some people have told me that after changing the font size, it didn't change the text on the icon. I'm not sure why that is. I've tried to duplicate it, but wasn't able to.

Test The Icon

> If you have the files on the History page sorted by the most recent date at the top of the list, the L5 New Classes letter (icon) document should be at the top of the list. If the arrow to the right of the Date column on the History page is pointing down, then you have the files sorted in the order that I am referring to. If you are having trouble seeing the entire file name, close the Help system on the right.

1. Double-click on the icon in the document. The New Classes Spreadsheet should open.
2. Close the spreadsheet and the letter. When prompted to save changes to the letter, click Yes.

How To Add An Icon To A Document Using The Insert Object Option

You may find this method easier to add an icon to a document.

1. Save the New Classes Information Letter as `L5 Insert Object (linked)`.
2. Click on the blank line after the second paragraph and press Enter, then press the Tab key twice.
3. Insert ⇒ Object. Select the option **CREATE FROM FILE**, then click the Browse button. Navigate to your folder and double-click on the New Classes Spreadsheet file.
4. Select the **LINK** and **DISPLAY AS ICON** options, then click the Change Icon button and select the **DEFAULT** icon option.
5. Click OK to close the Change Icon dialog box. Click OK to close the Insert Object dialog box and save the changes.
6. If you double-click on the icon, the spreadsheet will open. Close the spreadsheet and word processing documents.

Test The Linked And Embedded Documents

Now that you have created documents that have linked and embedded objects, it's time to see how they work. In order to do this, you need to modify the document that is linked or embedded. In the exercises that you linked or embedded an object, you always used the same file, the New Classes Spreadsheet. You will modify this spreadsheet to see how the linked document that you created will change and the embedded document that you created will stay the same.

Modify The Source File

1. Open the New Classes Spreadsheet.
2. Click in cell C6. Type `500` and press Enter.
3. Save the change and close the spreadsheet.

Test The Change Made To The Spreadsheet

You will now get to see what the difference is between linked and embedded documents by opening some of the documents that you created earlier in this lesson.

1. Open the L5 New Classes Letter (linked) document. You should see the new price of $500 in cell C6 (the first price).

2. Open the L5 New Classes Letter (embedded) document. You should see the original price of $350 in cell C6.

3. Close both of the word processing documents and open the New Classes Spreadsheet.

4. Click in cell C6. Type `350` and press Enter, then save the change and close the spreadsheet.

How To Link A Chart To A Word Processing Document

Just like you can link spreadsheets to a word processing document, you can also link a variety of other types of documents including charts.

1. Open the Class Schedule for March spreadsheet, then View ⇒ Chart. You should now see the chart.

2. Edit ⇒ Copy.

3. Save the L4 New Classes Letter document as `L5 New Classes Letter (with chart).`

4. Click on the blank line after the second paragraph and press the Enter key. Edit ⇒ Paste Special, then select the Paste Link option and click OK. Your letter should have the chart shown in Figure 5-21. As you can see, the chart is a bit large for the document.

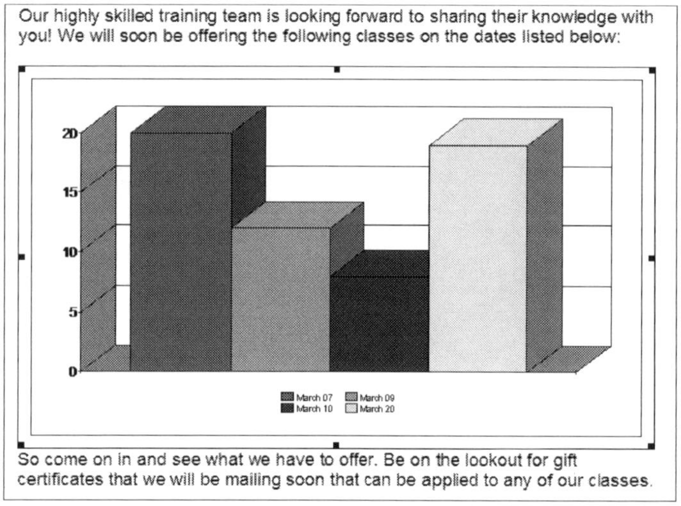

Figure 5-21 Chart added to the letter

How To Resize A Chart

You will see a border that has squares around the chart as shown above in Figure 5-21. This is called a **FRAME**.

1. If you don't see the frame, click anyplace on the chart. Place the cursor on the square in the lower right corner of the frame. The mouse pointer will change to a double arrow as illustrated in Figure 5-22.

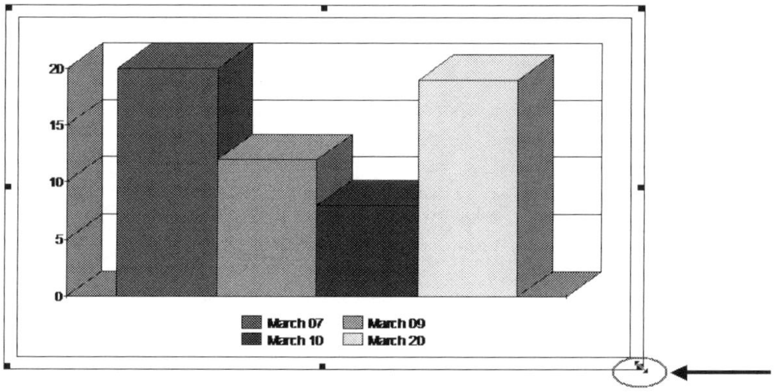

Figure 5-22 Mouse pointer in position to resize the chart

2. Press the left mouse button and drag the mouse up and over to the left until the chart is the size that you want, then click on a blank space on the document to deselect the chart.

3. Insert a blank line below the chart. Press the up arrow key until the cursor is to the left of the chart. You should see a large blinking cursor to the left of the chart as shown in Figure 5-23.

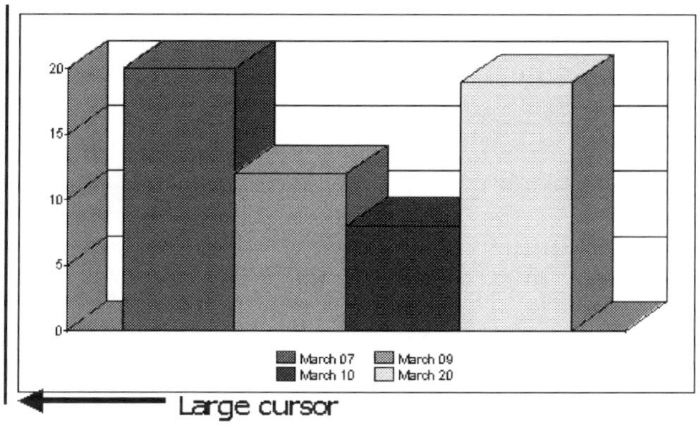

Figure 5-23 Large cursor illustrated

4. Press the Tab key. The chart should have moved to the right. Save the changes. Close the letter and the spreadsheet.

> You could also click on the chart and click the **INCREASE INDENT** button on the toolbar to move the chart.

How To Move (Drop & Drag) Text

Drop and drag is a term that you may have heard before, but were not quite sure what it meant. It means to move content from one section of a document to another section. It works the same way that cut and paste works. You can use either to accomplish the same task.

1. Open the L5 Term Paper (with footnotes) document. The cursor should be in front of the first word in the document. Hold down the left mouse button and drag the cursor to the right until the first sentence is highlighted, as shown in Figure 5-24.

> The "Black Sox"[1] scandal threatens to undermine the prestige and popularity of America's national pastime. Eight members of last year's Chicago White Sox baseball team are indicted in September for fraud in connection with last year's 5-to-3 World Series loss to Cincinnati.

Figure 5-24 First sentence highlighted

2. Move the cursor over the highlighted text. Hold down the left mouse button and drag the highlighted text to the end of the second paragraph. Press the space bar. Your document should look like the one shown in Figure 5-25.

Did you notice that the footnote changed from one to two after the words Black Sox? Refer back to Figure 5-24 and Figure 5-11, then look at the document on your screen. When you move parts of a document that contain a footnote to another location, Works will automatically renumber the footnotes.

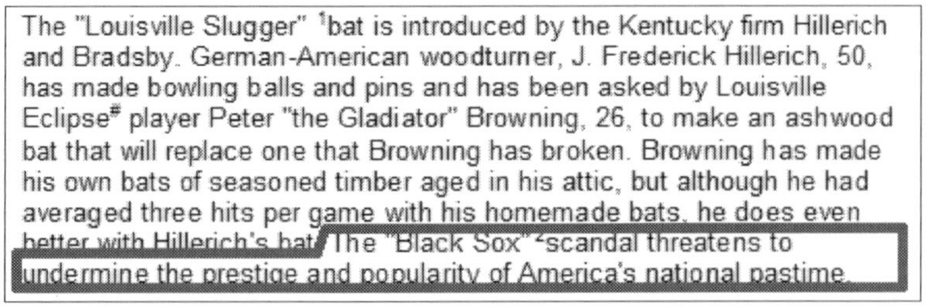
The "Louisville Slugger" [1]bat is introduced by the Kentucky firm Hillerich and Bradsby. German-American woodturner, J. Frederick Hillerich, 50, has made bowling balls and pins and has been asked by Louisville Eclipse[#] player Peter "the Gladiator" Browning, 26, to make an ashwood bat that will replace one that Browning has broken. Browning has made his own bats of seasoned timber aged in his attic, but although he had averaged three hits per game with his homemade bats, he does even better with Hillerich's bat. The "Black Sox" [2]scandal threatens to undermine the prestige and popularity of America's national pastime.

Figure 5-25 Sentence moved to the end of the second paragraph

How To Set Paragraph Alignment

You can set the paragraph alignment in one of four ways.

Figure 5-26 shows each of the paragraph alignment options.

Figure 5-26 Paragraph alignment options

① **ALIGN LEFT** is how the paragraph that you are reading is aligned. All of the characters are aligned vertically on the left margin. This is the default alignment of Works and every other word processing package that I have used.

② **ALIGN RIGHT** is the opposite of Align Left. All of the characters are aligned vertically on the right margin.

③ **CENTERED** alignment has each line in the paragraph centered between the left and right margins.

④ **JUSTIFIED** alignment is a combination of the Left and Right alignment. All of the lines in the paragraph are aligned on the right and the left. Some novels use this type of paragraph alignment.

1. Place the cursor anyplace in the first paragraph. Click the **ALIGN RIGHT** button on the toolbar. The paragraph will change to the right alignment format. Click the Center button. The paragraph is now centered.

2. Right-click in the first paragraph and select Paragraph. You will see the dialog box shown in Figure 5-27. Notice the alignment options. This is another way to set the paragraph alignment. In the **ALIGNMENT** section of the Format Paragraph dialog box select Justified, then click OK. The first paragraph should have the Justified paragraph format.

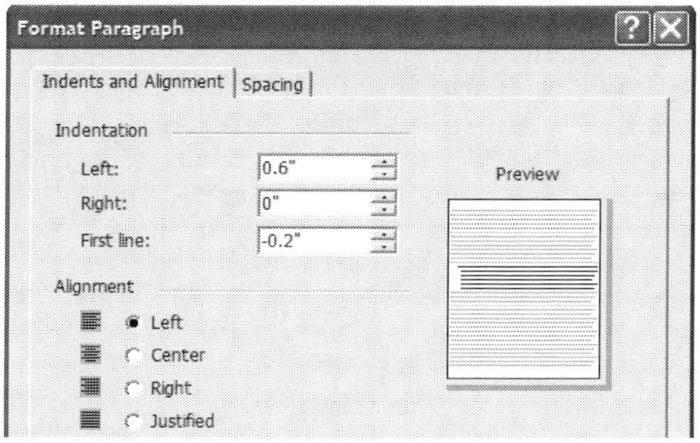

Figure 5-27 Format Paragraph dialog box

Indent Paragraph Option

The Indent Paragraph options are similar to the Paragraph alignment options that you just learned about. Paragraph alignment options are used more than Indent formatting options. The two most popular indent options have buttons on the Formatting toolbar. Refer back to Lesson 4, Figure 4-1 and Table 4-2 for the Indent button options for a review, if necessary.

The top half of Figure 5-27 above, shows the Indentation options. Figure 5-28 illustrates the three basic types of indentation.

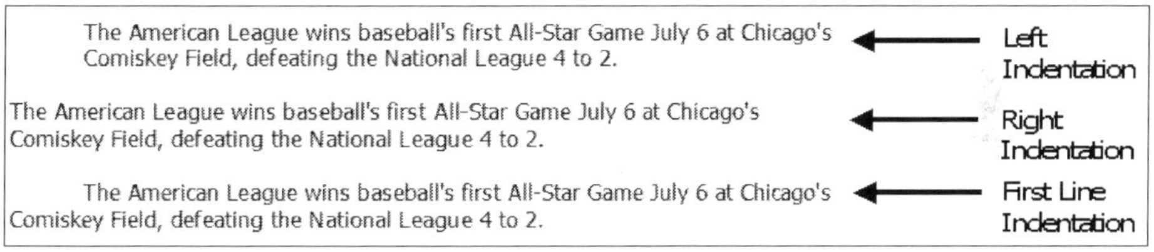

Figure 5-28 Indentation options illustrated

Unlike paragraph alignment, you can use more than one indentation option on the same paragraph at the same time. Figure 5-29 shows what is known as a **HANGING INDENT**.

To create this type of indentation, enter a positive number in the **LEFT** indentation field and negative number in the **FIRST LINE** field as shown earlier in Figure 5-27.

> The American League wins baseball's first All-Star Game July 6 at Chicago's Comiskey Field, defeating the National League 4 to 2. The American League wins baseball's first All-Star Game July 6 at Chicago's Comiskey Field, defeating the National League 4 to 2.

Figure 5-29 Hanging indent illustrated

Paragraph Spacing

There are three types of paragraph spacing available in the word processor. The one that you are probably most familiar with is **LINE** spacing. The two other paragraph spacing options allow you to add space before and after the line of text that they are applied to.

Line Spacing

Line spacing refers to the amount of space between each line in a paragraph. Paragraph spacing options are on the Format Paragraph dialog box, on the **SPACING** tab.

1. Right-click in the second paragraph and select Paragraph. On the Spacing tab, you should see the options shown in Figure 5-30. You will see an option called **LINE SPACING**. It is currently set to Single, which is the default.

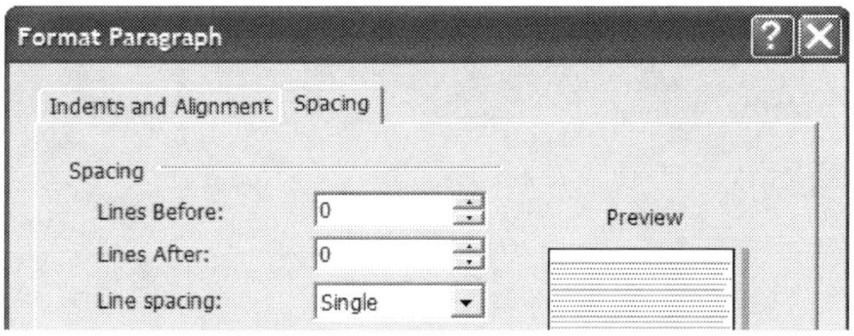

Figure 5-30 Spacing options

2. Open the Line Spacing drop-down list and select **DOUBLE**, then click OK. The second paragraph should now be double spaced.

3. Click the **UNDO** button on the toolbar to return the paragraph to its original format.

Before And After Line Spacing Options

These options do exactly as their names imply. The **LINES BEFORE** option will add space before the line of text that you select. The **LINES AFTER** option will add space after the line of text that you select. These options are most often used with section headings in a document.
All of the section headings in this workbook use both of these spacing options. Figure 5-31 illustrates the **BEFORE** and **AFTER** line spacing options.

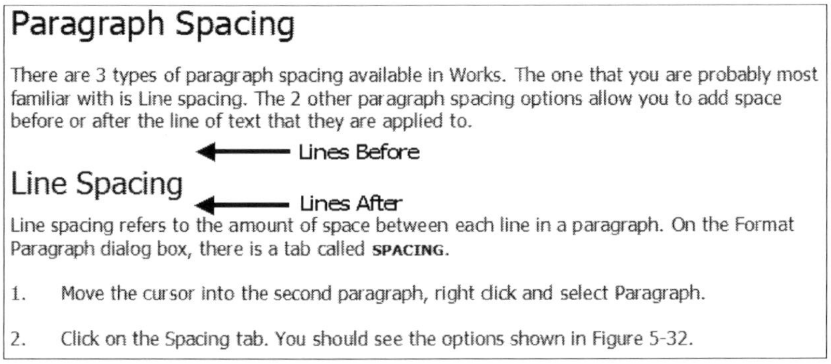

Figure 5-31 Lines Before and Lines After options illustrated

The Zoom Option

From time to time you may have the need to view a document smaller or larger than the default 100% zoom level. If so, there are several options that you can select from. Follow the steps below to change the zoom setting in a word processing document.

1. View ⇒ Zoom. You will see the dialog box shown in Figure 5-32.

   As you can see in Figure 5-32, the 100% option is selected. The 75% option will reduce the size of the information displayed on the screen.

   The 200% option will make the document appear larger on the screen. You can also select a custom zoom level. These zoom settings are the same ones that are in the Print Preview window. I used a custom zoom of 125% to take some of the screen shots in this workbook.

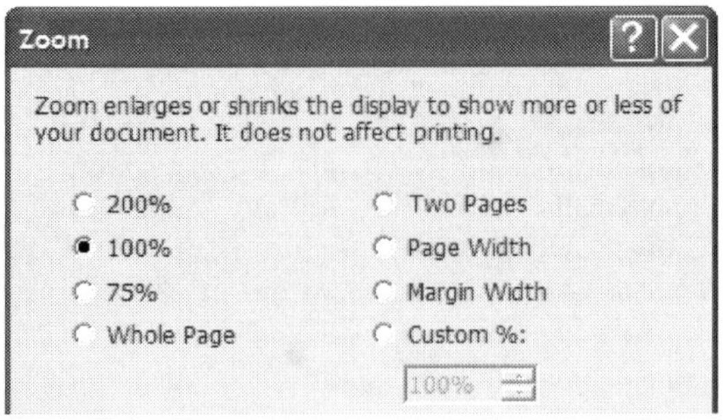

Figure 5-32 Zoom dialog box

2. Close the document, but do not save the changes.

Test Your Skills

1. Save the Term Paper document as `L5(skills)`.

   - Double space the first paragraph.
   - Add the date to the right corner of the header.
   - Add the word PAGE and the page number in the right corner of the footer.
   - Add two Auto Number footnotes in the third paragraph.
   - Add two Custom Mark footnotes in the fourth paragraph.
   - Move the sentence with the second Custom Mark footnote to the end of the first paragraph.
   - Insert the chart shown earlier in Figure 5-21.
   - Create a hanging indent in the second paragraph.

TABLE OF CONTENTS, TEMPLATES & HYPERLINKS

In this lesson you will learn how to do the following:

- ☑ Create a Table Of Contents
- ☑ Add borders and shading
- ☑ Create a template
- ☑ Use WordArt
- ☑ Save word processing documents as HTML web pages
- ☑ Create hyperlinks

LESSON 6

How To Create A Table Of Contents

Some types of documents that you will create may require a Table Of Contents. There is no built-in tool for this, but you can create one manually using options on the Page Setup and Tabs dialog boxes.

Edit The Document

Something that needs to be done is to create a blank page at the beginning of the document for the Table of Contents. The document also needs page numbers.

1. Save the Table Of Contents document as `L6 Table Of Contents`.

2. Add three blank lines to the beginning of the document.

3. Place the cursor on the blank line above the first paragraph of the document. Insert ⇒ Break ⇒ Page Break. This will add a new page at the beginning of the document for the Table Of Contents page. If you needed another page for a cover page, you could add it now.

Set The Page Number And Footer Options

In order for the document to not print the page number on the first page, which is the page the Table Of Contents is on, you have to let Works know that is what you want to do.

1. Move the cursor to the top of the first page. (The first page is blank.) File ⇒ Page Setup.

2. On the Other Options tab, change the **STARTING PAGE NUMBER** to zero. Select the option **NO FOOTER ON FIRST PAGE**. Your dialog box should have the settings shown in Figure 6-1. Click OK. This option will prevent the page number from printing on the Table Of Contents page of the document.

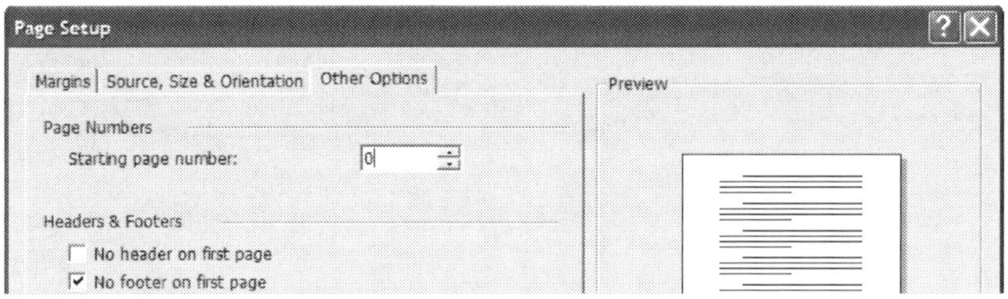

Figure 6-1 Page Setup - Other Options tab

Add Page Numbers To The Document

1. View ⇒ Header and Footer.

2. Click the **SWITCH BETWEEN HEADER AND FOOTER** button on the Header and Footer toolbar. The cursor should be in the footer section on page 2. The reason that the cursor is in the footer on page 2, instead of page 1 is because you selected the option to not have a footer on the first page of the document.

3. Press the Tab key once, then click the **INSERT PAGE NUMBER** button on the Header and Footer toolbar. The document should now have page numbers.

4. Close the Header and Footer toolbar and save the changes. If you preview the document, you will not see a page number on the first page of the document, which is blank. This is what you want.

Tab Stops

The tab stop option is needed to align the page numbers in the Table of Contents.

1. Move the cursor to the first line on the first page of the document and type `Table Of Contents`, then press the Enter key twice.

2. Highlight the text that you just typed and change the font size to 16, then press the right arrow key three times.

3. Format ⇒ Tabs. You should see the dialog box shown in Figure 6-2. In the **TAB STOP POSITION** field, type `4.5"`. This means that you want the first tab at the 4.5 inch mark. This gives you plenty of room to type in the entries for the Table of Contents before the page numbers.

The tab stop that you are setting is for the page numbers in the Table Of Contents. The Table Of Contents would look best if the page numbers are right aligned. The alignment options specify the alignment that will occur at the tab stop that you are creating.

The first three alignment options on the dialog box work the same as the paragraph alignment options that you learned about in a previous lesson. The **DECIMAL** alignment option is used when you need to line up numbers that have a decimal point.

When you press the Tab key to move to the tab stop that you set, the space will be filled with periods. This is the option that is used the most, but you are free to use any of the leader options.

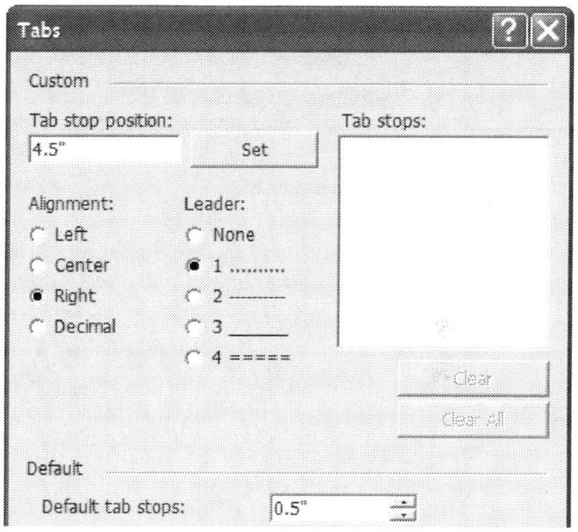

Figure 6-2 Tabs dialog box

4. In the Alignment section on the Tabs dialog box, select **RIGHT**, then select **LEADER 1**. Your dialog box should have the options selected that are shown above in Figure 6-2.

5. Click the **SET** button. You should see 4.5 in the **TAB STOPS** section (to the right of the **SET** button) in the dialog box. Click OK.

Create The Table Of Contents

You are now ready to create the Table Of Contents. By now you would have determined what items you want to include in the Table Of Contents.

1. Type `Chicago White Sox` and press the Tab key, then type `1`. The space before the page number should have filled in with periods. Press Enter.

2. Add the Table Of Contents entries shown in Table 6-1 to your document. When you are finished, your Table Of Contents should look like the one shown in Figure 6-3.

Table Of Contents Entries	Page
Louisville Slugger	2
Baseball's American League	3
Baseball Hall of Fame	5
World Series	6
Toronto Blue Jays	6

Table 6-1 Entries for the Table Of Contents

Table Of Contents

Chicago White Sox 1
Louisville Slugger 2
Baseball's American League 3
Baseball Hall of Fame 5
World Series 6
Toronto Blue Jays 6

Figure 6-3 Completed Table Of Contents

> As you may have figured out, if any of the items in the Table Of Contents moves to another page or is deleted, you will have to manually make the changes in the Table Of Contents.

3. Preview the document. As you will see, there is no page number on the Table Of Contents page. There are page numbers on the other pages of the document which is what you want.
   Save the changes and close the document.

Templates

A template is a document that can be used over and over. A fax cover sheet is an example of a document that you could create and save as a template. Templates look like regular documents. The difference is in how you save them. Earlier, you created a fax cover page using the wizard. Now you will learn to create a fax cover page template from scratch.

Create A Fax Cover Page Template

1. Open a new word processing document and press the Enter key twice, then move the cursor back up to the first line and click the Bold button. Press the Caps Lock key on your keyboard.

2. Type `FAX COVER PAGE` and click the Center button, then highlight the text and change the font size to 20.

3. Press the right arrow key twice, then press the Enter key four times. Change the font size to 12. Type `DATE`, then tab to the 3 inch mark and type `# OF PAGES`.

4. Press the Enter key three times and type `TO`. Tab to the 3 inch mark and type `FROM`. Finish your document so that it looks like the one shown in Figure 6-4.

FAX COVER PAGE

DATE # OF PAGES

TO FROM

FAX#

SUBJECT

Figure 6-4 Fax cover page

How To Add A Border Around Text

1. Press the Enter key four times and type `NOTES`. Press the Enter key three times.

> The reason that you are adding these blank lines now, is so that if you have to type below the border that you are about to create, you will be able to.

2. Highlight the word **NOTES**. Format ⇒ Borders and Shading.

3. Open the **LINE STYLE** drop-down list and select the first double border option as illustrated in Figure 6-5, then click OK.

The **BORDER STYLE** options on the right side of Figure 6-5, let you select where you want to place the border. The default option is **OUTLINE**, which is what is selected. If you did not want a border on all four sides, you would select the options below the Outline option to indicate where you want the border lines.

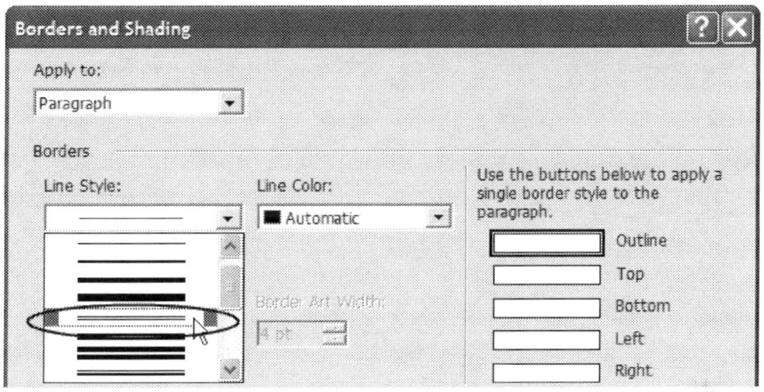

Figure 6-5 Line Style option illustrated

4. Click to the right of the word Notes and press the Enter key four times, then turn the Caps Lock off. Your document should look like the one shown in Figure 6-6. The Notes box will get larger as you enter more text in it.

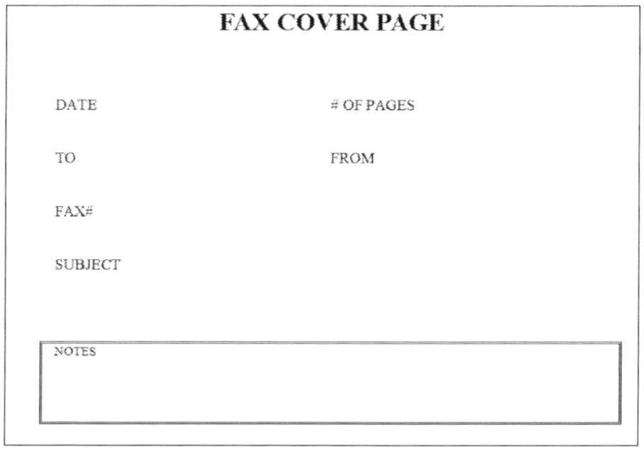

Figure 6-6 Border added to the Notes field

How To Add Shading To Text

1. Highlight the words **FAX COVER PAGE** at the top of the document, then Format ⇒ Borders and Shading. Select the same **LINE STYLE** option that you did in the previous exercise.

2. Open the **FILL STYLE** drop-down list and select the lightest gray shading color option as illustrated in Figure 6-7. Click OK. Your document should look like the one shown in Figure 6-8.

Notice that all of the **BORDER STYLE OPTIONS** on the right side of the dialog box are filled in with the **LINE STYLE** option that you selected. This lets you know where the border will appear. This is a good way to check to make sure that you have selected the border location options that you want.

The options shown on the right side of the dialog box illustrate that the border will be placed on all four sides of the paragraph, which is what you want. If the dialog box had the border style options illustrated in Figure 6-9, the border would only appear above and below the paragraph, not on all four sides.

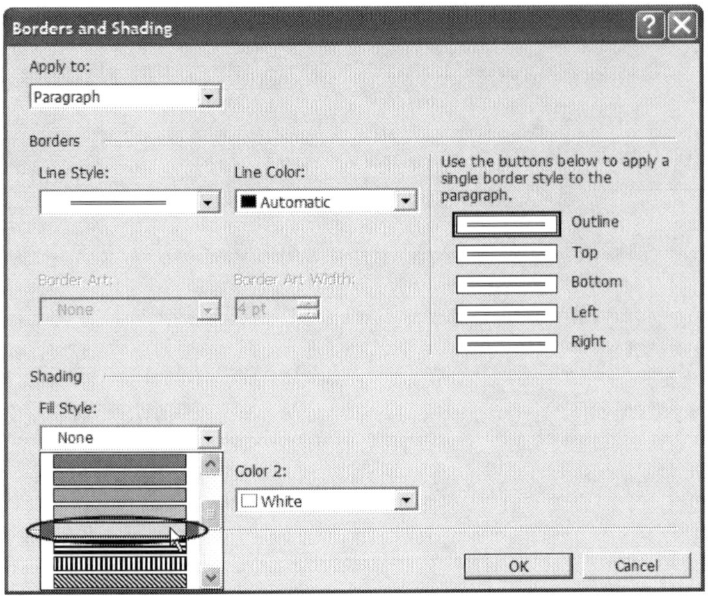

Figure 6-7 Fill Style option illustrated

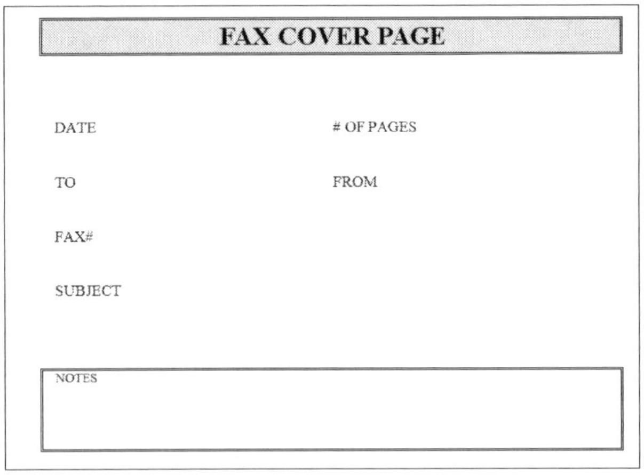

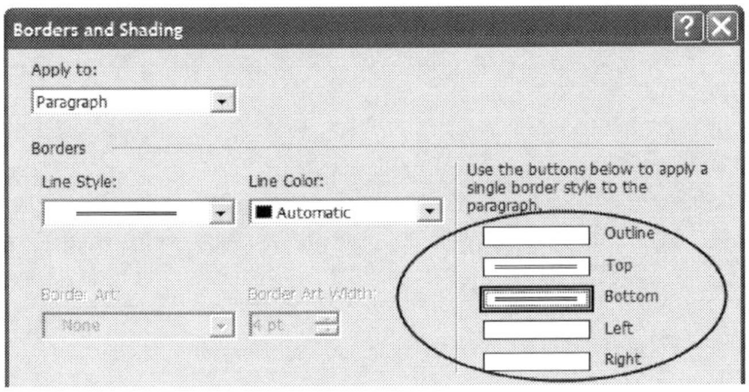

Figure 6-9 Top and bottom border locations illustrated

Figure 6-8 Border and shading added to the title of the document

Save The Document As A Template

1. Click Save, then open the **SAVE AS TYPE** drop-down list and select **WORKS TEMPLATE.**

> If you clicked the Template button you could also save the document as a template. The difference is that you do not have the option of selecting the folder that the template is saved in. I don't know about you, but I prefer to know where the files are that I create.

2. Navigate to your folder. Type `Fax Cover Page Template` as the file name and click Save.

3. Close the document, then click the Task Launcher button on the taskbar.

4. Click on the Tasks link on the Task Launcher, then click on the **PERSONAL TEMPLATES** category. You should see the Fax Cover Page Template as an option, as shown in Figure 6-10 on the right.

The templates that you create will be listed in this task category, regardless of where you save them on your hard drive. When you open a template, a new document will open and a copy of the template is placed in the new document. If you have created templates in Works before going through this workbook, you will see them listed in this category also.

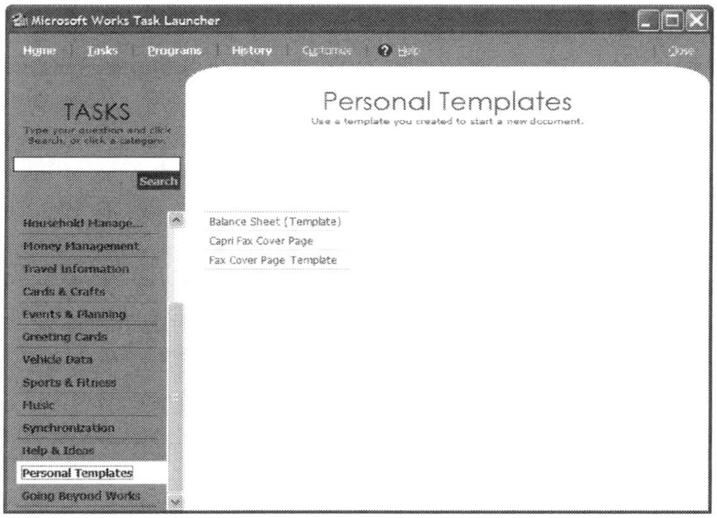

Figure 6-10 Personal Templates

Using The Template That You Created

1. Click on the Fax Cover Page Template option, then click the **START THIS TASK** link. Look in the upper left corner of the document. You will see the words **UNTITLED DOCUMENT**. This lets you know that this is a new document. If you open an existing document, you would see the document name in the upper left corner of the window.

2. Click to the right of the Date field and type `1/1/04`.

> A word of caution. Templates do not always keep the template text where you typed it when you created the template. Often, you will have to re-adjust the template text. The reason this happens is because there is no option to keep the text from moving around on the page. If Works had an option to add fields to word processing documents, it would prevent the text in the template from moving around in the document.

3. Change the date to `1/29/04`. Notice that the # Of Pages field moved. To put the field back where it belongs, move to the end of the date that you just typed and press the Delete key.

4. Click Save. Navigate to your folder and type `L6 Test Fax Cover Page` as the file name, then close the document. Every time that you open the Fax Cover Page Template document, you will get a new copy of it.

WordArt Toolbar

WordArt allows you to create text with special effects. Some of the effects in WordArt include changing the spacing between characters, flipping text sideways, shading and rotating text. Figure 6-11 shows the WordArt toolbar. Table 6-2 explains the purpose of each button. Many of these options work the same as they do for regular text.

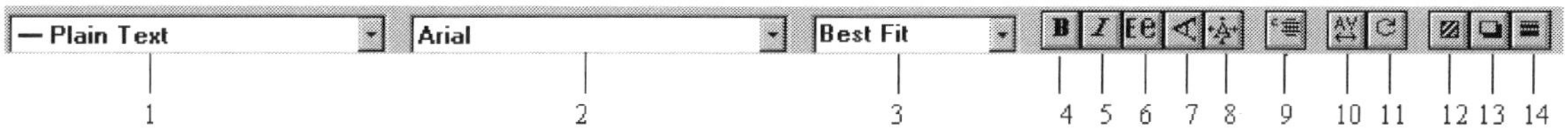

Figure 6-11 WordArt toolbar

Button	Purpose
1	**Shape** allows you to select a shape for the WordArt. Figure 6-13 shows all of the shapes.
2	**Font** lists all of the available fonts.
3	**Font Size** lists all of the available font sizes for the font that is selected.
4	**Bold** will make the WordArt bold.
5	**Italic** will make the WordArt italic.
6	**Even Height** will make all of the letters (upper and lower case) the same height.
7	**Flip** turns letters on their side, as shown at the bottom of Figure 6-18.
8	**Stretch** will stretch the WordArt vertically and horizontally until it fills the frame.
9	**Align** allows you to select the type of alignment for the text.
10	**Spacing Between Characters** allows you to add or remove spaces between individual characters in a word.
11	**Rotation** turns the WordArt to any angle.
12	**Shading** adds a background color to the WordArt.
13	**Shadow** adds a shadowing effect to the WordArt. Figure 6-15 shown later, shows the effects that you can use.
14	**Border** adds a border to the WordArt.

Table 6-2 WordArt toolbar buttons explained

Creating WordArt

1. Open a new word processing document and click the **INSERT WORDART** button on the Standard toolbar. You will see the Enter Your Text dialog box.

2. Type `Computer Book Sale` in the **ENTER YOUR TEXT HERE** dialog box as shown in Figure 6-12, then close the dialog box by clicking on the **X** in the upper right corner.

Figure 6-12 Text added to the dialog box

How To Create A Shadow Special Effect

1. Open the **SHAPE** drop-down list. You will see the options shown in Figure 6-13. Select the Wave shape in the last column, fourth one down. The Shape drop-down list should have **WAVE 2** in it, where you see "Plain Text" in the figure.

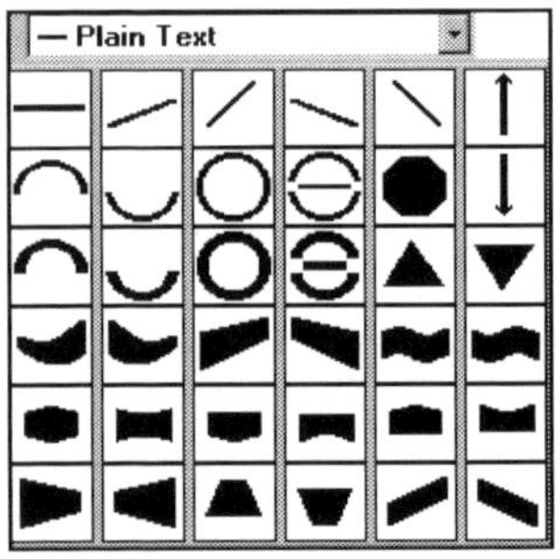

Figure 6-13 Shape drop-down list options

2. Open the Font Size drop-down list (It says Best Fit) and select 32. The dialog box shown in Figure 6-14 appears, asking you to resize the WordArt object. Click Yes.

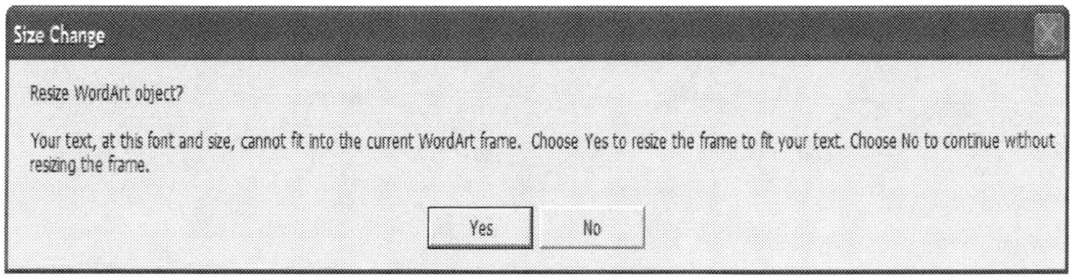

Figure 6-14 Size change dialog box

3. Click the **SHADOW** button on the toolbar. You should see the dialog box shown in Figure 6-15. Click the third button from the right.

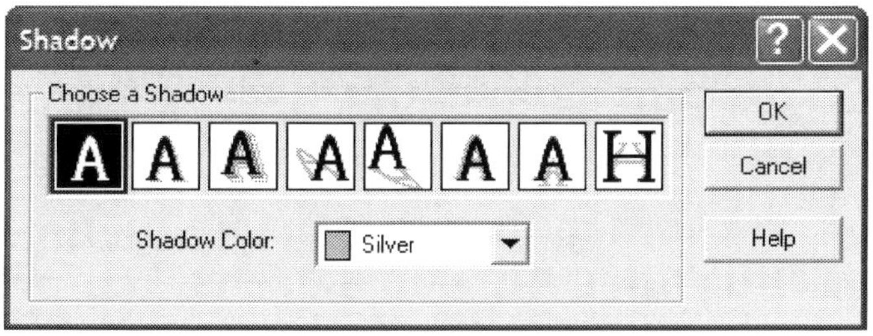

Figure 6-15 Shadow dialog box

4. Change the **SHADOW COLOR** to Red and click OK. Click Yes when prompted to resize the WordArt object. The text should be black and red. Your WordArt should look like the one shown in Figure 6-16. Click on a blank space on the document so that the WordArt is not selected.

Figure 6-16 WordArt with the shadow effect applied

Flip And Rotation WordArt Options

The flip and rotation options allow you to turn WordArt in any direction that you want.

1. Move four or five lines down the page past the WordArt that you just created, then click the WordArt button on the toolbar and type `This Is Flip` in the dialog box. Close the dialog box.

2. Change the font size to `30`. Click Yes to resize the Word Art object.

3. Click the **FLIP** button on the WordArt toolbar. Click Yes to resize the Word Art object, then click the **ROTATION** button. You will see the dialog box shown in Figure 6-17.

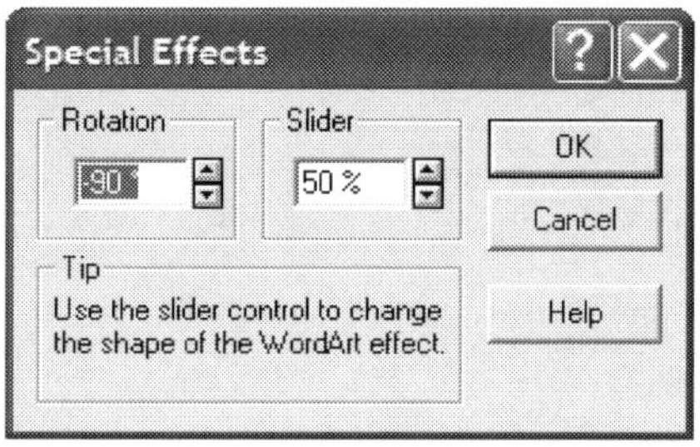

Figure 6-17 Special Effects dialog box

4. Click the Up arrow on the **ROTATION** field until the number changes to 0 (zero), then click OK. Click Yes when prompted to resize the WordArt. Your document should look like the one shown in Figure 6-18.

Figure 6-18 Flipped and rotated text illustrated

5. Save the document as `L6 WordArt Fun`, then close it.

How To Turn A Word Processing Document Into A Web Page

Hopefully the heading for this section hasn't scared you off if you have heard that creating web pages is difficult. HTML is one of the languages that web pages are created with and is one of the most popular languages used to create web pages.

1. Save the Term Paper document as `L6 Web Term Paper`.

2. Open the Save As Type drop-down list and select **HTML DOCUMENT** as shown in Figure 6-19. Click Save. You will see the message shown in Figure 6-20.

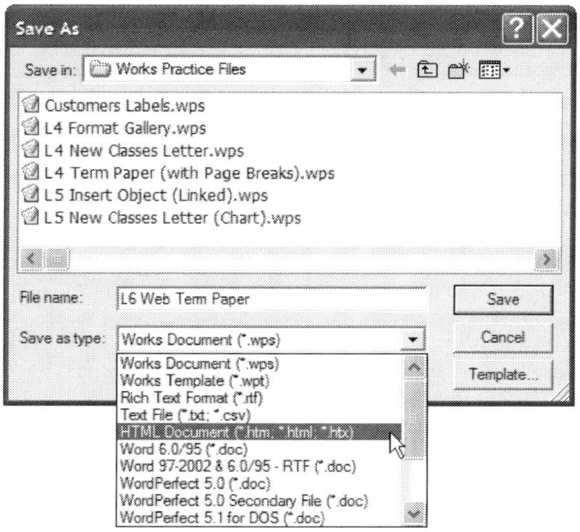

Figure 6-19 HTML file type option illustrated

HTML does not use all of the formatting that Works uses. HTML is a programming language that has rules that must be followed.

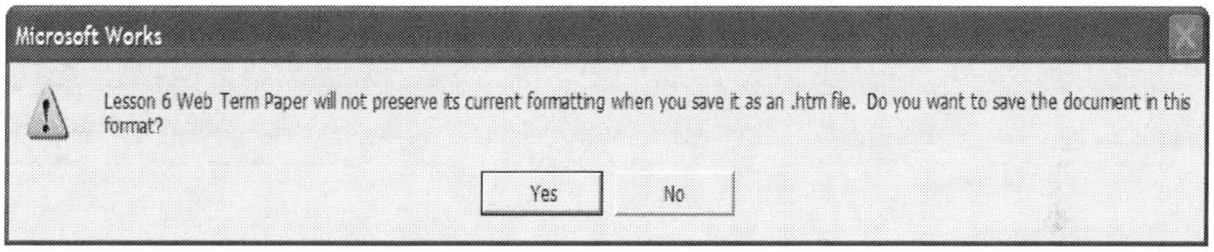

Figure 6-20 HTML formatting warning message

The dialog box above in Figure 6-20 is letting you know that some of the formatting that the document has cannot be converted to HTML format and will be lost when saved in HTML format. The only real option that you have at this point is to save the document and then edit it, so that it conforms to HTML standards.

3. Click Yes, then close the L6 Web Term Paper document. When prompted to save the changes to the document, click Yes.

If you look at the L6 Web Term Paper document you will realize that the formatting the message in Figure 6-20 was referring to is the spacing of the document. All of the blank lines between the paragraphs have been removed. To fix this, you would add the blank lines between paragraphs back to the document. What I've noticed is that you really can't save an existing document in HTML format. If you need to create a web page, my advise is to use another software package.

Interestingly enough, unlike Excel spreadsheets, you cannot save the spreadsheets in Works as web pages.

Adding Hyperlinks To A Word Processing Document

More than likely you have been to a web site and saw links that let you send an email or links that will take you to another web page or web site. These "links" are really called **HYPERLINKS**. There are three types of hyperlinks that you can create in a word processing document. Each type will let you link to something different as described below.

① Web site or file on the Internet.
② An email address.
③ A file on your hard drive.

Create A Link To A Web Site

You may be very familiar with this type of link, because you probably use it more than any of the other types of links.

1. Save the Term Paper document as `L6 Hyperlinks`.

2. Highlight the text **LOUISVILLE SLUGGER** in the second paragraph. Insert ⇒ Hyperlink. You should see the **INSERT HYPERLINK** dialog box.

There are three pieces of information that you have to provide in order to create a hyperlink. You have to provide what you want to link to. This is the top section of the Insert Hyperlink dialog box. You have to provide the location of what you want to link to, which is done in the middle section of the dialog box. The last thing that you have to provide is the text that you want to use for the link.

In this exercise, the hyperlink text information is already filled in because you selected the text to use before opening the dialog box. I would recommend that you select the text for this type of hyperlink before opening the dialog box because doing that would be one less step that you have to complete.

The default option **A WEB SITE OR FILE ON THE INTERNET** is what you want to link to, so you can skip the top section. The middle section is where you enter the Internet address to go to, when the link is clicked on. The choices are an Internet Address or an email address. The middle section will change, based on the option you select at the top of the dialog box. In this exercise you want the Louisville Slugger link to go to a web site.

3. Click after the **HTTP://** in the Internet Address field and type `www.slugger.com`. Your dialog box should have the options selected that are shown in Figure 6-21. Click OK. The words **LOUISVILLE SLUGGER** should now be a hyperlink as shown in Figure 6-22.

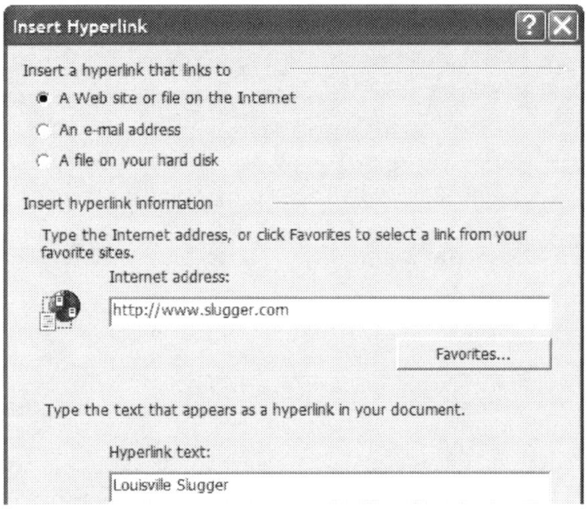

Figure 6-21 Options for a web site address hyperlink

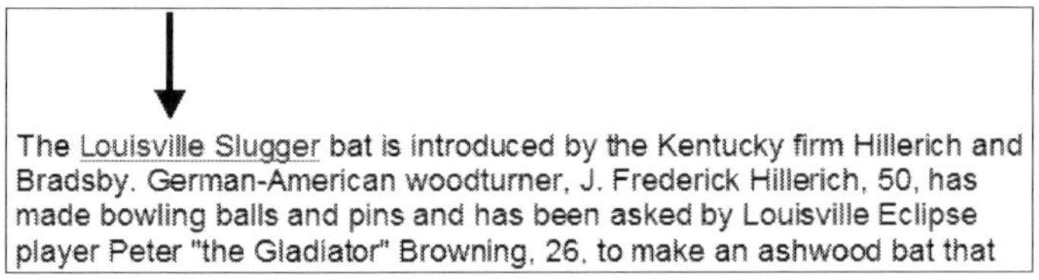

Figure 6-22 Web site address hyperlink illustrated

If you have a document that has a hyperlink like the one shown above in Figure 6-22 and you want to know what web site it is referencing, hold your mouse pointer over the link and the web site address will be displayed, as shown in Figure 6-23.

Figure 6-23 Web site address illustrated

4. Save the changes. If you want to test the link, make sure that your computer is connected to the Internet. Once connected, click on the link that you just created and the web site www.slugger.com will open.

Create An Email Address Link

An email address link will open a new email window in the email software that the person who clicks on the link has. This means that if I'm using Outlook Express as my email software, the email window that will open for me would be in Outlook Express. If you are using a different email package and click on the same email address link, the email software that you use would open. When the email window opens, the email address that you provide on the Insert Hyperlink dialog box will automatically be added to the **TO** field of the email.

In this exercise, you will create a hyperlink using your own email address. If you do not have an email address, you can make one up to complete this exercise.

1. Add a blank line at the top of the L6 Hyperlinks document and place the cursor on the blank line, then Insert ⇒ Hyperlink. Select the option, **AN E-MAIL ADDRESS** at the top of the dialog box. Notice that the other two sections of the dialog box changed from the previous exercise.

2. After the words **MAILTO:** in the **E-MAIL ADDRESS** field, type your email address.

Notice that the **HYPERLINK TEXT** field was filled in for you automatically. You could use this as the text for someone to click on to send you an email. The problem with this is that many people may not know that this link is for sending an email. It would be easier to know what the link was for, if the hyperlink text was more informative. You could use "Click here to send me an email" as the text.

If you wanted to get the email address from your address book, you would click the **ADDRESS BOOK** button.

This would open your address book. The address book shown in Figure 6-24 is the one that comes with Outlook Express.

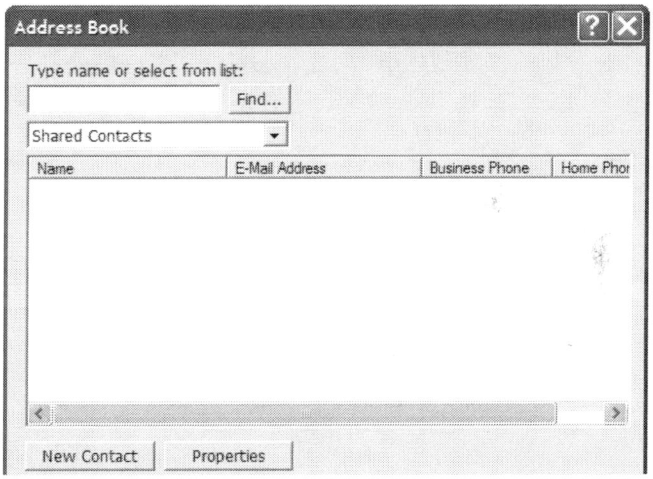

Figure 6-24 Outlook Express address book

3. Type `Click here to send me an email` in the **HYPERLINK TEXT** field. Your dialog box should have the options selected that are shown in Figure 6-25. Click OK. Your document should have an email address hyperlink similar to the one shown in Figure 6-26.

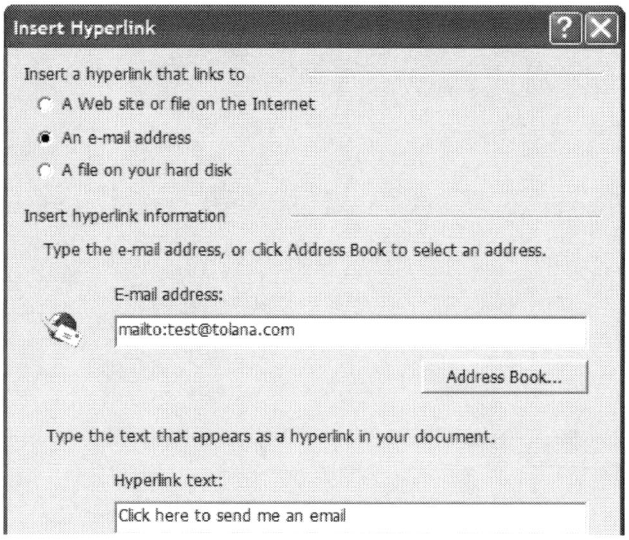

Figure 6-25 Options for an email address hyperlink

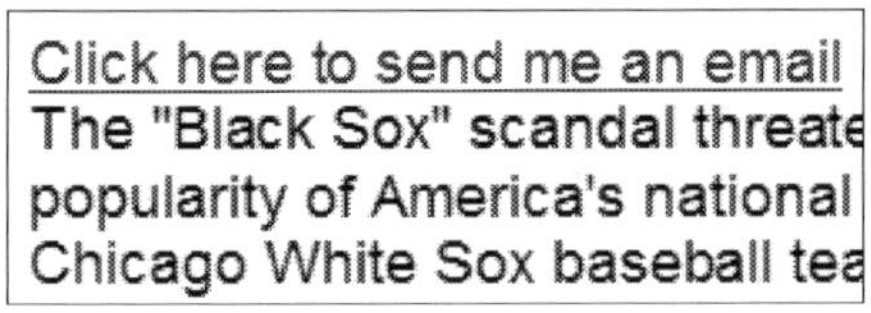

Figure 6-26 Email address hyperlink added to the document

4. Save the changes. If you click on the email address link, your email software should open. You should see the email address that you entered in the **TO:** field as shown in Figure 6-27.

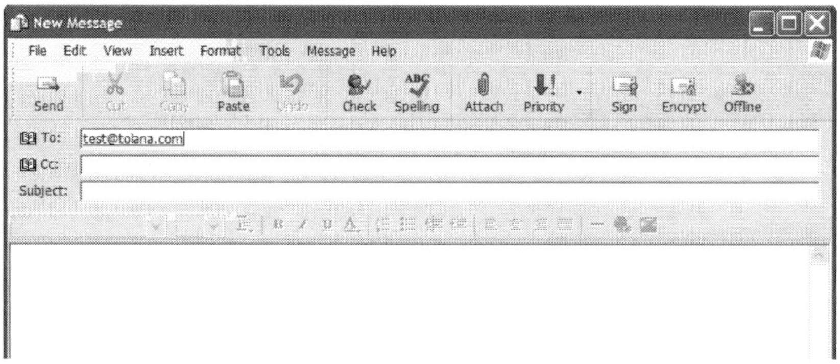

Figure 6-27 Email address in the TO: field illustrated

Create A Link To A File On Your Hard Drive

Out of the three types of hyperlinks that are available in Works, creating a link to a file on your hard drive is probably the least used. The reason is because only people that have access to your hard drive will be able to access the file that this link points to. This type of link could be useful though, if you have files that you use on a regular basis and the files are saved in several different folders on your hard drive.
In this exercise, you will create a link in the L6 Hyperlinks document that points to a document on your hard drive.

1. Add two blank lines above the email link at the top of the document, then place the cursor on the first blank line in the document. Type `Link to the version with page breaks.` Highlight the words that you just typed.

2. Insert ⇒ Hyperlink, then select the third option **A FILE ON YOUR HARD DISK**, at the top of the Insert Hyperlink dialog box. The hyperlink information section of the dialog box is now prompting you to select a file on your hard drive.

3. Click the **BROWSE** button and navigate to your folder in the Open dialog box. When you find the folder, double-click on it so that the folder name is in the **LOOK IN** field at the top of the dialog box.

4. Scroll through the files and double-click on the file, L4 Term Paper (with page breaks). If you do not see this file, select another file in the folder. Your dialog box should look like the one shown in Figure 6-28. You may have a different path in the **FILE PATH** field, which is ok.

The text in the **HYPERLINK TEXT** field is what you selected before opening the dialog box. If you made a mistake or want to use different text you could change it here.

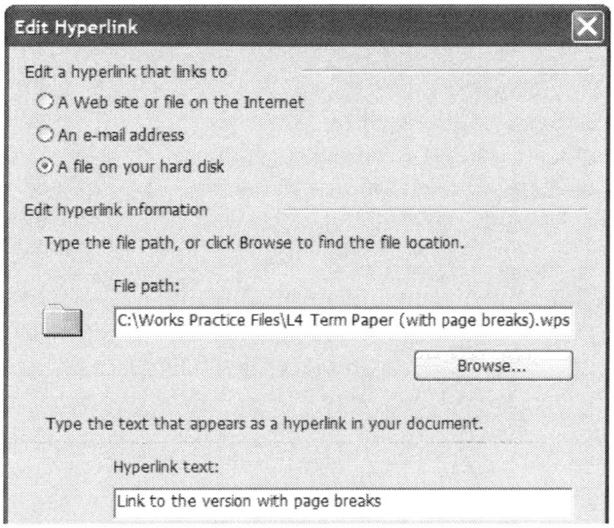

Figure 6-28 Options for a file on your hard drive hyperlink

5. Click OK. You should now have a link at the top of your document. Save the changes.

6. Click on the link now. The L4 Term Paper (with page breaks) document or the document that you selected, should open. Close both of the documents that are open.

How To Edit A Hyperlink

If you need to edit a hyperlink follow the steps below. You do not have to edit any of the links that you created in the previous exercises. For now you can read how to edit a hyperlink should you have the need in the future to do so.

1. Right-click on the hyperlink that you need to edit and select Hyperlink as shown in Figure 6-29.

Figure 6-29 Hyperlink shortcut menu option illustrated

2. The Insert Hyperlink dialog box will open for the hyperlink that you selected to edit. Make the changes that you need and click OK, then save the changes.

Test Your Skills

1. Open the Table of Contents document and save it as `L6(skills)`.

    - Highlight six phrases other than those listed earlier in Table 6-1 and change their color to red. Select phrases on different pages in the document.
    - Create a table of contents that uses the right alignment and Leader 2 options.
    - Set the tab stop at 4 inches.
    - Add page numbers in the header.
    - Create the table of contents heading so that it looks like the one shown earlier in Figure 6-3.
    - Create a table of contents for the six phrases that are in red in the document.
    - Create a hyperlink that points to www.baseballhalloffame.org for the words Baseball Hall Of Fame on page 5.
    - Create a hyperlink that points to the Class Schedule for March spreadsheet at the top of page 1.

MAIL MERGE, LABELS AND ENVELOPES

Works has a mail merge wizard that is similar to the label wizard that you used earlier in this workbook. In this lesson you will learn to create a mail merge from scratch. You will also learn how to do the following:

- ☑ Create a mail merge letter using a database
- ☑ Create filters for mail merge documents
- ☑ Create mailing labels
- ☑ Add clip art to a label
- ☑ Create envelopes
- ☑ Sort the records that will print in the mail merge letter

LESSON 7

Mail Merge Basics

A mail merge will allow you to print customized letters, labels and envelopes. Suppose you need to send the same Welcome package to 20 new customers or a cover letter and resume to 20 potential employers. You could open the letter, type in the name and address, print it and repeat this process for each customer or your could create a mail merge. To create a mail merge, you need two things:

① A list of names and addresses that you want to print.

② A document to print the names and addresses with. This document could be a form letter, label or envelope.

> A mail merge is not limited to names and addresses. You can merge any information that is stored in a spreadsheet, database or address book into a document.

Create A Mail Merge Letter Using A Database

In this exercise you will learn how to create a mail merge letter from scratch and how to use names and addresses in a database. If you have names and addresses in a spreadsheet, instead of selecting a database, you would select the spreadsheet. I think it is easier to already have the body of the letter created that you want to use for the mail merge before adding the fields. This is how you will complete this exercise. On your own you are free to create the letter at the same time that you create the merge.

1. Save the L5 New Classes Letter (linked) document as `L7 Mail Merge Letter`.
2. Click on the line above the word Dear. Tools ⇒ Mail Merge ⇒ Open Data Source.
3. Click the **MERGE INFORMATION FROM ANOTHER TYPE OF FILE** button shown in Figure 7-1. Open the Customers Database file. You will see the dialog box shown in Figure 7-2.

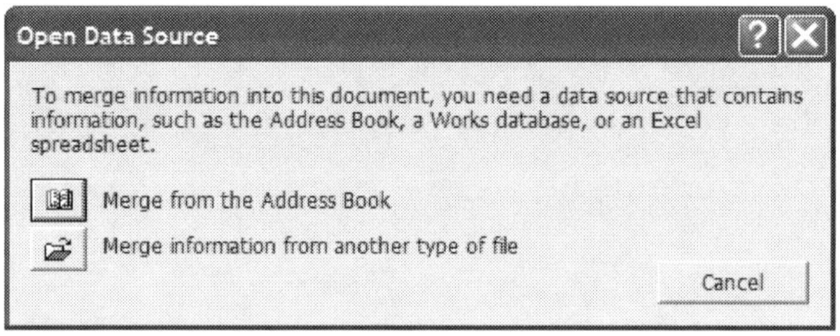

Figure 7-1 Open Data Source dialog box

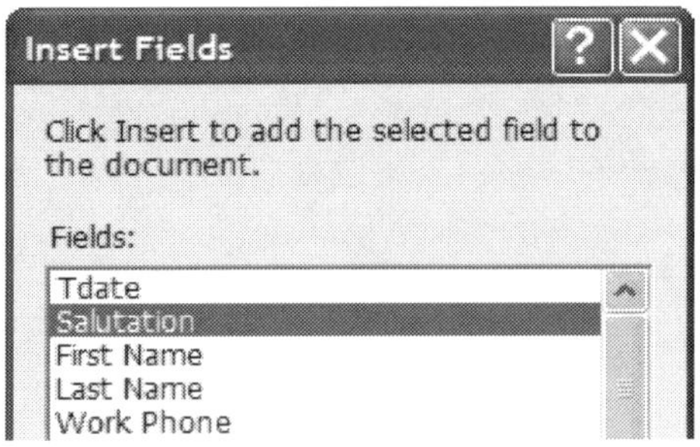

Figure 7-2 Insert Fields dialog box

4. Add the fields in Table 7-1 to the mail merge document, then close the Insert Fields dialog box.

Fields To Add
Salutation
First Name
Last Name
Company
Address
City
State
Zip Code

Table 7-1 Fields to add to the mail merge document

How To Modify The Fields

The way the mail merge fields are on the letter now is not how you want them to print. If you do not modify the layout of the fields before you print the letter, the letters will look like the one shown in Figure 7-3.

Capri Book Company
302 Main St ♦ ♦ Laurel, CT 06868 ♦ USA
Phone (203) 555-1418 ♦ Fax (203) 555-1419 ♦ Email me@xyz.com
MsTinaJones30 Long StFt LaudFL32991
Dear ,
As owner of Capri Book Company, I want to express my sincere appreciation for the business you have brought us over the years. In response to numerous

Figure 7-3 Letter without the fields rearranged

1. Move the cursor to the end of the Salutation field and press the space bar. This will add a space between the Salutation and First name fields. Add a space between the First and Last name fields.

2. Click in front of the Company field and press Enter.

> You can move to the next field by pressing the right arrow key on your keyboard or by using your mouse.

3. Rearrange the fields so that your letter looks like the one shown in Figure 7-4. There should be two blank lines after the merge fields, before the word Dear. Save the changes.

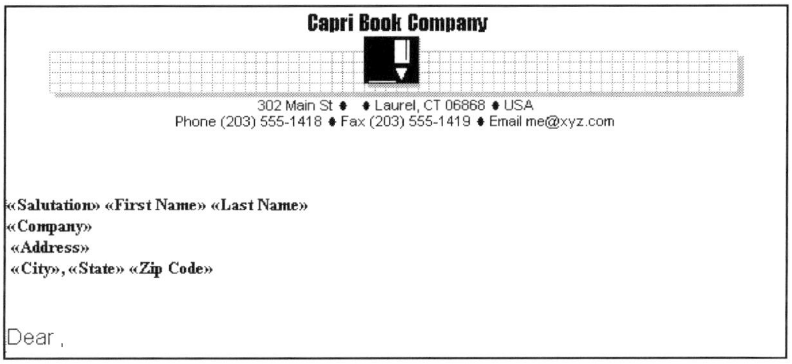
Capri Book Company
302 Main St ♦ ♦ Laurel, CT 06868 ♦ USA
Phone (203) 555-1418 ♦ Fax (203) 555-1419 ♦ Email me@xyz.com
«Salutation» «First Name» «Last Name»
«Company»
«Address»
«City», «State» «Zip Code»
Dear ,

Figure 7-4 Fields rearranged in the letter

How To Change The Font And Size Of The Fields

1. Highlight all of the fields. Change the font to Arial, so that the fields will be the same as the text in the body of the letter.

2. With the fields still highlighted, change the font size to 12, then click the Bold button to turn the bold formatting off.

How To Personalize The Greeting Line

The person's name needs to be added after the word Dear in the letter.

1. Click on a blank space in the letter to deselect all of the inserted fields, then right-click on the **SALUTATION** field as shown in Figure 7-5 and select **COPY**.

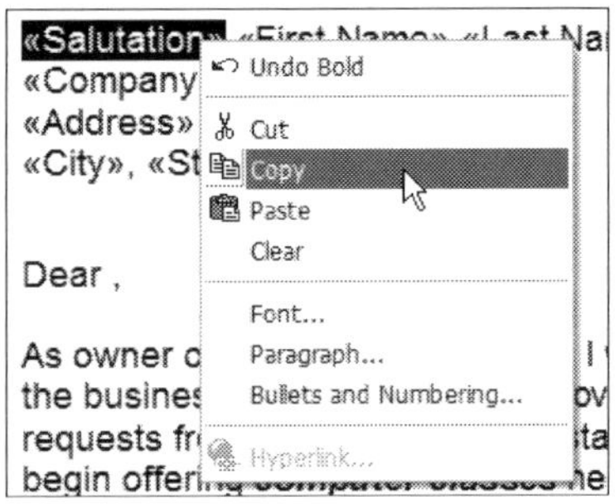

Figure 7-5 Field selected to be copied

2. Click in front of the comma after the word **DEAR** and press the space bar, then right-click and select Paste. The Salutation field should now be after the word Dear.

3. Press the space bar. Copy the Last Name field and place it after the Salutation field that you just added. Your letter should look like the one shown in Figure 7-6. Save the changes.

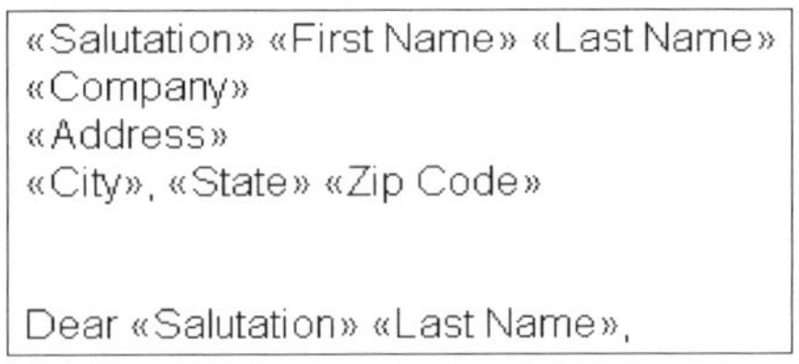

Figure 7-6 Fields added to the greeting line of the letter

Check The Layout Of The Letter

Now that these fields have been added, you need to make sure that the layout is the way that you want it. The best way to determine this is to preview the letters.

1. Click the Print Preview button.

Scroll through the letters. You may see that each letter takes up two pages. This is not what you want, so you need to modify the letter. If your letters are not two pages each, you can read through this exercise in case you have to fix this in the future.

2. Click the **CLOSE** button in the Print Preview window, then scroll down to the end of the letter. If the letter is taking up two pages, you can tell by looking in the lower left corner of the window, where you will see the total number of pages as shown in Figure 7-7.

Figure 7-7 Total number of pages in the document

3. File ⇒ Page Setup, then change all four margin settings to 1" as shown in Figure 7-8 and click OK.

One inch margins are often the standard for letters.

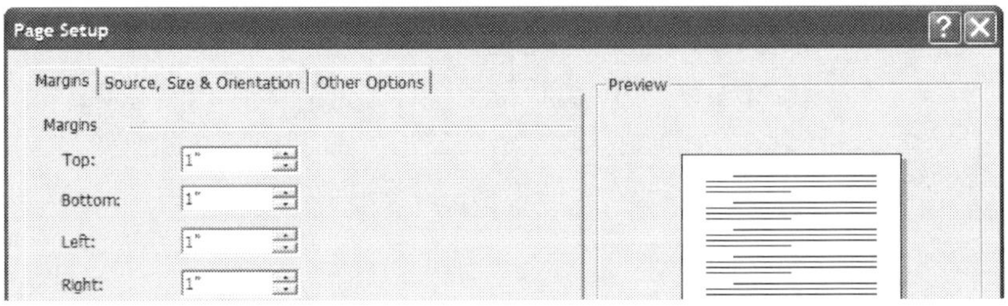

Figure 7-8 Margin options changed

4. Save the changes. If you preview the letters now, each letter should only take one page.

Custom Paper Settings

From time to time you may have the need to use a different size paper, other than 8.5 x 11 or 11 x 14. If you do, follow the steps below to select the custom paper settings that you need. You do not need to complete these steps now.

1. Open the document that you need to print on custom paper.
2. File ⇒ Page Setup. On the Source, Size & Orientation tab open the **SIZE** drop-down list to look for the paper size that you need. If you see the size that you need, select it and click OK. If you do not see the size that you need, select the **CUSTOM SIZE** option highlighted in Figure 7-9.

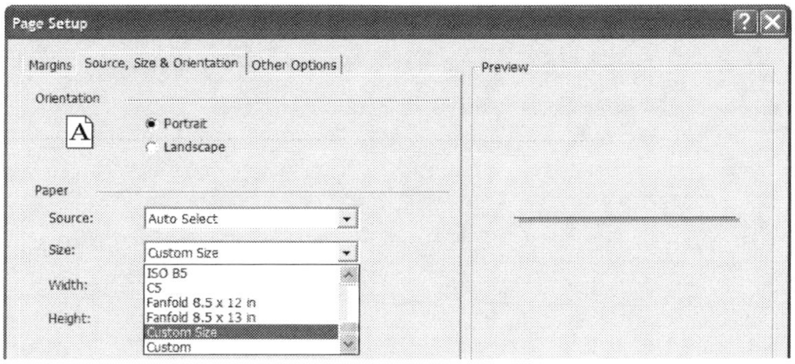

Figure 7-9 Custom size selected

3. Change the **WIDTH** and **HEIGHT** options to the custom size that you need. Figure 7-10 shows the width set to seven inches and the height set to five inches. Click OK and save the changes.

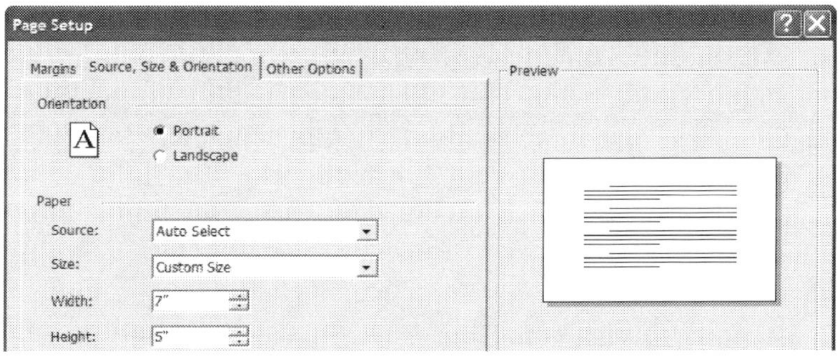

Figure 7-10 Width and height options changed

Creating A Mail Merge Document With A Filter

In a previous exercise you created a mail merge document and used a database as the source of the names and addresses for the letter. If the database has thousands of names and addresses, you may not want to send the letter to everyone in the database. The way to narrow down the names in the database that you send the letter to is to create a filter. A filter will only print letters for the names that match the criteria that you create.

In this exercise you will build on the mail merge document that you created earlier in this lesson by creating a filter for the database. The filter that you will create will be for all customers that have purchased computer books.

The Customers Database has a list of names that have been categorized by the type of books that they have purchased, as shown in Figure 7-11.

✔		First Name	Last Name	Work Phone	Company	Address	City	State	Zip Code	Category
	1	Tina	Jones	(609)364-2500		30 Long St	Ft Laud	FL	32991	Computer
	2	Jamie	Walker	(908)652-9609		997 Lenox Dr	Reno	NV	32883	Mystery
	3	Stuart	Thomas	(718)503-0331		90A Jersey Ave	Orlando	FL	32761	Sports
	4	Todd	Green	(203)452-1300		41 Jefferson Rd	Tampa	FL	32672	Biography
	5	Glen	Carter	(407)471-0159		1 Edward Dr	Las Vegas	NV	60022	Sports
	6	Kelly	Fontaine	(702)825-9787	Jersey Bank	272 Rt 64	Cherry Hill	NJ	07458	Computer
	7	Brenda	Taylor	(610)967-7308	Symphony C&L	500 Point Rd	Ft Lee	NJ	08663	Sports
	8	Steve	Smith	(702)947-8701	Big Design	2200 Research Way	Bronx	NY	11201	Computer
	9	Clair	Walsh	(215)909-8882	Two of A kind	892 Main St	Menden	CT	06403	Mystery
	10	Tina	Walker	(702)703-0101		123 Main St	Stamford	CT	06402	Computer
	11	Tom	Smith	(215)909-1885		45 Jericho Ave	Wilton	CT	06405	Sports
	12	Fred	Amos	(215)327-7079		19 Rodney	Westwood	CT	06403	Biography
	13	Amy	Gardner	(610)664-4646		132 W Park Ave	Wilson	NJ	07403	Mystery
	14	Louis	Riker	(702)667-3053		23 Essex Pl	Tappan	CT	06402	Biography
	15	Brian	Bark	(610)554-3002		300 Winston Pl	Norwood	NY	10023	Computer
	16	Robert	Emerson	(908)587-6422	New Real Estate	200 Mountain Ave	Ft. Laud	FL	32847	Mystery
	17	Peter	Young	(718)505-4259	Elmwood Sales	188 William St	Bogota	NV	32881	Sports
	18	Randi	Sherwood	(718)505-3388	Hi-Tech Inc	777 Broad Ave	Ramsey	PA	19001	Computer
	19	Carrie	Downing	(407)987-4563	Financial Services	63 Maple Ave	Glen Rock	NV	32888	Computer

Figure 7-11 Database categories illustrated

Because you already have the letter created to send to the computer book buyers and have attached the letter to a database, the easiest way to create a filter for computer book buyers is to open the existing mail merge document and save it with a new file name and then create the filter.

Several months from now the file name will help you remember what type of customer this letter was mailed to. You may want or need to use this letter for a different mail merge in the future. For example, next week you may want to send this letter to mystery book buyers. You can do one of two things. You could change the filter on this letter, or you could save this letter with a new name and change the filter on the new document. This way, you would have a version for mystery book buyers and one for computer book buyers. If you customize any of the body of the letter for a specific category of book buyer, you would need two letters.

Create The Filter

1. Save the L7 Mail Merge Letter document as
   `L7 Mail Merge Letter (Filter=ComputerBooks).`

2. Tools ⇒ Mail Merge ⇒ Filter and Sort. You will see the dialog box shown in Figure 7-12.

Selecting the fields to filter on is how you narrow down the records in the database that will print when you print the mail merge document.

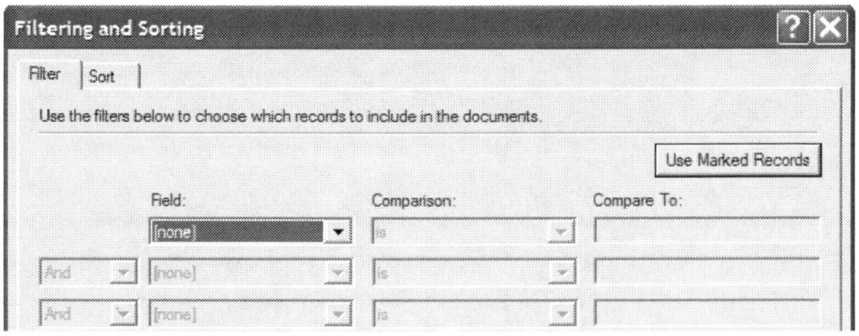

Figure 7-12 Filtering and Sorting dialog box

3. Open the first **FIELD** drop-down list and select **CATEGORY**.

The field names in the list are from in the database that you have associated with this document. The field **MARKED**, refers to records that may be marked in the database. You will learn about marked records in the database lesson.

The **COMPARISON** options allow you to select how you want the information in the field that you selected (in this example, the Category field), to compare to what you select or enter in the **COMPARE TO** field. The four comparison options are explained in Table 7-2.

Comparison	Select This Option If You . . .
Is	Want the data in the field to match what is in the Compare To field.
Is Not	Do not want the data in the field to match what is in the Compare To field, meaning that you want every record except those that have the value listed in the Compare To field.
Is Less Than	Want records that have a value less than what is in the Compare To field.
Is Greater Than	Want records that have a value greater than what is in the Compare To field.

Table 7-2 Comparison options explained

4. You only want to print records of customers that are computer book buyers. Based on the information in Table 7-2, you want to select **IS** in the Comparison field.

The only records that you want to have this filter find are ones that have "Computer" in the Category field, as shown earlier in Figure 7-11.

The values that you see in the **COMPARE TO** drop-down list are the values in the Category field in the database. Refer back to Figure 7-11 if you want to see the values in the Category field. This filter will only retrieve records that have **COMPUTER** in the Category field in the database.

5. Open the **COMPARE TO** drop-down list and select Computer. Your dialog box should have the options selected that are shown in Figure 7-13. Click OK. You should see the dialog box shown in Figure 7-14.

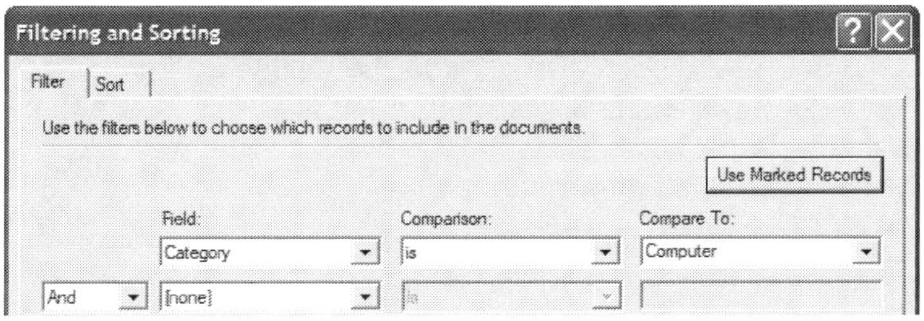

Figure 7-13 Filter options selected

Notice that seven records were retrieved from the database even though there are more records in the database. These are the records in the database where the category field has "Computer" in it. These seven records are the ones that will print in the mail merge letter.

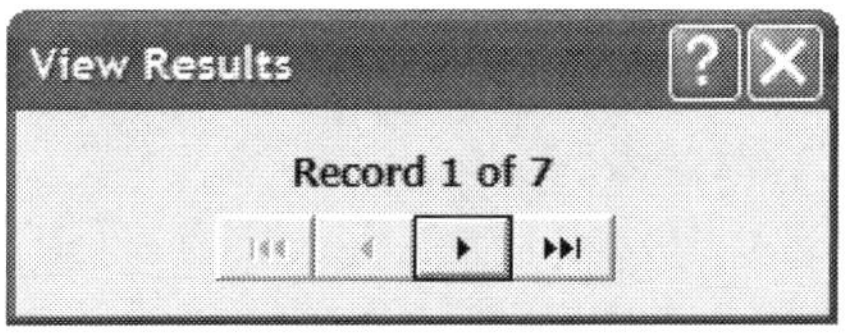

Figure 7-14 View Results dialog box with the records that meet the filter criteria

6. Close the View Results dialog box and save the changes. If you want to preview the letters, you can. When you are finished close the document.

If you know that there are records that will print that do not have information in all of the fields that you have added to the mail merge document you can fill in the data in the database or you can suppress the lines that have empty fields by selecting the option, **DON'T PRINT LINES WITH EMPTY FIELDS** on the Print dialog box as illustrated in Figure 7-15.

Look at the letter shown in Figure 7-16. There is no company name displayed because the record does not have any data in the Company field and the line for the Company name has been suppressed.

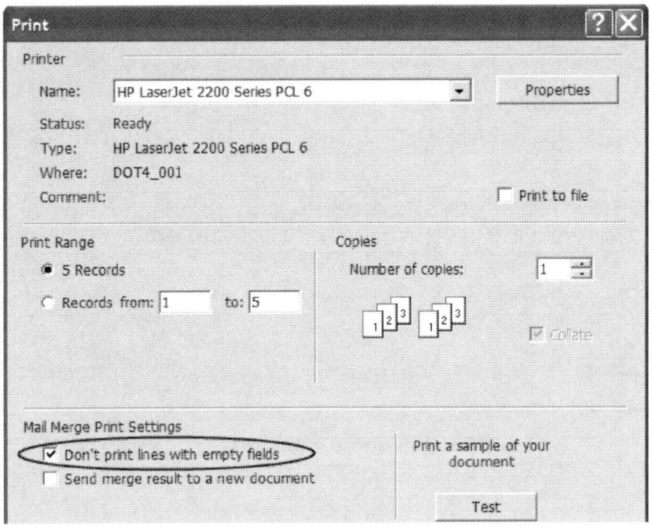

Figure 7-15 Suppress lines with empty fields option illustrated

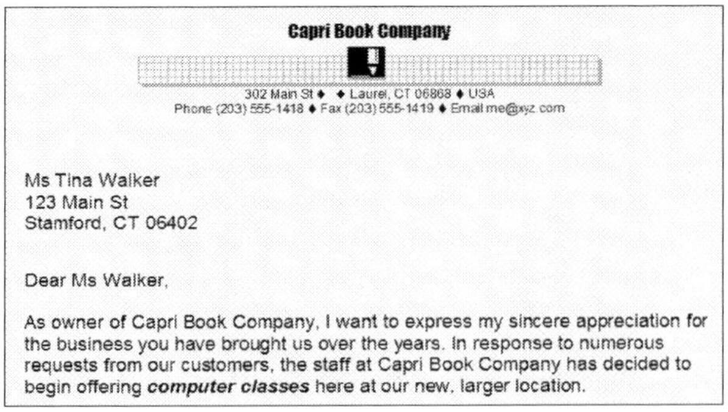

Capri Book Company

302 Main St ♦ ♦ Laurel, CT 06868 ♦ USA
Phone (203) 555-1418 ♦ Fax (203) 555-1419 ♦ Email me@xyz.com

Ms Tina Walker
123 Main St
Stamford, CT 06402

Dear Ms Walker,

As owner of Capri Book Company, I want to express my sincere appreciation for the business you have brought us over the years. In response to numerous requests from our customers, the staff at Capri Book Company has decided to begin offering ***computer classes*** here at our new, larger location.

Figure 7-16 Letter with the company name field suppressed

Create A Personalized Mail Merge Letter

Earlier you created a mail merge letter that printed all of the names in a database. You also created a filter to only print letters for customers in the database that matched the criteria that you created in the filter. Now you will take the mail merge process one step further.

Have you ever received a letter in the mail that had information about your last purchase or some other personal information besides your name and address? This is also done in the mail merge process and is what you will learn how to do in this exercise. You will create a mail merge letter that will print the dollar amount of the customers last order in the body of the letter. You only want to send this letter to customers whose last order was $50 or more. You will use an existing letter as the basis for this personalized letter, because it already has the database attached that you need to use.

1. Save the L7 Mail Merge Letter document as `L7 Mail Merge Letter (order amt $50 or more).`

2. Close the Insert Fields dialog box.

Create The Order Amount Filter

As stated earlier, this filter will only select customers whose last order was $50 or more. The database field that contains the comparison information is the Order Amount field.

1. Tools ⇒ Mail Merge ⇒ Filter and Sort. Open the first Field drop-down list and select the **ORDER AMOUNT** field.

2. Open the Comparison drop-down list and select **IS GREATER THAN**, then type `49.99` in the **COMPARE TO** field. Your dialog box should have the options selected that are shown in Figure 7-17.

> In the previous exercise, the **COMPARE TO** field was a drop-down list. The options for the Compare To field will change based on the field that you are doing the comparison on. The Order Amount field is a numeric field, which means that the information in the Compare To field must be numeric.

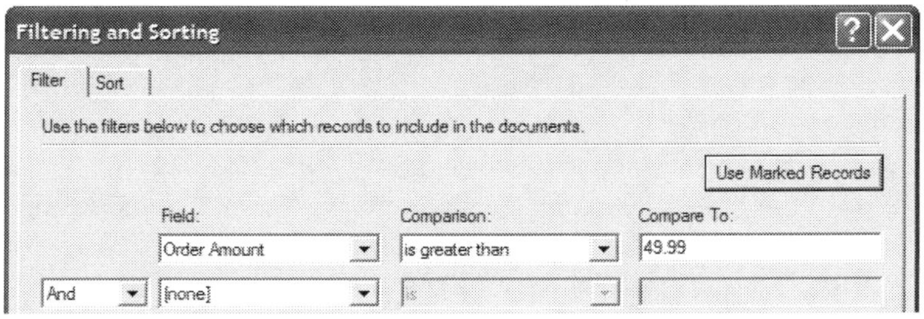

Figure 7-17 Order amount $50 or more filter

> I'm sure that you are asking yourself why couldn't you type 50 in the Compare To field? You can, but you would not get customers whose last order was exactly $50, because the **IS GREATER THAN** comparison knows that 50 is not greater than 50, so any records with $50 in the order amount field would be skipped. If you have used other software you may have seen the option, **IS GREATER THAN OR EQUAL TO.** In that case, you could type 50 in the Compare To field.

3. Click OK. If you want, you can preview the letters by clicking on the buttons on the View Results dialog box. Save the changes and leave the letter open.

There should be five records in the View Results dialog box. If you had typed 50 in the Compare To field, only four records would have been retrieved because one record in the database has an order amount of $50.

Personalize The Letter

The next task is to modify the body of the letter to let each customer know what their last order amount was, which is why they are receiving this offer.

1. Delete one of the blank lines above the word **DEAR** at the top of the letter, then scroll down to the paragraph after the table and place the cursor in front of the paragraph.

2. Type `Because your last order was $`, then press the space bar.

3. Tools ⇒ Mail Merge ⇒ Insert Fields. Double-click on the Order Amount field, then close the Insert Fields dialog box.

4. Type `, you will receive an additional 15% discount`. Your letter should look like the one shown in Figure 7-18. There should be a space after the comma. Save the changes.

> Because your last order was $ «Order Amount», you will receive an additional 15% discount. So come on in and see what we have to offer. Be on the lookout for gift certificates that we will be mailing soon that can be applied to any of our classes.

Figure 7-18 Order Amount field and text added to the letter

View The Letters

If you look in the lower left corner of the word processing window and see that the letter is two pages, delete the blank lines after the word "Sincerely". The filter that you created is suppose to only print letters for customers whose last order was $50 or more.

1. Click the Print Preview button. The letter on page 1 is for Stuart Thomas, whose last order was $75, which is greater than $50. If you look at the rest of the letters, you will see that they meet the criteria of the filter.

2. Close the Print Preview window.

Mail Merge Printing Options

Notice that there is a blank line after the customers name. This blank line is there because this record does not have any data in the Company field. It doesn't look very professional to have a blank line in the address portion of the document. Fortunately, there is a way to suppress blank lines from printing in mail merge documents, which you learned about earlier. The Print dialog box shown earlier in Figure 7-15 has options for mail merge documents. Table 7-3 explains the mail merge printing options.

Option	What It Does
Don't print lines with empty fields	Suppresses blank lines.
Send merge result to a new document	Saves the result of a mail merge document in a new document. This option is helpful if you have a need to save a copy of the actual letters that you print, that contain the merged information.

Table 7-3 Mail merge print options

These mail merge print options are only available when you have a mail merge document open. Each time that you print a mail merge document you have to select these options if you need them because they are not saved with the document.

1. Open the Print dialog box (File ⇒ Print) and select the option, Don't print lines with empty fields. Click the Preview button on the Print dialog box. Go through the letters and you will not see a blank line on the letters that do not have a company name, as shown in Figure 7-19.

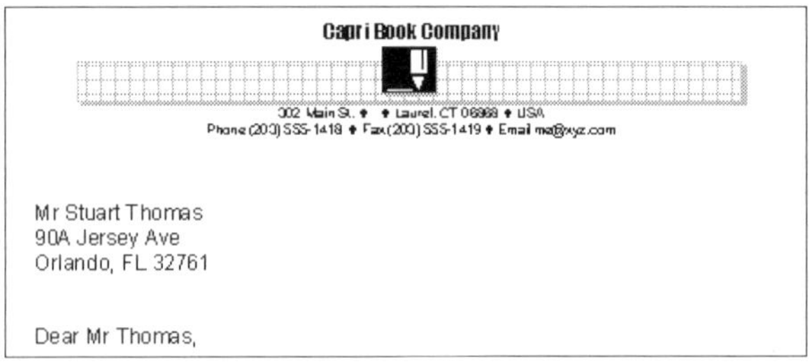
Capri Book Company
302 Main St. ♦ ♦ Laurel, CT 06868 ♦ USA
Phone (203) 555-1418 ♦ Fax (203) 555-1419 ♦ Email ma@xyz.com

Mr Stuart Thomas
90A Jersey Ave
Orlando, FL 32761

Dear Mr Thomas,

Figure 7-19 Letter with the company name line suppressed

2. Go to the second letter. The order amount for Tina Walker is $50, which also meets the filter criteria **IS GREATER THAN $49.99.**

3. Click Close. Save the changes and leave the document open.

How To Insert A Date Field

One thing that is missing from the mail merge letters that have been created so far in this lesson is a date.

1. Place the cursor two lines above the first salutation field in the document. Insert ⇒ Date and Time, then select the second date format.

2. Check the option Automatically update when printed and click the Insert button.

3. Change the font and size of the date field to Arial 12. Turn off the bold. Your letter should look like the one shown in Figure 7-20. Save the changes and leave the document open.

January 17, 2005

«Salutation» «First Name» «Last Name»
«Company»
«Address»
«City», «State» «Zip Code»

Dear «Salutation» «Last Name»,

As owner of Capri Book Company, I want to express my sincere appreciation for the business you have brought us over the years. In response to numerous requests from our customers, the staff at Capri Book Company has decided to begin offering ***computer classes*** here at our new, larger location.

Figure 7-20 Date field added to the letter

How To Send The Merge Results To A New File

You may have a need to save the result of the mail merge. If so, follow the steps below.

1. Open the mail merge document that you want to save the result of. In this exercise open the L7 Mail Merge Letter (order amt $50 or more) document, if it is not already open.

2. File ⇒ Print, then select the option, **SEND MERGE RESULTS TO A NEW DOCUMENT** and click OK.

You will now see a new document that has a copy of the letter for each customer record that meets the filter criteria. The way that you know that this is a new document is by looking in the upper left corner of the window. You will see the words "Untitled Document". If you had a need to further customize some letters but not all of them, you could do that in this copy of the mail merge letters and print the letters from this document instead of from the original mail merge document.

3. Click Save and type `L7 Merge results in a new document` as the file name and close both of the documents.

Creating Labels

In Lesson 3 you created labels with the wizard. Now you will learn how to add a filter to a label document, how to add clip art to a label and how to make multiple copies of one label.

Creating Labels With Filters

In previous versions of Works, you could use the filter that you created for the mail merge letter document for the labels also. For some reason this functionality has been removed. This means that you have to create the same filter for the labels document that you did for the mail merge letter document, if you want to print labels (or envelopes) for the same names that you will print mail merge letters for.

1. Open a new word processing document. Tools ⇒ Labels, then select the **MAILING LABELS** option and click OK.

2. Select Avery label size 5163, then click the **NEW DOCUMENT** button.

3. Click the Merge information from another type of file button.

4. Open the Customers Database file and add the fields in Table 7-4 to the mailing label. Don't forget to add spaces between the fields that need them and add a comma after the City field.

Fields To Add
Salutation
First Name
Last Name
Company
Address
City
State
Zip Code

Table 7-4 Fields for the mailing label

5. Save the document. Type `L7 Labels (order amt $50 or more)` as the file name. Leave the document open.

Add Text To A Label

So far, the only thing that you have added to a mail merge document is fields from a database. That is about to change. The labels in this exercise are for letters that will announce a private sale. It would be a great idea to let the recipients know right on the label that this mailing contains information about a private sale. Adding text to your label is another way to customize your mailings.

1. Place the mouse pointer in front of the Salutation field on the label and press Enter.

2. On the blank line above the Salutation field type `*Private Sale*`. Your label should look like the one shown in Figure 7-21.

Private Sale
«Salutation» «First Name» «Last Name»
«Company»
«Address»
«City», «State» «Zip Code»

Figure 7-21 Label layout with text added

Creating A Filter For The Labels

Just like you created a filter for the mail merge letter, you can create filters for labels.
The process is exactly the same.

1. Tools ⇒ Mail Merge ⇒ Filter and Sort. Open the first Field drop-down list and select the **ORDER AMOUNT** field.

2. Open the Comparison drop-down list and select **IS GREATER THAN**, then type `49.99` in the **COMPARE TO** field. Your dialog box should have the options shown earlier in Figure 7-17. Click OK.

3. Close the View Results dialog box. Save the changes and leave the document open.

Previewing The Labels

1. Open the Print dialog box and select the option, Don't print lines with empty fields.

2. Preview the document. You should see the five labels for the customers whose last order was $50 or more, as shown in Figure 7-22. Click the Close button.

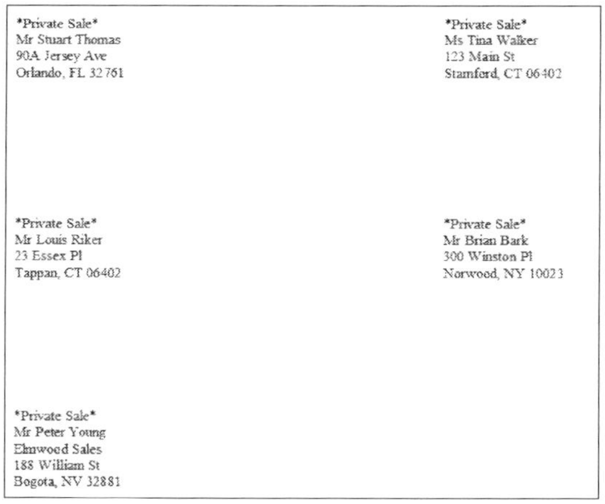

Figure 7-22 Labels in print preview

Add Clip Art To A Label

If you have a logo or another graphic that you want to include on your labels, you can do so by following the steps below. In this exercise you will add a graphic that comes with Works to the labels.

Select The Clip Art

1. Save the L7 Labels (order amt $50 or more) document as `L7 Labels (with clip art).`

2. Click in front of the **PRIVATE SALE** line, then Insert ⇒ Picture ⇒ Clip Art. You will see the dialog box shown in Figure 7-23.

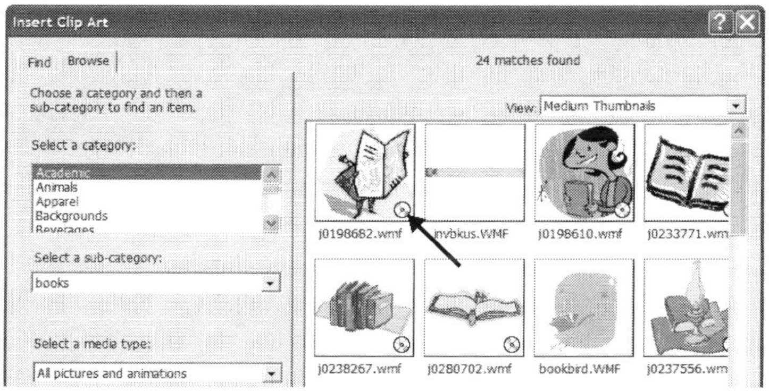

Figure 7-23 Insert Clip Art dialog box

> Clip art that has a disk icon in the lower right corner of the image, as illustrated above in Figure 7-23, means that the image is not installed on your hard drive. You can install these files by selecting the file and inserting the Works CD in the CD drive.

3. On the **BROWSE** tab select the **ACADEMIC** category, then select the **BOOKS** sub-category.

4. Select the file, bookbird.wmf or another file that does not have a disk in the lower right corner and click the **INSERT** button.

> The **FIND** tab on the Insert Clip Art dialog box will let you search for clip art by using keywords. All of the clip art that comes with Works have keywords. Type in the keyword that describes the type of clip art that you are looking for in the **TYPE A KEYWORD** field. Then click the **SEARCH** button. The clip art that has the keyword that you entered will be displayed on the right side of the dialog box as shown in Figure 7-24. The keyword used in the search is "newspaper".

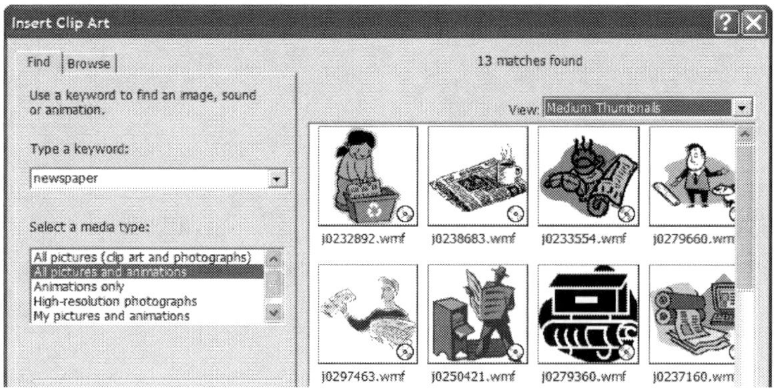

Figure 7-24 Result of the keyword search

Resize The Clip Art

As you can see, the size of the clip art is too large for the label and needs to be resized.

1. Right-click on the clip art on the label and select **FORMAT OBJECT**.

2. On the Size tab change the **HEIGHT** and **WIDTH** to `0.5`", as shown in Figure 7-25, then click OK.

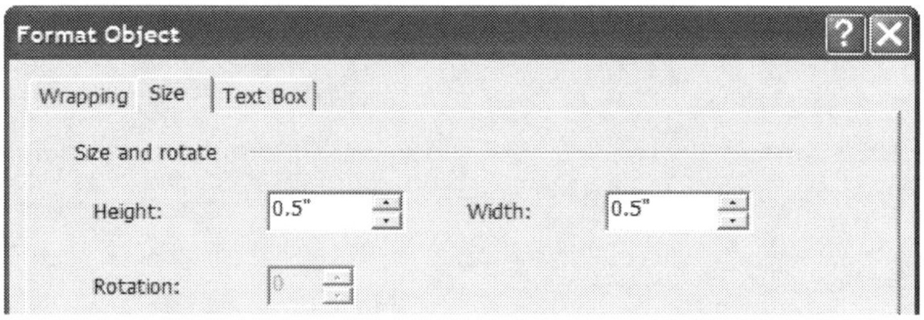

Figure 7-25 Size options on the Format Object dialog box

Select The Print Options

1. File ⇒ Print.

   Notice that the number of records that will print is shown in the **PRINT RANGE** section on the Print dialog box as illustrated in Figure 7-26. If you decided that you didn't want to print all five records, you could specify which of the records you wanted to print by using the From and To options.

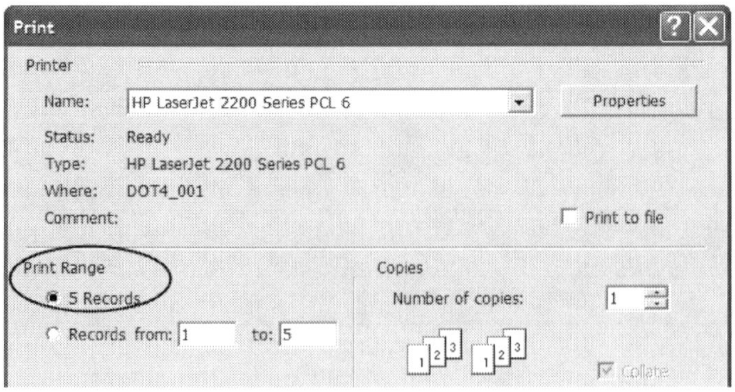

Figure 7-26 Print Range illustrated

2. Select the option, Don't print lines with empty fields on the Print dialog box, then preview the labels. They should look like the ones shown in Figure 7-27.

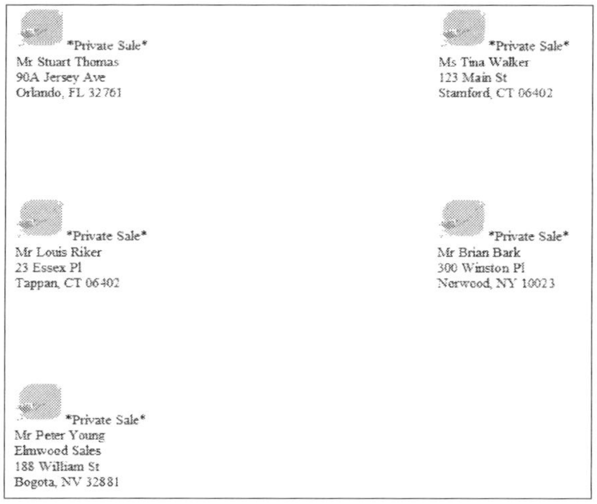

Figure 7-27 Labels with clip art added

3. Save the changes and close the document.

How To Create Multiple Copies Of One Label

You may have a need to print more than one copy of the same label. This type of label is probably most used for creating return address labels. The major difference between this type of label and the ones that you have created so far in this lesson is that this label is usually not attached to a database.

Even if you need to create a sheet of labels based off of a single name and address in a database or spreadsheet, it is quicker to just type the information right on the label, then it is to go through all of the steps to get the information from another source like a database, spreadsheet or address book.

1. Open a new word processing document.
2. Tools ⇒ Labels, then select the **RETURN ADDRESS LABELS** option on the Labels dialog box and click OK.
3. Select Avery label 5660, then click the **NEW DOCUMENT** button.
4. Type `Capri Book Company` and press Enter. Type `302 Main Street` and press Enter. Type `Laurel, CT 06868`.
5. Save the document as `L7 Sheet of labels (with the same address)`. Preview the document. You should see three columns of the same address label as shown in Figure 7-28. Close the document.

Figure 7-28 Multiple labels

> You cannot create labels and envelopes in the same document. The best work around that I have found is to have two versions of the same document if you need to print labels and envelopes. I save one document as filename (labels) and the other as filename (envelopes).

How To Create Envelopes

Creating envelopes is very similar to creating labels.

1. Open a new word processing document. Tools ⇒ Envelopes. You will see the dialog box shown in Figure 7-29.

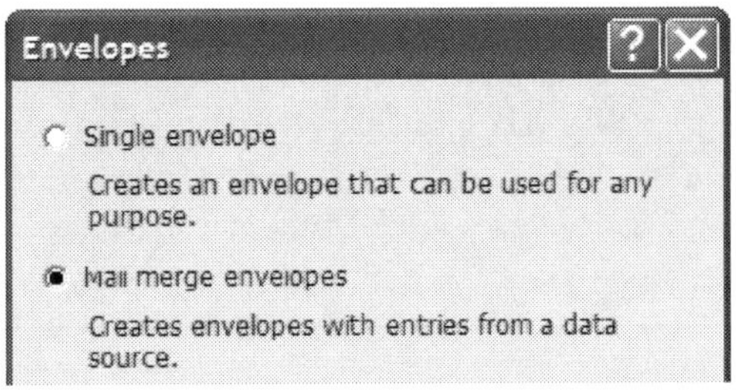

Figure 7-29 Envelopes dialog box

2. Select the **MAIL MERGE ENVELOPES** option and click OK, then select the **SIZE 10** envelope if it is not already selected.

If the envelope size that you need is not in the **ENVELOPE SIZE** drop-down list, you can create a custom envelope size, just like you can create a custom paper or label size. Figure 7-30 shows the custom Envelope Size dialog box.

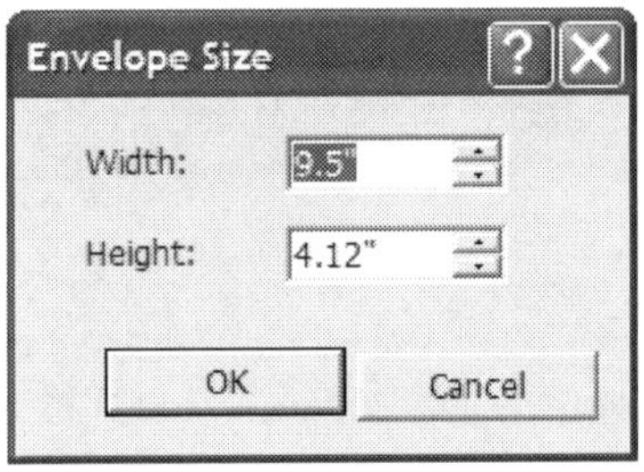

Figure 7-30 Envelope Size dialog box

3. Click the New Document button, then click the Merge information from another type of file button.

4. Select the Customers Database file and click the Open button, then add the fields in Table 7-5 to the envelope. Don't forget to add a space between the fields that need them. Add a comma after the City field. Your envelope should look like the one shown in Figure 7-31.

Fields To Add
Salutation
First Name
Last Name
Company
Address
City
State
Zip Code

Table 7-5 Fields to add to the envelope

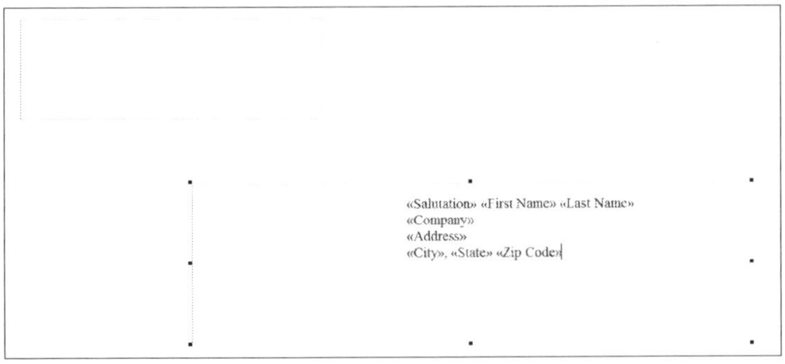

Figure 7-31 Envelope layout

5. Save the document. Type `L7 Envelopes (order amt $50 or more)` as the file name. Leave the document open.

Adding The Return Address

In the upper left corner of the envelope shown above in Figure 7-31, you will see a square. This is the return address section of the envelope.

1. Click in the **RETURN ADDRESS** section of the envelope and type `Capri Book Company`, then press Enter.

2. Type `302 Main Street`. Press Enter and type `Laurel, CT 06868`. Save the changes and leave the document open.

Creating A Filter For Envelopes

If you preview the envelopes you will see one for each record in the Customers database. If you only need to print envelopes for specific records in the database, you need to create a filter. You create the filter for envelopes the same way that you do for the letters and labels.

1. Tools ⇒ Mail Merge ⇒ Filter and Sort. Open the first Field drop-down list and select the Order Amount field.

2. Open the Comparison drop-down list and select **IS GREATER THAN**, then type `49.99` in the Compare To field. Your dialog box should look like the one shown earlier in Figure 7-17. Click OK.

3. Close the View Results dialog box and save the changes. Click the Preview button, then click OK. Your envelope should look like the one shown in Figure 7-32. Close the document.

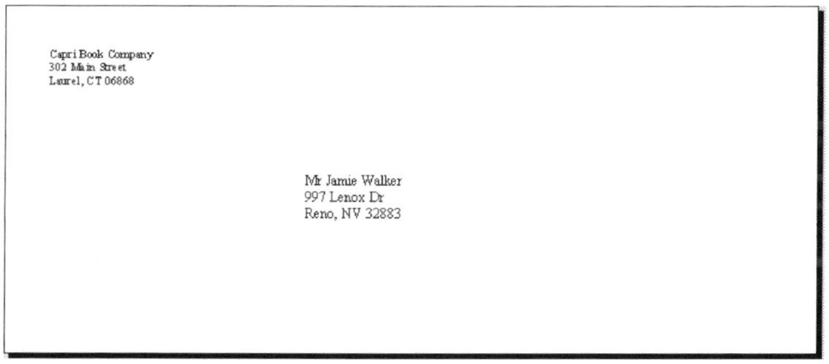

Figure 7-32 Completed envelope

You can add clip art to envelopes the same way that you can for letters and labels.

Sorting Records

You may have a need to sort the records in the database so that the letters, labels or envelopes print in a certain order. One reason to sort records is if you are doing a bulk mailing. To send envelopes via bulk mail, the addresses must be sorted in zip code order.

The steps below will show you how to sort the records in a letter, label or envelope mail merge document. In this exercise you will sort the records in ascending order by zip code.

1. Open the document that you want to sort. For this exercise, open the L7 Mail Merge Letter (Filter=ComputerBooks) document. Close the Insert Fields dialog box.

2. Tools ⇒ Mail Merge ⇒ Filter and Sort. On the **SORT** tab open the **SORT BY** drop-down list and select the Zip Code field. If the **ASCENDING** option is not already selected across from the Sort by field, select it now. The Sort tab should have the options selected that are shown in Figure 7-33.

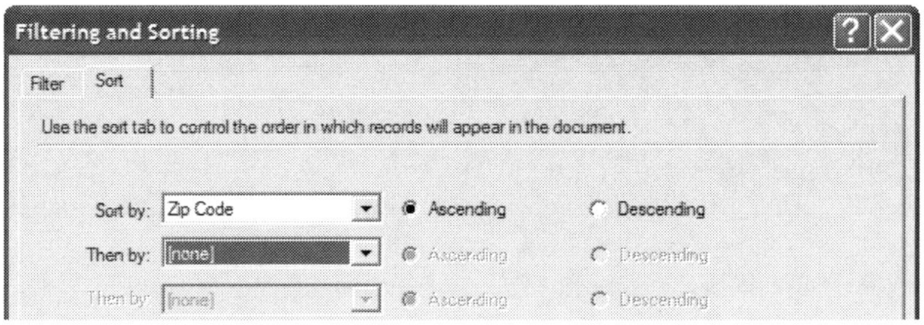

Figure 7-33 Sort tab options

3. Click OK and close the View Results dialog box.

4. File ⇒ Save As. Type `L7 Mail Merge Letter (sorted by zip code)` as the file name. If you preview the records you will see that they are in ascending order by zip code. Close the document.

Test Your Skills

1. Save the L5 New Classes Letter (linked) document as `L7(skills)`.

   - Create a mail merge using the fields shown earlier in Table 7-5.
   - Create a filter to display all of the records in the state CT.
   - Send the merge results of the CT filter to a new document named `L7(skills 1)`.

2. Save the L5 New Classes Letter (linked) document as `L7 order amt less than 30`.

   - Create a filter to display all records that have an order amount less than $30.

ADVANCED WORD PROCESSING TECHNIQUES

In this lesson you will learn how to create a table, create columns of text, that can be used as the layout for a brochure or newsletter, wrap text around clip art and how to use Note-It.

In previous lessons you linked and embedded spreadsheets in word processing documents. Now you will learn how to create a table in a word processing document. Tables created in a word processing document are similar to spreadsheets. You will also learn how to do the following:

- ☑ Add a watermark to a document
- ☑ Create page borders
- ☑ Use the Auto Correct option

LESSON 8

How To Create A Table

1. Save the New Classes Information Letter as `L8 New Classes Letter (with table).`

2. Move the cursor to the blank line after the second paragraph and press Enter, then click the **INSERT TABLE** button on the toolbar. You should see the dialog box shown in Figure 8-1.

   The Insert Table dialog box will let you select the number of rows and columns for the table, as well as, a format. Click on a few of the formats so that you can get an idea of what the different table formats look like.

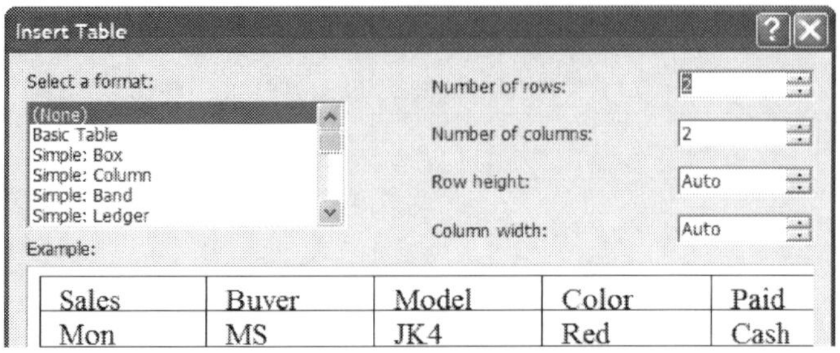

Figure 8-1 Insert Table dialog box

3. Change the **NUMBER OF ROWS** to 4 by clicking on the up arrow at the end of the field.

4. Change the **NUMBER OF COLUMNS** to 3, then select the **PROFESSIONAL BAND** format and click OK.

5. Type the information in Table 8-1 into the table in the letter. The table should look like the one shown in Figure 8-2.

To move from one column to the next, press the Tab key or the arrow key that points in the direction that you want to move.

Class	Price	Next Class Starts
Works	$295	February 10
Word	$495	February 12
Access	$1,295	February 10

Table 8-1 Information to enter in the table

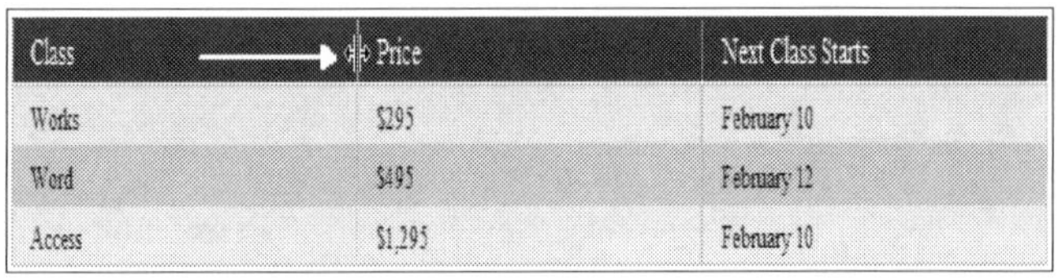

Class	Price	Next Class Starts
Works	$295	February 10
Word	$495	February 12
Access	$1,295	February 10

Figure 8-2 Class schedule table

Resize The Table

In Figure 8-2 above, the columns are too wide. They need to be made smaller.

1. Place the cursor on the bar between the Class and Price columns as illustrated above in Figure 8-2. The cursor will change to a double headed arrow. Hold the left mouse button down and drag the mouse pointer to the left, so that it is closer to the Class column heading.

2. Place the mouse pointer on the bar before the Next Class Starts column and drag it closer to the Price column heading, then place the mouse pointer at the end of the Next Class Starts column. Drag the mouse pointer to the left. Your table should look like the one shown in Figure 8-3.

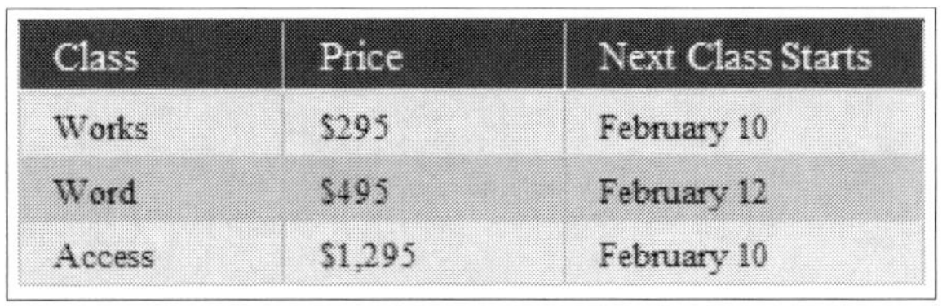

Class	Price	Next Class Starts
Works	$295	February 10
Word	$495	February 12
Access	$1,295	February 10

Figure 8-3 Table resized

Format The Table Columns

The table would look better if the column headings were centered. The data in the Next Class Starts column would also look better if it was centered.

1. Highlight the Class and Price column headings, then click the Center button on the toolbar. Both headings should now be centered.

2. Highlight the first date in the **NEXT CLASS STARTS** column, then click the Center button. Repeat this step for the other two start dates.

> I tried selecting all three date cells at one time and then clicked the Center button. When I did that, the entire table moved to the center of the row. I don't know if this is a bug or if that is the way the Center option is suppose to work with more than one cell selected in a table.

3. Highlight the entire table and click the **INCREASE INDENT** button on the toolbar three times. The table should look like the one shown in Figure 8-4. Save the changes and close the document.

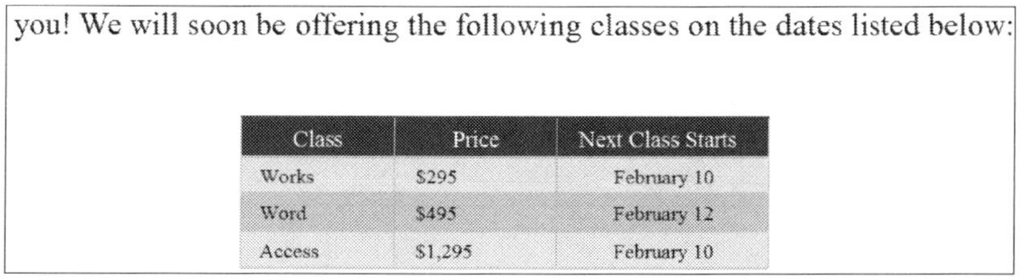

Figure 8-4 Completed table

How To Insert A Spreadsheet Into A Word Processing Document

In the last few exercises you added and edited a table in a word processing document. Tables in the word processor have a lot of features, but if you find that you need more functionality, you should insert a spreadsheet into the word processing document. If this is the case, you can follow the steps below.

1. Open a new or existing word processing document that you want to add a spreadsheet to, then click the **INSERT SPREADSHEET** button on the Standard toolbar or Insert ⇒ Spreadsheet.

You will see that the word processing menu and toolbars go away. In place of them, the spreadsheet application takes over inside of the word processing application as shown in Figure 8-5.

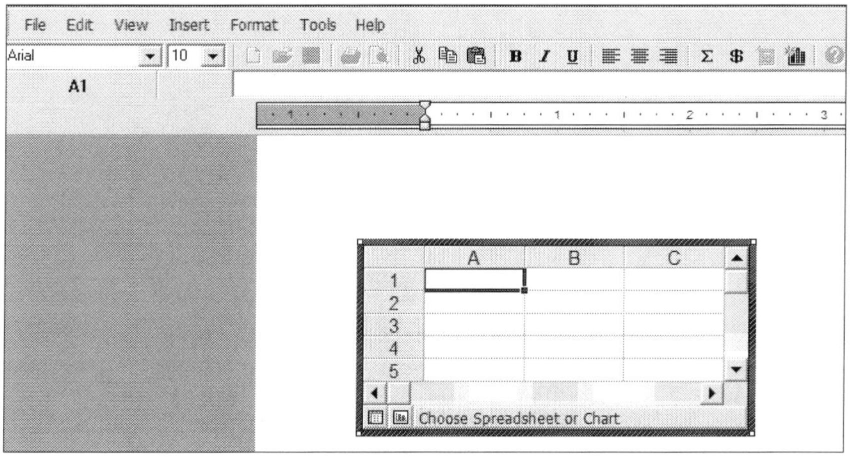

Figure 8-5 Spreadsheet application in the word processing application

2. Make the spreadsheet window larger by dragging one of the four corners out, then add the data to the spreadsheet and save the changes.

Creating Multi-Column Documents

Multi-column documents can be used to create brochures and newsletters. Multi-column documents look like pages in a phone book, magazine or newspaper. You can set the number of columns and the amount of space between the columns. Based on the number of columns that you select, the width of the columns are automatically created.

How To Set Up Columns In A Document

1. Open a new word processing document. Format ⇒ Columns. You should see the Format Columns dialog box.

2. Change the Number of columns to `3`, then change the **SPACE BETWEEN** field to `0.25"`. You have to type this number in because it is not one of the default options in the list.

> The **SPACE BETWEEN** field determines how much white space will be between each column. You can also have a line between the columns.

3. If the **LINE BETWEEN COLUMNS** option is not checked, check it now. The dialog box should have the options selected, that are shown in Figure 8-6. Click OK. The document should now have three columns. Leave the document open while completing the next exercise.

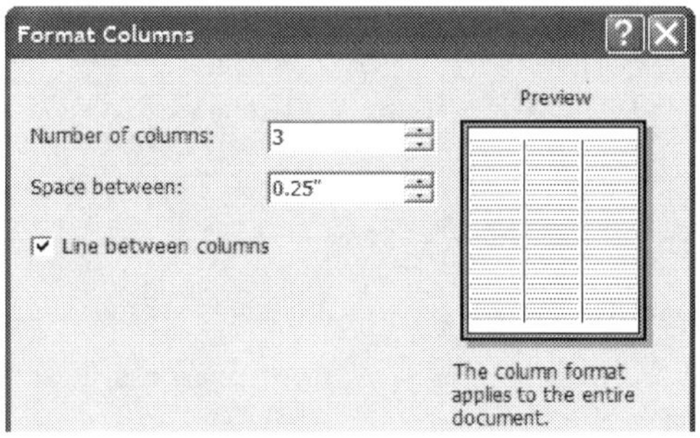

Figure 8-6 Format Columns dialog box

How To Copy And Paste Text From Another Document

Rather than have you type in information to see how the multi-column feature works, you will copy text from another document and paste it into this document.

1. File ⇒ L8 New Classes Letter (with table) document from the bottom of the File menu or open it from the History tab.

2. Highlight the first two paragraphs of the letter. Right-click on the highlighted paragraphs and select Copy, then close the document.

3. Right-click in the new document in the left column and select Paste. Your document should look like the one shown in Figure 8-7.

4. If you want to put text into the second and third columns of the document, place the cursor at the end of the text that you just pasted in the document and press the **CTRL** and **V** keys three times. Preview the document. It should look like the one shown in Figure 8-8.

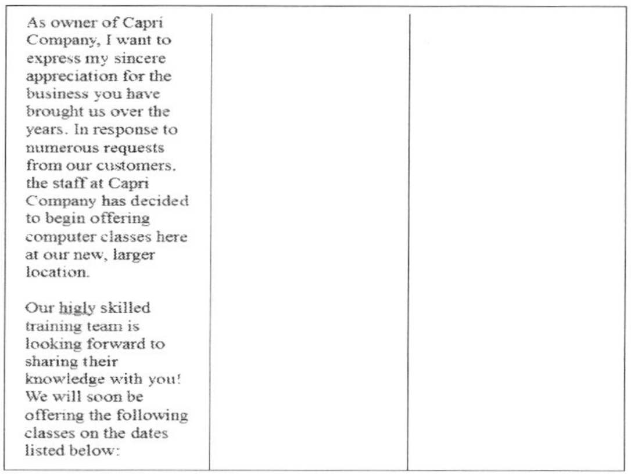

As owner of Capri Company, I want to express my sincere appreciation for the business you have brought us over the years. In response to numerous requests from our customers, the staff at Capri Company has decided to begin offering computer classes here at our new, larger location.

Our higly skilled training team is looking forward to sharing their knowledge with you! We will soon be offering the following classes on the dates listed below:

Figure 8-7 Text added to the first column

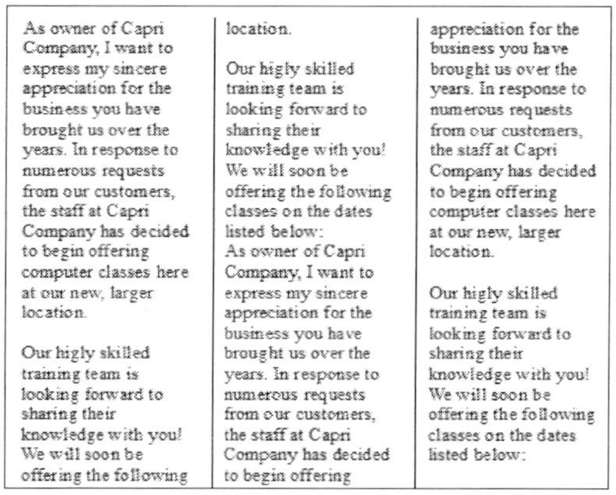

As owner of Capri Company, I want to express my sincere appreciation for the business you have brought us over the years. In response to numerous requests from our customers, the staff at Capri Company has decided to begin offering computer classes here at our new, larger location.

Our higly skilled training team is looking forward to sharing their knowledge with you! We will soon be offering the following

location.

Our higly skilled training team is looking forward to sharing their knowledge with you! We will soon be offering the following classes on the dates listed below:
As owner of Capri Company, I want to express my sincere appreciation for the business you have brought us over the years. In response to numerous requests from our customers, the staff at Capri Company has decided to begin offering

appreciation for the business you have brought us over the years. In response to numerous requests from our customers, the staff at Capri Company has decided to begin offering computer classes here at our new, larger location.

Our higly skilled training team is looking forward to sharing their knowledge with you! We will soon be offering the following classes on the dates listed below:

Figure 8-8 Multi-column document with text

5. Close the document and save it as `L8 Multi Column Exercise`.

How To Create Columns In An Existing Document

If you have already created a document and now have the need to change the layout to columns, you can do that easily by following the steps below.

1. Save the Term Paper document as `L8 Term Paper (with columns & clip art)`.
2. Follow the steps in the section, **HOW TO SET UP COLUMNS IN A DOCUMENT**, earlier in this lesson to add columns to this document.
3. Click the Print Preview button. Your document should look like the one shown above in Figure 8-9. Click the Close button on the Print Preview window, then save the changes and leave the document open.

How To Add Clip Art To A Multi-Column Document

1. In the second column of the L8 Term Paper document, click on the blank line after the first paragraph and press Enter. Click the **INSERT CLIP ART** button on the toolbar.
2. Select the Sports & Leisure category, then select the Baseball sub-category. Double-click on the clip art that you want to use. If you do not have this category, select any piece of clip art.
3. Resize the clip art by placing the mouse pointer on the square in the lower right corner of the frame. Press the left mouse button and drag the mouse diagonally up and over to the left to make the frame around the clip art smaller.
4. With the clip art still selected, click the **CENTER** button. Your document should look similar to the one shown in Figure 8-9. Save the changes and close the document.

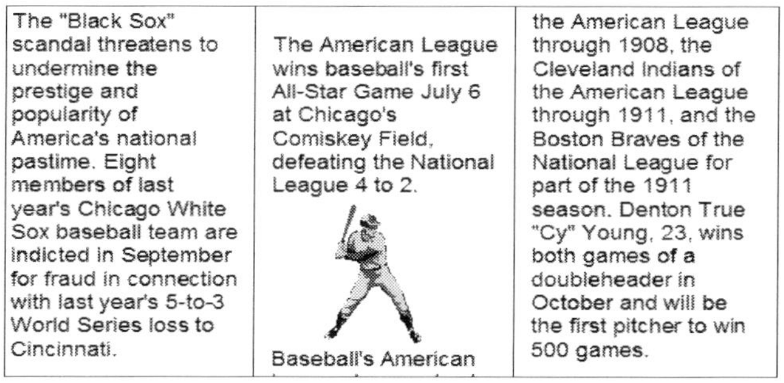

The "Black Sox" scandal threatens to undermine the prestige and popularity of America's national pastime. Eight members of last year's Chicago White Sox baseball team are indicted in September for fraud in connection with last year's 5-to-3 World Series loss to Cincinnati.

The American League wins baseball's first All-Star Game July 6 at Chicago's Comiskey Field, defeating the National League 4 to 2.

Baseball's American

the American League through 1908, the Cleveland Indians of the American League through 1911, and the Boston Braves of the National League for part of the 1911 season. Denton True "Cy" Young, 23, wins both games of a doubleheader in October and will be the first pitcher to win 500 games.

Figure 8-9 Clip art added in the column

Wrap Text Around Clip Art

You may have the need to wrap text around a piece of clip art or another object. Works has three style wrap options and two text placement options that you can use to wrap text around clip art.

Style Options

The three style options discussed below determine how the text will be wrapped around the object.

① **IN LINE WITH TEXT** puts the object into the line of text. The object is treated like a character on the line. Text will be above and below the object.
② **SQUARE** wraps the text around the frame of the object.
③ **TIGHT** wraps the text around the object.

Text Placement Options

The two text placement options discussed below are only available with the **SQUARE** and **TIGHT STYLE** options that were discussed above.

① **NO TEXT ON THE LEFT** will only wrap text on the right side of the clip art.
② **NO TEXT ON THE RIGHT** will only wrap text on the left side of the clip art.

How To Use The Style Options

1. Save the Term Paper document as `L8 Term Paper (with text wrap).`

2. Place the cursor before the word **PETER** on the fourth line in the second paragraph, then click the Insert Clip Art button on the toolbar. Double-click on the clip art that you want to add to the document.

3. Format ⇒ Object. Click the **SQUARE** button style shown in Figure 8-10, then click OK. Your document should look like the one shown in Figure 8-11.

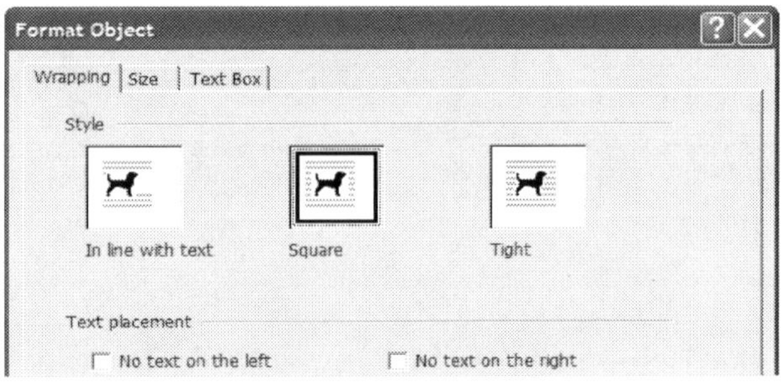

Figure 8-10 Format Object dialog box

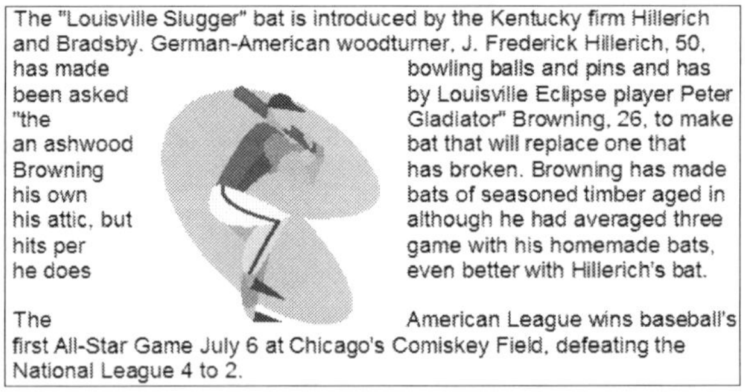

The "Louisville Slugger" bat is introduced by the Kentucky firm Hillerich and Bradsby. German-American woodturner, J. Frederick Hillerich, 50, has made bowling balls and pins and has been asked by Louisville Eclipse player Peter "the Gladiator" Browning, 26, to make an ashwood bat that will replace one that Browning has broken. Browning has made his own bats of seasoned timber aged in his attic, but although he had averaged three hits per game with his homemade bats, he does even better with Hillerich's bat.

The American League wins baseball's first All-Star Game July 6 at Chicago's Comiskey Field, defeating the National League 4 to 2.

Figure 8-11 Text wrapped around the object using the square style

How To Use The Text Placement Options

1. Right-click on the clip art and select **FORMAT OBJECT**, then select the **TIGHT** wrapping style. This option places the text closer to the clip art.

2. Select the **NO TEXT ON THE RIGHT** text placement option and click OK. Your document should look like the one shown in Figure 8-12. If you wanted less white space on the left side of the clip art, you would have to edit the clip art and remove some of the white space that is around the clip art.

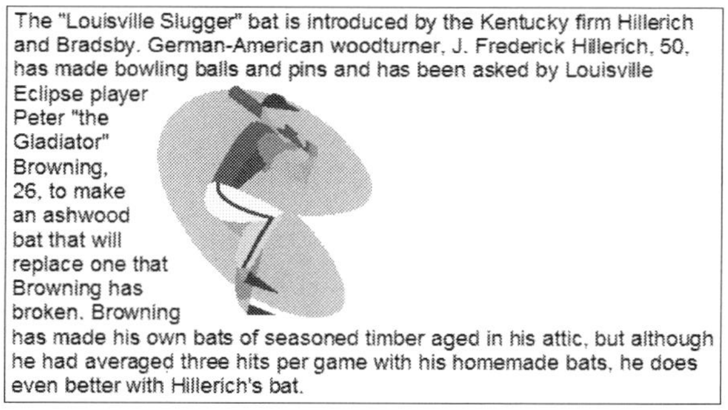

The "Louisville Slugger" bat is introduced by the Kentucky firm Hillerich and Bradsby. German-American woodturner, J. Frederick Hillerich, 50, has made bowling balls and pins and has been asked by Louisville Eclipse player Peter "the Gladiator" Browning, 26, to make an ashwood bat that will replace one that Browning has broken. Browning has made his own bats of seasoned timber aged in his attic, but although he had averaged three hits per game with his homemade bats, he does even better with Hillerich's bat.

Figure 8-12 Tight text wrapping style and text placement options illustrated

How To Wrap Text Around Clip Art

1. Right-click on the clip art and select **FORMAT OBJECT**.

2. Select the **TIGHT** style, then clear any other options that are selected on the **WRAPPING** tab and click OK. Your document should look like the one shown in Figure 8-13. Notice that the text is closer to the clip art.

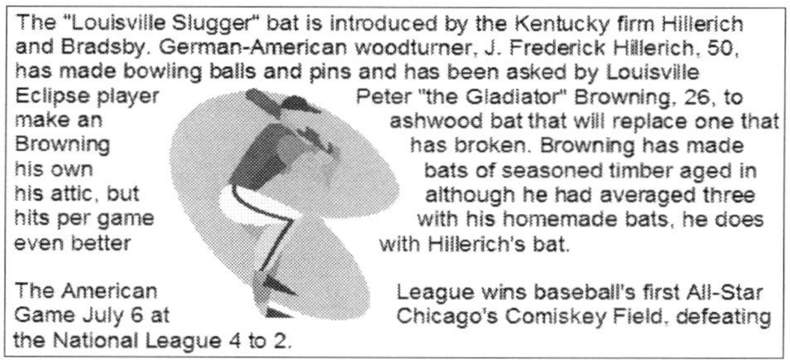

The "Louisville Slugger" bat is introduced by the Kentucky firm Hillerich and Bradsby. German-American woodturner, J. Frederick Hillerich, 50, has made bowling balls and pins and has been asked by Louisville
Eclipse player Peter "the Gladiator" Browning, 26, to
make an ashwood bat that will replace one that
Browning has broken. Browning has made
his own bats of seasoned timber aged in
his attic, but although he had averaged three
hits per game with his homemade bats, he does
even better with Hillerich's bat.

The American League wins baseball's first All-Star
Game July 6 at Chicago's Comiskey Field, defeating
the National League 4 to 2.

Figure 8-13 Tight text wrapping style around the clip art illustrated

3. Save the changes and close the document.

How To Add A Title To A Multi-Column Document

If you are creating a newsletter or brochure, you may want to add a title across the columns of the document. This is accomplished by using WordArt.

1. Save the L8 Term Paper (with columns & clip art) document as `L8 Term Paper(with title across columns)`.

2. If the cursor is not in the first position on the first line of the document, place it there now, then click the **INSERT WORDART** button on the toolbar.

3. Type `Baseball Term Paper` in the WordArt dialog box, then close the dialog box.

4. Open the **SHAPE** drop-down list and select the fourth shape in the fifth column. The drop-down list should have **WAVE 1** in it.

5. Open the Font Size drop-down list and select 20. Click Yes to resize the WordArt object, then click on a blank space in the document to deselect the WordArt.

6. Right-click on the Word Art and select Format Object, then click the **SQUARE** option and click OK.

7. Place the cursor on the middle square on the right side of the frame of the Word Art, as illustrated in Figure 8-14, then drag it to the right until it touches the right border of the document, as shown in Figure 8-15. Save the changes and close the document.

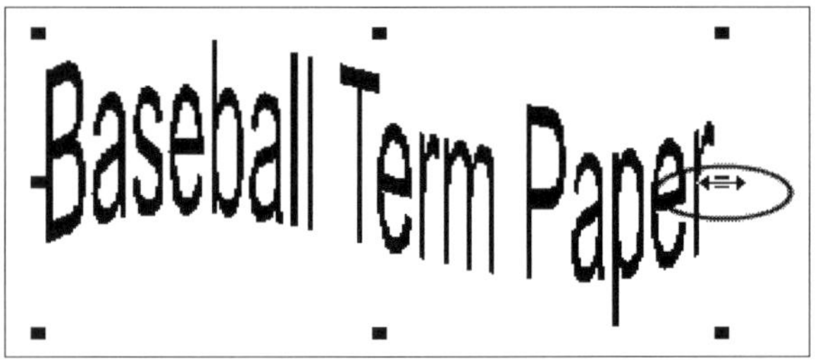

Figure 8-14 Cursor in position to move the WordArt

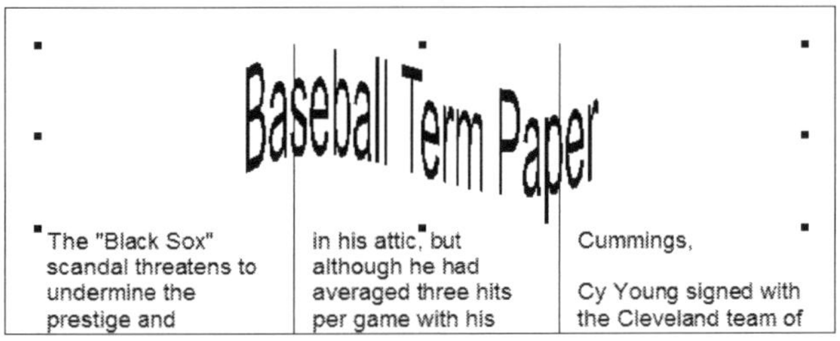

Figure 8-15 WordArt stretched across the columns

If the Word Art in your document is not at the top of the page as shown above in Figure 8-15, drag the Word Art up to the top of the page.

Adding Borders And Shading To Text

Borders are often used to make certain parts of a document stand out. An example of borders and shading added to text are the tip boxes like the one shown above. In Works, the borders can be single, double, bold or a colored line. You can also place borders on the left, right, top or bottom of a paragraph. An example of a partial border is the single line at the top of this page, right below the page header information.

1. Save the L8 Term Paper (with columns & clip art) document as `L8 Term Paper (with borders & shading).`

2. Format ⇒ Columns. Change the Number of columns option to 1 and click OK.

3. Press the Enter key twice at the beginning of the first paragraph, then type `Baseball Term Paper` on the first line of the document.

4. Change the font size to 24, then move the cursor to the beginning of the title.

5. Format ⇒ Borders and Shading. You should see the Borders and Shading dialog box. Select the third style from the bottom of the **LINE STYLE** drop-down list, then open the **LINE COLOR** drop-down list and select Red.

6. Select the third style from the bottom of the **FILL STYLE** drop-down list. Your dialog box should have the options selected that are shown in Figure 8-16. Click OK.

7. Click the Center button on the toolbar. Your document should look like the one shown in Figure 8-17. You should see a striped box, with a red dotted line around the title of the document. Save the changes and leave the document open.

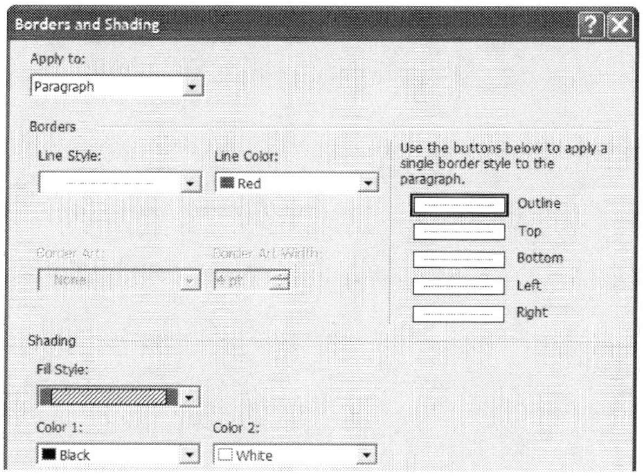

Figure 8-16 Border and Shading options

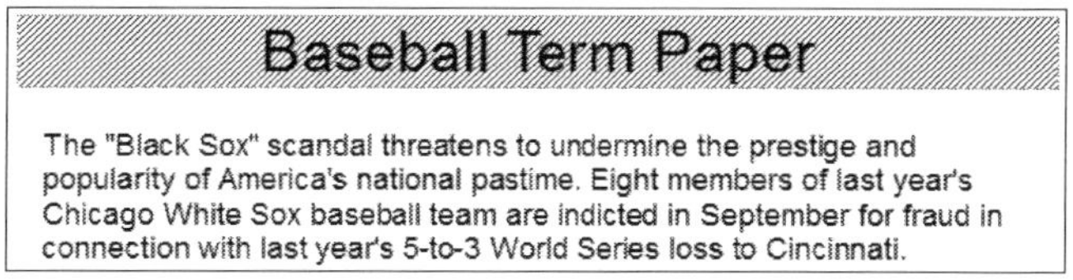
Baseball Term Paper

The "Black Sox" scandal threatens to undermine the prestige and popularity of America's national pastime. Eight members of last year's Chicago White Sox baseball team are indicted in September for fraud in connection with last year's 5-to-3 World Series loss to Cincinnati.

Figure 8-17 Borders and shading added to the title of the document

Add Additional Border And Shading Options To The Document

1. Scroll down and highlight the first two paragraphs under the clip art.

2. Format ⇒ Borders and Shading. Select the Line Style option below the word **NONE** in the drop-down list, then change the **LINE COLOR** to Blue.

3. In the Borders section, click in the box next to **LEFT** and **RIGHT** illustrated in Figure 8-18. There should not be a blue line in the left and right border options. Click OK. You should see a blue line above and below the two paragraphs that you highlighted.

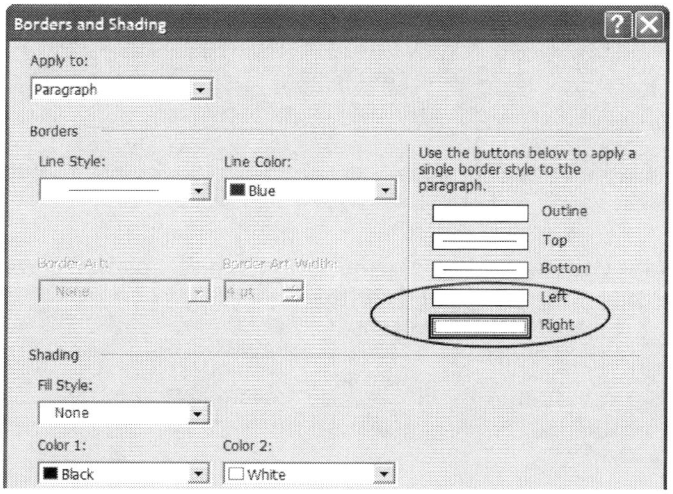

Figure 8-18 Single border options illustrated

4. Highlight the paragraph below the two paragraphs that you just added borders to.

5. Format ⇒ Borders and Shading. Select the double line option in the **LINE STYLE** drop-down list, then open the **FILL STYLE** drop-down list and select the lightest gray option. It's the one right above the fill styles with designs.

6. Open the **COLOR 1** drop-down list and select Yellow, then click OK. Your document should look like the one shown in Figure 8-19. The bottom paragraph should have a double lined border around it and it should have yellow shading. Save the changes and close the document.

> Baseball's American League is organized by teams whose annual pennant winner will compete beginning in 1903 with the top team of the 25-year-old National League in World Series championships.
>
> Baseball's curve ball pitch is invented by Brooklyn, N.Y., pitcher William Arthur Cummings.
>
> Cy Young signed with the Cleveland team of the National League to begin an outstanding pitching career that will continue for nearly 23 years: with Cleveland through 1898, the St. Louis Cardinals through 1900, the Boston Red Sox of the American League through 1908, the Cleveland Indians of the American League through 1911, and the Boston Braves of the National League for part of the 1911 season. Denton True "Cy" Young, 23, wins both games of a doubleheader in October and will be the first pitcher to win 500 games.

Figure 8-19 Paragraph with a border and fill color added

Adding Borders To Clip Art

So far in this lesson you have added clip art to documents, wrapped text around clip art and added borders to text. Now you will learn how to add borders around clip art.

1. Open a new word processing document and add two pieces of clip art to the document, then make each piece of clip art much smaller.

2. Right-click on the first piece of clip art and select **FORMAT OBJECT**. You should see the Format Object dialog box. Select the **SQUARE** wrapping style and click OK.

3. Format ⇒ Borders and Shading. If the **BORDER ART** option on the Borders and Shading dialog box is dimmed out, close the dialog box and repeat the steps above again.

4. Open the Border Art drop-down list and select a border that you like, then select the smallest **BORDER ART WIDTH** size by clicking on the arrow until the numbers stop changing. Click OK. The first piece of clip art should have the border around it that you selected.

5. Right-click on the second piece of clip art and select Format Object, then select the **TIGHT** wrapping style and click OK.

6. Format ⇒ Borders and Shading. Open the Border Art drop-down list and select a border that you like. Select a different border option for this piece of clip art then the one you used for the other piece of clip art.

7. Select the Border Art Width size that you want and click OK. Click on a blank space in the document to deselect the clip art. There should be borders around both pieces of clip art similar to those shown in Figure 8-20.

Figure 8-20 Borders added to the clip art

8. Save the document. Type `L8 Borders around clip art` as the file name. Leave the document open.

Adding A Page Border To A Document

In the previous exercise you added borders around clip art. In this exercise you will add a border to the page. Adding a border to a page requires fewer steps then adding borders around clip art.

1. Format ⇒ Borders and Shading. Open the **APPLY TO** drop-down list and select Page. The Border Art drop-down list should now be available.

2. Open the Border Art drop-down list and select a border that you like. Select the Border Art Width size that you want and click OK. You should now have a border around the entire page, similar to the one shown in Figure 8-21. Save the changes and close the document.

Figure 8-21 Border added to the page

Using Note-It

Note-It allows you to add comments to a document. A graphic is added to the document that lets the reader know that there is a note attached. Double-clicking on the graphic will open the note.
Using Note-It is like using yellow post-it notes, which you may be familiar with. The only difference is that the note is represented graphically.

How To Create A Note-It Object

1. Save the Term Paper document as `L8 Term Paper(with Note-It).`

2. Place the cursor at the end of the first paragraph. Insert ⇒ Object. Select Microsoft Note-It in the **OBJECT TYPE** list, then select the option **DISPLAY AS ICON**.

3. Click the **CHANGE ICON** button and type `Needs more` in the Label field at the bottom of the dialog box shown in Figure 8-22. Click OK to close the Change Icon dialog box, then click OK to close the **INSERT OBJECT** dialog box. You should see the dialog box shown in Figure 8-23.

Figure 8-22 Change Icon dialog box

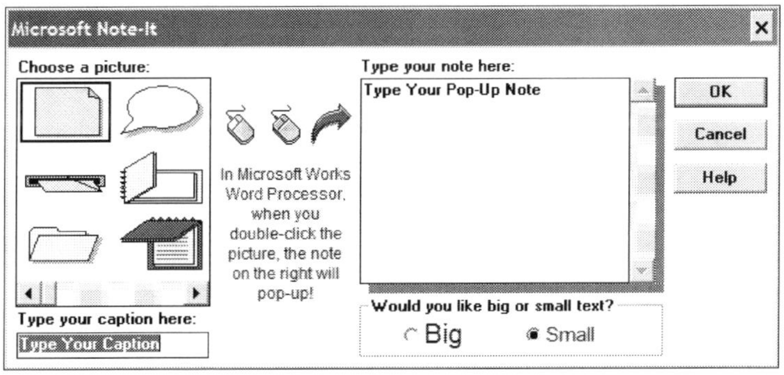

Figure 8-23 Microsoft Note-It dialog box

In previous versions of Works, you could select a picture and enter a caption for it on the Note-It dialog box shown above in Figure 8-24. For some reason, this feature does not work in this version of Works or maybe it's just my copy of the software that doesn't work.

4. Type `Don't forget to add the year to this game` in the **TYPE YOUR NOTE HERE** field. Click OK, then make the graphic smaller.

How To Read A Note

1. Double-click on the graphic. Your document should look like the one shown in Figure 8-24. The note is at the top of the document window.

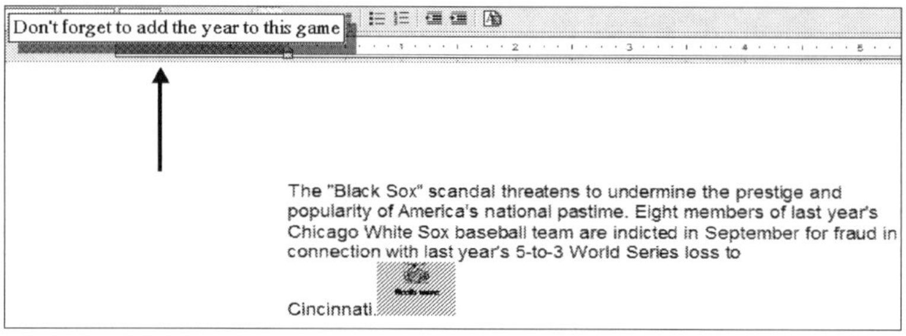

Figure 8-24 Note illustrated

2. When you are finished reading the note, press Enter or click any place in the document to close the note. Save the changes and close the document.

To delete a note from a document, highlight the graphic and press the Delete key.

NEW Creating A Watermark

Watermarks are most often used to display a graphic or text, usually in gray scale behind the regular text in a document. You may have seen a document that has the word "draft" in gray on a document, slanting towards the upper right corner of the page.

Works does not allow you to type text to use as a watermark. If you wanted to use text, like the word "Draft" as a watermark, you would have to create the text and save it as a graphic. Being the nice person that I am, I created a graphic with the word "Draft", that you can use to complete this exercise.

1. Save the Term Paper document as `L8 Term Paper(with watermark).`

2. Insert ⇒ Watermark. Select the **PICTURE WATERMARK** option, then click the **SELECT PICTURE** button.

3. Navigate to your folder and select the file, draft_watermark.gif as shown in Figure 8-25, then click the **INSERT** button.

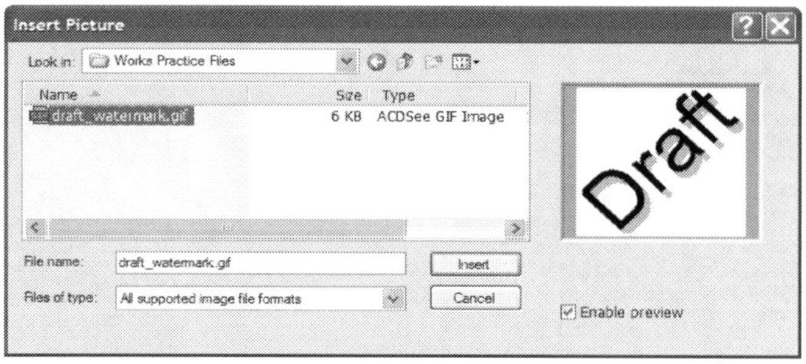

Figure 8-25 Watermark graphic selected

4. Select the middle button in the **POSITION** section of the Insert Watermark dialog box as illustrated in Figure 8-26. Click the **APPLY** button. Move the dialog box out of the way so that you can see more of the watermark. Click OK and preview the document. Your document should look like the one shown in Figure 8-27.

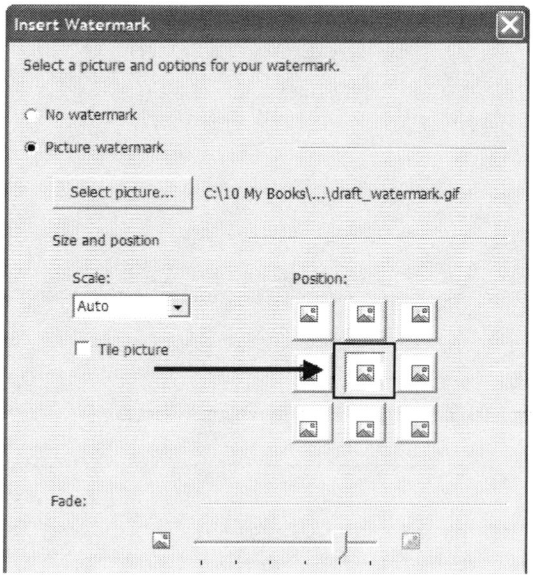

Figure 8-26 Watermark options

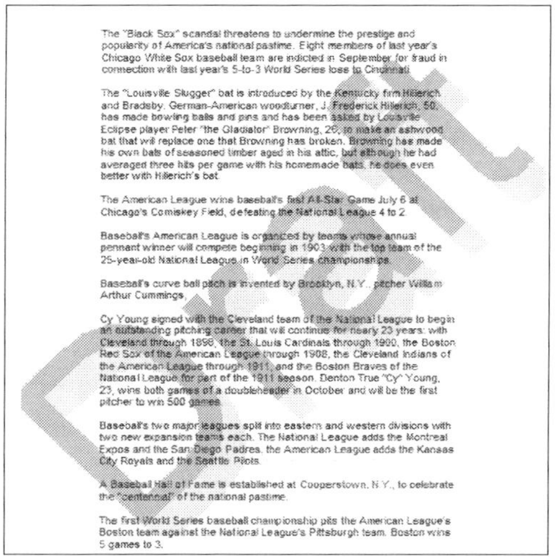

The "Black Sox" scandal threatens to undermine the prestige and popularity of America's national pastime. Eight members of last year's Chicago White Sox baseball team are indicted in September for fraud in connection with last year's 5-to-3 World Series lose to Cincinnati.

The "Louisville Slugger" bat is introduced by the Kentucky firm Hillerich and Bradsby. German-American woodturner, J. Frederick Hillerich, 50, has made bowling balls and pins and has been asked by Louisville Eclipse player Peter "the Gladiator" Browning, 26, to make an ashwood bat that will replace one that Browning has broken. Browning has made his own bats of seasoned timber aged in his attic, but although he had averaged three hits per game with his homemade bats, he does even better with Hillerich's bat.

The American League wins baseball's first All-Star Game July 6 at Chicago's Comiskey Field, defeating the National League 4 to 2.

Baseball's American League is organized by teams whose annual pennant winner will compete beginning in 1903 with the top team of the 25-year-old National League in World Series championships.

Baseball's curve ball pitch is invented by Brooklyn, N.Y., pitcher William Arthur Cummings.

Cy Young signed with the Cleveland team of the National League to begin an outstanding pitching career that will continue for nearly 23 years: with Cleveland through 1898, the St. Louis Cardinals through 1900, the Boston Red Sox of the American League through 1908, the Cleveland Indians of the American League through 1911, and the Boston Braves of the National League for part of the 1911 season. Denton True "Cy" Young, 23, wins both games of a doubleheader in October and will be the first pitcher to win 500 games.

Baseball's two major leagues split into eastern and western divisions with two new expansion teams each. The National League adds the Montreal Expos and the San Diego Padres, the American League adds the Kansas City Royals and the Seattle Pilots.

A Baseball Hall of Fame is established at Cooperstown, N.Y., to celebrate the "centennial" of the national pastime.

The first World Series baseball championship pits the American League's Boston team against the National League's Pittsburgh team. Boston wins 5 games to 3.

Figure 8-27 Watermark added to a document

Insert Watermark Dialog Box Options Explained

① The **SIZE AND POSITION** options allow you to resize the watermark graphic if needed, to be in proportion with the size of the page.

② The **FADE** sliding scale option allows you to adjust the color of the graphic. You can make the graphic darker or lighter then the original.

③ Clicking the **APPLY** button will let you preview the watermark before you close the Insert Watermark dialog box. Once you have the watermark the size and color that you want, click OK.

> If you need to change a watermark option after you have added it to the document you can, by following the steps above.

5. Save the changes and close the document.

The Auto Correct Option

This option will automatically correct some typing errors. Works comes with several auto correct entries. If you find that you are constantly making the same spelling error, you could create an auto correct entry for it. Works comes with a lot of auto correct entries that you may have already used and not have known. Figure 8-28 shows the Auto Correct dialog box.

If you open the Auto Correct dialog box (Tools ⇒ AutoCorrect) and scroll down the list shown in Figure 8-28, you will see - - > in the **REPLACE** column and a right arrow in the **WITH** column. If you type what is in the Replace column in a document, it will be replaced with what is in the With column. If you want, you can type – – > in the document now.

One of the most commonly misspelled words is the word **AND**. As you scroll down the list, look for the word **AND** in the second column.

Auto Correct can be useful if you like using shortcuts. Suppose you do not want to type out the days of the week. You could create an auto correct entry that would allow you to type *mon* and have it automatically replaced with "Monday". If you use a symbol on a regular basis that is not already in the list, you can create an auto correct entry for it.

Another example of when to create an Auto Correct entry is when you need to use the same phrase. This sentence, "Your document should look like the one shown in Figure" is probably the most used sentence in this workbook. Instead of typing it over and over, I created an auto correct entry for it.

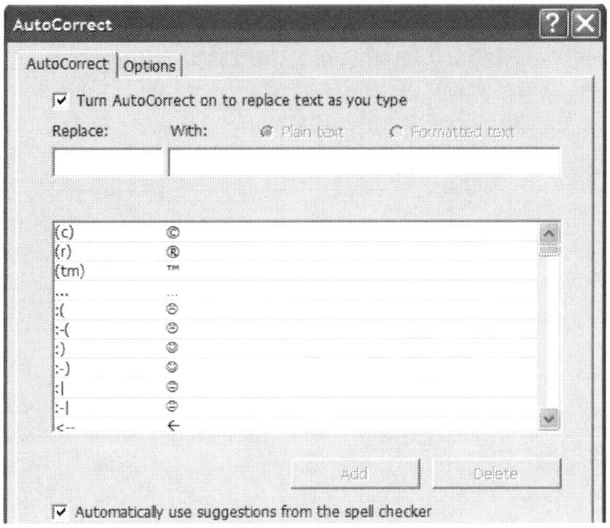

Figure 8-28 Auto Correct dialog box

How To Create An Auto Correct Entry

1. Open a new word processing document, if one is not already open. Tools ⇒ AutoCorrect. If the option **TURN AUTOCORRECT ON TO REPLACE TEXT AS YOU TYPE** is not checked, check it now.

2. Type `tue` in the **REPLACE** field, then press the Tab key and type `Tuesday` in the **WITH** field. Your dialog box should have the options shown in Figure 8-29.

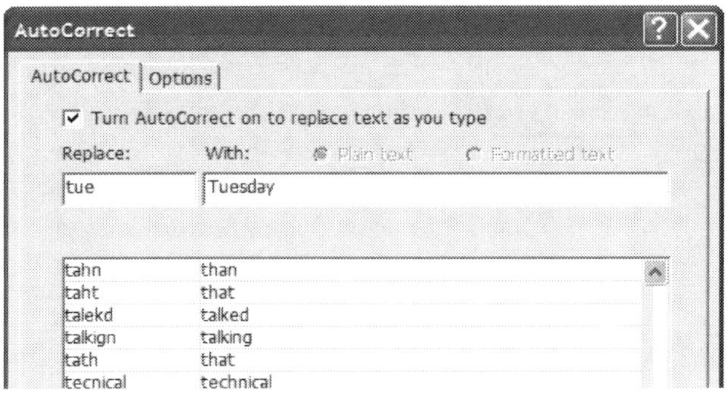

Figure 8-29 New Auto Correct entry

When creating a new auto correct entry, what you type in the Replace field cannot already be in the list. If it is, you will overwrite the existing Auto Correct entry.

3. Click Add, then click OK. Type `tue` and press the space bar. You should now see the word Tuesday.

How To Create An Auto Correct Entry For A Symbol

Creating an auto correct entry for a symbol will save time if you use the symbol frequently. I use the ⇒ symbol frequently in this workbook. Having an Auto Correct entry for it saves me a lot of time. Follow the steps below to create this type of Auto Correct entry.

1. Insert ⇒ Special Character. Open the Font drop-down list and select **SYMBOL**, if it is not already selected. Double-click on the symbol shown in Figure 8-30, then click Close.

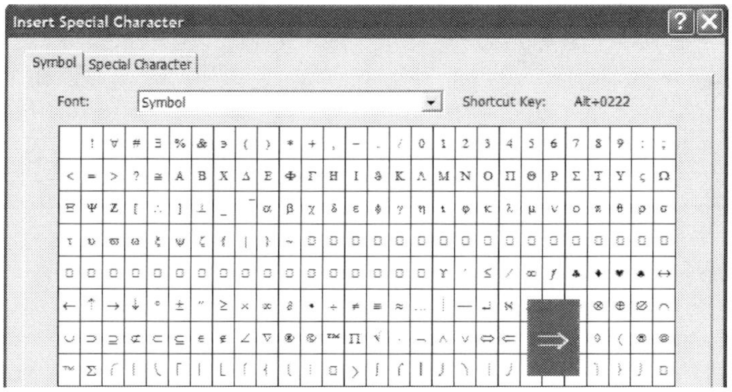

Figure 8-30 Symbol selected

2. Highlight the symbol in the document and change the font to Tahoma. Change the **FONT SIZE** to 10.

> You can use whatever font and font size that you want. I use Tahoma, font size 10, as the default. This workbook also uses the Tahoma font, which is why I selected this font and size for the arrow symbol. You should select the font and size that you use most.

3. Make sure that the symbol is still highlighted. Tools ⇒ Auto Correct. The arrow symbol should be in the **WITH** field. Type `>chk` in the Replace field. Do not put a space between the > and the letter C. Your dialog box should have the options shown in Figure 8-31.

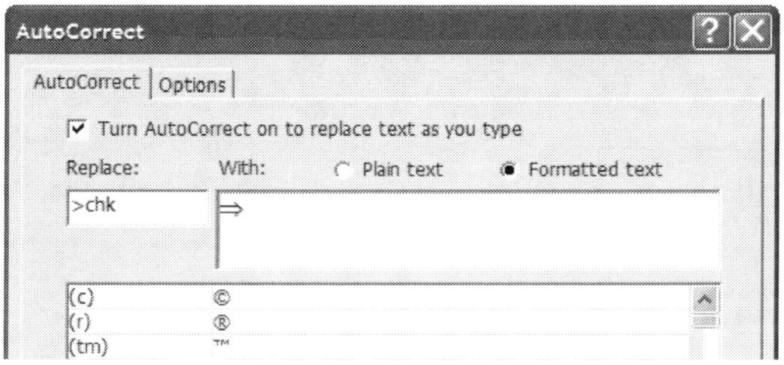

Figure 8-31 Auto Correct entry for the arrow symbol

4. Click Add, then click OK.

5. To use the symbol auto correct entry, type `>chk` and press the space bar. You should see the arrow. Close the document, but do not save the changes.

Test Your Skills

1. Save the Term Paper document as `L8(skills)`.

    - Create a four column document with lines between each column.
    - Paste text from the Term Paper document into the L8 (skills) document to fill all four columns.
    - Add a piece of clip art in the first column. Use the Tight style option.
    - Add a border to the document.
    - Add the watermark graphic shown earlier in Figure 8-25 to the document.

SPREADSHEET BASICS

In this lesson you will learn how to use the spreadsheet application. You will create a spreadsheet from scratch. You will also learn the following spreadsheet formatting techniques:

- ☑ Inserting rows and columns
- ☑ Changing column widths
- ☑ Changing number formats
- ☑ Changing the alignment of cells
- ☑ Adding borders and shading
- ☑ Auto Format feature

LESSON 9

Parts Of A Spreadsheet

Figure 9-1 illustrates the parts of a spreadsheet. Table 9-1 explains each item that is illustrated.

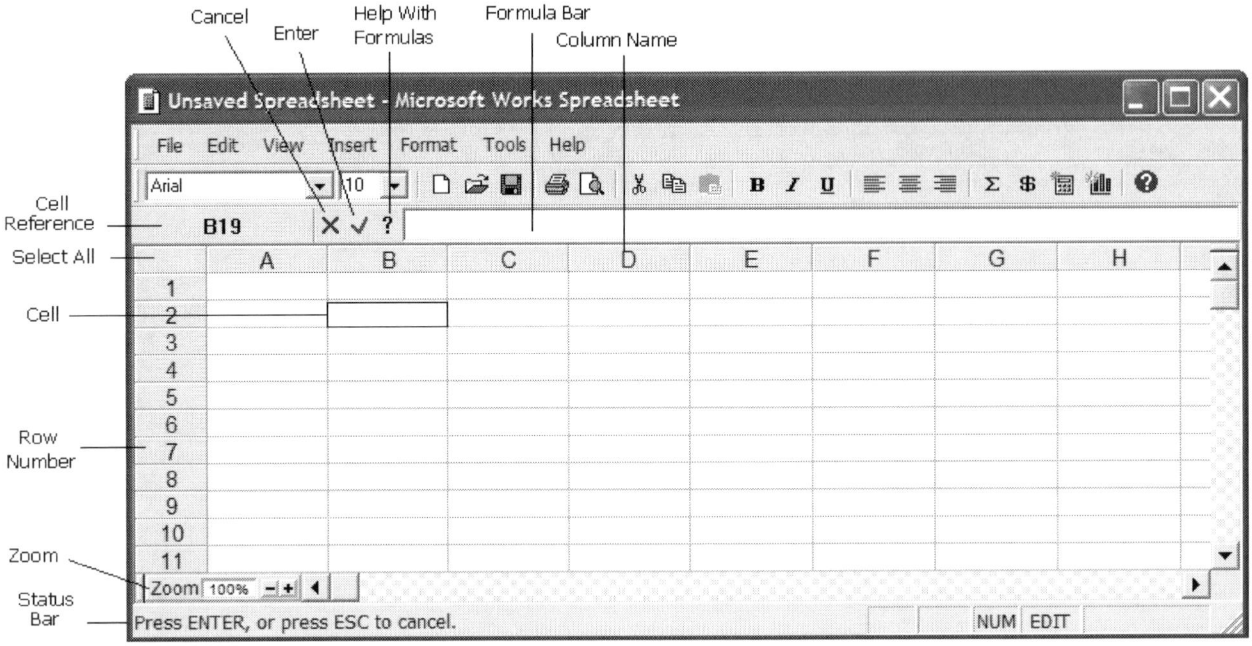

Figure 9-1 Parts of a spreadsheet illustrated

Part	Description
Cancel	Deletes the information that you just entered in the spreadsheet.
Cell	The place where you enter information in a spreadsheet.
Cell Reference	Lets you know what cells are selected.
Column Name	Clicking on the column name lets you select the entire column.
Enter	Works the same as pressing the Enter key.
Formula bar	You can view, enter and edit formulas or data here. This is the same as typing in a cell.
Help With Formulas	Opens the Help System.
Row Number	Clicking on the row number lets you select the entire row.
Select All	Clicking in this square will select (highlight) the entire spreadsheet.
Status bar	Provides a description of the command that is selected and other information about the option.
Zoom	Lets you adjust how large or small the spreadsheet is displayed on the screen.

Table 9-1 Parts of a spreadsheet explained

Spreadsheet Toolbar And Menu

Before you begin creating spreadsheets you should familiarize yourself with the spreadsheet menu and toolbar. Figure 9-2 shows the spreadsheet toolbar.

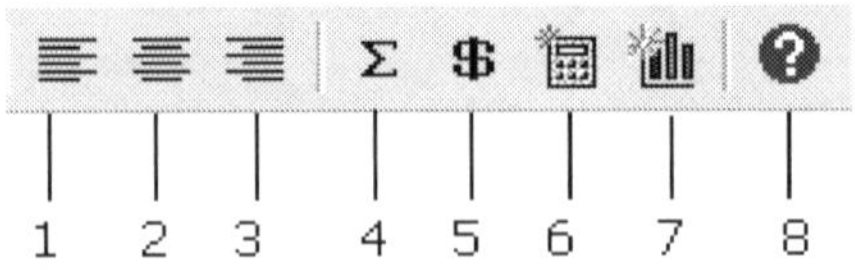

Figure 9-2 Spreadsheet toolbar

Table 9-2 explains the purpose of each toolbar button.
Figure 9-3 shows the spreadsheet menu.
Table 9-3 explains the menu options.

Button	Purpose
1	Left aligns the selected text. This is the default alignment.
2	Centers the selected text between the margins.
3	Right aligns the selected text.
4	Auto Sum automatically sums (adds) a row or column of numbers.
5	Automatically formats the selected cells with the $x,xxx.xx currency format.
6	Easy Calc is a wizard that helps you create formulas.
7	Lets you to create a chart based on the data selected in the spreadsheet.
8	Opens the Help System.

Table 9-2 Spreadsheet toolbar buttons explained

Figure 9-3 Spreadsheet menu

Menu	Purpose
File	Used for opening, saving, creating and printing spreadsheets.
Edit	The commands on this menu will let you copy, paste and cut, as well as, select rows and columns, fill a range of cells and replace data.
View	Change how the spreadsheet is displayed on the screen. There are options for creating charts, headers and footers.
Insert	Insert rows, columns, page breaks, functions and range names.
Format	Format numbers, cell borders, adjust row and column height and freeze titles.
Tools	Contains the spell check tool and the chart options.
Help	Opens the Help System.

Table 9-3 Spreadsheet menu options explained

Change The Size Of The Toolbar

If the default size of the toolbar on the spreadsheet application is too small, you can make it larger by following the steps below.

1. Open the spreadsheet application.
2. View ⇒ Toolbar ⇒ Use Large Icons, as shown in Figure 9-4.

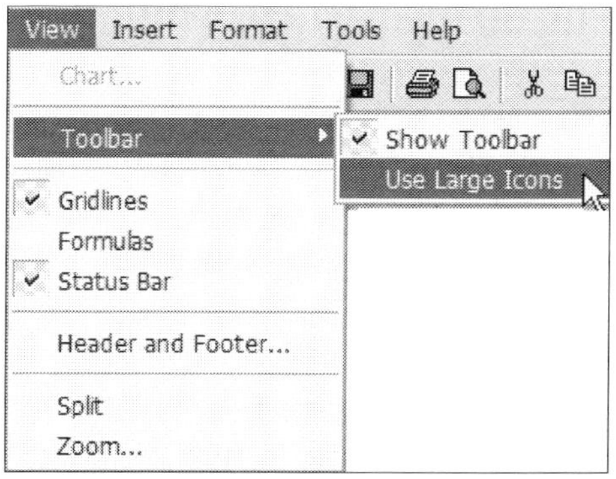

Figure 9-4 Use Large Icons option illustrated

Gridlines

Some people prefer to work on spreadsheets without the gridlines. If this is how you prefer to work, follow the steps below to turn the gridlines off.

1. View ⇒ Gridlines, as shown in Figure 9-5. Figure 9-6 shows a spreadsheet without the gridlines.

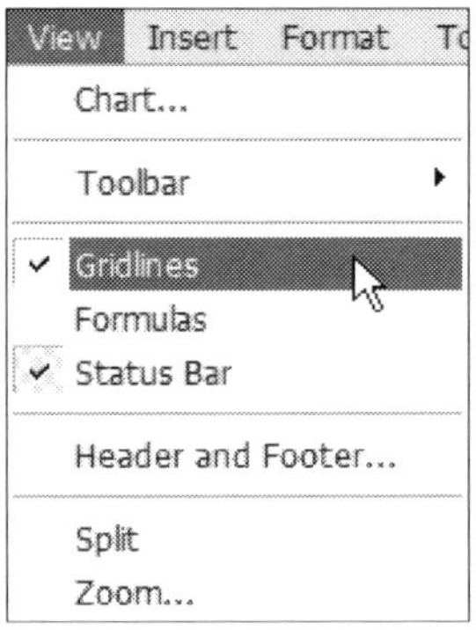

Figure 9-5 Gridlines option illustrated

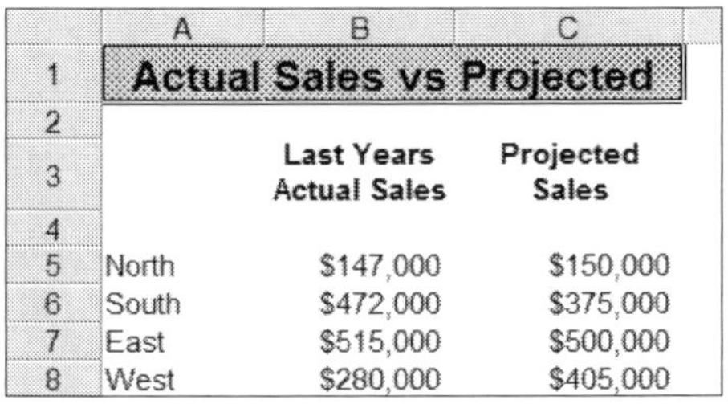

Figure 9-6 Spreadsheet without the gridlines

Turning off the gridlines in the spreadsheet does not prevent the gridlines from printing on paper.

Zoom Options

Earlier you learned how to make the toolbar buttons larger. You can also make the spreadsheet larger or smaller. As shown earlier in the lower left corner of Figure 9-1, the zoom level is set to 100%, which is the default. The easiest way to zoom in or out is to click on the plus or minus buttons to the right of the zoom percent.

1. Click on the word **ZOOM**. You will see the shortcut menu shown in Figure 9-7.

   View ⇒ Zoom, will also open the Zoom dialog box.

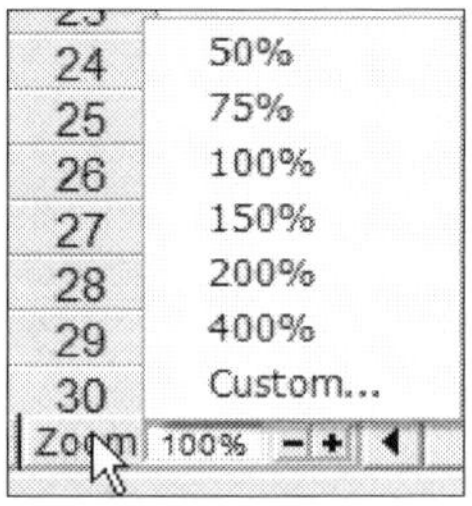

Figure 9-7 Zoom shortcut menu

2. Select the **CUSTOM** option on the Zoom shortcut menu. You will see the dialog box shown in Figure 9-8. This dialog box will allow you to select a custom zoom option if none of the preset options are what you need.

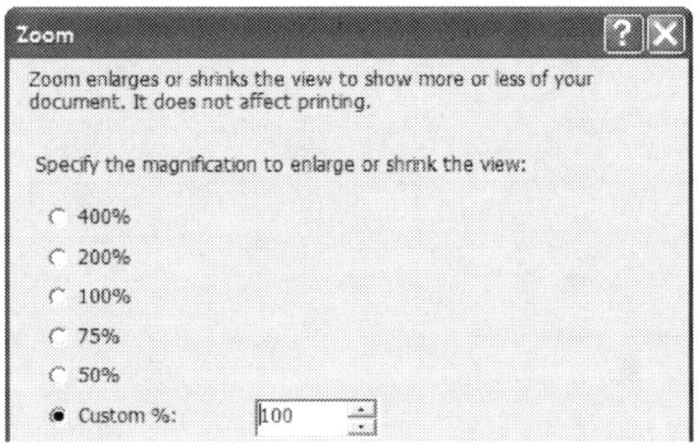

Figure 9-8 Zoom dialog box

Select Cells, Rows And Columns

Selecting Cells

To select a cell, put the cursor in the cell that you want to enter new information in or edit existing information. This is sometimes called **HIGHLIGHTING**. This is very similar to highlighting text that you learned about in the word processing lessons. In the upper left corner of the spreadsheet you will see the cell address, cell name or range that you have selected, as shown in Figure 9-9. In Figure 9-9, the cell B3 is selected.

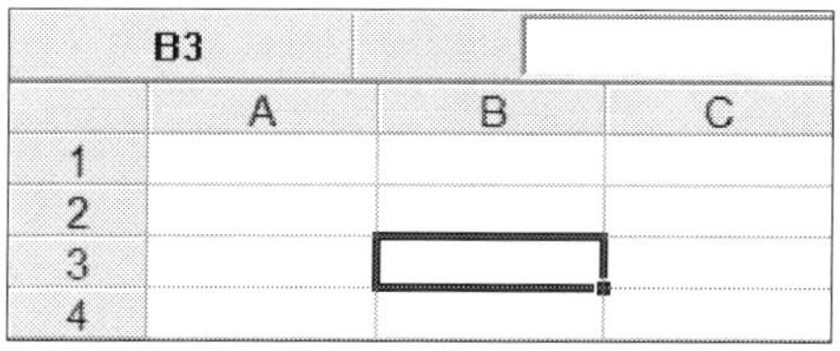

Figure 9-9 Cell selected and address illustrated

Selecting Rows

To select an entire row, click on the row number on the left side of the spreadsheet. Figure 9-10 shows that row 2 is selected.

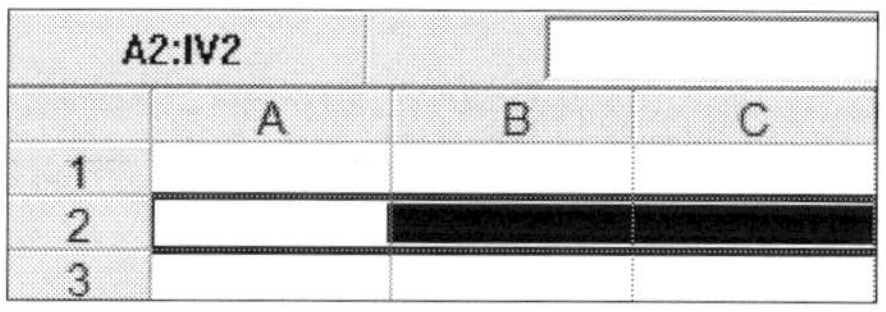

Figure 9-10 Row 2 selected

Selecting Columns

To select an entire column click on the column letter, which is also called the column heading, as shown in Figure 9-11.

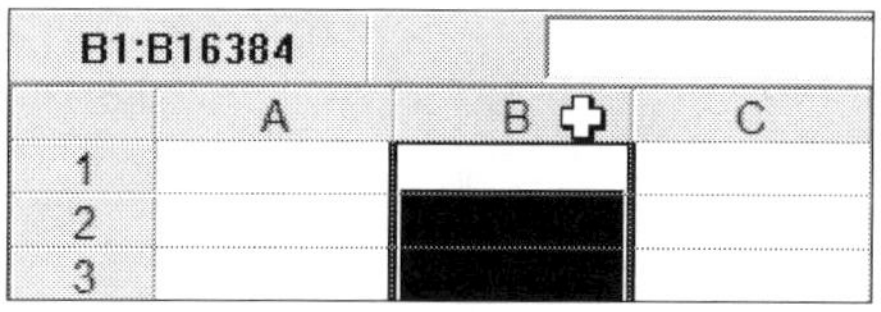

Figure 9-11 Column B selected

Select A Range Of Cells

You can select a group of adjacent cells. If you wanted to select the range A2 to D5, (which includes the following cells, A2, A3, A4, A5, B2, B3, B4, B5, C2, C3, C4, C5, D2, D3, D4 and D5) click in cell A2, hold down the left mouse button and drag the mouse across to column D and then down to row 5. Your spreadsheet would look like the one shown in Figure 9-12.

Throughout the spreadsheet lessons, you will see instructions like: **HIGHLIGHT THE RANGE A2 TO D5**. This means that you should select the cells that are in the range, similar to what is shown in Figure 9-12. If you aren't sure whether you have selected the correct range of cells, you can look in the Cell Reference section of the spreadsheet window.

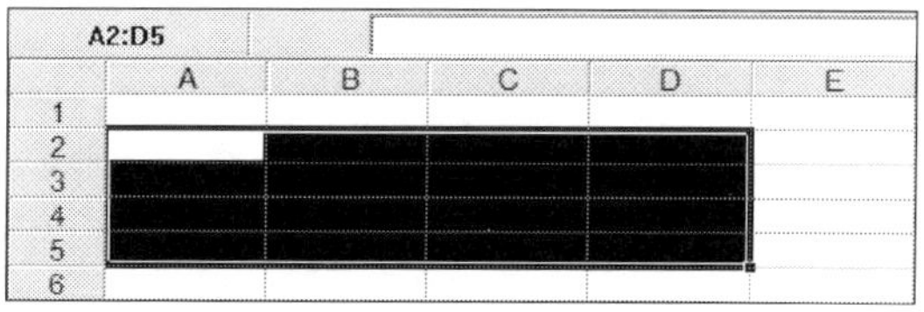

Figure 9-12 Cell range A2 to D5 selected

Select Cells Using The Keyboard

With more and more people using laptops, I think that a discussion on how to select cells using the keyboard is necessary. The easiest way to select cells without using a mouse is to follow the steps below.

1. Place the cursor in the first cell of the range that you want to select, then press and hold down the **SHIFT** key.

2. Use the arrow keys on your keyboard to move to the right and then down to select the cells in the range that you need. After you have selected all of the cells, release the Shift key.

> In the instructions above, instead of holding down the Shift key, you can press the **F8** key. If you use the F8 key, you do not have to hold the F8 key down like you do the Shift key to select cells.

Create Your First Spreadsheet

Spreadsheets can have up to 256 columns and 16,384 rows.

1. Open a new spreadsheet if one is not already open. In cell A1 type `Actual Sales vs Projections` and press Enter.

2. Type `Actual` in cell B3, then type `Projected Sales` in cell C3.

> In addition to entering or modifying existing data in a cell, you can add or modify data in the Formula bar which was illustrated earlier in Figure 9-1.

3. Add the data in Table 9-4 to the spreadsheet. When you are finished, your spreadsheet should look like the one shown in Figure 9-13.

Cell	Data
A4	North
A5	South
A6	East
A7	West
B4	123000
B5	424000
B6	394000
B7	210000
C4	150000
C5	400000
C6	375000
C7	225000

Table 9-4 Data to add to the spreadsheet

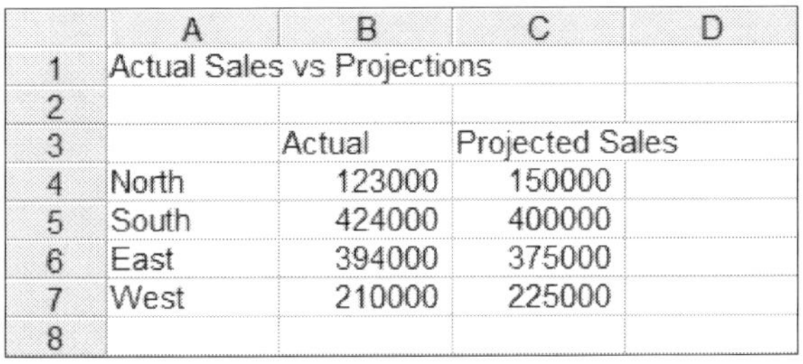

	A	B	C	D
1	Actual Sales vs Projections			
2				
3		Actual	Projected Sales	
4	North	123000	150000	
5	South	424000	400000	
6	East	394000	375000	
7	West	210000	225000	
8				

Figure 9-13 Actual Sales vs Projections spreadsheet

Change The Column Width

The default column width on spreadsheets is 10 characters. You may often find that the default column width size does not meet your needs. The Projected Sales title in cell C3 is an example of this.

There are several ways to adjust the column width. The easiest way is to drag the column border to the right to make the column wider. Another way is to open the Columns Width dialog box shown in Figure 9-14. (Format ⇒ Column Width) You can type in the width that you want or select the option to fit the widest text in the column.

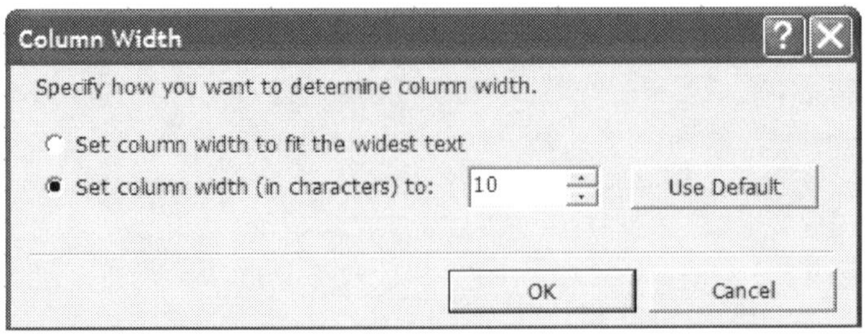

Figure 9-14 Column Width dialog box

1. Place the cursor on the line between columns C and D as illustrated in Figure 9-15. The cursor will change and you will see the word **ADJUST**.

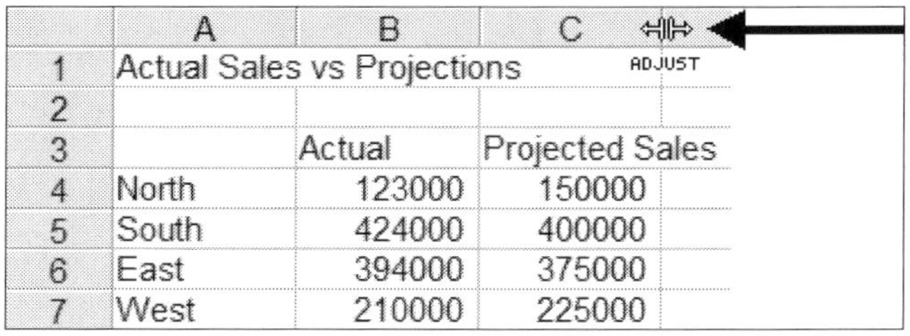

Figure 9-15 Cursor in position to change the column width

2. Hold down the left mouse button and drag the mouse to the right until you go past the end of the Projected Sales title.

3. Save the spreadsheet. Type `L9 Actual Sales vs Projected` as the file name.

Change The Row Height

Just like the column width can be changed, the row height can also be changed.

1. Place the cursor on the line between rows 3 and 4 as illustrated in Figure 9-16.

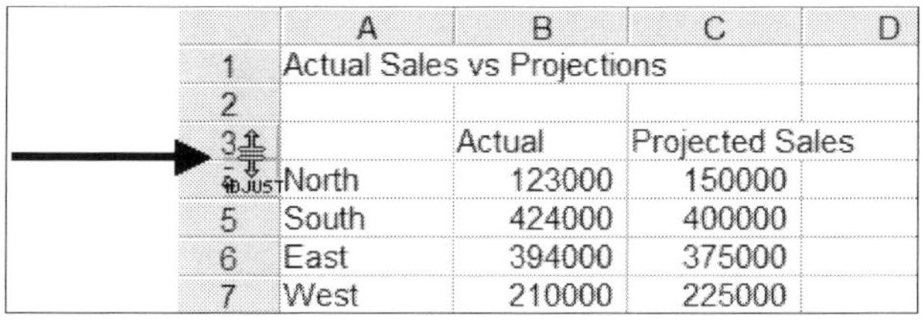

Figure 9-16 Cursor in position to change the row height

2. Hold down the left mouse button and drag the mouse down to the middle of row 4.

Insert Rows

1. Right-click on row 4 (in the tan area on the left) and select **INSERT ROW**, as shown in Figure 9-17. There should be a blank row between the column titles and the first row of data.

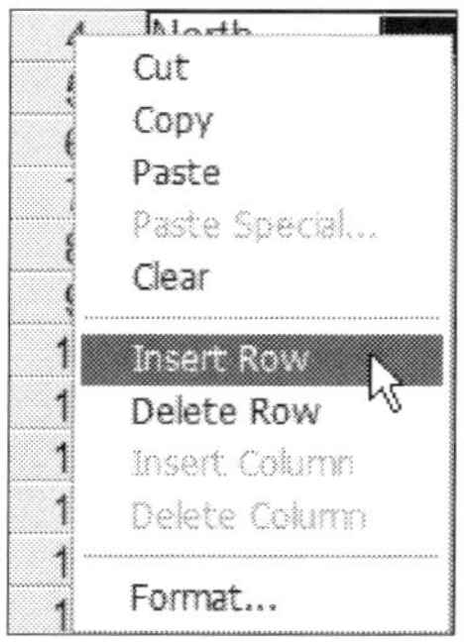

Figure 9-17 Spreadsheet shortcut menu

Insert Columns

1. Right-click on column B and select **INSERT COLUMN** as shown in Figure 9-18. There should be a blank column after column A.

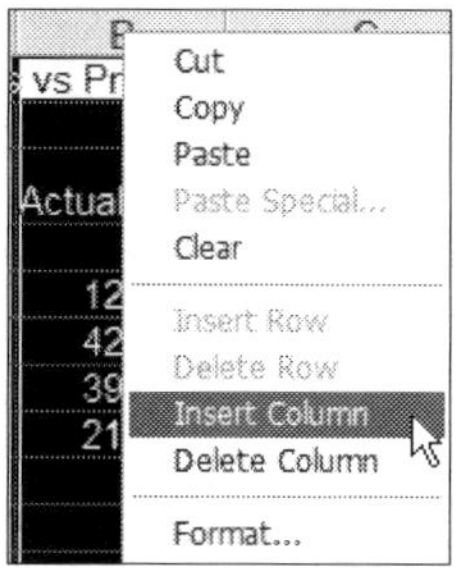

Figure 9-18 Selected column illustrated

Delete A Column

1. Right-click on the column heading (in this exercise, column B) that you want to delete and select **DELETE COLUMN**. Deleting a row works the same way.

Number Formats

When you enter numbers in a spreadsheet, no formatting is applied by default. You can add commas, dollar and percent signs. You can also format dates and times. The numbers in columns B and C would look better and be easier to read if they were formatted.

1. Highlight the range B5 to C8 as shown in Figure 9-19, then right-click on the highlighted cells and select Format. You will see the dialog box shown in Figure 9-20. It may take a few seconds for the dialog box to open.

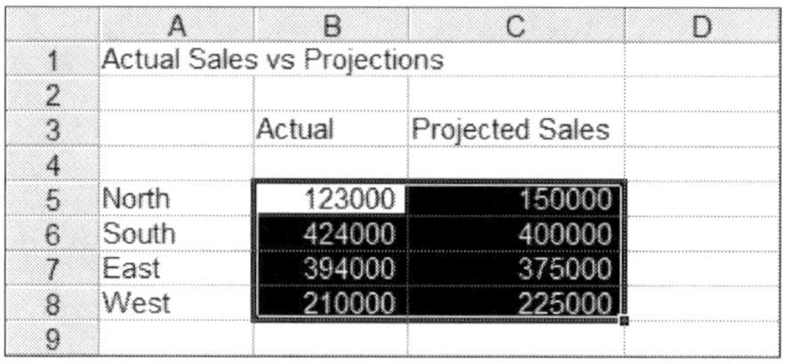

Figure 9-19 Cells selected to format

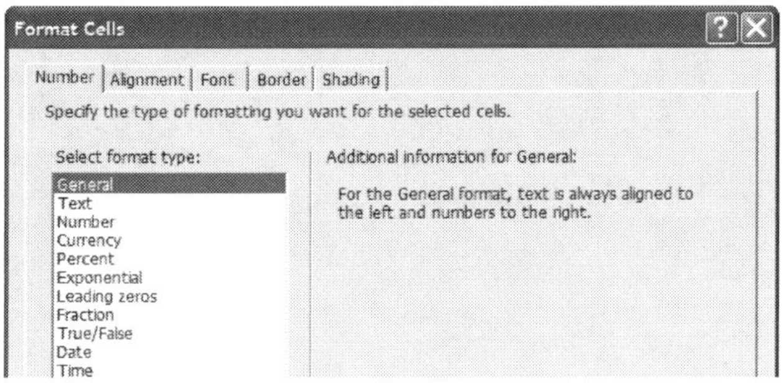

Figure 9-20 Format Cells dialog box

Format ⇒ Number, will also open the Format Cells dialog box.

2. Click on the Currency format. Make sure the **SHOW NEGATIVE NUMBERS IN RED** option is selected.

The default number of decimal places is two. It is probably a good idea to always select the **SHOW NEGATIVE NUMBERS IN RED** option as shown in Figure 9-21, in case you enter negative numbers or create formulas that could produce negative numbers. Selecting this option forces negative numbers to appear in red on the spreadsheet. The Format Cells dialog box also allows you to modify alignment, font, border and shading options.

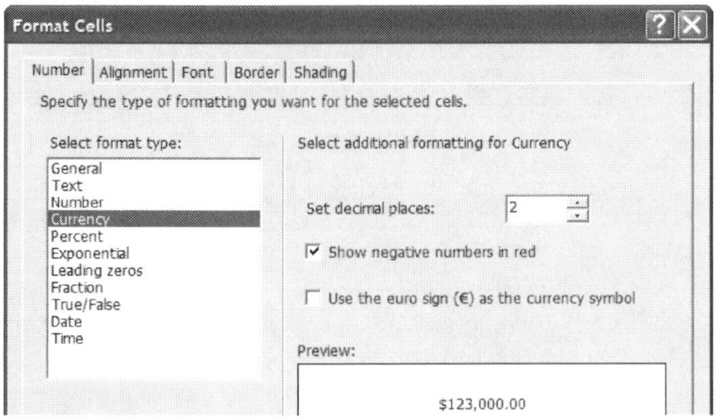

Figure 9-21 Currency options illustrated

3. Click on each of the tabs now so that you can become familiar with the options. The options selected on each tab are the default formatting options. Figures 9-22 to 9-25 show the options on these tabs.

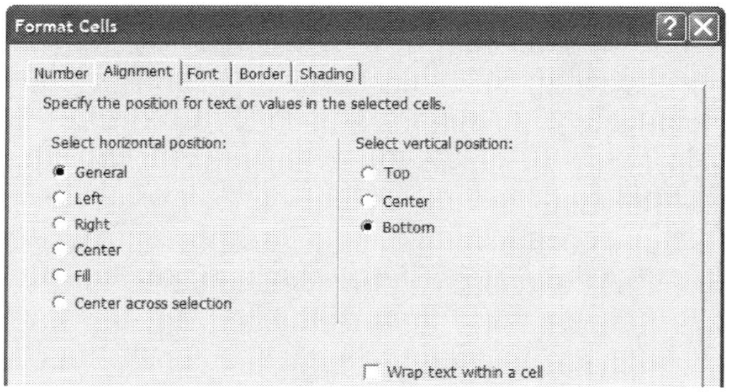

Figure 9-22 Alignment tab options

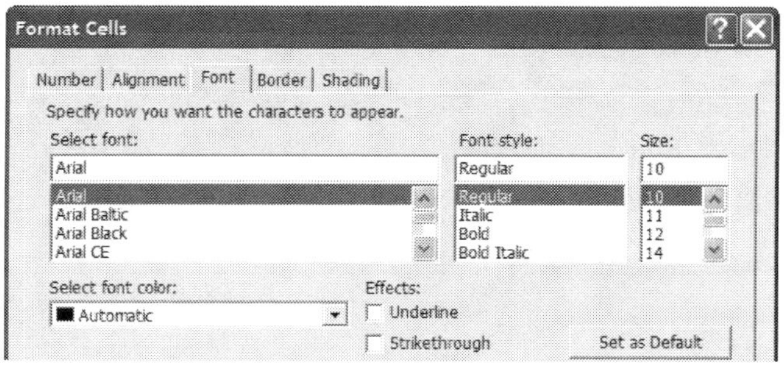

Figure 9-23 Font tab options

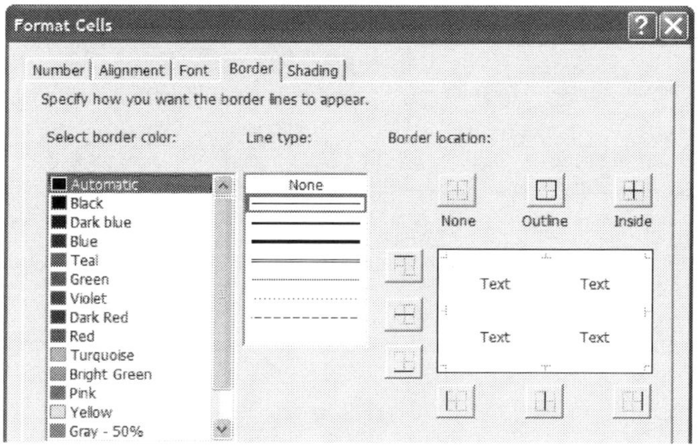

Figure 9-24 Border tab options

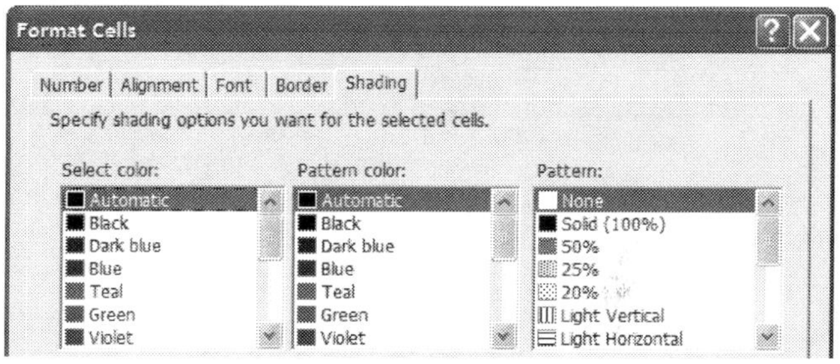

Figure 9-25 Shading tab options

4. Click OK. You should see the pound signs in column B, as shown in Figure 9-26. The pound signs let you know that the data is too large for the width of the cell. Place the cursor between columns B and C. Hold down the left mouse button and drag the mouse to the right until the numbers in column B are visible. Save the changes and leave the spreadsheet open.

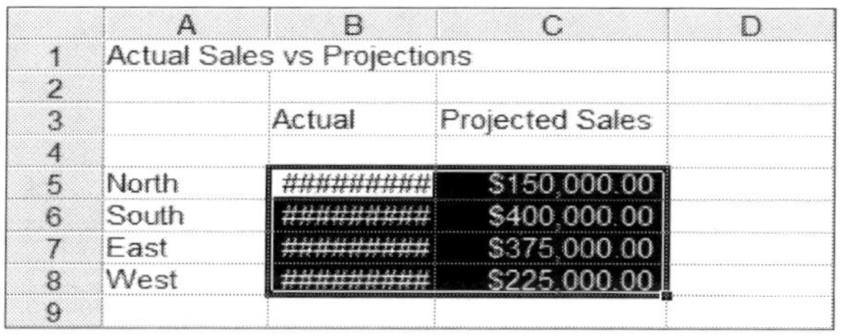

Figure 9-26 Cell width that is too small

Formatting Text In A Spreadsheet

You can format text in a spreadsheet just like you can in a word processing document.

1. Highlight cells B3 and C3, then click the Bold button on the toolbar. With the cells still highlighted, right-click on them and select Format.

2. On the Alignment tab select **CENTER** as the horizontal position, then click OK. The titles should now be centered in the cells.

Yes, you could have centered the text using the Center button on the toolbar, but I wanted to demonstrate how to use some of the options on the Format Cells dialog box.

Center Text Across Cells

The **CENTER ACROSS SELECTION** option is on the Alignment tab of the Format Cells dialog box. This option allows you to automatically spread the contents of one cell across several cells in a row.

1. Highlight the range A1 to C1, then Format ⇒ Alignment.

> This is the same as right-clicking on the highlighted cells and selecting Format.

2. Select the **CENTER ACROSS SELECTION** option.

3. Click on the Font tab and change the **FONT STYLE** to bold, then click OK. The title should now be centered across columns A, B and C. Your spreadsheet should look like the one shown in Figure 9-27. The text appears to be in cells A1, B1 and C1. Click in cell A1. Look in the **FORMULA BAR** and you will see that the title is only in this cell.

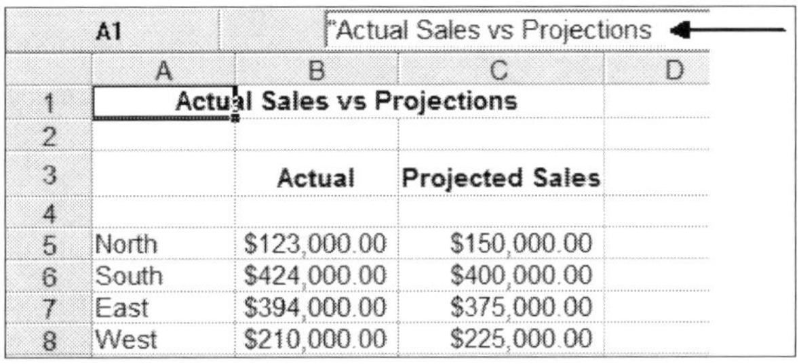

Figure 9-27 Text centered across cells and contents of cell A1 illustrated in the Formula bar

Adding Borders And Shading

1. Highlight the range A1 to C1, then right-click on the highlighted cells and select Format. On the Font tab change the size to 14.

2. On the Border tab select the fourth **LINE TYPE**, then click the **OUTLINE** button in the Border location section on the Format Cells dialog box as illustrated in Figure 9-28.

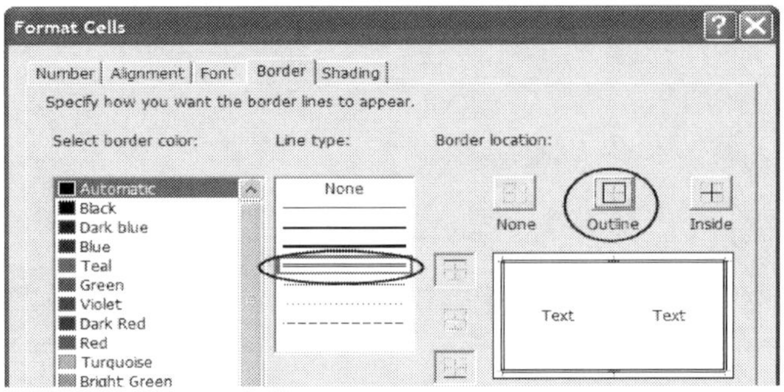

Figure 9-28 Line type and border location illustrated

3. Change the **BORDER COLOR** to Black. On the Shading tab change the **SELECT COLOR** to Yellow. This is the background color.

4. Select the fourth **PATTERN** (20%) and click OK. The title should now have a double black line border and a yellow background. Your spreadsheet should look like the one shown in Figure 9-29. Save the changes and leave the spreadsheet open.

	A	B	C
1	Actual Sales vs Projections		
2			
3		Actual	Projected Sales
4			
5	North	$123,000.00	$150,000.00
6	South	$424,000.00	$400,000.00
7	East	$394,000.00	$375,000.00
8	West	$210,000.00	$225,000.00

Figure 9-29 Borders and shading added to the spreadsheet

How To Wrap Text In A Cell

The wrap text feature is useful when you have more information then will fit on one line in a cell. This feature is primarily used for text.

1. Right-click on cell C3 and select Format. On the Alignment tab select the **WRAP TEXT WITHIN A CELL** option, then click OK.

2. Make row 3 longer. The text in cell C3 should now be on two lines in the cell, as shown in Figure 9-30. If not, adjust the width of column C. Save the changes.

	A	B	C
1	Actual Sales vs Projections		
2			
3		Actual	Projected Sales
4			
5	North	$123,000.00	$150,000.00
6	South	$424,000.00	$400,000.00
7	East	$394,000.00	$375,000.00
8	West	$210,000.00	$225,000.00

Figure 9-30 Wrap text feature illustrated

The Replace Command

This command will search for the text that you specify and replace it with what you want. The Replace command in the spreadsheet application works very similar to how it works in the word processing application.

> If you only want to search a specific portion of the spreadsheet, select it first and then follow the steps below.

1. Edit ⇒ Replace. You should see the **FIND AND REPLACE** dialog box. In the **FIND WHAT** field type `Projections`.

2. Press the Tab key and type `Projected`. The **SEARCH BY** options shown in Figure 9-31 let you select the direction that the search will take, either row by row or column by column.

If you want to see each match before it is changed, click the Find Next button. If you want the information replaced every place that it exists in the spreadsheet, click the Replace All button.

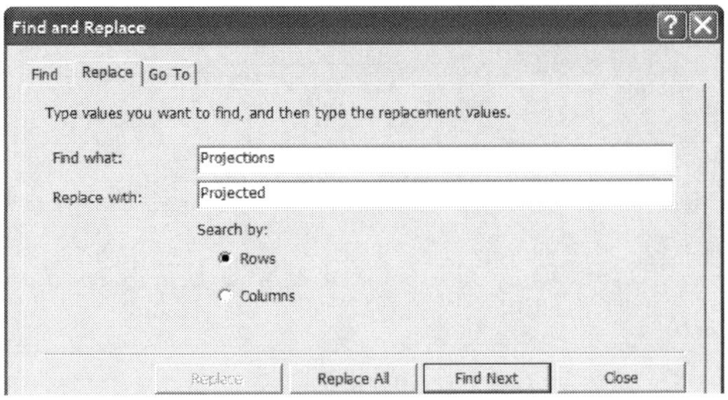

Figure 9-31 Replace options

3. Click the Replace All button. The word **PROJECTIONS** should have been replaced with the word **PROJECTED** in the title.

How To Edit Text Or Data In A Cell

There are two ways to edit data in a cell. You can re-type the contents of the cell or you can only change the portion of data in the cell that needs to be changed.

1. Click in cell B3 and press the **F2** key.

2. Using the left arrow key, move the cursor so that it is between the quote (") and the A, as shown in Figure 9-32.

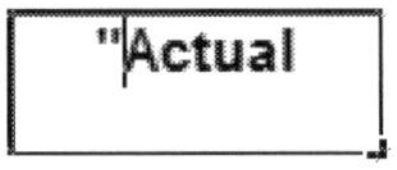

Figure 9-32 Cursor in position to edit the information in the cell

3. Type `Current` and press the space bar. Press the **END** key, then press the space bar.

4. Type `Sales`, then press Enter. Wrap the text in this cell. If you need help, refer back to the section, "How To Wrap Text In A Cell". Your spreadsheet should look like the one shown in Figure 9-33.

	A	B	C
1	**Actual Sales vs Projected**		
2			
3		**Current Actual Sales**	**Projected Sales**
4			
5	North	$123,000.00	$150,000.00
6	South	$424,000.00	$400,000.00
7	East	$394,000.00	$375,000.00
8	West	$210,000.00	$225,000.00

Figure 9-33 Completed spreadsheet

5. Save the changes and leave the spreadsheet open.

Auto Format

If you do not want to format a spreadsheet manually you can use the Auto Format option to change the appearance of the spreadsheet. There are 19 Auto Format styles. To use one of the Auto Format styles, create the spreadsheet and select the Auto Format style that you want. You can also use an Auto Format style on a spreadsheet that you have already formatted.

How To Format The Entire Spreadsheet

1. Save the L9 Actual Sales vs Projected spreadsheet as `L9 Actual Sales (with auto format).`

2. Highlight the range A1 to C8. Format ⇒ Auto Format. You will see the dialog box shown in Figure 9-34.

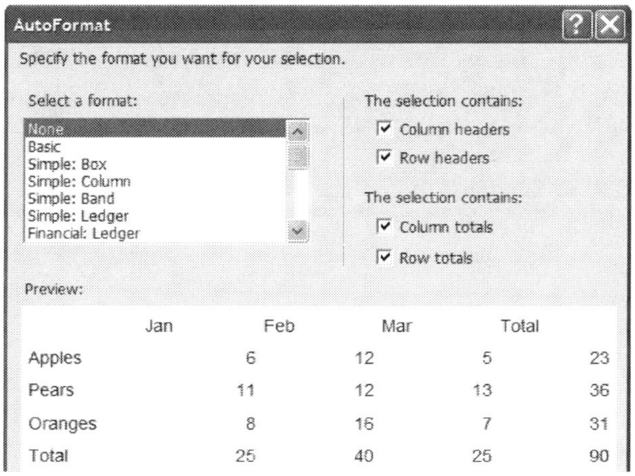

Figure 9-34 Auto Format dialog box

3. Select the **SIMPLE LEDGER** format, then clear the **COLUMN TOTALS** and **ROW TOTALS** options.

> You should only leave the **COLUMN TOTALS** and **ROW TOTALS** options checked if the last row or last column of your spreadsheet actually has totals. If you leave these options checked, the last row and column will have different formatting then the rest of the spreadsheet, like the one shown in Figure 9-35.

As you can see, the format shown in Figure 9-35 is not the correct format for the spreadsheet that you are currently working on because your spreadsheet does not have totals in the last row or last column.

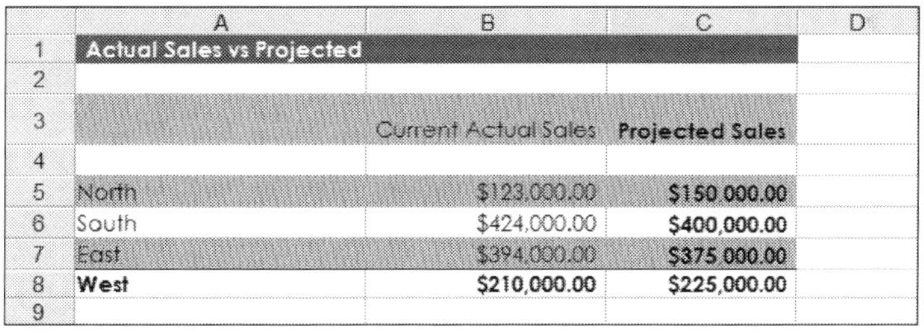

Figure 9-35 Auto Format applied with the column and row total options selected

4. Click OK. Your spreadsheet should look like the one shown in Figure 9-36. Save the changes and close the spreadsheet.

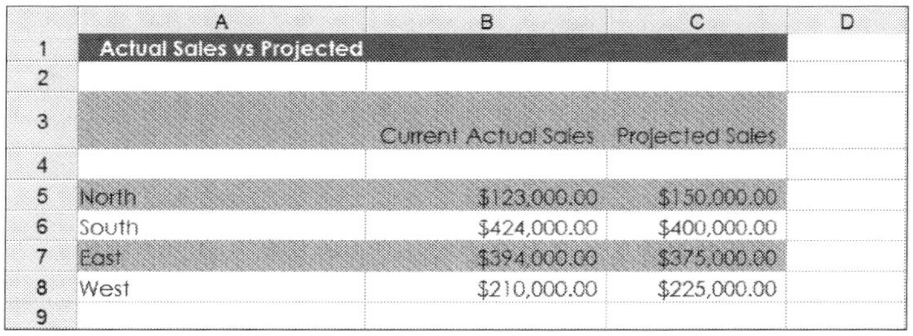

Figure 9-36 Spreadsheet with an Auto Format applied

How To Format Part Of The Spreadsheet

You can also apply an Auto Format style to a portion of the spreadsheet. The only difference is that you have to select the portion of the spreadsheet that you want to format before opening the Auto Format dialog box.

1. Save the L9 Actual Sales vs Projected spreadsheet as `L9 Actual Sales (partial auto format).`

2. Highlight the range A3 to C8. Format ⇒ Auto Format, then select the **ELEGANT: COLUMN** format and click OK. The spreadsheet title should still be the same. Only cells A3 to C8 should have changed, as shown in Figure 9-37. Save the changes and close the spreadsheet.

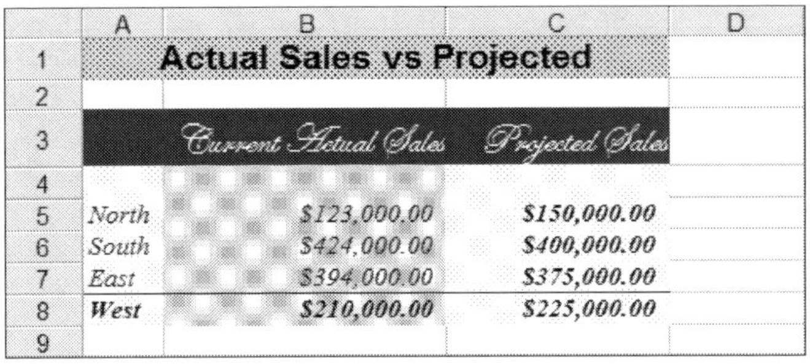

	A	B	C	D
1	Actual Sales vs Projected			
2				
3		Current Actual Sales	Projected Sales	
4				
5	North	$123,000.00	$150,000.00	
6	South	$424,000.00	$400,000.00	
7	East	$394,000.00	$375,000.00	
8	West	$210,000.00	$225,000.00	
9				

Figure 9-37 Part of the spreadsheet formatted

Copying Cells

The Copy command allows you to select the entire spreadsheet or a portion of it and place it someplace else in the same spreadsheet or in another spreadsheet.

1. Open the L9 Actual Sales vs Projected spreadsheet and highlight the range A6 to B7.

2. Right-click on the highlighted cells and select Copy, then right-click in cell E11 and select Paste.

3. Make column F wider so that the numbers are displayed. Your spreadsheet should look like the one shown in Figure 9-38.

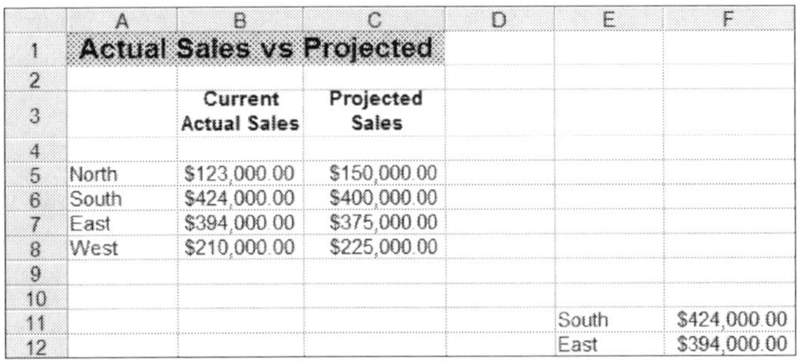

	A	B	C	D	E	F
1	Actual Sales vs Projected					
2						
3		Current Actual Sales	Projected Sales			
4						
5	North	$123,000.00	$150,000.00			
6	South	$424,000.00	$400,000.00			
7	East	$394,000.00	$375,000.00			
8	West	$210,000.00	$225,000.00			
9						
10						
11					South	$424,000.00
12					East	$394,000.00

Figure 9-38 Cells copied

You can double-click on the line between columns F and G to make the column wider.

How To Copy Cells From One Spreadsheet To Another

1. Highlight the range C3 to C8, then right-click on the highlighted cells and select Copy.

2. Click the **NEW** button on the toolbar. A new spreadsheet will open. Right-click in cell A3 and select Paste. The data should now be in the new spreadsheet. Make column A wider.

3. Slide the new spreadsheet down so that you can also see the Actual Sales vs Projected spreadsheet, as shown in Figure 9-39.

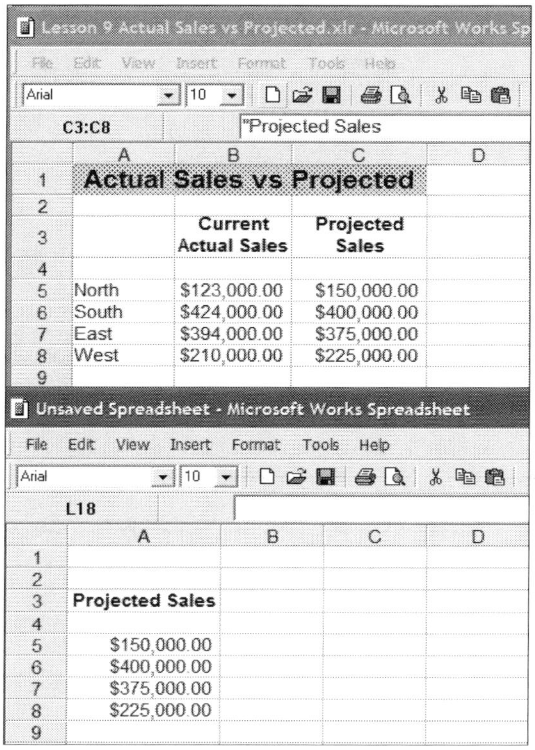

Figure 9-39 Cells copied to a new spreadsheet

How To Move Cells

1. Highlight the range A5 to A8 in the bottom spreadsheet shown above in Figure 9-39, then right-click on the highlighted cells and select Cut.

2. Right-click in cell A9 in the bottom spreadsheet and select Paste. The data now starts in cell A9. Close the bottom spreadsheet, but do not save the changes.

3. Highlight the range E11 to F12 in the L9 Actual Sales vs Projected spreadsheet, then press the Delete key. Save the changes.

Range Names

Range names allow you to reference a cell or a group of cells by a name, instead of the cell name. If you needed to reference the Current Actual Sales for all regions, you would refer to it as B3:B8. You could create a range name like Actual_Sales to reference these cells. You can use range names in formulas, which will make the formulas easier to read.

Other Reasons To Use Range Names

- ☑ If you had a formula that subtracted Projected Sales from Actual Sales, the formula would be easier to read if it looked like this, **NORTH_SALES - PROJECTED_SALES** instead of **B5 - C5**.
- ☑ If you type in the wrong cell address in a formula, you may not notice it as fast as you would if you were using range names in the formula.

> Range names can have a maximum of 15 characters and can include letters, numbers and the underscore. You cannot have spaces in range names.

Creating Range Names

1. Save the L9 Actual Sales vs Projected spreadsheet as `L9 Actual Sales(with range names).`

2. Highlight the range B5 to B8. Insert ⇒ Range Name. You should see the dialog box shown in Figure 9-40. Type `Actual_Sales` in the Name field, then click OK.

Figure 9-40 Range Name dialog box

Works tries to help by suggesting a range name for you. In Figure 9-40 above, that is why you see the word **NORTH** in the Name field.

3. Highlight the range C5 to C8, then Insert ⇒ Range Name. Type `Projected_Sales` in the Name field, then click OK.

4. Highlight cell B7. Insert ⇒ Range Name. Type `East_Sales` in the Name field, then click OK.

5. Insert ⇒ Range Name. Your dialog box should have all of the range names shown in Figure 9-41. Close the dialog box and save the changes.

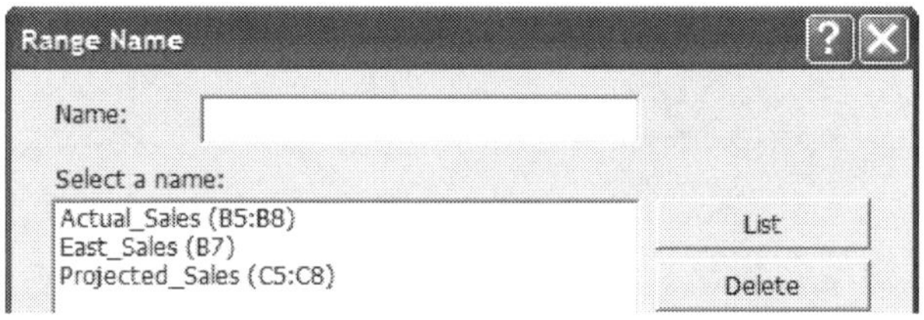

Figure 9-41 Range names that you created

Notice that the cell ranges are shown to the right of the range name. This is helpful if you do not remember which cells the range name is referring to.

The Go To Command

This command works the same in the spreadsheet application as it does in the word processing application.

1. Edit ⇒ Go To. You will see the dialog box shown in Figure 9-42.

The **GO TO** field is used to enter a cell that you want to go to. This feature is probably most helpful when you are working with a very large spreadsheet. If the spreadsheet had a defined print area, you would see the print area name listed in the **SELECT A RANGE NAME** section of the dialog box. You will learn how to create print areas in Lesson 11.

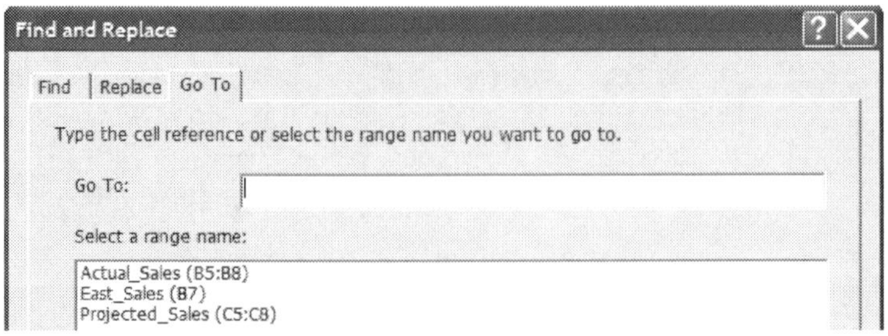

Figure 9-42 Go To tab on the Find and Replace dialog box

If the spreadsheet has range names, you will see them on the Go To tab. If you select a range name in the dialog box and click the Go To button, the range area will be highlighted on the spreadsheet.

2. Close the L9 Actual Sales (with range names) spreadsheet.

How To Convert Spreadsheet Data To Database Format

Doing mail merges and creating reports in a database is much easier then doing these tasks in a spreadsheet. You may have the need to convert a spreadsheet into a format that can be used in a database. The format that spreadsheets and databases can both read is **csv**.

1. Open the Customers spreadsheet. File ⇒ Save As. In the Save As Type drop-down list select **TEXT & COMMAS**, as shown in Figure 9-43.

The Text & Commas format will keep spreadsheet data in the row and column format when you use the data in a database. You will loose formatting like bold or italic. This is ok because you can format the data when you print a report from the database.

Later you will open this file in a database. The other formatting that could be lost is in the zip code field. Zip codes that start with a zero, will drop the first zero if they were not entered with an apostrophe as the first character in the spreadsheet.

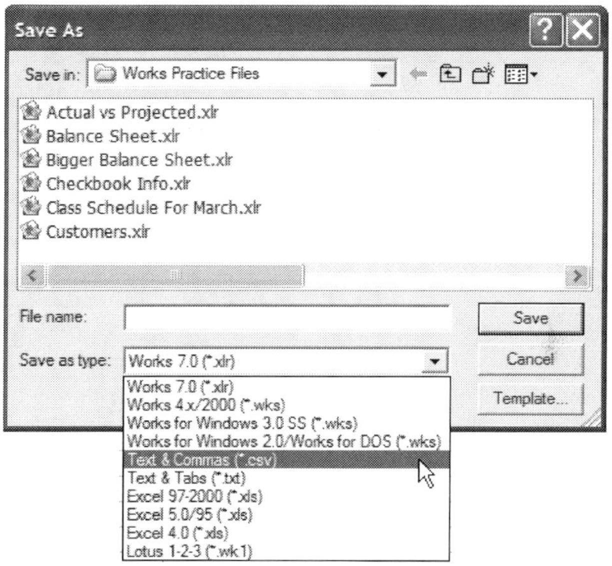

Figure 9-43 Save as type options illustrated

2. Type `Customer (in csv format)` as the file name and press Enter. When prompted, click OK to save without formatting. Close the spreadsheet.

Test Your Skills

1. Save the L9 Actual Sales vs Projected spreadsheet as `L9(skills)`.

   - Create range names for the following sections of the spreadsheet:
     West_Actual Sales
     East_both (East actual and projected sales)
     East_west (East and west projected sales)

   - Format rows 7 and 8 with the Financial ledger format.
   - Create the subtitle, `For this year and last year` in cell A2.
   - Center the subtitle across columns A, B and C.

FORMULAS AND FUNCTIONS

Formulas and functions are the real power of spreadsheets. You have probably heard the term **NUMBER CRUNCHING**. Formulas and functions allow you to do number crunching. In this lesson you will learn how to do the following:

- ☑ Copy and move formulas
- ☑ Use the Fill Right, Fill Down, Easy Calc and AutoSum features
- ☑ Use Range Names in formulas

LESSON 10

What Are Formulas And Functions?

A **FORMULA** performs a calculation (like addition, subtraction or multiplication) on cells in the spreadsheet. You create formulas. The result of the formula is placed in a cell.

FUNCTIONS are pre-built formulas that come with Microsoft Works and other spreadsheet packages. Functions are often more complex than formulas that you create. Examples of functions include **NOW**, which returns the current date and time. **PV** is a function that calculates the present value of an annuity. There are over 70 functions that came with Works. You can also use functions in your formulas.

> All formulas and functions must begin with an equal sign.

Creating Formulas Manually

In this exercise you will learn how to create a formula to calculate the Total Assets for each month. The formula is Cash + Inventory + Receivables = Total Assets. The cells needed for this calculation are in rows 6 to 8 on the spreadsheet.

1. Save the Balance Sheet spreadsheet as `L10 Modified Balance Sheet.`

2. Click in cell B10. Type `= B6 + B7 + B8` and press Enter. Your spreadsheet should look like the one shown in Figure 10-1.

> You should not type spaces in the formula. If you do, Works will automatically remove them. I use spaces in this workbook to make the formulas easier to read. You do not have to type the cell letter as a capital letter. You can type them in lower case letters they will automatically be converted to a capital letter once you press the Enter key.

The formula that you typed in is at the top of Figure 10-1.

If you need to modify the formula, press the F2 key. You can edit the formula in the cell or you can click in the **FORMULA BAR** and modify the formula there. You can also enter and edit non formula data in the Formula bar.

B10 =B6+B7+B8

	A	B	C	D	E
1					
2					
3					
4					
5	Current Assets				
6	Cash	17580	12100	74770	44425
7	Inventory	31783	45700	21006	12230
8	Receivables	59560	27500	54321	34567
9					
10	Total Assets	108923			
11					
12					
13	Avg Cash				YTD Cash
14	Avg Inventory				YTD Inventory
15	Avg Mthly Receivables				YTD Receivables

Figure 10-1 Formula entered in cell B10

3. Click in cell F13 and type `= B6 + C6 + D6 + E6 + F6` and press Enter.

This formula will calculate the amount of year to date cash that the company has. Data will be added to column F later in this lesson. In the next lesson you will add the columns for the other months.

How To Copy Formulas Using The Fill Right Command

The formula that you created in cell B10 is the same formula that is needed for columns C and D. The only difference is that the column letter is different. You could type the same formula in cell C10 and D10 or you could use the Fill Right command which will copy the formula to cells C10 and D10.

1. Highlight the range B10 to D10. Your spreadsheet should look like the one shown in Figure 10-2. Edit ⇒ Fill Right. This command will copy the formula in cell B10 and place a copy of it in cells C10 and D10.

You may be thinking that the formula in cells C10 and D10 will be the same as the formula in cell B10. The **FILL RIGHT** command copies the formula and automatically modifies it for the other columns that are highlighted. Works is designed to think that you want the same formula that you used with the fill command, but that you want it to add the data in cells in the column that is being filled. Therefore, it automatically changes the column letter in the formula.

B10:D10 =B6+B7+B8

	A	B	C	D	E
1					
2					
3					
4					
5	Current Assets				
6	Cash	17580	12100	74770	44425
7	Inventory	31783	45700	21006	12230
8	Receivables	59560	27500	54321	34567
9					
10	Total Assets	108923			
11					

Figure 10-2 Range of cells to be filled illustrated

2. Click in cell D10. Look at the formula in the Formula bar. You should see **=D6 + D7 + D8**. Your spreadsheet should look like the one shown in Figure 10-3. Save the changes and leave the spreadsheet open.

	A	B	C	D	E
1					
2					
3					
4					
5	Current Assets				
6	Cash	17580	12100	74770	44425
7	Inventory	31783	45700	21006	12230
8	Receivables	59560	27500	54321	34567
9					
10	Total Assets	108923	85300	150097	

Figure 10-3 Formula copied to other cells

Easy Calc Wizard

The Easy Calc Wizard allows you to create basic and complex formulas without typing in the formula. I'm sure that this will make you very happy. Easy Calc helps eliminate any typographical errors on your part. You can however, type in the formulas while using the Easy Calc wizard. In this exercise you will create a formula to calculate the inventory total for the year.

1. Click the **EASY CALC** button on the toolbar or Tools ⇒ Easy Calc. You will see the dialog box shown in Figure 10-4. Select the **ADD** Common function, if it is not already selected and click Next. You will see the dialog box shown in Figure 10-5.

Figure 10-4 displays the types of formulas and functions that you can create using Easy Calc. The **OTHER** button will let you create formulas using the more advanced functions like **NOW** that was discussed earlier in this lesson.

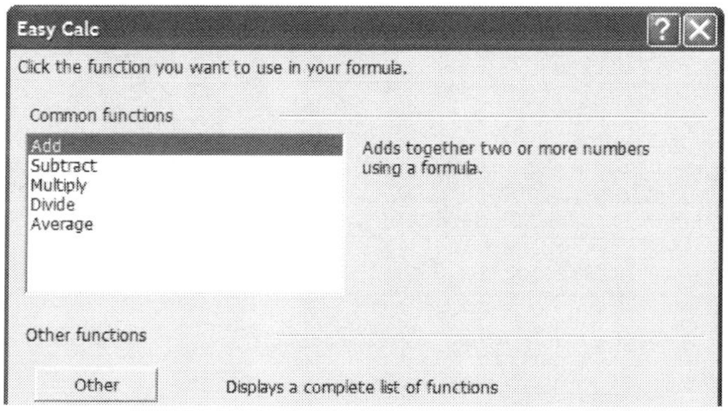

Figure 10-4 Easy Calc dialog box

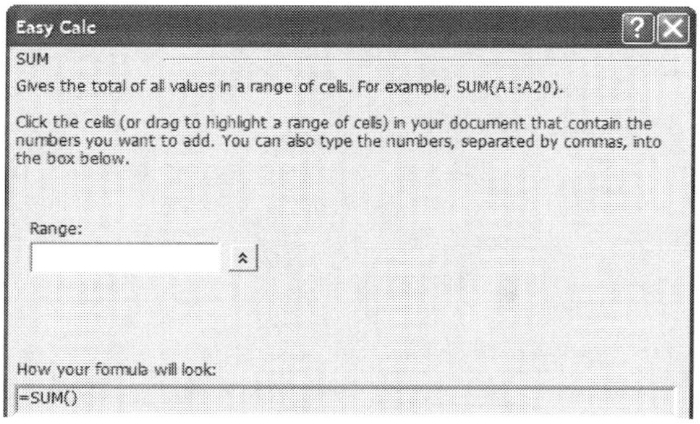

Figure 10-5 Easy Calc Sum dialog box

2. Move the Easy Calc dialog box down so that you can see rows 1 to 7 on the spreadsheet, then highlight the range B7 to M7.

The dialog box will temporarily disappear while you are highlighting cells on the spreadsheet.

The reason that you selected this range is to account for all 12 months. The **RANGE** on the dialog box should read B7:M7, as shown in Figure 10-6. If you wanted, you could have typed in the range instead of highlighting the range on the spreadsheet.

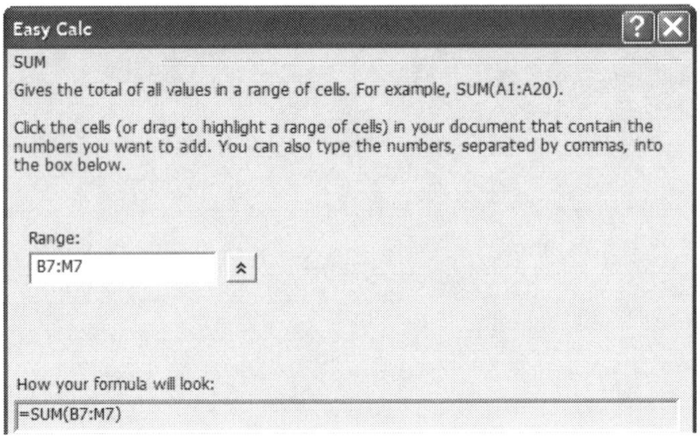

Figure 10-6 Range selected

3. Click Next. You are prompted to select the cell that you want to store the result of the formula in. Click in cell F14 in the spreadsheet, or type `F14` in the **RESULT AT** field on the dialog box shown in Figure 10-7.

   If you discover that the formula that you created is not what you want, click the Back button to make the necessary changes to the formula.

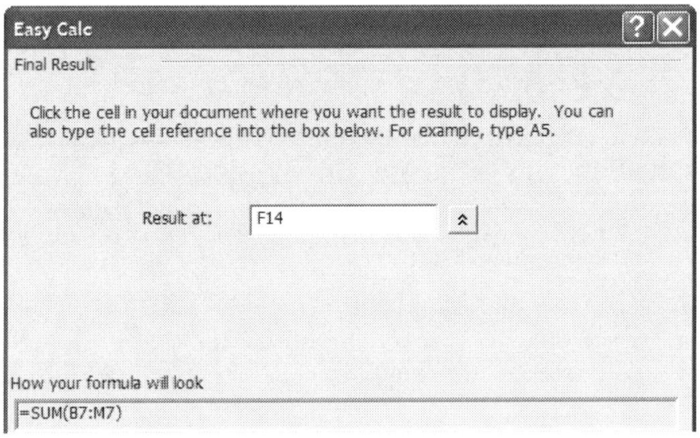

Figure 10-7 Result cell for calculation selected

4. Click the Finish button on the Easy Calc dialog box. You should have the value **110719** in cell F14. Save the changes and leave the spreadsheet open.

The Auto Sum Option

The Auto Sum option is used to add the values in two or more adjacent cells. Auto Sum is most often used to add columns of data like cells B6 to B8 and place the result in B10. You can also use Auto Sum to add rows of data. In this exercise you will use the Auto Sum option to calculate the YTD Receivables. (YTD stands for Year To Date).

1. Click in cell F15, then click the Auto Sum button on the toolbar. This is where you want the result placed. I find it easier to click in the cell where I want the formula placed before creating the formula.

The range F13 to F14 is automatically highlighted because Works thinks that this is the range that you want to sum. The range that you really want to sum is B8 to M8. You can type the range that you want in the highlighted section of the formula, or you can highlight the cells in the spreadsheet.

> Notice as you highlight the cells, that the cell range in the formula in cell F15 changes as you select more cells.

2. Highlight the cell range B8 to M8 as shown in Figure 10-8, then press Enter or click the Auto Sum button. The number **175948** should be in cell F15.

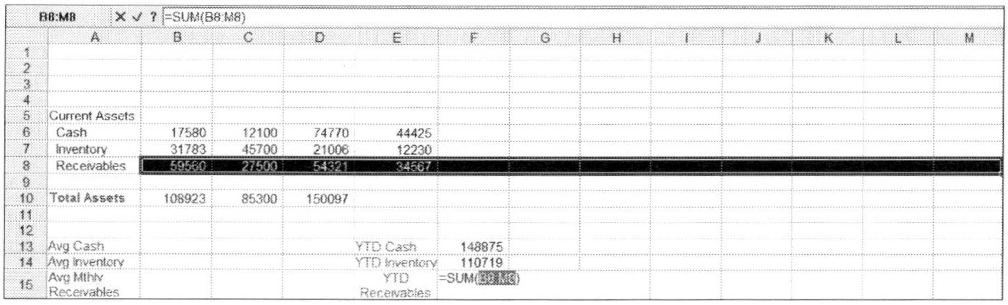

Figure 10-8 Range selected for the Auto Sum formula

3. Save the changes and leave the spreadsheet open.

Calculating Averages

In this exercise you will create two "Average" formulas. Average formulas add all of the values in a range of cells and divide the sum by the number of values (cells) used in the formula. The first formula that you will create is the Average Cash Amount. You will create this formula manually. The second formula that you will create is the Average Inventory Amount. You will create this formula using Easy Calc.

Create An Average Formula Manually

1. In cell B13 type `=Sum(B6:F6)/5`. Don't press Enter. Your formula should look like the one shown in Figure 10-9.

The formula shown in Figure 10-9 will sum (add) the values in cells B6, C6, D6, E6 and F6 and divide that value by five, which is the total number of cells that you are calculating the average for.

`=SUM(B6:F6)/5`

Figure 10-9 Formula bar for cell B13

If this spreadsheet was set up to calculate the average for 12 months, the formula would be **=SUM(B6:M6)/12**.

2. Press Enter. The number **29775** should be in cell B13.

Create An Average Formula Using Easy Calc

1. Click the Easy Calc button on the toolbar, then select the **AVERAGE** function and click Next.

2. Highlight the range B7 to F7 on the spreadsheet or type `B7:F7` in the **RANGE** field, then click Next.

3. Click in cell B14 or type `B14` in the Result at field, then click Finish. The number **27679.75** should be in cell B14.

4. Copy the formula in cell B14 to cell B15 by highlighting cells B14 and B15. Edit ⇒ Fill Down. Your spreadsheet should look like the one shown in Figure 10-10. Save the changes and leave the spreadsheet open.

	A	B	C	D	E	F
1						
2						
3						
4						
5	Current Assets					
6	Cash	17580	12100	74770	44425	
7	Inventory	31783	45700	21006	12230	
8	Receivables	59560	27500	54321	34567	
9						
10	Total Assets	108923	85300	150097		
11						
12						
13	Avg Cash	29775			YTD Cash	148875
14	Avg Inventory	27679.75			YTD Inventory	110719
15	Avg Mthly Receivables	43987			YTD Receivables	175948

Figure 10-10 Average formulas added to the spreadsheet

How To Create A Formula Using A Range Name

In the previous lesson you created range names in a spreadsheet. Range names allow you to reference cells with a meaningful name, instead of by cell names.

1. Click in cell E10 and type `=Sum(April_Assets)`, then press Enter. The Range name April_Assets references cells E6 to E8.

This is not a range that you created in the previous lesson. I created the range April_Assets among others and saved them in the spreadsheet, while writing the book. I'm telling you this because I don't want you to think that you missed an exercise, or worse, that I left something out of the book.

Viewing Range Names On The Spreadsheet

If you create several range names in a spreadsheet you may want to see a list of them while you are working, without having to open the Range Name dialog box. To display range names on the spreadsheet, follow the steps below.

1. Click in cell A18. Insert ⇒ Range Name, then click the **LIST** button.

2. Make column A wider if necessary. Your spreadsheet should look like the one shown in Figure 10-11.

If you had selected a portion of the spreadsheet that already had data in it, you would overwrite the data when the range name list was added to the spreadsheet. If this happens, click No and select a portion of the spreadsheet where there is no data.

When you are finished creating or editing a spreadsheet, you can delete the range name list from the spreadsheet unless you need it to stay on the spreadsheet.

	A	B	C
1			
2			
3			
4			
5	Current Assets		
6	Cash	17580	12100
7	Inventory	31783	45700
8	Receivables	59560	27500
9			
10	Total Assets	108923	85300
11			
12			
13	Avg Cash	29775	
14	Avg Inventory	27679.75	
15	Avg Mthly Receivables	43987	
16			
17			
18	Cash	B6:F6	
19	April_Assets	E6:E8	
20	Inventory	B7:F7	

Figure 10-11 Range name list added to the spreadsheet in rows 18 to 20

> If you create new range names after displaying the list on the spreadsheet, the new range names will not automatically be displayed in the spreadsheet. You will have to follow the steps above to re-display the Range name list.

Add More Data To The Spreadsheet

1. Add the data in Table 10-1 to the spreadsheet. As you enter these values, watch how the values in fields that have formulas change. For example, the values in cells F13 and B14 will change.

Cell	Value
F6	68222
F7	18450
F8	57833

Table 10-1 New data for the spreadsheet

2. Copy the formula in cell D10 to cells E10 and F10. Your spreadsheet should look like the one shown in Figure 10-12.

	A	B	C	D	E	F
5	Current Assets					
6	Cash	17580	12100	74770	44425	68222
7	Inventory	31783	45700	21006	12230	18450
8	Receivables	59560	27500	54321	34567	57833
9						
10	Total Assets	108923	85300	150097	91222	144505
11						
12						
13	Avg Cash	43419.4			YTD Cash	217097
14	Avg Inventory	25833.8			YTD Inventory	129169
15	Avg Mthly Receivables	46756.2			YTD Receivables	233781
16						
17						
18	Cash	B6:F6				
19	April_Assets	E6:E8				
20	Inventory	B7:F7				

Figure 10-12 More data and formulas added to the spreadsheet

3. Delete the Range name list in cells A18 to B20, then save the changes.

How To View All Formulas On A Spreadsheet

To verify that the formulas are correct, it would be helpful to see all of the formulas on the spreadsheet at the same time. The cells that have formulas will show the formulas and not the values.

1. View ⇒ Formulas. Your spreadsheet should look like the one shown in Figure 10-13.

	A	B	C	D	E	F
5	Current Assets					
6	Cash	17580	12100	74770	44425	68222
7	Inventory	31783	45700	21006	12230	18450
8	Receivables	59560	27500	54321	34567	57833
9						
10	Total Assets	=B6+B7+B8	=C6+C7+C8	=D6+D7+D8	=SUM(April_Assets)	=SUM(F6:F8)
11						
12						
13	Avg Cash	=SUM(Cash)/5			YTD Cash	=B6+C6+D6+E6+F6
14	Avg Inventory	=AVG(Inventory)			YTD Inventory	=SUM(B7:M7)
15	Avg Mthly Receivables	=AVG(B8:F8)			YTD Receivables	=SUM(B8:M8)

Figure 10-13 Formulas displayed on the spreadsheet

2. View ⇒ Formulas, to hide the formulas. Save the changes and close the spreadsheet.

Functions

As stated earlier in this lesson, functions are built-in formulas that you can use to save time.
The statistical functions covered in the rest of this lesson are among the more popular functions that are used.

The Inventory spreadsheet that you will use keeps track of the quantity, cost, markup, sales price and profit per book, as well as, averages and the number of book titles that are on hand.

Count Function

This function will count the number of cells in the range. It does not count the contents of the cells.
If you need to know how many book titles are listed on a spreadsheet, you would use the Count function.

1. Save the Inventory spreadsheet as `L10 Inventory (with functions).`
2. Click in cell B13, then click the Easy Calc button. Click the **OTHER** button on the Easy Calc dialog box. You will see the dialog box shown in Figure 10-14.

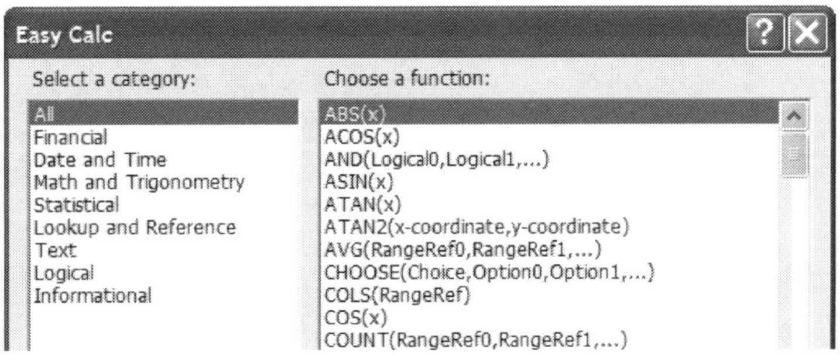

Figure 10-14 Easy Calc function dialog box

3. Select the **STATISTICAL** category, then select the **COUNT** function on the right. This function will count the number of cells in the range that you select.
4. Click the Insert button, then highlight the range B7 to B12 on the spreadsheet and click Next.

This range is ok, even though cell B12 is blank. The Count function only counts cells that have a formula, text, number, the value N/A or ERR in it.

If you do not want the result to be placed in the cell specified in the Result at field shown in Figure 10-15, in this case cell B13, you can change it on the **FINAL RESULT** window of the Easy Calc dialog box. Because you selected cell B13 before you started to add the function to the spreadsheet, the wizard remembered it.

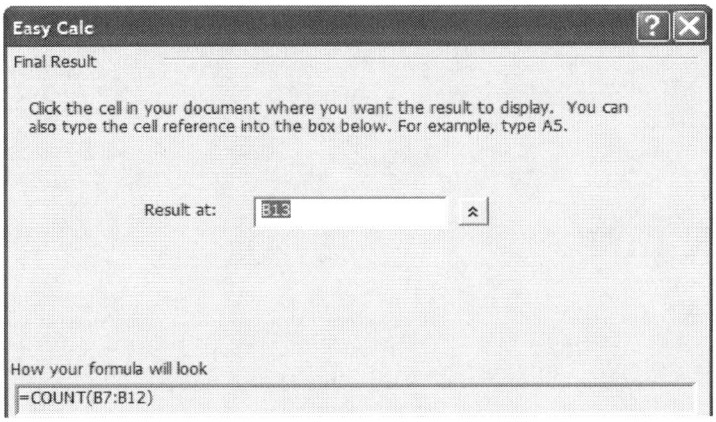

Figure 10-15 Final Result window of the Easy Calc wizard

5. Click Finish. Your spreadsheet should look like the one shown in Figure 10-16. There are five book titles listed in the spreadsheet. Save the changes and leave the spreadsheet open.

	A	B	C	D	E	F
5	Name Of Book	Quantity	Cost	Markup %	Sale Price	Book Profit
6						
7	Learning Multimedia	8	$12.00	0.05		
8	The New Way To Surf	7	$6.98	0.04		
9	Works Made Easy	9	$9.95	0.09		
10	Leearning Works	4	$7.98	0.075		
11	Surfing The Net	12	$5.95	0.03		
12						
13	# Of Titles On Hand	5				

Figure 10-16 Count function illustrated

AVG Function

The AVG function calculates the average value of a range of numbers. In this exercise you will calculate the average percent that books are marked up.

1. Click in cell D15 and open the **EASY CALC** dialog box, then click the Other button.
2. Select the **STATISTICAL** category, then select the **AVG** function.
3. Click the Insert button. Change the range to `D7:D11`, then click Next.
4. Click Finish because you want the result placed in cell D15. The number **0.057** should be in cell D15.

MIN Function

The MIN function will evaluate all of the values in the range that you specify and find the lowest value in the range. In the Inventory spreadsheet this function would be useful if you wanted to know which book had the least number of copies on hand or which book cost the least. In this exercise you will use the MIN function to find the book that has the lowest markup percent.

1. Click in cell D16 and open the Easy Calc dialog box, then click the Other button.
2. Select the Statistical category, then select the **MIN** function.
3. Click the Insert button. Change the range to `D7:D11`, then click Next.
4. Click Finish. The number **0.03** should be in cell D16. If you look at the five values in the Markup % column you will see that 0.03 is the lowest value in the column.

Now that you have used a few of the functions in the Inventory spreadsheet you may be saying that you could do these calculations in your head. This is true for a spreadsheet that does not have a lot of data like the one that you are currently working on. What if the Inventory spreadsheet had 500 or more books in it? It may not be so easy to determine which title had the least number of copies on hand or which book cost the least. If you wanted to keep the stats on your favorite sports team or if you coach a sports team for children, being able to easily maintain their averages would save you a lot of time.

MAX Function

The MAX function will evaluate all of the values in the range that you specify and find the highest value in the range. In this exercise you will use the MAX function to find the book that has the largest markup percent.

1. Click in cell D17 and open the Easy Calc dialog box, then click the Other button.
2. Select the Statistical category, then select the **MAX** function.
3. Click the Insert button. Change the range to `D7:D11`, then click Next.

4. Click Finish. The number **0.09** should be in cell D17.

STD Function

The Standard Deviation function (STD) calculates the mean (average) value in the range of cells selected and then calculates how far from the mean each value in the range of cells that you have selected is. In this exercise you will calculate the standard deviation for the cost of the books.

1. Click in cell C19 and open the Easy Calc dialog box, then click the Other button.
2. Select the Statistical category, then select the **STD** function.
3. Click the Insert button. Change the range to `C7:C11`, then click Next.
4. Click Finish. The number **2.1637874** should be in cell C19. Your spreadsheet should look like the one shown in Figure 10-17. Save the changes.

	A	B	C	D	E	F
5	Name Of Book	Quantity	Cost	Markup %	Sale Price	Book Profiit
6						
7	Learning Multimedia	8	$12.00	0.05		
8	The New Way To Surf	7	$6.98	0.04		
9	Works Made Easy	9	$9.95	0.09		
10	Leearning Works	4	$7.98	0.075		
11	Surfing The Net	12	$5.95	0.03		
12						
13	# Of Titles On Hand	5				
14						
15	Average Markup			0.057		
16	Minimum Markup			0.03		
17	Maximum Markup			0.09		
18						
19	Cost Deviation		2.1637874			

Figure 10-17 Functions added to the spreadsheet

Calculate The Sales Price

In this exercise you will create a formula manually to calculate the sales price of each book. The sales price equals the cost times the markup percent plus the cost.

1. Create a formula in cell E7 that calculates the sales price. You can use any method that you want. The number **12.60** should be in cell E7.

The first task that you need to complete is to calculate 5% of the cost. Multiplying C7 times D7 will give you the markup amount in dollars. Next you have to add the markup amount to the cost of the book. Therefore, the formula is =(C7*D7)+C7.

2. Copy the formula to cells E8 to E11.

> Use the Fill Down command on the Edit menu to copy the formula to the cells listed in the step above.

Using parenthesis in a formula determines the order of how the formula is calculated. The portion of a formula inside the parenthesis is calculated together. In the sales price exercise that you just completed, the value in cell C7 is multiplied by the value in cell D7. The sum of that calculation is added to the value in cell C7. The result is placed in cell E7.

Calculate The Profit

The Book Profit column represents the profit for each book sold. The formula is Sales Price minus Cost.

1. Create a formula in cell F7 to calculate the book profit.

> The formula is in the Formula bar in Figure 10-18. You can use the Fill Down option on the Edit menu to copy the formula.

2. Copy this formula to cells F8 to F11. Your spreadsheet should look like the one shown in Figure 10-18.

F7 =E7-C7

	A	B	C	D	E	F
5	Name Of Book	Quantity	Cost	Markup %	Sale Price	Book Profit
6						
7	Learning Multimedia	8	$12.00	0.05	12.60	0.60
8	The New Way To Surf	7	$6.98	0.04	7.26	0.28
9	Works Made Easy	9	$9.95	0.09	10.85	0.90
10	Leearning Works	4	$7.98	0.075	8.58	0.60
11	Surfing The Net	12	$5.95	0.03	6.13	0.18
12						
13	# Of Titles On Hand	5				
14						
15	Average Markup			0.057		
16	Minimum Markup			0.03		
17	Maximum Markup			0.09		
18						
19	Cost Deviation		2.1637874			

Figure 10-18 Book profit formula added to the spreadsheet

3. Highlight the range A5 to F19 and apply the **FINANCIAL LEDGER** Auto Format, then clear the Row totals option shown in Figure 10-19.

If you leave the **ROW TOTALS** option checked, the numbers in the Book Profit column in the spreadsheet will be bold. The Auto Format is set up to bold the last column selected in the spreadsheet that the formatting will be applied to because the Auto Format thinks that the last column is a total. In the Preview section of Figure 10-19 there is no total column. Figure 10-20 shows a total column because the Row totals option is checked.

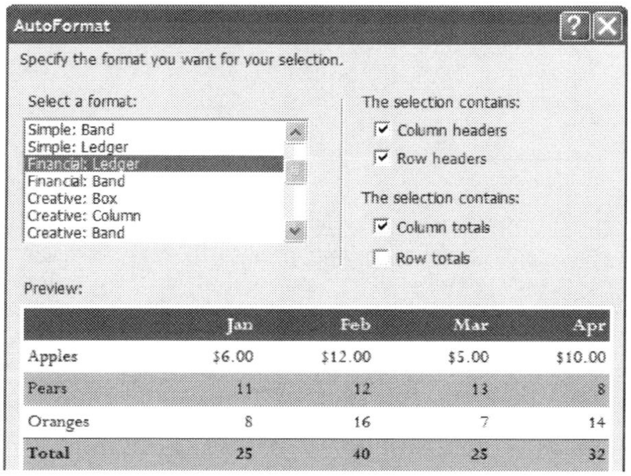

Figure 10-19 Modified Auto Format options

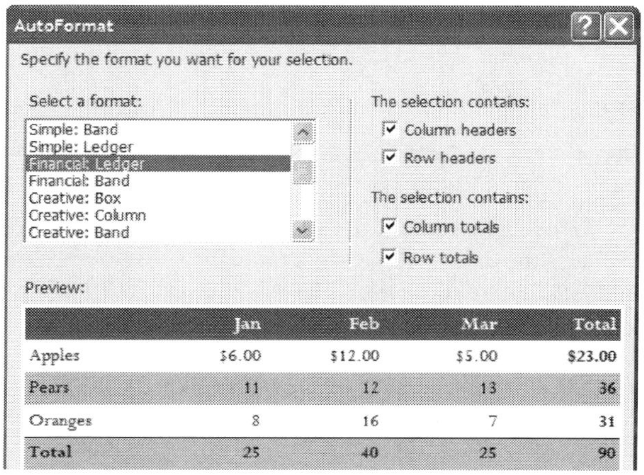

Figure 10-20 Default Auto Format options illustrated

4. Click OK. Your spreadsheet should look like the one shown in Figure 10-21. Save the changes and close the spreadsheet.

	A	B	C	D	E	F
4						
5	Name Of Book	Quantity	Cost	Markup %	Sale Price	Book Profiit
6						
7	Learning Multimedia	8	$12.00	0.05	12.60	0.60
8	The New Way To Surf	7	$6.98	0.04	7.26	0.28
9	Works Made Easy	9	$9.95	0.09	10.85	0.90
10	Leearning Works	4	$7.98	0.075	8.58	0.60
11	Surfing The Net	12	$5.95	0.03	6.13	0.18
12						
13	# Of Titles On Hand	5				
14						
15	Average Markup			0.057		
16	Minimum Markup			0.03		
17	Maximum Markup			0.09		
18						
19	Cost Deviation		2.16378742			

Figure 10-21 Inventory spreadsheet with an Auto Format applied

> If you wanted to change the green background of row five on the spreadsheet, you would select the range A5:F5, right-click and select Format. On the Shading tab change the background to the color that you wanted. You can do the same thing for the other rows in the spreadsheet.

Test Your Skills

1. Save the Bigger Balance Sheet as `L10(skills)`.

   - Add the data in Table 10-2 to the spreadsheet.

Cell	Data
A39	Avg Payroll
A40	Min Phone
A41	Max Toner

Table 10-2 Data to add to the spreadsheet

   - Create a formula to calculate the average payroll for all 12 months. Place the result in cell B39.
   - Create a formula to calculate the minimum phone costs for all 12 months. Place the result in cell B40.
   - Create a formula to calculate the maximum toner cost for all 12 months. Place the result in cell B41.

SPREADSHEET FORMATTING TECHNIQUES

In this lesson you will learn another way to automatically fill in rows and columns in a spreadsheet. Just when you thought that you had learned all of the formatting techniques for spreadsheets, you find out that there's more. You will learn how to do the following:

- ☑ Add headers and footers to a spreadsheet
- ☑ Hide columns
- ☑ Freeze cells
- ☑ Sort data
- ☑ Use the spell checker
- ☑ Add a page break to a spreadsheet
- ☑ Save a spreadsheet as a template

LESSON 11

Auto Fill

Auto Fill is another way to copy the value in a cell to other cells in the spreadsheet. If you are creating a personal income statement for the year you need to include your mortgage payment amount for each month. You could type the value in one cell and copy it 11 times to other cells or you could use Auto Fill. In the previous lesson you learned the basics of this command. In this lesson you will learn more about Auto Fill.

1. Open a new spreadsheet. In cell B3, type `2300` and press Enter.

2. Place the cursor on the lower right corner of cell B3. The cursor will change and you should see the word **FILL** as shown in Figure 11-1. Hold down the left mouse button and drag the mouse to cell F3. All of the cells should have 2300 in it.

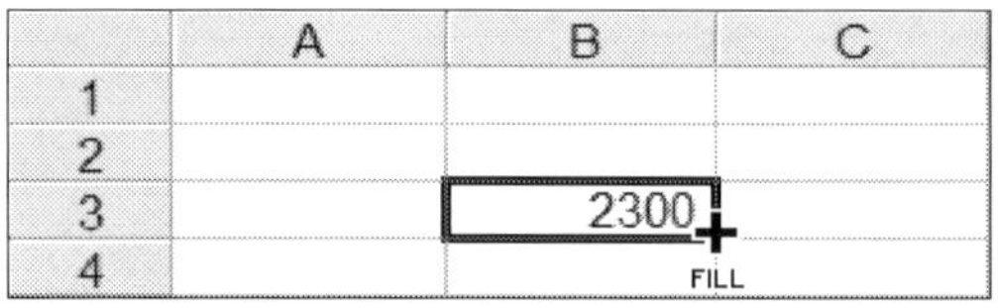

Figure 11-1 Cursor in the Auto Fill position

3. With the cells still selected, change the format of the cells to comma, with no decimal places. (**HINT:** Format ⇒ Number)

4. You can also fill down. Select cell E3. Move the mouse to the **FILL** position. Drag the mouse down to cell E5. Cells E4 and E5 should now be filled in with the same number as shown in Figure 11-2.

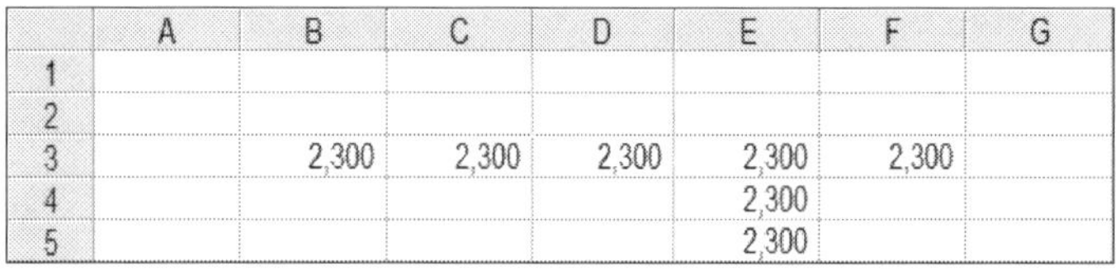

Figure 11-2 Cells filled in with the Auto Fill option

Using Auto Fill To Fill In More Than One Column Or Row

You can use Auto Fill to fill in several columns or rows at the same time. Pay attention to the case (upper and lower) in the first step below.

1. Type `TEST1` in cell A4. Type `TestA` in cell B4. Type `Test3` in cell C4.

2. Make cell A4 bold. Change the format color in cell B4 red. (**HINT:** Format ⇒ Font)

3. Add a **LINE TYPE** border to cell C4.

4. Highlight the range A4 to C4. Place the cursor in the lower right corner of cell C4. Press the left mouse button and drag the mouse down to row 7. Your spreadsheet should look like the one shown in Figure 11-3. Notice that each column retained its formatting. Also notice that the numbers incremented in columns A and C.

5. Change cell B6 to `Test4`, then highlight the range A6 to C6 and use the Auto Fill option to fill in cells D6 to G6. Notice that the numbers incremented, as shown in Figure 11-4.

6. Save the changes. Type `L11 Fun with Auto Fill` as the file name. Leave the spreadsheet open.

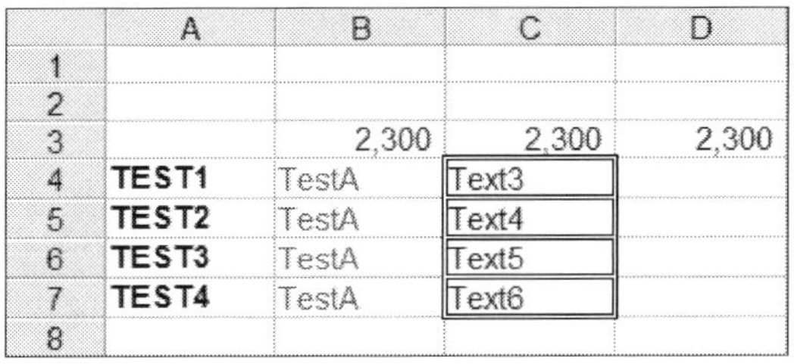

Figure 11-3 Auto Fill result for step 4

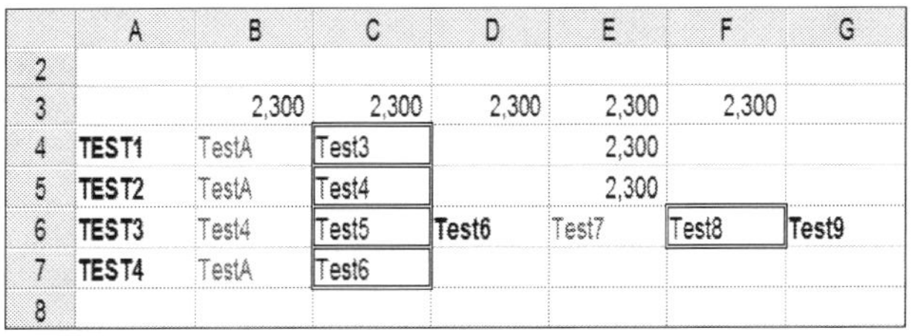

Figure 11-4 Auto Fill result for step 5

Fill Series

Fill Series is similar to Auto Fill because Fill Series fills in cells based on the criteria that you select. The difference is that Fill Series fills in cells with a pattern, similar to the pattern that was created with the Auto Fill example shown above in Figure 11-4.

Using Fill Series With Days Of The Week

1. Type `Monday` in cell A8 and press Enter.

2. Highlight the range A8 to A12. Edit ⇒ Fill Series. On the Fill Series dialog box, click OK. You should see Monday through Friday in cells A8 to A12.

Using Fill Series With Numeric Dates

1. Type `2/15/04` in cell B8 and press Enter.

2. Highlight the range B8 to B12. Edit ⇒ Fill Series. You will see the dialog box shown in Figure 11-5.

   The value that you enter in the **INCREASE BY** field will increment the value in cell B8. If you leave the value at one, you will get dates in sequential order.

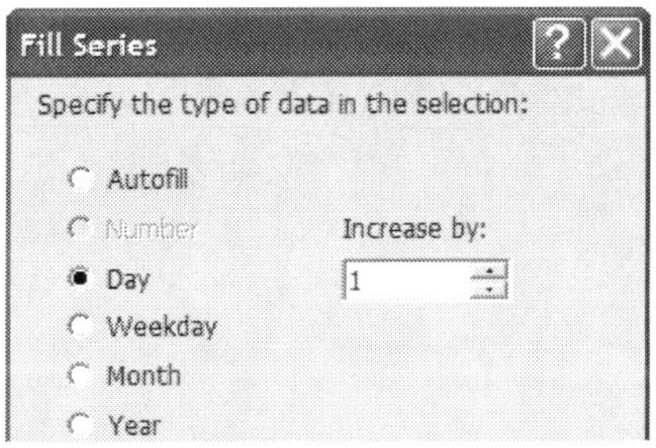

Figure 11-5 Fill Series dialog box

3. Change the Increase by value to 2 and click OK. The dates filled in should be every other date.

Using Fill Series With Months

1. Type `January` in cell C11 and press Enter.

2. Highlight the range C11 to F11. Edit ⇒ Fill Series and select Month.

3. Change the Increase by value to 3 and click OK. The months April, July and October should have filled in. Save the changes and close the spreadsheet.

Modify The Bigger Balance Spreadsheet

This exercise shows you how to use many of the features that you have learned about spreadsheets.

1. Save the Bigger Balance Sheet spreadsheet as `L11 Bigger Balance Sheet.`

2. Auto Fill cells B4 to M4 with the months of the year, starting with January.

3. Place a black border below the months, then center the months in the cells.

> To place the border below the cells, highlight the range. Format ⇒ Border. Select the Bottom border location option as illustrated in Figure 11-6.

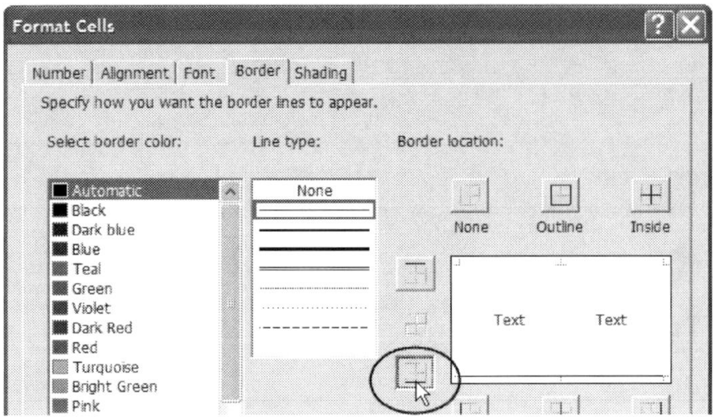

Figure 11-6 Border option illustrated

4. Type `Balance Sheet` in cell A1 and make the cell bold. Type `Current Assets, Income & Expenses` in cell A2, then make cell A2 Italic.

5. Center cells A1 and A2 across columns A to M. Use the **CENTER ACROSS SELECTION** option, then insert a row after row 2. The top portion of your spreadsheet should look like the one shown in Figure 11-7. Save the changes and leave the spreadsheet open.

> You can center both cells at the same time. If you need help, refer back to Lesson 9 "Center Text Across Cells".

	A	B	C	D	E	F	G	H	I
1						**Balance Sheet**			
2						*Current Assets, Income & Expenses*			
3									
4									
5		January	February	March	April	May	June	July	August
6									
7	Current Assets								
8	Cash	17580	12100	74770	44425	74770	17580	44425	12500
9	Inventory	31783	45700	21006	12230	21006	37874	12230	45700
10	Receivables	59560	27500	54321	34567	54321	59560	44567	27500
11									
12	Total Assets	108923	85300	150097	91222	150097	115014	101222	85700

Figure 11-7 Modified balance sheet

Freezing Columns And Rows

Freezing columns and rows is extremely useful when you are working with spreadsheets that are wider or longer than your computer screen. In Figure 11-7 above, you would have to scroll to the right to see the data for the months September to December. You would have to scroll down to see the Expense data portion of the spreadsheet.

Often, when you do a lot of scrolling you may forget the column or row title names. Works allows you to freeze columns and rows so that when you scroll, the column and row headings are always visible on the screen. If you freeze the row titles in column A, they will always be visible on your screen no matter how far to the right you scroll.

How To Freeze Rows

The most logical row to freeze in the spreadsheet shown above in Figure 11-7 is row 6. That way, when you scroll down the page you will always be able to see the months. To freeze rows, place the cursor in the cell under the last row that you want to freeze. To freeze rows 1 to 6, you would place the cursor in cell A7.

1. Save the L11 Bigger Balance Sheet spreadsheet as `L11 Balance Sheet(frozen rows).`

2. Click in cell A7. Format ⇒ Freeze Titles. Scroll down the spreadsheet until you see row 36, the Total Expenses row. You can still see rows 1 to 6, even though you are at the end of the spreadsheet.

Notice that there is a line at the bottom of row 6, as shown in Figure 11-8. This lets you know that the rows above it are frozen.

	A	B	C	D	E	F	G	H	I
1						Balance Sheet			
2						Current Assets, Income & Expenses			
3									
4									
5		January	February	March	April	May	June	July	August
6									
7	Current Assets								
8	Cash	17580	12100	74770	44425	74770	17580	44425	12500
9	Inventory	31783	45700	21006	12230	21006	37874	12230	45700
10	Receivables	59560	27500	54321	34567	54321	59560	44567	27500
11									
12	Total Assets	108923	85300	150097	91222	150097	115014	101222	85700

Line indicating that rows are frozen

Figure 11-8 Frozen rows illustrated

3. Save the changes and close the spreadsheet.

How To Freeze Columns

You can freeze columns so that when you have to scroll to the right, you can still see the headings that are in the first few columns of the spreadsheet. To freeze columns, click in row 1, in the column after the last column that you want to freeze. If you need to always see columns A and B on the spreadsheet, you would click in cell C1.

1. Save the L11 Bigger Balance Sheet spreadsheet as `L11 Balance Sheet(frozen column).`

2. Click in cell B1. Format ⇒ Freeze Titles. Your spreadsheet should look like the one shown in Figure 11-9. The frozen column line is after column A. Scroll to the right until you see the data for November and December. Notice that column A is still visible.

	A	B	C	D	E	F	G	H	I
1						Balance Sheet			
2						Current Assets, Income & Expenses			
3									
4									
5		January	February	March	April	May	June	July	August
6									
7	Current Assets								
8	Cash	17580	12100	74770	44425	74770	17580	44425	12500
9	Inventory	31783	45700	21006	12230	21006	37874	12230	45700
10	Receivables	59560	27500	54321	34567	54321	59560	44567	27500
11									
12	Total Assets	108923	85300	150097	91222	150097	115014	101222	85700

Figure 11-9 Frozen column illustrated

3. Save the changes and close the spreadsheet.

Freezing Rows And Columns In The Same Spreadsheet

You can freeze rows and columns in the same spreadsheet. This is probably the most used freeze option. To freeze rows and columns, click under the last row that you want to freeze and to the right of the last column that you want to freeze. If you want to freeze column A and rows 1 to 6, you would click in cell B7.

1. Save the L11 Bigger Balance Sheet spreadsheet as
   `L11 Balance Sheet(frozen rows & columns).`

2. Click in cell B7. Format ⇒ Freeze Titles. Your spreadsheet should look like the one shown in Figure 11-10. The frozen column line is after column A. The frozen row line is below row 6. Scroll to the right until you see the data for November and December. Notice that column A is still visible. Scroll down the spreadsheet until you see row 36. You can still see column A and rows 1 to 6, even though you are at the end of the spreadsheet.

	A	B	C	D	E	F	G	H	I
1						Balance Sheet			
2						Current Assets, Income & Expenses			
3									
4									
5		January	February	March	April	May	June	July	August
6									
7	Current Assets								
8	Cash	17580	12100	74770	44425	74770	17580	44425	12500
9	Inventory	31783	45700	21006	12230	21006	37874	12230	45700
10	Receivables	59560	27500	54321	34567	54321	59560	44567	27500
11									
12	Total Assets	108923	85300	150097	91222	150097	115014	101222	85700

Figure 11-10 Frozen rows and columns

An easy way to remember what cell to click in when freezing rows and columns in the same spreadsheet is to visualize where the frozen lines should be. If you wanted to always see columns A, B and C and rows 1 to 12, click in cell D13. Click in the row below the row that you want to freeze. In this example row 13. Because you want to see columns A, B and C, click in column D.

3. Save the changes and close the spreadsheet.

How To Remove Frozen Rows Or Columns

For most actions you can use the Undo option on the Edit menu. The Undo option is not available for the Freeze Titles option.

To remove the frozen rows or columns, Format ⇒ Freeze Titles. This will undo the Freeze Titles option and remove the check mark that is illustrated in Figure 11-11.

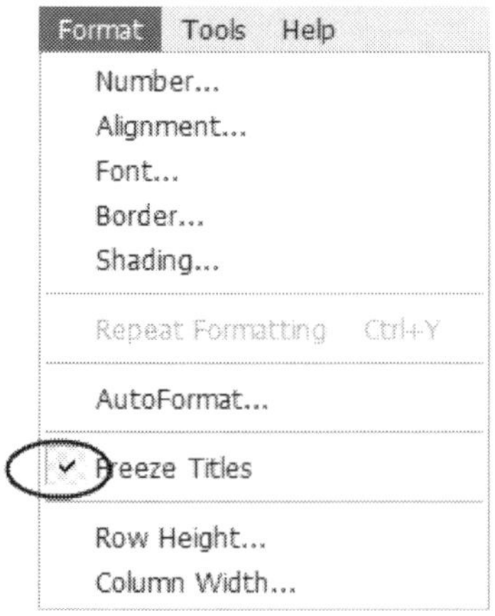

Figure 11-11 Freeze Titles option illustrated

Hiding Rows And Columns

Hiding rows and columns is another way to work with large spreadsheets. You can hide rows and columns that you do not need to see or do not want to print. Often, rows or columns that have confidential information like social security numbers are hidden when printed. To hide a row, set the **ROW HEIGHT** property to zero. To hide a column, set the **COLUMN WIDTH** property to zero.

How To Hide A Row

1. Save the L10 Inventory (with functions) spreadsheet as `L11 Hidden rows & columns.`

2. Highlight rows 15 to 17. Format ⇒ Row Height, then change the option **SET ROW HEIGHT (IN POINTS) TO** 0 (zero). Your dialog box should look like the one shown in Figure 11-12.

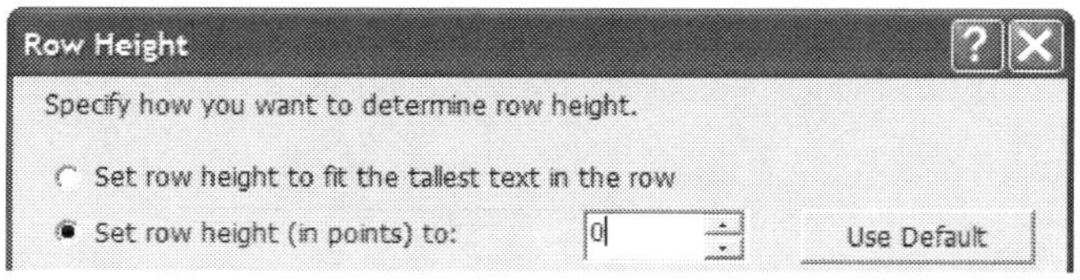

Figure 11-12 Row Height dialog box

> If you change your mind after hiding rows and want to display them again with their default value of 12, you can click the **USE DEFAULT** button shown above in Figure 11-12.

3. Click OK. Your spreadsheet should look like the one shown in Figure 11-13. The thick line that you see between rows 14 and 18, lets you know that rows are hidden. This line does not print.

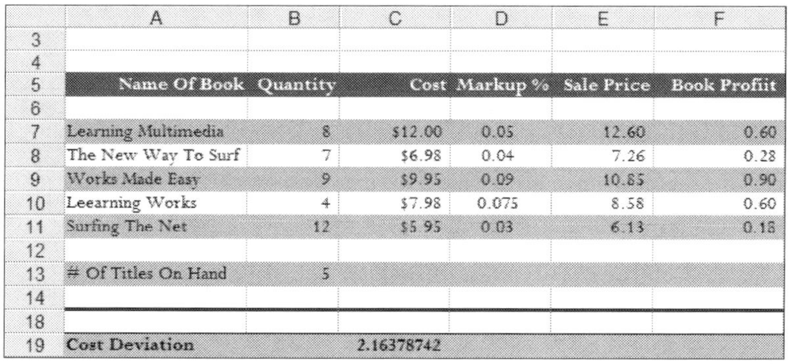

	A	B	C	D	E	F
3						
4						
5	Name Of Book	Quantity	Cost	Markup %	Sale Price	Book Profit
6						
7	Learning Multimedia	8	$12.00	0.05	12.60	0.60
8	The New Way To Surf	7	$6.98	0.04	7.26	0.28
9	Works Made Easy	9	$9.95	0.09	10.85	0.90
10	Leearning Works	4	$7.98	0.075	8.58	0.60
11	Surfing The Net	12	$5.95	0.03	6.13	0.18
12						
13	# Of Titles On Hand	5				
14						
18						
19	Cost Deviation		2.16378742			

Figure 11-13 Hidden rows illustrated

How To Hide A Column

Hiding a column works the same way that hiding rows works.

1. Highlight column D. Format ⇒ Column Width, then change the option **SET COLUMN WIDTH (IN CHARACTERS) TO** 0 (zero) and click OK. Your spreadsheet should look like the one shown in Figure 11-14. Column D is now hidden.

> If you change your mind after hiding columns and want to display them again with their default value of 10, you can click the **USE DEFAULT** button on the Column Width dialog box.

	A	B	C	E	F
3					
4					
5	Name Of Book	Quantity	Cost	Sale Price	Book Profiit
6					
7	Learning Multimedia	8	$12.00	12.60	0.60
8	The New Way To Surf	7	$6.98	7.26	0.28
9	Works Made Easy	9	$9.95	10.85	0.90
10	Leearning Works	4	$7.98	8.58	0.60
11	Surfing The Net	12	$5.95	6.13	0.18
12					
13	# Of Titles On Hand	5			
14					
18					
19	Cost Deviation		2.16378742		

Figure 11-14 Hidden column illustrated

2. Save the changes.

How To Restore Hidden Columns

To restore a hidden column, follow the steps below.

1. Highlight the column to the left and to the right of the column (or columns) that you want to restore. In this exercise, highlight columns C and E.

2. Format ⇒ Column Width. Click the **USE DEFAULT** button if you want to restore the column width to its original size. If you want to restore the column to a different size, type the size that you want in the Set column width (in characters) to field.

3. Click OK or press Enter. Column D should now be restored.

How To Restore Hidden Rows

Restoring rows is very similar to restoring columns. Follow the steps below to restore the rows that you hid earlier in this lesson.

1. Highlight rows 14 and 18.

2. Format ⇒ Row Height, then type `12` in the Set row height (in points) to field. Click OK. Rows 15, 16 and 17 should have been restored.

3. Close the spreadsheet but do not save the changes. You want this spreadsheet to still have the hidden rows and columns, in case you want to refer back to it later.

Sorting Data In A Spreadsheet

Sorting allows you to arrange the data in a more meaningful way. If you are entering names and addresses in a spreadsheet of people that want to sign up for various classes, more than likely you will enter the names in the order that people sign up for a class and not in the order by the class they are signing up for. If you sort the spreadsheet by the class each person signed up for the names will be grouped by class. You can sort on any column on the spreadsheet.

Sorting The Entire Spreadsheet

1. Save the Customers spreadsheet as `L11 Customers(sorted)`.

You must select the entire spreadsheet or the portion of the spreadsheet that you want to sort.

2. Highlight the range A1 to I20. Your spreadsheet should look like the one shown in Figure 11-15. Tools ⇒ Sort. You will see the dialog box shown in Figure 11-16. Table 11-1 explains the sort options.

Figure 11-15 Range selected to be sorted

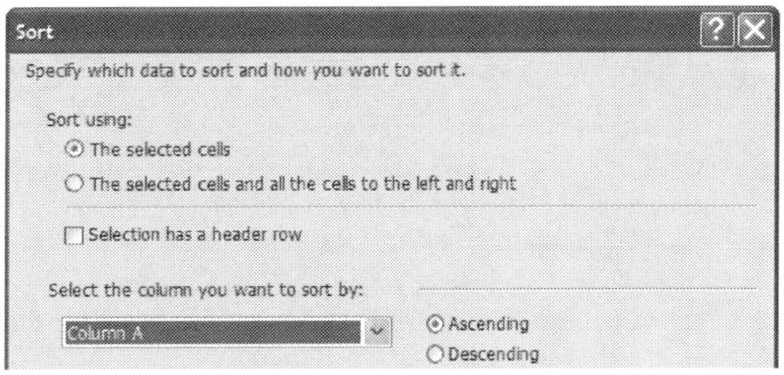

Figure 11-16 Sort dialog box

> Clicking on the empty square above row 1 will select the entire spreadsheet, which is quicker then highlighting the spreadsheet.

Sort Option	**What The Option Does**
Sort Using	Lets you select which cells will be sorted.
Selection has a header row	Select this option if the first row of the spreadsheet has column names as shown earlier in Figure 11-15. Selecting this option will not sort the first row, which is what you want most of the time. If the first row does not have column names or is not selected, do not select this option. If you did not select this option for the spreadsheet shown earlier in Figure 11-15, the first row would be sorted like all of the other rows that are highlighted. For example, if you were sorting the spreadsheet shown earlier in Figure 11-15 by Column B, the Last name column, row 1 would be sorted alphabetically like the other rows. With the header row option selected, the contents of row 1 will stay at the top of the spreadsheet, which is usually what you want.
Sort By options (3)	These drop-down fields will let you select the column or columns that you want to sort on. You can sort on a maximum of three columns.
Ascending/ Descending	These options determine the order of the sort. If you want to sort a column in low to high order (A to Z or 1 to 10), select **ASCENDING**. If you want to sort a column in high to low order (Z to A or 10 to 1), select **DESCENDING**.

Table 11-1 Sort options explained

> If you select the Header row option, you will see the column heading names (the contents in row 1) in the Sort by drop-down lists instead of Column A, Column B etc, as shown above in Figure 11-16. It will probably be easier to select the columns that you want to sort on by using this option.

3. Select the first **SORT USING** option shown above in Figure 11-16, then check the option **SELECTION HAS A HEADER ROW**.

4. Open the first **SORT BY** drop-down list and select Last Name. This will sort the spreadsheet by the Last Name field. Figure 11-17 shows the options that you should have selected.

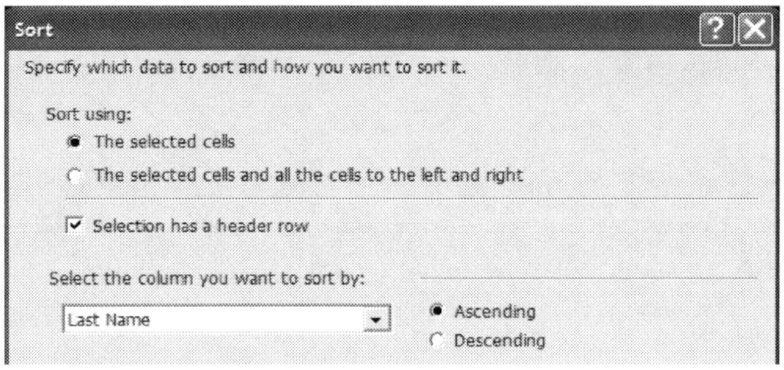

Figure 11-17 Sort options

5. Click the **SORT** button. Your spreadsheet should look like the one shown in Figure 11-18. Figure 11-19 shows what the spreadsheet would look like if the Selection has a header row option was not selected. The column names are not in row 1, they are in row 10.

	A	B	C	D	E	F	G	H	I
1	First Name	Last Name	Phone	Company	Address	City	State	Zip Code	Category
2	Fred	Amos	(215)327-7079		19 Rodney	Westwood	CT	06403	Biography
3	Brian	Bark	(610)554-3002		300 Winston Pl	Norwood	NY	10023	Computer
4	Glen	Carter	(407)471-0159		1 Edward Dr	Las Vegas	NV	60022	Sports
5	Carrie	Downing	(407)987-4563	Financial Services	63 Maple Ave	Glen Rock	NV	32888	Computer
6	Robert	Emerson	(908)587-6422	New Real Estate	200 Mountain Ave	Ft. Laud	FL	32847	Mystery
7	Kelly	Fontaine	(702)825-9787	Jersey Bank	272 Rt 64	Cherry Hill	NJ	07458	Computer
8	Amy	Gardner	(610)664-4646		132 W Park Ave	Wilson	NJ	07403	Mystery
9	Todd	Green	(203)452-1300		41 Jefferson Rd	Tampa	FL	32672	Biography
10	Tina	Jones	(609)364-2500		30 Long St	Ft Laud	FL	32991	Computer
11	Louis	Riker	(702)667-3053		23 Essex Pl	Tappan	CT	06402	Biography
12	Randi	Sherwood	(718)505-3388	Hi-Tech Inc	777 Broad Ave	Ramsey	PA	19001	Computer
13	Steve	Smith	(702)947-8701	Big Design	2200 Research Way	Bronx	NY	11201	Computer
14	Tom	Smith	(215)909-1885		45 Jericho Ave	Wilton	CT	06405	Sports
15	Brenda	Taylor	(610)967-7308	Symphony C&L	500 Point Rd	Ft Lee	NJ	08663	Sports
16	Stuart	Thomas	(718)503-0331		90A Jersey Ave	Orlando	FL	32761	Sports
17	Jamie	Walker	(908)652-9609		997 Lenox Dr	Reno	NV	32883	Mystery
18	Clair	Walker	(215)909-8882	Two of A kind	892 Main St	Menden	CT	06403	Mystery
19	Tina	Walker	(702)703-0101		123 Main St	Stamford	CT	06402	Computer
20	Peter	Young	(718)505-4259	Elmwood Sales	188 William St	Bogota	NV	32881	Sports

Figure 11-18 Spreadsheet sorted in Last Name order

	A	B	C	D	E	F	G	H	I
1	Fred	Amos	(215)327-7079		19 Rodney	Westwood	CT	06403	Biography
2	Brian	Bark	(610)554-3002		300 Winston Pl	Norwood	NY	10023	Computer
3	Glen	Carter	(407)471-0159		1 Edward Dr	Las Vegas	NV	60022	Sports
4	Carrie	Downing	(407)987-4563	Financial Services	63 Maple Ave	Glen Rock	NV	32888	Computer
5	Robert	Emerson	(908)587-6422	New Real Estate	200 Mountain Ave	Ft. Laud	FL	32847	Mystery
6	Kelly	Fontaine	(702)825-9787	Jersey Bank	272 Rt 64	Cherry Hill	NJ	07458	Computer
7	Amy	Gardner	(610)664-4646		132 W Park Ave	Wilson	NJ	07403	Mystery
8	Todd	Green	(203)452-1300		41 Jefferson Rd	Tampa	FL	32672	Biography
9	Tina	Jones	(609)364-2500		30 Long St	Ft Laud	FL	32991	Computer
10	First Name	Last Name	Phone	Company	Address	City	State	Zip Code	Category
11	Louis	Riker	(702)667-3053		23 Essex Pl	Tappan	CT	06402	Biography
12	Randi	Sherwood	(718)505-3388	Hi-Tech Inc	777 Broad Ave	Ramsey	PA	19001	Computer
13	Steve	Smith	(702)947-8701	Big Design	2200 Research Way	Bronx	NY	11201	Computer
14	Tom	Smith	(215)909-1885		45 Jericho Ave	Wilton	CT	06405	Sports
15	Brenda	Taylor	(610)967-7308	Symphony C&L	500 Point Rd	Ft Lee	NJ	08663	Sports
16	Stuart	Thomas	(718)503-0331		90A Jersey Ave	Orlando	FL	32761	Sports
17	Jamie	Walker	(908)652-9609		997 Lenox Dr	Reno	NV	32883	Mystery
18	Clair	Walker	(215)909-8882	Two of A kind	892 Main St	Menden	CT	06403	Mystery
19	Tina	Walker	(702)703-0101		123 Main St	Stamford	CT	06402	Computer
20	Peter	Young	(718)505-4259	Elmwood Sales	188 William St	Bogota	NV	32881	Sports

Figure 11-19 Spreadsheet sorted without the Selection has a header row option selected

How To Sort On Two Columns

In this exercise you will sort on the Last Name and First Name fields.

1. Highlight the range A2 to I20, then Tools ⇒ Sort. In the first Sort by drop-down list, select Column B.

2. In the second Sort by drop-down list, select column A. Figure 11-20 shows the options that you should have selected. Because the first row is not highlighted in the spreadsheet, you do not have to select the header row option on the dialog box. Click the **SORT** button. Your spreadsheet should look like the one shown in Figure 11-21. Look at rows 17 to 19. The three people with the last name Walker are in alphabetical order by their last and first names.

Notice that the Sort by options are the column letters instead of the column names.

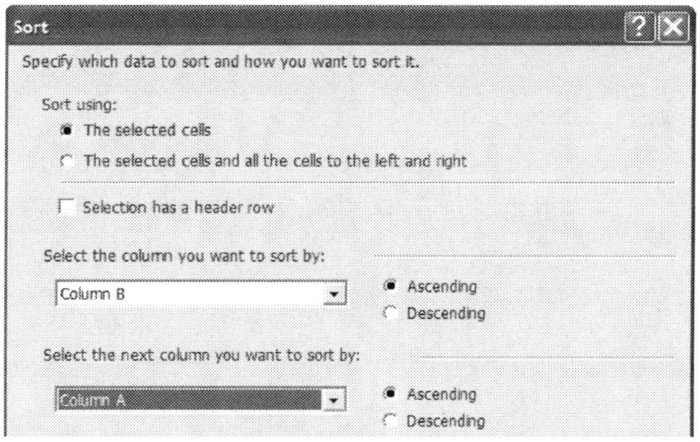

Figure 11-20 Two column sort options selected

	A	B	C	D	E	F	G	H	I
1	First Name	Last Name	Phone	Company	Address	City	State	Zip Code	Category
2	Fred	Amos	(215)327-7079		19 Rodney	Westwood	CT	06403	Biography
3	Brian	Bark	(610)554-3002		300 Winston Pl	Norwood	NY	10023	Computer
4	Glen	Carter	(407)471-0159		1 Edward Dr	Las Vegas	NV	60022	Sports
5	Carrie	Downing	(407)987-4563	Financial Services	63 Maple Ave	Glen Rock	NV	32888	Computer
6	Robert	Emerson	(908)587-6422	New Real Estate	200 Mountain Ave	Ft. Laud	FL	32847	Mystery
7	Kelly	Fontaine	(702)825-9787	Jersey Bank	272 Rt 64	Cherry Hill	NJ	07458	Computer
8	Amy	Gardner	(610)664-4646		132 W Park Ave	Wilson	NJ	07403	Mystery
9	Todd	Green	(203)452-1300		41 Jefferson Rd	Tampa	FL	32672	Biography
10	Tina	Jones	(609)364-2500		30 Long St	Ft Laud	FL	32991	Computer
11	Louis	Riker	(702)667-3053		23 Essex Pl	Tappan	CT	06402	Biography
12	Randi	Sherwood	(718)505-3388	Hi-Tech Inc	777 Broad Ave	Ramsey	PA	19001	Computer
13	Steve	Smith	(702)947-8701	Big Design	2200 Research Way	Bronx	NY	11201	Computer
14	Tom	Smith	(215)909-1885		45 Jericho Ave	Wilton	CT	06405	Sports
15	Brenda	Taylor	(610)967-7308	Symphony C&L	500 Point Rd	Ft Lee	NJ	08663	Sports
16	Stuart	Thomas	(718)503-0331		90A Jersey Ave	Orlando	FL	32761	Sports
17	Clair	Walker	(215)909-8882	Two of A kind	892 Main St	Menden	CT	06403	Mystery
18	Jamie	Walker	(908)652-9609		997 Lenox Dr	Reno	NV	32883	Mystery
19	Tina	Walker	(702)703-0101		123 Main St	Stamford	CT	06402	Computer
20	Peter	Young	(718)505-4259	Elmwood Sales	188 William St	Bogota	NV	32881	Sports

Figure 11-21 Result of the two column sort

How To Move A Column

To help make seeing the results of the next sort easier, it would help if the **CATEGORY** column was the first column in the spreadsheet. This is not a requirement. It will just help make the result of this exercise easier to see.

1. Right-click on column I and select **CUT**, as shown in Figure 11-22.

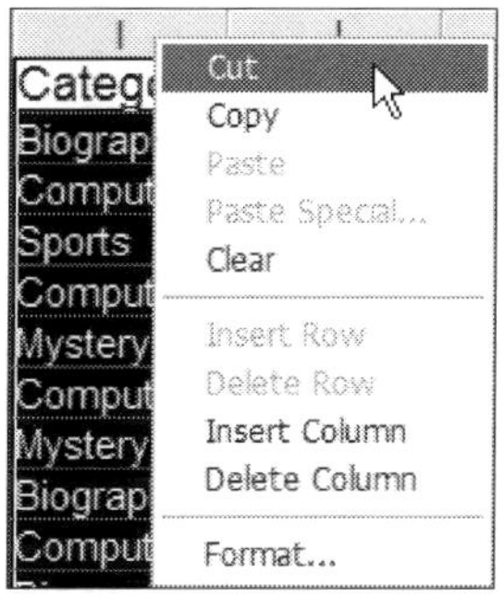

Figure 11-22 Spreadsheet shortcut menu

2. Right-click on column A and select Paste. The Category column should now be in column A.

How To Sort On Three Columns

In this exercise you will sort the spreadsheet by category. Within each category, you will sort the data by the last and first names.

1. Click in the square above the row numbers to highlight the entire spreadsheet, then Tools ⇒ Sort. Select the Header row option.

2. In the first Sort by drop-down list select Category, if it is not already selected, then in the second Sort by drop-down list select Last Name.

3. In the last Sort by drop-down list select First Name, then click the Sort button. Your spreadsheet should look like the one shown in Figure 11-23. The records are sorted on all three fields. Notice that the names are in order by the last and first name columns in each category. Save the changes and close the spreadsheet.

	A	B	C	D	E	F	G	H	I
1	Category	First Name	Last Name	Phone	Company	Address	City	State	Zip Code
2	Biography	Fred	Amos	(215)327-7079		19 Rodney	Westwood	CT	06403
3	Biography	Todd	Green	(203)452-1300		41 Jefferson Rd	Tampa	FL	32672
4	Biography	Louis	Riker	(702)667-3053		23 Essex Pl	Tappan	CT	06402
5	Computer	Brian	Bark	(610)554-3002		300 Winston Pl	Norwood	NY	10023
6	Computer	Carrie	Downing	(407)987-4563	Financial Services	63 Maple Ave	Glen Rock	NV	32888
7	Computer	Kelly	Fontaine	(702)825-9787	Jersey Bank	272 Rt 64	Cherry Hill	NJ	07458
8	Computer	Tina	Jones	(609)364-2500		30 Long St	Ft Laud	FL	32991
9	Computer	Randi	Sherwood	(718)505-3388	Hi-Tech Inc	777 Broad Ave	Ramsey	PA	19001
10	Computer	Steve	Smith	(702)947-8701	Big Design	2200 Research Way	Bronx	NY	11201
11	Computer	Tina	Walker	(702)703-0101		123 Main St	Stamford	CT	06402
12	Mystery	Robert	Emerson	(908)587-6422	New Real Estate	200 Mountain Ave	Ft. Laud	FL	32847
13	Mystery	Amy	Gardner	(610)664-4646		132 W Park Ave	Wilson	NJ	07403
14	Mystery	Clair	Walker	(215)909-8882	Two of A kind	892 Main St	Menden	CT	06403
15	Mystery	Jamie	Walker	(908)652-9609		997 Lenox Dr	Reno	NV	32883
16	Sports	Glen	Carter	(407)471-0159		1 Edward Dr	Las Vegas	NV	60022
17	Sports	Tom	Smith	(215)909-1885		45 Jericho Ave	Wilton	CT	06405
18	Sports	Brenda	Taylor	(610)967-7308	Symphony C&L	500 Point Rd	Ft Lee	NJ	08663
19	Sports	Stuart	Thomas	(718)503-0331		90A Jersey Ave	Orlando	FL	32761
20	Sports	Peter	Young	(718)505-4259	Elmwood Sales	188 William St	Bogota	NV	32881

Figure 11-23 Result of the three column sort

The Spell Checker

A lot of information in a spreadsheet is numeric. Row and column names are primarily text, which means that there can be typos. The Spell Checker works the same in a spreadsheet as it does in a word processing document. Numeric only fields are skipped during the spell check process. If you did check fields that had numbers, every numeric field would be considered a spelling error.

1. Open the L10 Inventory (with functions) spreadsheet, then press the F7 key to start the Spell Checker. You should see the dialog box shown in Figure 11-24.

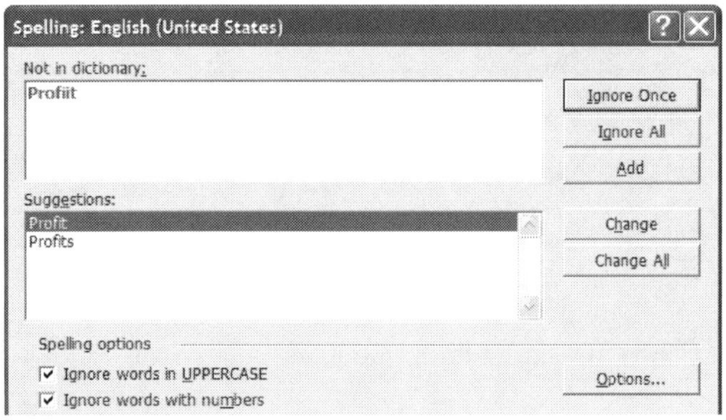

Figure 11-24 Spelling dialog box

Tools ⇒ Spelling, is another way to start the spell checker.

2. To accept the highlighted word in the **SUGGESTIONS** box, click the Change or Change All button now.

3. Another misspelled word was found. The word in the Suggestions box is the word that you want, so click the Change or Change All button. Click OK on the Spelling check is complete dialog box. Save the changes and close the spreadsheet.

Headers And Footers

In this exercise you will learn how to add information to the header and footer sections of a spreadsheet.

1. Open the L11 Balance Sheet (frozen rows & columns) spreadsheet.

2. View ⇒ Header and Footer.

The dialog box shown in Figure 11-25 allows you to create your own header and footer information. The **NO HEADER ON FIRST PAGE** and **NO FOOTER ON FIRST PAGE** options allow you to specify whether or not you want the header or footer information to print on the first page of the spreadsheet.

Each of the drop-down lists (Left, Center, Right) on the Header and Footer dialog box have options that you can select, as shown in Figure 11-26. You can also type in text.

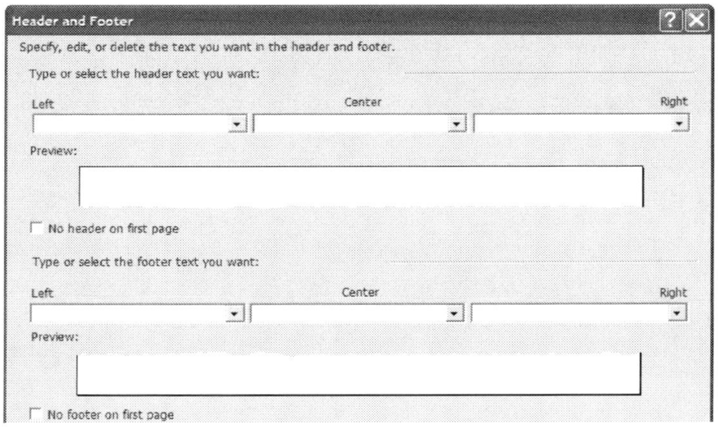

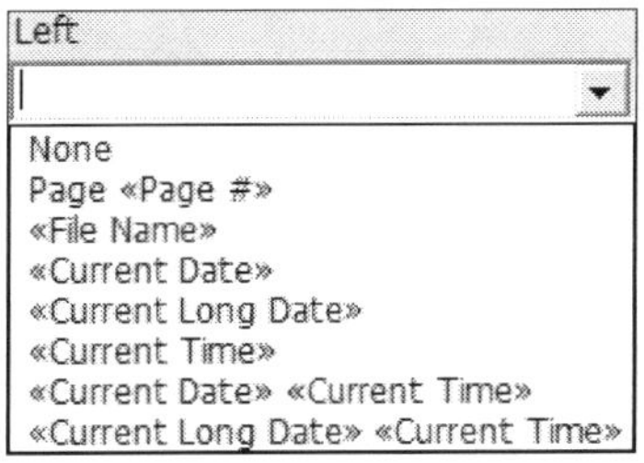

Figure 11-26 Default header and footer options

Figure 11-25 Header and Footer dialog box

> Left, Center and Right refer to the location in the header and footer that the information will be placed.

Add Information To The Header Section Of The Spreadsheet

1. In the header section type `**CONFIDENTIAL**` in the **LEFT** field.

2. In the header section type `Internal` in the **RIGHT** field.

This will cause **CONFIDENTIAL** to be printed in the upper left corner of the spreadsheet and the word INTERNAL in the upper right corner of the spreadsheet.

Add Information To The Footer Section Of The Spreadsheet

1. Open the **LEFT** drop-down list in the footer section and select <<File Name>>. Open the **CENTER** drop-down list and select <<Current Date>>.

2. Open the **RIGHT** drop-down list in the footer section and select Page <<Page #>>. Figure 11-27 shows the options that should be selected. Click OK.

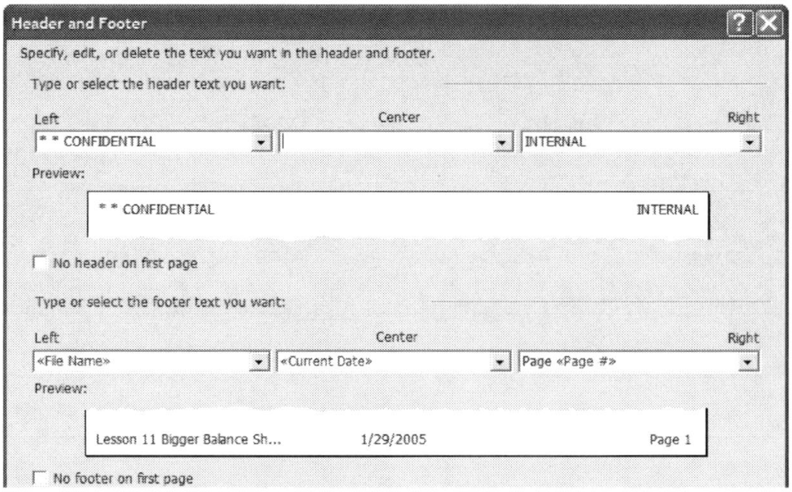

Figure 11-27 Completed Header and Footer dialog box

Notice that the options that you selected or typed in are shown in the **PREVIEW** sections of the dialog box shown above in Figure 11-27.

View Header And Footer Information

Unlike word processing documents, you cannot see what the header and footer information will look like in the normal view of the spreadsheet. To view header and footer information, the spreadsheet has to be in Print Preview.

1. Preview the document. Click on the document to make it larger. It should look like the one shown in Figure 11-28.

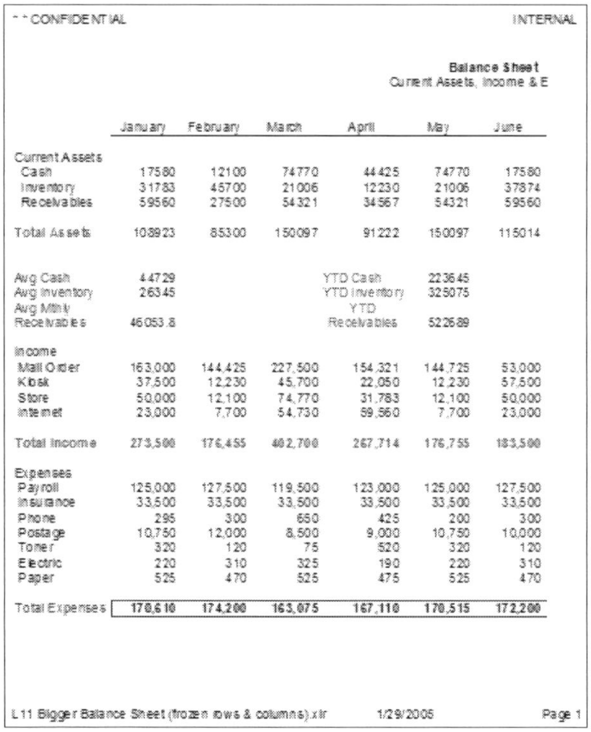

* * CONFIDENTIAL INTERNAL

Balance Sheet
Current Assets, Income & E

	January	February	March	April	May	June
Current Assets						
Cash	17580	12100	74770	44425	74770	17580
Inventory	31783	45700	21006	12230	21006	37874
Receivables	59560	27500	54321	34567	54321	59560
Total Assets	108923	85300	150097	91222	150097	115014
Avg Cash	44729			YTD Cash	223645	
Avg Inventory	26345			YTD Inventory	325075	
Avg Mthly Receivables	46053.8			YTD Receivables	522689	
Income						
Mail Order	163,000	144,425	227,500	154,321	144,725	53,000
Kiosk	37,500	12,230	45,700	22,050	12,230	57,500
Store	50,000	12,100	74,770	31,783	12,100	50,000
Internet	23,000	7,700	54,730	59,560	7,700	23,000
Total Income	273,500	176,455	402,700	267,714	176,755	183,500
Expenses						
Payroll	125,000	127,500	119,500	123,000	125,000	127,500
Insurance	33,500	33,500	33,500	33,500	33,500	33,500
Phone	295	300	650	425	200	300
Postage	10,750	12,000	8,500	9,000	10,750	10,000
Toner	320	120	75	520	320	120
Electric	220	310	325	190	220	310
Paper	525	470	525	475	525	470
Total Expenses	170,610	174,200	163,075	167,110	170,515	172,200

L11 Bigger Balance Sheet (frozen rows & columns).xlr 1/29/2005 Page 1

Figure 11-28 Balance sheet in portrait view

2. Click Close.

How To Change The Page Orientation

You will notice that you can only see the first six months on the page. The page orientation needs to be changed.

1. File ⇒ Page Setup. On the Source, Size & Orientation tab, select the **LANDSCAPE** option and click OK.

2. Preview the document. It should look like the one shown in Figure 11-29. This looks a little better, but you still can't see all of the months. To fix this, you will need to change the margins.

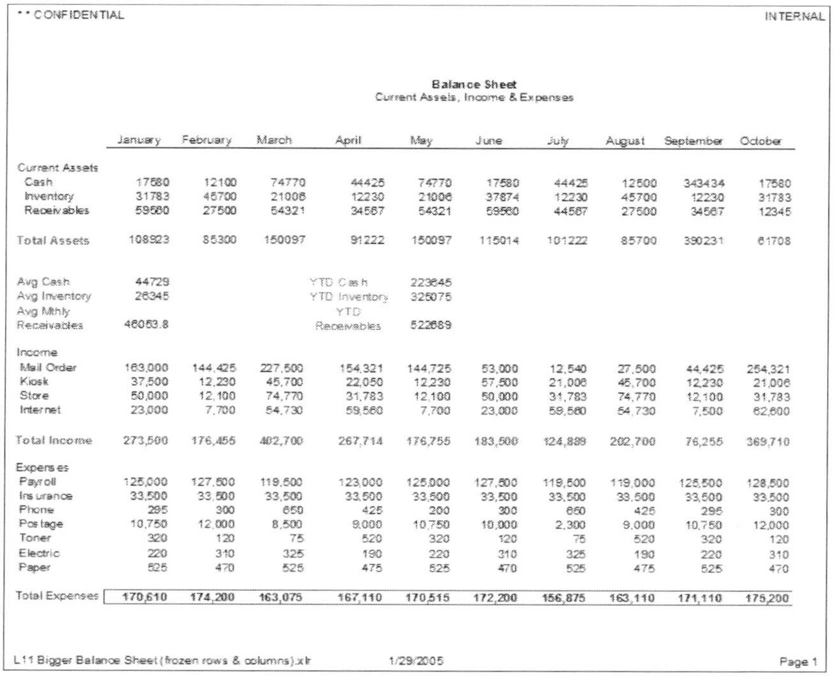

** CONFIDENTIAL INTERNAL

Balance Sheet
Current Assets, Income & Expenses

	January	February	March	April	May	June	July	August	September	October
Current Assets										
Cash	17580	12100	74770	44425	74770	17580	44425	12500	343434	17580
Inventory	31783	45700	21006	12230	21006	37874	12230	45700	12230	31783
Receivables	59560	27500	54321	34567	54321	59560	44567	27500	34567	12345
Total Assets	108923	85300	150097	91222	150097	115014	101222	85700	390231	61708
Avg Cash	44729			YTD Cash	223645					
Avg Inventory	26345			YTD Inventory	325075					
Avg Mthly Receivables	46053.8			YTD Receivables	522689					
Income										
Mail Order	163,000	144,425	227,500	154,321	144,725	53,000	12,540	27,500	44,425	254,321
Kiosk	37,500	12,230	45,700	22,050	12,230	57,500	21,006	45,700	12,230	21,006
Store	50,000	12,100	74,770	31,783	12,100	50,000	31,783	74,770	12,100	31,783
Internet	23,000	7,700	54,730	59,560	7,700	23,000	59,560	54,730	7,500	62,600
Total Income	273,500	176,455	402,700	267,714	176,755	183,500	124,889	202,700	76,255	369,710
Expenses										
Payroll	125,000	127,500	119,500	123,000	125,000	127,500	119,500	119,000	125,500	128,500
Insurance	33,500	33,500	33,500	33,500	33,500	33,500	33,500	33,500	33,500	33,500
Phone	295	300	650	425	200	300	650	425	295	300
Postage	10,750	12,000	8,500	9,000	10,750	10,000	2,300	9,000	10,750	12,000
Toner	320	120	75	520	320	120	75	520	320	120
Electric	220	310	325	190	220	310	325	190	220	310
Paper	525	470	525	475	525	470	525	475	525	470
Total Expenses	170,610	174,200	163,075	167,110	170,515	172,200	156,875	163,110	171,110	175,200

L11 Bigger Balance Sheet (frozen rows & columns).xlr 1/29/2005 Page 1

Figure 11-29 Balance sheet in landscape view

3. Click the Close button and go back into Page Setup. On the Margins tab change the left and right margins to `0.4"`. Figure 11-30 shows the options that you should have selected. Click OK.

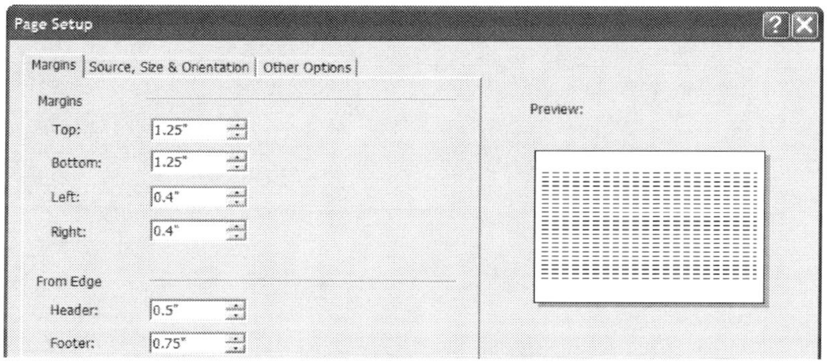

Figure 11-30 Modified margin settings

4. Preview the document. It should look like the one shown in Figure 11-31. If you want, you can print the spreadsheet.

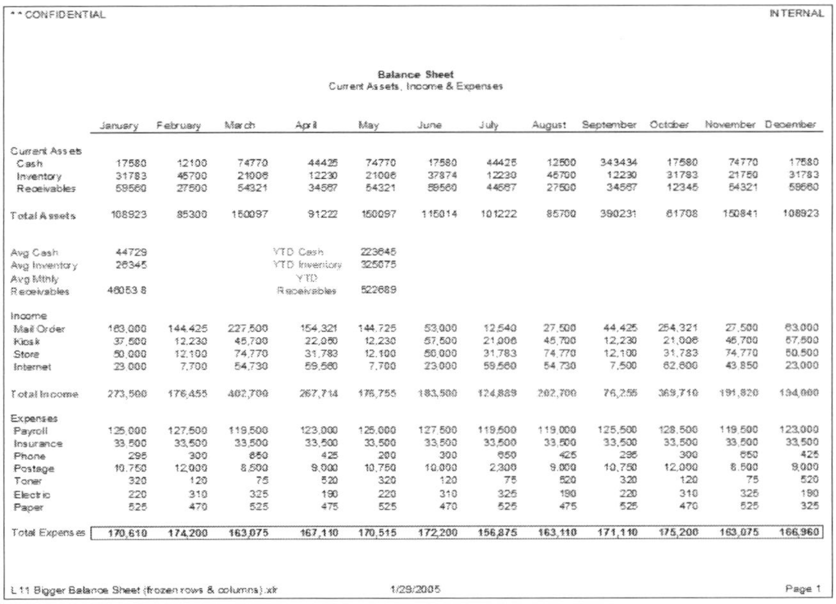

** CONFIDENTIAL INTERNAL

Balance Sheet
Current Assets, Income & Expenses

	January	February	March	April	May	June	July	August	September	October	November	December
Current Assets												
Cash	17580	12100	74770	44425	74770	17580	44425	12500	343434	17580	74770	17580
Inventory	31783	45700	21006	12230	21006	37874	12230	45700	12230	31783	21750	31783
Receivables	59560	27500	54321	34567	54321	59560	44567	27500	34567	12345	54321	59560
Total Assets	108923	85300	150097	91222	150097	115014	101222	85700	390231	61708	150841	108923
Avg Cash	44729			YTD Cash	223645							
Avg Inventory	26345			YTD Inventory	325075							
Avg Mthly Receivables	46053 8			YTD Receivables	522689							
Income												
Mail Order	163,000	144,425	227,500	154,321	144,725	53,000	12,540	27,500	44,425	254,321	27,500	63,000
Kiosk	37,500	12,230	45,700	22,050	12,230	57,500	21,006	45,700	12,230	21,006	45,700	57,500
Store	50,000	12,100	74,770	31,783	12,100	50,000	31,783	74,770	12,100	31,783	74,770	50,500
Internet	23,000	7,700	54,730	59,560	7,700	23,000	59,560	54,730	7,500	62,600	43,850	23,000
Total Income	273,500	176,455	402,700	267,714	176,755	183,500	124,889	202,700	76,255	369,710	191,820	194,000
Expenses												
Payroll	125,000	127,500	119,500	123,000	125,000	127,500	119,500	119,000	125,500	128,500	119,500	123,000
Insurance	33,500	33,500	33,500	33,500	33,500	33,500	33,500	33,500	33,500	33,500	33,500	33,500
Phone	295	300	650	425	200	300	650	425	295	300	650	425
Postage	10,750	12,000	8,500	9,000	10,750	10,000	2,300	9,000	10,750	12,000	8,500	9,000
Toner	320	120	75	520	320	120	75	520	320	120	75	520
Electric	220	310	325	190	220	310	325	190	220	310	325	190
Paper	525	470	525	475	525	470	525	475	525	470	525	325
Total Expenses	170,610	174,200	163,075	167,110	170,515	172,200	156,875	163,110	171,110	175,200	163,075	166,960

L11 Bigger Balance Sheet (frozen rows & columns).xlr 1/29/2005 Page 1

Figure 11-31 Balance sheet completed

If you want to print gridlines or the row and column headings, go into Page Setup and click on the options shown in Figure 11-32 that you need.

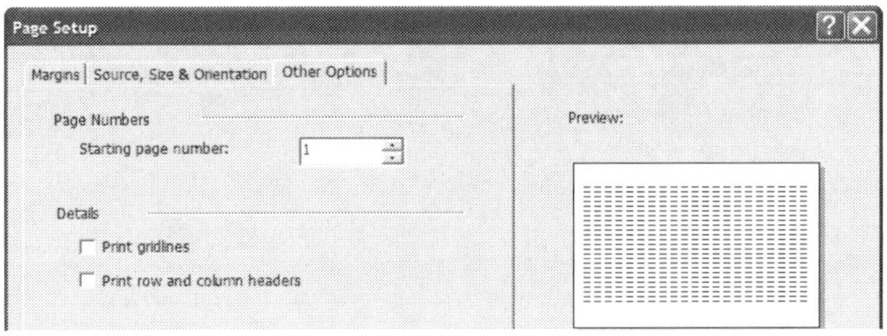

Figure 11-32 Gridlines, row and column header options

5. Click OK and save the changes.

Adding Page Breaks

The spreadsheet does not display page breaks like the word processor does. Unless you preview the spreadsheet in Print Preview before you print it, you will not know what data will be printed on the next page. The way around this is to insert manual page breaks. You can insert horizontal and vertical page breaks.

Insert A Page Break

1. Click in cell B27. Insert ⇒ Insert Page Break.

If you make a mistake, immediately open the Edit menu and select Undo Insert Page Break.

2. In the dialog box shown in Figure 11-33, select the option **ABOVE THE SELECTED CELL**, if it is not already selected and click OK. You should see a dotted line below row 26. This is the page break mark.

If you wanted to insert a vertical page break you would select the option, **TO THE LEFT OF THE SELECTED CELL**.

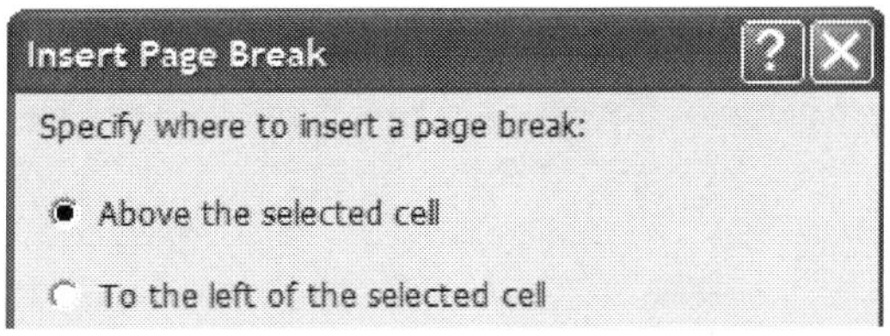

Figure 11-33 Insert Page Break dialog box

View The Page Break Results

1. Preview the spreadsheet. On the first page you should see the Assets and Income sections of the spreadsheet. Press the **PAGE DOWN** key or click the Next button on the toolbar. You should see the Expenses section on the second page.

2. Click Close and save the changes.

How To Delete A Page Break

If you want to keep the page break in your document, skip this exercise.

1. Highlight row 27. Insert ⇒ Delete Page Break. The page break will be removed.

> Because you have a frozen column, the row will not appear highlighted as you may expect. Instead, cell A27 will be highlighted. If you look in the upper left corner of the spreadsheet you will see the range A27:IV27. This lets you know that the entire row has been selected.

2. Save the changes and leave the spreadsheet open.

How To Save A Spreadsheet As A Template

The spreadsheet that you have open now would make a good template. It has formulas, frozen rows and columns. To be used as a template, a lot of the data in the range B8 to M34 has to be deleted, so that you start off with an empty spreadsheet.

1. Delete the data in the following ranges: B8 to M10, B20 to M23 and B28 to M34. Your spreadsheet should look like the one shown in Figure 11-34.

If you were going to use this spreadsheet for real, you would have to modify the formulas in cells B15 to B17. When you created these formulas, they were set up to only account for five months and not 12 months. The reason that you see the error in the **AVERAGE** fields is because there is no data in the spreadsheet.

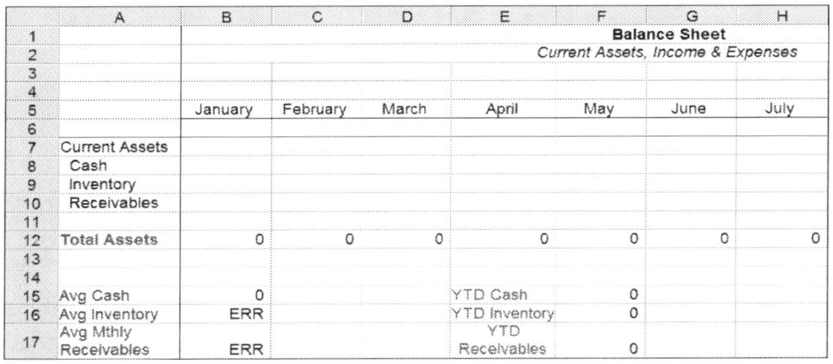

	A	B	C	D	E	F	G	H
1							Balance Sheet	
2							*Current Assets, Income & Expenses*	
3								
4								
5		January	February	March	April	May	June	July
6								
7	Current Assets							
8	Cash							
9	Inventory							
10	Receivables							
11								
12	Total Assets	0	0	0	0	0	0	0
13								
14								
15	Avg Cash	0			YTD Cash	0		
16	Avg Inventory	ERR			YTD Inventory	0		
17	Avg Mthly Receivables	ERR			YTD Receivables	0		

Figure 11-34 Balance Sheet template

2. File ⇒ Save As. Click the **TEMPLATE** button and type `Balance Sheet (Template)` as the file name as shown in Figure 11-35.

When you saved the Fax Cover page word processing document as a template, you had the option of saving it in your folder or any folder that you wanted to. If you open the Save As type drop-down list, you will see that there is no option to save the spreadsheet as a template. I don't know about you, but I think that there should be more consistency between the word processing and spreadsheet applications.

The spreadsheet that you are working on now probably is not what you would want as the default spreadsheet template. In Figure 11-35 there is an option to make this the default template. Do not check this option.

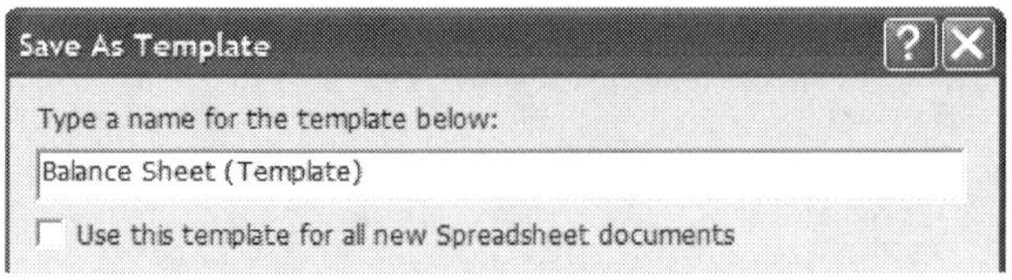

Figure 11-35 Save As Template dialog box

If you needed or wanted to use specific settings like font, font size or margins, as the basis for all of your spreadsheets, you would create an empty spreadsheet that has these options set to what you want and then save it as the default template that all new spreadsheets would be created from.

This is when you would check the option, **USE THIS TEMPLATE FOR ALL NEW SPREADSHEET DOCUMENTS**, shown above in Figure 11-35. Remember that checking this option, replaces the template that you currently see when you open a new spreadsheet.

3. Click OK, then close the L11 Balance Sheet (frozen rows & columns) spreadsheet, but do not save the changes.

4. Open the Task Launcher, then click on the Tasks link. Click on the Personal Templates link. You should see the Balance Sheet template that you just created as shown in Figure 11-36.

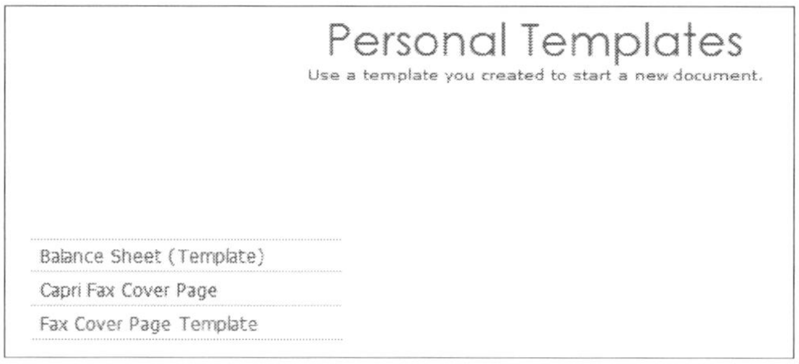

Figure 11-36 Personal Templates

5. Click on the link for the Balance Sheet (Template) shown above in Figure 11-36, then click the **START THIS TASK** link. You should see an empty spreadsheet as shown earlier in Figure 11-34. Close the spreadsheet, but do not save the changes.

Spreadsheet Printing Options

In the last two lessons you created and modified several spreadsheets, but you may not have printed any on your own. In this exercise you will learn about the spreadsheet printing options. The majority of the spreadsheet printing options are identical to the word processing printing options. What follows are the options that are only available in the spreadsheet application.

Viewing Charts

In a previous lesson you learned one way to view charts. You can also view charts as they will look when printed, which may be a little different then the way you see the chart when you are working on it.
To view a chart the way that it will look when printed, follow the steps below.

1. Open a spreadsheet that has a chart. To walk through this exercise, open the Class Schedule For March spreadsheet.

2. View ⇒ Chart, then View ⇒ Display As Printed. You will see some differences between this version of the chart and the one you saw when you first opened the chart. Close the chart and spreadsheet. When prompted to save the changes, click No.

Creating A Print Area

Some of the spreadsheets that you have modified are really large. Sometimes you may only need or want to print a certain part of the spreadsheet. To only print a certain part of the spreadsheet, you have to create what is known as a **PRINT AREA**. When a spreadsheet has a print area associated with it, only the portion of the spreadsheet that is in the print area will print. Follow the steps below to create a print area.

1. Save the L11 Bigger Balance Sheet spreadsheet as `L11 Balance Sheet (with print area).`

2. Highlight the range A1 to G17. File ⇒ Print Area ⇒ Set Print Area, as shown in Figure 11-37. Click Yes, when prompted to set the print area, then save the changes.

If you wanted to use the Print Area option to print a portion of the spreadsheet once, you should not save the spreadsheet after you create the print area. Because you saved the print area in this exercise, every time that you print this spreadsheet, only the portion of the spreadsheet that is defined in the print area will print until you clear the print area option.

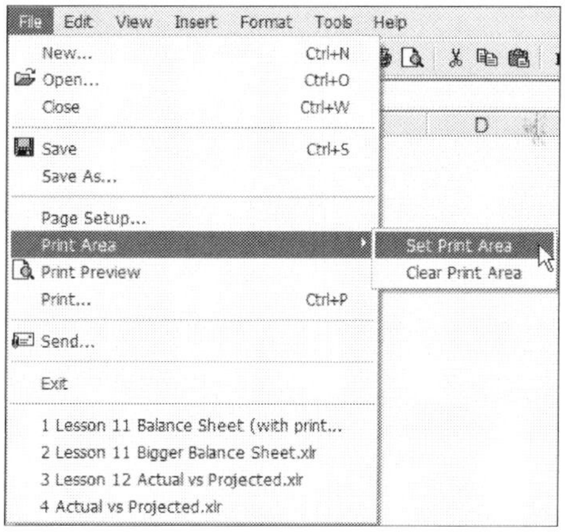

Figure 11-37 Print Area menu options

3. Preview the spreadsheet. You will only see the portion of the spreadsheet (in this exercise, cells A1 to G17) that is included in the print area.

How To Remove A Print Area

If you have created a print area and no longer need it or want to change the print area, follow the steps below.

1. Open the spreadsheet that has the print area.

2. File ⇒ Print Area ⇒ Clear Print Area. If you want to create a different print area, create it now.

3. Save the changes and close the spreadsheet.

Test Your Skills

1. Save the L10 Inventory (with functions) spreadsheet as `L11(skills)`.

    - Freeze Column A and rows 1 to 5.
    - Create a print area for the range A5 to F13.
    - Insert a page break after row 13.
    - Add the words "Inventory Spreadsheet" in the upper left corner of the header.
    - Add the current long date in the upper right corner of the header.
    - Add the word "Page" and the page number in the center of the footer.

2. Save the Customers Spreadsheet as `L11(skills 2)`.

    - Sort the spreadsheet by the Category and State fields.
    - Create a print area for the range D1 to I20.

CHART BASICS

Charts allow you to represent spreadsheet data in a visual format. Representing data in chart format should make the data easier to understand. Works has a wizard that you can use to create charts. There are 12 types of charts that you can create including pie, bar and line charts. In this lesson you will learn the following:

☑ How to create a variety of charts
☑ Basic chart formatting techniques

LESSON 12

Charts Overview

Charts are linked to data in a spreadsheet and are saved with the spreadsheet. You can create up to eight charts for each spreadsheet. If you change data in the spreadsheet, any charts that are based off of the data that is changed is automatically updated.

Chart Types

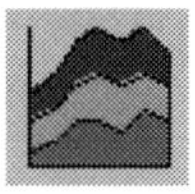

Area charts show how the data has changed over a period of time. Figure 12-1 shows how the four types of income (mail order, store, kiosk and Internet) make up the total income and how the income changes over the months.

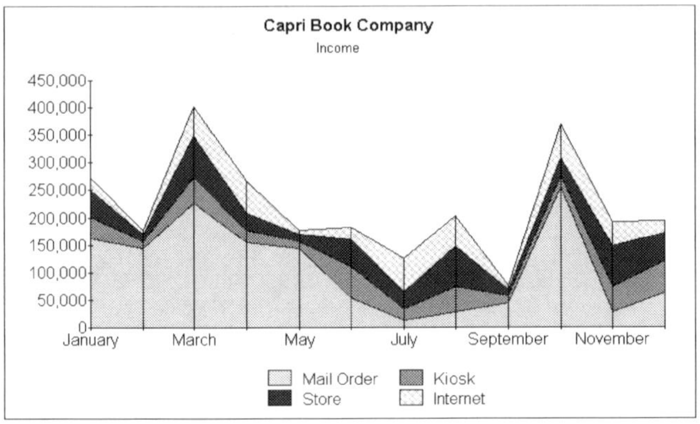

Figure 12-1 Area chart

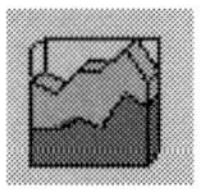

3D Area charts are similar to area charts. The difference is that the data is displayed in 3D format.

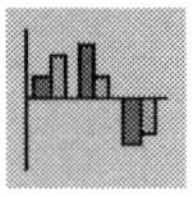

Bar charts, as shown in Figure 12-2 compare data in intervals of time. This is probably the most used chart type. **STACKED BAR** charts show each item as a percent of the total.

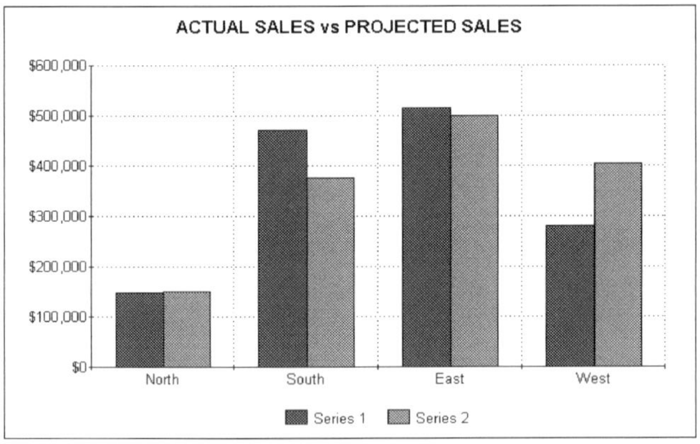

Figure 12-2 Bar chart

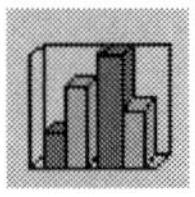

3D Bar charts show data values side by side, separately or stacked.

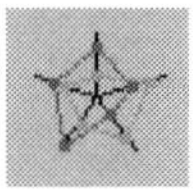

Radar charts compare sets of data relative to a center point and shows how far the data is from the standard.

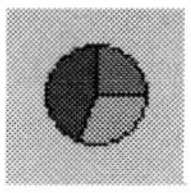

Pie charts only show information for one point in time. Figure 12-3 shows the various types of income for July.

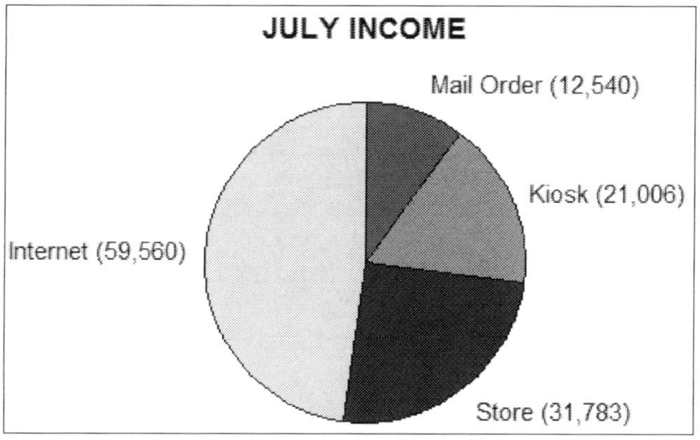

Figure 12-3 Pie chart

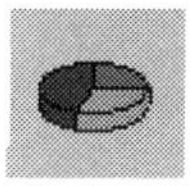

3D Pie charts look similar to pie charts. The difference is that they have the 3D effect, as shown in Figure 12-4.

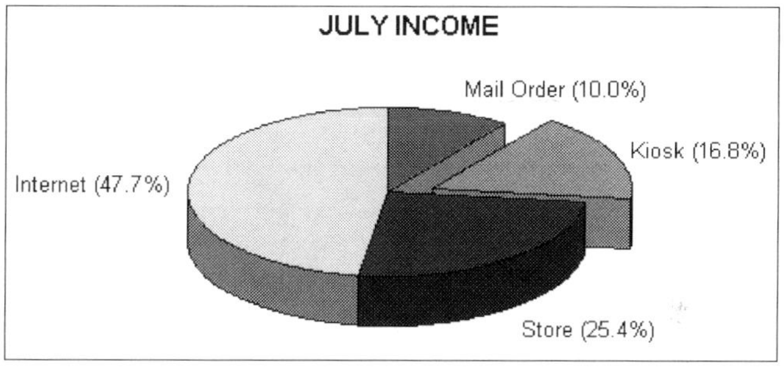

Figure 12-4 3D Pie chart

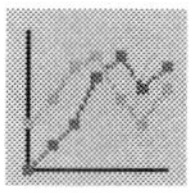

Line charts show trends and changes over a period of time. The markers show the exact values. In Figure 12-5, the data is represented with lines.

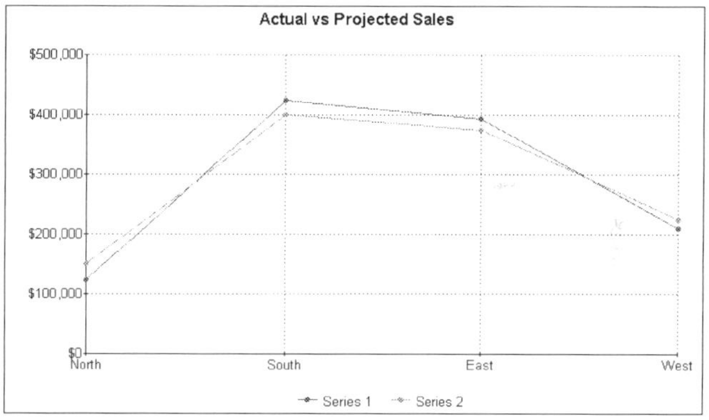

Figure 12-5 Line chart

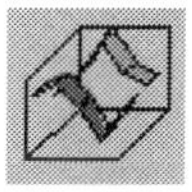

3D Line charts are similar to line charts. 3D line charts are often used when the data lines cross each other frequently. This makes a line chart easier to read.

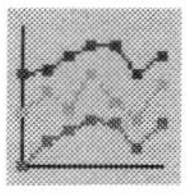

Stacked Line charts add the values of one line to another line and illustrate the flow of data.

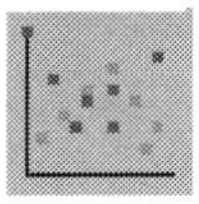

X-Y (Scatter) charts show how two values are related (like salary and job title) and how a change in one value effects the other value, as shown in Figure 12-6.

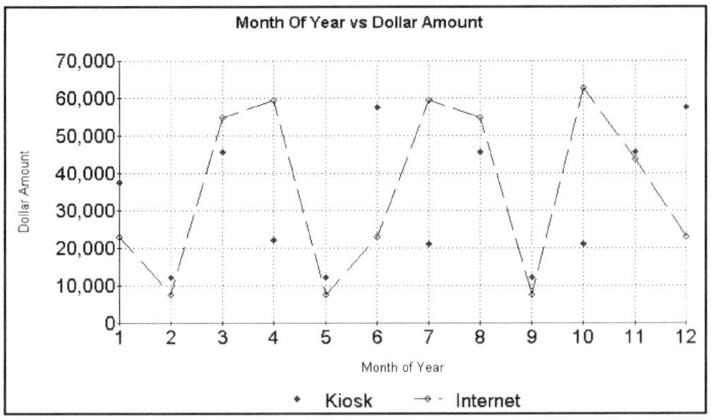

Figure 12-6 X-Y (Scatter) chart

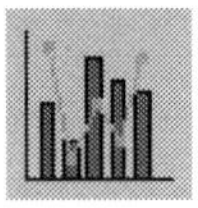

Combination charts allow you to combine bar and line chart types in the same chart. Figure 12-7 shows a combination chart.

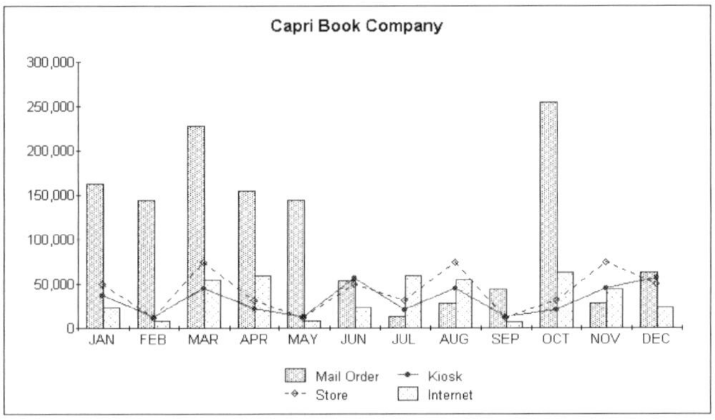

Figure 12-7 Combination chart

Parts Of A Chart

Charts can contain all or any of the options discussed below. These options can be added or deleted as needed. Figure 12-8 illustrates the parts of a chart.

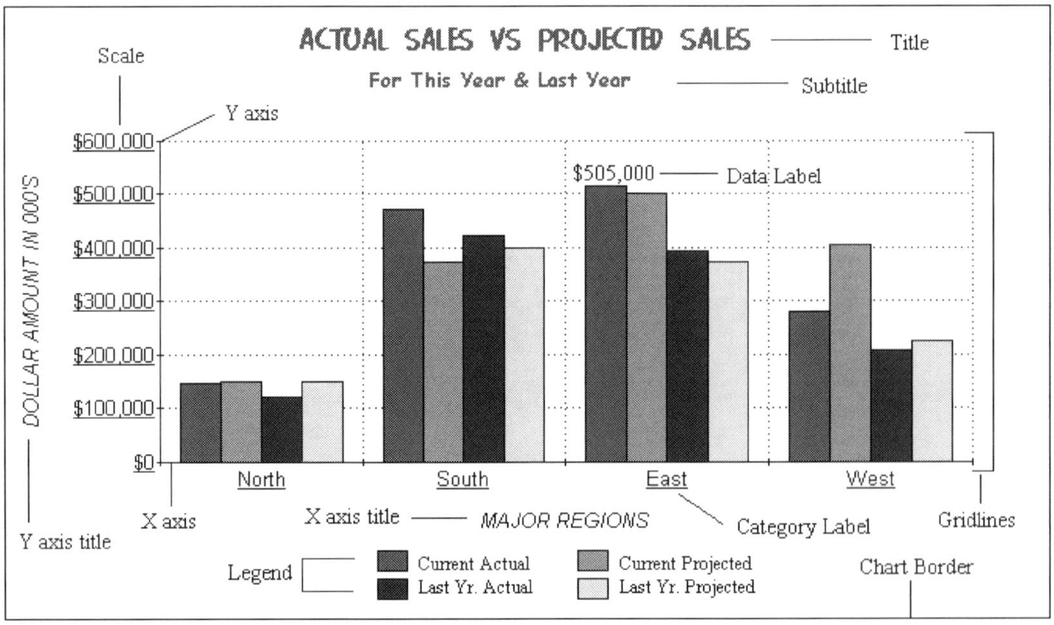

Figure 12-8 Parts of a chart illustrated

Chart Options Explained

The parts of the chart illustrated above in Figure 12-8 are explained below.

Title and **Subtitle** are a description of what type of data the chart is displaying.

X and **Y Axis** represent the vertical axis (Y) and horizontal axis (X) on the chart. The X axis often represents quantities or percents.

Category Label defines the type of data that is displayed.

Data Labels show the exact value of the data.

Grid Lines make the chart easier to read if the values are close in range. You can have horizontal and vertical gridlines.

Scale shows the unit of measurement. The scale range is taken from the data that you select in the spreadsheet. The scale is automatically created for you.

Borders go around the entire chart.

The **Legend** is used to help make the chart easier to read. Legends are color coded representations of the different data items on the chart.

Chart Menu And Toolbar

Before you begin creating charts you should familiarize yourself with the chart menu and toolbar. Figure 12-9 shows the chart menu. Table 12-1 explains the menu options.
Figure 12-11 shows the chart toolbar. Table 12-2 explains the purpose of each button.

Figure 12-9 Chart menu

Menu	Purpose
File	Used for opening, saving, creating and printing charts.
Edit	The commands on this menu let you modify various parts of the chart.
View	Lets you select another chart that is associated with the spreadsheet, switch to the spreadsheet and view the chart as it will look when printed. There are also options for creating headers and footers.
Format	Allows you to format fonts, add color to the chart and change the horizontal and vertical axis options.
Tools	Allows you to rename, delete and duplicate charts.
Window	Allows you to display the chart and spreadsheet side by side, as shown in Figure 12-10.
Help	Opens the Help System.

Table 12-1 Chart menu options explained

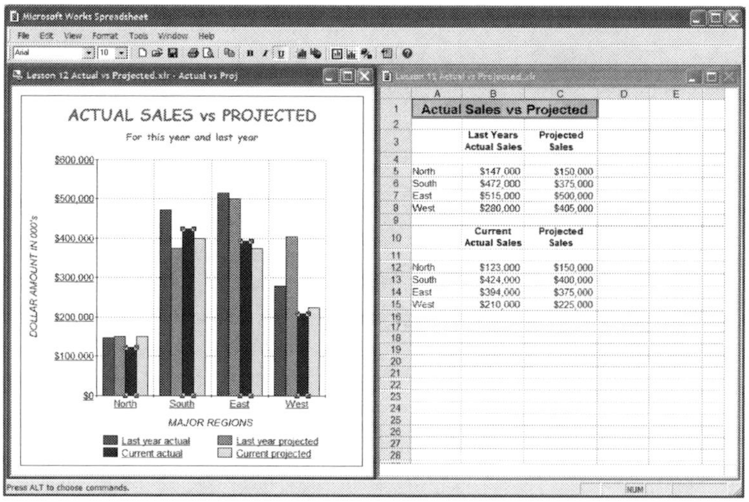

Figure 12-10 Chart and spreadsheet side by side

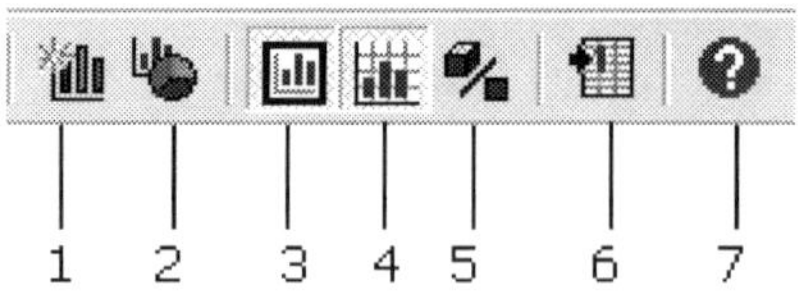

Figure 12-11 Chart toolbar

Button	Purpose
1	Opens the New Chart dialog box.
2	Opens the Chart Type dialog box, which lets you select the type of chart that you want to create.
3	Adds or removes the border around the chart.
4	Adds or removes gridlines on the chart.
5	Changes the chart that is open into a 3-D chart.
6	Opens the spreadsheet and takes you to the first series of data that is used in the chart.
7	Opens the Help System.

Table 12-2 Chart toolbar buttons explained

Selecting Data To Chart

Most of the time you will select more columns than rows when you create a chart.
In Figure 12-12, the categories are taken from cells A1 to A4. The individual rows of data are placed on the Y axis. Cells B1 to B4 will go on the Y axis. You can have up to six data ranges on the Y axis.

	A	B
1	North	$123,000.00
2	South	$424,000.00
3	East	$394,000.00
4	West	$210,000.00

Figure 12-12 X and Y axis data illustrated

If you include row and column headings in the data that you select to chart, they are automatically placed in the chart legend and the labels on the X axis. Data from columns are placed on the X axis and data in rows is placed on the Y axis of charts. If you select more rows than columns, just the opposite occurs. Rows are placed on the X axis and columns are placed on the Y axis.

If the rows and columns that you want to chart are next to each other, you can select them at the same time when you create the chart. If they are not next to each other, you will have to add one series of data to the chart and then go back and select another series.

Create A Bar Chart

The first chart that you will create is a bar chart. There could be an entire book on creating charts, so in an effort to cover as many topics as possible, some will be combined.

1. Save the Actual vs Projected spreadsheet as `L12 Actual vs Projected`.

2. The first thing that you will do is chart the sales for last year. Highlight the range A5 to C8 as shown in Figure 12-13. Click the **NEW CHART** button on the toolbar. You should see the dialog box shown in Figure 12-14. This is where you select the chart type and some of the options for the chart.

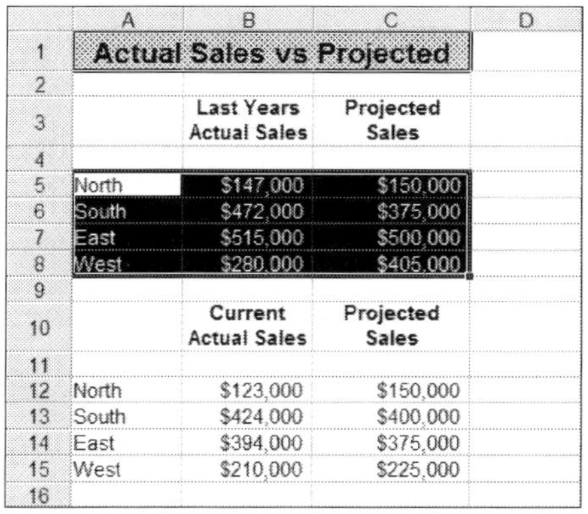

Figure 12-13 Range highlighted to chart

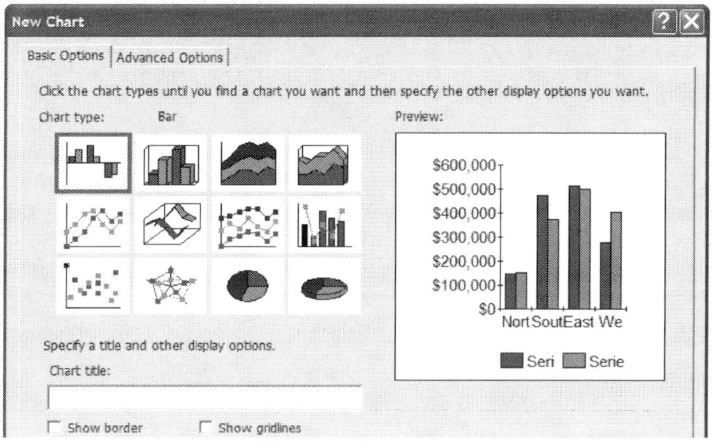

Figure 12-14 New Chart dialog box

3. Select the Bar chart type if it is not already selected, as shown above in Figure 12-14. Type `ACTUAL SALES vs PROJECTED SALES` in the **CHART TITLE** field.

How To Add A Border And Gridlines To The Chart

Gridlines are used in charts to make them easier to read.

1. Check the **SHOW BORDER** and **SHOW GRIDLINES** options in the lower left corner of the New Chart dialog box, then click OK. Your chart should look like the one shown in Figure 12-15. Each bar represents one cell of data. Notice that the legend at the bottom of the chart was automatically created.

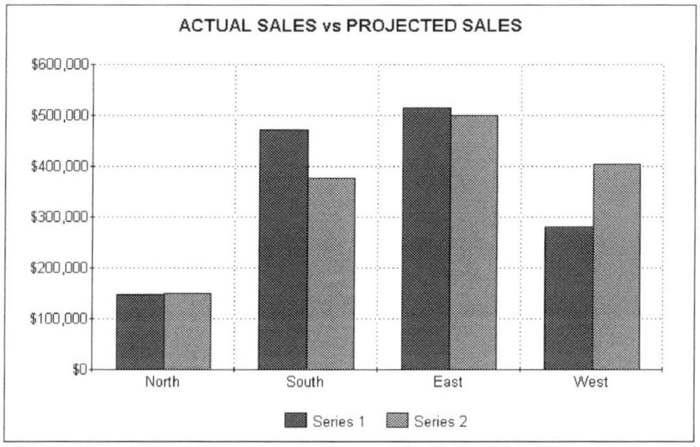

Figure 12-15 Sales chart

How To Add Another Series Of Data To The Chart

This chart is suppose to show the relationship of actual and projected sales for the current year and the previous year. So far you have added last years sales information to the chart, which is one series of data.

The data for the current year is not next to the data for last year in the spreadsheet, so you have to add this data separately to the chart. In order to do this, you need to look at the spreadsheet to get the range for the current years data.

1. View ⇒ Spreadsheet. The range for the current actual sales is B12 to B15. The range for the current projected sales is C12 to C15.

2. Window ⇒ L12 Actual Sales vs Projected.xlr - Chart1.

3. Edit ⇒ Series. Your dialog box should look like the one shown in Figure 12-16. Notice that the first two series are filled in. The first series is for last years actual sales. The second series is for last years projected sales. Type `B12:B15` in the third field, then press the Tab key. Type `C12:C15` in the fourth field and click OK. Your chart should look like the one shown in Figure 12-17. The way the chart is now, it is impossible to know which bars in the chart are for which year.

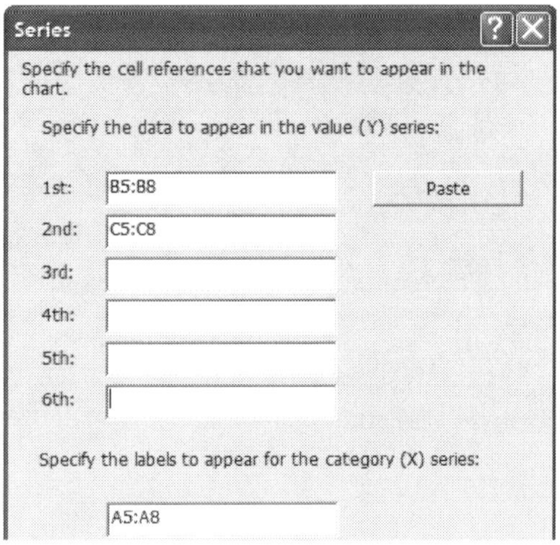

Figure 12-16 Series dialog box

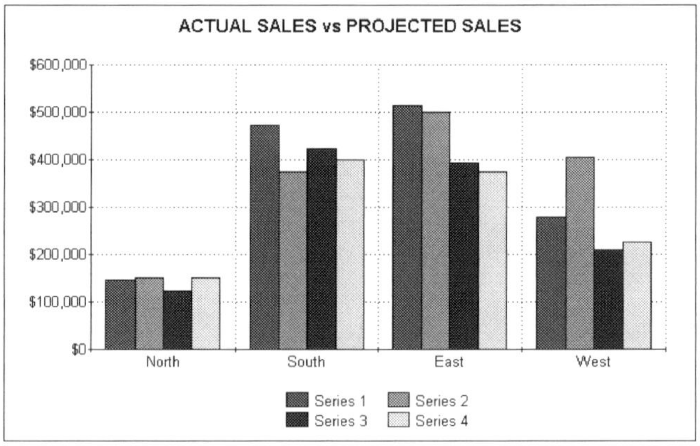

Figure 12-17 Second series of data added to the chart

How To Add Titles To The Chart

Adding titles to a chart is optional. Often you will want to use the same title that already exists in a cell or cells in the spreadsheet. If this is the case, you can type in the cell name (like A1) that has the title that you want to use.

1. Edit ⇒ Titles. You should see the Titles dialog box. In the Chart title field you will see the title that you typed in on the New Chart dialog box. Press the Tab key and type `For this year and last year` in the Chart subtitle field.

> The **HORIZONTAL (X) AXIS TITLE** field is used for the description of the category across the bottom of the chart. The **VERTICAL (Y) AXIS TITLE** field is used for the description of the category down the left side of the chart.

2. Press the Tab key and type `MAJOR REGIONS` in the Horizontal (X) axis title field. Press the Tab key and type `DOLLAR AMOUNT IN 000's` in the Vertical (Y) axis title field. The 000 is zero's. Your dialog box should look like the one shown in Figure 12-18. Click OK. Your chart should look like the one shown in Figure 12-19. Notice that the chart has gridlines and a border.

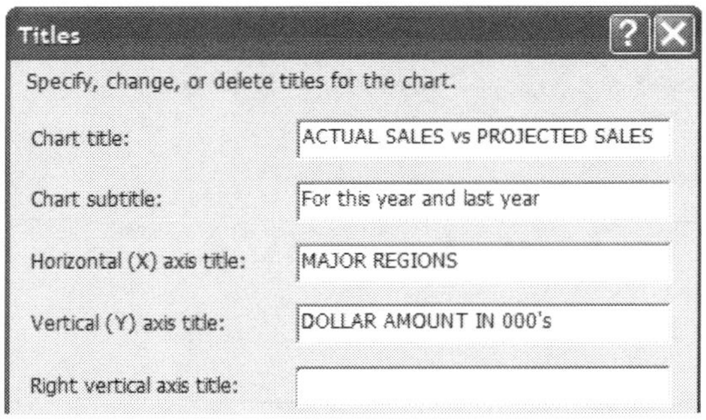

Figure 12-18 Titles dialog box options

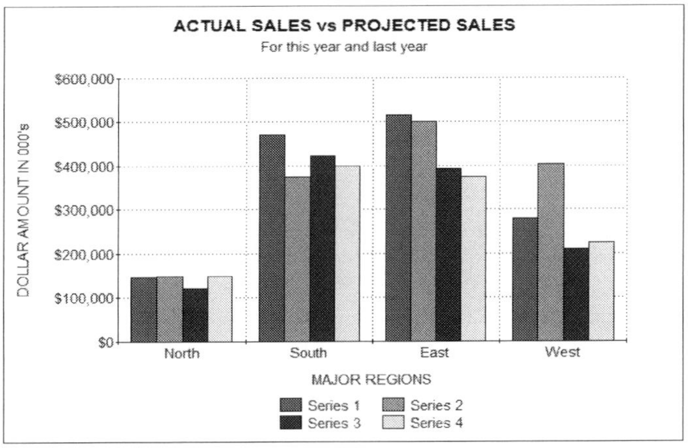

Figure 12-19 Chart with the titles added

Add Legend Labels To The Chart

Currently, the legend labels are named Series 1 to 4. The problem is that you do not know what they represent. In this exercise you will modify the legend labels so that they will make more sense to anyone that reads the chart.

1. Edit ⇒ Legend/Series Labels. Select the option, **USE VALUES IN SPREADSHEET FOR SERIES LABELS.** Notice that only four value series fields are available. That's because you have four series of data on the chart. If you had five or six series of data, that number of value series fields would be available for you to fill in.

2. Press the Tab key and type `Last year actual` in the 1st value series field. Press the Tab key and type `Last year projected` in the 2nd value series field.

3. Press the Tab key and type `Current actual` in the 3rd value series field. Press the Tab key and type `Current projected` in the 4th value series field. Your dialog box should look like the one shown in Figure 12-20. Click OK. Your chart should look like the one shown in Figure 12-21.

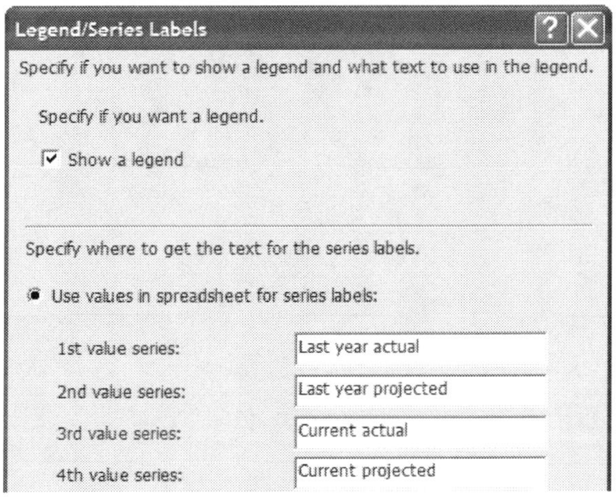

Figure 12-20 Legend/Series Labels dialog box filled in

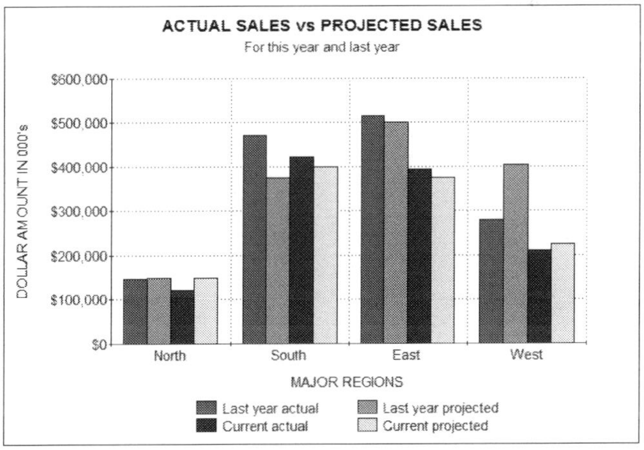

Figure 12-21 Chart with modified legend

Modify The Fonts On The Chart

1. Right-click on the chart title Actual Sales vs Projected Sales, then select Font as shown in Figure 12-22, then select a font that will stand out. I selected the Comic Sans MS font, but you can use any font that you want.

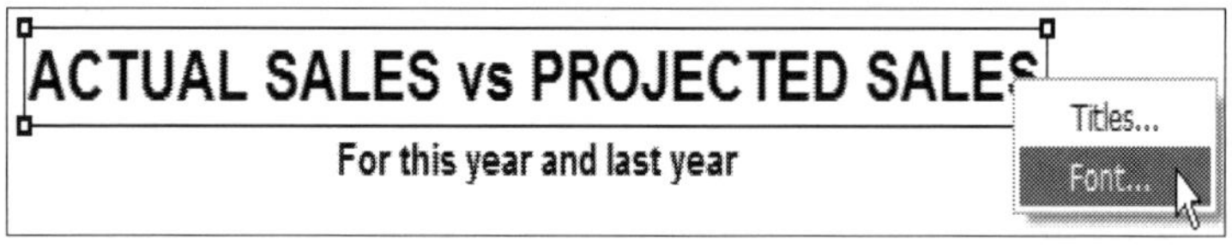

Figure 12-22 Chart title selected

2. Make the font style bold and change the font size to 16, then change the font color to red. Your Font dialog box should look similar to the one shown in Figure 12-23. Click OK.

If you forget what portion of the chart you are modifying, you can look in the **ELEMENT TO FORMAT** section of the Font dialog box. The portion that is highlighted is the one that you are working on.

Usually the font size of subtitles is smaller than the chart title, but you can make the subtitle any size that you want.

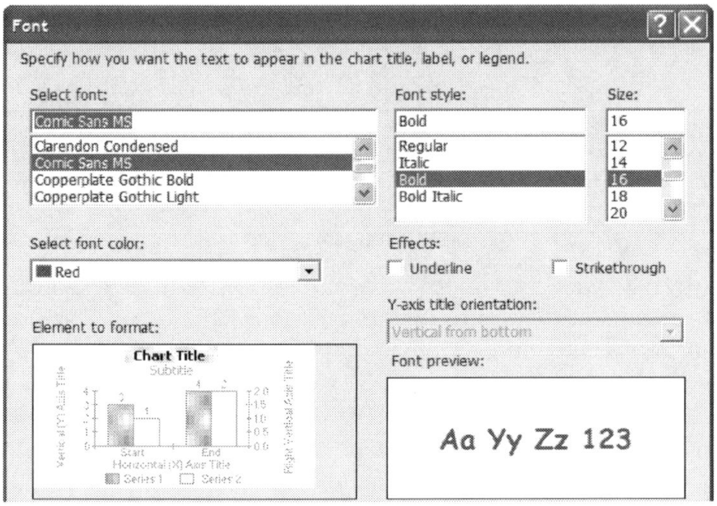

Figure 12-23 Font options selected

3. Right-click on the subtitle and select Font. Change the font and color to the same that you used for the title, then change the font size to 10 and click OK.

4. Right-click on any of the three chart items listed below and select Font. Check the **UNDERLINE** effect option as shown in Figure 12-24 and click OK. The dollar amounts, categories and legend should all be underlined.

- ☑ A dollar amount (ex. $400,000) on the vertical axis.
- ☑ A category (North, South, East or West) on the horizontal axis.
- ☑ One of the four legend series options.

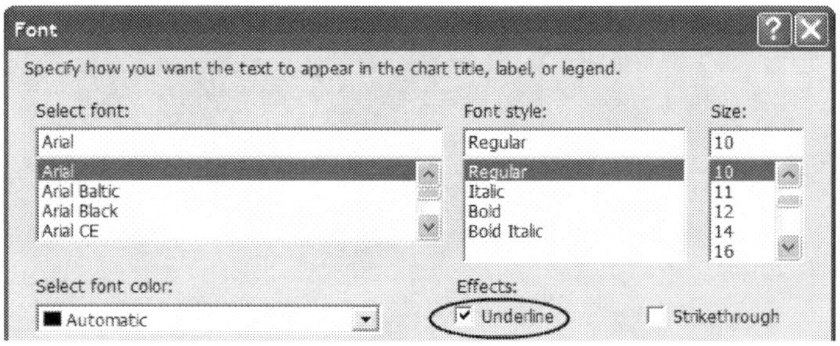

Figure 12-24 Underline effect illustrated

5. Right-click on either of the following axis titles and select Font. Change the Font style to Italic and click OK. Your chart should look like the one shown in Figure 12-25. Normally, you may not add this much formatting to a chart. It's done here so that you can see how to modify various parts of the chart.

☑ Vertical axis title (Dollar Amount in 000's).
☑ Horizontal axis title (Major Regions).

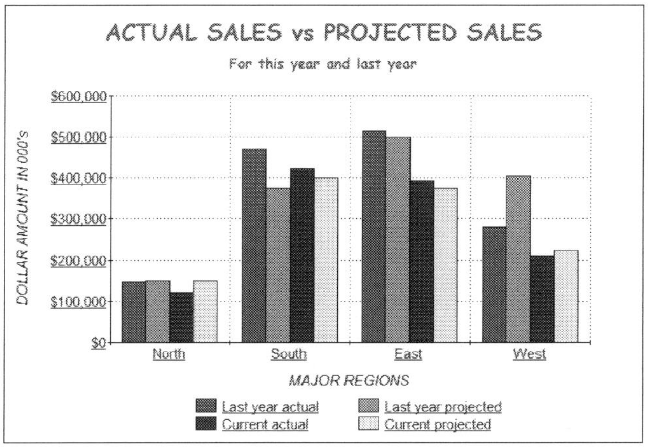

Figure 12-25 Chart titles modified

How To Rename A Chart

Every chart that you create is automatically named. Look in the upper left corner of the chart window to see the default chart name. The chart shown above in Figure 12-25 is named Chart1. Giving the chart a more descriptive name is a good idea, especially if you will create more than one chart for the spreadsheet. Renaming charts is optional.

The chart name can have a maximum of 15 characters.

1. Tools ⇒ Rename Chart. Type `Actual vs Proj` in the **TYPE A NEW NAME FOR THE CHART** field, as shown in Figure 12-26.

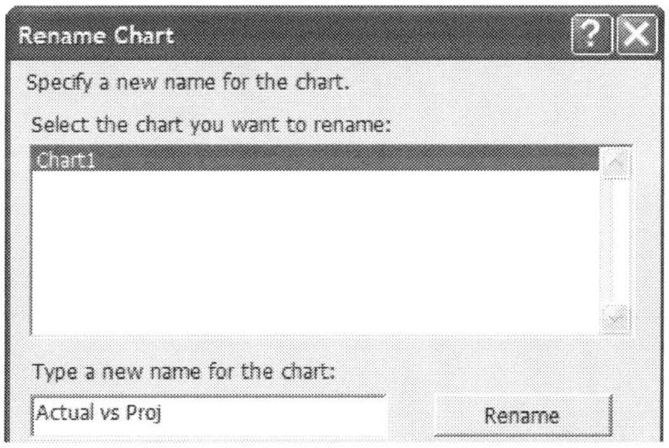

Figure 12-26 Rename Chart dialog box

2. Click the **RENAME** button, then click OK.

3. Save the changes. Close the chart (File ⇒ Close). The spreadsheet should still be open.

How To Create A Chart Based On An Existing Chart

You may have a need to use an existing chart in a different way. The chart that you just created includes data for the current and previous years. If you only want to see data for one of the years, you could create a new chart from scratch or you can modify an existing chart.

How To Duplicate A Chart

The duplicate chart feature is similar to the Save As feature in the word processor and spreadsheet applications.

1. Tools ⇒ Duplicate Chart. If there was more than one chart listed in the Duplicate Chart dialog box, you would select the one that you want to duplicate. Since there isn't, click the Duplicate button.

2. Click on the Chart1 chart and type `Last Years Data` in the Type a new name for the chart field. You should have the options shown in Figure 12-27. Click OK.

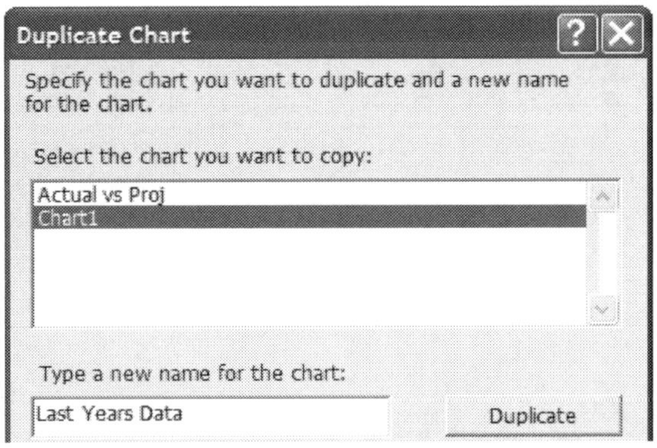

Figure 12-27 Duplicate Chart dialog box

Modify The Chart

The following items need to be modified on the new chart. You will complete these tasks in the remainder of this lesson.

- ☑ Remove the current years data.
- ☑ Change the charts subtitle.
- ☑ Add data labels.
- ☑ Change the fill patterns and colors.
- ☑ Change the font size of the Data Labels.
- ☑ Change the chart type.

How To Remove Data From A Chart

1. View ⇒ Chart. Select the Last Years Data chart and click OK.

2. Edit ⇒ Series. The Series dialog box contains the data for all of the bars on the chart. Delete the data in the 3rd and 4th series fields. These fields contain the current years data. Click OK. The current years data should not be on the chart. Notice that the legend has also changed.

Change The Charts Subtitle

1. Right-click on the chart subtitle and select Titles.

2. Type `For last year` as the new chart subtitle as shown in Figure 12-28 and click OK.

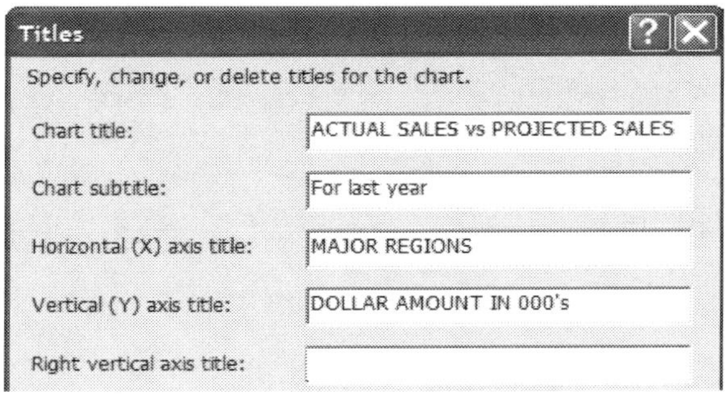

Figure 12-28 Modified chart subtitle

Add Data Labels To The Chart

Data labels will show the actual value for each category. Just by looking at the bars on the chart, you cannot tell the exact amount that the bar represents unless the top of the bar ends at one of the lines on the axis.

1. View ⇒ Data Labels. Select the option **SHOW DATA LABELS IN THE CHART**, as shown in Figure 12-29. Click OK. Numbers should now be above each bar on the chart.

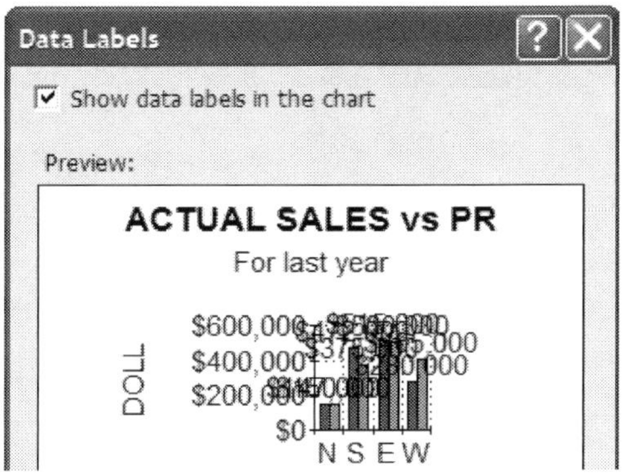

Figure 12-29 Data Labels dialog box

Change The Fill Pattern And Colors On The Chart

Changing fill patterns and colors will make the chart more appealing and hopefully, easier to read.

1. Format ⇒ Shading and Color. You will see the dialog box shown in Figure 12-30.

On this dialog box you can change the colors and patterns of the chart. Because you right-clicked on the Store slice of the pie, the third slice series is automatically selected.

If you want to change more than one slice, make the changes for one slice of the pie, click the Format button, then make the changes for another slice of the pie.

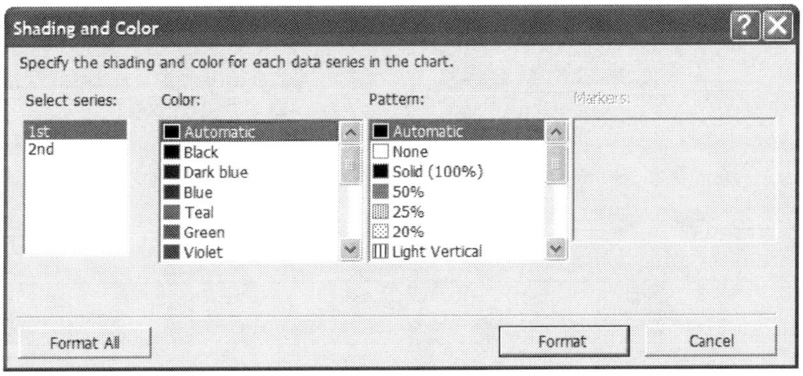

Figure 12-30 Shading and Color dialog box

Shading And Color Dialog Box Options Explained

① The **SELECT SERIES** option refers to the individual series of data on the chart. Each section on the chart has its own series on this dialog box. If you were working on a pie chart, each series would be a slice of the pie chart. I think that the Select Series section of the dialog box would be easier to work with if the names in the legend were used, if the chart had them. This would let you know which series you were working on without having to guess or look at the chart.

② The **COLOR** options will let you change the colors of the series of data on the chart. The default is Automatic.

③ The **PATTERN** options contain designs that you can use to fill the inside of bars, slices of a pie, the line style or area of a chart.

④ **MARKERS** are only available for line and mixed line charts, which you will create in the next lesson.

If you move the dialog box away from the chart you can see the changes that you make when you click the Format button. After you make all of the changes for a series of data, you have to click the Format button before making changes to another series of data.

2. Select Blue in the Color section, then click the **FORMAT** button.

3. Select the 2nd series and change the color to Dark Blue, then change the pattern to Light Vertical. Click the Format button. Click Close. Your chart should look like the one shown in Figure 12-31. Save the changes.

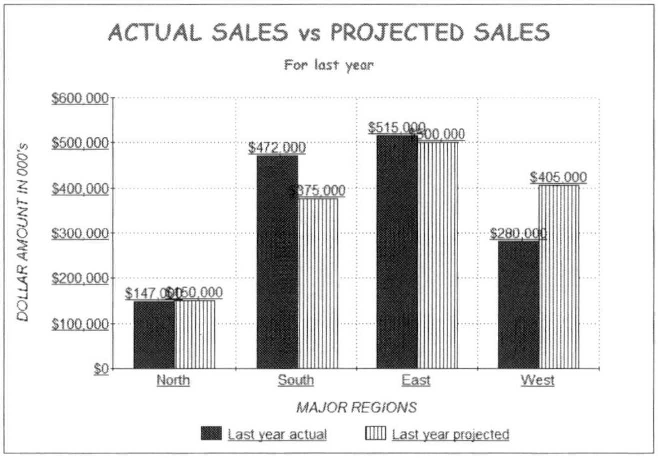

Figure 12-31 Fill pattern modified

Change The Font Size Of The Data Labels

As you can see in Figure 12-31 above, the data labels for some columns are hard to read because they overlap. You can easily fix this by following the steps below.

1. Right-click on one of the data labels as shown in Figure 12-32 and select Font.

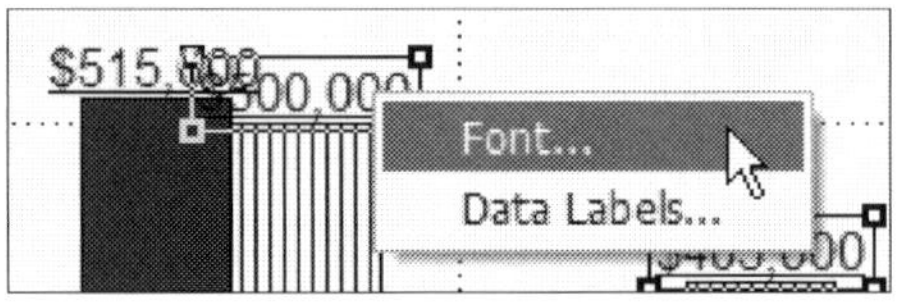

Figure 12-32 Data label selected to be modified

2. Change the font size to 8 and click OK. You should be able to see all of the data labels clearly. Save the changes.

Change The Chart Type

You can change the chart type if you want to see the data a different way. In this exercise you will change the chart to a 3D bar chart.

1. Tools ⇒ Duplicate Chart. Select the Last Years Data chart, if it is not already selected and type `Last Year In 3D` in the field at the bottom of the Duplicate Chart dialog box. Click the Duplicate button, then click OK.

2. View ⇒ Chart. Select the Last Year in 3D chart and click OK.

3. Click the **CHART TYPE** button on the toolbar, then select the **3-D BAR** chart type on the Basic Types tab. It is the second button from the left in the first row, as shown in Figure 12-33.

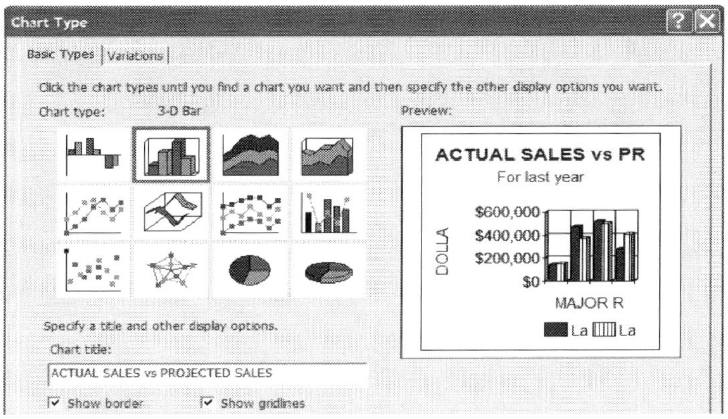

Figure 12-33 3-D bar chart type illustrated

4. On the Variations tab select the chart type in the bottom right corner as shown in Figure 12-34, then click OK. Your chart should look like the one shown in Figure 12-35.

The options on the Variations tab, are other "looks" that the chart can have. The chart options on the first row are the "stacked" options that I mentioned earlier.

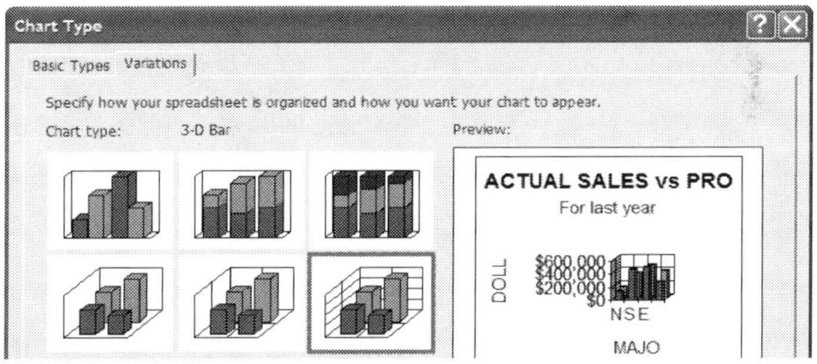

Figure 12-34 Variations tab options

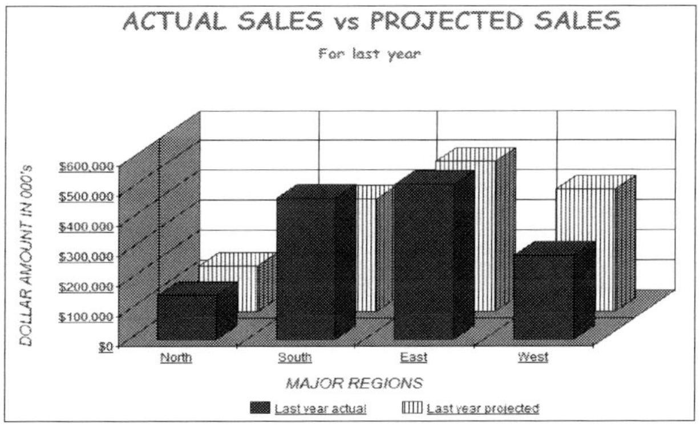

Figure 12-35 3-D chart

Modify The 3-D Chart

1. Format ⇒ Shading and Color. Select Yellow in the Color section, then click the Format button and select the 2nd series.

2. Change the color to Gray -25% and click the Format button, then click Close. Your chart should look like the one shown in Figure 12-36.

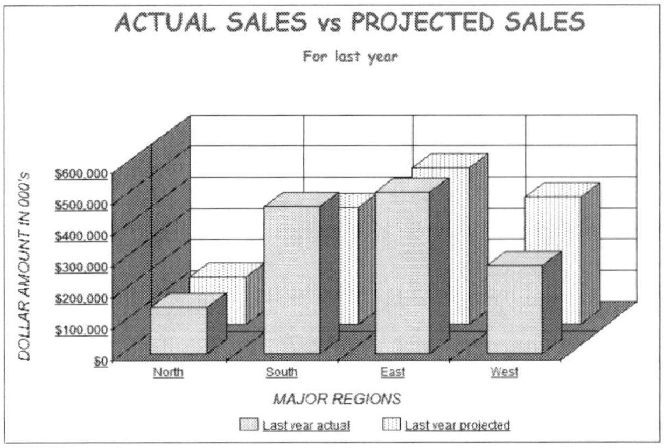

Figure 12-36 3-D chart with shading and color added

3. Close the charts and spreadsheet, then save the changes.

Test Your Skills

1. Save the Actual vs Projected spreadsheet as `L12(skills)`.

   - Create a bar chart with gridlines and a border for the current years sales data.
   - Format the chart so that it looks like the one shown earlier in Figure 12-31.
   - Name the chart, `This years data`.
   - Duplicate the chart that you just created. Save it as `This Year 3D`.
   - Change the chart to a 3D bar chart. Use the second variation in the second row.
   - Format the chart by changing the colors of the bars on the chart.
   - Duplicate the This Years Data chart. Save it as `3D Stacked`.
   - Change the chart type to 3D stacked.

ADVANCED CHART TECHNIQUES

In the lesson you will learn how to do the following:

- ☑ Create and modify pie, line, combination and area charts
- ☑ Use cell contents as labels

LESSON 13

Create A Pie Chart

The pie chart that you will create will illustrate the four sources of income for the month of July.

1. Save the L11 Bigger Balance Sheet spreadsheet as `L13 Charts`.

2. Highlight the range H20 to H23. Click the New Chart button on the toolbar, then select the Pie chart type illustrated in Figure 13-1.

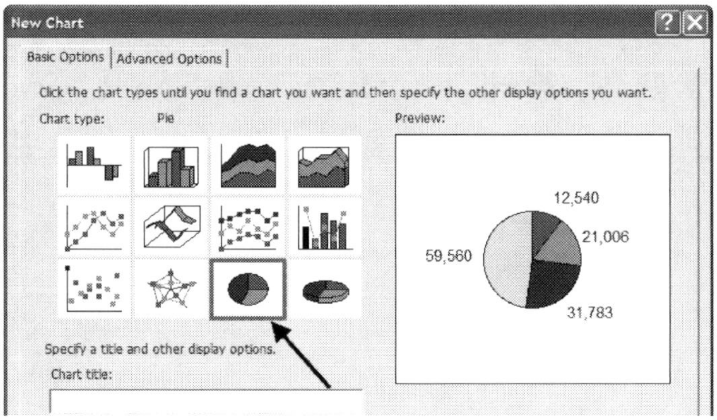

Figure 13-1 Pie chart type selected

3. Type `JULY INCOME` in the **CHART TITLE** field and click OK.

Advanced Chart Options

It is very possible that you may never need to modify the default advanced chart options. If you do, click on the **ADVANCED OPTIONS** tab on the New Chart dialog box. You will see the options shown in Figure 13-2. Some chart types have different advanced options. Figure 13-3 shows the advanced options for a bar chart.

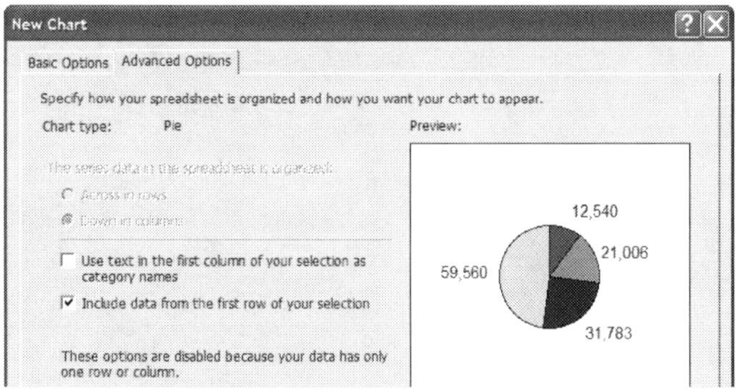

Figure 13-2 Advanced pie chart options

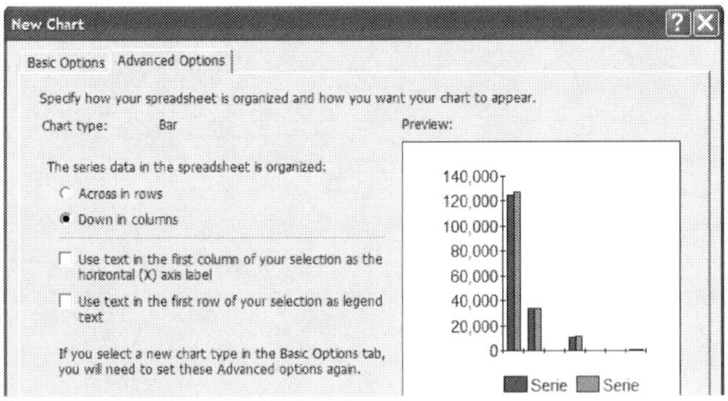

Figure 13-3 Advanced bar chart options

How To Use Cell Contents As Labels

You can use the contents of cells on the spreadsheet as labels on a chart. This is useful if you think you may change the column or row headings in the spreadsheet after the chart has been created. Using the **CELL CONTENTS AS LABELS** option will automatically update the labels on your chart if the corresponding cells on the spreadsheet change.

1. Edit ⇒ Series.

2. Type A20:A23 in the **SPECIFY THE LABELS TO APPEAR FOR THE CATEGORY (X) SERIES** field as shown at the bottom of Figure 13-4. This will add the contents of these cells to the chart. The range A20 to A23 is the range that has the values for the data labels. Click OK.

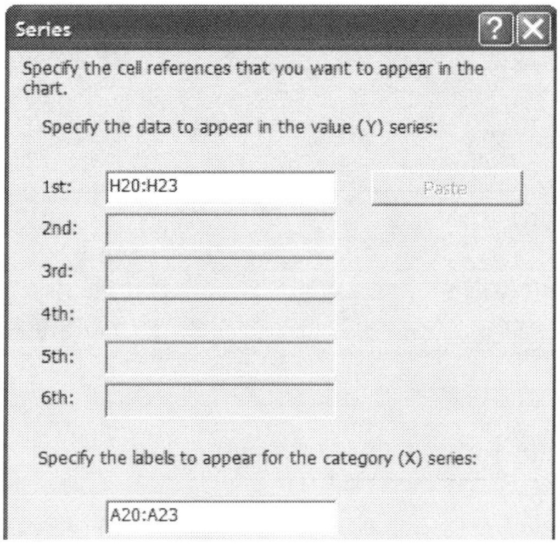

Figure 13-4 Category label range entered

How To Add Data Labels

Pie charts can have two labels for each slice of the chart. You can display the row or column heading, which you created in the previous exercise and you can display the actual value that the slice of the pie is representing.

1. View ⇒ Data Labels.

The values in the two label sections can display a variety of information about the data that the chart represents. In the 1st label drop-down list, notice that the category labels that you created in the previous exercise are selected.

2. Open the 2nd label drop-down list and select the **DATA VALUES** option. This option will print the numeric equivalent of the bar or in this case, the slice of the chart. Your dialog box should have the options selected that are shown in Figure 13-5. Click OK. Your chart should look like the one shown in Figure 13-6.

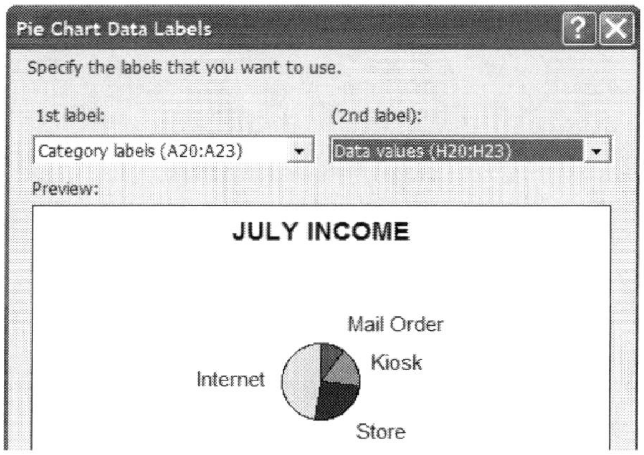

Figure 13-5 Pie Chart Data Labels dialog box options

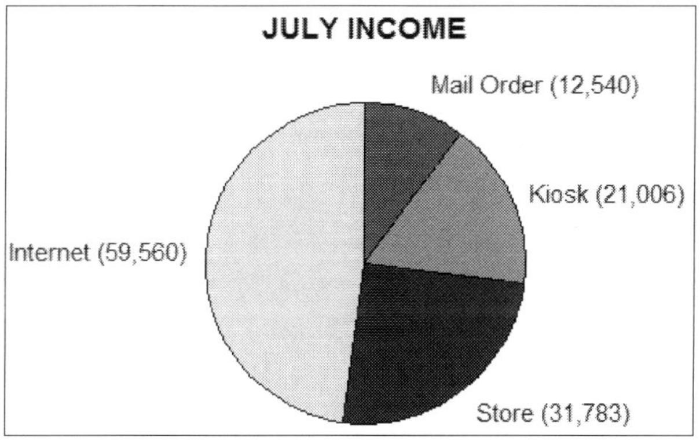

Figure 13-6 Pie chart with data labels added

3. Tools ⇒ Rename Chart. Type July Income Pie in the field at the bottom of the dialog box. Click the Rename button, then click OK.

How To Explode A Slice Of The Pie

Exploding a slice of the pie means to move a slice of the pie away from the rest of the pie.

1. Right-click on the Store slice of the pie and select Shading and Color. You will see the Shading and Color dialog box.

Do you remember me saying in the previous lesson that the "Select" section of the Shading and Color dialog box would be easier to work with if it used names from the legend or in this case, the pie slice name? This is a perfect example of what I mean. You really have no idea which slice of the pie series 1, 2, 3 or 4 is. To me, its little features like this that cause frustration.

2. Change the **PATTERN** to Light Down Diagonal, then check the **EXPLODE SLICE** option. Click the Format button. Don't close the Shading and Color dialog box. Your chart should look like the one shown in Figure 13-7. It will not have the border shown in the figure. I added the border for illustration purposes. In the next exercise you will add a border to the chart.

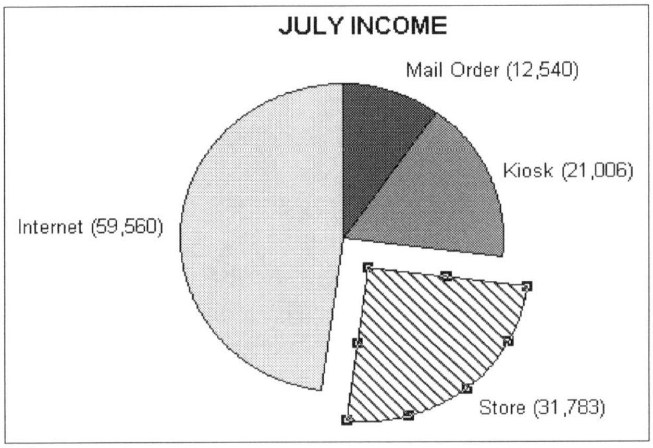

Figure 13-7 Pie chart with an exploded slice

3. Select **SLICE 1** on the Shading and Color dialog box and change the color to Gray -25%. Click the Format button. Click Close, then save the changes.

How To Turn The Chart Into A 3-D Chart

In the previous lesson you learned how to change the bar chart type. Changing a chart type is basically the same, regardless of the type of chart that you start off with. 3-D charts seem to be one of the more popular chart types.

How To Duplicate An Existing Chart

The 3D chart that you will create in this exercise will be based off of the July Income chart that you just created. Instead of creating the 3D chart from scratch, it is sometimes easier to duplicate an existing chart and modify it as needed.

1. Tools ⇒ Duplicate Chart. Type `July Income 3-D` in the field at the bottom of the dialog box.

2. Click the Duplicate button, then click OK.

Change The Chart To A 3-D Chart

1. View ⇒ Chart. Select the July Income 3-D chart and click OK.

2. Click the 3-D button on the toolbar as shown in Figure 13-8.

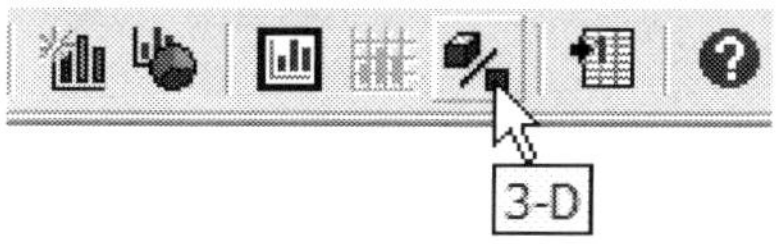

Figure 13-8 3-D button illustrated

3. Click the Chart Type button, then check the **SHOW BORDER** option and click OK.

Modify The 3-D Chart

1. Right-click on the Mail Order slice of the chart and select Shading and Color.

2. Change the pattern to **TRELLIS**, then click the Format button. Select **SLICE 2** and change the color to White.

3. Click the Format button, then click Close. Your chart should look like the one shown in Figure 13-9. Save the changes. Close both charts, but leave the spreadsheet open.

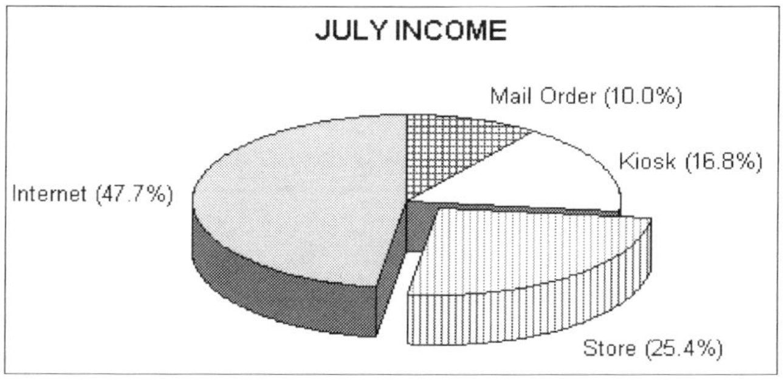

Figure 13-9 3-D Pie chart

If you want to see what a chart that you have created will look like in a different chart type, click the chart type button that corresponds to the chart that you want to see (like 3D Area). Your chart will change to the type that you selected. As soon as you are finished viewing the new format, select **UNDO CHART TYPE** from the Edit menu to return to the original version of the chart.

Create An Area Chart

As discussed in the previous lesson, area charts show how the data has changed over a period of time. In this exercise you will create an area chart and learn how to use the frequency option.

1. Highlight the range A20 to M23 on the L13 Charts spreadsheet, then click the New Chart button and select the Area chart type. (It's the third option on the first row.)

2. Type `Capri Book Company` as the chart title, then check the Show Border option and click OK. Your chart should look like the one shown in Figure 13-10.

The chart looks good as it is.
One thing that is missing is that you do not know what the range is.
If the month names were across the bottom of the chart, you would know what the markers across the bottom of the chart represent. This would make the chart easier to understand.

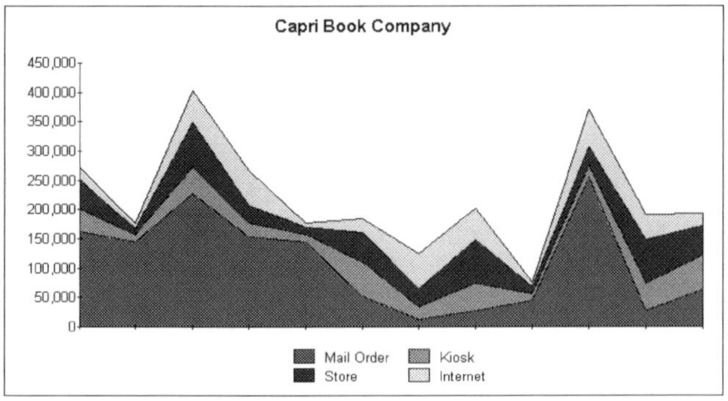

Figure 13-10 Area chart

Add A Subtitle To The Chart

1. Edit ⇒ Titles.

2. Type `Income` in the Chart subtitle field and click OK.

Add Category Labels Across The Bottom Of The Chart

The values for the months are in cells B5 to M5.

1. Edit ⇒ Series.

2. Type `B5:M5` in the **CATEGORY (X) SERIES** field at the bottom of the dialog box and click OK.

If you cannot see the full names for all 12 months across the bottom of the chart, you have the three options that are listed below that can be used to modify the category labels.

① Make the font size smaller.
② Type in the abbreviated month names in the spreadsheet and insert them in the chart.
③ Change the label frequency.

How To Change The Font Size Of The Category Labels

1. Click on any of the month names and change the font size to 8.

Rename The Chart

1. Tools ⇒ Rename Chart. Type `Income-Fontsize` as the chart name.

2. Click the Rename button, then click OK and save the changes.

How To Create Abbreviated Month Names For A Chart

In this exercise you will modify the chart to show abbreviated month names across the bottom of the chart. Once you changed the font size of the category labels you were able to see the entire month name. If that did not solve the problem of not being able to see the entire category label, you could abbreviate the labels, which would make them easier to read. This is what you will learn how to do in this exercise.

Duplicate The Chart

1. Tools ⇒ Duplicate Chart. Select the Income-Fontsize chart.

2. Type `Income Months` as the chart name, then click the Duplicate button. Click OK and save the changes.

Create The Abbreviated Month Names

The spreadsheet currently does not have the month names in abbreviated format, so you have to create them on the spreadsheet.

1. Window ⇒ L13 Charts.xlr. Highlight the range B41 to M41. Yes, these cells are empty.
2. Right-click on the highlighted cells and select Format. Select the **TEXT** format type and click OK.
3. Type `JAN` in cell B41, then fill the range B41 to M41 with the abbreviated months. (Edit ⇒ Fill Series). Abbreviated month names should be in cells B41 to M41. Save the changes.

Add The Abbreviated Month Names To The Chart

1. View ⇒ Chart, then select the Income Months chart and click OK.
2. Right-click on any of the month names and change the font size to 12.
3. Edit ⇒ Series. Type `B41:M41` in the Category (X) Series field at the bottom of the dialog box. This range points to the abbreviated month names that you just created in the spreadsheet. Click OK. Your chart should look like the one shown in Figure 13-11. Save the changes to the chart.

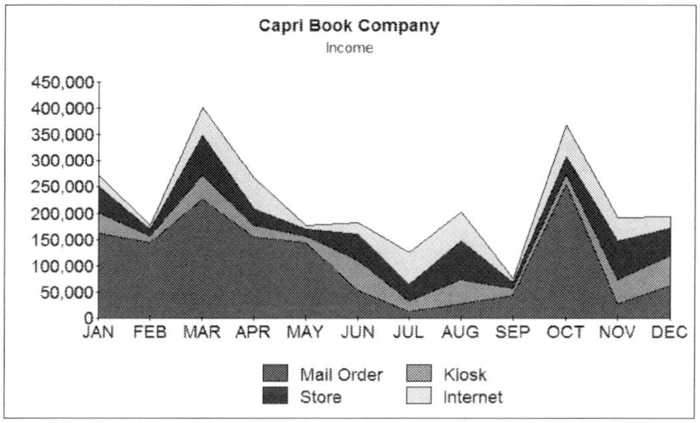

Figure 13-11 Area chart with abbreviated names

How To Change The Label Frequency

Label frequency refers to the number of labels that are shown across the bottom of the chart. The area chart may be easier to read if all 12 months were not shown across the bottom of the chart. This is what the frequency refers to - how many times something is displayed on the chart.

Duplicate The Chart

1. Tools ⇒ Duplicate Chart. Select the Income-Fontsize chart.
2. Type `Income FRQ/GRID` as the name for the new chart. (FRQ/Grid is an abbreviation that I made up for frequency and gridlines).
3. Click the Duplicate button, then click OK.

Change The Label Frequency

1. View ⇒ Chart. Select the Income FRQ/GRID chart and click OK.

2. Right-click on one of the months and select the Horizontal (X) Axis option. You should see the dialog box shown in Figure 13-12.

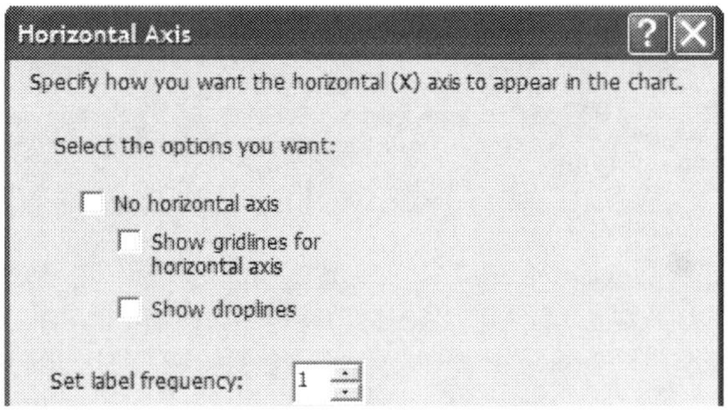

Figure 13-12 Horizontal Axis dialog box

3. Change the Label Frequency to 2 and click OK. Your chart should look like the one shown in Figure 13-13. You should only see every other month across the bottom of the chart.

As you saw in Figure 13-12 above, you can add gridlines and droplines to your chart.

DROPLINES are lines that go from the data point to the X axis and show where one marker ends and another one starts.

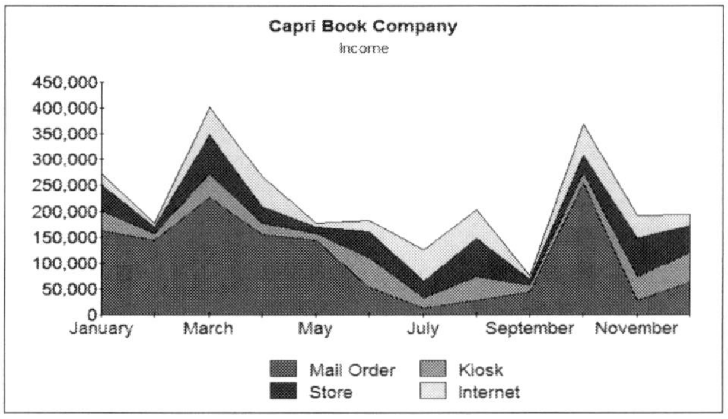

Figure 13-13 Label frequency modified

4. Open the Horizontal X Axis dialog box again and add the droplines. Your chart should look like the one shown in Figure 13-14.

Droplines can be useful to show each month on this chart when only every other month's name is shown across the bottom of the chart. For example, the dropline between January and March is referencing February's data.

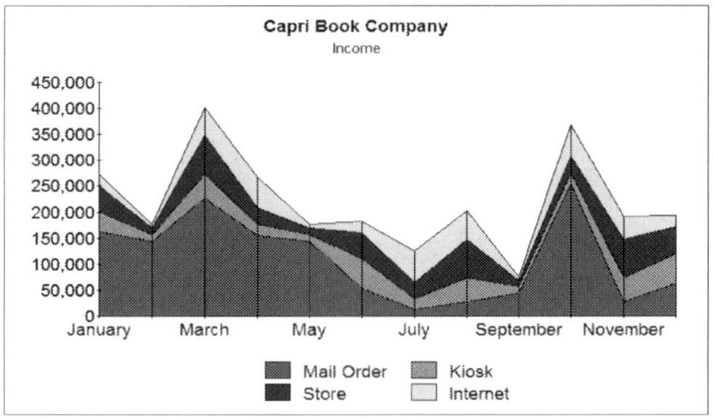

Figure 13-14 Droplines added to the chart

How To Add Gridlines To A Chart

Sometimes it is helpful to see vertical and horizontal gridlines on a chart.

1. Open the Horizontal X Axis dialog box. Select **SHOW GRIDLINES FOR HORIZONTAL AXIS** and click OK.

2. Format ⇒ Vertical (Y) Axis. Select the option, **SHOW GRIDLINES FOR VERTICAL AXIS** as shown in Figure 13-15. Click OK. Your chart should look like the one shown in Figure 13-16.

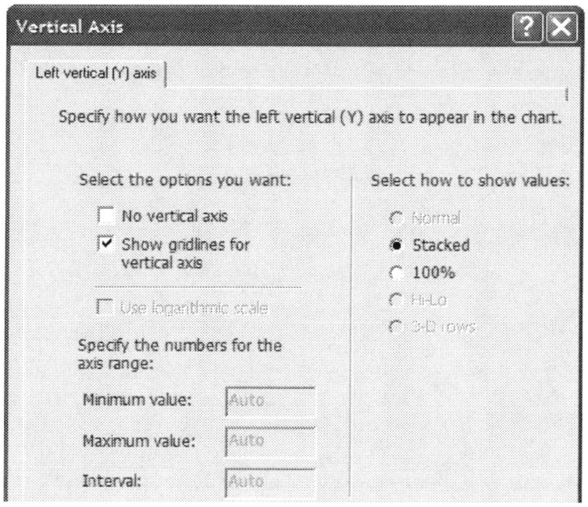

Figure 13-15 Vertical Axis dialog box

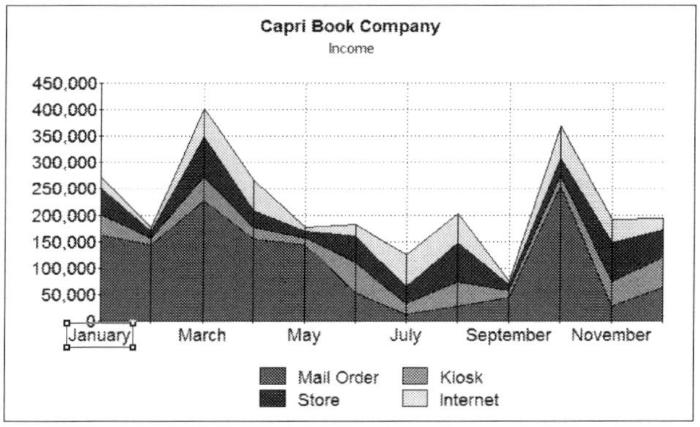

Figure 13-16 Horizontal and vertical gridlines added to the chart

3. Save the changes to the chart and spreadsheet, then close the spreadsheet.

Create A Line Chart

Line charts are often used when you want to see a trend in the data, opposed to each actual value that the chart is created from.

1. Save the L12 Actual vs Projected spreadsheet as `L13 Actual vs Projected`.

2. Highlight the range A12 to C15, then click the New Chart button.

3. Select the Line chart type (It's the first option in the second row.) and type `Current Actual vs Projected Sales` as the chart title.

4. Check the Show border and Show gridines options, then click OK. Your chart should look like the one shown in Figure 13-17.

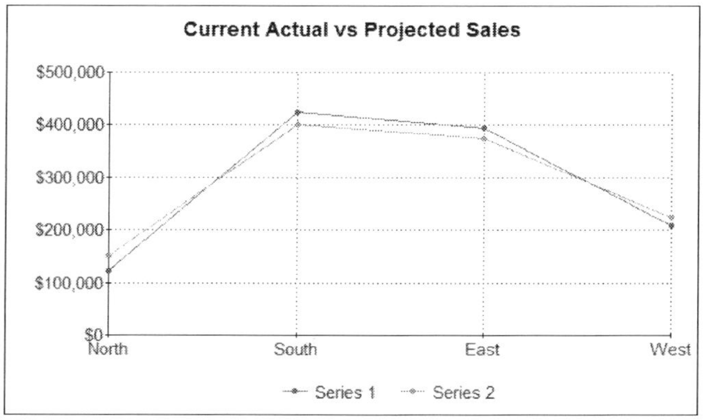

Figure 13-17 Line chart

Modify The Line Chart

1. Edit ⇒ Legend/Series Labels. Select the option, **USE VALUES IN SPREADSHEET FOR SERIES LABELS** and type `Actual Sales` in the 1st value series field.

2. Type `Projected Sales` in the 2nd value series field. Your dialog box should have the options shown in Figure 13-18. Click OK. The legend should have changed. Save the changes.

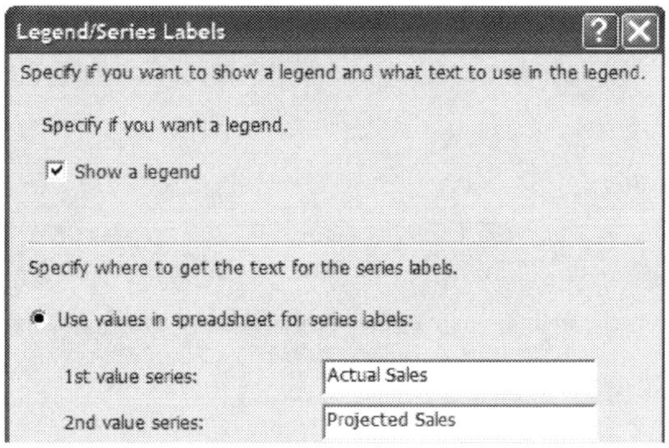

Figure 13-18 Legend/Series Labels dialog box with the options filled in

How To Verify And Rename The Data In A Chart

How do you know that you are adding the right name to the right line in the chart? Charts are created from the spreadsheet in the order that the data appears. You would not see data from column H before data from column B in the chart. To make sure that the labels on the chart are correct, you need to confirm that the actual sales amount is less than the projected sales amount for the North.

1. Window ⇒ L13 Actual vs Projected.xlr.

The actual current sales amount in cell B12 is $123,000 and the projected sales amount in cell C12 is $150,000 for the North. $123,000 is less than $150,000, which lets you know that you have labeled the lines in the chart correctly.

2. Window ⇒ Actual vs Projected.xlr-Chart1.
3. Tools ⇒ Rename Chart. Select Chart1, if it is not already selected and type `Act Proj Line` as the chart name. (This is short for Actual Projected Line Chart.)
4. Click the Rename button, then click OK. Save the changes.

Create A 3-D Line Chart

In this exercise you will create a 3-D line chart that is based off of an existing line chart.

1. Duplicate the Act Proj Line chart. Type `Act/Proj 3D` as the file name for the new chart.
2. Open the Act/Proj 3D chart, then click the Chart type button on the toolbar.
3. Select the 3-D Line chart option as illustrated in Figure 13-19. On the **VARIATIONS** tab, select the third chart option in the first row as illustrated in Figure 13-20. Click OK. Your chart should look like the one shown in Figure 13-21. Save the changes and close the chart.

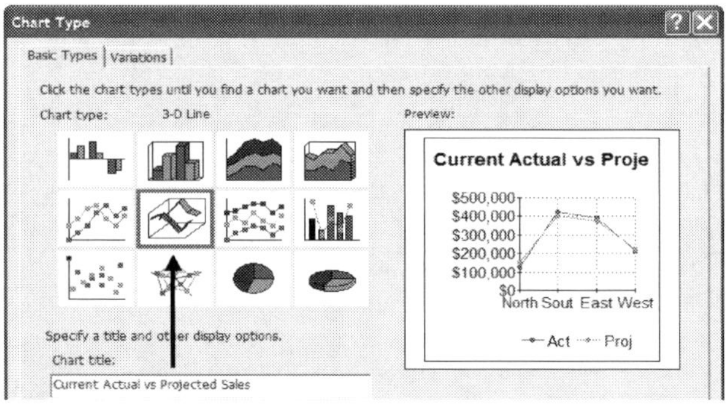

Figure 13-19 3-D Line chart option illustrated

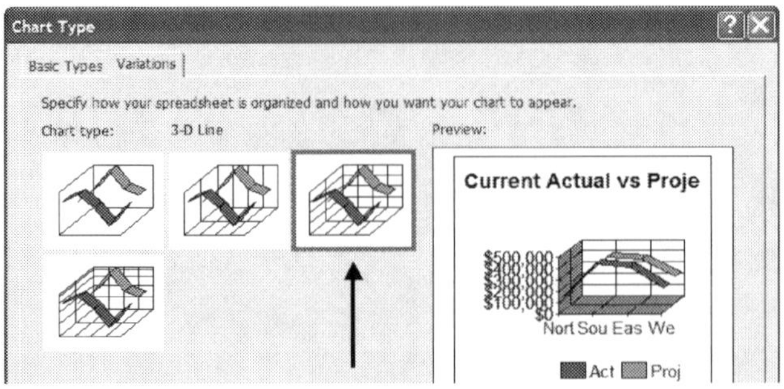

Figure 13-20 3-D Line chart variation options

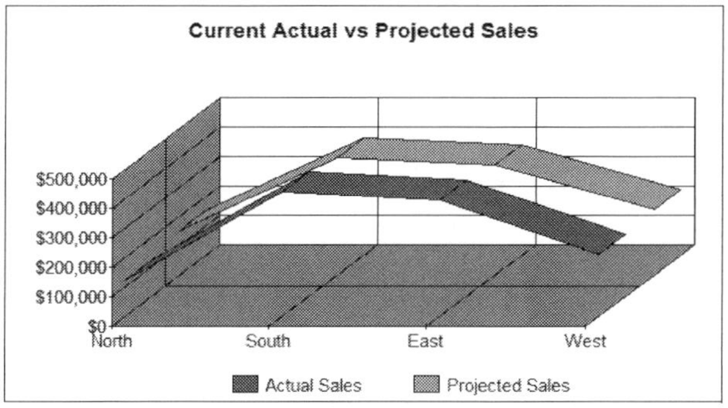

Figure 13-21 3-D Line chart

Create A 3-D Bar Chart

Earlier I mentioned that you can change the chart type of an existing chart to a different chart type. In this exercise you will create a 3-D bar chart from an existing line chart.

1. Duplicate the Actual vs Proj chart. Type `Actual 3D` as the file name for the new chart.
2. Open the Actual 3D chart and click the Chart Type button on the toolbar.
3. Select the 3-D Bar option (It's the second option in the first row.). On the Variations tab select the third chart type in the second row.
4. Click OK. Your chart should look like the one shown in Figure 13-22. Save the changes. Close the charts and the spreadsheet.

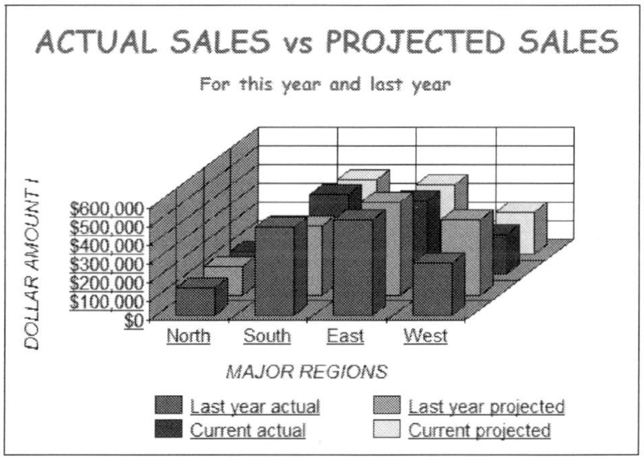

Figure 13-22 3-D Bar chart

Create A Combination Chart

As you learned in the previous lesson, combination charts are a mixture of line and bar charts.

1. Open the L13 Charts spreadsheet and highlight the range A20 to M23 on the spreadsheet, then click the New Chart button and select the Combination chart type. (It's the last option in the second row.)
2. Type `Capri Book Company` as the chart title. Check the Show Border option and click OK.

Modify The Combination Chart

The chart on your screen is pretty hard to read. It would look better if the following changes were made. The next few exercises will walk you through completing all of these tasks.

- ☑ One of the line series on the chart was a bar.
- ☑ Abbreviated months were across the bottom of the chart.
- ☑ The lines had distinguishable markers for easy reference.
- ☑ Add vertical gridlines.
- ☑ Add header and footer information.

Change A Line Series To A Bar Series

1. Format ⇒ Line and Bar. You should see the dialog box shown in Figure 13-23. Each value can be a line or a bar. As shown in Figure 13-23, only the 1st value (Y) series is a bar.

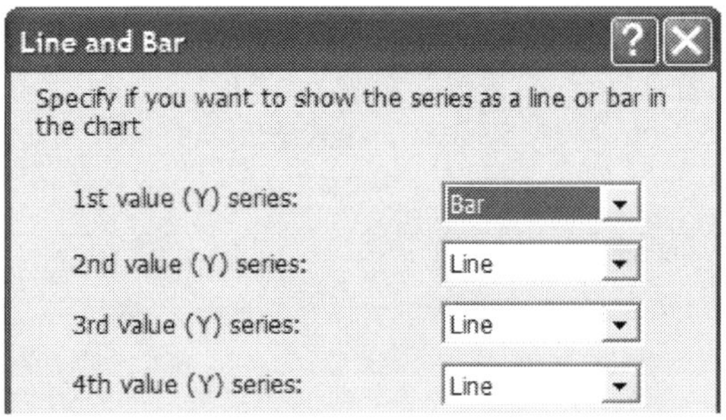

Figure 13-23 Line and Bar dialog box

2. Select the Bar option for the 4th value and click OK. You should now see two bars of data and two lines of data on the chart.

Add Months Across The Bottom Of The Chart

1. Edit ⇒ Series.

2. Type `B41:M41` in the Category (X) Series field at the bottom of the Series dialog box. You created the abbreviated month names earlier in this lesson. Click OK. Your chart should look like the one shown in Figure 13-24.

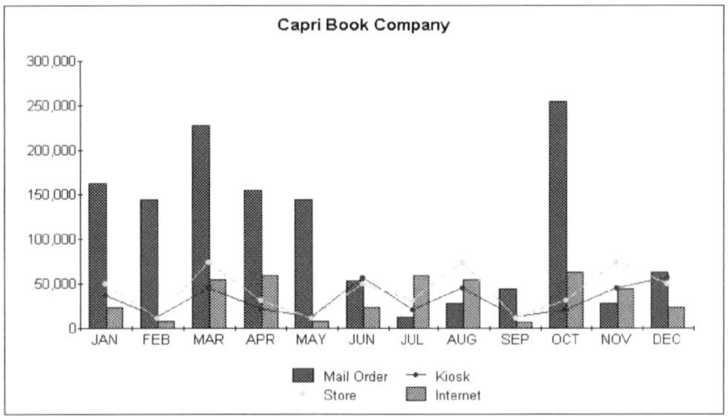

Figure 13-24 Months added across the bottom of the chart

Add Markers To A Chart

1. Right-click on the yellow line in the chart and select Shading and Color. The third series should be highlighted on the dialog box.

2. Change the color to Black, then change the **LINE STYLE** to Dotted, which is the next to last Line style option shown in Figure 13-25.

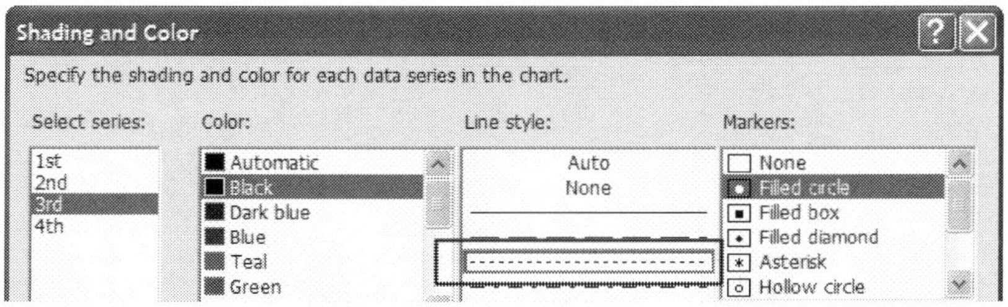

Figure 13-25 Line style option illustrated

3. Change the **MARKER** to Hollow diamond, then click the Format button.

Change The Shading And Color Options For Other Series On The Chart

1. Select the 4th series and change the **COLOR** to Gray -25%, then change the **PATTERN** to Light Grid. Click the Format button.

2. Select the 1st series and change the **PATTERN** to 50%, then click the Format button. Click Close. Your chart should look like the one shown in Figure 13-26.

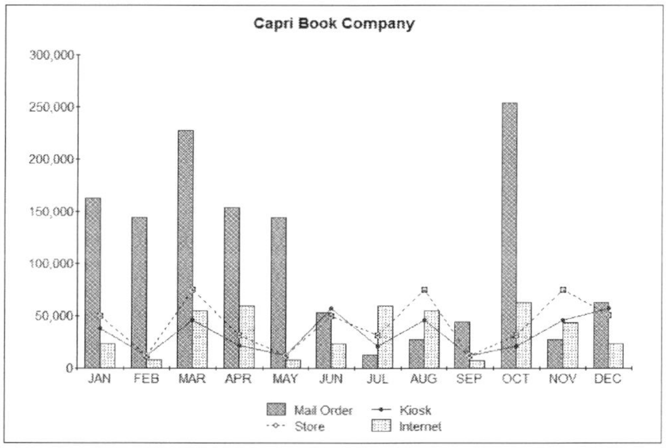

Figure 13-26 Colors and markers modified on the chart

Add Vertical Gridlines

1. Format ⇒ Vertical (Y) Axis.

2. Check the Show gridlines for vertical option and click OK. Your chart should look like the one shown in Figure 13-27.

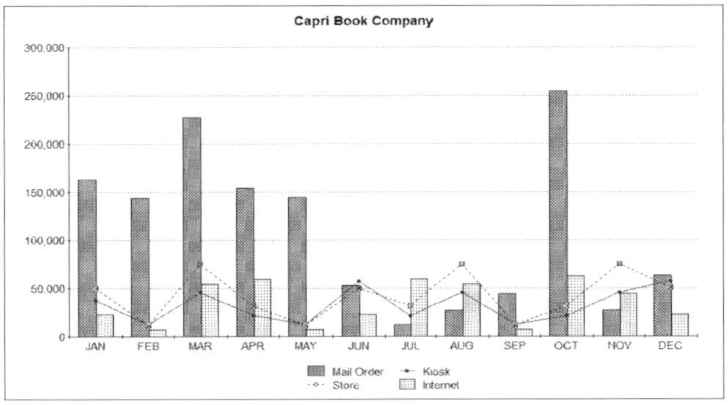

Figure 13-27 Vertical gridlines added to the combination chart

Add Header And Footer Information To A Chart

You can add headers and footers to charts, just like you can add them to spreadsheets or word processing documents.

1. View ⇒ Header and Footer.

2. Type `Confidential Information` in the Left Header field, then type `Internal Use Only` in the Left Footer field and click OK.

> To view the header and footer information on a chart, you have to go into Print Preview.

3. Rename the Chart1 chart. Type `Income Combo` as the chart name.

4. Edit ⇒ Titles. Type `Income Combo Chart` as the chart subtitle and click OK, then save the changes.

Printing Charts

Before you print a chart, it is a good idea to preview it to check the layout. Usually, the chart looks good in design view. The chart may not look the same in print preview.

1. View the chart that you just created. You should see that the chart looks a little squished.

2. Go into Page Setup and change the orientation to **LANDSCAPE**, then click OK. Preview the chart. It should look like the one shown in Figure 13-28. Save the changes. Close the chart and spreadsheet.

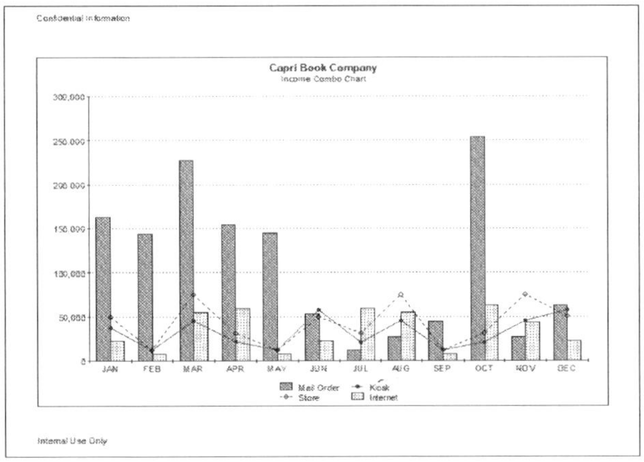

Figure 13-28 Income combo chart

For practice you can print out a few charts as they are, then change the orientation or margin options and print them again to see which options work best with the various types of charts that you have created.

Test Your Skills

1. Save the Inventory spreadsheet as `L13(skills)`.

   - Create an area chart.
   - Add drop lines and gridlines.
   - Name the chart `Area_Skills`.

2. Duplicate the area chart that you created above and change it to a 3-D line chart similar to the one shown earlier in Figure 13-21.

   - Name the duplicate chart `3D_Area_Skills`.

DATABASE BASICS

In this lesson you will be introduced to databases. You will learn how to do the following:

- ☑ Create a database from scratch
- ☑ Change field sizes, number formats and field alignments

LESSON 14

What Is A Database?

A database is a collection of related information. A products database will have one record for each product that a company sells. Each record will contain information about one product like the product number, product name, price, quantity on hand and quantity on order. Each piece of information in the record is stored in a field. Fields are similar to columns in a spreadsheet.

Before you create a database you should plan it out on paper by listing all of the fields that you will need. You should take into consideration what you will use the database for. If you will be printing business letters, you may need a field to store the persons title, in addition to their name and address.

Database Toolbar And Menu

Works comes with database templates that you can use as is, or modify to meet your needs. Figure 14-1 shows the database toolbar and Table 14-1 explains the purpose of each button. Figure 14-2 shows the database menu. Table 14-2 explains the menu options.

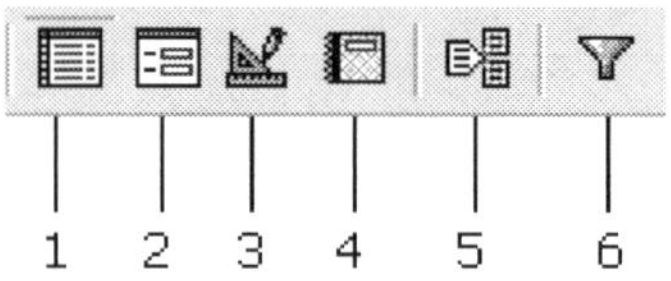

Figure 14-1 Database toolbar

Button	Purpose
1	**List View** lets you view the data in a database in spreadsheet format.
2	**Form View** lets you view and enter the data on a form, one record at a time.
3	**Form Design** lets you modify the form.
4	**Report View** lets you view and modify a report.
5	**Insert Record** lets you add a new record to the database.
6	**Filters** lets you create, use or modify a filter.

Table 14-1 Database toolbar buttons explained

Figure 14-2 Database menu

Menu	Purpose
File	Used for opening, saving, creating and printing databases.
Edit	The commands on this menu will let you copy, paste and cut, as well as, select records and fields, fill in a range of cells and replace data.
View	Change how the database is displayed on the screen.
Record	Add records and fields, as well as, sort the database.
Format	Format numbers, alignment, fonts, adjust record height and change the field width.
Tools	Contains the spell check tool and the report options like creating, renaming and deleting.
Help	Opens the Help System.

Table 14-2 Database menus explained

Database And Spreadsheet Similarities

As you will see, the database window has a lot of the same characteristics that the spreadsheet window has. Below are some of the similarities that databases and spreadsheets have.

- ☑ They look similar.
- ☑ You can use formulas and functions.
- ☑ The row height and column width can be adjusted.
- ☑ Search and replace.
- ☑ Fill Series options.

If you have used other software packages to create a database, the one thing that you will notice is that the database package in Works does not allow you to create multiple tables in the database.

Database Customizations And Options

There are some features that you can change in the database application as discussed below.

Customizations

The one feature that you can customize in the database application is the toolbar. You can add or remove buttons. This is a read-only exercise, meaning that you will not add or remove any buttons on your toolbar now. If you have the need to add or remove buttons on the toolbar later, you can come back to this section and modify your toolbar as needed.

1. Open a new database by clicking on the Programs link on the Task Launcher. Select **WORKS DATABASE**, then click on the **START A BLANK DATABASE** link.

2. Click the **ADD** button on the Create Database dialog box, then click **DONE**.

3. Tools ⇒ Customize Toolbar. You will see the dialog box shown in Figure 14-3.

   The **CATEGORIES** on the left side of the dialog box correspond to the menu options on the database window.

   When you click on a category, the buttons that you can add to the toolbar will be displayed in the **TOOLBAR BUTTONS** section of the dialog box.

   The option **REMOVE FONT NAME AND POINT SIZE FROM THE TOOLBAR** will hide the font name and font size options on the toolbar.

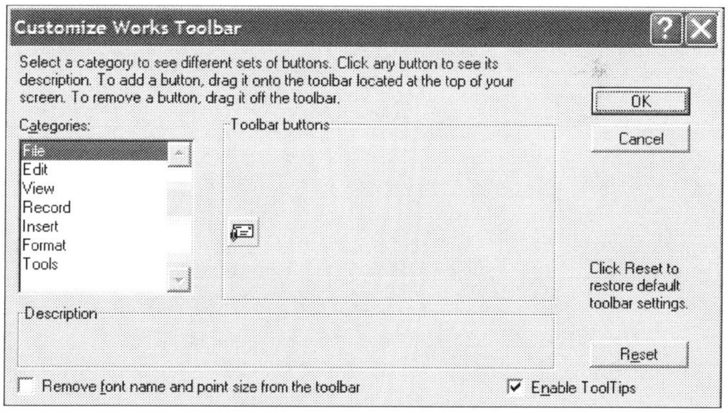

Figure 14-3 Customize Works Toolbar dialog box

   If you don't want to see the tool tips in the database application clear the option, **ENABLE TOOLTIPS** in the lower right corner of the dialog box.

4. Click on the **RECORD** category. You should see the toolbar buttons shown in Figure 14-4.

If you wanted to add a button to the toolbar, drag it from the dialog box up to the toolbar where you want to place it.

If you want to remove a button from the toolbar, click on the button that you want to remove on the toolbar and drag it off the toolbar. You have to do this when the Customize Works Toolbar dialog box is open.

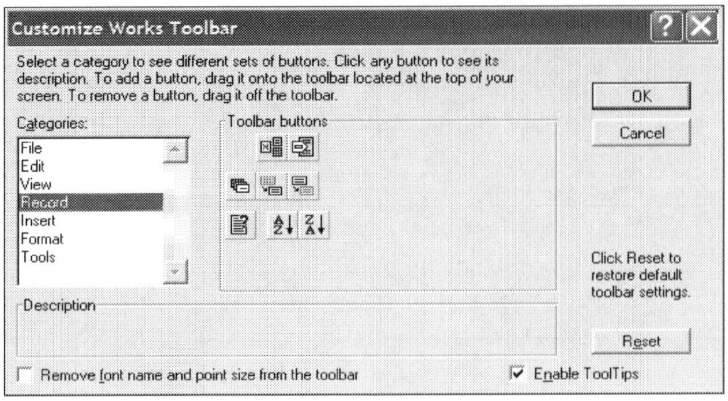

Figure 14-4 Record menu toolbar button options illustrated

5. For now close the dialog box by clicking Cancel.

Options

The options allow you to change how you work with a database. You do not have to make any changes now. You can read about the options that are available. You can come back to this section and make any changes that you need.

1. Tools ⇒ Options. Click on the General tab.

   The options shown in Figure 14-5 let you change the unit of measure, the format that you want to send a database in, if you send it in an email and the dictionary that you want to use.

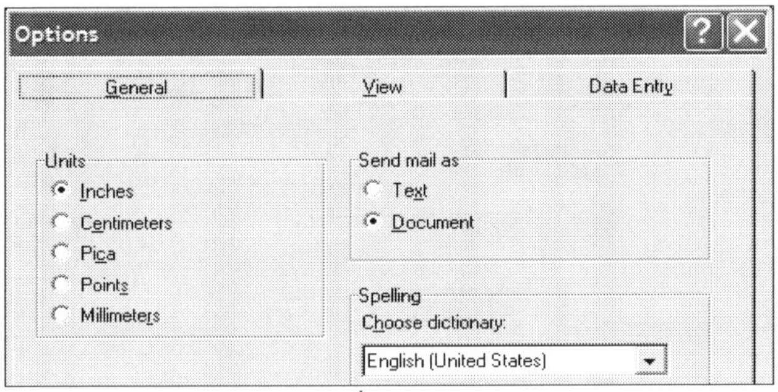

Figure 14-5 General tab options

2. Click on the View tab.

   The choices shown in Figure 14-6 let you select options that can help you when you are using a database. These options provide additional help.

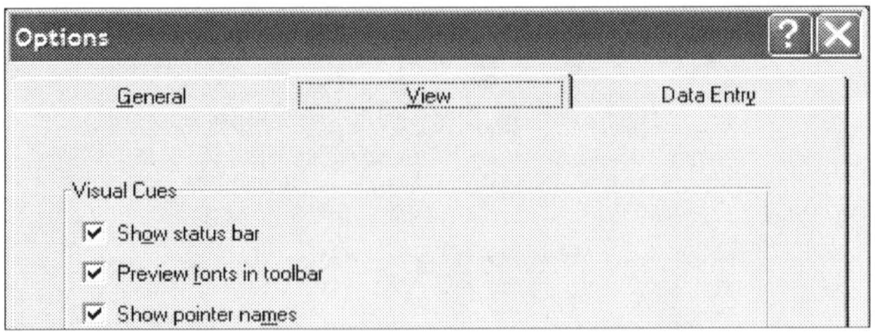

Figure 14-6 View tab options

3. Click on the Data Entry tab.

The choices shown in Figure 14-7 let you select options that you can use when typing information into the database.

The **CELL DATA ENTRY MODES** options determine the places that you can enter data in the List view.

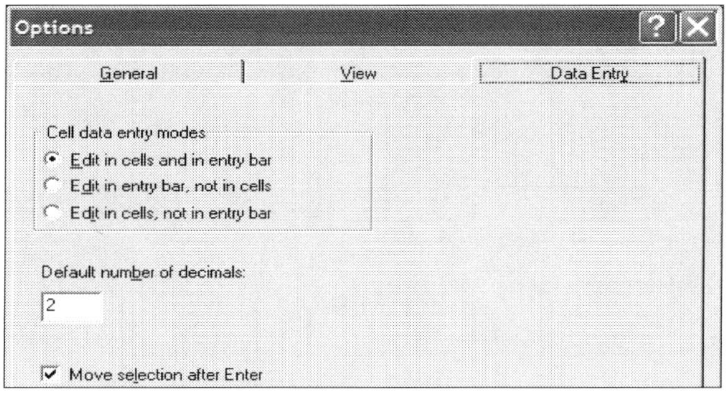

Figure 14-7 Data Entry tab options

Figure 14-8 shows the Entry bar in the database window. The Entry bar should look familiar because it is similar to the Formula bar in the spreadsheet application.

Figure 14-8 Entry bar illustrated

4. Close the Options dialog box. Close the database, but do not save the changes.

Create A Database From Scratch

In this exercise you will create a Products database. This database will store all of the products for a company.

1. Click on the **DATABASE** icon on the Home Page of the Task Launcher, then select the **BLANK DATABASE** option if it is not already selected, as shown in Figure 14-9.

As shown in Figure 14-9, there are three types of databases that you can open in Works, as discussed below.

① Select the **BLANK DATABASE** option when you want to create a new database.
② Select the **TEMPLATE** option when you want to create a new database that is based off of a database template. The database template can be one of the default ones that comes with Works as shown in Figure 14-10 or a database template that you create.
③ Select the **EXISTING** option when you want to open a database that has already been created.

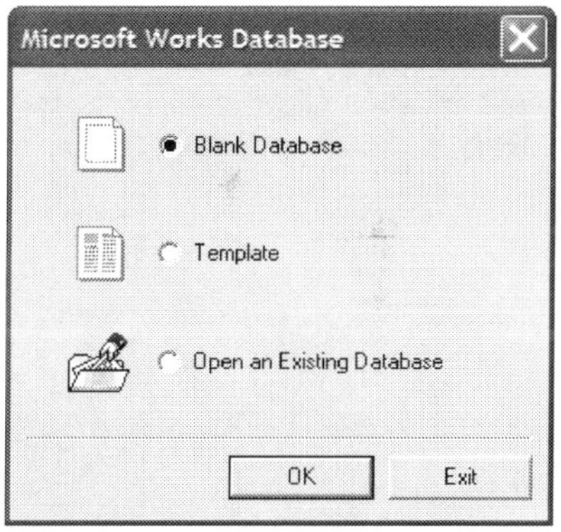

Figure 14-9 Database options

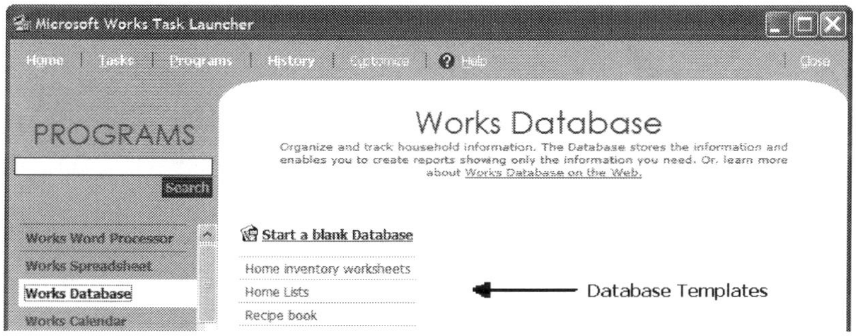

Figure 14-10 Database templates that come with Works

2. Click OK. You will see the dialog box shown in Figure 14-11.

   This dialog box lets you add fields to the database and specify the format for each field. Field formats will be explained later in the lesson.

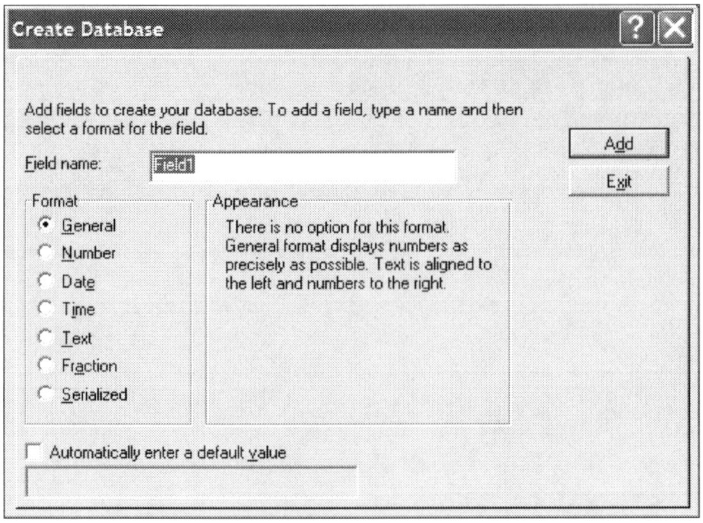

Figure 14-11 Create Database dialog box

Database field names can be a maximum of 15 characters.

3. Type `Product Number` in the Field name field and select the Text format.

The reason that you are selecting the Text format instead of the number format is because the product number will contain special characters like a dash, like product number CH-100.

4. Click Add. The Product Number field should be visible as a column in the database window.

Field Formats Explained

There are seven field formats that you can select from as described below. Each field type allows you to store a different type of data.

① **General** any type of text or numeric value can be stored in this field format.

You may be thinking that to make things easy you should use the General format for all of the fields that you create. Just the opposite is true. You should only use the General format if none of the field formats discussed below is appropriate.

② **Number** allows you to enter numeric values.
③ **Date** allows you to enter dates in several formats.
④ **Time** allows you to enter times in several formats.
⑤ **Text** allows you to enter text or numeric values that may contain special characters, like parenthesis in phone numbers.
⑥ **Fraction** allows you to enter fractions like ½ or ¼.
⑦ **Serialized** format will automatically fill in sequential numbers each time a new record is added to the database. A good use of this format would be in an invoice database, where each invoice requires a unique number.

Add More Fields To The Database

1. Type `Product Name` in the Field name field on the Create Database dialog box and select the Text format, then click **ADD**.

2. Type `Qty On Hand` in the Field name field and select the Number format.

3. In the **APPEARANCE** section select 1,234.56 and change the **DECIMAL PLACES** to `0` (zero) as shown in Figure 14-12.

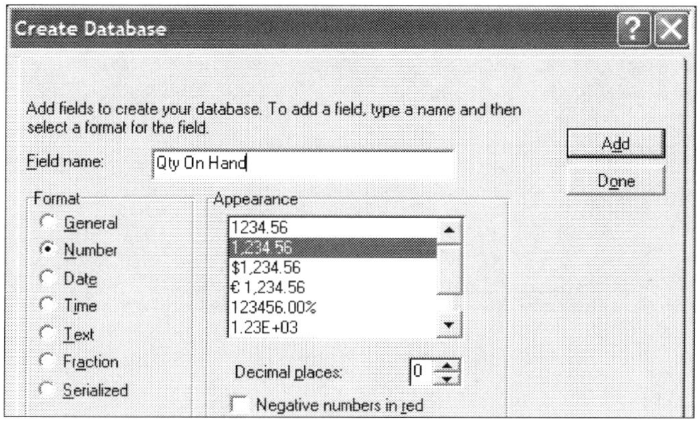

Figure 14-12 Decimal places set to zero

4. Click Add, then add the three fields in Table 14-3 to the database. When you are finished, do not click the **DONE** button. You will add more fields to the database in the next exercise.

Field Name	Format	Appearance	Decimal Places
Price	Number	$1,234.56	2
Cost	Number	$1,234.56	2
Date Ordered	Date	mm/dd/yyyy (1)	

Table 14-3 Fields to add to the database

(1) It's the first option in the list.

How Create A Default Value For A Field

If the option **AUTOMATICALLY ENTER A DEFAULT VALUE** is selected for a field, each record added to the database would have the default value automatically filled in the field. This will save time during data entry because data would not always have to be entered into the field. If the default value is not what you need for a particular record, you can type over it.

An example of a when to use a default value is if you are entering names and addresses and they are all in the same state. You could enter the two character abbreviation for the state as the default value. Every address that you enter will automatically have the state field filled in.

1. Type `Qty On Order` in the Field name field and select the Number format.

2. Select the appearance 1,234.56, then change the decimal places to zero.

The reason that you have to set the decimal places to zero is because you only want to allow whole numbers in the Qty On Order field. For example, you would not order 5.75 copies of a book.

3. Check the option Automatically enter a default value, then type `25` in the field below this option. Figure 14-13 shows the options that you should have selected.

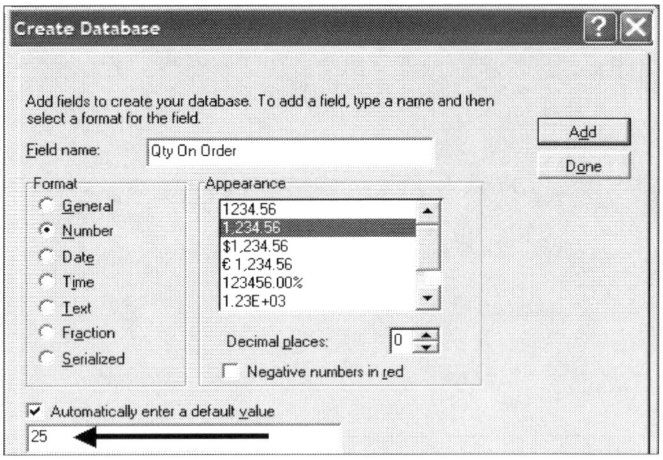

Figure 14-13 Default value entered

4. Click the Add button, then click the Done button. Your database should look like the one shown in Figure 14-14.

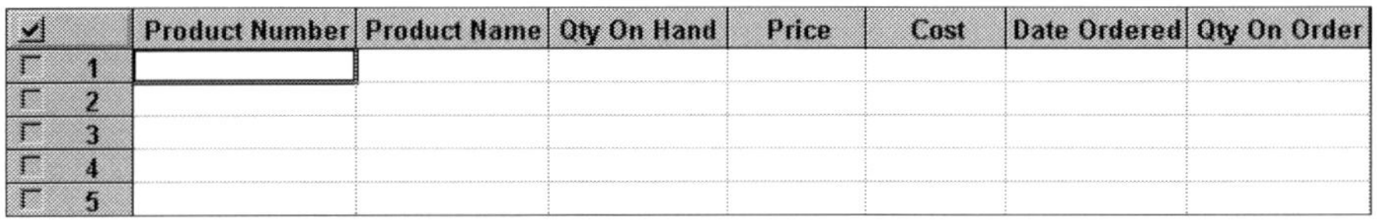

Figure 14-14 Database in List view

5. Click Save, then navigate to your folder and type `L14 Products Database` as the file name.

How To Modify A Field Name

If you noticed that you made a mistake in the field name, follow the steps below to correct it. If you haven't made any mistakes so far in this exercise, you can read through this section now to become familiar with how to modify a field, should the need arise in the future.

1. Click on the field name that you need to change, then Format ⇒ Field. You will see the dialog box shown in Figure 14-15.

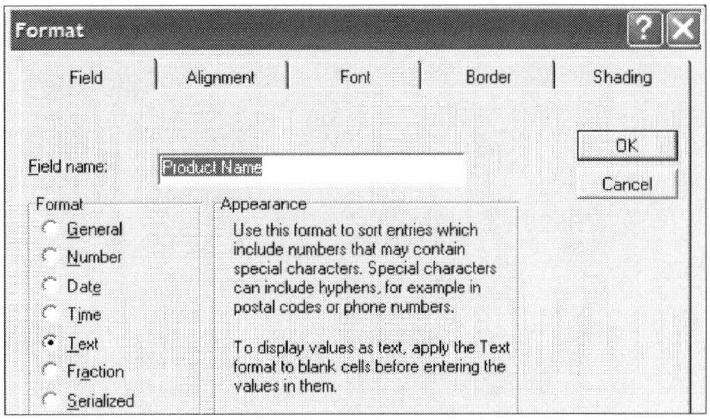

Figure 14-15 Format dialog box

2. Make the changes to the field name, then click OK.

Changing Field Format Defaults

Many of the default formats for fields may not be what you need. The dialog box shown above in Figure 14-15 displays tabs for alignment, font, border and shading formats. Figures 14-16 to 14-19 show the options that are available on each of these tabs. The **WRAP TEXT** alignment option shown in Figure 14-16 if selected, will force the data in the field to automatically wrap if the data is longer than the width of the field. This works the same way as the wrap text feature in the spreadsheet application.

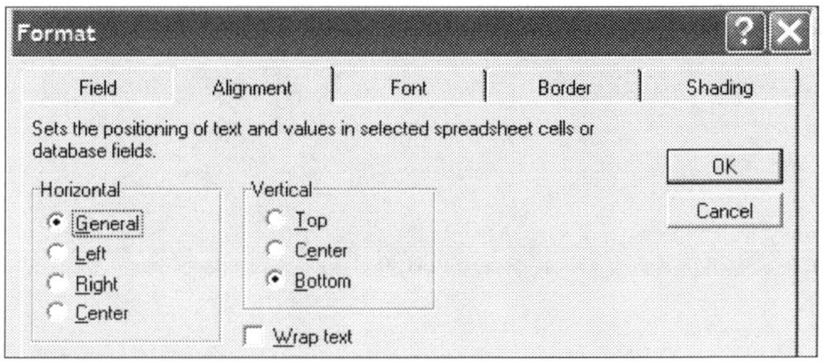

Figure 14-16 Alignment tab options

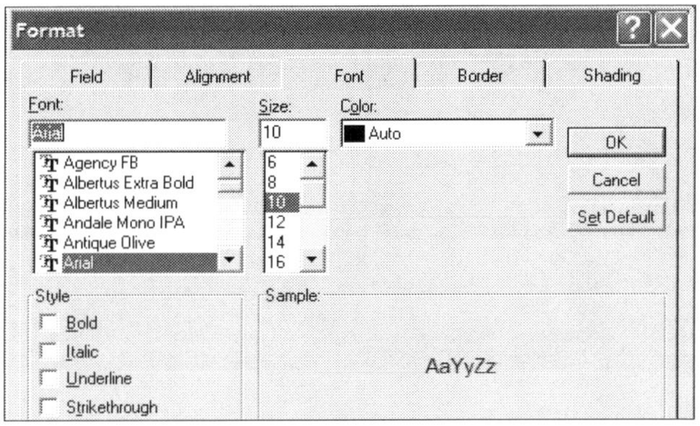

Figure 14-17 Font tab options

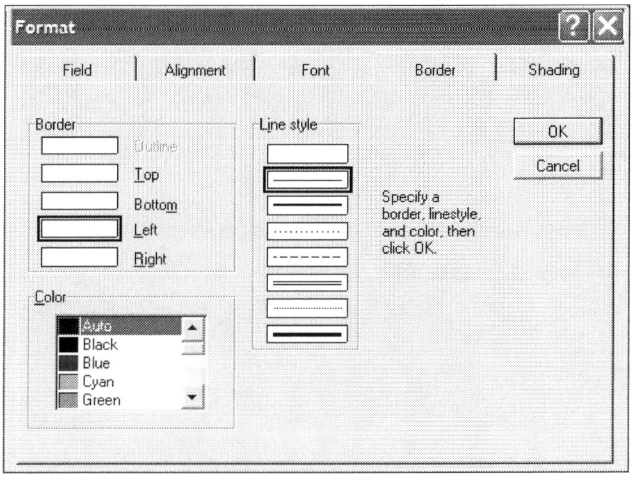

Figure 14-18 Border tab options

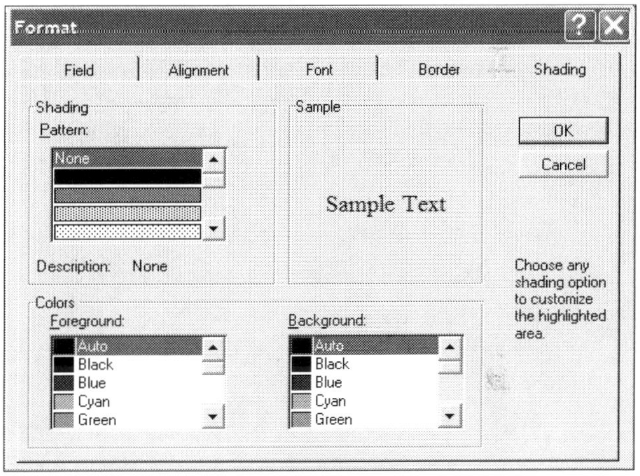

Figure 14-19 Shading tab options

1. Click on the Product Number column heading. Format $\Rightarrow$ Field.

2. On the Alignment tab **RIGHT** for the Horizontal position and click OK.

Selecting this option for the Product Number field will cause the data that is entered in the field to be right aligned, just like the feature does in a word processing or spreadsheet file.

3. Save the changes and leave the database open.

How To Copy Records From One Database To Another

1. Open the Products database. (This is not the database that you just created. This is the one that you downloaded from the web site for this workbook.)

2. Click in the first row of the Product Number field, then scroll down until row 21 is highlighted. Scroll to the right without letting go of the mouse button until the Qty On Order column is highlighted, as shown in Figure 14-20.

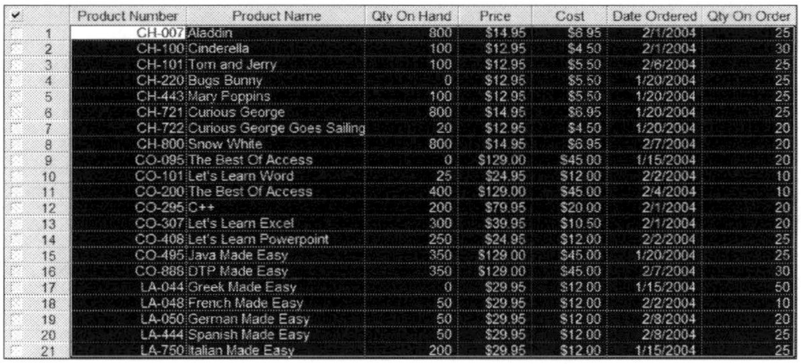

	Product Number	Product Name	Qty On Hand	Price	Cost	Date Ordered	Qty On Order
1	CH-007	Aladdin	800	$14.95	$6.95	2/1/2004	25
2	CH-100	Cinderella	100	$12.95	$4.50	2/1/2004	30
3	CH-101	Tom and Jerry	100	$12.95	$5.50	2/6/2004	25
4	CH-220	Bugs Bunny	0	$12.95	$5.50	1/20/2004	25
5	CH-443	Mary Poppins	100	$12.95	$5.50	1/20/2004	25
6	CH-721	Curious George	800	$14.95	$6.95	1/20/2004	25
7	CH-722	Curious George Goes Sailing	20	$12.95	$4.50	1/20/2004	20
8	CH-800	Snow White	800	$14.95	$6.95	2/7/2004	20
9	CO-095	The Best Of Access	0	$129.00	$45.00	1/15/2004	20
10	CO-101	Let's Learn Word	25	$24.95	$12.00	2/2/2004	10
11	CO-200	The Best Of Access	400	$129.00	$45.00	2/4/2004	10
12	CO-295	C++	200	$79.95	$20.00	2/1/2004	20
13	CO-307	Let's Learn Excel	300	$39.95	$10.50	2/1/2004	20
14	CO-408	Let's Learn Powerpoint	250	$24.95	$12.00	2/2/2004	25
15	CO-495	Java Made Easy	350	$129.00	$45.00	1/20/2004	25
16	CO-888	DTP Made Easy	350	$129.00	$45.00	2/7/2004	30
17	LA-044	Greek Made Easy	0	$29.95	$12.00	1/15/2004	50
18	LA-048	French Made Easy	50	$29.95	$12.00	2/2/2004	10
19	LA-050	German Made Easy	50	$29.95	$12.00	2/8/2004	20
20	LA-444	Spanish Made Easy	50	$29.95	$12.00	2/8/2004	25
21	LA-750	Italian Made Easy	200	$29.95	$12.00	1/15/2004	25

Figure 14-20 Data highlighted to be copied

3. Right-click on the highlighted cells and select **COPY** as shown in Figure 14-21.

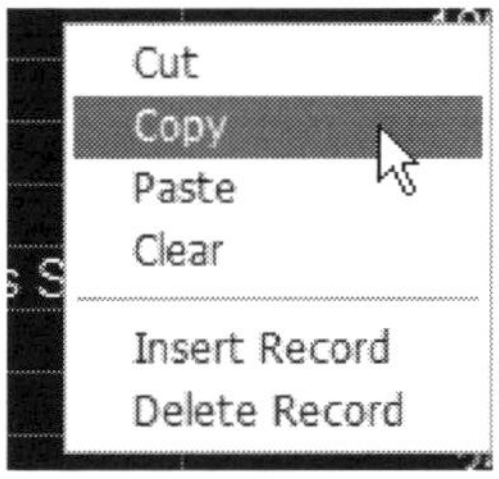

Figure 14-21 Shortcut menu illustrated

4. Switch to the L14 Products database, then right-click in the first row of the Product Number field and select Paste. The records you copied should be in the database that you created.

5. Save the changes to the L14 Products database. Close the Products database. When prompted to save the large clipboard contents, click No.

How To Enter Records In A Database

1. Click the **FORM VIEW** button on the toolbar and move to record 22 by clicking on the button illustrated in Figure 14-22 in the bottom left corner of the database window. You should see a blank record.

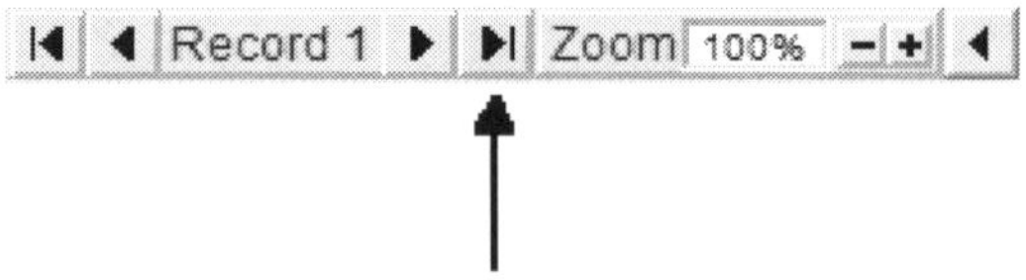

Figure 14-22 Form view navigation buttons illustrated

2. Add the information in Table 14-4 to the database. To move from field to field, press the Tab key.

In This Field	Type This
Product Number	CO-500
Product Name	Works Made Easy
Qty On Hand	275
Price	129
Cost	45
Date Ordered	1/24/2004
Qty On Order	30

Table 14-4 Data for the new record

Notice that the Qty On Order field had the value 25 in it automatically. That's because you set up a default value for this field when you created the database.

3. Save the changes and close the database.

Adding, Deleting, Renaming And Moving Fields

After you have added a few records to the database you may discover that you need more fields or don't need some fields. Some fields may need to be renamed to be more meaningful. Many of the features that you will learn how to delete in this lesson like field protection, you will learn how to create in the next lesson.

How To Delete Fields

1. Save the Customer Address Book database as `L14 Customer Address Book`.

2. If you scroll to the right you will see many fields (columns) that do not have data. Right-click on the Middle name column heading. The entire column should now be highlighted. Select the **DELETE FIELD** option.

3. Click OK when asked to permanently delete this information, then delete each of the fields in Table 14-5.

If two or more fields are side by side, you can delete them at the same time if you highlight the columns before right-clicking on them.

Fields To Delete
Position
Business Type
Country
Date filled
Backorders
Backords filled
Description
Job Completed
Service Person
Title

Table 14-5 Fields to delete

4. Save the changes and leave the database open.

How To Turn Off Field Protection

The fields that you just deleted were pretty straight forward because they did not have any protection. Some fields in the L14 Customer Address Book database have protection that must be changed before the field can be deleted. In this exercise you will learn how to remove protection from a field.

1. Open the L14 Customer Address Book database, if it is not already open.

2. Click on the Tdate field name. Format ⇒ Protection. You will see the dialog box shown in Figure 14-23.

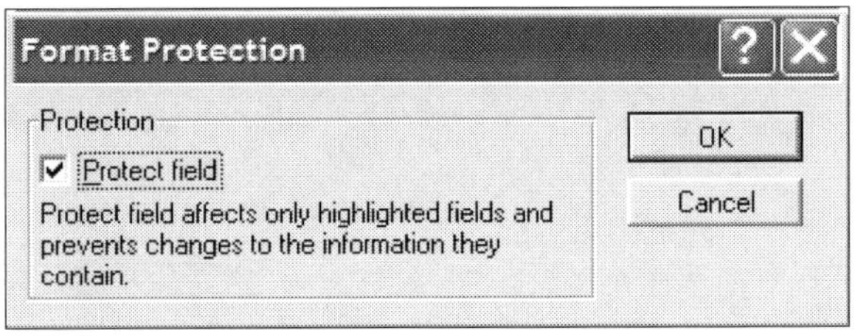

Figure 14-23 Format Protection dialog box

3. Clear the Protection field option and click OK, then click in a cell to deselect the column.

How To Delete Protected Fields

The reason that you would protect a field is because you do not want the information in the field to be changed by anyone that uses the database. If you try to delete information in a field that is protected, you will see the message shown in Figure 14-24. This dialog box lets you know that the field is protected and that the information in the field can't be changed. If you want to change information in the field or delete the field, you have to turn the protection off first.

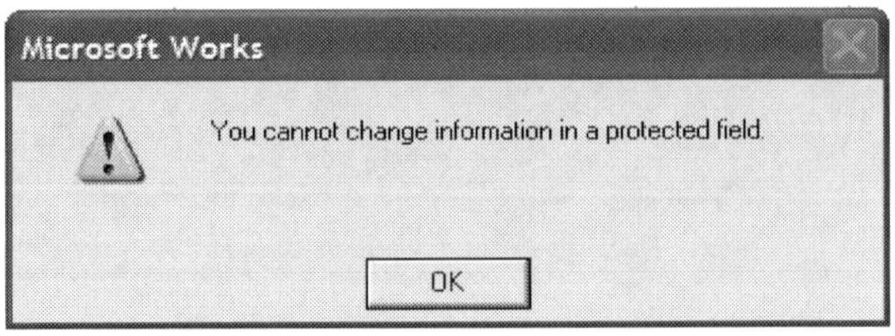

Figure 14-24 Protected field warning

1. Highlight the Order Test and Backorder Test columns, then Format ⇒ Protection.

As you can see both of these fields are protected, which means that you could not delete information in them until the protection is removed. The Formula bar shown in Figure 14-25 displays the Order Test field filter.

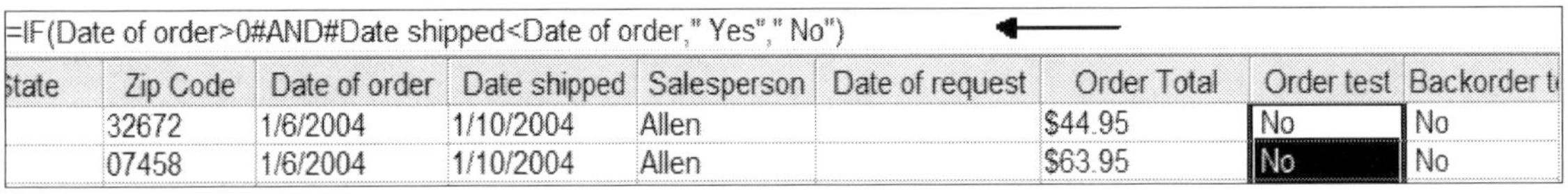

State	Zip Code	Date of order	Date shipped	Salesperson	Date of request	Order Total	Order test	Backorder t
	32672	1/6/2004	1/10/2004	Allen		$44.95	No	No
	07458	1/6/2004	1/10/2004	Allen		$63.95	No	No

Figure 14-25 Filter for the Order Test field

2. Turn off the protection on the Order Test and Backorder Test fields and click OK, then delete these fields and save the changes.

How To Rename Fields

The Date of Request field in the Customer Address Book database will now be used to track the next time customers should be contacted about a special promotion. This means that the field name needs to be changed to make it easier to know what type of information is being stored in the field.

1. Select the Date of Request field.

2. Format ⇒ Field, then type `Next Contact On` as the new field name and click OK. As shown in Figure 14-26, the field has been renamed. Save the changes.

Salesperson	Next Contact On	Order Total
Allen		$44.95
Allen		$63.95
Allen		$12.95

Figure 14-26 Date of Request field renamed to Next Contact On

How To Add Fields

You can add fields at the end of the database or between existing fields. In this exercise you will learn how to add fields to an existing database.

1. Click on the Work Phone column. Record ⇒ Insert Field. You should see the options shown in Figure 14-27.

> Select the **BEFORE** option if you want to insert the new field before (to the left of) the field that is highlighted in the database. Select the **AFTER** option if you want the new field to be inserted after (to the right of) the highlighted field.

You can also insert a new field by right-clicking on a column heading and selecting Insert field and then select Before or After.

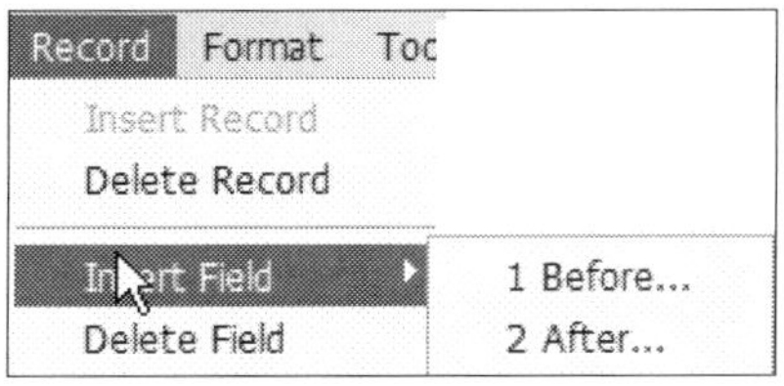

Figure 14-27 Insert Field options

2. Select **AFTER**. Type `Fax Number` in the Field name field, then select the Text format.

3. Click Add, then click Done. Your database should look like the one shown in Figure 14-28.

Work phone	Fax Number	Category
(203)452-1300		Biography
(702)825-9787		Computer
(718)505-4259		Computer
(718)505-4259		Computer

Figure 14-28 Fax Number field added to the database

4. Insert a field named **EMAIL ADDRESS** before the Date Of Order field. Use the Text format for the field. Save the changes.

How To Modify The Data Entry Form

When you create a database, a data entry form is automatically created. Most of the time you will have to modify the data entry form so that it meets your needs. Now that fields have been added, deleted and modified in the L14 Customer Address Book database, the data entry form needs to be modified. It is a good idea to create as many of the fields in the database as possible before modifying the data entry form.

Form Design View

This view of the database allows you to modify the layout and appearance of the data entry form. You can move fields around, add color, borders and shading to the form.

1. Click the **FORM DESIGN** button on the toolbar. The top half of your form should look like the one shown in Figure 14-29.

As you can see, the form needs some work before it can be used to enter information into the database. One thing that needs to be done is to delete what is not needed.

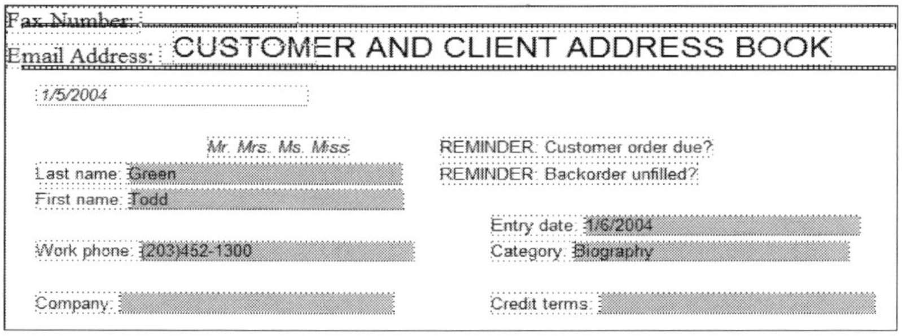

Figure 14-29 Customer and client address book data entry form

2. Hold down the left mouse button and draw a box around the two field titles that start with the word **REMINDER**. Both field titles should now be highlighted as illustrated in Figure 14-30. Press the Delete key.

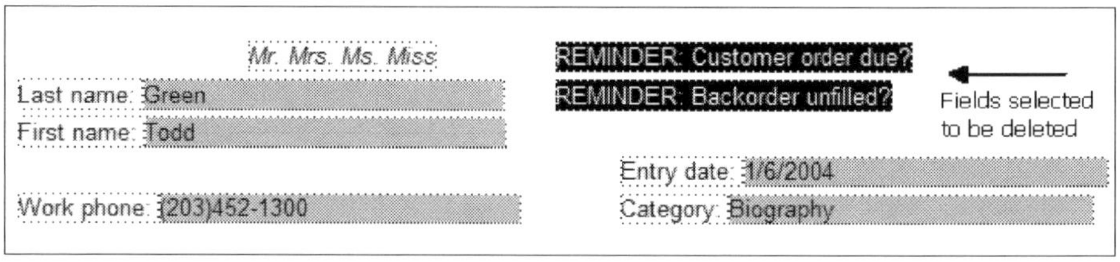

Figure 14-30 Fields highlighted to be deleted

3. Delete the field titles in Table 14-6. To delete a single field title, click on it, then press the Delete key. The Yes/No and Date titles are in the Orders section of the form, as shown in Figure 14-31.

Titles To Delete
Mr. Mrs. Ms. Miss
Yes/No
Date

Table 14-6 Field titles to delete

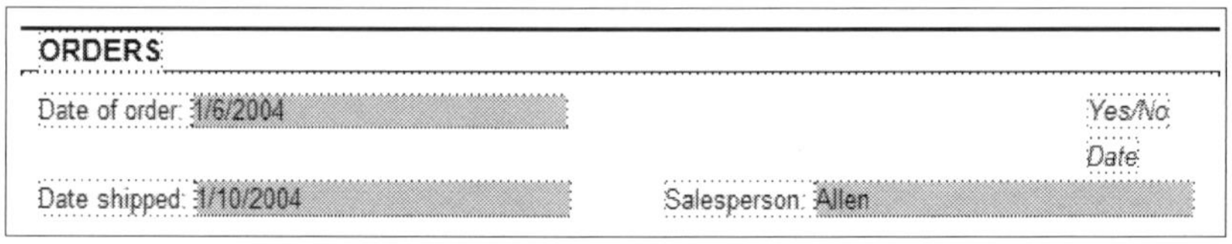

Figure 14-31 Orders section of the form

How To Move Fields Around On A Form

The primary reasons that you would move the fields around on a form is to make the form look better and to make the form easier to use.

1. Click on the First name field. The cursor should have changed to **DRAG** as shown in Figure 14-32. Hold the left mouse button down and drag the First name field above the Last name field.

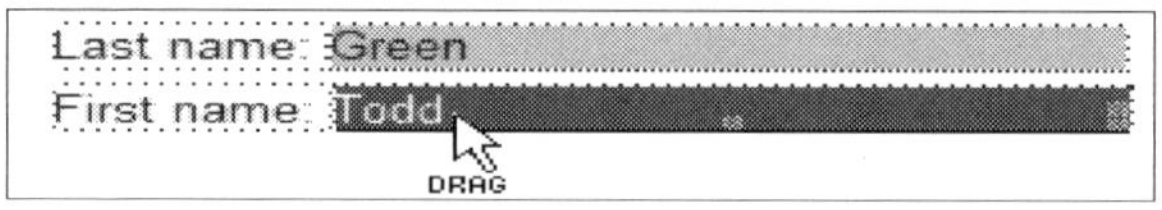

Figure 14-32 Cursor in position to move a field

2. Move the Work Phone field across from the First name field.

3. In the upper left corner of the form you should see the Fax Number and Email Address fields that you added to the database. Select the Fax Number field and move it below the Work Phone field, then select the Email Address field and move it below the Fax Number field. Change the font to Arial and the font size to 8 on both of these field titles.

4. Rearrange the other fields in this section of the form so that it looks like the one shown in Figure 14-33.

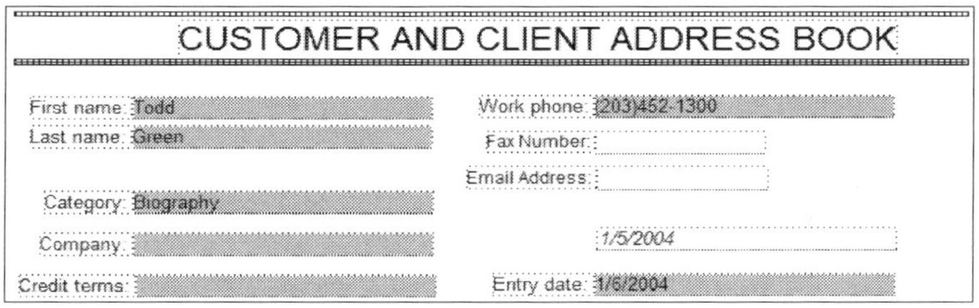

Figure 14-33 Fields rearranged on the form

How To Insert A Label

The field above the Entry date field does not have a label. Without a label you do not know what data is stored in this field.

1. Insert ⇒ Label. Type `Today's Date` in the field as shown in Figure 14-34, then click the **INSERT** button.

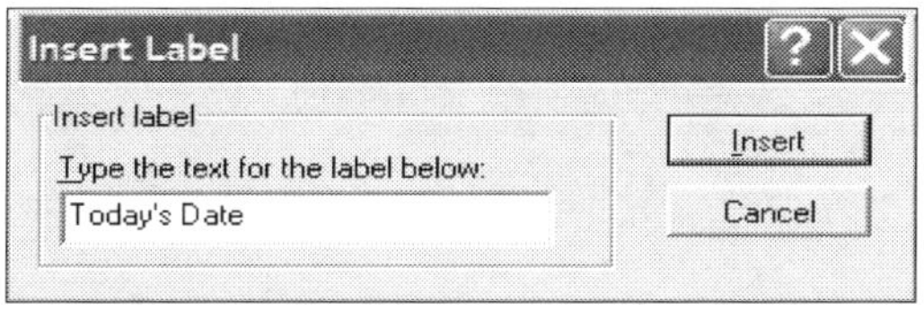

Figure 14-34 Insert Label dialog box

2. Move the label in front of the field above the Entry date field. Your form should look like the one shown in Figure 14-35. Save the changes.

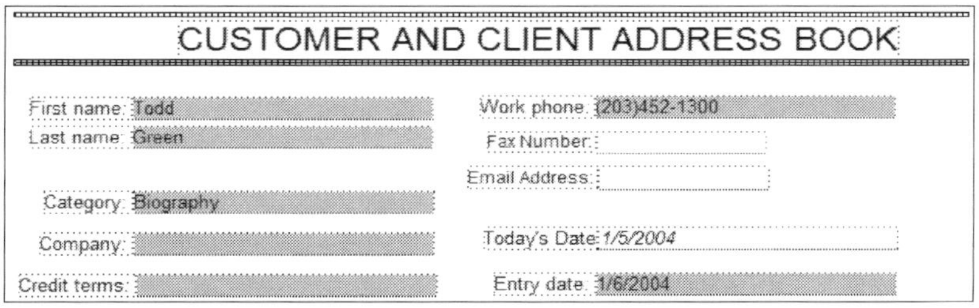

Figure 14-35 Today's Date label added to the form

In case you are scratching your head about the title for this field, Today's date doubles as the date the person became a customer.

How To Change The Form Title

The forms title needs to be changed because the database only has customers in it.

1. Click on the forms title. The title should now be in the Formula bar as shown in Figure 14-36. Press the F2 key.

Figure 14-36 Form title in Edit mode

2. Delete the words **AND CLIENT** in the Formula bar, then press Enter.

How To Add Clip Art To A Form

Just like you can add clip art to a word processing document, clip art can be added to a database form. WordArt and other objects can also be added to database forms.

1. Draw a box around the form title and all of the fields in the top section of the form as shown in Figure 14-37. Everything in the top section should be highlighted.

> To draw this box, place the mouse in the upper left corner of the form and drag the mouse to the right and then down until you have all of the fields inside of the box that you are drawing.

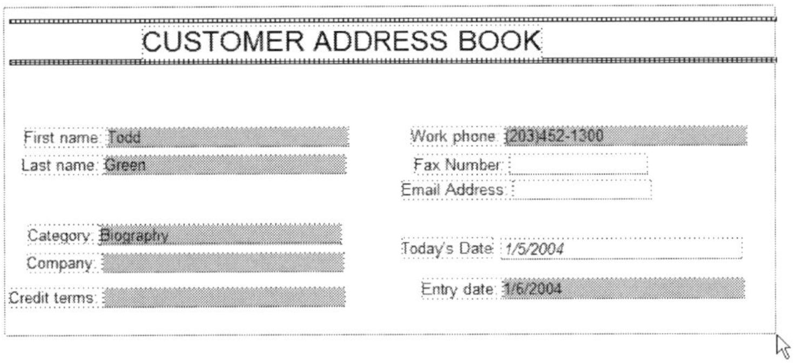

Figure 14-37 Box drawn around the top section of the form

2. Drag everything down about one inch from the top of the form, then click on the top row of the form. (You won't see anything.)

3. Insert ⇒ Clip Art. Select the Academic category, then select the Books sub-category.

4. Double-click on the bookbird.wmf file. If you do not have this piece of clip art, select a different one. Resize and center the clip art so that your form looks like the one shown in Figure 14-38.

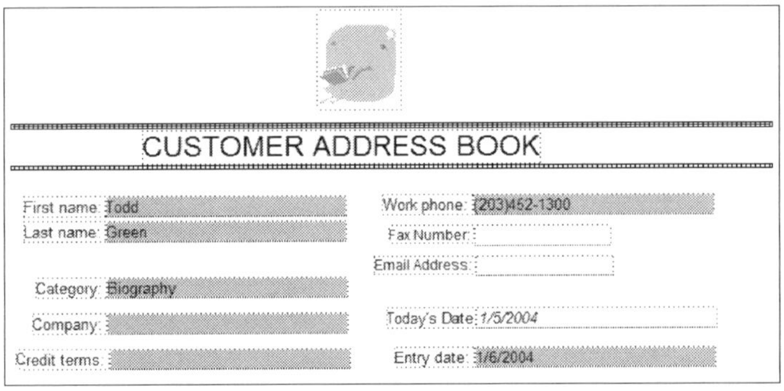

Figure 14-38 Clip art added to the form

Rearrange The Rest Of The Data Entry Form

1. Rearrange the Address, Orders and Service sections of the form, so that they look like the ones shown in Figure 14-39.

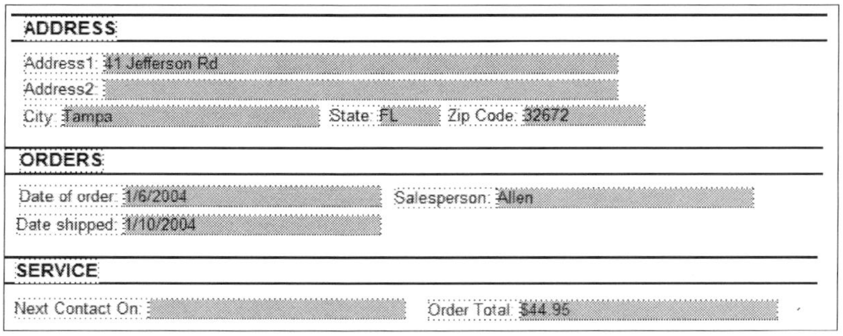

Figure 14-39 Address, Orders and Service sections of the form rearranged

2. Make the State and Zip Code fields smaller. With the cursor in the **RESIZE** position shown in Figure 14-40, hold down the left mouse button and drag the mouse to the left to make the field smaller. Save the changes.

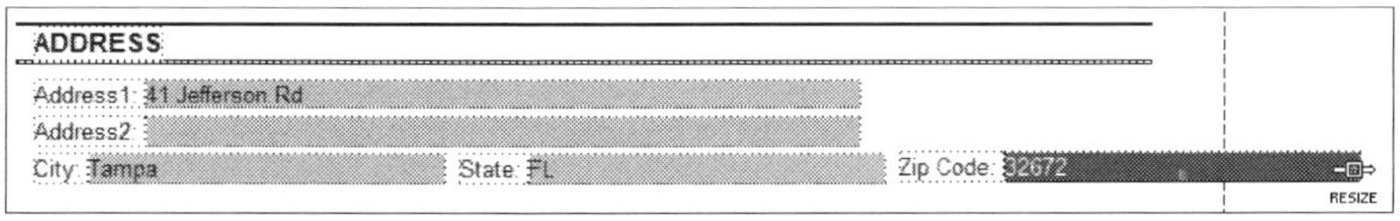

Figure 14-40 Zip Code field selected to be resized

How To Modify The Tab Order

Tab order refers to the order that the Tab key uses to go from field to field on the data entry form. If the fields are arranged on a form in a different order then they are in List View, you will have to change the tab order on the data entry form.

Test The Current Tab Order On The Form

1. Click the Form View button on the toolbar.

2. Click in the First name field, then press the Tab key eight times. Notice how the cursor jumps around on the form.

Modify The Tab Order

1. Click the **FORM DESIGN** button, then Format ⇒ Tab Order.

   The fields in your dialog box may be in a different order then the ones shown in Figure 14-41. Your dialog box shows the current tab order of your form.

   To change the order, select a field in the **SET TAB ORDER** list and click the Up or Down button to move the field to the correct position. The first field in the list should be the first field that you want to enter data in on the form.

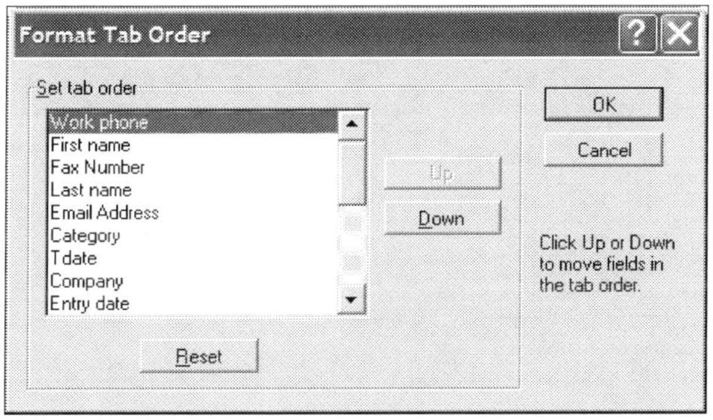

Figure 14-41 Format Tab Order dialog box

2. Select the Work Phone field and click the **UP** or **DOWN** button until the field is right below the Last name field, then select the Company field and click the Up or Down button until the field is right below the Category field.

3. Move the Credit terms field so that it is right below the Company field. As needed, rearrange the remaining fields in each section of the data entry form so that they are in the order listed in each step below.

4. As you tab through the fields, this is the order that you should have in the top section of the form: First name, Last name, Work Phone, Fax Number, Email Address, Category, Company, Credit Terms, Today's Date, Entry Date.

5. The tab order for the Address section should be Address 1, Address 2, City, State, Zip Code.

6. The tab order for the Orders section should be Date of order, Date shipped, Salesperson.

7. The tab order for the Service section should be Next Contact On, Order Total. Click OK to close the Format Tab Order dialog box, then click the Form View button.

8. Click in the First name field. Press the Tab key until you get to the end of the form. The cursor should go from field to field without jumping all over the form like it did earlier. Save the changes.

How To Change The Shading Of A Field

As shown earlier in Figure 14-38, some fields have a shaded data entry field and some do not. To keep the look of the fields consistent, some of the field borders need to be changed.

> I've noticed that the fields that are not shaded are the ones added after the database is first created.

1. Click the Form Design button, then click on the data portion of the Fax Number field as illustrated in Figure 14-42.

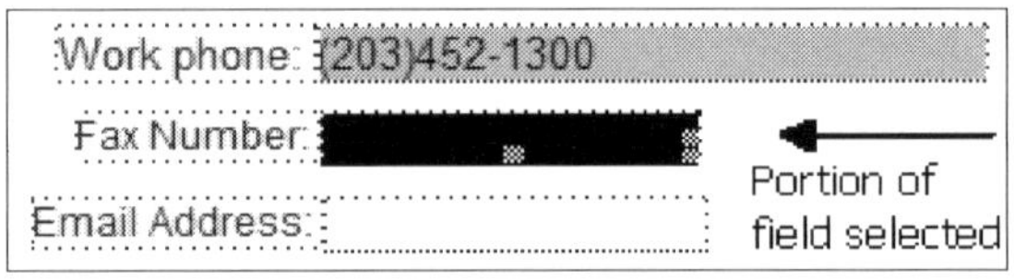

Figure 14-42 Data portion of the field illustrated

2. Format ⇒ Shading. Select Light Gray for the **FOREGROUND** and **BACKGROUND** color.

3. Click on the first gray bar in the **PATTERN** section. The description underneath should be **SOLID (100%)** as shown in Figure 14-43.

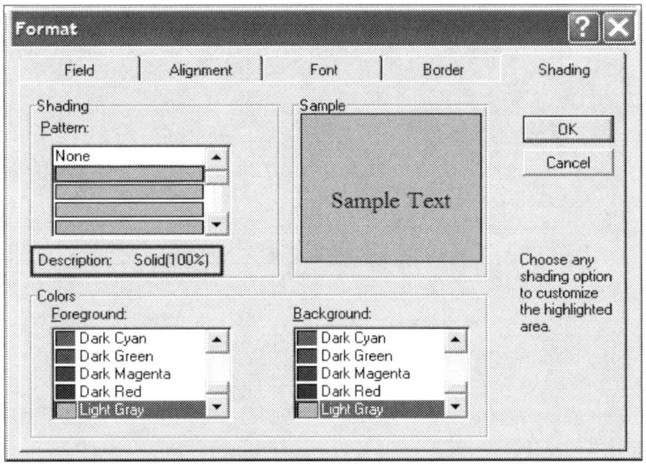

Figure 14-43 Shading options selected

4. Click OK. Repeat these steps for the Email Address and Today's Date fields. When you are finished, your form should look like the one shown in Figure 14-44. Save the changes and leave the form open.

If you select both of these fields first, you can change the shading options for both fields at the same time. You can click on one field, then press and hold down the Shift key to select additional fields.

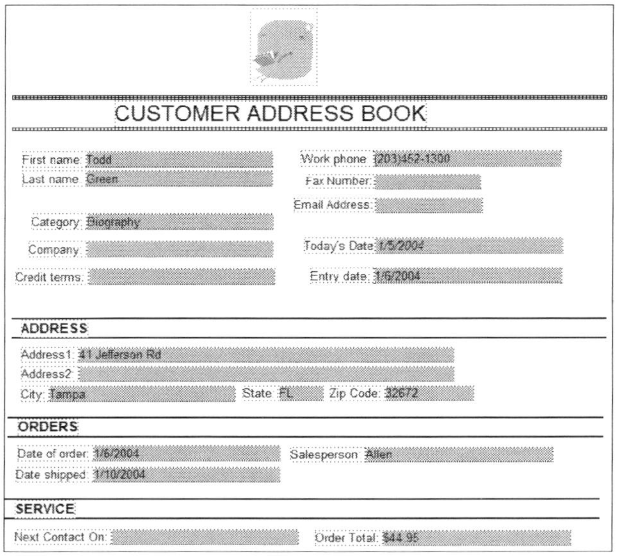

Figure 14-44 Completed customer address book data entry form

The Go To Dialog Box

The Go To dialog box works a little differently in the database application then it does in the word processing and spreadsheet applications.

1. Click on the List View button.

2. Edit ⇒ Go To.

The Go To dialog box lets you go to a specific record or field, as shown in Figure 14-45.

Enter the record number that you want to view in the **GO TO** field or select a field that you want to go to in the record that is selected, from the **SELECT A FIELD** section of the dialog box.

I'm sure that the developers of Works had a purpose in mind for this feature, but so far I haven't been able to figure out what it is.

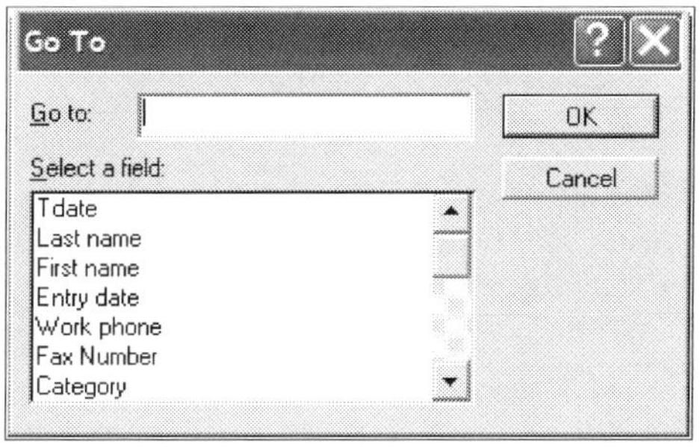

Figure 14-45 Go To dialog box

Test Your Skills

1. Create a data entry form for the L14 Products database. Save the database as `L14(skills)`. The data entry form should look like the one shown in Figure 14-46. Make sure that the tab order is correct.

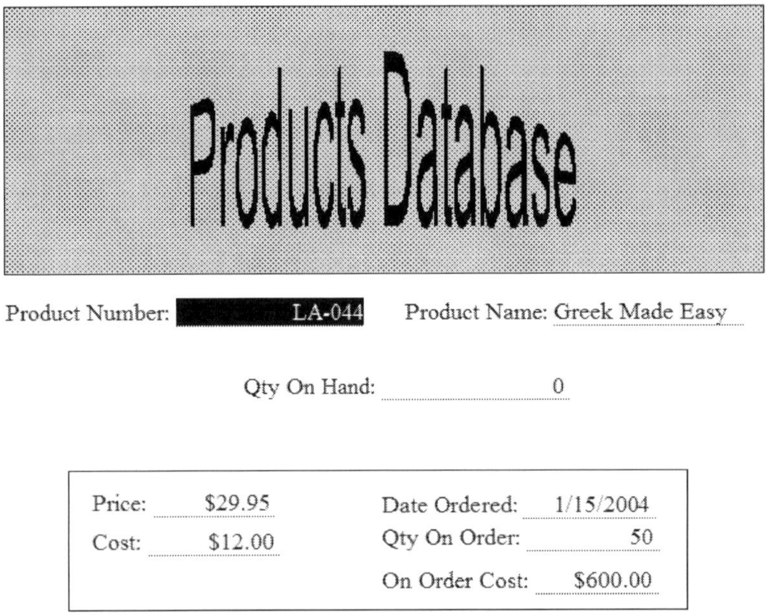

Figure 14-46 Products data entry form

DATABASE SORTING, FILTERS & FORMULAS

In this lesson you will learn how to do the following:

- ☑ Sort records in a database
- ☑ Create filters
- ☑ Create formulas
- ☑ Protect fields
- ☑ Add information to headers and footers
- ☑ Convert databases into spreadsheet format
- ☑ Mark records

LESSON 15

Sorting

Sorting allows you to view the data in the database in a more meaningful way by rearranging the records in the order that you specify. You can sort the records on up to three fields at one time. When you sort the records, they do not physically "move" around in the database. Sorting records is temporary. If you sort the records in a database today, you will have to resort them again tomorrow if you need to see the records in the same order again.

Sort The Database On One Field

In this exercise you will learn how to sort the records on one field. Often, this may be all that is necessary to see the data in the order that you want.

1. Save the L14 Customer Address Book database in List View as `L15 Customer Address Book.`

2. Record ⇒ Sort Records. You should see the Sort Records dialog box. Select Category in the **SORT BY** drop-down list and click OK. Your database should look like the one shown in Figure 15-1. The records are now in order (sorted) by category.

✔	Tdate	Last name	First name	Entry date	Work phone	Fax Number	Category
1	1/5/2004	Green	Todd	1/6/2004	(203)452-1300		Biography
2	1/9/2004	Smith	Tom	1/10/2004	(215)909-1885		Biography
3	1/16/2004	Wilson	Helen	1/16/2004	(610)967-7308		Biography
4	1/14/2004	Downing	Carrie	1/16/2004	(407)987-4563		Biography
5	1/6/2004	Fontaine	Kelly	1/6/2004	(702)825-9787		Computer
6	1/11/2004	Young	Peter	1/11/2004	(718)505-4259		Computer
7	1/21/2004	Davis	Martin	1/21/2004	(718)505-4259		Computer
8	1/5/2004	Jones	Tina	1/6/2004	(609)364-2500		Computer
9	1/6/2004	Smith	Steve	1/10/2004	(702)947-8701		Computer
10	1/10/2004	Gardner	Amy	1/10/2004	(610)664-4646		Computer

Figure 15-1 Records sorted by the category field

Sort The Database On Multiple Fields

In this exercise you will sort the database on three fields. One of these fields will be sorted in descending order. This sort will display the records by salesperson. Under each salesperson, the records will be sorted in date order and within date order, the order totals will be in descending order.

1. Sort the database by Salesperson, **THEN BY** Date of order, **THEN BY** Order Total in descending order. Figure 15-2 shows the options that you should have selected. Click OK. Your database should look like the one shown in Figure 15-3.

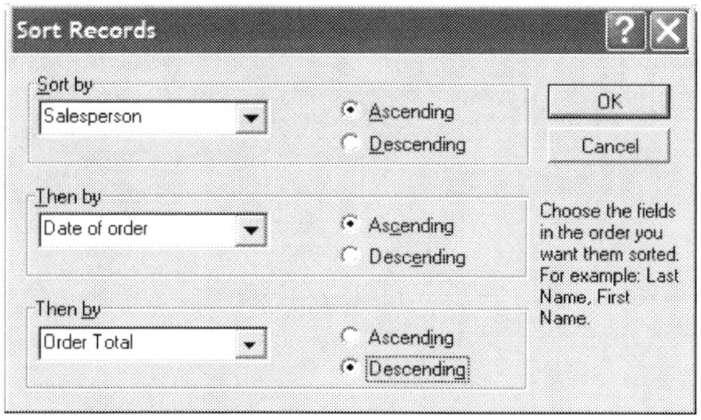

Figure 15-2 Sorting options selected

Date of order	Date shipped	Salesperson	Next Contact On	Order Total
1/6/2004	1/10/2004	Allen		$63.95
1/6/2004	1/10/2004	Allen		$44.95
1/11/2004	1/18/2004	Allen		$12.95
1/21/2004	1/22/2004	Allen		$62.00
1/10/2004	1/10/2004	Altec		$34.99
1/10/2004	1/15/2004	Altec		$12.95
1/15/2004	1/21/2004	Altec		$50.00
1/18/2004	1/18/2004	Altec		$75.00
1/6/2004	1/10/2004	Brown		$34.99
1/10/2004	1/16/2004	Brown		$34.99
1/10/2004	1/11/2004	Brown		$21.95
1/16/2004	1/16/2004	Brown		$12.95

Figure 15-3 Database sorted on three fields

As you can see in Figure 15-3 above, the records are first sorted by salesperson. Each salespersons records are then in order by the date of order field and within each date of order, the records are in order by the order total, from high to low (descending order).

Filters

Filters are similar to sorting in that you can rearrange how the records in the database are displayed. When you filter records only the records that meet the filter criteria are displayed in the database window. Filters can be saved, which means that you do not have to recreate the filter over and over again, each time you need to use it. Filters are more flexible than sorting because you can use more than three fields.

> Filter names can contain a maximum of 15 characters.

Create An Easy Filter

There are two types of filters that you can create: Easy filters and Formula filters. Easy filters allow you to create filters through point and click. Unless you know for sure that your filter will need a formula, try creating an Easy filter first. If you only wanted to see customers in the State of Nevada, you would create an Easy filter to only show records where the State was equal to NV.

1. Open the L15 Customer Address Book database, if it is not already open.

2. Tools ⇒ Filters. Type `State = NV` in the **FILTER NAME** dialog box as shown in Figure 15-4 and click OK.

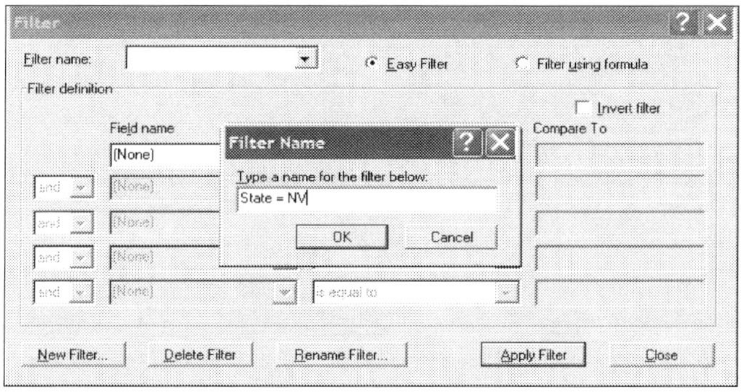

Figure 15-4 Filter Name dialog box

3. Open the **FIELD NAME** drop-down list and select the State field, then type `NV` in the **COMPARE TO** field. The Filter dialog box should have the options shown in Figure 15-5.

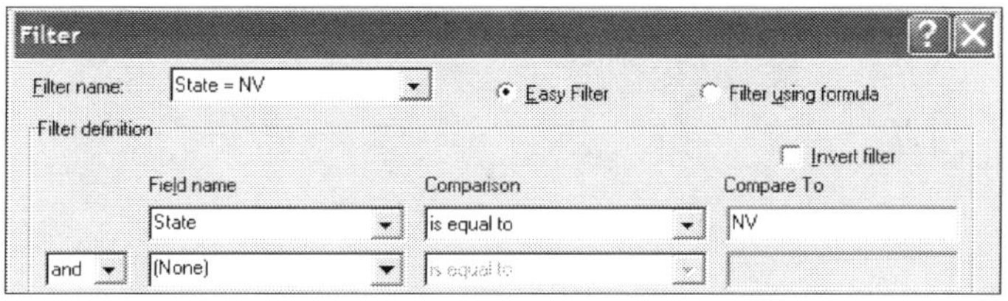

Figure 15-5 Options for the State = NV filter

4. Click the **APPLY FILTER** button and scroll to the right so that you can see the zip code field. Your database window should look like the one shown in Figure 15-6.

The numbers down the left side of the database window are the numbers of the records that match the criteria of the filter. The criteria in this exercise is that the records have NV in the State field.

✓		Address1	Address2	City	State	Zip Code
	3	188 William St		Bogota	NV	32881
	4	188 William St		Bogota	NV	32881
	9	1 Edward Dr		Las Vegas	NV	60022
	19	997 Lenox Dr		Reno	NV	32883
	25	63 Maple Ave		Glen Rock	NV	32888

Figure 15-6 Result of State = NV filter applied to the database

5. To see all of the records again, Record ⇒ Show ⇒ All Records.

Create A Filter For A Specific Zip Code Range

In this exercise you will create a filter for zip codes that begin with a zero.

1. Create a new filter and name it Zip Code. Tools ⇒ Filters. Click the **NEW FILTER** button.
2. Select the appropriate field in the Field Name drop-down list, then select the appropriate Comparison operator from the drop-down list.
3. Enter the appropriate value in the Compare To field and apply the filter. You should see the records shown in Figure 15-7. If you do not see the same records, compare your filter to the one shown in Figure 15-8.

	Address1	Address2	City	State	Zip Code
1	272 Rt 64	Suite 124	Cherry Hill	NJ	07458
5	892 Main St	5th Floor	Menden	CT	06403
6	19 Rodney		Westwood	CT	06403
8	892 Main St		Menden	CT	06403
10	23 Essex Pl		Tappan	CT	06402
11	123 Main St		Stamford	CT	06402
12	272 Rt 64	Suite 124	Cherry Hill	NJ	07458
13	45 Jericho Ave		Wilton	CT	06405
14	500 Point Rd		Ft Lee	NJ	08663
17	500 Point Rd		Ft Lee	NJ	08663
21	132 W Park Ave		Wilson	NJ	07403

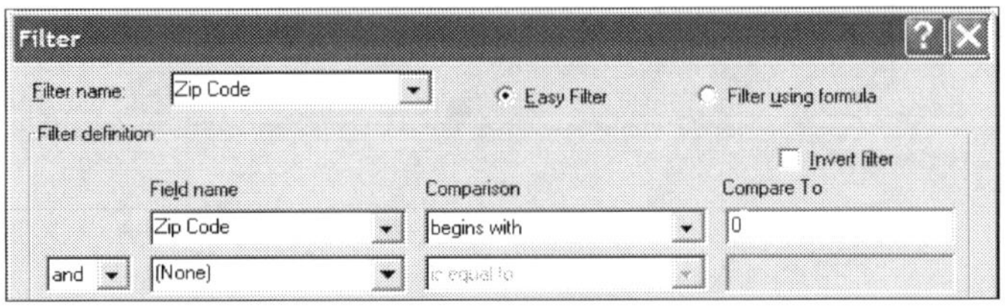

Figure 15-8 Zip Code filter options

Figure 15-7 Result of the Zip Code filter applied to the database

> Don't forget to show all of the records when you have finished viewing the results of the filter.

Create A More Complex Filter

The filter that you will create in this exercise will find records that meet all three of the following criteria.

① Orders for the Salesperson with the last name Brown.
② Orders that have an order date between January 9, 2004 and January 18, 2004.
③ Orders that do not have a credit term.

Create The Salesperson Criteria

1. Tools ⇒ Filters. Click the New Filter button.
2. Type `Order Date` as the Filter name and click OK.
3. Open the Field name drop-down list and select Salesperson, then type `Brown` in the Compare To field.

The **AND** operator to the left of the second Field name drop-down list allows you to select how you want each line of the filter to relate to the other lines in the filter. Your choices are **AND** and **OR**.

When you want two or more conditions in the Filter Definition section of the dialog box to be met, use the **AND** operator between the conditions that must be met. Use the **OR** operator if you want each filter criteria to be met independently of each other.

Create The Order Date Criteria

1. Open the next Field name drop-down list and select Date of order.

2. Open the Comparison drop-down list and select **IS GREATER THAN OR EQUAL TO**, then type `1/9/04` in the Compare To field.

3. Open the third Field name drop-down list and select the Date of order field.

4. Open the Comparison drop-down list and select **IS LESS THAN OR EQUAL TO**, then type `1/18/04` in the Compare To field.

The reason that you have two rows of criteria for the order date is because you need to find all orders **BETWEEN** the date range 1/9/04 and 1/18/04.

> When you need to create filter criteria to find records between two values (like the order date criteria above), you should list the lowest value first (in this exercise 1/9/04) and the highest value in the range last (in this exercise 1/18/04).

If you only wanted orders for a specific date or orders before or after a specific date, you would only have to enter the Order Date field once in the Field Definition section of the Filter dialog box.

Create The Credit Terms Criteria

1. Open the fourth Field name drop-down list and select the Credit terms field.

2. Open the Comparison drop-down list and select **IS BLANK**. Figure 15-9 shows the options that you should have selected.

Yes, believe it or not, this is an Easy Filter. Hopefully you see how versatile Easy Filters are.

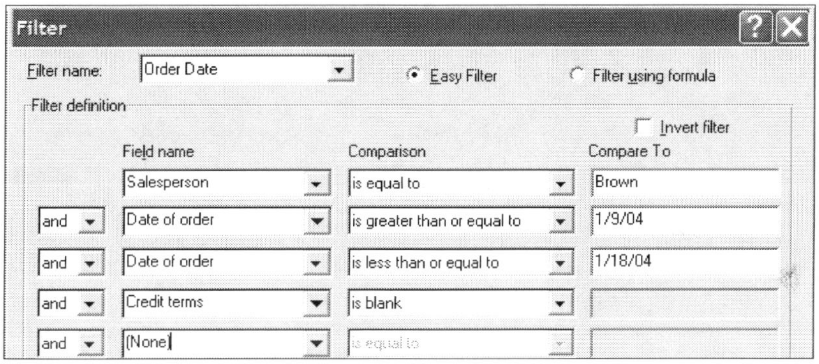

Figure 15-9 Options for the Order Date filter

3. Click the Apply Filter button. Records 10, 11 and 12 should be displayed, as shown in Figure 15-10.

✔	Tdate	Last name	First name	Entry date	Work phone	Fax Number	Category
10	1/10/2004	Riker	Louis	1/10/2004	(702)667-3053		Sports
11	1/6/2004	Walker	Tina	1/10/2004	(702)703-0101		Sports
12	1/15/2004	Morgan	Sarah	1/16/2004	(702)825-9787		Mystery

Figure 15-10 Result of the Order Date filter applied to the database

If you have other records displayed, go back and check your filter criteria and make the necessary changes so that your filter options match those shown above in Figure 15-9, then re-apply the filter.

Salesperson Brown has four sales in the database. The reason the fourth sale, record nine, was not displayed when you applied the filter is because the date of the order is 1/6/04. This date does not fall within the date range (1/9/04 to 1/18/04) of the filter.

4. Display (show) all of the records. Save the changes and close the database.

> To keep the filters that you create, you have to save the database when you are finished creating a filter.

Formulas

You can enter formulas in database fields just like you can enter them in spreadsheet cells. The first formula that you will create will calculate the cost for each product in the database. The second formula that you will create will calculate the next date each customer should be contacted.

Calculate The On Order Cost Amount

1. Save the L14 Products Database in List View as `L15 Products Database`. There is no field for the total cost of each product that is on order. You will create this field now.

2. Right-click on the Qty On Order field heading. Select Insert Field ⇒ After, as shown in Figure 15-11.

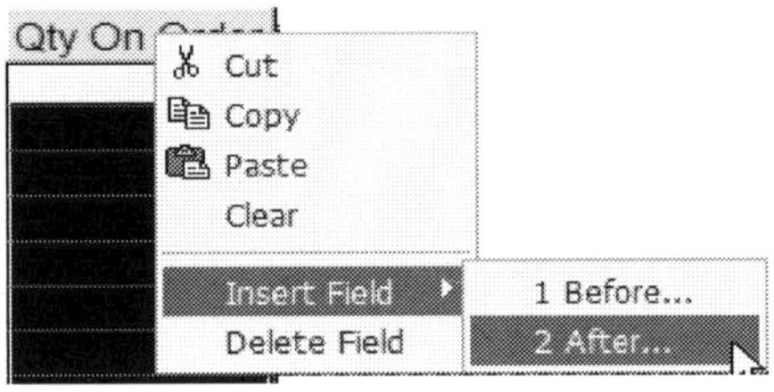

Figure 15-11 Menu options illustrated

3. Type `On Order Cost` in the Field name and select the Number format.

4. Select the $1,234.56 **APPEARANCE**. Click Add, then click Done. You should now see the new field in the database.

5. The cursor should be in the On Order Cost field. Type `= Cost * Qty On Order`.
   The formula in the **ON ORDER COST** field should look like the one shown in Figure 15-12.
   Press Enter. The formula is copied to every record in the database. Your database should look like the one shown in Figure 15-13. Save the changes and close the database.

Qty On Order	On Order Cost
25	=Cost*Qty On Order
30	
25	

Figure 15-12 On Order Cost formula added to the field

✓		Product Name	Qty On Hand	Price	Cost	Date Ordered	Qty On Order	On Order Cost
	1	Aladdin	800	$14.95	$6.95	2/1/2004	25	$173.75
	2	Cinderella	100	$12.95	$4.50	2/1/2004	30	$135.00
	3	Tom and Jerry	100	$12.95	$5.50	2/6/2004	25	$137.50
	4	Bugs Bunny	0	$12.95	$5.50	1/20/2004	25	$137.50

Figure 15-13 Result of the On Order Cost formula applied to the database

Calculate The Next Contact Date

This formula will calculate a date, 30 days greater than the date in the Date of order field. The goal is to contact customers 30 days after they have placed an order.

1. Open the L15 Customer Address Book database in List View and scroll to the right so that you can see the Next Contact On field.

2. Click in the first Next Contact On field and type `= Date of Order + 30`. The formula should look like the one shown in Figure 15-14. Press Enter. Your database should look like the one shown in Figure 15-15.

Next Contact On	Order Total
=Date Of Order + 30	$44.95
	$63.95

Figure 15-14 Formula added to the Next Contact On field

Date of order	Date shipped	Salesperson	Next Contact On
1/6/2004	1/10/2004	Allen	February 05, 2004
1/6/2004	1/10/2004	Allen	February 05, 2004
1/11/2004	1/18/2004	Allen	February 10, 2004
1/21/2004	1/22/2004	Allen	February 20, 2004
1/10/2004	1/15/2004	Altec	February 09, 2004

Figure 15-15 Result of the Next Contact On formula applied to the database

How To Modify The Format Of A Field

As you can see in Figure 15-15 above, the date in the Next Contact On field is 30 days greater than the Date of order. The date format of the field needs to be changed, so that it is the same format as the other date fields in the database.

1. Click the Next Contact On field column heading. Format ⇒ Field. Select the first option in the Appearance section on the Field tab and click OK. The Next Contact On field should look like the one shown in Figure 15-16.

Date of order	Date shipped	Salesperson	Next Contact On
1/10/2004	1/11/2004	Brown	2/9/2004
1/10/2004	1/16/2004	Brown	2/9/2004
1/16/2004	1/16/2004	Brown	2/15/2004
1/10/2004	1/11/2004	Faulk	2/9/2004

Figure 15-16 Format of the Next Contact On field modified

2. Save the changes and leave the database open.

Headers And Footers

One reason that you would want to add header or footer information to a database is because you plan to print the database just as it is, instead of creating a report. You will learn how to create reports in the next lesson.

1. View ⇒ Headers and Footers.

2. Type `Customer Information Database` in the Header field, then type `Do Not Distribute` in the Footer field as shown in Figure 15-17 and click OK.

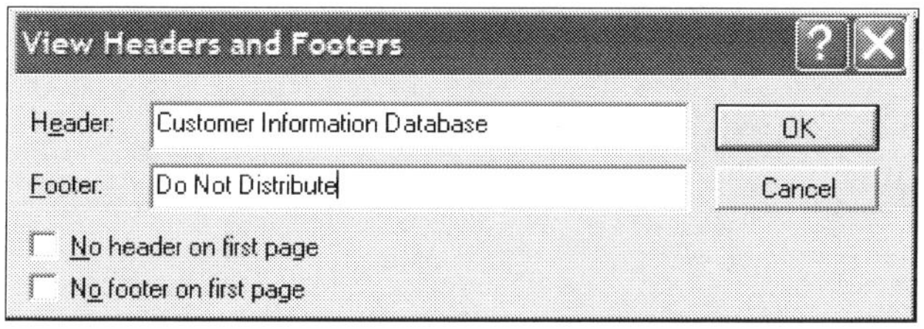

Figure 15-17 View Headers and Footers dialog box

3. File ⇒ Page Setup. On the Margins tab change the Top margin to `1"`.

4. On the Other Options tab select the options, **PRINT GRIDLINES** and **PRINT RECORD AND FIELD LABELS**, then click OK.

5. Click the Print Preview button on the toolbar. Your report should look like the one shown in Figure 15-18.

   Notice that you can't see all of the fields on one page.

   You should change the orientation to landscape and change the margins to see all of the fields.

   You may have to print this on legal paper to get all of the fields on one page. If you scroll down you will see the footer information that you entered.

Customer Information Database

	Tdate	Last name	First name	Entry date	Work phone	Fax Number	Category
1	1/5/2004	Green	Todd	1/6/2004	(203)452-1300		Biography
2	1/6/2004	Fontaine	Kelly	1/6/2004	(702)825-9787		Computer
3	1/11/2004	Young	Peter	1/11/2004	(718)505-4259		Computer
4	1/21/2004	Davis	Martin	1/21/2004	(718)505-4259		Computer
5	1/10/2004	Amos	Fred	1/10/2004	(215)327-7079		Sports
6	1/6/2004	Walsh	Clair	1/10/2004	(215)909-8882		Mystery
7	1/14/2004	Sherwood	Randi	1/15/2004	(718)505-3388		Sports
8	1/16/2004	Smith	Shaun	1/18/2004	(215)909-8882		Mystery
9	1/6/2004	Carter	Glen	1/6/2004	(407)471-0159		Sports
10	1/10/2004	Riker	Louis	1/10/2004	(702)667-3053		Sports
11	1/6/2004	Walker	Tina	1/10/2004	(702)703-0101		Sports
12	1/15/2004	Morgan	Sarah	1/16/2004	(702)825-9787		Mystery
13	1/9/2004	Smith	Tom	1/10/2004	(215)909-1885		Biography
14	1/16/2004	Wilson	Helen	1/16/2004	(610)967-7308		Biography
15	1/11/2004	Emerson	Robert	1/11/2004	(908)587-6422		Mystery
16	1/5/2004	Jones	Tina	1/6/2004	(609)364-2500		Computer
17	1/6/2004	Taylor	Brenda	1/9/2004	(610)967-7308		Sports
18	1/5/2004	Thomas	Stuart	1/6/2004	(718)503-0331		Sports
19	1/5/2004	Walker	Jamie	1/6/2004	(908)652-9609		Mystery
20	1/10/2004	Gardner	Amy	1/10/2004	(610)664-4646		Computer
21	1/6/2004	Smith	Steve	1/10/2004	(702)947-8701		Computer
22	1/16/2004	Thomas	Brian	1/16/2004	(702)947-8701		Computer
23	1/20/2004	Jones	Sylvia	1/21/2004	(908)587-6422		Sports
24	1/10/2004	Bark	Brian	1/10/2004	(610)554-3002		Computer
25	1/14/2004	Downing	Carrie	1/16/2004	(407)987-4563		Biography

Do Not Distribute

Figure 15-18 Customer Address Book database in Print Preview

> If you want to view other pages of the database report, click the **NEXT** button in the Print Preview window. If you want to make the report larger on the screen, click the **ZOOM IN** button.

6. Click Cancel when you are finished viewing the report and save the changes.

Protecting Fields

In the previous lesson you learned how to remove protection from a field. Now you will learn how to add protection to a field. When you have data that you do not want to be changed, you should protect the field. Usually fields that you would protect are fields that you do not enter data in, like an invoice number field or fields that have a calculation.

In the L15 Customer Address Book database, the Next Contact On field should be protected because this field is updated when the Date of order field is filled in. There is no reason to change the data in the Next Contact On field.

1. Highlight the Next Contact On column. Format ⇒ Protection. Check the **PROTECT FIELD** option, then click OK.

2. Change the Date of order field on the first record to `1/3/2004` and press Enter. Notice that the Next Contact On date field changed to 2/2/2004 from 2/5/2004.

3. Click in the Next Contact On field in row 1 and try to change the date. You will see the message shown in Figure 15-19. This message lets you know the field is protected and that you can't change the information in it. Press Enter or click OK. Save the changes and leave the database open.

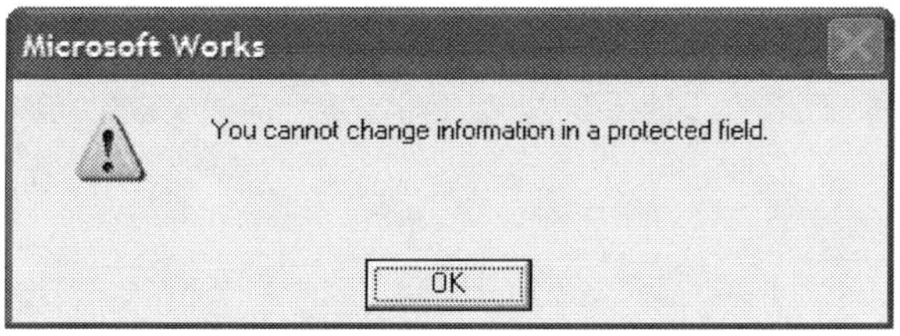

Figure 15-19 Protected field warning message

How To Use Spreadsheet Data In A Database

In a previous lesson you saved a spreadsheet in CSV format. Now you will use the data in the CSV file in a database.

1. File ⇒ Open. Navigate to your folder and open the Files of Type drop-down list and select **ALL FILES (*.*)**, then double-click on the file, Customer (in csv format).

2. Click the List View button on the toolbar.

You will see that the some of the zip codes only have four digits instead of five. That is because the first digit is a zero. When numeric data is converted, zero's at the beginning of a number are dropped unless they were entered in cells that have a text format or entered with an apostrophe as the first character in the cell.

Notice that the field names are Field 1, Field 2, etc. The field names need to be changed to something more meaningful, so that whoever uses the database will know what type of data should be entered in each field.

The first record (row 1) contains the field names.

3. Highlight the Field 1 column. Format ⇒ Field.

4. Type `First Name` in the Field name field, then change the Format to text. Click OK. Repeat the steps above for the remaining fields.

5. Once you have renamed all of the fields, right-click on a field in the first row and select **DELETE RECORD**. The first record should now be deleted.

6. Save the changes. Notice that the file will be saved as a database instead of a spreadsheet, as illustrated in Figure 15-20. Close the database. The spreadsheet will be saved in database format.

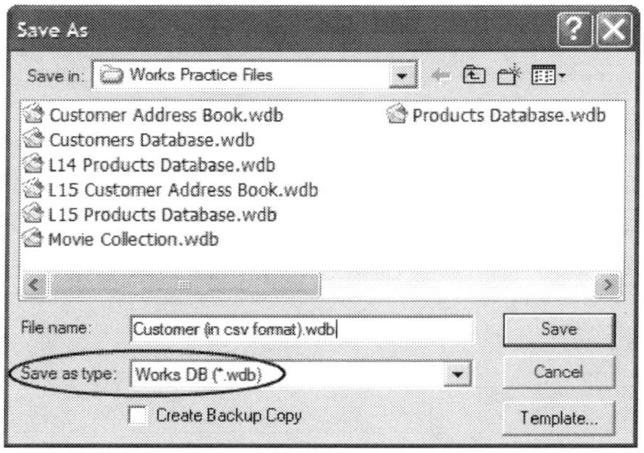

Figure 15-20 Database save options illustrated

> If you wanted to create another copy of the database or a backup copy, you would check the **CREATE BACKUP COPY** option, shown above in Figure 15-20.

How To Convert Data To Spreadsheet Format

Using formulas in a database is not as flexible as it is in a spreadsheet. If the need arises to use data in a database in a spreadsheet, you can do so in a few easy steps.

1. Save the L15 Customer Address Book database as `L15 Customer Address Book (in csv format)`, then select Text & Commas from the **SAVE AS TYPE** drop-down list as shown in Figure 15-21.

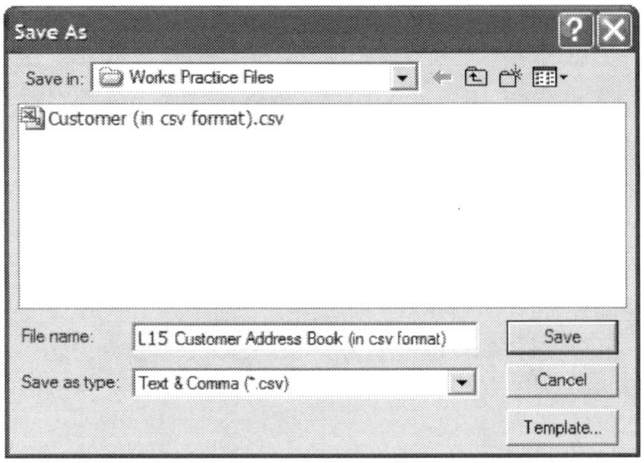

Figure 15-21 Save As Type option

2. Click Save, then click OK to save without formatting the spreadsheet and close the database.

Marking Records

This option allows you to select records that would be hard to select by sorting or filtering the database. Marking records is used when you want to select records at random. You can show, hide or print marked records. The left most column in List View shows whether or not a record is marked. If there is a check mark in the column, the record is marked.

How To Mark Records

1. Open the L15 Products Database.

2. Put a check mark on records 2, 5 and 18. Your database should look like the one shown in Figure 15-22.

✓		Product Number	Product Name	Qty On Hand	Price
	1	CH-007	Aladdin	800	$14.95
✓	2	CH-100	Cinderella	100	$12.95
	3	CH-101	Tom and Jerry	100	$12.95
	4	CH-220	Bugs Bunny	0	$12.95
✓	5	CH-443	Mary Poppins	100	$12.95
	6	CH-721	Curious George	800	$14.95
	7	CH-722	Curious George	20	$12.95
	8	CH-800	Snow White	800	$14.95
	9	CO-095	The Best Of Ac	0	$129.00
	10	CO-101	Let's Learn Wo	25	$24.95
	11	CO-200	The Best Of Ac	400	$129.00
	12	CO-295	C++	200	$79.95
	13	CO-307	Let's Learn Exc	300	$39.95
	14	CO-408	Let's Learn Pow	250	$24.95
	15	CO-495	Java Made Eas	350	$129.00
	16	CO-888	DTP Made Eas	350	$129.00
	17	LA-044	Greek Made Ea	0	$29.95
✓	18	LA-048	French Made E	50	$29.95

Figure 15-22 Marked records

How To Only Show Marked Records

1. Record ⇒ Show ⇒ Marked Records. You should only see the three records that you just marked.

2. Clear record 18 by clicking in the check box to the left of the record.

3. Record ⇒ Show ⇒ Marked Records. You should only see records 2 and 5.

How To Show Unmarked Records

This option will let you show records that are not marked.

1. Record ⇒ Show ⇒ Unmarked records. You should see all of the records except for records 2 and 5.

How To Print Marked Records

To print marked records, they have to be visible on the screen.

1. Mark records 16, 19 and 21, then show the marked records. You should see the records shown in Figure 15-23.

✓	Product Number	Product Name	Qty On Hand	Price	Cost	Date Ordered	Qty On Order	On Order Cost
✓ 2	CH-100	Cinderella	100	$12.95	$4.50	2/1/2004	30	$135.00
✓ 5	CH-443	Mary Poppins	100	$12.95	$5.50	1/20/2004	25	$137.50
✓ 16	CO-888	DTP Made Eas	350	$129.00	$45.00	2/7/2004	30	$1,350.00
✓ 19	LA-050	German Made E	50	$29.95	$12.00	2/8/2004	20	$240.00
✓ 21	LA-750	Italian Made Eas	200	$29.95	$12.00	1/15/2004	25	$300.00

Figure 15-23 Marked records

2. Click the Print Preview button. You should only see the five records that are marked, that are shown above in Figure 15-23. Go back to List View.

How To Unmark All Records

This option will redisplay all of the marked records.

1. Click in the check box that is at the top of the marked record column. In Figure 15-23 above, it's the check box to the left of the Product Number column heading. All of the check marks should disappear.

2. Close the database, but do not save the changes.

Test Your Skills

1. Save the L15 Products database as `L15(skills)`.

   - Create a filter called `Qty_On_Hand` that will show all records that have a Qty On Hand between 100 and 400 and a price between $15 and $100.
   - Create a filter called `Order_Date` that has an order date greater than 1/15/04 and the Qty On Hand is less than 300.

DATABASE REPORT BASICS

This lesson will teach you how to create reports and edit report definitions. The Reports Creator is the wizard that is used to create reports. Reports allow you to print data in a more meaningful way then you can just printing records in the database without any formatting. The biggest advantage of creating reports is that you can select the fields that you want to print. In the previous lesson you created a report in a database, but you could not modify the report.

You learned how to sort records and learned that you could not save the sort. You also learned how to create filters. Reports allow you to sort records, create filters and place the fields that you want in a report and save it. These are the benefits of creating reports.

LESSON 16

Create A Customers By State Report

This report will print the customers in state order. Within each state, the customers names will be sorted in alphabetical order by last name, then by first name.

Select The Database

1. Save the L15 Customer Address Book database as `L16 Customer Reports.`

2. Tools ⇒ Report Creator. Type `Cust By State` in the dialog box shown in Figure 16-1, then click OK. You will see the dialog box shown in Figure 16-2.

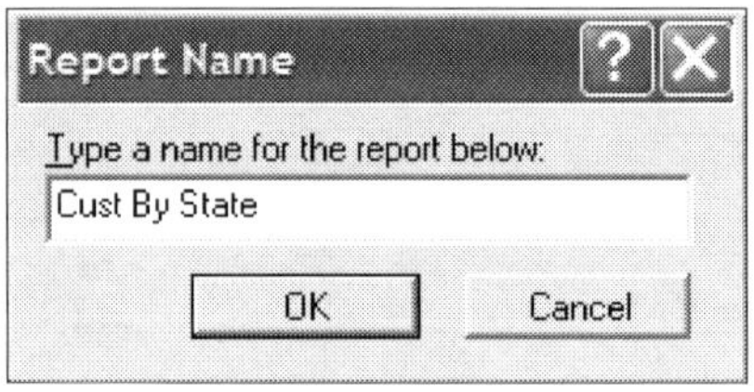

Figure 16-1 Report Name dialog box

> Works will automatically assign a default name to each report that you create, like Report 1, Report 2, etc. Report names can have a maximum of 15 characters.

Figure 16-2 shows the Report Creator wizard. Clicking the Next button will take you to the next tab at the top of the dialog box. You can also click on the tab itself. You do not have to select options on each of the tabs. You do not have to select options in the same order that the tabs are in.

The exception to this is the options on the Grouping tab. You have to select a field on the Sorting tab before you can select options on the Grouping tab.

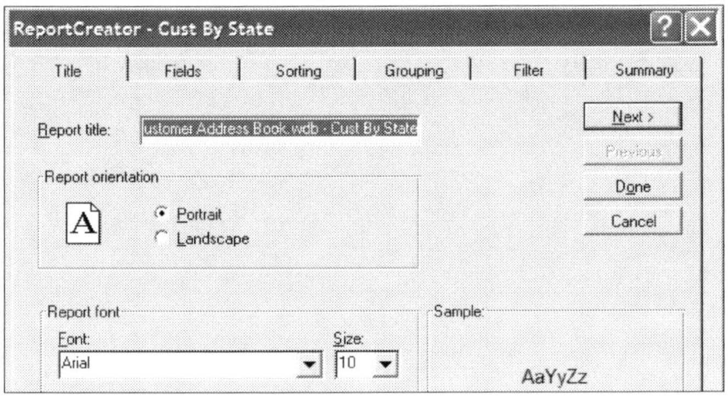

Figure 16-2 Report Creator dialog box

This exercise will walk you through the options on each tab so that you can become familiar with them and learn what the reporting options are.

> You can accept the report title that is automatically created or you can type in your own report title. The report title will print at the top of the report. Report titles can contain a maximum of 255 characters.

Add The Title And Select The Page Orientation

1. Type `Customers In State Order` in the **REPORT TITLE** field.

2. Change the **REPORT ORIENTATION** to landscape and click Next.

Select The Fields For The Report

The order that you add the fields to the **FIELD ORDER** list is the order that they will print on the report, from left to right.

1. Select the First name field in the **FIELDS AVAILABLE** list, then click Add.

You can also double-click on the field in the Fields available list to add it to the Field order list instead of selecting the field and clicking the Add button. You may find this easier or faster.

2. Add the following fields to the Field order list: Last name, Company, Address1, Address2, City, State and Zip Code.

Take your time adding the fields to the report. If you add a field by mistake, select it in the Field order list, then click the **REMOVE** button. If you add a field out of order, there isn't an option to rearrange them on the dialog box shown below in Figure 16-3. This means that you would have to remove the fields that are not in the right order and add them back in the correct order. The other option is to rearrange the fields on the Report Definition window. This may not be a good option either, especially if many of the fields have summary fields associated to them. The summary fields would also have to be moved.

Display Options

The display options discussed below allow you to add additional information to the report automatically, instead of adding the information manually.

① **SHOW FIELD NAMES AT TOP OF EACH PAGE** If this option is selected, the field names will be printed in bold at the top of each page.
② **SHOW SUMMARY INFORMATION ONLY** This option is used to print counts and totals, like the number of customers in a state, without printing each customer record on the report.

1. Make sure the first **DISPLAY OPTION** is selected, as illustrated in Figure 16-3. This figure also shows the fields that should be in the Field order section of the dialog box for this report. Click Next.

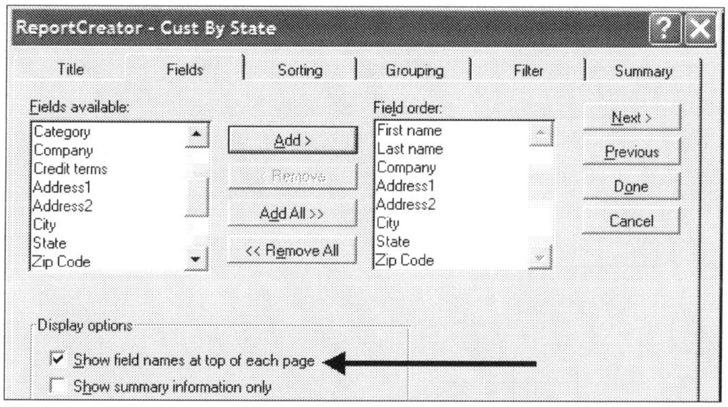

Figure 16-3 Fields tab options

Select The Fields To Sort On

This report will be sorted by State. Within each state, the records will be sorted in last and first name order. The fields that you sort on are the fields that you can group by. Grouping will be explained later in this lesson.

1. On the Sorting tab, select State from the **SORT BY** drop-down list, then select Last name from the second drop-down list.

2. Select First name from the last drop-down list. Your dialog box should have the options shown in Figure 16-4. Click Next.

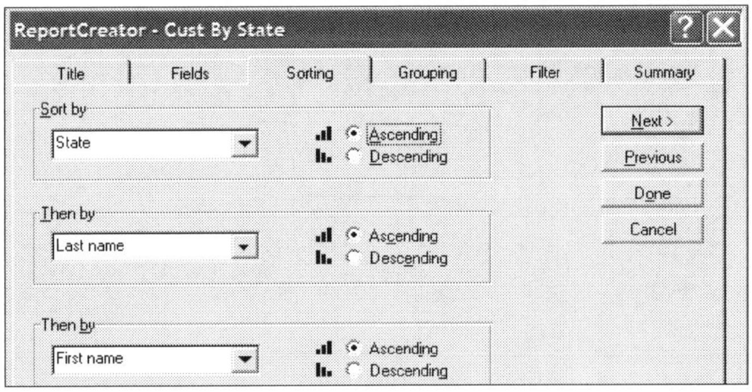

Figure 16-4 Sorting tab options

Grouping Options

Grouping options determine what will happen with the records in each group. In this report you will be grouping the records by State. There are four grouping options: When contents change, Use first letter only, Show group heading and Start each group on a new page. Each of these options are explained below.

Grouping Options Explained

① The **WHEN CONTENTS CHANGE** option will cause a blank line to be inserted when the value in the field that you are grouping on changes. In this report you are grouping by State. Once all of the records for one state have printed, a blank line will be inserted before records for the next state prints. This option must be selected if you want to use any of the other grouping options that are discussed below.

② The **USE FIRST LETTER ONLY** option is similar to the When contents change option. A blank line will be inserted when the first character of the value in the field that you are grouping on changes. This option is very useful if you wanted to print a phone list report. If you were going to print all of the records in the Customer Address Book database by last name and selected the Use First Letter Only option, after all of the records printed for one letter of the alphabet, a blank line would be inserted before the next group of records printed, as shown in Figure 16-5. Notice that when the first letter of the last name changes, there is a blank line.

③ The **SHOW GROUP HEADING** option will force the field that you are grouping on to print when the group value changes. This is useful when you want to only print the group name once, instead of on each detail line of the report.

④ The **START EACH GROUP ON A NEW PAGE** option will start (print) each group on a new page in the report.

Last name	First name	Company	Address1	City	State
Amos	Fred		19 Rodney	Westwood	CT
Bark	Brian		300 Winston Pl	Norwood	NY
Carter	Glen		1 Edward Dr	Las Vegas	NV
Davis	Martin	Elmwood Sales	188 William St	Bogota	NV
Downing	Carrie	Financial Services	63 Maple Ave	Glen Rock	NV
Emerson	Robert	New Real Estate	200 Mountain Ave	Ft. Laud	FL
Fontaine	Kelly	Jersey Bank	272 Rt 64	Cherry Hill	NJ
Gardner	Amy		132 W Park Ave	Wilson	NJ
Green	Todd		41 Jefferson Rd	Tampa	FL
Jones	Sylvia	New Real Estate	200 Mountain Ave	Ft. Laud	FL
Jones	Tina		30 Long St	Ft Laud	FL

Figure 16-5 Use first letter only grouping option illustrated

Select The Grouping Options

1. On the Grouping tab select the options, When contents change and Start each group on a new page in the **GROUP BY STATE** section. Figure 16-6 shows the options that should be selected. Click Next.

Notice that the grouping options appear for each of the three fields that you are sorting on. If you were only sorting on one field, the grouping options would only be available for that one field. In other words, you can't group on fields that you aren't sorting on. If you needed to select grouping options for the first or last name fields, you would select them now.

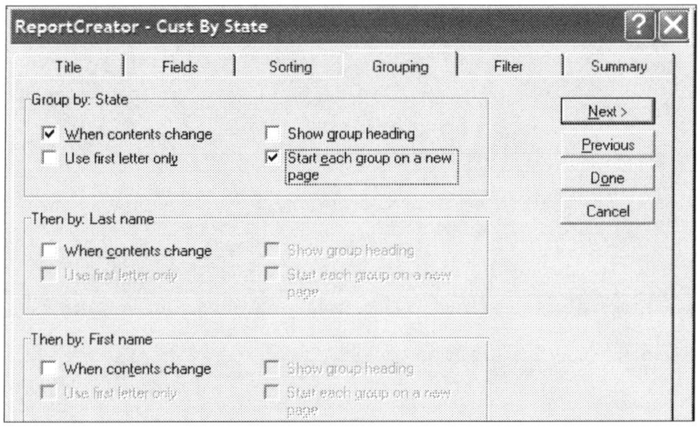

Figure 16-6 Grouping tab options

Select The Filter

Use a filter when you only want to print specific records in the database. Figure 16-7 shows the Filter options. There are two default filter options that you can also select in addition to creating your own filters or using existing filters in the database. They are discussed below.

The other filters shown in Figure 16-7 are ones that you created in a previous lesson. You can also modify existing filters in the database from this dialog box.

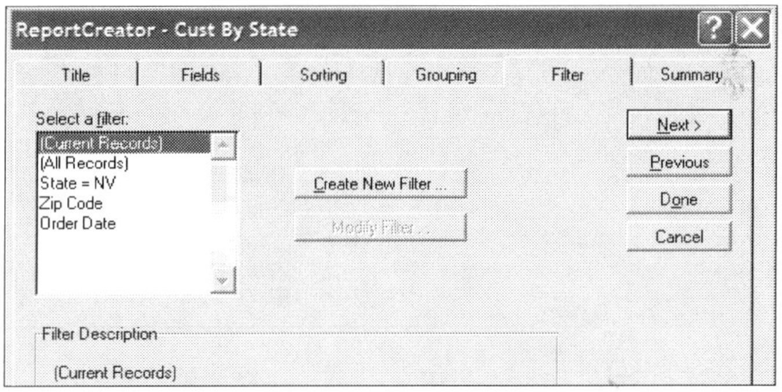

Figure 16-7 Filter tab options

Default Filter Options

① **(CURRENT RECORDS)** will not print any records that are hidden. If you have five records hidden before you run the report, they will not print on the report.
② **(ALL RECORDS)** will print all records whether or not they are hidden.

Create A New Filter

The filter that you will create in this exercise will be used as criteria for the report. The other criteria that you will use in this report is the sorting and grouping options that you selected on previous tabs. The purpose of this filter is to only display records that do not have an email address. By creating this filter only records that do not have an email address will be printed on the report. In this database no record currently has an email address, so all of the records will print.

1. Click the Create New Filter button and type `Email is Empty` on the Filter Name dialog box, then click OK.

2. Select the Email Address field in the Field name drop-down list.

3. Select **IS BLANK** in the Comparison drop-down list, then click OK. The Email is Empty filter should be selected on the Report Creator dialog box. Click Next.

Select The Summary Information

The Summary tab options allow you to specify what type of summary information if any, you want to include on the report. If you wanted a count of the number of records by state you would select the State field and the **COUNT** summary type. If you wanted this count to print at the end of each group, you would select the option **AT END OF EACH GROUP**.

> Most summary options do not work on text fields. The Summary type **COUNT** is an exception. It will count the number of records in a group.

1. Select the State field in the **SELECT A FIELD** list and clear the option, **SHOW SUMMARY NAME**.

2. Select the Summary type **COUNT**, then select the Display summary options, **AT END OF EACH GROUP** and **UNDER EACH COLUMN**. Figure 16-8 shows the options that you should have selected.

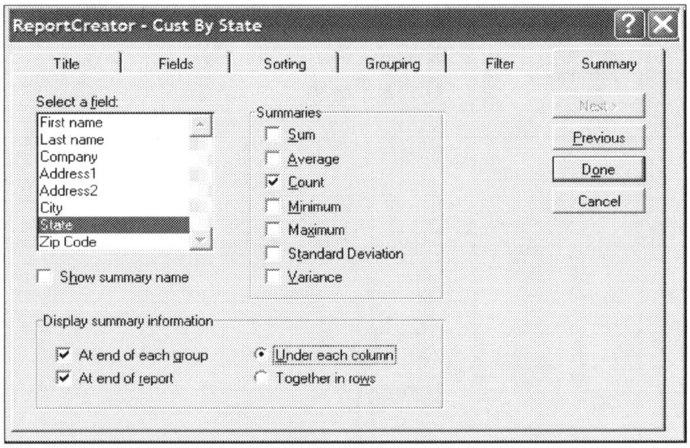

Figure 16-8 Summary tab options on the Report Creator dialog box

Display Summary Information Options

These four options work in conjunction with the options that you select in the **SUMMARIES** section of the dialog box shown above in Figure 16-8.

① **AT END OF EACH GROUP** will create a total when the value in the group changes from the previous record. If you wanted to know how many customers in the database purchased a specific type of book, you would group on the category field and select the count summary option. After all of the records in one category have printed on the report, totals will print for that category. This will happen each time the data in the category field changes.

② **AT END OF REPORT** will create a grand total at the end of the report. The grand total that is created depends on which field is selected.

③ **UNDER EACH COLUMN** will place the summary information under the column of data that is being totaled.

④ **TOGETHER IN ROWS** will place the summary information in rows, instead of columns on the report.

Preview The Report

1. Click Done, then click the **PREVIEW** button on the dialog box shown in Figure 16-9 to view the report. Your report should look like the one shown in Figure 16-10.

> The **MODIFY** button shown in Figure 16-9 will open the Report Definition window that you will use later in this lesson.

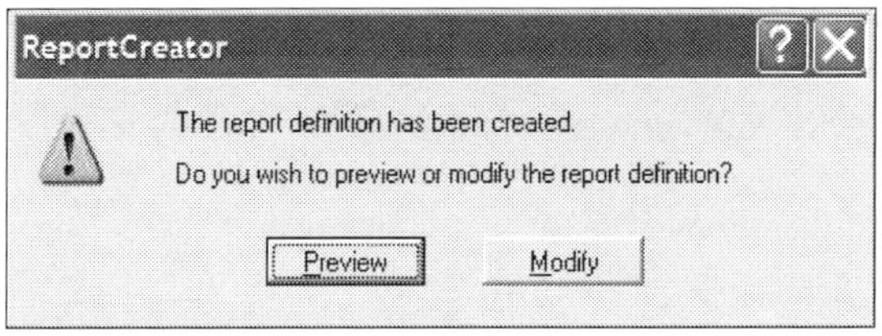

Figure 16-9 Report Preview/Modify dialog box

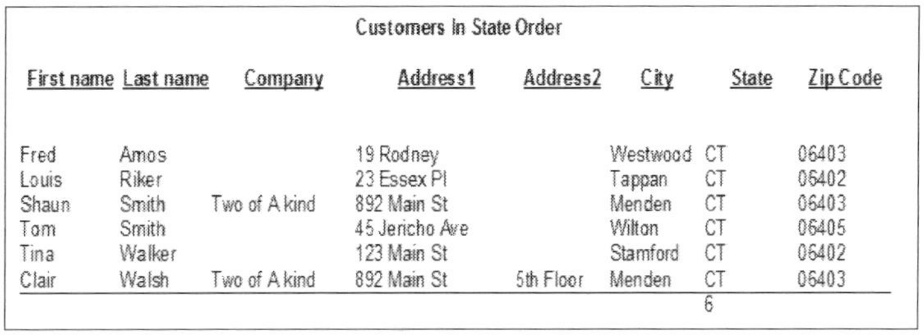

Customers In State Order

First name	Last name	Company	Address1	Address2	City	State	Zip Code
Fred	Amos		19 Rodney		Westwood	CT	06403
Louis	Riker		23 Essex Pl		Tappan	CT	06402
Shaun	Smith	Two of A kind	892 Main St		Menden	CT	06403
Tom	Smith		45 Jericho Ave		Wilton	CT	06405
Tina	Walker		123 Main St		Stamford	CT	06402
Clair	Walsh	Two of A kind	892 Main St	5th Floor	Menden	CT	06403
						6	

Figure 16-10 Customers In State Order report

2. Click the Next button on the Print Preview window to see the next page of the report. As you can see, this report needs a little work. The fields are not lined up under the titles. Close the Preview window. You should see the Report Definition window shown in Figure 16-11.

Not bad for your first report, but in the next few exercises you will learn how to modify this report to make it look better.

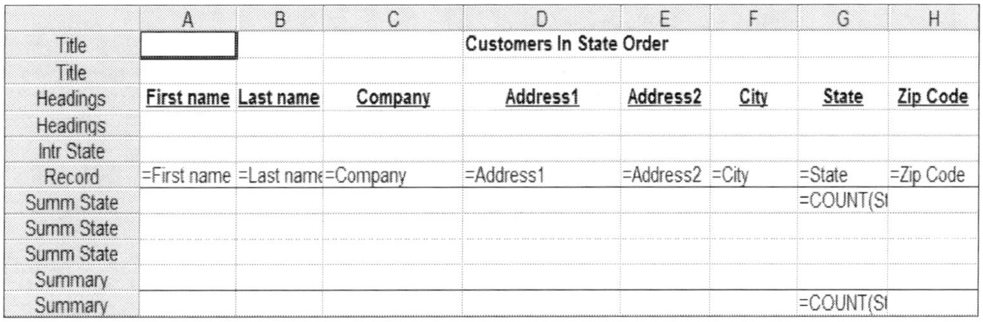

	A	B	C	D	E	F	G	H
Title				Customers In State Order				
Title								
Headings	First name	Last name	Company	Address1	Address2	City	State	Zip Code
Headings								
Intr State								
Record	=First name	=Last name	=Company	=Address1	=Address2	=City	=State	=Zip Code
Summ State							=COUNT(St	
Summ State								
Summ State								
Summary								
Summary							=COUNT(St	

Figure 16-11 Report Definition window

Report Definition Window

The Report Definition window allows you to modify the report. Each row above in Figure 16-11 has a label. The labels are on the left side of the window. Each label type is a separate section of the report. Table 16-1 explains each section of the report.

Section	Purpose
Title	Titles print at the top of the first page of the report. If you want the title to print on every page of the report, it has to be placed in the headings section. Placing the title in the headings section is optional.
Headings	Usually contain the field titles and any information that you want to print on every page of the report. You can accept the default field titles or you can change them as needed.
Intr	(and a field name) If a field is in this row, a blank line will be printed between groups.
Record	Fields in this section will print for every record that meets the criteria if any, that has been selected. This is known as the detail section of the report.
Summ	(and a field name) This section is used to print statistical information that you select on the Report Creator Summary tab. You can also create your own calculations and place them on the report. This section will print at the end of each group.
Summary	Calculations and other data in this section of the report, print at the end of the report. This section prints once at the end of the report.

Table 16-1 Report Definition window sections explained

Modify The Customers In State Order Report

The next few exercises will show you how to use the Report Definition window to modify the Customers In State Order report.

Modify The Heading Section Of The Report

1. Click on the first Headings row on the left side of the Report Definition window. The entire row should be highlighted, as shown in Figure 16-12. Right-click on the highlighted headings and select Format.

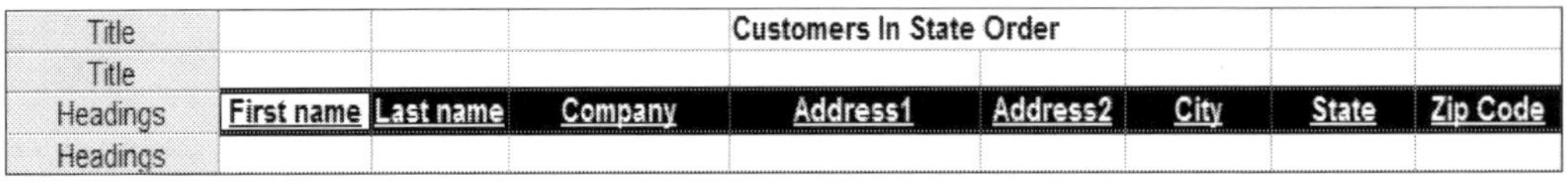

Figure 16-12 First headings row highlighted

2. On the Alignment tab you should see the dialog box shown in Figure 16-13. Select **LEFT** as the Horizontal position. These options should be familiar from the spreadsheet lessons.

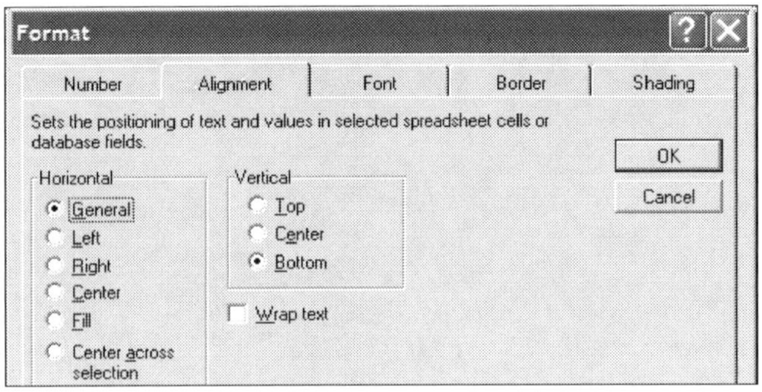

Figure 16-13 Alignment tab options

3. Click OK. Make the First name, Last name, Address 2 and City columns wider, the same way you would in a spreadsheet.

Modify The Summ Section Of The Report

1. Type `Total For -` on the first **SUMM STATE** row in column E. This is creating a label for the count field in column G in the Summ State section of the report. Right align this cell.

2. Type `= State` on the first **SUMM STATE** row in column F.

"Total For - " is a label that you are creating for the count of customers in each state.

"= State" is the field that you are using to count (sum).

If you are a little confused, this will be cleared up in a few minutes when you see how these changes modify the report.

3. Highlight the first Summ State row, then change the font size to 12.

The report would look better if there wasn't a page break after each state. The light gray dotted line that you see between the last two Summ State rows is the page break indicator.

4. Highlight the last two Summ State rows as shown in Figure 16-14, then right-click on the highlighted rows and select **DELETE ROW**.

	A	B	C	D	E	F	G	H
Title				Customers In State Order				
Title								
Headings	First name	Last name	Company	Address1	Address2	City	State	Zip Code
Headings								
Intr State								
Record	=First name	=Last name	=Company	=Address1	=Address2	=City	=State	=Zip Code
Summ State					Total For -	=State	=COUNT(	
Summ State								
Summ State								
Summary								
Summary							=COUNT(S	

Figure 16-14 Summ State rows highlighted

Change The Report Margin Settings

Now that some fields have been made wider, all of the fields will not fit on the page with the current margin settings.

1. File ⇒ Page Setup. On the Margins tab change the left and right margins to 1", then click OK. Preview the report. It should look like the one shown in Figure 16-15.

If you look below the detail records for CT, you will see the label that you created earlier and a total count of the customers in the State column.

Customers In State Order

First name	Last name	Company	Address1	Address2	City	State	Zip Code
Fred	Amos		19 Rodney		Westwood	CT	06403
Louis	Riker		23 Essex Pl		Tappan	CT	06402
Shaun	Smith	Two of A kind	892 Main St		Menden	CT	06403
Tom	Smith		45 Jericho Ave		Wilton	CT	06405
Tina	Walker		123 Main St		Stamford	CT	06402
Clair	Walsh	Two of A kind	892 Main St	5th Floor	Menden	CT	06403
				Total For -	CT	6	
Robert	Emerson	New Real Estate	200 Mountain Ave		Ft Laud	FL	32847
Todd	Green		41 Jefferson Rd		Tampa	FL	32672
Sylvia	Jones	New Real Estate	200 Mountain Ave		Ft. Laud	FL	32847
Tina	Jones		30 Long St	Apt 2	Ft Laud	FL	32991
Stuart	Thomas		90A Jersey Ave		Orlando	FL	32761
				Total For -	FL	5	
Kelly	Fontaine	Jersey Bank	272 Rt 64	Suite 124	Cherry Hill	NJ	07458
Amy	Gardner		132 W Park Ave		Wilson	NJ	07403
Sarah	Morgan	Jersey Bank	272 Rt 64	Suite 124	Cherry Hill	NJ	07458
Brenda	Taylor	Symphony C&L	500 Point Rd		Ft Lee	NJ	08663
Helen	Wilson	Symphony C&L	500 Point Rd		Ft Lee	NJ	08663
				Total For -	NJ	5	
Glen	Carter		1 Edward Dr		Las Vegas	NV	60022
Martin	Davis	Elmwood Sales	188 William St		Bogota	NV	32881
Carrie	Downing	Financial Services	63 Maple Ave		Glen Rock	NV	32888
Jamie	Walker		997 Lenox Dr		Reno	NV	32883
Peter	Young	Elmwood Sales	188 William St		Bogota	NV	32881
				Total For -	NV	5	
Brian	Bark		300 Winston Pl		Norwood	NY	10023
Steve	Smith	Big Design	2200 Research Way		Bronx	NY	11201
Brian	Thomas	Big Design	2200 Research Way	5th Floor	Bronx	NY	11201
				Total For -	NY	3	

Figure 16-15 Modified report

> Earlier I mentioned the term **DETAIL RECORDS**. Figure 16-15 above displays six detail records for the state of CT. Each detail record represents one record in the database.

2. Click the Next button on the Print Preview window. You will see the number 25 on the report without a title. This number is the total number of customer records that are on the report. Close the preview window.

Modify The Summary Section Of The Report

In this exercise you will create a label for the count field in the summary section of the report. Usually the totals in the summary section of the report as known as grand totals.

1. Type `Total # of Customers -` in column E on the last **SUMMARY** row.

2. Preview the report, then go to page 2 of the report. Page 2 of the report should look like the one shown in Figure 16-16.

Did you notice that the second page of the report does not have the report title at the top of the page like the first page does? If you want the report title to print on every page, it has to be placed in the Headings section of the Report Definition window.

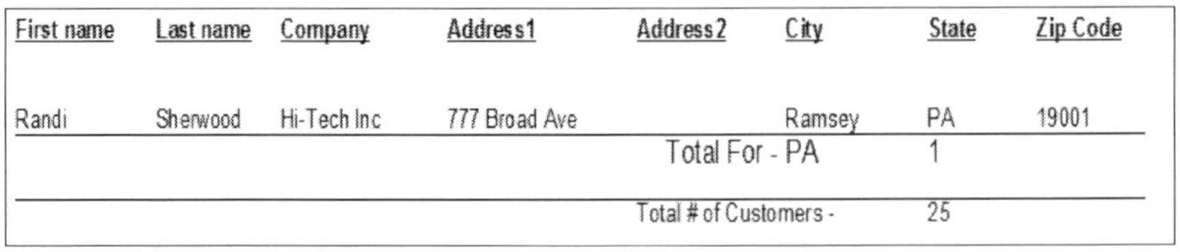

First name	Last name	Company	Address1	Address2	City	State	Zip Code
Randi	Sherwood	Hi-Tech Inc	777 Broad Ave		Ramsey	PA	19001
				Total For - PA		1	
				Total # of Customers -		25	

Figure 16-16 Second page of the report

3. Go back to the Report Definition window. Click Save and leave the database open.

Create The Sales In Nevada Report

This report will display all of the customers in Nevada. It will also show the total amount (sum) of the orders per salesperson, as well as, how many orders (count) per salesperson there are from customers in Nevada. The report will be sorted by Salesperson and then by Order Date.

1. Open the L16 Customer Reports database, if it is not already open.
2. Tools ⇒ Report Creator. Type `Sales In NV` as the report name, then click OK.
3. Type `Customer Sales In Nevada` as the report title, then click Next.
4. Add the following fields to the Field order list: First name, Last name, Date of order, Salesperson and Order Total.
5. Sort the report by Salesperson, then by Date of order and click Next.
6. Select the option **WHEN CONTENTS CHANGE** as the Salesperson Group by option, then click Next.
7. Select the filter **STATE = NV** as shown in Figure 16-17, then click Next. You created this filter in a previous exercise.

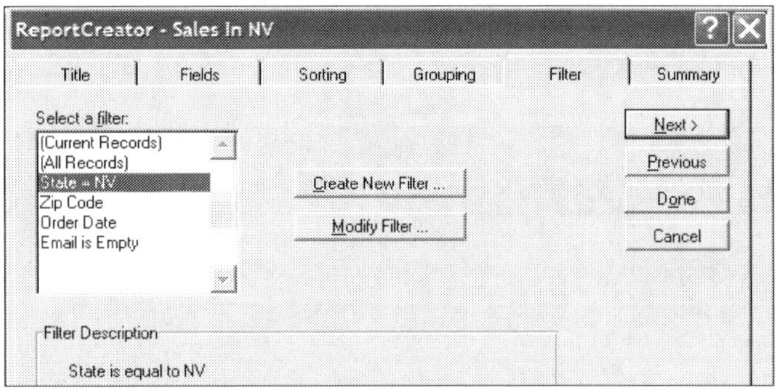

Figure 16-17 Filter selected for the report

8. Select the Order Total field on the Summary tab and select the Summary options **SUM** and **COUNT**. This will tell you how many records there are and the total dollar amount of orders for each salesperson.
9. Select the options At end of each group, At end of report and Under each column in the Display summary information section of the dialog box. Click Done and preview the report. Your report should look like the one shown in Figure 16-18. Close the Preview window.

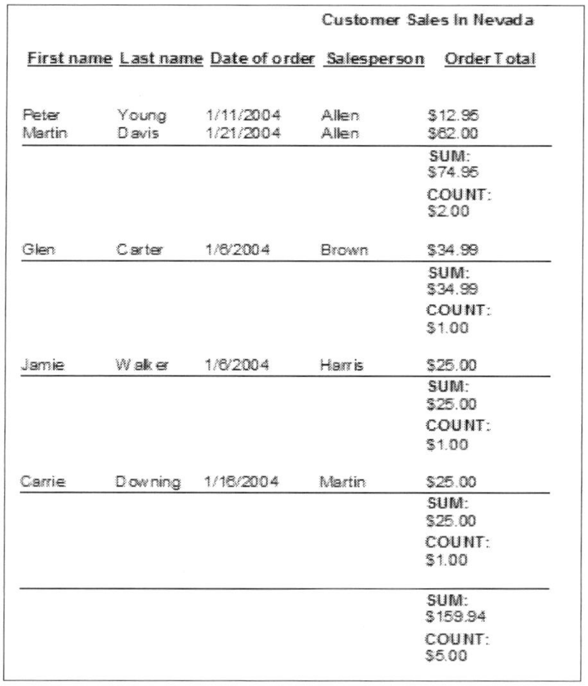

Customer Sales In Nevada

First name	Last name	Date of order	Salesperson	Order Total
Peter	Young	1/11/2004	Allen	$12.95
Martin	Davis	1/21/2004	Allen	$62.00
				SUM: $74.95
				COUNT: $2.00
Glen	Carter	1/6/2004	Brown	$34.99
				SUM: $34.99
				COUNT: $1.00
Jamie	Walker	1/6/2004	Harris	$25.00
				SUM: $25.00
				COUNT: $1.00
Carrie	Downing	1/16/2004	Martin	$25.00
				SUM: $25.00
				COUNT: $1.00
				SUM: $159.94
				COUNT: $5.00

Figure 16-18 Customer Sales In Nevada report

Modify The Sales In Nevada Report

As you can see, the report needs to be modified so that it will look more professional.

1. Make the First name and Last name columns wider.

2. Delete the four **SUM** and **COUNT** field titles in column E.

3. Modify the Summ Salesperson and Summary sections by completing the two tasks below. When you are finished, the layout should look like the one shown in Figure 16-19.

   ① Type the text in column C in the Summ Salesperson and Summary sections of the report.
   ② Select and cut the formulas, then paste them where they need to be.

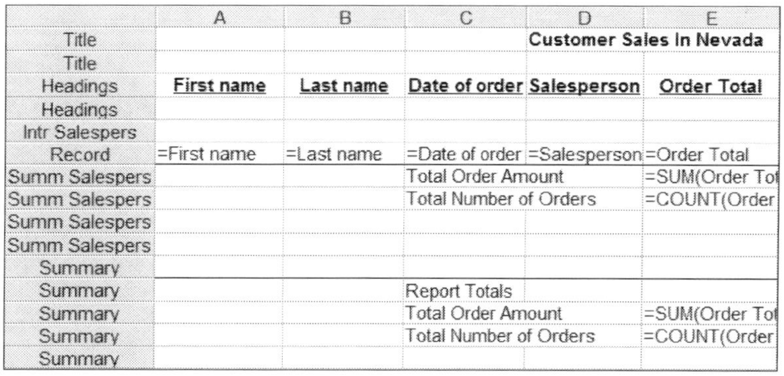

	A	B	C	D	E
Title				Customer Sales In Nevada	
Title					
Headings	First name	Last name	Date of order	Salesperson	Order Total
Headings					
Intr Salespers					
Record	=First name	=Last name	=Date of order	=Salesperson	=Order Total
Summ Salespers			Total Order Amount		=SUM(Order To
Summ Salespers			Total Number of Orders		=COUNT(Order
Summ Salespers					
Summ Salespers					
Summary					
Summary			Report Totals		
Summary			Total Order Amount		=SUM(Order To
Summary			Total Number of Orders		=COUNT(Order
Summary					

Figure 16-19 Modified report

4. Save the changes and leave the report open.

Format The Fields

1. Right-click on the first **= COUNT** formula in column E and select Format.

2. Select the Comma format, then change the Decimal places to zero and click OK.

3. Repeat these steps for the other Count field in column E.

4. Preview the report. It should look like the one shown in Figure 16-20.

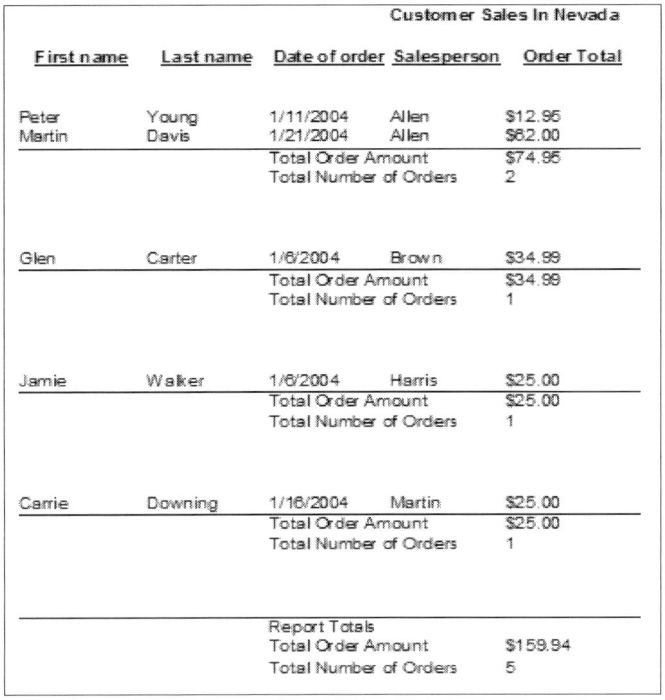
Customer Sales In Nevada

First name	Last name	Date of order	Salesperson	Order Total
Peter	Young	1/11/2004	Allen	$12.95
Martin	Davis	1/21/2004	Allen	$62.00
		Total Order Amount		$74.95
		Total Number of Orders		2
Glen	Carter	1/6/2004	Brown	$34.99
		Total Order Amount		$34.99
		Total Number of Orders		1
Jamie	Walker	1/6/2004	Harris	$25.00
		Total Order Amount		$25.00
		Total Number of Orders		1
Carrie	Downing	1/16/2004	Martin	$25.00
		Total Order Amount		$25.00
		Total Number of Orders		1
		Report Totals		
		Total Order Amount		$159.94
		Total Number of Orders		5

Figure 16-20 Modified Customer Sales In Nevada report

5. Close the Preview window. If you want to make any changes to the report you can make them now. Save the changes and leave the database open.

How To Duplicate A Report

Often, you will create a report and would like to also view it sorted or grouped differently or with a different filter. You can duplicate a report and make any changes that you want to the duplicate copy. This is similar to duplicating a chart in a spreadsheet.

1. Tools ⇒ Duplicate Report. Select the Sales in NV report.

2. Type `Sales By Rep` in the **TYPE A NAME BELOW** field as shown in Figure 16-21.

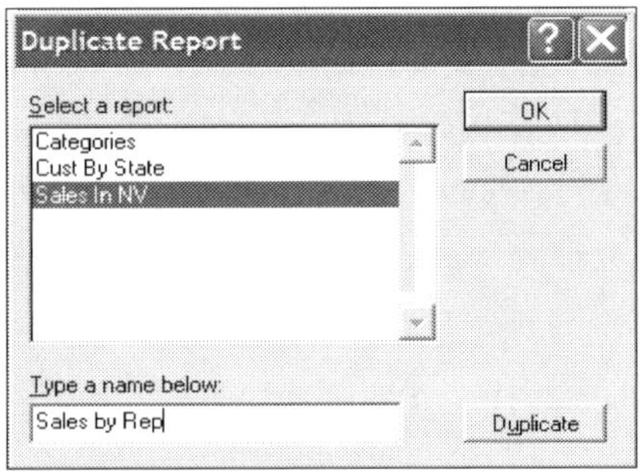

Figure 16-21 Duplicate Report dialog box

3. Click Duplicate, then click OK.

Modify The Duplicate Report

1. View ⇒ Report. Select the Sales By Rep report and click the **MODIFY** button.

2. In column A, type `Sales By Rep` in the first **TITLE** row.

3. Change the font size to 14 and make the title bold, then delete the other report title in the first Title row.

How To Center The Title Across The Row

This is very similar to centering text across cells in a spreadsheet.

1. Highlight columns A through E in the first Title row, then right-click on the highlighted row and select Format.

2. On the Alignment tab select the **CENTER ACROSS SELECTION** option, then click OK. The title should now be centered across the first row. Save the changes.

Modify The Field Alignment

1. Highlight all of the fields in the **RECORD**, **SUMM** and **SUMMARY** report sections in column E, then right-click on the highlighted fields and select Format.

2. On the Alignment tab select the Right **HORIZONTAL ALIGNMENT** option, then click OK.

Modify The Report Settings

The report that this one is duplicated from only printed records where the State is equal to Nevada. You want the Sales By Rep report to print all of the records in the database. To have all of the records in the database print in this report you need to change the filter.

1. Format ⇒ Report Settings. The options on the dialog box shown in Figure 16-22 allow you to change the Sorting, Grouping and Filter options.

2. Select the **(ALL RECORDS)** filter and click Done. Preview the report. It should look like the one shown in Figure 16-23.

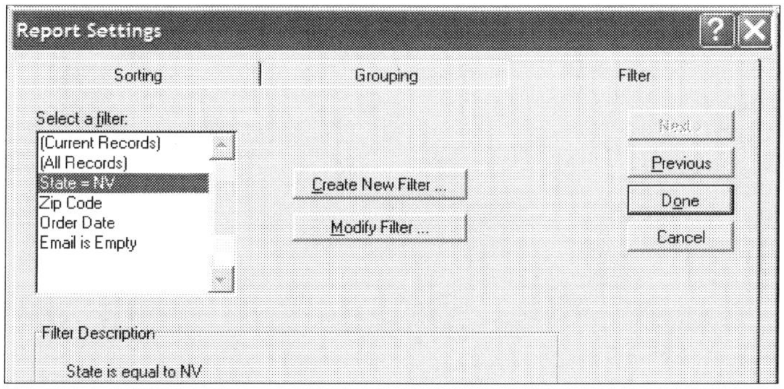

Figure 16-22 Report Settings dialog box

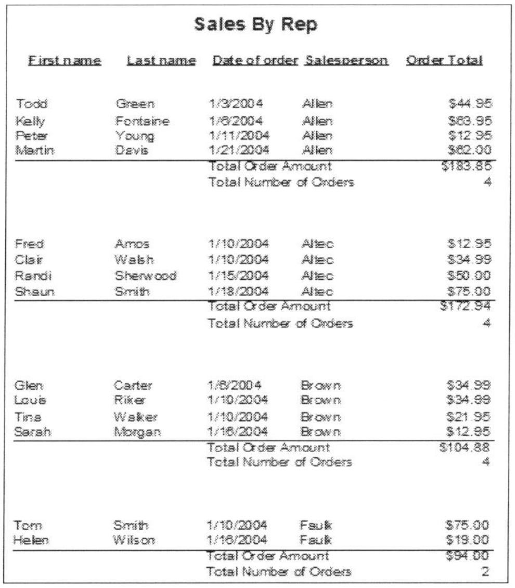

Sales By Rep

First name	Last name	Date of order	Salesperson	Order Total
Todd	Green	1/3/2004	Allen	$44.95
Kelly	Fontaine	1/6/2004	Allen	$63.95
Peter	Young	1/11/2004	Allen	$12.95
Martin	Davis	1/21/2004	Allen	$62.00
		Total Order Amount		$183.85
		Total Number of Orders		4
Fred	Amos	1/10/2004	Altec	$12.95
Clair	Walsh	1/10/2004	Altec	$34.99
Randi	Sherwood	1/15/2004	Altec	$50.00
Shaun	Smith	1/18/2004	Altec	$75.00
		Total Order Amount		$172.94
		Total Number of Orders		4
Glen	Carter	1/6/2004	Brown	$34.99
Louis	Riker	1/10/2004	Brown	$34.99
Tina	Walker	1/10/2004	Brown	$21.95
Sarah	Morgan	1/16/2004	Brown	$12.95
		Total Order Amount		$104.88
		Total Number of Orders		4
Tom	Smith	1/10/2004	Faulk	$75.00
Helen	Wilson	1/16/2004	Faulk	$19.00
		Total Order Amount		$94.00
		Total Number of Orders		2

Figure 16-23 First page of the Sales By Rep report

3. Click Next. The second page of your report should look like the one shown in Figure 16-24. You can print the report if you want to. Save the changes and close the report.

First name	Last name	Date of order	Salesperson	Order Total
Steve	Smith	1/10/2004	Harris	$85.00
		Total Order Amount		$189.99
		Total Number of Orders		4
Brian	Thomas	1/16/2004	Jones	$63.95
Sylvia	Jones	1/21/2004	Jones	$34.99
		Total Order Amount		$98.94
		Total Number of Orders		2
Brian	Bark	1/10/2004	Martin	$44.95
Carrie	Downing	1/16/2004	Martin	$25.00
		Total Order Amount		$69.95
		Total Number of Orders		2
		Report Totals		
		Total Order Amount		$1,151.50
		Total Number of Orders		25

Figure 16-24 Second page of the Sales By Rep report

Test Your Skills

1. Save the L16 Customer Reports database as `L16(skills)`.

   - Create the report shown earlier in Figure 16-5.
   - Duplicate the Sales By Rep report. Name the new report `January Sales`.
   - Create a filter for the January Sales report to only display orders between 1/1/2004 and 1/31/2004 based on the Date of order field.

ADVANCED REPORT TECHNIQUES

In this lesson you will create reports to show the products on order, products on order by date, and a sales report by salesperson. You will also learn how to do the following:

- ☑ Add borders to rows on a report
- ☑ Add information to the header and footer sections of a report

LESSON 17

Create The Products On Order Report

In this exercise you will create a report to show all of the products that are low on stock and have been reordered.

1. Save the L15 Products database as `L17 Product Reports`.
2. Tools ⇒ Report Creator. Type `On Order` as the report name, then click OK.
3. Type `Products On Order` in the Report title field, then change the font to Century Gothic and click Next.
4. Add the following fields to the report. Product Name, Cost, Qty On Order, On Order Cost and Date Ordered. Click Next and sort the report by Product Name.

Add The Summary Information For The Product Name Field

1. On the Summary tab select the Product Name field. Select the Count summary type. This summary type will display the total number of products that have been reordered.
2. Turn off the **SHOW SUMMARY NAME** option, then select the **UNDER EACH COLUMN** Display Summary option. Figure 17-1 shows the Summary tab options that you should have selected.

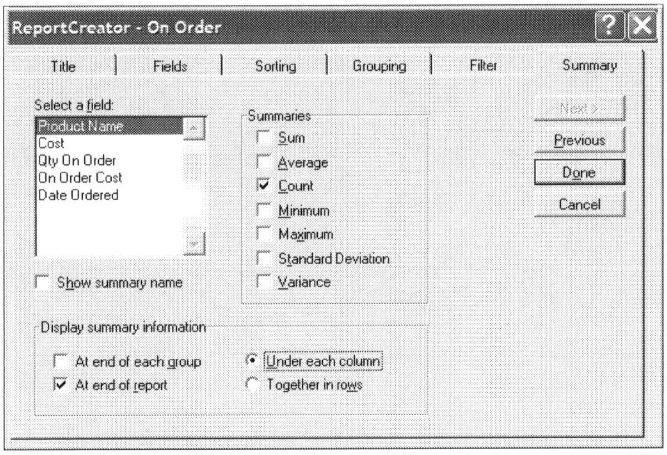

Figure 17-1 Summary tab options for the Product Name field

Add Summary Information To More Than One Field On A Report

You just finished creating summary information for the Product Name field. This report would be more effective if other fields on the report also had summary information. In this exercise you will create summary information for the Qty On Order and On Order Cost fields.

1. Select the Qty On Order field, then select the **SUM** Summary type. This summary will display the total number of pieces that are being reordered.

Notice in Figure 17-1 above, how the options that you selected for the Product Name field have been cleared from the dialog box now that you have selected another field. Each time you click on a different field name, the options from the previous field that you have selected are cleared. This is how you can add summary information for more than one field on a report.

2. Select the On Order Cost field. Select the Sum Summary type. This summary will display the total dollar amount for all of the product pieces that are being reordered. Click Done and preview the report, which should look like the one shown in Figure 17-2.

Products On Order

Product Name	Cost	Qty On Order	On Order Cost	Date Ordered
Aladdin	$6.95	25	$173.75	2/1/2004
Cinderella	$4.50	30	$135.00	2/1/2004
Tom and Jerry	$5.50	25	$137.50	2/6/2004
Bugs Bunny	$5.50	25	$137.50	1/20/2004
Mary Poppins	$5.50	25	$137.50	1/20/2004
Curious Georg	$6.95	25	$173.75	1/20/2004
Curious Georg	$4.50	20	$90.00	1/20/2004
Snow White	$6.95	20	$139.00	2/7/2004
The Best Of Ac	$45.00	20	$900.00	1/15/2004
Let's Learn Wo	$12.00	10	$120.00	2/2/2004
The Best Of Ac	$45.00	10	$450.00	2/4/2004
C++	$20.00	20	$400.00	2/1/2004
Let's Learn Exc	$10.50	20	$210.00	2/1/2004
Let's Learn Pov	$12.00	25	$300.00	2/2/2004
Java Made Ea	$45.00	25	$1,125.00	1/20/2004
Works Made E	$45.00	30	$1,350.00	1/24/2004
DTP Made Eas	$45.00	30	$1,350.00	2/7/2004
Greek Made E	$12.00	50	$600.00	1/15/2004
French Made E	$12.00	10	$120.00	2/2/2004
German Made	$12.00	20	$240.00	2/8/2004
Spanish Made	$12.00	25	$300.00	2/8/2004
Italian Made E	$12.00	25	$300.00	1/15/2004
22		515	$8,889.00	

Figure 17-2 Products On Order report

3. Close the Preview window and save the changes.

Modify The Products On Order Report

The Products on order report looks pretty good as it is. The next few exercises will show you how to modify a few sections of the report.

Modify The Report Title

1. Center the report title across the top of the report.

2. Change the font size of the report title to 16, then make the report title bold and change the color to Red.

How To Center A Column Of Data

1. Right-click on the Qty On Order field in the **RECORD** row and select Format. On the Alignment tab change the Horizontal alignment to Center, then click OK.

2. Repeat the step above for the Sum (Qty On Order) field in the Summary row.

3. Make columns C, D and E wider.

How To Add A Border To The Record Row

1. Highlight columns A through E on the Record row, then right-click on the highlighted columns and select Format.

2. On the Border tab click on the **OUTLINE** Border option, then select the second **LINE STYLE** option illustrated in Figure 17-3. Click OK and save the changes.

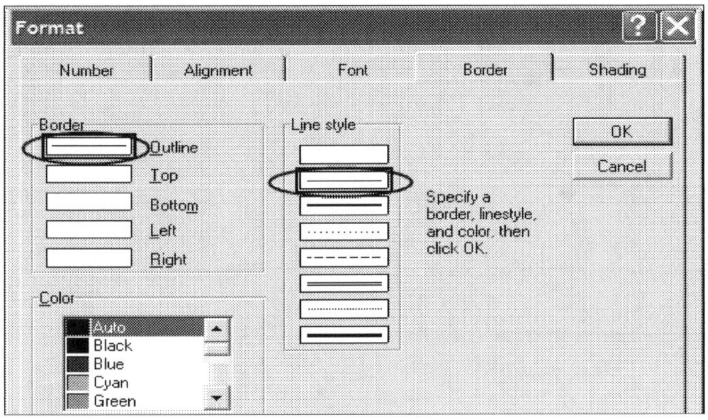

Figure 17-3 Border options illustrated

Modify The Summary Section

1. Move the **COUNT (PRODUCT NAME)** field from column A to column B in the Summary row.

2. Type `Number of Products on order` in column A on the second Summary row, then make column A wide enough to see the text that you just entered in the column.

3. Delete the first Summary row by right-clicking on the label and selecting Delete Row as shown in Figure 17-4. Preview the report. It should look like the one shown in Figure 17-5. Save the changes and leave the report open.

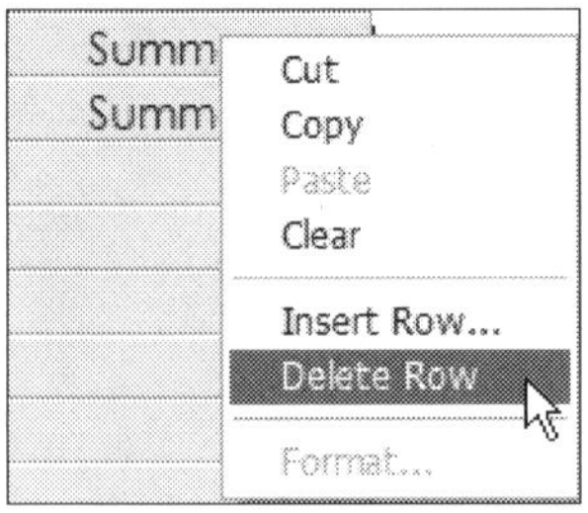

Figure 17-4 Option to delete the summary row illustrated

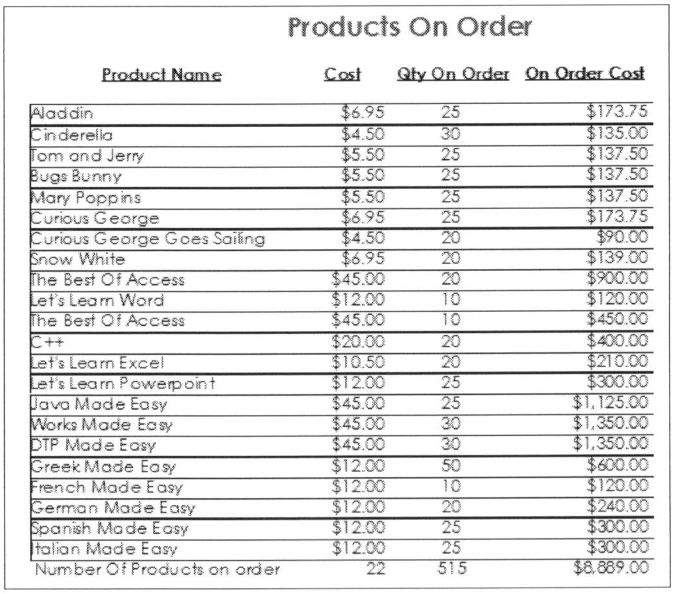

Products On Order

Product Name	Cost	Qty On Order	On Order Cost
Aladdin	$6.95	25	$173.75
Cinderella	$4.50	30	$135.00
Tom and Jerry	$5.50	25	$137.50
Bugs Bunny	$5.50	25	$137.50
Mary Poppins	$5.50	25	$137.50
Curious George	$6.95	25	$173.75
Curious George Goes Sailing	$4.50	20	$90.00
Snow White	$6.95	20	$139.00
The Best Of Access	$45.00	20	$900.00
Let's Learn Word	$12.00	10	$120.00
The Best Of Access	$45.00	10	$450.00
C++	$20.00	20	$400.00
Let's Learn Excel	$10.50	20	$210.00
Let's Learn Powerpoint	$12.00	25	$300.00
Java Made Easy	$45.00	25	$1,125.00
Works Made Easy	$45.00	30	$1,350.00
DTP Made Easy	$45.00	30	$1,350.00
Greek Made Easy	$12.00	50	$600.00
French Made Easy	$12.00	10	$120.00
German Made Easy	$12.00	20	$240.00
Spanish Made Easy	$12.00	25	$300.00
Italian Made Easy	$12.00	25	$300.00
Number Of Products on order	22	515	$8,889.00

Figure 17-5 Completed Products On Order report

4. Click Cancel, then save the changes and leave the report open to complete the next exercise.

Add Header And Footer Information

As you will see, the header and footer options are limited in the database application, when compared to the options available in the word processing or spreadsheet applications. There are codes available that you can use to insert the date, page number and a few other features. Table 17-1 contains a list of header and footer codes that you can use in reports. These codes are shortcuts. For example, you can type **&P** instead of typing the word **PAGE** when you want to print a page number. Headers and footers basically work the same way in reports as they do in spreadsheets. You do not have to type capital letters as shown in the **TYPE THIS** column in Table 17-1. I did it to make it easier for you to read.

If You Want To . . .	Type This
Print the current date in short format	&D
Print the current date in long format	&N
Print the current time	&T
Print the page number	&P
Print the file name	&F
Print one ampersand	&&
Left align characters	&L
Right align characters	&R
Center characters	&C

Table 17-1 Header and footer codes

1. View ⇒ Headers and Footers. Type `Purchasing Dept` in the Header field.

2. Type `&L &D &R &P` in the Footer field. Your dialog box should look like the one shown in Figure 17-6.

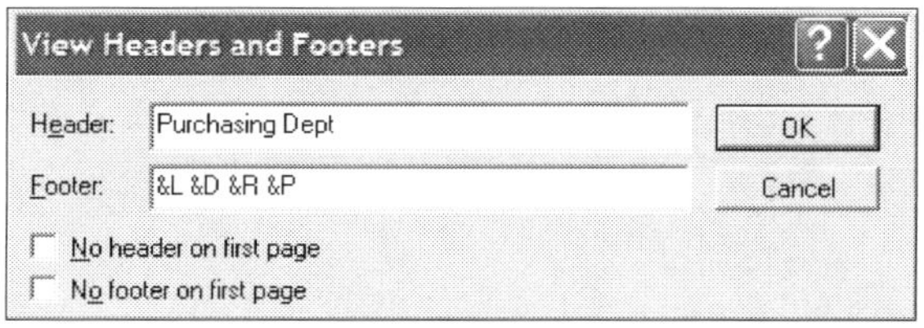

Figure 17-6 View Headers and Footers dialog box

3. Click OK and preview the report. You should see the header and footer information shown in Figure 17-7. Notice the date and page number at the bottom of the report.

Notice the date and page number at the bottom of the report.

Purchasing Dept

Products On Order

Product Name	Cost	Qty On Order	On Order Cost
Aladdin	$6.95	25	$173.75
Cinderella	$4.50	30	$135.00
Tom and Jerry	$5.50	25	$137.50
Bugs Bunny	$5.50	25	$137.50
Mary Poppins	$5.50	25	$137.50
Curious George	$6.95	25	$173.75
Curious George Goes Sailing	$4.50	20	$90.00
Snow White	$6.95	20	$139.00
The Best Of Access	$45.00	20	$900.00
Let's Learn Word	$12.00	10	$120.00
The Best Of Access	$45.00	10	$450.00
C++	$20.00	20	$400.00
Let's Learn Excel	$10.50	20	$210.00
Let's Learn Powerpoint	$12.00	25	$300.00
Java Made Easy	$45.00	25	$1,125.00
Works Made Easy	$45.00	30	$1,350.00
DTP Made Easy	$45.00	30	$1,350.00
Greek Made Easy	$12.00	50	$600.00
French Made Easy	$12.00	10	$120.00
German Made Easy	$12.00	20	$240.00
Spanish Made Easy	$12.00	25	$300.00
Italian Made Easy	$12.00	25	$300.00
Number Of Products on order	22	515	$8,889.00

2/1/2005 1

Figure 17-7 Report with header and footer information added

4. Save the changes and leave the database open.

Create The Orders By Date Report

This report will print the products that are on order based on the date that they were ordered. The report will be grouped by the Order date. Totals will be printed for each order date.

1. Tools ⇒ Report Creator. Type `Orders By Date` as the report name, then click OK.
2. On the **FIELDS** tab add the following fields to the report: Product Name, Qty On Order, On Order Cost and Date Ordered, then click Next.
3. Select Date Ordered as the field to sort by, then sort by the Product Name field and click Next.
4. Select When contents change as the Date Ordered group by option, then click Next.
5. Select the (All Records) filter and click Next.
6. Select the Product Name field, then select the **COUNT** summary type and turn off the Show summary name option. Select the options At end of each group and Under each column.
7. Select the Qty On Order field, then select the **SUM** summary type.
8. Select the On Order Cost field, then select the Sum summary type. Click Done, then preview the report. It should look like the one shown in Figure 17-8.

L17 Product Reports.wdb - Orders By Date

Product Name	Qty On Order	On Order Cost	Date Ordered
Greek Made Ea	50	$600.00	1/15/2004
Italian Made Ea	25	$300.00	1/15/2004
The Best Of Acc	20	$900.00	1/15/2004
3	95	$1,800.00	
Bugs Bunny	25	$137.50	1/20/2004
Curious George	25	$173.75	1/20/2004
Curious George	20	$90.00	1/20/2004
Java Made Easy	25	$1,125.00	1/20/2004
Mary Poppins	25	$137.50	1/20/2004
5	120	$1,663.75	
Works Made Ea	30	$1,350.00	1/24/2004
1	30	$1,350.00	

Figure 17-8 Orders By Date report

Modify The Orders By Date Report

1. Change the report title to `Products Database - Orders By Date`. Center the report title across the first row of the report, then change the report title font size to 14.
2. Left align the Product Name heading.
3. Move the **= COUNT (PRODUCT NAME)** field in the Summ Date Ordered and Summary sections to column B below the =Sum (Qty On Order) field. Left align the Count fields that you just moved.
4. In column A in the second **SUMM DATE ORDERED** field, type `Number of Products Ordered`.
5. In column A in the second **SUMMARY** row, type `Total Pieces Ordered`.
6. In column A in the third Summary row, type `Total # of Products Ordered`.

7. Make column A wide enough to see all of the text that you just added to the report, then make column C wider. Your Report Definition window should look like the one shown in Figure 17-9. Preview the report. It should look like the one shown in Figures 17-10 and 17-11.

	A	B	C	D
Title	Products Database - Orders By Date			
Title				
Headings	Product Name	Qty On Order	On Order Cost	Date Ordered
Headings				
Intr Date Orde				
Record	=Product Name	=Qty On Orde	=On Order Cost	=Date Ordere
Summ Date Orde		=SUM(Qty On	=SUM(On Order (	
Summ Date Orde	Number of Products Ordered	=COUNT(Proc		
Summary				
Summary	Total Pieces Ordered	=SUM(Qty On	=SUM(On Order (	
Summary	Total # of Products Ordered	=COUNT(Proc		

Figure 17-9 Report Definition window

Products Database - Orders By Date

Product Name	Qty On Order	On Order Cost	Date Ordered
Greek Made Easy	50	$600.00	1/15/2004
Italian Made Easy	25	$300.00	1/15/2004
The Best Of Access	20	$900.00	1/15/2004
	95	$1,800.00	
Number of Products Ordered 3			
Bugs Bunny	25	$137.50	1/20/2004
Curious George	25	$173.75	1/20/2004
Curious George Goes Sailing	20	$90.00	1/20/2004
Java Made Easy	25	$1,125.00	1/20/2004
Mary Poppins	25	$137.50	1/20/2004
	120	$1,663.75	
Number of Products Ordered 5			
Works Made Easy	30	$1,350.00	1/24/2004
	30	$1,350.00	
Number of Products Ordered 1			
Aladdin	25	$173.75	2/1/2004
C++	20	$400.00	2/1/2004
Cinderella	30	$135.00	2/1/2004
Let's Learn Excel	20	$210.00	2/1/2004
	95	$918.75	
Number of Products Ordered 4			

Figure 17-10 Page 1 of the Orders By Date report

Product Name	Qty On Order	On Order Cost	Date Ordered
Total # of Products Ordered	22		

Figure 17-11 Page 2 of the Orders By Date report

8. Save the changes and close the database.

Create The Sales Rep Report

This exercise will show you how to create a report that will group the data by Sales Rep. Within each sales rep group, the detail records will be sorted in order of when the customers should be contacted next.

1. Save the L16 Customer Reports database as `L17 Customer Reports`.

2. Tools ⇒ Report Creator. Type `Sales Rep` as the report name, then click OK.

3. Type `Sales Rep Totals` as the report title, then click Next.

4. Add the following fields to the report: First name, Last name, Next Contact On, Category and Order Total, then click Next.

5. Sort by Salesperson, then click Next.

6. On the Grouping tab, select the When contents change and Show group heading options.

These options will display the sales rep's name above all of the customers that they need to contact. If you needed to distribute this report to each sales rep, you would want to add a page break after each sales reps data, so that each sales reps information would start printing at the top of a new page. This would make it easier to distribute the report pages to the sales reps.

Add The Summary Information To The Report

1. On the Summary tab select the Order Total field. Select the Sum, Average and Count Summary options. Clear the Show summary name option.

2. Select the options At end of each group and Under each column. The Summary tab should have the options selected that are shown in Figure 17-12.

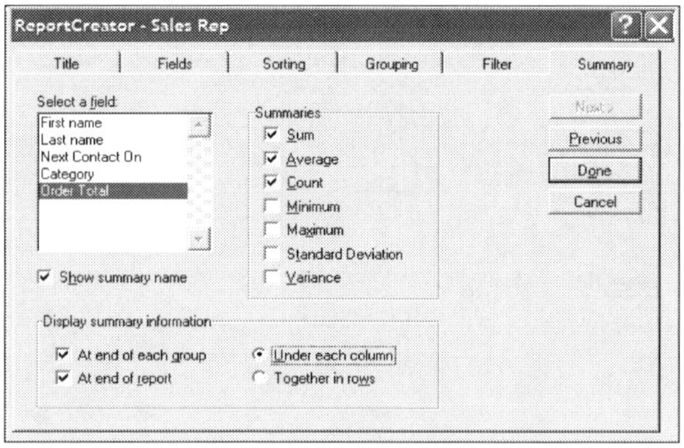

Figure 17-12 Summary tab options

3. Click Done, then preview the report. Your report should look like the one shown in Figure 17-13. Save the changes and leave the report open.

Sales Rep Totals

First name	Last name	Next Contact On	Category	Order Total
Allen				
Todd	Green	2/2/2004	Biography	$44.95
Kelly	Fontaine	2/5/2004	Computer	$63.95
Peter	Young	2/10/2004	Computer	$12.95
Martin	Davis	2/20/2004	Computer	$62.00
				$183.85
				$45.96
				$4.00
Altec				
Fred	Amos	2/9/2004	Sports	$12.95
Clair	Walsh	2/9/2004	Mystery	$34.99
Randi	Sherwood	2/14/2004	Sports	$50.00
Shaun	Smith	2/17/2004	Mystery	$75.00
				$172.94
				$43.24
				$4.00

Figure 17-13 Sales Rep Totals report

Modify The Sales Rep Totals Report

The first thing that you should notice is that all of the total fields are lined up under each other. The report would look better and would be easier to read if these totals were spread out.

1. Center the report title across the first row of the report.
2. Right align the Next Contact On, Category and Order Total fields in the **RECORD** row.
3. Make the First name, Last name and Category columns wider.
4. Move the Salesperson field from the Intr Salesperson row to column B in the first Summ Salesperson row under the Last Name field.
5. Type `Totals For` in column A in the first Summ Salesperson row.
6. Rearrange the total fields in the Report Definition window to look like the ones shown in Figure 17-14.

	A	B	C	D	E
Title			Sales Rep Totals		
Title					
Headings	First name	Last name	Next Contact On	Category	Order Total
Headings					
Intr Salespers					
Record	=First name	=Last name	=Next Contact On	=Category	=Order Total
Summ Salespers	Totals For	=Salesperson			=SUM(Order Tot
Summ Salespers				=AVG(Order Tota	
Summ Salespers				=COUNT(Order T	
Summ Salespers					
Summ Salespers					
Summ Salespers					
Summary					
Summary					=SUM(Order Tot
Summary				=AVG(Order Tota	
Summary				=COUNT(Order T	
Summary					
Summary					
Summary					

Figure 17-14 Fields rearranged in the Report Definition window

7. Make column C wider, then add the field titles shown in Figure 17-15 in column C in the Summ Salesperson and Summary sections.

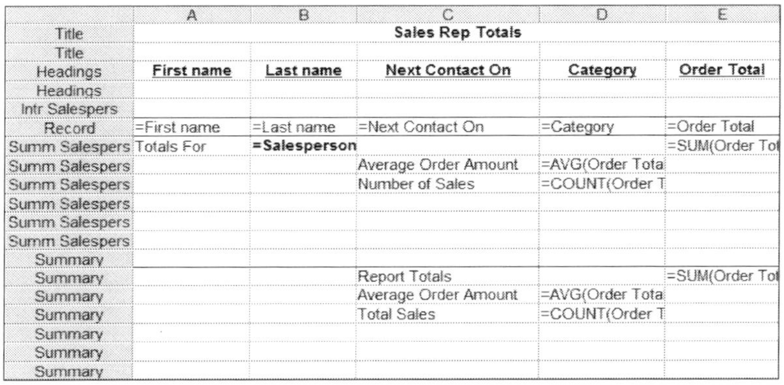

	A	B	C	D	E
Title			Sales Rep Totals		
Title					
Headings	First name	Last name	Next Contact On	Category	Order Total
Headings					
Intr Salespers					
Record	=First name	=Last name	=Next Contact On	=Category	=Order Total
Summ Salespers	Totals For	=Salesperson			=SUM(Order Tot
Summ Salespers			Average Order Amount	=AVG(Order Tota	
Summ Salespers			Number of Sales	=COUNT(Order T	
Summ Salespers					
Summ Salespers					
Summ Salespers					
Summary					
Summary			Report Totals		=SUM(Order Tot
Summary			Average Order Amount	=AVG(Order Tota	
Summary			Total Sales	=COUNT(Order T	
Summary					
Summary					
Summary					

Figure 17-15 Field titles added to the report

8. Right align all of the total fields in the Summ and Summary sections of the report.
9. Change the format type of the **=COUNT** fields to Number Comma, with zero decimal places. Save the changes.

Add And Remove Lines On A Report

1. Select the first three Summ Salesperson rows in columns A through E, then right-click and select Format.
2. On the Border tab, click on the **OUTLINE** border option, then click OK.
3. Select the Intr Salesperson row, then right-click and select Format.
4. On the Border tab, click on the **BOTTOM** border option twice, so that the box is clear, as illustrated in Figure 17-16.

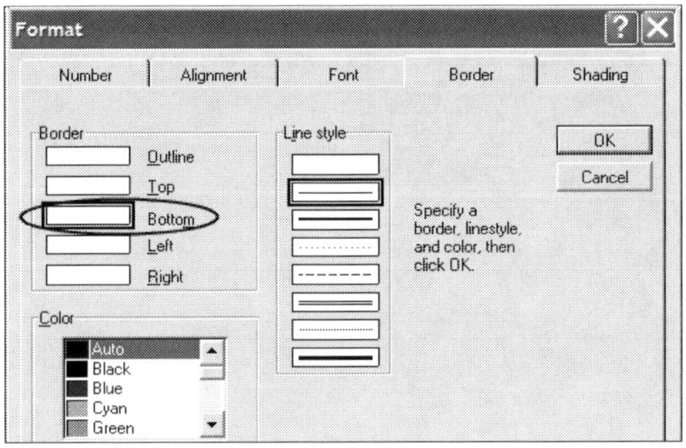

Figure 17-16 Border options changed

5. Click OK and preview the report. It should look like the one shown in Figures 17-17 and 17-18. Save the changes and close the database.

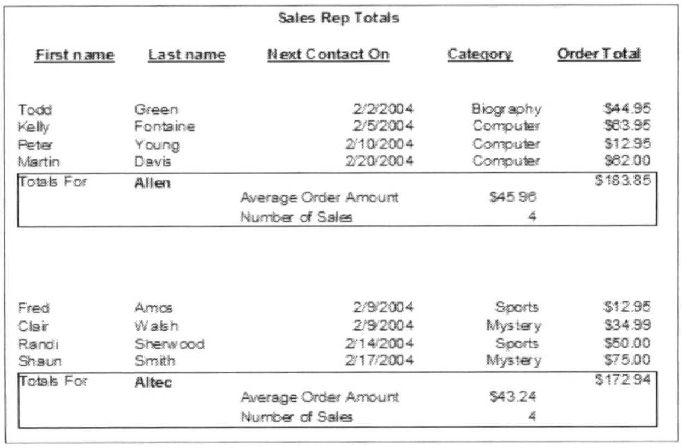

Sales Rep Totals

First name	Last name	Next Contact On	Category	Order Total
Todd	Green	2/2/2004	Biography	$44.95
Kelly	Fontaine	2/5/2004	Computer	$63.95
Peter	Young	2/10/2004	Computer	$12.95
Martin	Davis	2/20/2004	Computer	$62.00
Totals For	Allen			$183.85
		Average Order Amount	$45.96	
		Number of Sales	4	
Fred	Amos	2/9/2004	Sports	$12.95
Clair	Walsh	2/9/2004	Mystery	$34.99
Randi	Sherwood	2/14/2004	Sports	$50.00
Shaun	Smith	2/17/2004	Mystery	$75.00
Totals For	Altec			$172.94
		Average Order Amount	$43.24	
		Number of Sales	4	

Figure 17-17 Page 1 - Sales Rep Totals report

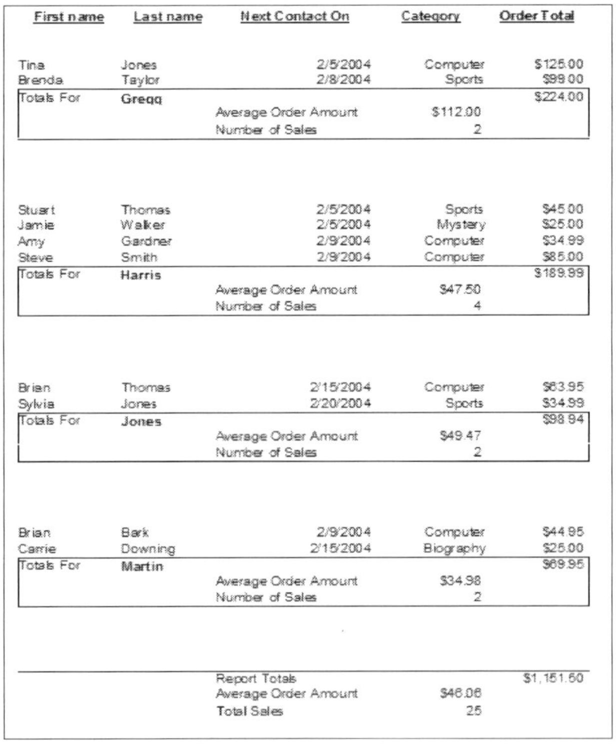

First name	Last name	Next Contact On	Category	Order Total
Tina	Jones	2/5/2004	Computer	$125.00
Brenda	Taylor	2/8/2004	Sports	$99.00
Totals For	Gregg			$224.00
		Average Order Amount	$112.00	
		Number of Sales	2	
Stuart	Thomas	2/5/2004	Sports	$45.00
Jamie	Walker	2/5/2004	Mystery	$25.00
Amy	Gardner	2/9/2004	Computer	$34.99
Steve	Smith	2/9/2004	Computer	$85.00
Totals For	Harris			$189.99
		Average Order Amount	$47.50	
		Number of Sales	4	
Brian	Thomas	2/15/2004	Computer	$63.95
Sylvia	Jones	2/20/2004	Sports	$34.99
Totals For	Jones			$98.94
		Average Order Amount	$49.47	
		Number of Sales	2	
Brian	Bark	2/9/2004	Computer	$44.95
Carrie	Downing	2/15/2004	Biography	$25.00
Totals For	Martin			$69.95
		Average Order Amount	$34.98	
		Number of Sales	2	
		Report Totals		$1,151.50
		Average Order Amount	$46.06	
		Total Sales	25	

Figure 17-18 Page 2 - Sales Rep Totals report

Test Your Skills

1. Save the L17 Customer Reports database as `L17(skills)`.

   - Duplicate the On Order report. Name the duplicate report `20_On_Order`.
   - Create a filter for the 20_On_Order report called `Qty_On_Order_20` that finds records that the Qty On Order field equals 20.
   - Add a subtitle to the report to indicate the Qty On Order equals 20.
   - Remove the header information from the report.

THE CALENDAR

In this lesson you will learn how to use the following features of the calendar:

- ☑ Calendar views
- ☑ The default calendar options
- ☑ Creating, viewing and modifying appointments
- ☑ The View Reminders dialog box
- ☑ Creating and using appointment categories
- ☑ Printing the calendar

LESSON 18

Calendar Overview

The calendar has several features that you can use to help stay organized. These features include looking at the calendar in different views, creating appointments and setting reminders. You can also print your calendar.

> **MSWKSCAL.WCD** is the file that holds all of the calendar entries that you create. If you create a lot of entries in the calendar you may want to back this file up from time to time.

Calendar Views

The first place that you will see the calendar is on the right side of the Home page of the Task Launcher as shown in Figure 18-1.

The Appointments view, shown on the right side of Figure 18-1, provides an overview of the current months calendar. For a more detailed view and to use the majority of the calendar features, you have to open the calendar and use one of the views discussed below.

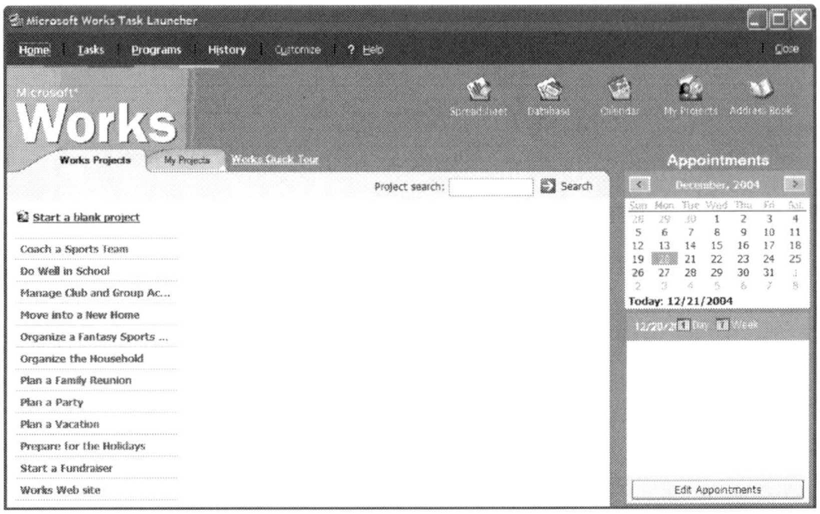

Figure 18-1 Calendar on the Home page of the Task Launcher

The bottom half of the Appointments section will display appointments for the day or week that you click on in the calendar. After you create appointments, you can come back to this page and view them. Dates that have at least one appointment will be bold on the calendar.

> The **EDIT APPOINTMENTS** button will open the calendar.

1. Click on the **CALENDAR** icon on the Home page. If your email software opens, close it and the calendar will open. You should see the calendar shown in Figure 18-2. If you have already used the calendar, you may have a different view showing then the one shown in Figure 18-2. The Day view lets you see all of the appointments for a particular day.

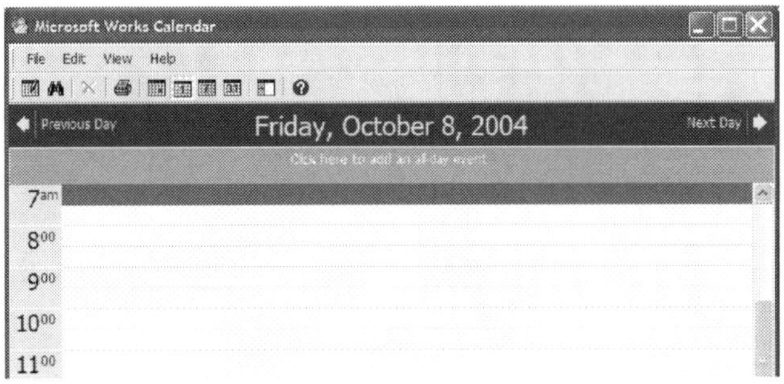

Figure 18-2 Day view of the calendar

> The **PREVIOUS** arrow button to the left of the date in the calendar shown above in Figure 18-2 will go back one day, one week or one month, depending on the calendar view that is currently open. The **NEXT** arrow button to the right of the date will go to the next day, the next week or the next month, depending on the calendar view that is currently open.

2. View ⇒ Week. You should see the view shown in Figure 18-3. This view will let you see all of the appointments for one week at the same time.

3. View ⇒ Month. You should see the view shown in Figure 18-4. This view will let you see all of the appointments for an entire month at the same time.

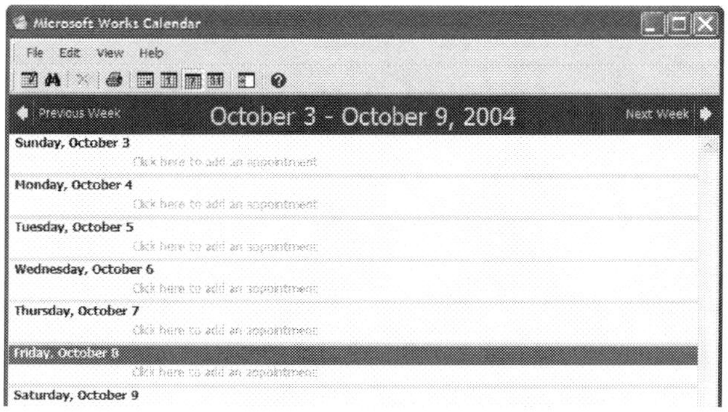

Figure 18-3 Week view of the calendar

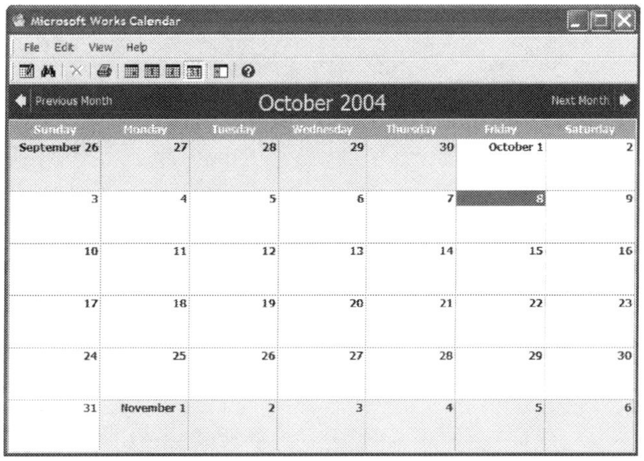

Figure 18-4 Month view of the calendar

Calendar Toolbar And Menu

You should familiarize yourself with the calendar toolbar and menu. Like the other applications in Works, the buttons on the toolbar are probably the ones that you will use most. Figure 18-5 shows the calendar toolbar. Table 18-1 explains the purpose of the buttons. Figure 18-6 shows the calendar menu. Table 18-2 explains the calendar menu options.

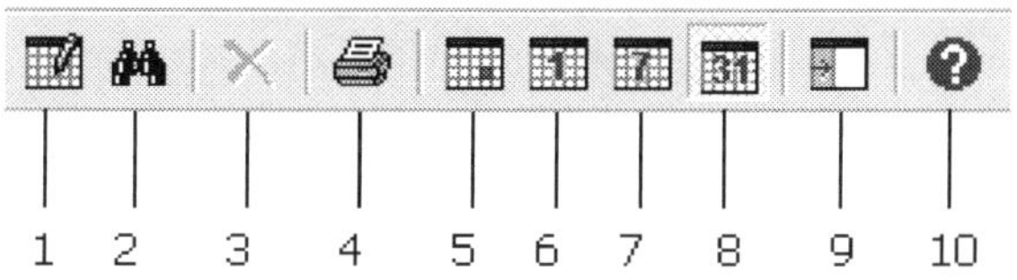

Figure 18-5 Calendar toolbar

Button	Purpose
1	Create a new appointment.
2	Opens the Find dialog box, which will let you search for an appointment.
3	Deletes an appointment or event.
4	Opens the Print dialog box so that you can print the calendar.
5	Takes you to "today" on the calendar. This is useful if your current calendar view is not the current day, week or month.
6	Opens the "Day" calendar view shown earlier in Figure 18-2.
7	Opens the "Week" calendar view shown earlier in Figure 18-3.
8	Opens the "Month" calendar view shown earlier in Figure 18-4.
9	Displays the category filters on the calendar window.
10	Opens the Help System.

Table 18-1 Calendar toolbar buttons explained

Figure 18-6 Calendar menu

Menu	Purpose
File	Open and create appointments, as well as, print the calendar.
Edit	Create and edit categories, update the calendar with birthday entries from your address book, find appointments and change the default calendar options.
View	Change how the calendar is displayed by selecting a different view, which you did earlier in this lesson, as well as, view reminders and categories.
Help	Opens the Help System.

Table 18-2 Calendar menu options explained

How To Change The Size Of The Toolbar

If the default size of the toolbar on the calendar is too small, you can make it larger by following the steps below.

1. Open the calendar if it is not already open.
2. View ⇒ Toolbar ⇒ Use Large Icons, as shown in Figure 18-7.

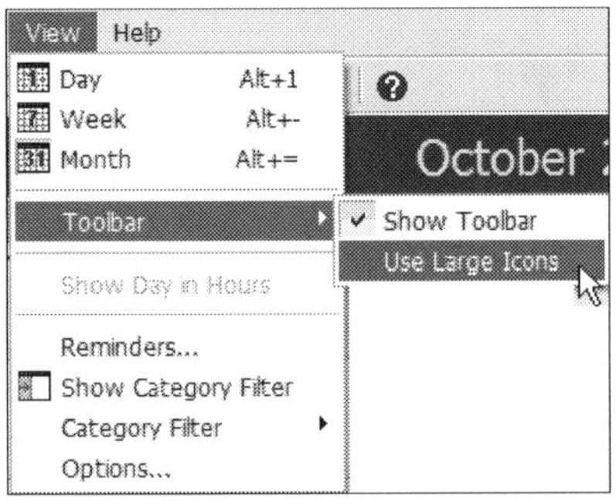

Figure 18-7 Use Large Icons option illustrated

Notice that you can also hide the toolbar, by clearing the **SHOW TOOLBAR** option shown above in Figure 18-7.

Calendar Options

The options discussed below will allow you to customize settings that will let the calendar work in a way that is best for you.

1. View ⇒ Options. You will see the dialog box shown in Figure 18-8.

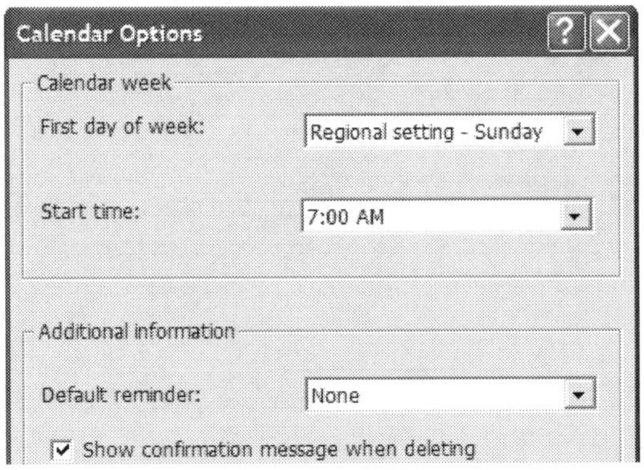

Figure 18-8 Calendar Options dialog box

① The **FIRST DAY OF WEEK** drop-down list will let you select which day you want the calendar to use as the first day of the week. The default is Sunday.
② The **START TIME** drop-down lists lets you select the earliest time that will be displayed on the daily calendar, shown earlier in Figure 18-2.
③ The **DEFAULT REMINDER** option lets you select how far in advance of an appointment or event that you want to be reminded of it. If you select a reminder time here, each time that you create a new appointment, this time will be filled in automatically. When you are creating or editing appointments, you have the option of changing the reminder time from what you select here.
④ The **SHOW CONFIRMATION MESSAGE WHEN DELETING** option, if checked will prompt you to see if you are sure that you really want to delete the item from your calendar.

2. Open the Default reminder drop-down list, select **15 MINUTES**, then click OK.

Appointments Overview

Appointments are probably the best reason to use the calendar. Because the appointment feature is very flexible, you can enter a variety of appointments. You can use appointments as a to do list. You can also create to-do lists in the Projects application that you will learn about in the next lesson.

If you assign a due date to a task in a project, an appointment and a reminder will automatically be created in the calendar, as you will see in the next lesson.

1. Click the New Appointment button on the toolbar (or File ⇒ New Appointment). You will see the dialog box shown in Figure 18-9.

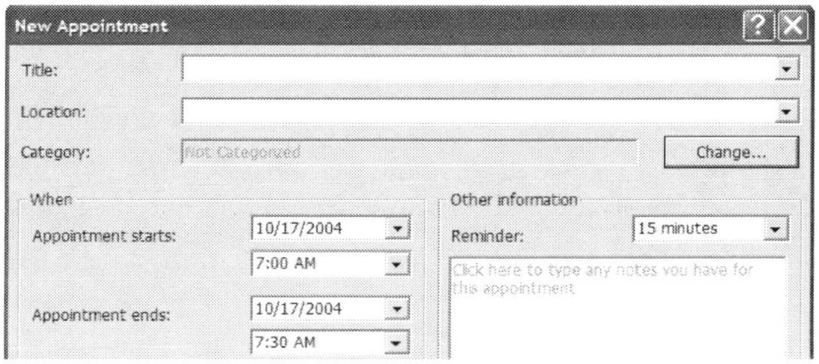

Figure 18-9 New Appointment dialog box

Most of the appointment fields are optional. At a minimum, you should fill in the title and start date.

① The **TITLE** field is what you want to name the appointment. The last seven appointment titles that you created will be in the drop-down list for this field. This is a free form field. It is a good idea to enter a title that makes sense to you.
② The **LOCATION** is where the appointment will take place.
③ The **CATEGORY** field will let you select a category for the appointment. You can use one of the categories shown in Figure 18-10 that comes with Works, or you can create your own category. To select a different category, click the **CHANGE** button on the New Appointment dialog box. The reason to select a category is if you think that you will want to view appointments that are similar. For example, if you have created several medical appointments, you may only want to view all of the medical appointments on the calendar at one time, instead of seeing all of your appointments. If you create a project, a category will automatically be created for the project.
④ The **APPOINTMENT START** and **END** fields let you select the day and time the appointment will start and end.

⑤ The **ALL-DAY EVENT** option if checked, will schedule the appointment for the entire day. Appointments scheduled for an entire day or more, like a three day conference, are called events. Other types of events include appointments that do not have a specific time.

⑥ The **MAKE THIS APPOINTMENT REPEAT** option if checked, will let you set the appointment up multiple times. An example of when to use this feature is for weekly meetings. This type of appointment is known as a **RECURRING** appointment. Recurring appointments can be daily, weekly, monthly or yearly. This is how you would set up birthday and anniversary reminders.

⑦ The **REMINDER** option determines how far in advance of the appointment start time that you will be notified. As shown earlier in Figure 18-9, 15 minutes is displayed by default. The reason is because that is the time that you selected earlier when setting up the default calendar options.

⑧ The **NOTES** field which is right below the Reminder field, is a free form field that you can enter any additional information about the appointment that you want.

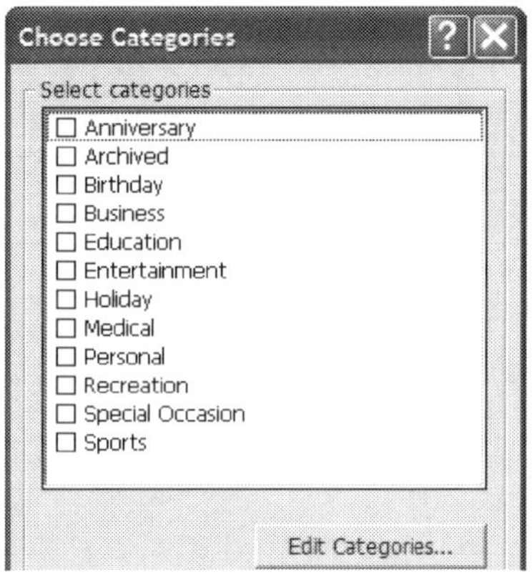

Figure 18-10 Default calendar category options

Create Your First Appointment

Now that you understand what each field on the appointment window means, it's time to create a few appointments. You will create several appointments and apply different options to the appointments.

1. Open the New Appointment dialog box, if it is not already open.

2. Type `My first appointment` in the **TITLE** field, then type `In my home office` in the **LOCATION** field.

3. Click the **CHANGE** button. (It's at the end of the Category field.) You should see the Choose Categories dialog box shown above in Figure 18-10. Select the **EDUCATION** category, then click OK.

4. The current date should be in the **APPOINTMENT STARTS** field. Open the time drop-down list in the Appointment starts section and select the time it will be 30 minutes from now. For example, if it is 9 PM now, you would select 9:30 PM.

5. The current date should be in the Appointment Ends field. If not, change it to the current date. Change the **APPOINTMENT ENDS** time to 1 hour from now.

6. Type `The purpose of this appointment is to test the reminder feature` in the **NOTES** field. Your appointment should look similar to the one shown in Figure 18-11. The only difference should be the dates and times. Click OK.

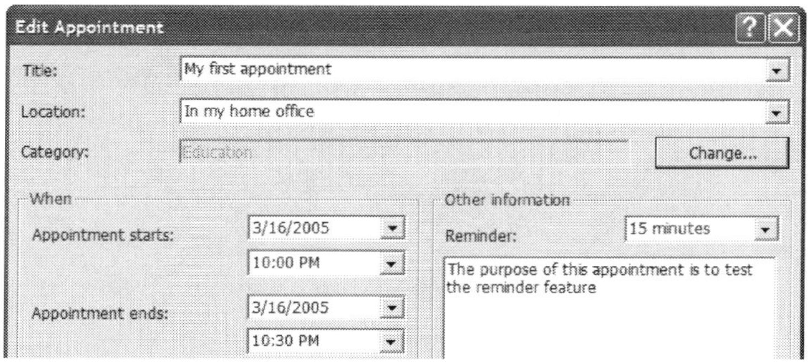

Figure 18-11 Completed appointment

View The Appointment That You Just Created

In 15 minutes, the View Reminders dialog box should appear on your screen with the appointment that you just created. When the View Reminder dialog box appears on your screen, go to the section called "View Reminders Dialog Box" later in this lesson. In the mean time, you can continue with the exercises. To view the appointment that you just created, follow the steps below.

1. Click on one of the calendar views. You will see the appointment that you just created, as shown in Figure 18-12. You should see a bell next to the appointment. This lets you know that there is a reminder set for the appointment.

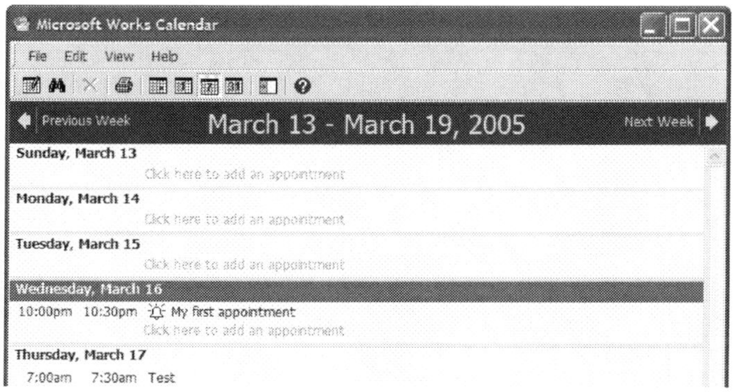

Figure 18-12 Appointment displayed in the weekly calendar view

2. If you double-click on the appointment, you will be able to see all of the details for the appointment. If you click on the Task Launcher button and look in the Appointments section, you will see the appointment that you just created, as shown in Figure 18-13.

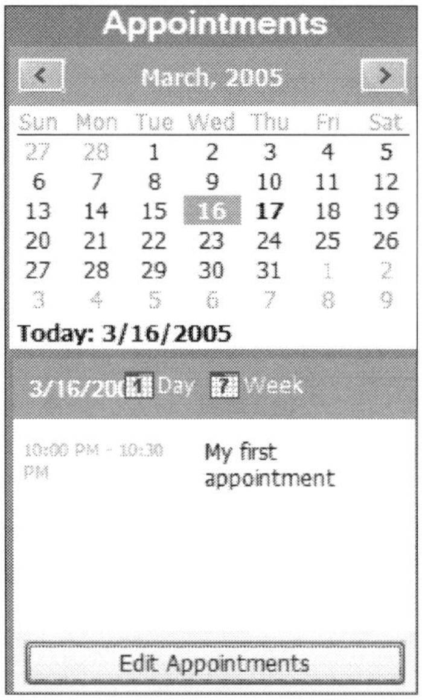

Figure 18-13 Appointment shown on the Home page of the Task Launcher

3. If you click the **EDIT APPOINTMENTS** button, the calendar will open to the view that you had open last.

View Reminders Dialog Box

If you are reading this section for the first time, hopefully that means that the View Reminders dialog box has appeared on your screen. If you set up the first appointment, but the View Reminders dialog box has not appeared on your screen, you may want to go to the next exercise and come back to this one when the View Reminders dialog box appears. Doing this will make it easier to follow along in this section, but the choice is yours.

> If it has been more than 15 minutes since you created the appointment shown earlier in Figure 18-11, you should go back and review your appointment to make sure that it looks like the one shown in Figure 18-11.

For appointments that you have set a reminder for, you will see the dialog box shown in Figure 18-14.

If you have several reminders set for the same time period, you will see multiple entries in this dialog box.

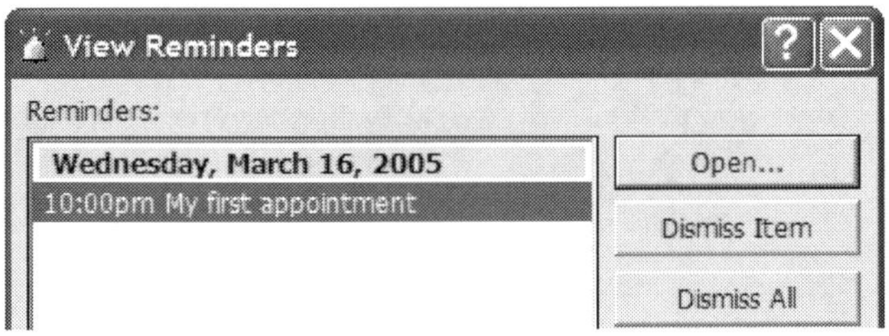

Figure 18-14 View Reminders dialog box

> Keep in mind that you can create appointments that overlap by time, which means that you can create an appointment that starts at 10 PM and ends at 11 PM and create an appointment that starts at 10:30 PM. The calendar application will not be warn you that you have created overlapping appointments.

View Reminders Dialog Box Options

This dialog box has three options that you can use to help manage the reminders that you create.

① The **OPEN** button will open the Edit Appointment dialog box shown in Figure 18-15. It looks like the New Appointment dialog box. You can view all of the appointment details on the Edit Appointment dialog box. You can also make changes to the appointment from this dialog box. If you make any changes on the Edit Appointment dialog box, click OK to save the changes.

② The **DISMISS ITEM** button will cancel the reminder that you select on the View Reminders dialog box. Using this option will allow you to cancel a reminder and leave the other reminders.

> Until you dismiss an appointment you will continue to be reminded of it on a daily basis. If you turn your computer on tomorrow you will receive a reminder about this appointment, if you do not dismiss it now.

③ The **DISMISS ALL** button will cancel all of the reminders that are displayed on the View Reminders dialog box at the time you click the Dismiss All button.

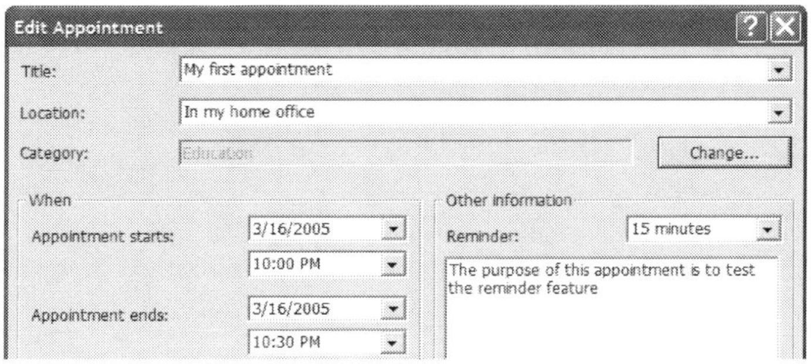

Figure 18-15 Edit Appointment dialog box

1. You can dismiss the reminder now or wait until tomorrow to dismiss it.

2. When you are finished, close any dialog boxes that you have open.

Create An All Day Event

1. Use the information in Table 18-3 to create an all day event. Your appointment should look like the one shown in Figure 18-16.

Title	All day event
Location	(leave it blank)
Category	Education
Start Date/Time	Tomorrow's date
End Date/Time	Tomorrow's date
All-day event	Check this option
Reminder	30 minutes
Notes	This is an all day event

Table 18-3 Information for an all day event

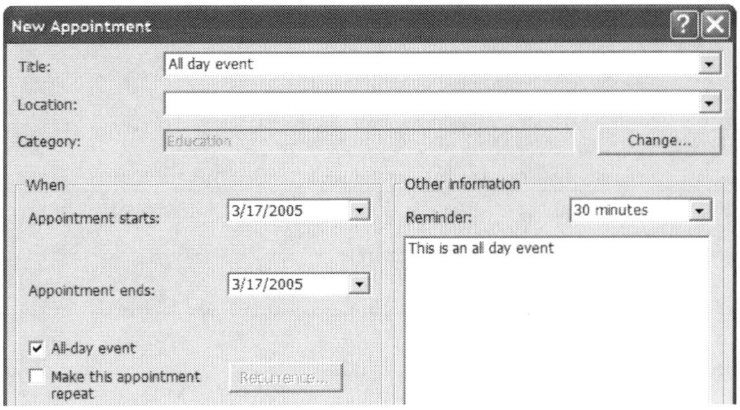

Figure 18-16 All day event appointment options

2. Click OK to save the appointment.

Create A Weekly Recurring Appointment

A recurring appointment is one that you want scheduled on a regular basis.

1. Use the information in Table 18-4 to create a weekly recurring appointment.

Title	Weekly recurring event
Location	At home
Category	Personal
Start Date/Time	2 days from today / 9 PM
End Date/Time	2 days from today / 10 PM
Reminder	15 minutes
Notes	Watch my favorite TV show

Table 18-4 Information for the weekly recurring appointment

2. Select the **MAKE THIS APPOINTMENT REPEAT** option.

3. Click the **RECURRENCE** button. You will see the Recurrence Options dialog box. Select the **END AFTER OCCURRENCES** option and change it to 6 as shown in Figure 18-17.

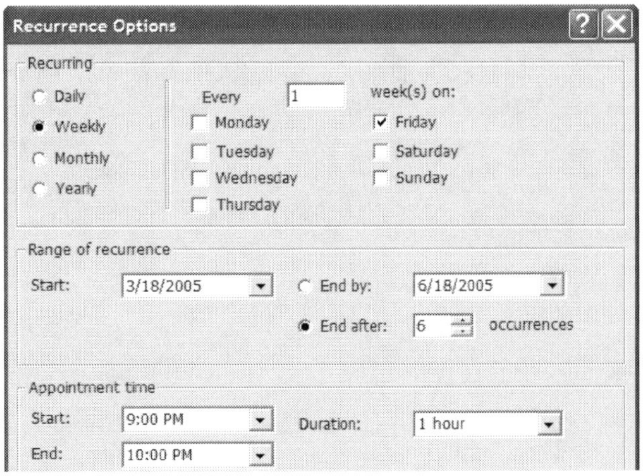

Figure 18-17 Recurrence options for a weekly recurring appointment

This means that you will be reminded to watch the TV show for the next six weeks.

4. Click OK to close the Recurrence Options dialog box. Your appointment should look similar to the one shown in Figure 18-18. Click OK.

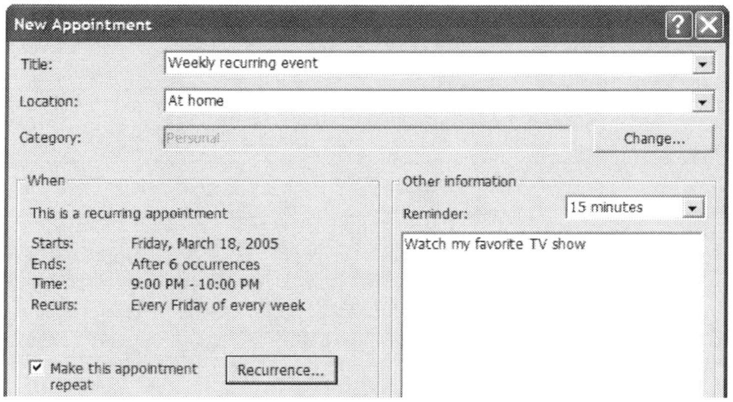

Figure 18-18 Weekly recurring appointment options illustrated

Create A Yearly Recurring Appointment

Creating a yearly recurring appointment is a good way to be reminded of birthdays and anniversaries.

1. Use the information in Table 18-5 to create a yearly recurring appointment.

Title	Friends birthday
Location	(leave blank)
Category	Birthday
Start Date/Time	Select the date, 8 days from today
Reminder	1 week
Notes	Birthday reminder.

Table 18-5 Information for the yearly recurring appointment

The reason that I had you set the start date eight days from today is so that tomorrow you will get a reminder for this yearly event. When you see the reminder for it, you can dismiss it so that you will not continue to be reminded of it.

2. Select the **MAKE THIS APPOINTMENT REPEAT** option.

3. Click the **RECURRENCE** button. Select the **YEARLY** recurring option on the Recurrence Options dialog box, then select the **ON** option, if it is not already selected.

The default yearly number of reminders is 10. If you needed a different number of years, you would change the **END AFTER OCCURRENCES** option to what you need.

4. Your dialog box should look similar to the one shown in Figure 18-19. Click OK. Your appointment should look similar to the one shown in Figure 18-20. Click OK.

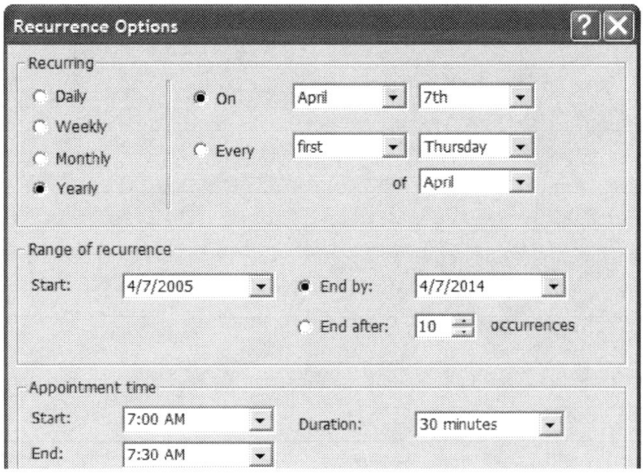

Figure 18-19 Recurrence options for a yearly recurring appointment

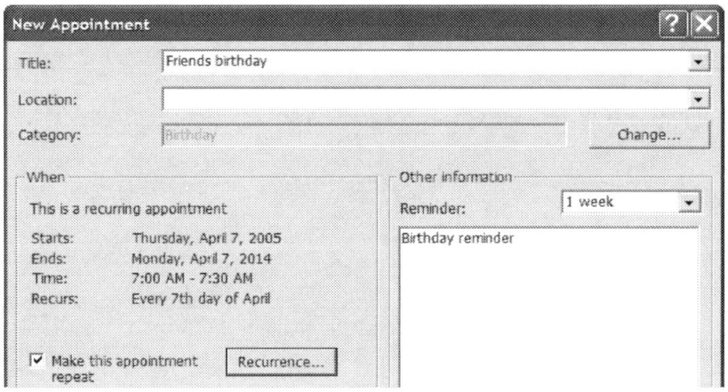

Figure 18-20 Yearly recurring appointment options illustrated

Modifying Recurring Appointments Overview

You may have a need to modify a recurring appointment. If so, you can follow the instructions below. In this exercise you will modify the weekly appointment that you created. You will change the time of the TV program, the title of the appointment and the number of occurrences.

1. In the weekly calendar view, locate the "Weekly recurring event" appointment that you created earlier in this lesson, similar to the one shown in Figure 18-21. When you locate the appointment, double-click on it. You will see the dialog box shown in Figure 18-22.

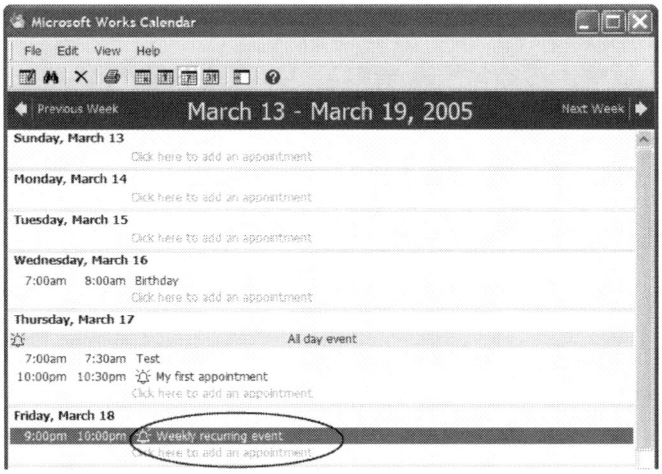

Figure 18-21 Weekly recurring event illustrated

As you can see in Figure 18-22, there are two options for modifying a recurring appointment. The first option, **OPEN THIS OCCURRENCE** will let you modify the occurrence of the appointment that you selected. You would select this option if you only wanted the changes that you are about to make, to only be applied to the appointment that you selected. This option will allow you to customize each occurrence of the appointment individually.

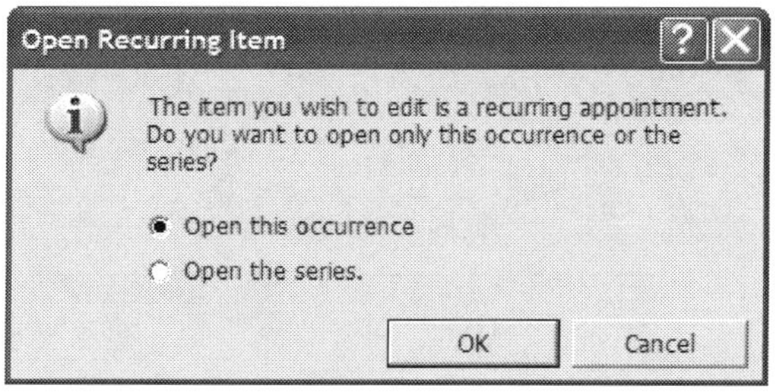

Figure 18-22 Open Recurring Item dialog box

The second option, **OPEN THE SERIES** will let you apply the changes that you are about to make to every occurrence of the appointment. The "Weekly recurring event" appointment that you created is scheduled for the next several weeks, as shown in Figure 18-23.

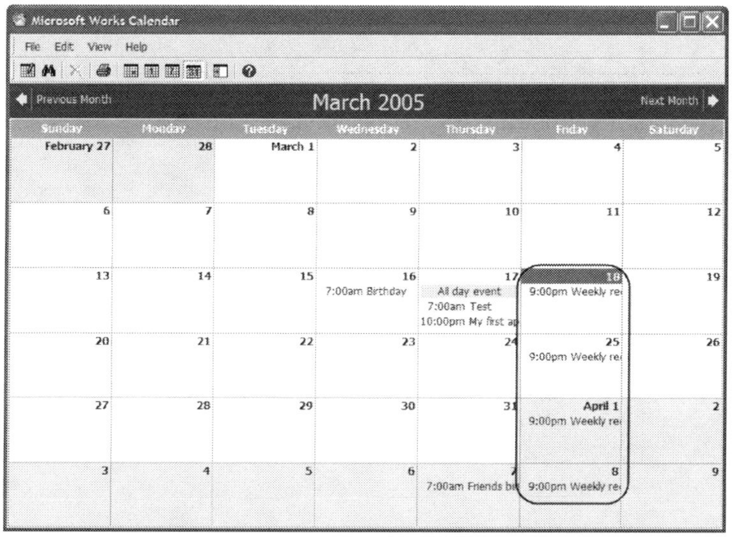

Figure 18-23 Weekly recurring appointment illustrated

2. Click Cancel on the Open Recurring Item dialog box.

Modify One Occurrence Of A Recurring Appointment

In this exercise you will modify one appointment from a recurring series of appointments. You will change the time for the second appointment in the series.

1. Right-click on the second "Weekly recurring event" appointment in the monthly calendar view and select **OPEN** as shown in Figure 18-24.

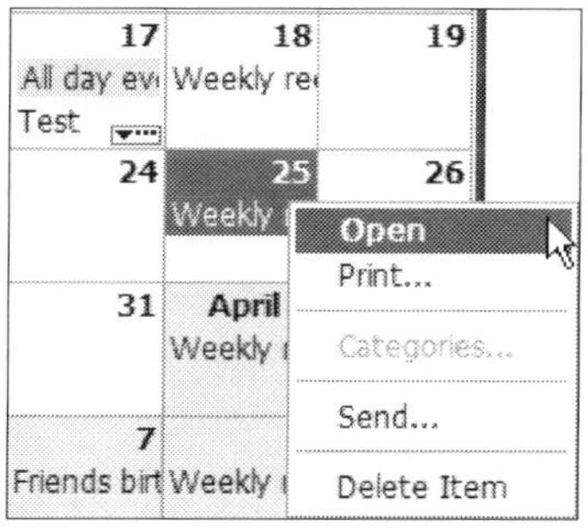

Figure 18-24 Calendar shortcut menu

2. You will see the Open Recurring Item dialog box that you saw earlier in Figure 18-22. Select the first option, if it is not already selected and click OK.

3. Change the **START TIME** to 10 PM. Your Edit Appointment dialog box should look like the one shown in Figure 18-25. The only difference should be the Start and End dates. Click OK.

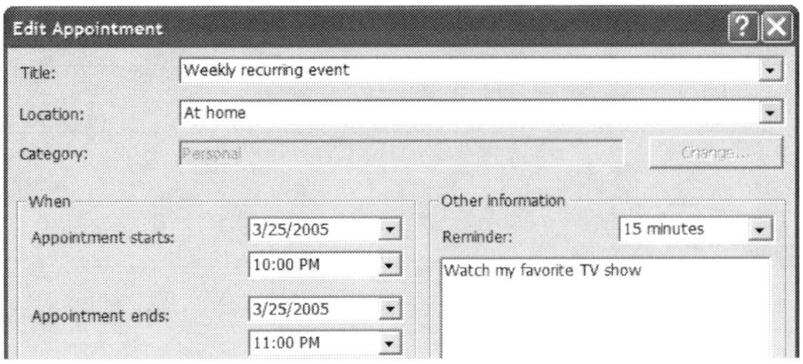

Figure 18-25 Changed Start and End times illustrated

Check The Appointment Changes

Now that you have changed one occurrence, you may think that the other appointments in the series have also changed. If you open any of the other appointments in the series you will see that the start time is still 9 PM and the end time is still 10 PM. To verify this, follow the steps below.

1. Right-click and select Open on any occurrence of the "Weekly recurring event", in the monthly calendar view, except for the second appointment.

2. Select the first option on the Open Recurring Item dialog box and click OK. You will see the dialog box shown in Figure 18-26. This dialog box still shows the original start and end times that you entered. Click Cancel to close the appointment.

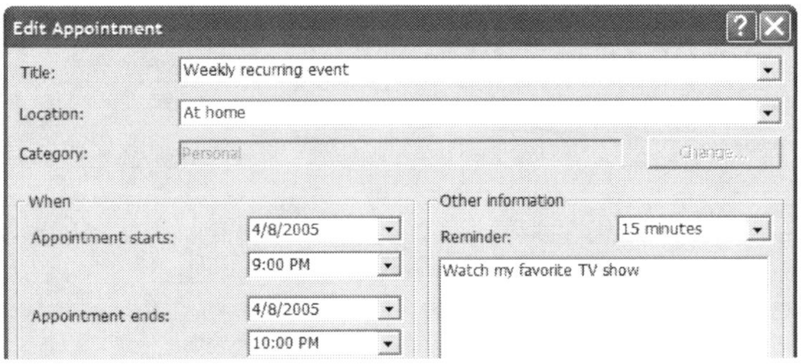

Figure 18-26 Appointment in series illustrated

Modify A Series Of Recurring Appointments

In this exercise you will modify all of the appointments in the series at one time. When you modify the series of appointments, any prior changes that you have made to individual appointments in the series could be lost, depending on which appointment in the series is selected as the one to make changes for all of the appointments in the series. The time change that you made earlier to the second appointment in the series, could be lost if it is not the appointment that is selected to make the changes to.

It is important to think about any changes that you may have to make to a series of recurring appointments. Any changes that need to be made to all of the appointments should be made first, otherwise you will have to make the same change multiple times. In this exercise, you will change the title of the appointment and the number of occurrences.

1. Right-click on the first weekly recurring event in the monthly calendar view and select **OPEN**. (You can select any appointment in the series.) You will see the Open Recurring Item dialog box. Select the second option, **OPEN THE SERIES** and click OK.

2. Change the **TITLE** to `Watch TV Show`.

3. Click the Recurrence button and change the **END AFTER OCCURRENCES** option to 12. Figure 18-27 shows the options that should be selected. Click OK. Your appointment should look like the one shown in Figure 18-28. Notice that the **ENDS** option has changed to 12 occurrences. Click OK to close the appointment window.

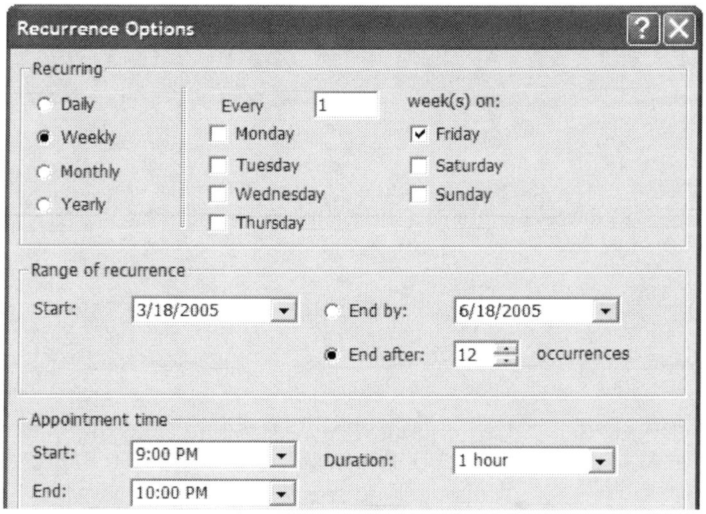

Figure 18-27 Modified recurrence options

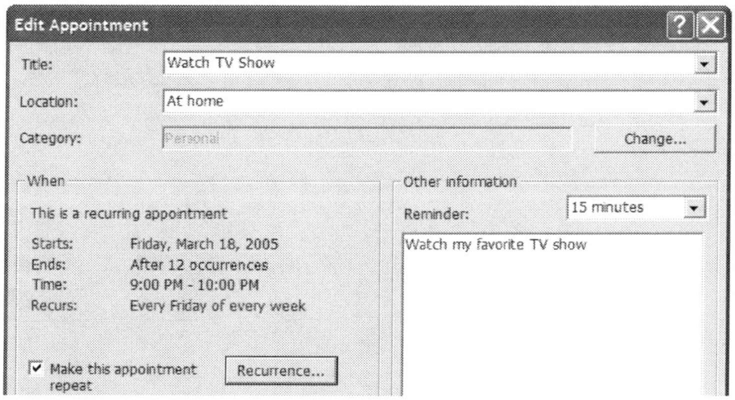

Figure 18-28 Modified appointment options

Check The Appointment Changes

Now that you have made changes to all of the appointments in the series, check the calendar and compare the differences shown in Figure 18-29 with the original appointment, shown earlier in Figure 18-23.

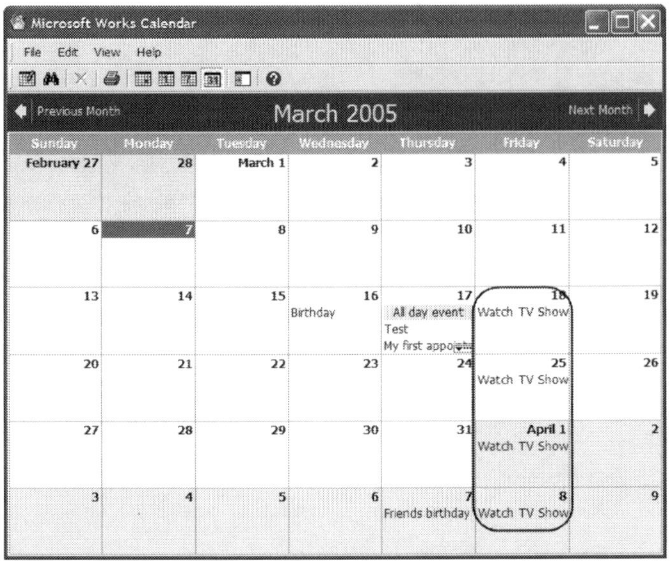

Figure 18-29 Modified weekly event illustrated

View Appointments On The Home Page

Earlier in the lesson, I mentioned that you can view appointments from the Home page at the bottom of the Appointments section. Now that you have created a few appointments you have something to view from the Home page. In the bottom portion of the Appointments section on the Home page, you can view appointments by day or by week.

View Appointments By Day

1. Go to the Home page of the Task Launcher. If you click on a date in the calendar that is bold and then click the **DAY** link, all of the appointments for that day will appear at the bottom of the Appointments section as shown in Figure 18-30.

View Appointments By Week

1. If you click on a date in the calendar that is bold and then click the **WEEK** link, all of the appointments for that week will appear at the bottom of the Appointments section as shown in Figure 18-31.

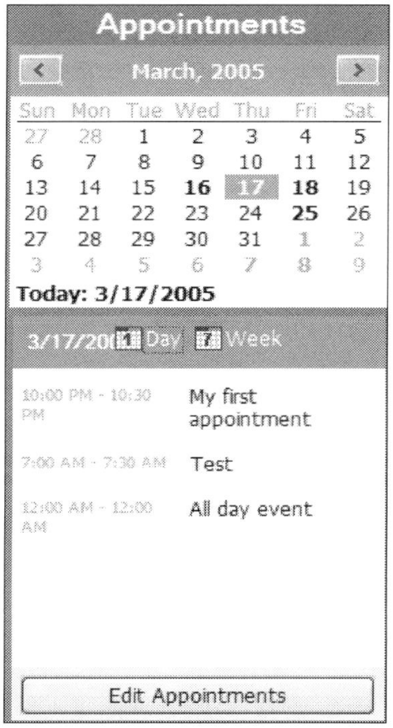

Figure 18-30 Appointments for one day illustrated

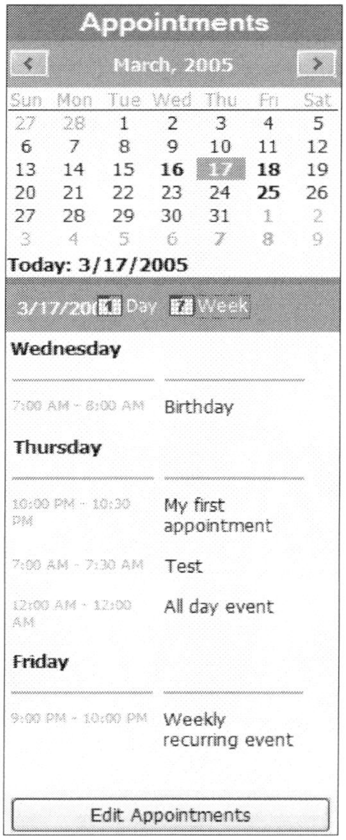

Figure 18-31 Appointments for one week illustrated

Categories

Categories are a way for you to group your appointments and events. The calendar has several categories that you can use that were shown earlier in Figure 18-10. If these options are not sufficient, you can create your own categories.

The reason that many people select a category for appointments is to be able to filter the appointments by category. An example of why this is helpful is if you only wanted to see all of the birthdays or anniversaries, or all of your weekly staff meetings.

Create More Appointments

For the category exercises to be more meaningful, you need a few more appointments. Create the three appointments in Table 18-6 in the same month that you created the other appointments in.

Appointment	1	2	3
Title	2nd friends birthday	Finish Lesson 18	Add new category
Category	Birthday	Education	(leave blank)
Start Date	1st of the month	3rd of the month	5th of the month

Table 18-6 Additional appointments

Adding, Modifying And Deleting Categories

In the next few exercises you will learn how to add, rename and delete categories.

Adding Categories

In this exercise you will learn how to add new categories to the existing list of categories.

1. Edit ⇒ Categories. You should see the Edit Categories dialog box. Type `My Category` in the field at the bottom of the dialog box shown in Figure 18-32.

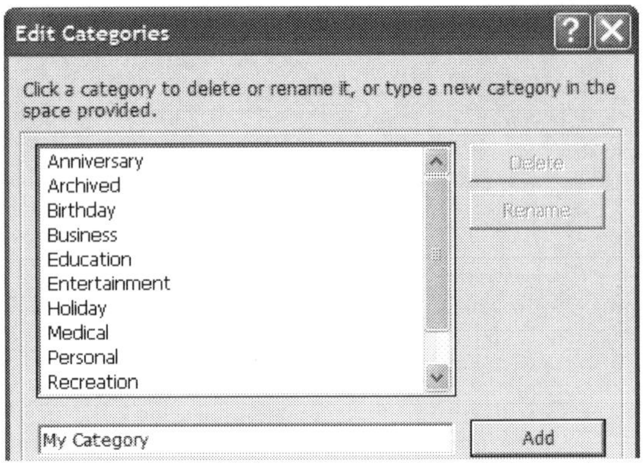

Figure 18-32 New category added

2. Click the **ADD** button. You should see the category that you just added, right below the Medical category.

3. Add the category `My 2nd Category` to the list.

Renaming Categories

You just noticed that the category that you just created should be My Last Category instead of My 2nd Category. You can rename the entry.

1. Click on the My 2nd Category option in the list and type `My Last Category` in the field at the bottom of the dialog box as shown in Figure 18-33.

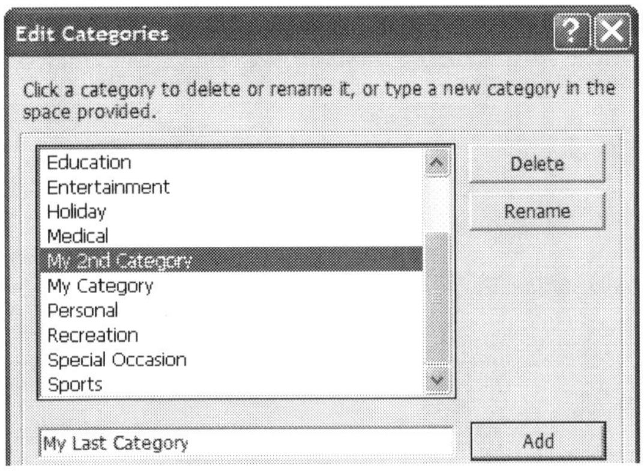

Figure 18-33 Category option selected to be renamed

2. Click the **RENAME** button.

Deleting Categories

You can just read through this exercise because there is no need to delete any categories.

1. If the Edit Categories dialog box shown above in Figure 18-33 is not open, open it now.

2. Click on the category that you want to delete, then click the **DELETE** button. Click OK.

> If you have a lot of appointments associated with categories, it is probably not a good idea to start deleting categories. If you delete a category that has appointments associated to it, you will see the message shown in Figure 18-34. This message is letting you know that you have at least one appointment associated to the category. If you still decide to delete the category, you can. The calendar has a filter that will display a list of appointments that do not have a category. You will learn about calendar filters later in this lesson.

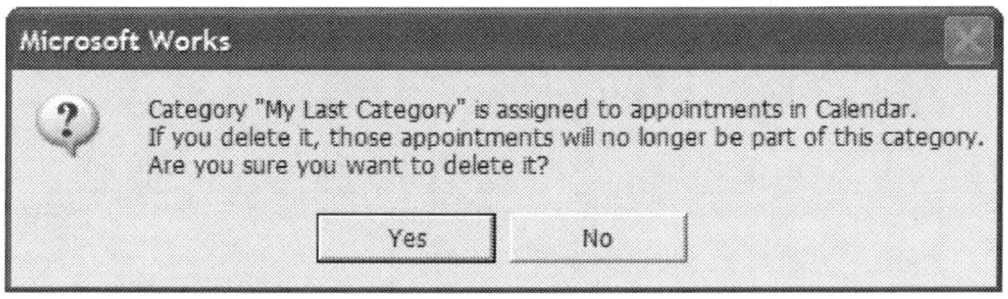

Figure 18-34 Category deletion warning message

Viewing Appointments

The two ways that you can view appointments are by scrolling through one of the calendar views, which you have already learned how to do in this lesson and by selecting (or deselecting) one or more categories of appointments that you want to view (or not view) by using the category filters.

View Appointments By Category

Now that you have added and modified categories, it's time to view the appointments by category. The best way to see a how the category feature works is in the month view of the calendar.

1. Open the calendar to the current months view or the month that has the appointments that you created in this lesson. Click the **CATEGORY FILTER** button on the toolbar. On the left you will see the category filters, as shown in Figure 18-35.

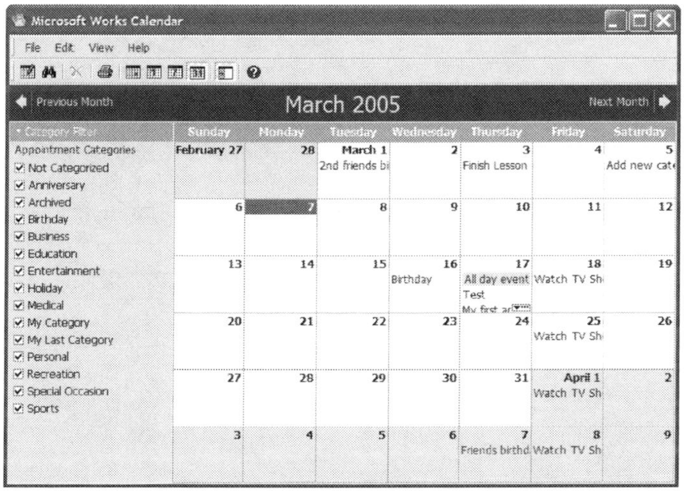

Figure 18-35 Category filters illustrated

2. If you clear the **EDUCATION** filter, you will see that the appointments for that category disappear from the calendar. The more filters that you clear, the fewer appointments you will see on the calendar.

Using The Find Option

The Find option is helpful when you have appointments spread out over several months. The three ways that you can find appointments are by **KEYWORD**, **TIME** and **CATEGORY**.

Find Appointments By Keyword

The keyword option will let you find appointments that have the keyword that you enter.

1. Click the **FIND** button on the toolbar or Edit ⇒ Find. You will see the Find dialog box.

2. Type the keyword that you want to search for. For this exercise, type `TV`.

You can select where you want the search to look for this keyword. Selecting the second option, **SEARCH TITLE AND NOTES** will search both of these fields for the keyword that you enter. This option will usually find more appointments.

3. Select the second option as shown in Figure 18-36, then click the **FIND NOW** button. You should see results similar to those shown in Figure 18-37.

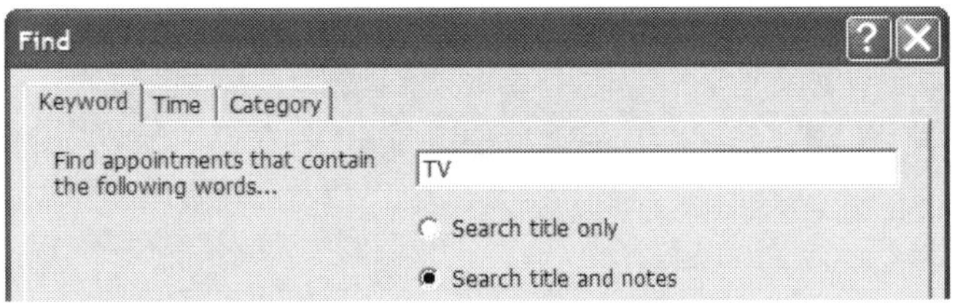

Figure 18-36 Keyword tab on the Find dialog box

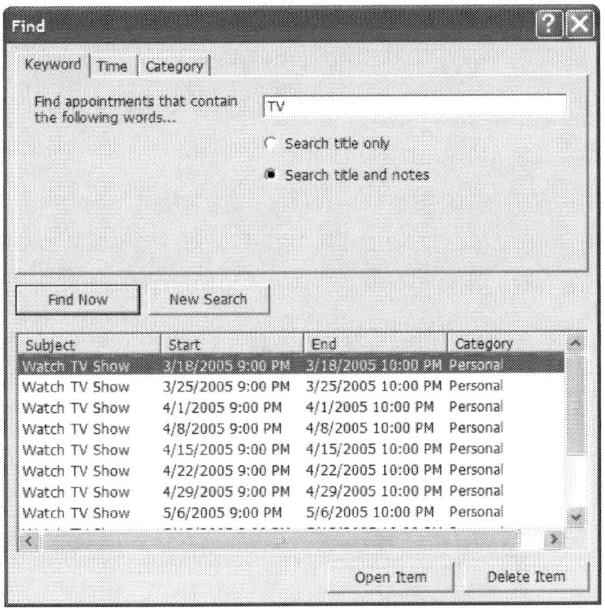

Figure 18-37 Result of the keyword search

At the bottom of Figure 18-37 are two buttons, **OPEN ITEM** and **DELETE ITEM**. They are explained below.

① If you select an appointment from the list and click the **OPEN ITEM** button, you will see the Edit Appointment dialog box shown earlier in Figure 18-28. You can edit the appointment in this dialog box. If you select an appointment from the search that is part of a series, you will see the Open Recurring Item dialog box shown earlier in Figure 18-22.

② If you select an appointment from the list and click the **DELETE ITEM** button, you will see the dialog box shown in Figure 18-38, if the appointment that you selected is part of a series. If you select an appointment that is not part of a series, you will see the dialog box shown in Figure 18-39.

Figure 18-38 Delete appointment dialog box for an appointment that is part of a series

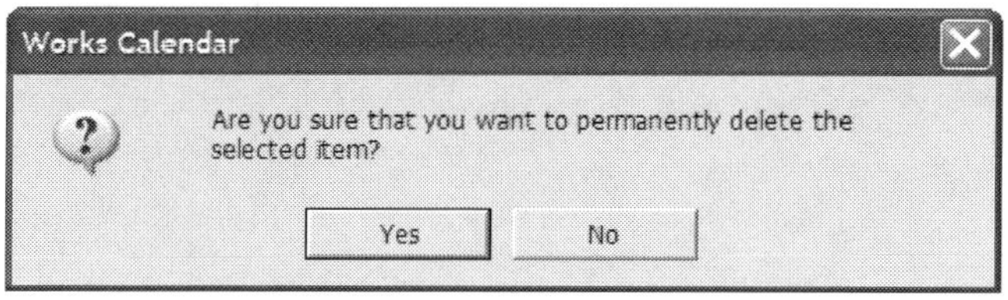

Figure 18-39 Delete appointment dialog box for an appointment that is not part of a series

4. If you want to perform another search, click the **NEW SEARCH** button shown earlier in Figure 18-37.

Find Appointments By Time

If you want to look for appointments in a certain time frame you can, by following the steps below. There are two time frames that you can select from **STARTS** and **ENDS**.

① The **STARTS** option will let you search for appointments based on the time that they start.

② The **ENDS** option will let you search for appointments based on the time that they end.

1. Open the Find dialog box. On the **TIME** tab open the first drop-down list and select Starts, then open the second drop-down list and select **NEXT MONTH**. Figure 18-40 shows the options that you should have selected. These options will search for all appointments that start next month.

2. Click the **FIND NOW** button. You will see results similar to those shown in Figure 18-41. Just like you can open and delete appointments from the Keyword tab, you can do the same from the Time tab.

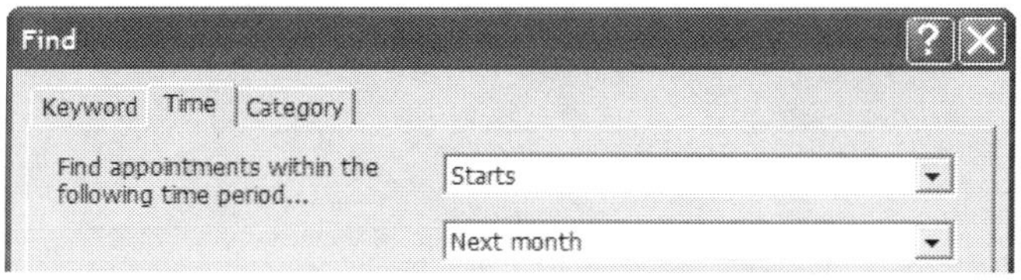

Figure 18-40 Time search options selected

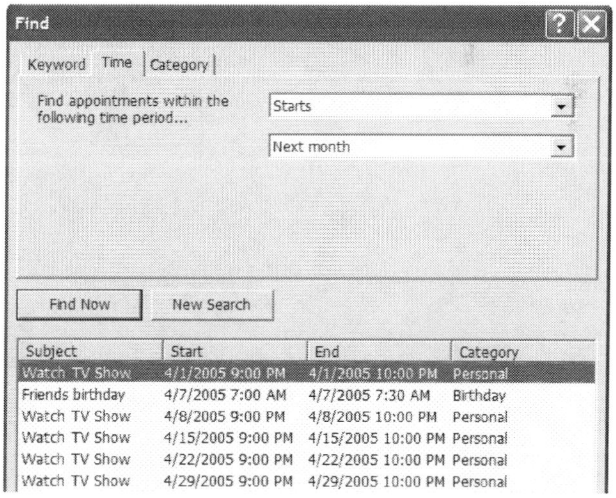

Figure 18-41 Results of the time search

Find Appointments By Category

The Category tab options work the same way that the category filters option works that you learned about earlier in this lesson.

1. Open the Find dialog box. On the **CATEGORY** tab you will see the options shown in Figure 18-42. From here you can select or deselect the categories that you want or do not want to see appointments for. When you are finished, close the Find dialog box.

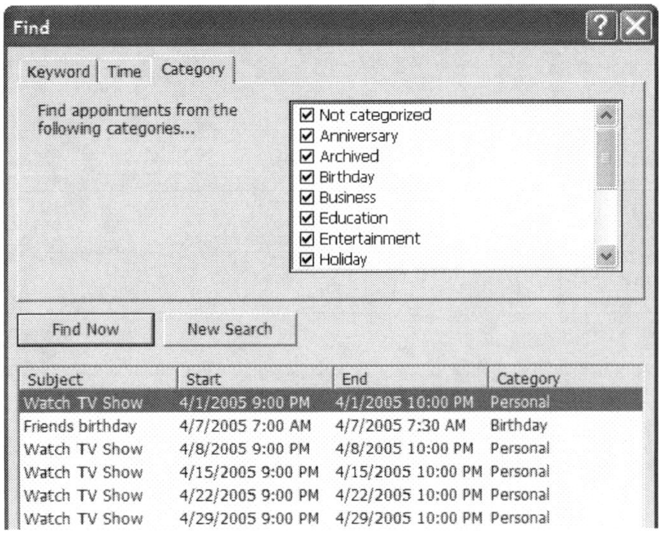

Figure 18-42 Result of the category search

If you use the Find category option, you have to clear the options on the Keyword and Time tabs first, unless you want them included as part of the category search.

2. When you are finished, close the Find dialog box.

Printing Calendars

Works provides several options for printing calendars as shown in Figure 18-43. The printing options are discussed below. The largest downside to printing calendars is that there is no print preview option. The only way to see the calendar is to print it.

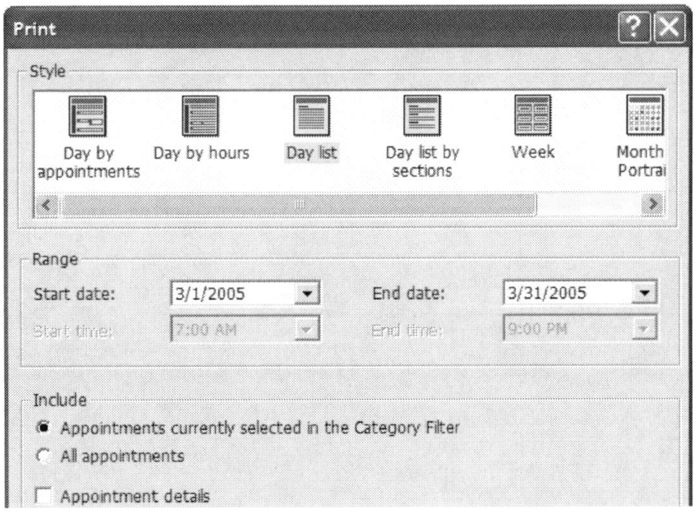

Figure 18-43 Calendar print options

① The **STYLE** options let you select the layout for the calendar that you want to print.
② The **RANGE** options let you select the date and time range for the calendar that you want to print.
③ The **INCLUDE** options let you select which appointments you want to print. You can use filters, which you have to select prior to opening the Print dialog box.

The **APPOINTMENT DETAILS** option is only available for certain calendar styles.

Test Your Skills

1. Create the appointments in Table 18-7.

Appointment	1	2
Title	3rd friends birthday	Complete Workbook
Category	Birthday	Education
Start Date	1st of the month	4th of next month

Table 18-7 Calendar appointments

2. Create the following two categories. `Test category 3` and `Test category 4`.
3. Assign the two appointments that you created in step 1 to Test category 4.
4. Dismiss all of the appointments that you created in this lesson.
5. Delete all of the appointments that you created in this lesson.

THE PROJECT ORGANIZER

The Project Organizer can be used as a blueprint or management tool for a project or event that has a lot of tasks associated with it. You can create your own project or you can use a project template that comes with Works and modify it as needed. In this lesson you will learn how to create a project based off of a template and how to create a project from scratch.

LESSON 19

The Project Organizer

As it's name indicates, the Project Organizer will help you keep the various projects that you are working on organized. The first exercise that you will work on will show you how to use a project organizer template and modify it to fit your needs.

Projects can have a few tasks or they can have hundreds of tasks. Keeping track of all of the tasks can be time consuming if they are not managed properly. Hopefully, you will see how using this tool can help you manage a project of any size.

Using A Project Organizer Template

The template that you will modify in this exercise is the fundraiser template. You will modify existing entries in the template, delete entries on the to do list and create new entries on the list. You will also associate documents that you have already created to a task, add a note to a task, select task due dates and select a project due date.

> Unlike other applications in Works, you cannot create a project template of your own. The work around that I have come up with is to create a project and enter the tasks that you would always need in a project and save it with a name similar to "My Mailing List Project Template", for example. Use a name that is appropriate for the type of template that you are creating. The reason that I use the word "template" as part of the file name is so that when I view the projects on the My Projects tab, I would know that it is a template and not a real project. You would open this project and then save it with another name.

Save A Copy Of An Existing Template

1. Click on the Programs link on the Works Task Launcher, then click on the **MY PROJECTS ORGANIZER** option. Click on the **START A FUNDRAISER** project illustrated in Figure 19-1.

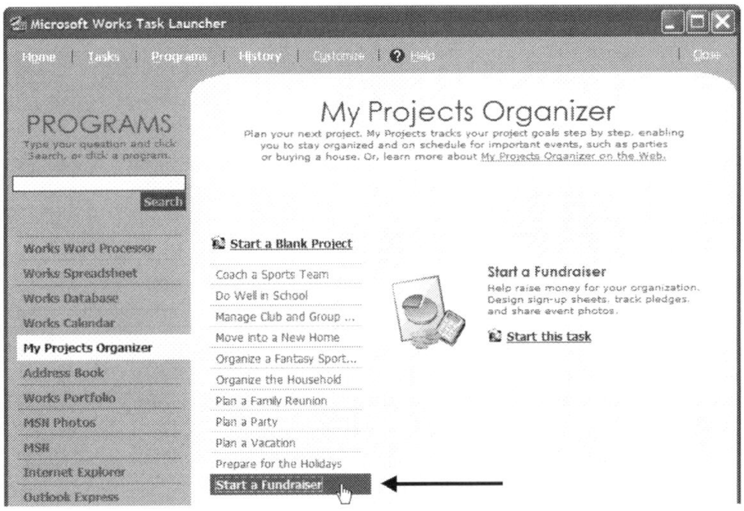

Figure 19-1 My Projects Organizer options illustrated

2. Click the **START THIS TASK** link. You will see the project template shown in Figure 19-2.

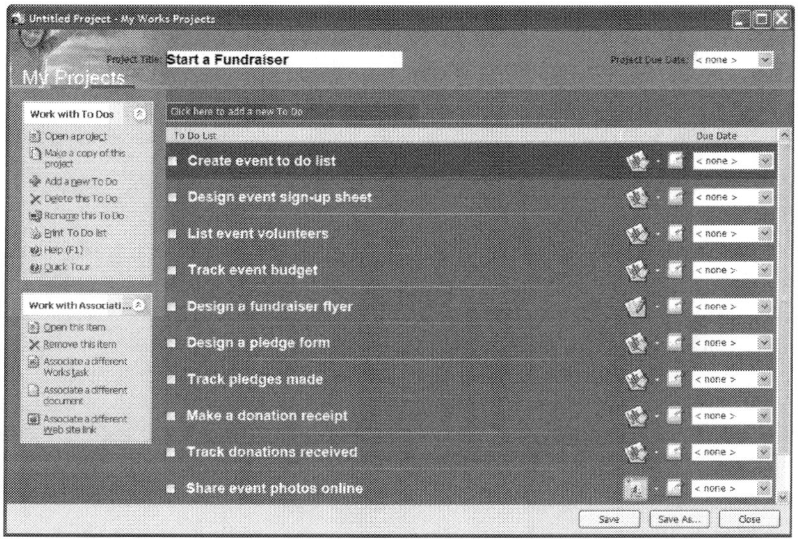

Figure 19-2 Fundraiser template

3. Click the **SAVE AS** button and navigate to your folder. Type `My Fundraiser Project` as the file name and press Enter or click Save.

> When you create and save a new project, a category filter is automatically created with the same name as the project, as illustrated in Figure 19-3. This will allow you view all of the tasks by due date in the calendar, by selecting the filter for the project.

Figure 19-3 Category filter for the project illustrated

Overview Of The Project Window

As you can see in Figure 19-2 shown earlier, there are a lot of options for the project. Below is an overview of the options for creating and modifying a project.

① **PROJECT TITLE** This is where you enter the name of the project. You should try to pick a descriptive name.

② **PROJECT DUE DATE** If the project has a date that it needs to be completed by, enter that date in this field.

③ **WORK WITH TO DO'S** This section of the project window contains the options for the tasks (The To Do's) of the project.

④ **WORK WITH ASSOCIATIONS** This section contains the options for attaching documents to tasks or removing documents from a task.

⑤ **TO DO LIST** This section lists all of the tasks for the project. Above the To Do list is an option called "Click here to add a new To Do". This is one way that you can create another task. To the left of each To Do item is a check box. When the task is completed, click in this box.

⑥ **ADDITIONAL ITEMS** These are the two buttons to the right of the task. The first button is for an attachment for the task. You will see different icons in this column depending on the type of file that is attached. The icons are the same as the ones you see on the home page of the Task Launcher for each application in Works. The last icon in this column (for the Share event photos online task) is one that you may not recognize. The yellow folder represents a link to a web site. If you click on the arrow at the end of one of these buttons, you will see the menu shown in Figure 19-4. These are the same options that are in the **WORK WITH ASSOCIATIONS** section of the project window. If you click on this button or select the **OPEN THIS ITEM** option shown in Figure 19-4, the file that is associated with the task will open.

The second button is for **NOTES** about the task. You can enter additional information, like the status of the task or any other information that needs to be included with the task. The icon shown in Figure 19-5 indicates that the there is no information in the Notes field. The icon shown in Figure 19-6 indicates that there is information in the Notes field. If you look closely, you will see that there is some writing on the icon in Figure 19-6.

⑦ **DUE DATE** If the task has a due date, you should enter it. Doing so will help you know the order that the tasks should be completed in.

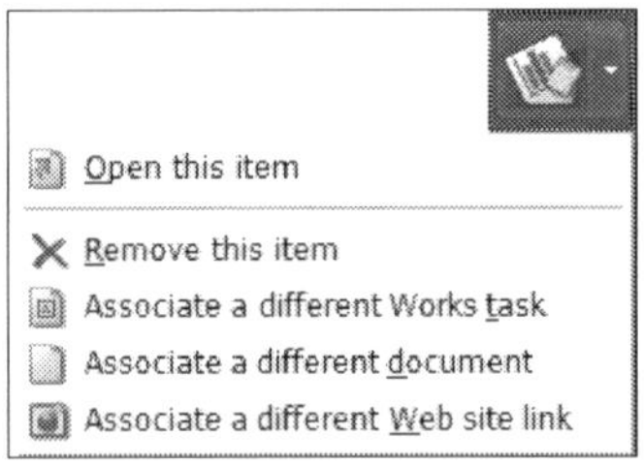

Figure 19-5 Empty notes field icon

Figure 19-6 Notes field with information icon

Figure 19-4 Work With Association options

Modify Existing Entries In The Project

In this exercise you will modify some of the entries and options that the template comes with, so that the project will meet your needs.

Modify The Project Title

The project title is in the upper left corner of the project window shown earlier in Figure 19-2. To modify the title follow the steps below.

1. Click in the Project Title field.

2. Highlight the text that is in the field and type `My Template Project`, then press Enter.

Modify The Project Due Date

Entering a project due date is optional. If the project that you are working on has a due date, you should fill it in. To fill in the project due date follow the steps below.

1. Open the drop-down list at the end of the Project Due Date field. You will see the calendar for the current month as shown in Figure 19-7.

If the project is due in the current month, click on the date in the calendar. If the project is due in a future month, click on the arrow to the right of the month and year, until you get to the month that the project is due, then select the day.

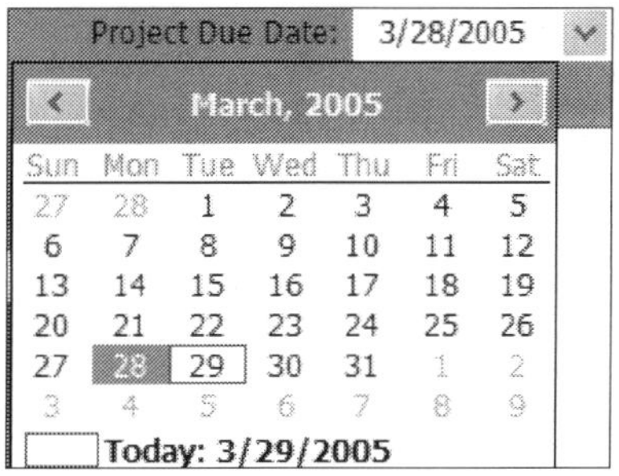

Figure 19-7 Project Due Date calendar

2. This project is due tomorrow, so click on tomorrow's date. Tomorrow's date should now be in the Project Due Date field.

3. Click the Save button to save the changes that you made to the project.

Modify An Existing Task

In the next few exercises, you will modify all of the options of an existing task. You will make the majority of the changes to the first task in the project.

Modify The Task Name

After you create a task, you may decide that the task name is not appropriate. If so, you can change the task name by following the steps below.

1. Click on the first task "Create event to do list", then click on the option **RENAME THIS TO DO** in the Work With To Do's section on the left side of the project window. The background of the task field should turn white.

2. Type `My modified task` in the field as shown in Figure 19-8, then press Enter.

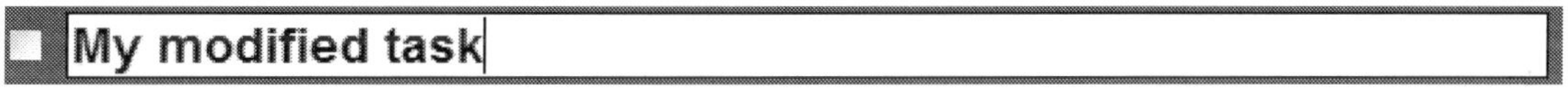

Figure 19-8 Task name modified

Modify The File Associated With A Task

In this exercise you will attach a word processing document to this task. The file that is currently associated with this task is a spreadsheet. If you click on the first button after the task name, you will see the file shown in Figure 19-9.

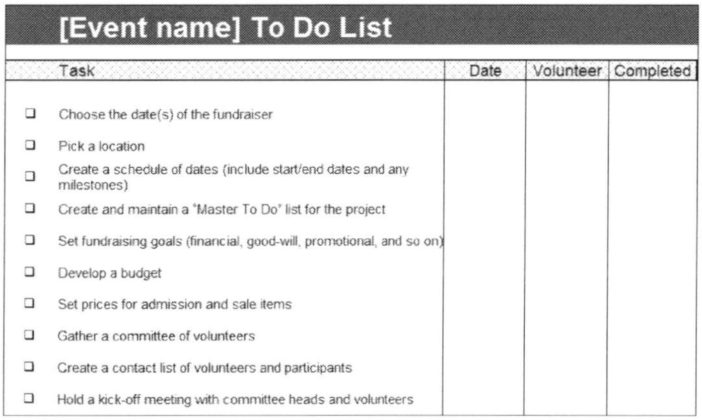

[Event name] To Do List

Task	Date	Volunteer	Completed
❑ Choose the date(s) of the fundraiser			
❑ Pick a location			
❑ Create a schedule of dates (include start/end dates and any milestones)			
❑ Create and maintain a "Master To Do" list for the project			
❑ Set fundraising goals (financial, good-will, promotional, and so on)			
❑ Develop a budget			
❑ Set prices for admission and sale items			
❑ Gather a committee of volunteers			
❑ Create a contact list of volunteers and participants			
❑ Hold a kick-off meeting with committee heads and volunteers			

Figure 19-9 File currently associated with the task

1. Click on the arrow at the end of the first button after the task name. You should see the menu shown earlier in Figure 19-4. Select the option **ASSOCIATE A DIFFERENT DOCUMENT**. You will see the Open dialog box.

2. Navigate to your folder. Select the L7 Mail Merge Letter (sorted by zip code) file, then click the Open button. Notice that the icon changed from a spreadsheet to a word processing icon. Save the changes.

> If you click on this icon the document that you created in Lesson 7 will open instead of the spreadsheet shown above in Figure 19-9.

Add Or Edit Information In The Note Field

Adding a new note or editing an existing note is the same process. The steps below will show you how to do both.

1. Click on the note icon that you want to add to or edit. You will see the window shown in Figure 19-10.

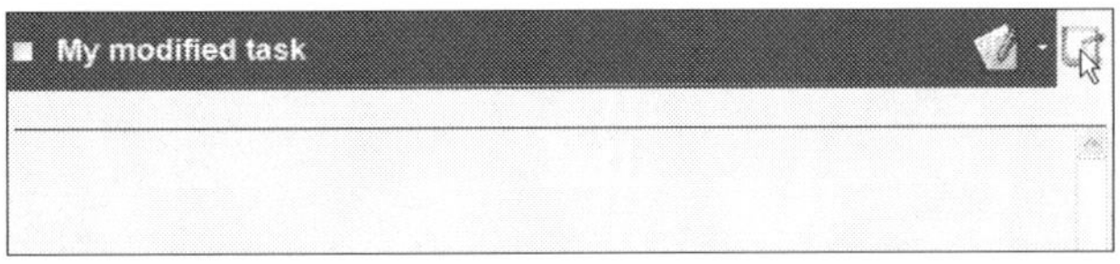

Figure 19-10 Note window

2. Type in the information that you want to include with the task or edit the information that is already in the Note field. For this exercise type `This is my first task`, then click the Note icon to close the window.

Add Or Edit The Task Due Date

Many, if not all tasks have a due date. Whether you enter a task due date is strictly up to you. If you have assigned a task a due date and need to change it, you can follow the steps below to change the due date.

> When you enter a task due date, the task is automatically added to your calendar. A reminder for the task is also automatically created.

1. Click on the arrow at the end of the **DUE DATE** field. You will see a calendar similar to the one shown earlier in Figure 19-7.
2. Select the date that the task is due. For this exercise select tomorrow's date, then save the changes.

> I don't know if this is a bug or if it's what the developers intended, but you can enter a task due date that is after the project due date.

Add Due Dates For The Other Tasks

In this exercise you will add due dates for the other tasks in this project, so that you can view the tasks in the calendar.

1. Open the Due Date drop-down list of the second task and select the first day of next month.

> To change the calendar to next month, click on the right arrow (the one after the date at the top of the calendar).

2. Open the Due Date fields for each of the remaining tasks and select the next day of next month. For example, the third task should be the second of next month. Each task should have a different date as shown in Figure 19-11.

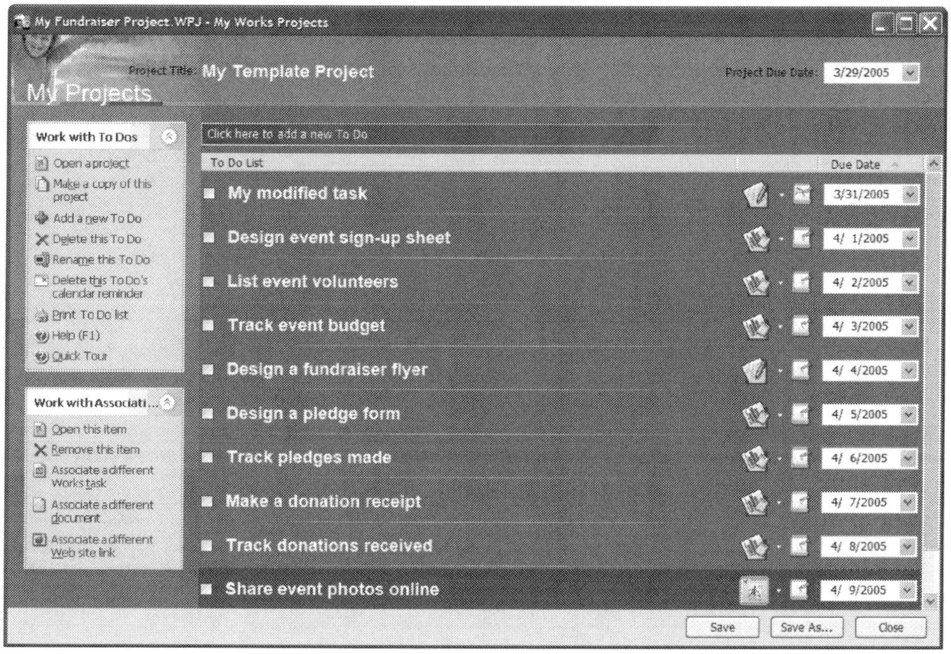

Figure 19-11 Due dates added to all of the tasks

3. Save the changes.

View Project Tasks In The Calendar

In this exercise you will view the tasks associated with this project in the calendar.

1. Open the calendar for next month. If the Category Filters are not visible on the left side of your calendar, click the **CATEGORY FILTERS** button on the toolbar.

2. Make sure the **MY TEMPLATE PROJECT** filter has a check mark next to it as illustrated in Figure 19-12.

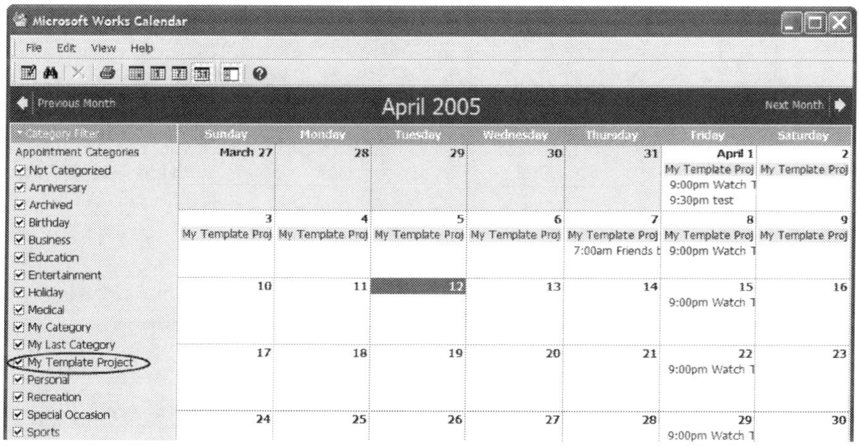

Figure 19-12 Calendar with filter option selected

3. Right-click on one of the tasks from the project in the calendar and select Open. You will see the dialog box shown in Figure 19-13. For now, close the Edit Appointment dialog box and the calendar.

If you need to edit any of the information for this task, you can make the changes on the Edit Appointment dialog box.

Notice that the **TITLE** field on the dialog box has the project name and the task name.

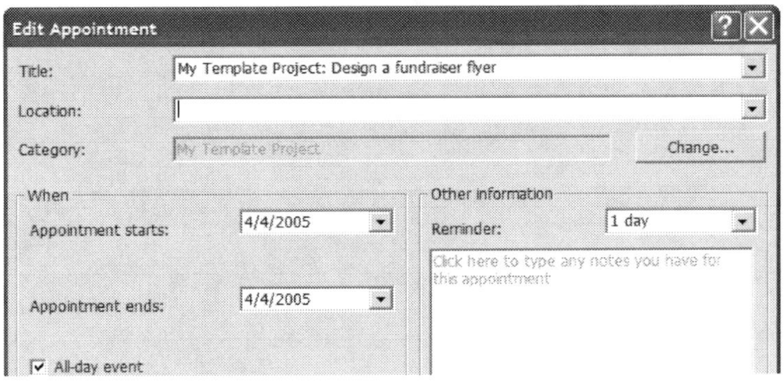

Figure 19-13 Edit Appointment dialog box

How To Delete Or Remove A Task Or Task Option

So far you have learned how to add and edit tasks, as well as, edit task options. In the next few exercises you will learn how to delete or remove a task or a task option.

Remove A Document Associated To A Task

In this exercise you will learn how to remove a document that is associated to a task. Doing this does not delete the document from your hard drive.

1. Click on the icon to the right of the first task in the To Do List and click the **REMOVE THIS ITEM** link in the Work With Associations section of the project window.

> You can also open the drop-down list for the field and select the **REMOVE THIS ITEM** option.

2. You will see the message shown in Figure 19-14. Click Yes. Notice that you see the icon shown in Figure 19-15. This icon lets you know that there is no document associated with this task on the To Do list.

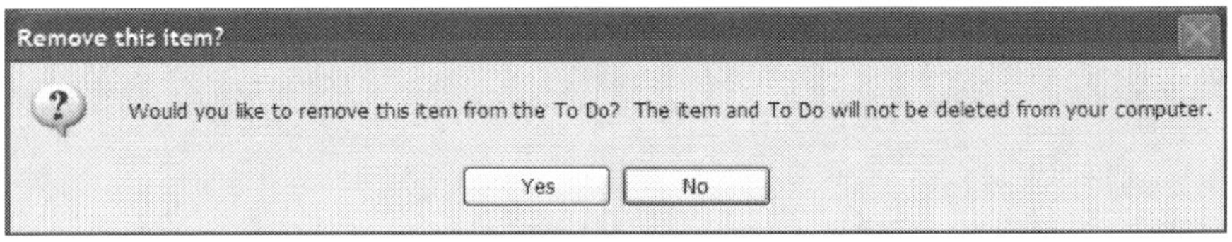

Figure 19-14 Remove this item message

Figure 19-15 No document associated with this task icon

Delete A Calendar Reminder For A Task

Earlier in this lesson you learned that if you add a date to a task, a calendar reminder is automatically created. There may be times when you do not want to be reminded of when a task is due. If so, you can follow the steps below to delete the calendar reminder for a project task.

> When you delete a calendar reminder, the task due date on the project window is automatically changed to **<NONE>**.

1. Select the first task in the To Do list if it is not already selected, then click on the link, **DELETE THIS TO DO'S CALENDAR REMINDER** in the Work With To Do's section of the project window. You will see the message shown in Figure 19-16. Click Yes. The calendar reminder will be deleted for this task.

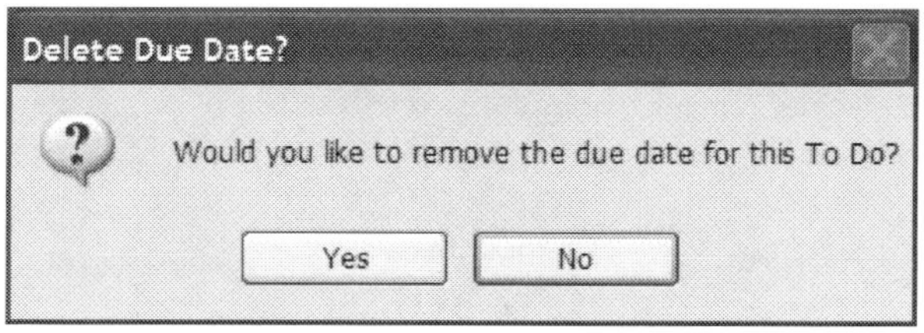

Figure 19-16 Delete due date message

2. Save the changes. If you look at the due date for the task, you will see <None> in the Due Date field.

How To Delete A Task

The primary reason to delete a task is because it is no longer needed in the project. If you need to delete a task from the To Do list, follow the steps below. Deleting a task in the project window will also delete it from the calendar.

1. Click on the task that you want to delete. In this exercise, click on the third task, **LIST EVENT VOLUNTEERS**.

2. Click on the link, **DELETE THIS TO DO** in the Work With To Do's section of the project window. You will see the message shown in Figure 19-17. Click Yes and the task will be deleted, then save the changes to the project.

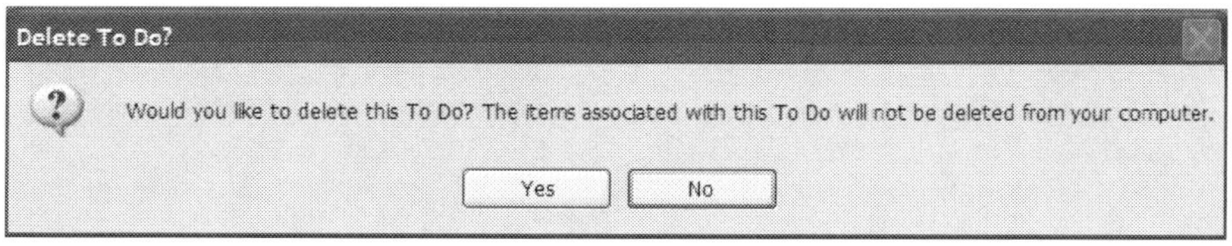

Figure 19-17 Delete To Do message

Available Options For A Task

Depending on what options you have added to a task and what options you have deleted from a task, the options in the **WORK WITH TO DO'S** and **WORK WITH ASSOCIATIONS** sections of the project window will change. If you refer back to Figure 19-11, you will see that both of these sections have all of the options available for the task that is selected. Compare the options available in Figure 19-11 to those available in Figure 19-18 and you will see that some options are not available.

The **DELETE THIS TO DO'S** calendar reminder option in the Work With To Do's section, is currently not available. The **OPEN THIS ITEM** and **REMOVE THIS ITEM** options in the Work With Associations section, are currently not available. The menu shown earlier in Figure 19-4 also has all of the options. The same menu is shown in Figure 19-19, but it has fewer options.

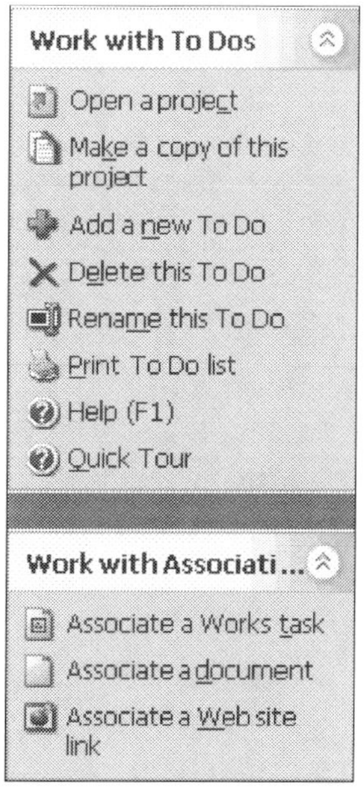

Figure 19-18 Work with To Do's and Associations sections illustrated

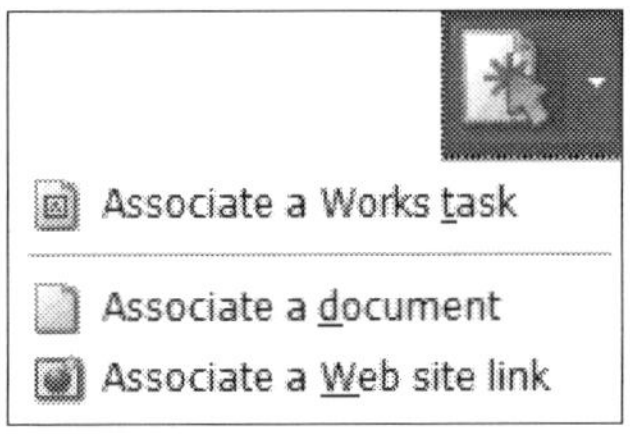

Figure 19-19 Menu with less options illustrated

Printing A Project

You do not have to print project now. You can read about the printing capabilities. The print feature in the project window is very limited. There are no layout options that you can select. Like the calendar, you cannot preview the To Do list before you print it. To print the To Do List, click on the Print To Do List link in the **WORK WITH TO DO'S** section of the project window.

How To Create A To Do Item

Creating a new task is easy. You can follow the steps below to create a new task for the project.

1. Click on the link **ADD A NEW TO DO** in the Work With To Do's section of the project window.

> Another way to add a To Do is to click on the words **CLICK HERE TO ADD A NEW TO DO** that is above the To Do List of tasks, as shown in Figure 19-20.

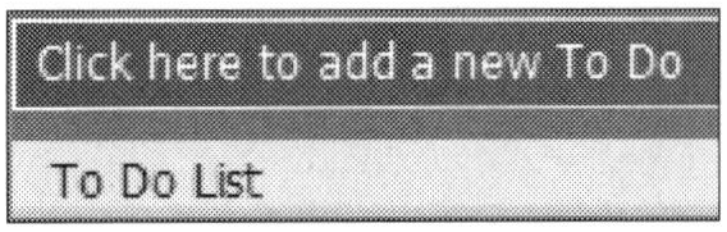

Figure 19-20 Another way to add a new To Do

2. Enter the name for the task in the white box, like the one you saw earlier in Figure 19-8.
3. To fill in the other options for the task, you can follow the steps in the "Add or Edit" sections, then save the changes and close the project window.

> The down side to adding additional to do's after the initial To Do's have been added to the project is that they are automatically placed at the end of the list. You can't insert a new To Do Item between existing tasks. The work around that I have come up with is to always add a Due Date for each task and sort the tasks in due date order. Doing this will rearrange the tasks in date order.

How To Create A Project

If you do not want to use a project template, you can create a project from scratch and add the tasks that you need. Once you create a new project, everything else is the same as what you learned earlier.
To create a new project follow the steps below.

1. Click on the Programs link on the Works Task Launcher, then click on the **MY PROJECTS ORGANIZER** option.
2. Click on the **START A BLANK PROJECT** link. You will see the new project shown in Figure 19-21.
3. Type `My 2nd Project` in the Project Title field, then click the Save button.
4. Navigate to your folder and type `My 2nd Project` as the file name. Press Enter or click Save.

Figure 19-21 New project

Add A New Document To A Task

Earlier you learned how to associate an existing document to a task. You can also create a new document while in the project window and associate it to a task.

1. Create a task named "Add new document" and press Enter.

2. Double-click on the task that you just created. You will see the dialog box shown in Figure 19-22 or the one shown in Figure 19-23. Both of these dialog boxes have the same features and functionality. They will let you create a new document and associate it with the task.

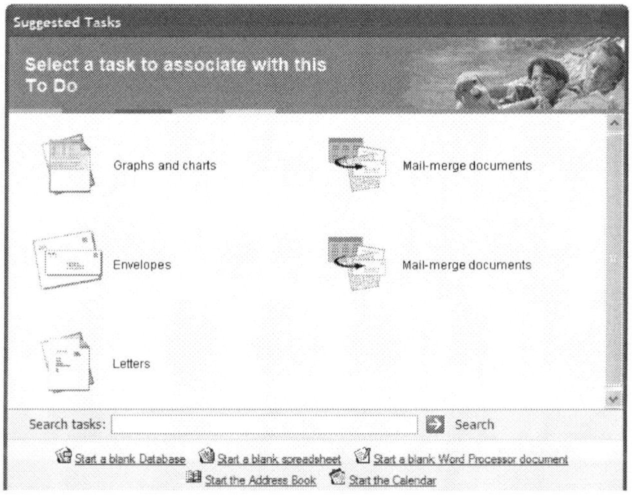

Figure 19-22 Suggested Tasks dialog box

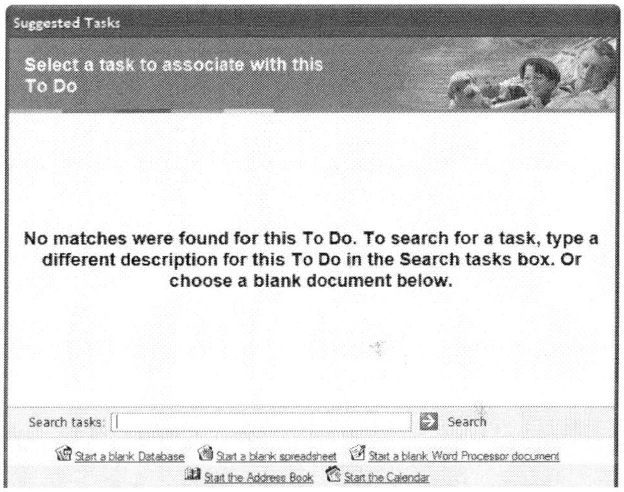

Figure 19-23 Another Suggested Tasks dialog box

Notice that you can also search for an existing file to associate to the task from both of these dialog boxes.

3. Click the **START A BLANK WORD PROCESSOR DOCUMENT** link. Notice that the icon changed to a word processing icon next to the task.

4. Click on the icon to the right of the task. A new word processing document will open. Save the empty document as `L19 Project`, then close the word processing application. Save the changes and close the project.

Viewing And Opening Projects From The Task Launcher

So far in this lesson you have created and edited projects and tasks, but you have not opened any. Like other applications in Works, you can open projects from the Home page of the Task Launcher by following the steps below.

1. Open the Task Launcher if it is not already open and click on the Home link.

On the home page of the Task Launcher you will see two project tabs: **WORKS PROJECTS** and **MY PROJECTS** as shown in Figure 19-24. The options on the Works Projects tab are the templates that you can select from. They are the same ones that you saw earlier in Figure 19-1.

If you need to search for a project, you can enter a keyword for the project in the **PROJECT SEARCH** field, shown in Figure 19-24.

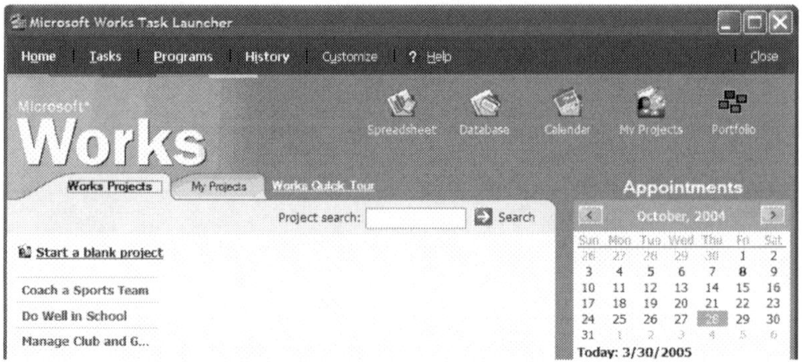

Figure 19-24 Project tabs illustrated

Notice that you can also start a blank (new) project from the Home page.

2. To view and open the projects that you have created, click on the **MY PROJECTS** tab. You will see the window shown in Figure 19-25. If you created projects prior to the ones that you created in this lesson, you will see them listed here as well.

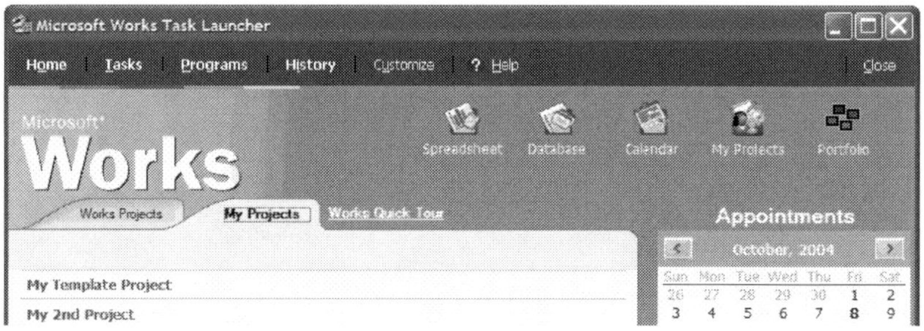

Figure 19-25 My Projects tab

3. Click on the link for the project that you want to open, then close the project when you are finished viewing it.

Test Your Skills

1. Create a new project and save it as `L19 Project (skills)`.

2. Add the two tasks in Table 19-1 to the project.

Task Name	Associated File	Note
Print the mail merge letter	L7 Mail Merge Letter.wps	Also print letters for computer book buyers.
Reorder books	L18 Inventory (with functions).xlr.	Order more computer books.

Table 19-1 Tasks to add to the project

3. Delete all of the calendar entries and categories that were created in this lesson.

INDEX

General

Templates

Word Processing

Spreadsheets

Functions

Charts

Databases

Database Reports

Calendar

Project Organizer

Made in United States
Orlando, FL
04 November 2026

90201483R00179